APOCALYPSE OF THE MODERN MIND

ALSO BY DANIEL JOSEPH POLIKOFF

CREATIVE NON-FICTION

Rue Rilke

Reset or Renaissance
Life, Liberty, and the Quest for Enlightenment in a Post-Covid World
Volume 1: Two Roads (An American Scholar's Covid Chronicle)

CRITICISM

In the Image of Orpheus: Rilke—A Soul History

POETRY

Dragon Ship

The Hands of Stars

TRANSLATION

Sonnets to Orpheus

Parzival/Gawain: Two Plays
an edited translation of *Der Gral* by A. M. Miller

APOCALYPSE
OF THE MODERN MIND

Covid and the Dialectic of Enlightenment

Reset or Renaissance
Volume II

Daniel Joseph Polikoff

Portal books ≈ 2025

Dedicated to the Memory of my Father

ALEXANDER POLIKOFF
1927–2025

Premier Advocate for the Public Interest
Tireless Champion of Humanity

2025
Portal books

An imprint of SteinerBooks/Anthroposophic Press, Inc.
834 Main Street PO Box 358, Spencertown, NY 12165
www.SteinerBooks.org

Library of Congress Control Number: 2024932575

ISBN: 978-1-938685-63-7

Printed in the United States of America
by Integrated Books International

CONTENTS

PART III: ORIGINAL RELATION

PART IV: SPIRITUAL DEMOCRACY

ACKNOWLEDGMENTS

I would like to thank my wife Monika for her love and support through difficult times, and for waking me up to realities I was initially not inclined to acknowledge. I would also like to thank John Scott Legg at SteinerBooks for stepping into the breach and providing *Reset or Renaissance* a foothold in the world, and standing behind its aim of seeking a new vision of what once was called the New World.

I owe Keiron Le Grice a debt of gratitude for his personal and professional support and preliminary feedback on the text. I owe Michael Martin the same for his invaluable aid in editing it. I would also like to thank my father Alexander for his lifelong example of unselfish dedication to the commonweal, tireless service to the cause of justice and truth in the public sphere, and keen analytic and legal acumen. I wish, too, to remember my mother, Barbara Garland Polikoff, for her unending love and dedication to poetic beauty, in life and literature alike.

I would recognize as well the courageous and caring individuals—physicians, nurses, researchers, journalists, and many others—who stood (and still stand) for truth and integrity in the midst of a hurricane of contrary opinion. Finally, I would acknowledge the courage and sacrifice of all who suffered through the dark night of the pandemic, especially those who have borne the burden of job loss or the (almost unimaginable) burden of personal injury to themselves or loved ones. Many have done so with a grace and fortitude exemplary of the nobility of human beings in times seemingly intent on crushing that pearl of great price forever.

Where there is no vision, the people perish.
The scholars are the priests of that thought that
establishes the foundations of the earth.

—Ralph Waldo Emerson, *The Method of Nature*

APOCALYPSE
OF THE MODERN MIND

RESET OR RENAISSANCE
VOLUME II

INTRODUCTION

Humanity today stands at a turning point in time, a crossroads demanding clear discrimination between the paths of good and evil. A pitched battle has long been underway between those heart-lit torches that guide humanity towards a more enlightened future and the obscure tools—now subtle, now brutal, now subtly brutal—that would deliver us into hands that crush us.

In point of fact, the forces of destruction appear ascendant today; even on the verge of triumph. Apocalyptic signs of crisis disfigure the face of the globe. Ecological degradation imperils the survival of life on earth; gross economic disparity grows ever worse, endangering the well-being of all; religious fundamentalism and widespread militarism foment intolerance and violence, tearing at the social fabric enfolding human existence. On all sides, the very sinews of the world seem stretched to the point of snapping whilst the flame of spirit appears nought but a feeble candle soon to be extinguished by the gale-force winds of fate.

This grave situation is both new and not new. The novel place in time wherein we find ourselves represents an advanced stage of developments long in the making. In the aftermath of the epochal disaster of World War II, Paul Brunton—one of the first 20th-century figures to bring Eastern wisdom into wide circulation in the West—authored a book titled *The Spiritual Crisis of Man.* On the first page, Brunton writes:

> Post-war times are noteworthy for their supreme suspense, for the unpleasant chaos and insecurity which grips whole countries or even continents, and for their state of continued crisis.... Never before were so many people plunged in so much uncertainty, so much perplexity and unsettlement. Signs of this condition are plenty and plain for all to read. The confusions come with the morning's breakfast. They move with terrific speed. Our newspapers give us in a single issue what was once the history of a whole month. Their pages dismay and distract us.[1]

Brunton could easily have penned these words today, except that the daily chaos may well not be encountered in a newspaper, but read or viewed on a screen. Meanwhile, the terrific speed of human affairs has accelerated beyond anything he could well have imagined and the crises (offspring, no doubt, of those to which Brunton alludes) are still more global and earthshaking.

How have we come to this pass? Why has human history taken such a dark turn, or marched so brazenly for so long down what may well be no generous boulevard but a deadly *cul-de-sac*? Why does the unfolding plot of humanity's life on earth look more and more like an ancient tragedy moving rapidly and inexorably toward its last devastating act?

The causes of the ubiquitous distress that so afflicts the globe today can hardly be superficial. On the contrary, these must be sought at the root of the matter: the dominant forms of culture that mold prevailing ideological norms and thus the conduct of life.

The emergencies confronting present-day humanity reflect not only drastic perturbations in the material order of things but critical developments in the history of consciousness. At the deepest level, the spiritual dilemma to which Brunton refers constitutes an intellectual crisis. Our predicament derives from our habitual mental construction of the nature of things: what we—whether consciously or not—hold to be, or not to be, true and real. The gist of the matter may be stated thus: today, we find ourselves face to face with the catastrophic deficiency of the belief systems that have largely dominated Western culture since the Renaissance and Reformation, the crippling insufficiencies inherent in the Modern worldview.

Those insufficiencies pervade and shape the texture of most every facet of human culture. They manifested spectacularly in Covid, spelling disaster on a previously unheard-of scale, the extent of which we have not yet begun to compass.

Not everyone, however, sees it that way, even with the benefit of hindsight. Therein lies a conundrum as well as a critical challenge.

~

On March 1, 2024, almost four years to the day after our son drove home from a CU Boulder campus newly emptied on account of Covid, I attended a book launch at the Mill Valley Library for New York author Eric Klinenberg's *2020: One City, Seven People, and the Year Everything Changed.*[2] Local residents filled the beautiful high-ceilinged, redwood-beam main reading room. The atmosphere was congenial, if not festive. In her introductory remarks, the library events coordinator confessed that, though a like occasion for a previous

Klinenberg book had gone swimmingly, the subject matter of *2020* gave the Events Committee serious pause. After all, who wants to dwell on the grueling Covid crisis we have finally left behind? Who does not want to turn that dark page and move on to another, less dismal chapter of life?

Eric Klinenberg offered another perspective. In his introductory remarks, he emphasized the importance of a retrospective look at the upheaval occasioned by the pandemic and the varied life lessons—psychological, social, political—taught by the travail of Covid-19. Many of those lessons involved the revelation of social inequalities yet to be redressed, such as the paradoxical treatment of "essential" workers whose lives were both dignified and callously disregarded during the pandemic.

I appreciated the human stories Klinenberg told. I could even go so far as to call the socially conscious values he espoused my own. Even so, amidst the hundred or so people gathered in the main reading room that evening, I felt myself to be a stranger, an alien presence in the library I had, as a resident of Mill Valley, frequented for over twenty-years.

The reader of my prior book[3] will know why. While I could honor Klinenberg's tales of the deeds performed by everyday people as they countered the hardships of the pandemic, I hold a profoundly different view of the relevant backstory, an entirely contrary understanding of the multifaceted phenomenon of Covid World itself.

Eric Klinenberg spoke as a staunch proponent of the officially authorized account of the Covid pandemic. As far as I could tell, everyone else in the room that night fell in that same category. Quite a few members of the audience were still wearing masks (a topic Klinenberg wrote and talked about at length), and I have little doubt that most all were "fully vaccinated" (whatever that might mean).

Klinenberg, moreover, while presenting himself as a social scientist, did not pretend to political non-partisanship. On the contrary, his remarks were seasoned with pointed barbs directed at those not securely ensconced in the liberal camp. It was, after all, those *others* who might well support the man who was, at the time, the presumptive Republican presidential nominee. Klinenberg—speaking the mind of many in that room and across the country—expressed an acute fear that Donald Trump would ride a populist wave to re-election in 2024 and, upon gaining the formidable power of the presidency once again, institute a dictatorial regime that would spell the effective end of democracy in America.

~

Problems of political philosophy—particularly the philosophy of democracy—are at the heart of *Apocalypse of the Modern Mind.* The issues the book explores (most explicitly in the concluding section titled "Spiritual Democracy") bear materially on the dangers inherent in right-leaning forms of authoritarianism. These typically grant undue power to a single (often, but not always, charismatic) individual. Examples in our time might include Victor Orbán in Hungary, Recep Erdogan in Turkey, and—potentially—Donald Trump.

The phenomenon of right-wing authoritarianism and the threat it poses to democracy, while critically illuminated by events related and arguments made in this book, is *not*, however, its chief subject or focus. That is because it was not right-wing authoritarianism that conjured Covid World. Nor is it right-wing authoritarianism that continues to legitimate and empower the persistently aggressive forces that did.[4]

The complex nexus of forces responsible for Covid World—the global vortex of power that some (with a nod to the iconic Wakowski brothers film) call the Matrix—represents a distinct species of authoritarian rule that (unlike some of the more populist-inflected right-leaning forms) does not openly represent itself as autocratic in character. It is this—for many persons, largely invisible—Matrix that the first two volumes of *Reset and Renaissance* seek to describe, define, and expose. The brand of leftward-leaning authoritarianism associated with it—one that typically features strong technocratic elements—poses no less of a threat to democracy than the right-wing kind that haunts my liberal Mill Valley neighbors. Indeed, it is my view that, for a variety of reasons, it is this formidable Matrix that probably represents the most clear and present danger, not only to democracy, but to humanity at large—the biological as well as spiritual integrity of our kind.

~

After Eric Klinenberg's talk and reading, I was one of the handful of persons who lined up to purchase a copy of his book. I had hoped to have an opportunity to converse with him, but he did not have time for any but the most cursory exchange. He did, however, sign my book. Under my name ("To Daniel") and above the stylish flourish of his initials, Klinenberg wrote:

In Solidarity!

This struck me as a peculiarly provocative phrase. How is it that he, and that whole room of intellectually wakeful persons could not only *believe*, but *take as an unquestionable given* that not only were they "right" about Covid, but that *any* rational, liberally-minded person would naturally be "in solidarity" with them in that regard?

The first volume of *Reset or Renaissance* sheds a good deal of light on that question, detailing a host of factors (the transformation of legacy media into a tool of corporate and state-sponsored propaganda, for instance) traceable to the machinery of the Matrix. Mentioned, too, are some contingent political reasons (e.g., fear and hatred of Trump) for the strict alignment of Democrats and Covid orthodoxy. In addition, however, to all the more proximate causes of Covid partisanship detailed in the prior volume, more deep-lying fault lines are at work here as well: age-old fractures—including the profound and ever-widening schism between science and religion—that have long riddled modern consciousness and deformed its development.

It is these underlying philosophical and ideological concerns (those crippling insufficiencies earlier cited) that shape the lineaments of modern consciousness so that my Mill Valley compatriots could be wholly convinced that they were and are right about Covid. In toeing the party line on the whole complex of issues comprising Covid World, they felt they were *upholding*, rather than *betraying*, the enlightened values of reason, science, freedom, social justice, and love for humanity to which the liberal creed is ostensibly pledged. The diabolical logic by which faith in those values, and investment in the methods of thought believed to serve them, turns into nightmarish betrayal, transforming liberalism into left-wing authoritarianism and democracy into autocracy, counts as the chief subject of not only the chapter titled "Leviathan: Enlightenment's Shadow," but the book as a whole.

Apocalypse of the Modern Mind, then, is not only about democracy. It is also, and even more fundamentally, a book about Enlightenment. Philosophically as well as historically, we do not have one without the other, at least within the context of the modern era. Enlightenment, moreover, comes first.

It come first because democracy is indeed a political *philosophy*, and cannot be well comprehended unless one's understanding is grounded in ideas that reach beyond the political per se. History itself reveals this clearly: the democratic impulse that emerged with such dramatic effect (first in America and later in Europe) grew out of a rich soil of ideas revolving around the most profound and far-reaching concerns: the status of divine and natural law and the relationship of the one to the other; the respective provinces of reason and of faith; the nature and destiny of humanity, and the sort of *progress* our kind not only could but should seek to realize in its quest for material prosperity and social harmony.

The ideas that underlie liberal democracy thus cannot be grasped in the absence of historical understanding that encompasses all the major concerns formative of modernity itself: the philosophical, religious, political, artistic, and scientific initiatives that marked the transition from the medieval to the modern era. It is in reviewing and recollecting that history that we can perhaps gain insight into the principles underlying the philosophy of democracy and (more generally) the truly *liberal* impulse that engendered modernity. It is that order of comprehension, as well, that enables vision of the counterfeit side of that precious coin: the *deformation* of liberal and democratic ideals implicit in what Theodore Adorno and Max Horkheimer call "the dialectic of enlightenment."

So it is that, while the first part of this book ("The Great Reset and the Dialectic of Enlightenment") examines 20th and 21st-century political and ideological currents that lead up to Covid World, its second part ("Modernity Dawns") aims to reconstruct, as lucidly as is possible in so few pages, the chief intellectual and cultural historical developments that catalyzed passage from the medieval to the modern world. The relevant transformations unfolded in the course of the latter part of the Middle Ages and the epochal movements that marked the fifteenth through eighteenth centuries: the European Renaissance, Protestant Reformation, Scientific Revolution, and Enlightenment. In these pages, you will encounter, in cameo, many of the trend-setting figures of those times: Aquinas and Ockham, Petrarch and Pico, Luther and Machiavelli, Kepler and Galileo, Bacon, Descartes, Locke, Voltaire and others.

Part II thus serves to frame the historical and philosophical landscape against which background all our more contemporary scenes—Covid among them—are staged. Its chapters revolve largely around the issue that defines the horizon of modernity: the promise and problem of human freedom, or (to give the concept a slightly more explicitly political twist) *liberty.*

From its inception, the democratic idea—historical accents upon property and aristocratic privilege notwithstanding—was a "liberal" one intent upon securing an unprecedented degree of sovereignty for the individual citizen and for the common person. That project—one inseparable from the concept of

Enlightenment itself—was, however, always vexed by its own shadow: potentially destructive tendencies inherent in the novel ideas about the human self, God, and nature that accompany the emergence of the nation state and the whole of modern culture.

The deficiencies inherent in the foundation of the modern worldview—one characterized, above all, by the sovereignty of science—figure as a chief topic in the middle parts of the book. Complementing inquiry into the destructive lines of force inherent in the machinery of modernity, I aim, with equal urgency, to recover the *constructive* forces at work in the liberal impulses birthed in the revolutionary era. *Apocalypse of the Modern Mind* thus strives to identify and elucidate *the dual legacy of the Enlightenment:* the genuine spiritual radiance that shines forth in the Age of Reason and the dark shadows cast by its brilliance. The book revolves around the riddle posed by that duplicity and endeavors to understand how the *same* historic movement responsible for many of the ideas that founded modern liberal democracy (including our operative notion of "liberty" itself) simultaneously prepares the ground for the technocratic authoritarianism that features as the dark underside of Covid World.

As the Emersonian aegis of Part III ("Original Relations") indicates, *Apocalypse* is concerned not only with the dark shadows that creep in under the door of our enlightened modernity, but also with radical solutions to the problems thus posed, solutions suggested by those bearers of a renewed Romantic or Transcendentalist idea of what enlightenment really means.

The final section of the book (Part IV: "Spiritual Democracy") brings the whole intricate tapestry of thought and action sketched in the prior parts back home to the current moment and place in time. If this last part contains a searing critique of the technocratic forms of political and cultural hegemony inherent in biomedical politics today, it does not stop there. To step *forward* toward a future that promises real freedom, it is necessary to go still further *back* in U.S. history: first to the momentous political debate preceding the American Revolution itself, and, finally, to the very seed of the democratic idea planted in the altogether revolutionary mind of Roger Williams.

Williams founded Providence Plantation, which (as the duly chartered Colony of Rhode Island) evolved into the first formal democracy in non-native America. Not coincidently, it was also this devoutly religious yet free-thinking Puritan who first conceived the (at the time, thoroughly iconoclastic) notion of the separation of church and state.

Roger Williams's seminal idea of religious freedom or "soul liberty" does not admit authoritarianism in any form: neither the monarchal and theocratical forms most prominent in his time, nor the technocratic species ascendant in our own. Nor would it, by any stretch of the imagination, countenance the one on account of fear of the other. *That,* I would suggest, is a history lesson for our time, one that should be studied in the main reading rooms of local libraries all across the country, if not across the world.

May this book—along with the prior volume of *Reset or Renaissance*—catalyze the kind of dialogue Eric Klinenberg and I did not but should have had.

~

A Note on the Chronology and Currency of the Text(s)

Apocalypse of the Modern Mind comprises the second volume of *Reset or Renaissance* and so is the sequel to the first volume, *Two Roads: An American Scholar's Covid Chronicle*. Most of Volume 2 was written in late 2021 and 2022, immediately following completion of the main body of the text of Volume 1. The Postscripts and Coda of Volume 1 were, however, written in 2023 while the final two chapters, Introduction and Afterword of Volume 2 were written in late 2023 and early 2024. Consistent with the chronicle style of the first volume, I generally refer to events current *at the time of composition* in the present tense.

Having now just finished with the editing of the original manuscript, I write this note in the changed political landscape of February 2025. The crushing weight of Covid World is no longer stooping our shoulders, while the worst fears of my Mill Valley neighbors have come true: Donald Trump is once again President of the United States.

This is no place to comment on the whirlwind of actions that followed upon his assumption of office, except to note that (along with the fade of the pandemic) some of those actions *seem* to put the urgency of certain concerns raised in this book in question.

The present book begins with a sketch of the vortex of power I call the Matrix, and the book unfolds a critique of the ideology, as well as the practical force, of the technocratic regime so named. The second Presidency of Donald Trump may represent a deflection of the Matrix as it operates through *certain* channels. This does not, however, diminish the relevance of this text as other channels remain in force or, like the "Stargate AI" project, are newly opened.

The crucial question remains: will the *mindset* underlying the Matrix prevail? Will technocracy continue to characterize the government of our institutions and so discolor the dreams of the People? Will the monarchical or theocratic attitudes discussed in the book's last chapters reemerge in reaction? Or will we find the path to the *spiritual democracy* that alone reflects the promise of the bright side of the Enlightenment heritage that birthed America, and kindled a beacon of liberty that still shines through fogs of war?

Time will tell. This book is my attempt to put a word in Time's ear.

PART I

THE GREAT RESET

AND THE

DIALECTIC OF ENLIGHTENMENT

CHAPTER 1

EVENT 201: LAUNCHING THE GREAT RESET

Author and cultural critic Charles Eisenstein has written a number of insightful essays on the topic of Covid. Nonetheless, I find myself taking serious issue with speculations he aired in his December 4, 2021, Substack posting.[5]

"The Human Family" records Eisenstein's Covid-related contemplations while basking in the afterglow of his family's Thanksgiving gathering. As far as Covid vaccines are concerned, Eisenstein's family scatters all over the map. Some champion vaccination; others just as vehemently oppose; others are in between. Despite these differences, Eisenstein and his clan enjoyed a lovely Thanksgiving unmarred by acrimony. Covid issues were not avoided, but never emerged as a contentious issue. How did Eisenstein and his family manage such temperance?

Calm prevailed in large part because (so Eisenstein surmises) everyone at the table felt secure in their standing as a valued member of the familial tribe. No one felt the need to convince anyone else of the rightness of their position in order to affirm their own identity. Eisenstein presents his family's gathering as a kind of prototype of how the fissures in society might close and form a bridge to a better future:

> I have a premonition about how the Covid rift in society will heal. The season of storms will end with a whimper. Neither side will admit they were wrong. Instead, everyone will quietly decide it wasn't that important. Mandates will peter out. People will stop caring who is vaccinated and who isn't.... Just as the public ceased to be terrified of terrorism (which like Covid was never quite the threat it was trumped up to be) so also will Covid fear fade into the background. Die-hard partisans on one side will say, "It was the vaccines that stopped it." On the other side they will say, "We finally reached natural herd immunity," or, "The virus has evolved to be less virulent." Most people won't care.[6]

Why does Eisenstein's imagination of Covid World fading gently as the night seem to me implausible, indeed, dangerously naive, especially for a thinker of his sophistication? That question can be answered with a single noun: The Matrix.

If the Covid controversies that vex society had originally been engendered by largely personal insecurities, Eisenstein's scenario might qualify as reasonable. Yet that assessment falls far short of any adequate description of the relevant sociopolitical reality. The conflicts at the war fronts described in the last chapter of the prior volume of *Reset or Renaissance*[7] were not instigated by ordinary people. While the public sphere does to some degree depend upon personal psychology and interpersonal dynamics, institutional and other higher orders of social organization represent distinct strata of reality that exert their own powerful sway. The turmoil that threatens democratic norms in Australia and Austria, in France, Germany, the U.S.A. and elsewhere, did not begin around a Thanksgiving table. Nor will it end there.

A complex system of power that works through an array of political and cultural institutions created Covid World and the controlling narrative that continues to shape its interpretation. I have already outlined many of the features of this Matrix, but here will endeavor a more formal description of this formidable force.

Here, in rudimentary form, is a diagram of the Matrix:

Industry/Corporate Interests (*e.g., Big Pharma, Big Tech*)

Government

Universities/Research Institutions *(Science)*

Health Care Systems *(Medicine)*

Media (*Legacy Media—Mainstream Press,*
Radio, Television. Social Media)

The Citizenry

The diagram schematically represents dynamics that helped create and sustain Covid World. It depicts a kind of pyramid of power flowing chiefly from the top down that works roughly as follows:

Big Pharma and its vested interests infiltrate governments by way of sheer financial leverage, massive lobbying efforts, and various mechanisms of corruption (e.g., revolving doors connecting the pharmaceutical industry and federal agencies). This results in the effective capture of critical government agencies that consequently no longer function independently and are rendered incapable of providing effective oversight. This negative influence ripples through government as a whole, conditioning executive, legislative, and even judicial opinion so that, to the extent this corruptive effect dominates, state power serves not to protect public health and welfare but (even if often unintentionally) to promote policies that benefit pharmaceutical companies and other related corporate interests.

Government agency directives and funds materially influence both science and medicine by way of relevant institutions. Grant money from agencies such as the National Institute of Health (NIH) or Center for Disease Control (CDC) support certain research projects and not others; journals charged (officially or unofficially) with supporting government policy exhibit marked biases in deciding what papers are accepted. Federal agencies (such as the CDC) enter the business of not merely setting guidelines, but publishing health protocols that dictate acceptable terms of medical practice. Treatment decisions favorable to Big Pharma are effectively mandated and divergence from recommended protocols precluded and even criminalized. Medical licensing boards fall in line, employing their power over professional livelihoods to ensure enforcement of government approved policies and protocols.

Technology platforms providing social media services are likewise conditioned by government directives, which may overtly or covertly coerce cooperation by threat of political disfavor, crippling fines, and relevant legislative action. This results in widespread censorship of online freedom of speech. Big Tech represents enormous corporate power that maintains varying degrees of operative independence from government. Even so, financial and ideological ties with pharmaceutical industry personnel and projects also materially influence relevant activity, including the use of algorithms to winnow what is too often carelessly classed as mis- or disinformation.

More traditional forms of media (press, radio, television) are heavily influenced if not controlled by pressure stemming from both government policy directives and corporate interest. Publishers and editors decline to publish stories that contest "expert" authority. Organs such as the TNI (The Trusted News Initiative), beholden to special interests, systematically review content in order to style what is presented as "true" to conform to a given controlling narrative. Radio and television channels, especially, are often directly subject to the financial power of Big Pharma, which heavily subsidizes programming.

This typically results in dissemination of propaganda and *de facto* censorship. The result is the presentation of a version of reality molded, not in the cauldron of truth and the crucible of debate, but in the pot-boiler of officially sanctioned (and often government and/or corporate funded) illusion.

The citizenry (We, the People) occupy the bottom or base of the pyramid. The information readily available to the People (and so the basis upon which to form opinions relevant to all things Covid) consequently arrives filtered through multiple levels of influence, all conditioned by the pervasive influence raying out from the apex of power.

The top-down flow of power inscribed in the form of this diagram represents an enormously important feature of the Matrix, one fundamentally incommensurate with democracy. At the same time, two important qualifications need be registered to form a more accurate image of the whole sociopolitical picture.

First: Big Pharma and the world of corporate interest; government (which would include, among other especially relevant organs, the intelligence agencies and the Department of the Defense); research institutions and other vehicles of science (including professional journals); health care systems and medical licensing boards; Big Tech and the social media platforms it provides, and mainstream press form *a more or less integrated crisscrossing array of influences, a true interlocking Matrix of Power* as much or more than any simply construed vertically configured system.

That said, the Matrix does remain hierarchically ordered, with its chief branches typically responsive to a central organizing intelligence. This brings us to the second critical qualification.

Another level of organization needs be added to the top-floor of the Matrix, at which *multinational organizations* such as the WHO (World Health Organization) and the WEF (World Economic Forum), as well as influential *private foundations* (The Rockefeller Foundation, The Bill and Melinda Gates Foundation) and, sometimes, associated *think tanks*, play a leading role in the whole system. These organization often join forces (if they are not already fused at the hip) with corporate interests to occupy what effectively constitutes a global apex of a highly centralized system of power. NGOs (non-governmental organizations), subject to varying degrees of control by vested interests, also play a significant role, their activities often furthering government and corporate agendas in disguised form.

Depending upon one's perspective, the whole picture—and particularly the huge sway of the constellation of forces at the top—may represent a best-, or a worst-case scenario. Whichever way one sees it (I will argue, strenuously, for the latter evaluation), this more or less coordinated array of forces represents a persistently potent reality, one that no private conversation over cranberry sauce will ever magically make disappear.

This Matrix possesses its own well-defined agenda. That agenda revolves around the motive that dictates most every aspect of corporate conduct: *monetary gain.* At the same time, the Matrix draws much of its potent force from other, less narrowly economic dimensions of human enterprise. Its *profit* motive (and here I borrow a pun from British podcaster Russell Brand) is soldered to a correlative and enabling *prophet(ic)* motive. The financial machinations of the Matrix are intrinsically and integrally linked to specific ideological commitments and geopolitical goals that, in sum, comprise nothing less than a comprehensive vision of a kind of New World Order. Chief proponents—most conspicuously, WEF founder Klaus Schwab and his collaborators—first proudly named the dramatic transformation thus envisioned *The Fourth Industrial Revolution*, but more recently (and more snappily) have rechristened their project *The Great Reset.*

What is the Great Reset, and what does this latest and greatest release from our Matrix rock stars have to do with Covid-19?

Let's begin with the second part of that question, the answer to which is relatively easy: *Just about everything.* A mountain of evidence points to the conclusion that actions sponsored by and deriving from the Matrix are responsible for: 1) Scientific gain-of-function research that engineered the Sars-CoV-2 virus and (whether through deliberate or unintentional release) led to the escape of the Covid virus in the vicinity of Wuhan; 2) Implementation of the whole Vaccine-Distance System of Covid response upon escape of the virus; 3) Crafting the controlling narrative that legitimates that response system; 4) All the ancillary measures (e.g., acts of censorship; sabotage of early treatment options) that continue to maintain that Vaccine-Distance System and its legitimating narrative in place by suppressing or beating back challenges to its veracity and authority; and 5) Promotion of measures (such as various social distancing rules as well as vaccine mandates and passports) that threaten to make official as well as unofficial rules and norms derivative of Matrix-influence a permanent feature of society.

This last clause brings us to a preliminary grasp of the idea of the Great Reset itself. As stated, it implies that widespread transformations (social, political, economic, psychological) instigated by the Matrix and originally introduced in response to Covid-19 may extend far beyond the pandemic and its immediate consequences. That extension is proposed in the form of a deliberate revisioning of a new post-pandemic world reality that is both (a) grounded in and fundamentally shaped by changes catalyzed by the pandemic, and (b) largely commensurate with the program of Schwab's Fourth Industrial Revolution or Great Reset. Accordingly, Schwab makes an equation of Covid-19 and the Great Reset into the very title of his latest book, *COVID-19: The Great Reset.*[8]

The word "Reset" denotes a closing down, a temporary termination of an entire system of operation followed by a re-opening of the system. The idea of *reset* differs materially from the sort of *restart* familiar in a computer context. Whereas the latter denotes a mere re-booting, reset implies that, while the system will be re-opened fairly quickly, the very ground of its activity will have been essentially altered and a new updated operating system installed.

The radical and even revolutionary character of that update can hardly be sufficiently accented here because we are speaking, in Schwab and his co-author Thierry Malleret's conception, not of any old reset, but of the *Great* Reset. Schwab and Malleret accordingly encourage us to imagine change of the greatest conceivable order of magnitude when contemplating the meaning of the phrase. Richard Ramsbotham, commenting upon Schwab and Malleret's book in an article titled "Covid-19 and 'The Great Reset': What is it All About and Where is it Heading" puts the gist of the matter succinctly: "There [*in Covid-19: The Great Reset*] we learn that Covid-19 is... the trigger for a complete reset of almost every single aspect of our lives."[9]

Schwab and Malleret's own words certainly bear out the apocalyptic dimensions of the envisioned transformation:

> Many of us are pondering when things will return to normal. The short response is: never.... Some analysts call it a major bifurcation, others refer to a deep crisis of "biblical" proportions.... Radical changes of such consequence are coming that some pundits have referred to a "before coronavirus" (BC) and "after coronavirus" (AC) era.[10]

The birth of Jesus Christ is not the only historical watershed Schwab and Malleret reference in order to image the world-transforming character of Covid-19. Noting that "epidemics throughout history have proven to be a force for lasting and radical change," our authors recite a litany of dramatic sociopolitical transformations catalyzed by pandemics. Suggesting that "the rise of the absolutist state, the gradual retreat of the church, and many other historical events...can be attributed in no small measure to pandemics," Schwab and Malleret cite Barbara Tuchman's specuation that the Black Death (which killed roughly a third of the European population) "may have been the unrecognized beginning of modern man."[11] Ramsbotham parses relevant passages:

> Comparing Covid-19 with the Black Death in the Middle Ages, Schwab asks: "If such profound social, political and economic changes could be provoked by the plague in the medieval world, could the Covid-19 pandemic mark the onset of a similar turning point?" And naming World War Two "the quintessential transformational war" he compares this also with Covid-19: "the magnitude of their transformative power is comparable" After a few pages of this he adds: "You get the point: we should take advantage of this unprecedented opportunity to reimagine our world."[12]

Schwab and Malleret's book naturally lobbies us to do that reimagining along the lines they envision and outline. I, however, find something deeply disingenuous in the whole proposition. Why? Not because I disagree with Schwab and Malleret's contention that the event of Covid-19 and humankind's response to it represent a critical crossroads in the history of humankind. I have said as much. The issue, however, lies in the question of the perspective from which one considers the matter and the path one might choose to take in response to the phenomenon.

The Great Reset gives the impression that the Covid-19 pandemic more or less appeared out of the blue, and that its authors are deliberating how to meet the challenges it poses from a largely objective and deeply humane perspective; one essentially unprejudiced by prior investments or special interests. If, however, we take the book and its authors (Schwab, remember, is the historic founder of the WEF) as representative of the interests of the Matrix, nothing could be further from the truth.

I have already stated that "a mountain of evidence" suggests that Matrix forces were deeply involved in creating both the conditions that eventually resulted in the escape of the Sars-CoV-2 virus and the system of response that dominated official Covid-19 policy world-wide. Let's touch briefly on the first claim before addressing, at length, the second.

On the one hand, Fauci's NIH did sponsor illegal gain-of-function research involving the coronavirus in the Laboratory of Virology in Wuhan, a facility repeatedly accused of falling far short of the safety standards proper to such dangerous research. Moreover, the first coronavirus cases reportedly involved lab personnel.

On the other hand, no reliable evidence (e.g., identification of a specific animal host) has surfaced to support the theory of natural zoonotic transmission, itself an exceptional circumstance as the jump from animal to human hosts faces diverse biological impediments. How fantastically improbable, then, is the supposition that the ongoing gain-of-function work with coronavirus at the Wuhan Lab had nothing whatsoever to do with the Covid-19 pandemic that just happened to originate in the immediate vicinity?

A great deal more has been written on the subject (including the coordinated Chinese and American coverup that aimed to discredit the lab leak theory),[13] and I will come back to it in a later chapter. Here, though, let's examine the evidence suggesting that—far from representing an unexpected occurrence—the Covid-19 pandemic was an event clearly foreseen and deliberately and thoroughly prepared for by personnel at the highest echelons of the Matrix.

Conspicuous verification of this remarkable fact is neither obscure nor hidden. On the contrary, it is an open secret: available, in plain view, for any and all to witness. To begin with, just (re)start your computer, and google: "Event 201."

A high-level wargame-like simulation staged by, and for the benefit of, a select group of business and political leaders, Event 201 convened in New York City just ten weeks before Covid-19 burst upon the world. What was the basis of the simulated scenario? *The eruption of a pandemic caused by a coronavirus.* And the purpose of this extraordinary exercise? *To educate those involved regarding how best to respond to such a situation.* As described by the Event 201 website: "Prominent individuals from global business, government, and public health were exercise players tasked with leading policy response to a fictional outbreak scenario in the Event 201 pandemic tabletop exercise."[14]

The Event 201 website (still proudly on view) provides informative practical details pertaining to the simulation—including its star-cast of sponsors—as well as a flavor of the larger intent shaping the elaborate proceedings:

The Johns Hopkins Center for Health Security in partnership with the World Economic Forum and the Bill and Melinda Gates Foundation hosted event 201, a high-level pandemic exercise on October 18, 2019, in New York, NY. The exercise illustrated areas where public/private partnerships will be necessary during the response to a severe pandemic in order to diminish large-scale economic and societal consequences.

Statement about nCoV and our pandemic exercise

In recent years, the world has seen a growing number of epidemic events, amounting to approximately 200 events annually. These events are increasing, and they are disruptive to health, economies, and society. Managing these events already strains global capacity, even absent a pandemic threat. Experts agree that it is only a matter of time before one of these epidemics becomes global—a pandemic with potentially catastrophic consequences. A severe pandemic, which becomes "Event 201," would require reliable cooperation among several industries, national governments, and key international institutions.[15]

Note, in particular, the constellation of power cited in this last sentence. Event 201 planners imagines private industry, national government, and international institutions as the parties primarily responsible for organizing any effective pandemic response. That power trio, along with influential private foundations such as the Bill and Melinda Gates Foundation (which sponsored Event 201), represents the constellation occupying the top floor of the Matrix, while the third Event 201 sponsor—The Johns Hopkins Center for Health Security—adds another key element of the integrated array of power and intelligence responsible for the shots heard around the world in the spring of 2020.

The cast of Event 201 participants mirrors the make-up of the sponsorship of the event, and constitutes a virtual who's who (or who is WHO) of top-level Matrix personnel. I provide a brief profile of some of the key players in the course of the ensuing discussion. A more thorough knowledge of the same can be obtained by clicking on the "Players" link on the Event 201 website and reviewing the profiles provided there, an exercise that proves an efficient means of obtaining a well-focused snapshot of the type of people that man the Matrix guns.

It is naturally worth noting that Event 201 took place only a few short months before the actual coronavirus "pandemic" turned the whole world upside down. Nor is temporal proximity the only eerie element of this coincidence. Many of the chief features of the system of Covid response enacted in

2020 track with almost surreal fidelity the strategies and tactics showcased and practiced at Event 201. In fact, some critics call Event 201 a dress rehearsal, the last, polished phase of preparation for a performance that will soon be publicly staged.

As a way of entering into the substance of the proceedings, let's briefly review some of the "7 Recommendations for Readiness"[16] answering to the "Joint Call for Pandemic Preparedness and Response," a document posted by the triumvirate of Event 201 sponsors in the aftermath of the simulation. The first reads:

> 1. Governments, international organizations, and businesses should plan now for how essential corporate capabilities will be utilized during a large-scale pandemic.

Note again the power trio (governments, international organizations, businesses) charged with responsibility for effective response. Note, too, most especially, the marked emphasis in this very first recommendation—one that sets the tone for all the rest—on "corporate capabilities" and their integration with government response.

The second recommendation reads:

> 2. Industry, national governments, and international organizations should work together to enhance internationally held stockpiles of medical countermeasures (MCMs) to enable rapid and equitable distribution during a severe pandemic.

The first two recommendations jointly envision groundwork preparing close cooperation between federal governments and pharmaceutical companies, chief providers of the MCMs mentioned in the second. The fourth and (to a lesser extent) the third reflect preoccupation with collaborative relationships between members of the power trio that might facilitate production and distribution of MCMs; most notably, the vaccines that are the first-mentioned form of such.

> 3. Countries, international organizations, and global transportation companies should work together to maintain travel and trade during severe pandemics.
>
> 4. Governments should provide more resources and support for the development and surge manufacturing of vaccines, therapeutics, and diagnostics that will be needed during a severe pandemic.

The first four recommendations thus all ultimately involve creating conditions conducive to what is finally explicitly named in the fourth: "Surge manufacturing of vaccines, therapeutics, and diagnostics." The Event 201 platform, as represented in these recommendations, presumes (or posits as axiomatic) that just this form of enterprise will constitute the chief line of defense in case of an outbreak, an eventuality the Event sponsors considered both inevitable and imminent.

The platform clearly adumbrates the most central plank of the strategy that shaped (with a few notable exceptions concentrated in relatively undeveloped areas of the world) governmental response to Covid-19 world-wide: namely, the vaccine-centric solution to the Covid challenge. Therapeutics are indeed mentioned in the same breath as vaccines, but still within the broader context of government and corporate industry collaboration. This implies that use of inexpensive, off-patent, repurposed drugs by physicians that would not require high-level coordination of Big Pharma and government (for instance, the widespread use of hydroxychloroquine or ivermectin) are not only excluded from the Event 201 strategic response plan, but are positively antithetical to it. Such initiatives do *not* depend upon the high-level collaboration of industrial innovation (Big Pharma inventing and developing new drugs that can be patented) and government (government contracts to purchase such products and implement their distribution).

This critical point is suggestive of a still more telling general truth: The Event 201 Response Plan, as reflected in the Seven Recommendations and the curricular content of the program as a whole, places *no emphasis whatsoever on academic (including scientific) integrity and freedom, local or independent medical expertise, the doctor-patient relationship, or good health practices.* Indeed, any mention of such initiatives, which are inherently for the most part independent of a centralized system of global control, are entirely excluded. One may accordingly infer that this class of actions (as in the aforementioned instance of the widespread use of repurposed drugs) contravenes the ideological and geopolitical program that—although hardly openly declared—underwrites the entire organization of Event 201.

Given the character of the event's sponsorship, this is hardly surprising. The influence of the players at or near the apex of the Matrix pyramid (corporate industry, multinational organizations such as the WEF, government agencies, and high-level research institutions) logically stands in an *inverse* relation to the quotient of power and responsibility accorded individual choice, medical or health freedom, and local control. The more weight given to the latter, the less central the role and degree of control exercised by the former, and vice versa.

This qualifies as a defining feature of the Matrix as it is presently organized and pervasively operative. Its founding ideological, sociopolitical, and psychological premises are antithetical to respect for intellectual impartiality, individual rights, freedom of choice, and local prerogative. The Matrix is, by nature, a centralized system of global control, the power of which feeds off the body politic. Nor are its ends and means commensurate with any citizenry which (eschewing the uniformity imposed by authoritarian forms of rule) aspires to democracy: governance "of, by, and for the people" and the honoring of civil rights and liberties.

I have not yet described the substantive agenda characteristic of Schwab's Fourth Industrial Revolution, and so, too, the Great Reset. Even so, the foregoing discussion discloses one defining feature of that program. Although its proponents will hardly openly acknowledge it, the agenda involves forms of sociopolitical transformation that entail a wholesale transfer of power from the individual and local (grassroots) level to a centralized system of a global elite, superbly represented by personnel in attendance at Event 201.

The fact, form and content of the entire simulation bears out the truth of that contention. Although I cannot cover the whole weekend long affair, the seventh and last recommendation, along with the text of the simulation session from which it emerged, offers especially telling (one might even say incriminating) evidence of the veracity of this claim. That last recommendation reads:

> 7. Governments and the private sector should assign a greater priority to developing methods to combat mis- and dis-information prior to the next pandemic response.

This is startling. Why should a group dedicated, in good faith, to the task of planning an effective pandemic response *presume* that official actions would incite *unwarranted* resistance? On what grounds might such a group simply *assume* the veracity of official story-lines and so automatically identify prospective dissent as "mis- and dis-information" that need be (and here the military metaphor is revealing) "*combated*"?

The recommendation takes as axiomatic that "governments and the private sector" (e.g., relevant industries, such as pharmaceutical, tech, and other corporate entities) possess a kind of monopoly on truth and insight into what is best for the public welfare. The recommendation does *not* advise that policymakers should be prepared to welcome critical input from scientists that work *independently* of government and industry, local doctors and health practitioners, the citizenry itself, and other sectors of society (e.g., advocacy groups and the like). It makes not the slightest gesture towards recognition that mounting an effective response to a pandemic requires the kind of willing participation of all involved best served by preserving the debate and dialogue proper to a democratic society; one open to a fair hearing of multiple points of view. Instead the recommendation urges the joint industry-government rulership to arm itself, in advance, with political and rhetorical weapons that will enable it effectively to delegitimize and silence any voices that might question the wisdom of its rule.

Correlatively, the 201 playscript reads as if it should be expected that official conduct will incite dramatic and radical resistance. This cannot but suggest that the Event 201 sponsors knew—in advance—that the system of pandemic response rehearsed in New York would, if implemented, sooner or later put government *at odds with the people.* According to the sociopolitical logic that underlies the proceedings, those contesting the official position need to be framed, not as conscientious citizens exercising lawful rights of freedom of speech and expression, but as enemies of the state and of the public good.

The entire transcript of the event bears out this disturbing conclusion.

The Event 201 simulation was organized into five topical segments: 1) an Introductory and Medical Countermeasure (MCM) discussion; 2) a Trade and Travel discussion; 3) a Finance discussion; 4) a Communications discussion; and 5) Hotwash and Conclusion. As indicated by the assignment of an entire segment to matters of communication, Event 201 lavished significant attention upon issues related to media and public relations management.

The Event website presents video coverage of each of the segments, and the *precís* of the Communications discussion presented on the Hotwash and Conclusions video conveys the gist of the conversation on that topic. The woman acting as narrator in this section (she does not herself act the role of one of the "players," but functions as a mouthpiece of its original conception) intones:

> Finally, government and the private sector should assign a greater priority to developing methods to combat mis- and dis-information related to pandemic response. Governments will need to partner with traditional and social media in order to research and develop nimble approaches to countering mis-information. For their part, media companies, we believe,

> should commit to ensuring that authoritative messages are prioritized and false messages suppressed.[17]

Clips devoted to communications on the highlight reel confirm and elaborate *the message of restrictive control,* and can also serve to introduce us to the type of personnel in attendance at Event 201.

According to his LinkedIn profile, Matthew Harrington is Global President and Chief Operating Officer at Edelmann,

> a global communications firm that partners with business and organizations to evolve, promote and protect their brands and reputations. A trusted C-suite adviser, Matthew is a specialist in corporate positioning and reputation management.[18]

Big Tech firms, including Bill Gates's brainchild Microsoft, represent Edelmann's most important client base, followed closely by multiple Big Pharma firms, including Pfizer, AstraZeneca, and Johnson & Johnson.[19]

Before Harrington's highlight moment, the screen lingers some moments on capital letters spelling out the message:

Misinformation Is Undercutting Efforts to Control the Pandemic

For his part, Harrington has this to offer on the topic:

> We're at a moment where the social media platforms have to step forward and recognize that the moment to assert that they are a technology platform and not a broadcaster is over. They in fact have to be a participant in broadcasting accurate information and partnering with the scientific and health communities to counterweight, if not flood the zone, of accurate information. Because to put the genii back in the bottle of the misinformation and disinformation is nigh impossible.[20]

Harrington's talk about "flooding the zone" foreshadows the tsunami of media attention that even today continues to inundate the populace, most of which serves to reinforce "authoritative messages" (Covid is a deadly, invisible, ubiquitous enemy; the vaccines are safe and effective, etc.). The social media censorship predicted and sanctioned by the general tenor of his remarks figures as one of the most disturbing and democracy-destroying features of the Covid landscape. Not only has, for instance, YouTube deplatformed whole programs (Brett Weinstein's *Dark Horse* podcast; Del Bigtree's *The Highwire*, and much, much more), Facebook and other mainstream social media services routinely scrub any postings considered unfriendly to the controlling narrative.[21] This practice includes such spectacularly inhumane actions as disappearing the cohort of vaccine-injured persons who were using Facebook to connect with and support each other.[22]

What if, however, tech companies do *not* step up to the plate and swing the "purifying" censer with sufficient force?

Lavan Thiru, Deputy Director at the Monetary Authority of Singapore, offers some tentative thoughts on that matter:

> One thing we haven't spoken about, and I'm wondering whether it is time to talk about this, is a step up on the part of the government on enforcement actions against fake news.[23]

Thiru's comments, like Harrington's, raise the question of how to distinguish "accurate" from "mis-" or "dis-" information"; "fake" from "real" news. Both merely assume that established authorities are in the position to make that determination more or less unilaterally, and may need to be empowered to enforce their views *whatever the cost to freedom of speech*—including the speech of independent researchers and experts whose views must be regarded as indispensable *if* the science guiding pandemic response is to reflect the most advanced, impartial, well-vetted inquiry. On the governmental front, moreover, censorial abuses of power lurk around the corner, legitimated by the *ideology of centralized control* that permeates every C-suite perfumed corner of Event 201.

A conversation involving Harringtom, Avril Haines, and Dr. Tom Inglesby sheds more dark light on the public relations matter at hand. In October 2019, Inglesby was director of the Johns Hopkins Center for Health Security, and an advisor to the NIH, Pentagon, and Department of Homeland Security. In early 2020 he moved over to the U.S. Department of Health and Human Services as senior advisor for its Covid-19 response, and so, like many other Event 201 participants, into a position directly responsible for Covid-19 management.

Avril Haines is another such individual. A former CIA Deputy Director, in April, 2021, President Biden appointed Haines as director of National Intelligence, in which capacity she ranks as one of the highest officials in charge of the U.S. pandemic response.

Addressing the matter of communications, Haines cautioned of "false information that is starting to actually hamper our ability to address the pandemic,"[24] suggesting that it might consequently be advisable to saturate media channels with proper messaging from reliable ("trusted") sources. Harrington responds:

> I think just to build a little bit on what Avril said...I think, as in previous conversations where we've talked about centralization around management of information or public health needs, there needs to be a centralized response around the communications approach that then is cascaded to informed advocates, represented in the NGO communities, the medical professionals, et cetera.[25]

Inglesby affirms the need for such centralization, while querying whether that strategy extends beyond national boundaries. "You mean," Inglesby asks in response to Harrington, "centralized international?" Harrington answers affirmatively that the capacity to gain access to pertinent information should be "...centralized on an international basis, because I think there needs to be a central repository of data facts and key messages."[26]

The conversation thus highlights the unbounded purview, the *global* character, of the centralized system of control envisioned by our blue-ribbon Matrix member Event 201 participants. Harrington's response to Inglesby, moreover, points to another salient feature of this system: its reliance upon the kind of extensive data collection dependent upon technologically advanced means of procurement and data processing.

Jane Halton, another participant, has occupied posts in both Australia's Health and Finance ministries and served as president of WHO's World Health Assembly. At present, she chairs Bill Gates's global Coalition for Epidemic Preparedness and, since March 2020, is a member of the Executive Board of the Australian national Covid-19 Coordination Commission.[27] Halton adds her two cents on the topic of communications, not only repeating control strategies already cited but—like Harrington, yet in a somewhat different manner—highlighting the critical role technology might play:

> I personally do not believe that trying to shut things down in terms of information is either practical or desirable. We do have a couple of strategies that are available to us, one of which is the flood strategy, the second of which is relying, and informing, and equipping trusted sources of information with the facts so they then can pass that on. But we also need to actually think about a technological answer to this.[28]

What is Halton referring to here? As Kennedy reports in his big Fauci book, off-camera, Halton informed her colleagues that the Gates Foundation was already hard at work inventing algorithms that would effectively winnow information on social media platforms to prevent dissemination of material that might be deemed harmful mis- or disinformation.[29]

This, remember, several months before Covid-19 burst upon the world-scene.

We verge here, as well, on that other chief characteristic of the agenda associated with the Great Reset. The centralized governance inherent to it requires sophisticated means of control that highly advanced technological systems are best suited to provide. The Fourth Industrial Revolution or Great Reset (insofar as it materializes) ushers in a form of world rule aptly termed *technocracy*. In the words of one of its harshest critics, "The backbone and infrastructure of technocracy is technology."[30]

The technocratic agenda, as advanced by the likes of Schwab and Bill Gates, represents a complex phenomenon involving systematic transformation of multiple interrelated dimensions of society. *COVID-19: The Great Reset* includes lengthy sections on Economic Reset, Societal Reset, Geopolitical Reset, Environmental Reset, and Technological Reset as well as a major part dedicated to Industry and Business, which treats of subjects such as the acceleration of digitalization, resilient supply chains, government and business, stakeholder capitalism, and ESG (environmental, social, and governance considerations).

While the book puts the whole Great Reset enterprise in the most positive imaginable light, its detractors take a sharply different view. Here is one critic's summary of the gist of the technocratic project, one that provides important historical context and opens a window on the integration of economic, technological, and political dimensions intrinsic to it:

> Technocracy is a resource-based economic system that began in the 1930s during the height of the Great Depression, when scientists and engineers got together to solve the nation's economic problems. It looked like capitalism and free enterprise were failing, so they decided to invent a new economic system from scratch. They called this system technocracy.
>
> Rather than being based on pricing mechanisms such as supply and demand, technocracy is based on resource allocation and social engineering through technology. Under this system, companies would be told what resources they're allowed to use, when, and for what, and consumers would be told what to buy.[31]

The original technocratic vision has been updated to include, as a vital and empowering component, new technological capacities:

> Artificial intelligence (AI), digital surveillance, and Big Data collection play very important roles, as does the digitization of industries and government, such as banking and health care. Together these technologies allow for the automation of social engineering and social rule, thereby doing away with the need for elected government leaders. Nations are to be led by unelected leaders who own all the world's resources and decide what is to become of them.[32]

This critique consciously slants the definition of "technocracy" to comport with the version endorsed by the WEF. More generally, though, one can understand "technocracy" as any system of rule wherein (often unelected) persons viewed as "experts," regarded as such because of the specialized (or technical) knowledge they possess in a given area, wield a disproportionate degree of power. They do so in part because informed decision making is presumed beyond the competence of the average citizen.

Of course, modern proponents of technocracy seldom if ever put the matter in terms as stark and unappealing as those sketched above. On the face of it, technocracy, as so described, appears profoundly antithetical not only to democracy, but to free market capitalism and the attachment to private ownership so deeply ingrained in the American psyche. Nonetheless, the putative aim of the technocratic system—at least in its new dress as the Great Reset—is governance of society in a form that not only provides the administrative capabilities requisite to meet the formidable crises facing the international community today (the capacity to respond efficiently to a pandemic, or meet the challenge of climate change), but additionally re-organizes human resources in a manner that serves both ecological and social justice.

When the WEF formally launched the Great Reset, it naturally did not speak of any degradation of organic system, *or* constriction of individual sovereignty, civil liberties, or human rights. On the contrary, it declared that the Great Reset

> will address the need for a more fair, sustainable and resilient future, and a new social contract centered on human dignity, social justice and where societal progress does not fall behind economic development.[33]

The new post-Covid edition of the Great Reset places still greater emphasis on the capacity of the proposed New World Order to address and rectify longstanding social and political inequalities. In pitching their system, Schwab and Malleret contend that such difficulties have already eroded trust in government and, indeed, the viability of the social contract that underwrites civil society *per se*. Schwab and Malleret:

> Today, the fundamental reasons underpinning the loss of faith in our social contracts coalesce around issues of inequality, the ineffectiveness of most redistribution policies, a sense of exclusion and marginalization, and a general sentiment of unfairness. This is why many citizens have begun to denounce a breakdown of the social contract, expressing more and more forcefully a general loss of trust in institutions and leaders.[34]

Schwab and Malleret further note that, in recent times, "populist and extremist parties" have often been able to capitalize on the "widespread exasperation" bred of such difficulties to win important elections. Schwab and Malleret, however, endorse a different form of redress:

> Although they are complex, the policy solutions do exist and broadly consist in adapting the welfare state to today's world by empowering people and by responding to the demands for a fairer social contract. Over the past few years, several international organizations and think tanks have adjusted to this new reality and outlined proposals on how to make it happen.[35]

Schwab and Malleret naturally accord the disruption occasioned by COVID-19 an important role in the envisioned transformation:

> The pandemic will mark a turning point by accelerating this transition. It has crystallized the issue and made a return to the pre-pandemic status quo impossible.[36]

The above passages suggest a few salient features of the special Schwab-Malleret brand of the Reset program. The respect accorded "international organizations and think tanks" rings with Matrix overtones, especially when one of the think tanks cited happens to be the World Bank. The conspicuous accent on state power also deserves special regard. The theme finds more explicit and extensive emphasis elsewhere in the book, which devotes an entire chapter to (and here I cite the chapter title): "The Return of 'Big' Government." There we read:

> One of the great lessons of the past five centuries in Europe and America is this: acute crises contribute to boosting the power of the state. It's always been the case and there is no reason why it should be different with the COVID-19 pandemic.[37]

As a passage from the same chapter discloses, the *political* fact of increased state power bears directly upon the very foundation of *economic* philosophy and policy, which in turn affects policies pertinent to the spheres of health and education:

> Almost overnight, the coronavirus succeeded in altering perceptions about the complex and delicate balance between the private and public realms in favour of the latter. It has revealed that social insurance is efficient and that offloading an ever-greater deal of responsibilities (like health and education) to individuals and the markets may not be in the best interests of society. In a surprising and sudden turnaround, the idea, which would have been anathema just a few years ago, that governments can further the public good while runaway economies without supervision can wreak havoc on social welfare may now become the norm. On the dial that measures the continuum between the government and the markets, the needle has decisively moved towards the left.[38]

Reading between the lines of this and other passages, one can hardly avoid an unpleasant conclusion. For all the upbeat and progressive sounding hoopla the Great Reset heralds as integral to the revolution it so names, its technocratic program sacrifices the human individual on the altar of the public good as the latter is defined by—not the will of We, the People, or the independent prerogative of the ordinary citizen—but the judgment of the select and privileged few whose interests ultimately find expression through the power of the state.

If this appears a hasty and undeserved conclusion, let's consider, for a moment, how a leading exemplar of Matrix political philosophy and policy and a co-sponsor of Event 201 generally *thinks* about human rights and, correspondingly, the relative merit of American and Chinese forms of governance in times of crisis.

In an August 2020 interview with *The Economist,*[39] Bill Gates offers these remarks in conversation with editor-in-chief Zanny Minton Beddoes:

> ***The Economist*** **(Minton Beddoes)**: What about China? Should we blame them...or should we praise them for the degree to which they got it under control internally?
>
> **Bill Gates:** They clearly made mistakes at the beginning.... But after that, in their typical, fairly authoritarian way, they did a very good job at suppressing the virus. There may have been a lot of individual rights that were violated there, but the overall macro effect that they achieved is kind of amazing!

> ***The Economist***: Now let's turn to the U.S.... Why has it done so badly?
>
> **Bill Gates** (smiling): Well, we believe in freedom. Individual freedom. We optimize for individual rights.

Richard Ramsbotham cites this exchange in his article, adding this relevant comment:

> Gates's response is unsettling because he isn't praising individual rights and freedoms, but almost laughing at them, as if to say, "Well, what kind of response can you expect from people who want freedom?"[40]

To anyone who knows anything about Gates and his Foundation, it goes without saying that much of the interview revolves around how to best kick-start a campaign of universal vaccination. Gates takes virtually for granted that such represents the only conceivable means of ending the pandemic. "To bring the epidemic to an end, we do need a vaccine."[41]

With respect to the question of human rights, the proponents of the Great Reset, often more politically savvy than Gates in *The Economist* interview, seldom acknowledge the extent to which their agenda is predicated upon the restriction of individual freedom. While this truth cannot be altogether hidden, it can be obscured and rhetorically trumped by reference to that other, supposedly greater good: *the collective welfare.*

Speaking as a political philosopher, I hold the dichotomy thus introduced to be a false one. *True community and social cohesion ultimately depend upon the humanity and moral conscience of free individuals,* not the kind of authoritarian coercion too often introduced in the name of the public good. Schwab and Malleret, however, *do* posit a rigid dualism, and make very clear which side they come down on in their role as heralds of the New World Order.

The following remarks regarding health insurance apply to sociopolitical life in general. Schwab and Malleret's squirmy sentences sound like a kinder and gentler version of Bill Gates:

> This is ultimately a moral choice about whether to prioritize the qualities of individualism or those that favour the destiny of the community. It is an individual as well as a collective choice (that can be expressed through elections), but the example of the pandemic shows that highly individualistic societies are not very good at expressing solidarity.[42]

For a book authored by two economists, *The Great Reset*, in fact, spends a surprising amount of time and effort debating matters of moral philosophy, openly acknowledging that, in a matter of such cataclysmic magnitude, such questions can in no wise be gainsaid. Their position with respect to these questions, however, remains disturbingly consistent, one-sidedly denigrating the value of individual rights. In a section titled "Moral Choices," Schwab and Malleret opine that, in a world shaken by the coronavirus, and so one that calls humanity to greater self-reflection,

> we could assume that we are now more individually aware of the fact that our decisions are infused with values and informed by moral choices. It might follow that, if (but it is a big "if") in the future we abandon the posture of self-interest that pollutes so many of our social interactions, we may be able to pay more attention to issues like inclusivity and fairness.[43]

Inclusivity and fairness: The words certainly have a pleasant ring. Yet is this not an instance of the wolf preaching gentleness to the lamb?

Another passage intimates what we could already guess readily enough: Those who stand to be *included* in the new social contract envisioned by The Great Reset, and who will thus qualify for "fair" treatment, are only those willing to obey the orders, issued by the authoritative ("expert") organs of global governance, that tell people what they must do if the world is to be saved from destruction:

> Will COVID-19 result in people withdrawing into themselves, or will it nourish their innate sense of empathy and collaboration, encouraging them towards greater solidarity? The examples of previous pandemics are not very encouraging, but this time there is a fundamental difference: we are all collectively aware that without greater collaboration, we will be unable to address the global challenges that we collectively face. Put in the simplest possible terms: if, as human beings, we do not collaborate to confront our existential challenges (the environment and the global governance free fall, among others) we are doomed. Thus, we have no choice but to summon up the better angels of our nature.[44]

The better angels of our nature? Let us be clear: Event 201, cosponsored by Gates and the WEF as well as Johns Hopkins, showcased the kind of measures Schwab and Malleret and Gates and their Matrix ilk endorse as necessary to inaugurate The Great Reset. As confirmed by the fact that many Event 201 participants (Inglesby, Haines, and Halton to mention three already cited) have subsequently played key roles in administrating the world wide Covid response, the Vaccine-Distance System of response actually implemented constitutes a real-time actualization of (early stages of) the Fourth Industrial

Revolution/Great Reset agenda. We are, that is, in the midst of the Matrix-sponsored experiment to realize, to the fullest possible extent, that agenda.

To this proposition may be added this critical correlate: We do not, therefore, need to take the likes of Gates, Malleret, and Schwab's word for what implementation of the Great Reset might actually look like, and what values it does or does not promote. Instead, we can, as good evidence-based researchers, examine our world today, considering all that has transpired and continues to manifest and so comprise sociocultural reality since March 2020, and evaluate for ourselves the objective merit and human value of the Matrix program.

Need I reiterate, after all that has already been shown and told, that such objective reality belies—blatantly contradicts—the progressive values and altruistic morality espoused by Matrix personnel? The official Covid-19 system of response has not in fact secured public health and welfare or renewed trust in public institutions, but rather had the opposite effect. It does not address economic and social inequalities in order to mend our disintegrating social contract or restore dignity to human being. Thus the Great Reset is not, in point of fact, a ticket to a better world free of fear and divisive conflict, but rather a covert operation, an unspoken declaration of war on science, nature, medicine, public health, democracy, and society itself.

I articulated many of the casualties of this war throughout the preceding volume of *Reset or Renaissance* and, by way of citation of *The Real Anthony Fauci,* recapitulated and summarized many of the same in the concluding chapter of *Two Roads*. Yet the war fronts are so broad (Schwab and Malleret's allusion to World War II may, after all, not be unjustified), I have not granted due attention to all major theatres, including the economic and class dimension of the war on society.

As we have seen, *COVID-19: The Great Reset* suggests that the touted Reset can serve to rectify the gross inequalities, economic as well as social, that afflict society today. If, however, we review the facts of the matter, it would not be amiss to employ yet again a phrase I have resorted to all too frequently: *Nothing could be further from the truth.* The economic upheaval occasioned by Covid-19 has indeed dramatically transformed the profile of the world's economy, but not at all in the direction of greater equity. Inevitably, the further economic disempowerment of the middle and lower classes has racial implications as well. Kennedy:

> During the COVID pandemic, Dr. Fauci served as ringmaster in the engineered demolition of America's economy. His lockdown predictably

shattered the nation's once-booming economic engine, putting 58 million Americans out of work, and permanently bankrupting small businesses, including 41 percent of Black-owned businesses, some of which took generations of investment to build.[45]

Lest you have any doubt who benefitted from the catastrophe, Kennedy fills in some of the predictable details:

> Dr. Fauci's business closures pulverized America's middle class and engineered the largest upward transfer of wealth in human history. In 2020, workers lost $3.7 trillion while billionaires gained $3.9 trillion. Some 493 individuals became new billionaires, and an additional 8 million Americans dropped below the poverty line. The biggest winners were the robber barons—the very companies that were cheerleading Dr. Fauci's lockdown and censoring his critics: Big Technology, Big Data, Big Telecom, Big Finance, Big Media behemoths (Michael Bloomberg, Rupert Murdoch, Viacom, and Disney), and Silicon Valley Internet titans like Jeff Bezos, Bill Gates, Mark Zuckerberg, Eric Schmidt, Sergey Brin, Larry Page, Larry Ellison, and Jack Dorsey.[46]

Did not Schwab and Malleret laud big government because "runaway economies without supervision can wreak havoc on social welfare"? It turns out, however, that, if you happen to be a private sphere mogul or entrepreneur, government power need not work to check your runaway train. In fact, if it's on your side of the track, it can pull the levers that sets your engine in motion and make sure it races powerfully on, unimpeded, into the future.

If you doubt the premises of my general argument here—doubt, for instance, that the measures inaugurated in response to Covid are engineered by the Matrix, or that they are intended to extend, indefinitely, into the future—digest this passage from *The Great Reset* on social distancing:

> In one form or another, social- and physical-distancing measures are likely to persist after the pandemic itself subsides.... After a while, the enduring concerns about technological unemployment will recede as societies emphasize the need to restructure the workplace in a way that minimizes close human contact. Indeed, automation technologies are particularly well suited to a world in which human beings can't get too close to each other.... Our lingering and possibly lasting fear of being infected with a virus (COVID-19 or another) will thus speed the relentless march of automation.... The process of automation was set in motion many years ago, but...the pandemic will fast forward the adoption of automation in the workplace and the introduction of more robots in our personal and

> professional lives. From the onset of the lockdowns, it became apparent that robots and AI were the "natural" alternative when human labour was not available. Furthermore, they were used...to reduce the health risks to human employees.[47]

I have laid great emphasis, in this book, on the "V" aspect of the Vaccine-Distance response system; but, as so splendidly exhibited here, the "D" (for distance) dimension plays an equally critical role in the Matrix-sponsored war on society. The Great Reset repeatedly touts the value of collaboration and the collective welfare. In reality, however, the practical measures (such as digitalization and automation) it endorses serve to *isolate and distance and estrange* one human being from another. The fear and aversion of our friends, family, neighbors and coworkers generated by the specter of Covid death turbocharges the "divide and conquer" tactic so integral to the Matrix and its quasi-military strategy.

A passage from Charles Eisenstein's inaugural coronavirus essay[48] helps make conscious for us how, in precise accord with Schwab and Malleret's Covid-19/Great Reset recipe, a host of social practices instituted in response to Covid threaten to become permanent features of a fundamentally altered landscape of human life and culture. As social distance—the psychical as well as physical separation of human beings from each other—constitutes the kernel of diversely related phenomena, Eisenstein takes it as his point of departure:

> Initially, the argument for social distancing was that it would save millions of lives by preventing a sudden surge of Covid cases from overwhelming the medical system. Now the authorities tell us that some social distancing may need to continue indefinitely, at least until there is an effective vaccine. I would like to put that argument in a larger context, especially as we look to the long term. Lest we institutionalize distancing and reengineer society around it, let us be aware of what choice we are making and why.[49]

Eisenstein expands the argument in a manner that makes the scale of sociological transformation already in process both clear in extent and emotionally palpable:

> The same goes for the other changes happening around the coronavirus epidemic. Some commentators have observed how it plays neatly into an agenda of totalitarian control. A frightened public accepts abridgments of civil liberties that are otherwise hard to justify, such as the tracking of everyone's movements at all times, forcible medical treatment, involuntary quarantine, restrictions on travel and the freedom of assembly, censorship

> of what the authorities deem to be disinformation, suspension of habeas corpus, and military policing of civilians. Many of these were underway before Covid-19; since its advent, they have been irresistible. The same goes for the automation of commerce; the transition from participation in sports and entertainment to remote viewing; the migration of life from public to private spaces; the transition away from place-based schools toward online education, the destruction of small business, the decline of brick-and-mortar stores, and the movement of human work and leisure onto screens. Covid-19 is accelerating preexisting trends, political, economic, and social.[50]

Eisenstein concludes these reflections with an ominous nod to what may all to easily become, as per Reset prescription, "the new normal":

> While all the above are, in the short term, justified on the grounds of flattening the curve (the epidemiological growth curve), we are also hearing a lot about a "new normal"; that is to say, the changes may not be temporary at all. Since the threat of infectious disease, like the threat of terrorism, never goes away, control measures can easily become permanent.[51]

This describes a quasi-military strategy, a war, on many fronts. A war, you may well ask, to what end? Profit, to be sure, but power as well—the power to make others play the part of pawns in some technocratic game.

Orwellian? To be sure. Here's a relevant passage from *1984*:

> The Party [read: The Matrix] seeks power entirely for its own sake. We are not interested in the good of others; we are interested solely in power. Not wealth or luxury or long life or happiness: only power, pure power. What pure power means you will understand presently. We are different from all the oligarchies of the past, in that we know what we are doing. All the others, even those who resembled ourselves, were cowards and hypocrites. The German Nazis and the Russian Communists came very close to us in their methods, but they never had the courage to recognize their own motives. They pretended, perhaps they even believed, that they had seized power unwillingly and for a limited time, and that just round the corner there lay a paradise where human beings would be free and equal. We are not like that. We know that no one ever seizes power with the intention of relinquishing it. Power is not a means, it is an end. One does not establish a dictatorship in order to safeguard a revolution; one makes the revolution in order to establish the dictatorship.[52]

Upon reading these last sentences, the dramatic declarations of paradigm change, of revolutionary transformation, inking the pages of *COVID-19: The*

Great Reset cannot but echo with a darker resonance. If you believe that the allusions to dictatorship here are beyond the pale of the Covid World created by the Matrix, you have not been paying sufficient attention to world affairs. All over the globe, Emergency Powers have been invoked to justify extraordinary authoritarian measures. As far as the consonance of such a dynamic with the hierarchal power structure of the Matrix is concerned, Luke Kemp, in an article titled "The Stomp Reflex: When Governments Abuse Emergency Powers," observes: "Emergency powers tend to only go one way: top-down. During an emergency, the knee-jerk reaction is always to reinforce those atop hierarchies." [53] For anyone devoted to democracy, Kemp's whole piece sets off loud alarm. Just one of many passages:

> A total of 32 countries have used militaries or military ordinances to enforce rules, which has not been without casualties.... Others have drawn on technology to gain government oversight. To monitor rule-breakers, 22 countries have used surveillance drones. Facial recognition programs have been expanded.[54]

These, though, are numbers and generalities. For a more visceral sense of what is going on, one need only look at footage from the internment camps for the unvaccinated set up in Australia, or—in that same country, pursuant to rules promulgated by, among others, Jane Halton of Event 201—watch persons who dare go unmasked on the streets body-slammed and violently wrestled to the ground by black-uniformed policemen, or gathered protesters singing of peace brutally besieged and dispersed by rubber bullets and water-cannons. In Austria, unvaccinated persons are essentially under house arrest and will soon be subject, for no other crime than refusal to get the jab, to fines of many *thousands* of euros and even jail time. Somewhere on the web, if it has not been disappeared, you can watch the cell-phone video of an airline stewardess showing the tiny cubicle in which she is being forcibly detained for twenty-one days in Hong Kong after landing there for a stop-over. Why? Because she is unvaccinated, or displaying Covid symptoms? No. She's both fully vaccinated and perfectly well (asymptomatic), but has been locked up like a criminal simply because a passenger on the flight to Hong Kong tested positive for Covid-19.

This is all news from abroad, but the news from the home front is hardly better. Americans, including this writer, continue to lose jobs and livelihood on account of personal health choices. Especially at risk are those highly qualified professionals most visibly and effectively contesting the official narrative and its practical implementation. Although few if any persons in the world are more accomplished in their areas of expertise *or* better positioned to address a wide array of medical and scientific questions pertaining to Covid-19 than Doctors Peter McCullough and Robert Malone, their advocacy of dissenting views has placed them squarely in the cross-hairs of Matrix gunners. Formal proceedings to revoke the licenses of both of these physicians have been instigated. Indeed, Dr. Peter McCullough, one of the most published physicians in history in his domain of expertise, is reportedly $150,000 in the hole on account of legal expenses incurred in defense of his medical license.[55]

This is intellectual and political tyranny. And it is the state, in coordination with other elements of the Matrix, that is creating the environment, the climate of opinion, making such previously unthinkable proceedings possible.

Still closer to the home front: Today is the 20th of December, 2021 and so the season of winter holidays. Ordinarily, I would be attending a number of the rich cultural events, including the Oakland Christmas Revels, that lend depth of meaning and a human face to the season. Yet I cannot attend a concert, or play, or performance of any kind. I cannot even view a movie at the local independent film center my wife and I have patronized, as subscribing members, for years. Nor can I, in San Francisco, eat in a restaurant, or workout in a gym, or take my son, who captained his high school varsity basketball team, to a Golden State Warriors game for Christmas, because I cannot show the proper papers.

These deprivations, while practically and psychologically severe, are nonetheless small sacrifices relative to those required of the unvaccinated (and even, as Hong Kong shows, the vaccinated) across the globe. Yet other local measures, both private and public, cut more deeply.

The dividing lines engendered by the government's disinformation campaign slice through families like a knife. My wife, son, and I have been disinvited to a family gathering at the house of close relatives who do not want unvaccinated persons compromising the "safety" of their home. The governor in my home state has promised a Covid-19 vaccine requirement for children to attend school. What is more tyrannical than forcing a parent who wishes to send their healthy young child to school (a child who is, statistically speaking, at no risk of serious illness or death by Covid) to subject their child to injection with a shoddily tested experimental drug proven to be, by any reasonable historical standard, extraordinarily dangerous?

I came across the Orwell passage on power cited earlier in another, later piece by Charles Eisenstein, this one titled "A Path Will Rise to Meet Us." It is no accident that everyone is writing about paths, and the necessity of choosing one or the other, today. Eisenstein himself is too alert and humane a writer to linger long in any turkey-induced stupor, and the complacency of his "Human Family" piece in any event cuts against the grain of most of his Covid reflections.

In "A Path Will Rise" Eisenstein evokes the psychology underlying the dynamics in play between government authorities and the populace today, construing the same on the model of an abusive relationship in which the power of the strong feeds off the fear-induced servility of the weak. The whole essay, like most all of Eisenstein's Covid work, is well worth reading for its sociopsychological probity. The following paragraph begins with one more quote from Orwell:

> "The more the Party is powerful, the less it will be tolerant: the weaker the opposition, the tighter the despotism." The Covid era has seen endless indignities, humiliations, and abuse heaped upon the public, each more outrageous than the last. It is as if someone is performing a psychological experiment to see how much people are willing to take. Let's tell them that masks don't work, and then reverse it and require them to mask up. Let's tell them they can't shake hands. Let's tell them they can't go near each other. Let's shut down their churches, choirs, businesses, and festivals. Let's stop them from gathering for the holidays. Let's make them inject poison into their bodies. Let's make them do it again. Let's make them do it to their children. Let's censor their first-hand stories as "false information." Let's feed them obvious absurdities to see what they'll swallow. Let's make promises and break them. Let's make the same promises again and break them again. Let's require authorization for their every movement. Wow, they're still going along with it? Let's see how much more they will take.[56]

A statement from a member of the European parliament corroborates both the tragic reality of the ascension of COVID-19-sponsored authoritarianism in the world today and, in closing, Eisenstein's analysis of social psychology:

> This message goes out to the people in Australia. My name is Christine Anderson. I'm a member of the European parliament, and I am answering your SOS call. I will do whatever I can to make it known to the world that your once free and liberal democracy has been transformed into a

> totalitarian regime which tramples on human rights, civil liberties, and the rule of law. I am imploring all of you around the world who still think your governments are looking out for your best interests: At no point in history have the people forcing the other into compliance been the good guys. The welfare of humanity has always been the alibi of tyrants.
>
> Do you not realize that this vaccine does not protect you from Covid? It does, however, protect you from governmental oppression. For now, that is. But don't think for even a second that this is not going to change tomorrow.
>
> I'm a German, and we once asked our grandparents how they could have just stood by in silence allowing a horrific totalitarian regime to come about. Anyone could have known. All they had to do was open their eyes and take a look. The vast majority chose not to. So, what will you tell your grandchildren. Will you tell them you didn't know? Will you tell them you were just following orders?
>
> You need to understand. It isn't about breaking the fourth wave. It is all about breaking people.[57]

At the moment, the power struggle between the authorities and the people pivots on the issue of vaccine mandates. Masking, especially the masking of children, should accede to the front line as well, but while you can always take off a mask (if not the effects of wearing one for weeks, months, or years on end), vaccination represents a largely irreversible violation of the right to bodily autonomy. Not only does such a mandate in and of itself constitute such a violation, the willingness of government (and a supporting cast of enabling citizens) to impose and enforce such a measure bears the broadest possible implications. While Christine Anderson minces no words in her cry of warning, the British podcaster Russell Brand gives temperate expression to the intellectual gist of the matter:

> The introduction of mandates and passes for an issue many people consider, at the moment, to be worthy of such regulation, could be applied down the line to anything. This is the thing about abetting authoritarianism and tyranny. At some point, it might be for things you agree with, but at some point, it might not be, because governments change, conditions change, the world changes. That's why it's imperative to have principles and values based upon something more than your own personal experiences and expedience.[58]

Brand's remarks echo those made by Ralph Waldo Emerson at the very end of that iconic, quintessentially American essay, "Self-Reliance":

> A political victory...raises your spirits, and you think good days are preparing for you. Do not believe it.... Nothing can bring you peace but the triumph of principles.[59]

Emerson's friend and fellow transcendentalist Henry David Thoreau expressed similar sentiments in his classic essay, "Civil Disobedience," the piece that inspired both Mahatma Gandhi and Martin Luther King, Jr.:

> Action from principle, the perception and the performance of right, changes things and relations; it is essentially revolutionary, and does not consist wholly with any thing which was.[60]

It is up to us which leaders we choose to follow: the Matrix-sponsored Generals of the Great Reset, or our true revolutionary forebears, the heralds of American Renaissance.

In so choosing, we would do well to remember that, as Albert Camus said, "The welfare of humanity is always the alibi of tyrants."

We, the People possess, and need reclaim, the power of self-determination. Despite the immense force wielded by the Matrix, its authority ultimately depends upon the consent and cooperation—the *obedience*—of ordinary persons, the citizens of the world.

Never believe the key to your fate, or the collective destiny of humankind, lies, billy-club-like, in the palm of someone else's hand.

Chapter 2

OF MOBS AND MARIONETTES

To many persons who trust in the essential integrity of government officials, health experts, and venerable news outlets (such as *The New York Times*), the image of a global agenda of economic, political, psychological, and social control may seem a surreal phantasm, a specter of evil that appears at infinite remove from the good faith act of undergoing vaccination or masking up to protect oneself and others from a deadly virus.

The success of the Matrix/Great Reset agenda depends—and dramatically so—upon just that illusion of remove.

The capacity of the Matrix to sustain that illusion hinges not only upon the deliberate strategy and tactics rehearsed at occasions such as Event 201 (including media control and censorship), but also upon predictable features of the popular mind-set.

It is both natural and comforting to assume that those invested with authority—even if humanly imperfect—largely *know* what they are doing, and *act* with the benefit of the community in mind. How else are we to feel secure, and—especially in the case of crises—be reasonably sure of what lead to follow? It is not only Matrix powers that want us to invest some central authority with superior wisdom and executive know-how; it is an innate tendency of the human soul, inherited from the state of utter dependence characteristic of childhood.

That, however, is only *more* reason to distrust this all-too-natural inclination. As Paul wrote: "When I was a child, I spoke as a child, I understood as a child, I thought as a child: but when I became a man, I put away childish things."[61]

It is relatively easy to be a good citizen and a credit to one's country if that simply means following orders…*until* one discovers that such complacency can all too easily lead to ever more dire straits, a brave new world irrevocably alien to almost all one has ever cherished.

The Matrix system of illusion banks, too, upon another property of the popular mind related to, yet not identical with, its Millgramesque faith in authority. Whereas the latter is essentially *idealist* in tenor (expressions of faith are always investment in an ideal image or form such as "the good father" or "health expert"), this ancillary property is pragmatic in nature. The Great Reset agenda, as I have described it, is grand indeed, and it may easily seem practically implausible that any elite cabal could hijack the machinery of national and international governance (not to mention virtually the whole of the medical establishment) to serve their own ends. Such a plot may well be the stuff of *conspiracy theory,* but (thus a great many sensible persons presume) can *hardly* reflect the truth underlying the current course of world affairs. Wildly improbable, the whole notion may doubtless be dismissed as the fabrication of disreputable factions of society, themselves possessed by a self-serving desire to upend the rule of responsible authorities.

It is integral to the power of the Matrix that Truth and Illusion trade places in the public imagination. As the substance of this book and countless other sources document, fact and reason could quickly destroy the credibility of the controlling narrative if Fact and Reason were not so violently and systematically both *suppressed* and *repressed*: *suppressed* by the manifold machinations of Matrix power (including censorship), and *repressed* by the (quite understandable) popular reluctance to recognize to what degree the darker side of our human nature has managed, by hook and by crook, to seize the levers of power. It accomplishes this less by the direct action of its few generals (although this is critical) than by way of the sometimes subtle, sometimes crude means by which it presses armies of ordinary citizens into service.

Did my citation of Orwell in the prior chapter—that passage portraying "The Party" as a heartless force intent wholly and solely upon Power for its own sake—seem more the stuff of dystopian fiction than historic fact? Did it evoke images of a degree of deliberate evil that one simply cannot attach to the vast majority of doctors, scientists, and public officials promoting vaccination and contagion control measures today? Qualms on that score are certainly understandable.

I may disagree, vehemently, with Bay Area Doctors Ghandi and Wachter with respect to mass vaccination,[62] but I have no grounds to believe that the motives of these professionals are less pure or well-intentioned than my own; or that they are somehow nefariously inhumane individuals. If the same could be said of countless others in this nation and abroad, and so of innumerable persons who perform vital public functions, how is it possible to sustain the counter-narrative I am advancing here—to uphold the claim that the official Vaccine-Distance system of response, in execution as well as conception, devolves from the Matrix's vortex of darkness?

In order to resolve the seeming contradiction between the common decency of most persons (including health professionals) and the immorality of the Matrix and its Great Reset program, one needs a modicum of understanding of how power operates in society. In particular, one need possess some sense of how it works in a global society that has become top-heavy and riddled with economic inequity.

The subject of the power lines that crisscross continents, countries, counties and neighborhoods is hugely complex; and while I have taken snapshots of some main cables in this opus, I can hardly chart the whole intricate nexus. I will, however, register some further observations that bear concretely upon pervasive molds of Matrix influence in the wake of Covid on two chief fronts: the economic or material, and (as I have already commenced in this chapter) the sociopsychological.

Matrix influence trickles—or even cascades—down from its global apex in the form of that magic elixir of power called money. How, realistically speaking, could the few conceivably so extend their sway over the many as to accomplish their stunningly ambitious, world-transformative goals? For the compliant, the carrot of virtue is sweetened by the sauce of dollars, while the stick of financial and professional loss threatens to smash those who resist the edicts handed down from on high.

Concomitantly, the political influence linked to the economic leverage exerted by the Matrix can scarcely be underestimated. Today, it is not only true that money talks; it also appears to have accrued the power to silence or otherwise crush voices of dissent in a manner historically associated with authoritarian regimes, but presumed foreign to democratic societies.

Virtually all the topics and scenarios covered in *An American Scholar's Covid Chronicle* bear witness to this disastrous development, including the suppression of early treatment options; media censorship; the consistent massaging and misrepresentation of scientific data; the discipline, dismissal, and even de-certification of disobedient doctors, and more. Let me here, by way of further update and amplification, cite two relevant instances of the impolitic sway of Big Pharma-tainted money flowing into and through U.S. government channels and so shaping—or rather autocratically dictating—public policy.

A healthcare policy analyst expert, A. J. DePriest is a Tennessean, one of twenty-eight who formed a small independent think tank and citizens' advocacy group called Tennessee Liberty Network. Tennessee Liberty does not identify with one or another end of the political spectrum, welcoming all "liberty-minded, conservative and classically liberal activists."[63] Its first project involved monitoring the disbursement of health care-related funds provided by the $2.2 trillion CARES (Coronavirus Aid, Relief, and Economic Security) Act signed into law in March 2020 by President Trump. The organization found little that was fishy in that department, but its work gained critical momentum when members began attending school board meetings soon after the passage of the second stupendous coronavirus relief bill, the $1.9 trillion American Rescue Plan (ARP) signed by President Biden in March of 2021.

A singular phenomenon sparked the interest of Tennessee Liberty members attending such meetings: the frequently witnessed spectacle of distraught parents (often, several at a given meeting) passionately pleading with school board members to rescind masking strictures so that their children would not have to bear the physical, emotional, and mental burden of constant mask-wearing. Even though the appeals were typically highly emotional, Tennessee Liberty observers noted that school board members consistently reacted with studied indifference and glassy-eyed stares that seemed to suggest that they had little or nothing to do with the matter at hand. After due investigative digging, Tennessee Liberty discovered the probable explanation for why school boards (which are, after all, comprised of human beings, many of whom are themselves parents) appeared so uniformly and callously unresponsive.

The reason was that the two coronavirus relief acts provided an unprecedented bonanza of government funding for school operation and improvement. In December of 2020, the CDC issued a report estimating that it would require $25 billion dollars to get every school in America up and running in compliance with necessary corona-related safety protocols. The CARES and ARP acts combined provided close to *eight times that figure: almost $200 billion* ($189.5) of ESSER (Elementary and Secondary School Emergency Relief) funds, the majority of which ($122 billion) flowed from ARP.[64] The mountain of money, however, came with strings attached.

A.J. DePries and her Tennessee Liberty colleagues discovered that, in order to qualify to receive their share of ESSER funds, school districts across the nation were required to submit a plan detailing how they intended to meet specific criteria spelled out by the CDC. Here is a relevant portion of the federal document outlining that provision and the specific requirements ("LEA" stands for "local educational agencies"—i.e., school districts):

> First, the requirement clarifies that an LEA's plan must include how it will maintain the health and safety of students, educators, and other school and LEA staff, and the extent to which it has adopted policies, and a description of any such policies, on each of the CDC's safety recommendations including: Universal and correct wearing of masks; modifying facilities to allow for physical distancing (e.g., use of cohorts/podding); handwashing and respiratory etiquette; cleaning and maintaining healthy facilities, including improved ventilation; contact tracing in combination with isolation and quarantine...diagnostic and screening testing; efforts to provide vaccinations to school communities.[65]

In conversation with Bigtree, DePries additionally clarifies that, in order to secure and maintain government funding, schools needed not only to submit the requisite district plans, but were required as well to prove their adequate implementation. Appropriate district plans were expected to be submitted *every six months* through September of 2023.

That means that a child in kindergarten at the outset of the pandemic in early 2020 would likely spend, under this edict, the better part of four years—including the whole of first, second, and third grades—either out of school altogether, or handicapped by masking.

Here's a relevant portion of the conversation between A.J. DePries and Bigtree. Note the latter's incredulity about the amount of money involved.

> **DB:** So when we are standing there as parents, at these school board meetings, and saying, "Get the masks off my kids. They're getting rashes on their face. They haven't seen their teacher smile. They're depressed. They are not interacting socially. I see them failing...," we just see those blank stares because that school board knows I'm not going to turn down...what is it? $10 million dollars, or $15 million dollars...to listen to **you.**
>
> **AJD:** Oh, **much** more than that. In Tennessee...Shelby County gets almost three-quarter billion dollars in Covid relief funds.
>
> **DB:** For education? To the schools?
>
> **AJD:** Yes, the Shelby County school system. For the Nashville public schools, it's a half-billion dollars in relief funds. BUT: to get that money they have to prove how they are fulfilling these requirements: Universal masking, contact tracing, isolation, quarantine, vaccination for all students, staff, and teachers. To get that money, they have to fulfill those requirements. That's what we discovered, and every state is doing it.[66]

Talk about top-down power. Anthony Fauci, who himself has conceded that masking confers little if any real protection from the virus,[67] and that its primary benefit is psychological, decides that school children in America should be masked through September 2023. The CDC follows orders, and the federal government uses massive amounts of tax-payer dollars to coerce school boards into enforcing useless but abusive policies. In so doing, it renders parents across the country powerless; without any real say as to how their children are to be treated for hours and hours of each and every school day for (not weeks or months but) *years* on end.

That's Matrix power at its most egregious.

That's *not* government of, by, and for the people. That's *not* democracy. That's despotism.

In her interview with Bigtree, DePries also addresses the pressing issue of hospital treatment of Covid. After attaining public recognition through its school board work, Tennessee Liberty began receiving calls for help from persons whose friends and loved ones were dying in hospitals on account of what these persons—like Kate Dalley[68]—regarded as ineffective and even dangerous treatment methods.

Unsurprisingly, Tennessee Liberty found that government health care policy followed a playbook similar to that applied to the schools, deploying huge sums of federal dollars to dictate institutional practices in a manner unresponsive to—and indeed destructive of—public welfare.

Swimming in the flood of federal funds allocated for Covid relief by CARES and ARP, not to mention resources channeled through the CMS, the federal government incentivized and even (by virtue of the threat of loss of funding) required hospitals to treat patients in a manner answerable, *not* to the discretion of individual patients and physicians free to employ the full range of treatment options supported by science, but to the narrowly restrictive protocols prescribed by the CDC, FDA and NIH. Fauci and his cohort's Big Pharma-tainted construction of Covid World (including what *to do* or *not to do* about it) was thus effectively written into law at the cost of not only billions of taxpayer dollars, but also the lives of untold persons thereby denied suitable treatment.

After embarking on its hospital-related work, Tennessee Liberty founded an associate organization called the Adam Group devoted to Covid education and patient advocacy. The group performs the kind of work that *should* be the province of responsible public health agencies. DePries:

> Our goal is to educate people as to how to prevent COVID because it is preventable, and how to treat COVID at home, because it can be treated at home without going to a hospital. Our number one goal is to keep people out of hospitals because we know what happens there. The advocacy work we do with people who are in hospitals...is the stuff of nightmares.[69]

Why? DePries explains that Tennessee hospitals received $166,000 dollars for the treatment of every Covid patient. That figure is not anomalous: it may even be on the low side: the comparable figures for Nebraska, West Virginia, and North Dakota were $379,000, $471,000, and $339,000. As with school monies, these are jaw-dropping figures, even for someone as knowledgeable about Covid politics as Del Bigtree, who inquires of DePries:

> **DB:** What do they have to do to get that money for that patient?
>
> **AJD:** They have to follow the NIH protocol for the treatment of COVID in hospitals.

After detailing how hospitals themselves often dissemble and veil that truth, DePries reaffirms:

> **AJD:** It all leads back to those NIH protocols. In those protocols, the only approved EUA drugs for use in hospitals of COVID is remdesivir.

If you want the full dope on remdesvir, you can read Kennedy's long section on the drug in *The Real Anthony Fauci.*[70] Not only is remdesivir entirely ineffective in the treatment of Covid, it is a toxic drug known (among other potential effects) to trigger renal or kidney failure, a fatal dysfunction that also happens to be a common effect of severe cases of Covid-19. In fact, Kennedy suggests that, just as many HIV deaths were likely caused by the ineffective and toxic AZT treatment promoted by Fauci at that time, it is quite likely that a signification portion of Covid deaths in the U.S. were actually attributable not to the disease itself, but to the Dr. Fauci-prescribed administration of the *only* drug authorized by the federal government for emergency use treatment of Covid.[71]

Neither DePries nor Bigtree is ignorant of the potential connection:

> **AJD:** And the reason other countries don't have the death rates we do, is that the United States, for the whole year of 2021, was the only country that was allowed to use remdesvir.

> **DB:** A failed Ebola drug that was so toxic, they said: "You're better off with Ebola. We are pulling it out of this trial."[72]

So, by all means, do all you can to stay out of the hospital, and keep your friends and family away, too. Because if they do enter one, the very normal, decent hospitalist who—trusting in the higher wisdom of the NIH and CDC as well as their own administrative superiors—simply follows orders, may well poison and kill them.

So much, for now, with respect to the material or economic means of Matrix control. Let's turn back again to the sociopsychological dimension of much of the population's willing participation in the mainstream Matrix agenda.

Once more, Charles Eisenstein can assist our learning curve here. It was Eisenstein who penned the paragraph cited in the prior chapter detailing (rather unforgettably) the abusive dynamics characterizing the power relation between government and the citizenry. In his continuation, Eisenstein recognizes that the evil intent inheres more *in the system itself* than in the minds and hearts of most who carry out its orders. The details of his description resonate all too well with DePries's images of school board members hung like puppets on the strings of government apparatus or hospital physicians deceasing patients with remdesivir and intubation:

> I have written the above as if the bullying powers were a bunch of cackling sadists delighting in the humiliation of their victims. That is not accurate. Most people staffing our governing institutions are normal, decent human beings. While it is also true that these institutions are hospitable environments for martinets, control freaks, and sadists, more often they turn people into martinets, control freaks, and sadists. These individuals are more symptom than cause of the generalized abuse of the public today. They are functionaries, playing the roles that a systematically abusive drama requires.

So far, Eisenstein's depiction spotlights the effective power of an abusive system itself, the operation that, as we have seen, often reflects superintendent economic factors. Now, though, Eisenstein pivots to the manner in which individuals in that system tend to *internalize its logic:*

> Causing suffering is not their root motivation; it is to establish control. The quest for power doubtless finds justification in the idea that it is all for the greater good. Yes, they think, it would be bad if evil people were in charge of the surveillance, censorship, and coercive apparatus, but

fortunately it is we, the rational, intelligent, far-seeing, science-based good guys who are at the helm.[73]

I am sure my erstwhile employers at Pacifica Graduate Institute did not see their requirement that I not only vaccinate, but register my status digitally so that it could be verified on my phone as an act of surveillance. Yet it *is* so, and an invasive one, but one evidently justified in their eyes because Pacifica administrators are, in their own minds, rational, intelligent, far-seeing, science-based good guys. (Joe Cambray, Pacifica's President,[74] holds a Ph.D. in chemistry from UC Berkeley.) Acting as such, they cannot really do wrong even when instituting what, from another perspective, may well be considered arbitrary and irrational *diktats* that do material and spiritual harm to staff and to students and play right into the hands of the Matrix agenda.

The next sentence of Eisenstein's essay expresses a profound and telling insight: "Through the absolute conviction by those who hold power that they are the good guys power transforms from a means to an end."

How are we to understand this? If I believe, without serious question, that mass vaccination and associated contagion control methods (masking, etc.) are the appropriate and necessary means of alleviating human suffering and death—indeed, the only viable methods available to us in the face of a deadly pandemic—I have little or no incentive to limit the exercise of power by means of which I seek to implement and enforce those measures. My intellectual and moral certainty, inflated by the magnitude of my responsibility with respect to what are perceived as matters of life and death, renders me carelessly dismissive of others' rights and sweeps away their qualms and questions as deluded or ethically irresponsible.

While more polite circles (such as at Pacifica) may be content to exercise autocratic power without flagrant ostracism or damning moral judgment, such relative temperance represents more the exception than the rule. More commonly, proponents of official policy regard dissent *not* as the product of rational reflection stemming from motives ethically sound as their own, but view it as indicative of a morally tainted, and even depraved, character. In traditional parlance, this means that such proponents see themselves and their actions as inherently virtuous while viewing the thoughts and deeds of those on the opposing side as bred of vice.

Here, we are verging on the moral set-up intrinsic to the Matrix psych-ops: the way the system works to provide *apparently* rational justification for intrinsically unethical abuses of power. It is this (im)moral master stroke that allow the members of its extensive supporting cast—perhaps the better part of the world population today—to carry out its reprehensible ends with a diabolically deformed "clean conscience."[75]

In writing these words, I myself am moved to a moment of critical self-reflection. Am not I myself, in writing this book, setting forth quite unequivocal opinions, and so guilty of like commission of the pride that is the ground of all vice—unquestioned certitude of the rightness and virtue of one's own stance, which licenses unreflective dismissal of not only others' deeply held views, but also their very being?

The question need be asked; and yet, no sooner have I put it to myself, than a retort arises in my mind. I may hold fast to my convictions, but, as regards Covid-world, I am, perforce, keenly aware of the rationale advanced by the other side, and continue to examine it in depth. Most importantly, it is not I, and my ilk, who are wielding those levers of power to silence and exile others, to suppress their views, and coerce them into performing actions violative of their rights of bodily autonomy—doing so, all the while, wrapped in a mantle of civic virtue.

This represents yet another critical, indeed, indispensable weapon of the Matrix psych-ops and its game of illusion. It banks, to be sure, upon the illimitable fear of death afflicting mortal human beings. The "pandemic of fear" qualifies as the *prima materia* of all Matrix operations; the prerequisite and ground of all its representations. Yet while despots and terrorists may rule by fear alone, leaders whose rule rests upon the perception of benevolence (their own self-perception, as well as that of the public) fence, too, with the foils of virtue, love, and righteousness. Consciously or not, Matrix minions manage—with the cleverness characteristic of the Master of all Illusion—to present what is, on the face of it, contrary to spiritual law and moral principle as right, good, and requisite for the protection of life.

Virtually without warning, all sorts of previously unthinkable things (remember Kennedy's list of the constitutional rights violated by our system of pandemic response[76]) are, in the name of humanity, christened as not only acceptable but also positively good.

In our Matrix-sponsored Covid-world, our new (ab)normal, Dr. Fauci, his Matrix cohort, and all those who believe in his Word, declare that it is good to love your neighbor, but bad to embrace or get anywhere close to him or her. It is good to cover little children's faces in constricting masks that obscure identity and free expression, impair breathing, and cripple all sorts of vital emotional communication. It is good to deny effective early treatment to ailing persons and good, too, to poison or intubate them in the hospitals despite the often fatal damage thus inflicted. It is good to punish and seek to extirpate accomplished physicians who, in their heartfelt quest to save lives, refuse to abide by protocols handed down from "health experts" who have never treated patients. It is good to allow only persons espousing authorized views to express their opinions in newspapers, radio, television, and social media platforms. It is good to attack and erase the existence of those vaccine-injured who seek to tell their stories and share the truth of their ruined lives. It is good to lock down society, close churches, and shutter businesses. It is good to force whole populations to undergo inoculation with an experimental drug that has already maimed and killed tens if not hundreds of thousands of persons. It is good to exclude, without sound scientific rationale, a whole class of persons from public life as if they were lepers, or bearers of a yellow star.

Such twisting of moral law, such nefarious manipulation of the human psyche, represents a chief canon in the Matrix arsenal. As it pertains not to the Matrix masterminds but to the populace at large, upon whose obedient cooperation the former ultimately depend, it may be regarded as a symptom of the phenomena recently christened "mass formation psychosis."[77] That unwieldy term denotes a sociopsychological pathology that results in people buying *en masse* into one or another narrative (e.g., "Jews are the cause of our country's ills") that has little or no basis in fact but nonetheless serves as a means of establishing and consolidating social identity—typically at the expense of some other *disfavored* class of persons. Mass formation psychosis springs up, like a dangerous mushroom, from the soil of four enabling conditions:

1. deficient social bonding and cohesion;
2. lack of any sense of intellectual coherence or sense-making in society;
3. free-floating anxiety; and
4. psychological discontent, frustration, and aggression associated with a deficient sense of both pleasure and higher purpose in life.[78]

Our present Covid-world amply fills all four conditions. The mainstream of the controlling Covid narrative distorts fact and reason, but adherence to it nevertheless furnishes a recognizable identity in the midst of a chaotic and increasingly terrifying world reality. The damnation of those who do not corroborate the story and so confirm the proffered identity—the vilification of Covid dissidents as conspiracy theorists, anti-vaxxers, right-wing extremists, and the like—consequently functions as a critical component of the social pathology that serves as the psychological ground of the Great Reset agenda.

The fourth and last pre-condition named above may be especially revealing insofar as inauguration of the Great Reset and its rapid acceleration by Covid-19 has launched—or fast-forwarded—society upon a historic trajectory of which it is largely unaware, and which We, the People, the citizenry of the world, have not consciously elected or deliberately chosen. The ground of the mass formation thus devolves, at the deepest levels of the collective psyche, from the distressing intimation that we are losing control of our lives and that we are being deprived of our sovereign power to participate in the creation of a future of our own making. Deep inside, we have the suspicion that the aircraft carrying our collective human destiny has been hijacked. We do not know by whom, exactly, or where we are headed, but in our gut cannot but fear the worst.

The condition, as described, is indeed a soul condition, a sociopsychological pathology. As such, it calls for therapeutic treatment, and, ultimately, a purging catharsis that may effect a liberating transformation. What that entails on the psychological level I cannot explore in depth here. Nonetheless, as the inner and outer worlds of the soul always mirror each other, our psychological situation inevitably finds expression, too, in objective correlatives, the *socio-political* circumstances bespeaking the individual self's standing in the world today.

How many times need it be repeated? *The welfare of humanity is always the alibi of tyrants.* The principle applies not only to political leaders, but to each and every person that inclines, out of fear or righteousness—or both—to impose his or her will upon another in defiance of true ethical principles and constitutional rights; a situation that naturally gathers force and consequence the more people flock together in that act and so exercise what John Stuart Mill memorably calls "the tyranny of prevailing opinion."[79]

Mill's phrase points in the direction of mass formation psychosis, which in turn is akin to what may be called more simply mob mentality. I have spoken of how Matrix psychology often manages to cast morally questionable deeds in a virtuous light; the dark flip-side of that same coin naturally entails often violent condemnation of those who do *not* conform to or uphold the Party line. That ostracism or "othering" typically achieves social confirmation of the rightness of one's deeds, even if these patently involve wronging other human beings by denying them a standing on par with one's own.

In fact, what is sometimes called "virtue signaling" today entertains a subtle connection with the practice of scapegoating so critical in the formation of the kind of group identity that crystallizes less around the sharing of common values than around the vilification of a common enemy. The demand for uniformity characteristic of such compromised species of identity formation inevitably involves uncritical group-think, and ultimately grounds itself in a rejection of reason and critical thinking. The moment anyone participating in any kind of mob stops to question their own assumptions, they cease ritually confirming those assumptions by unreflective repudiation of difference, and, as a result, instantly break from the herd.

In the 1950s, a certain specious form of American identity crystallized around the demonizing of all those stained by the taint of Communism. No serious engagement with Marxist thought was required in order to feel self-righteously justified in condemning those suspected of being Red. Indeed, so much as entertaining critical concerns respecting most any aspect of America's own resolutely capitalist ideology was enough to draw dangerous suspicion to oneself.

So it is again today, though now the hated enemies of the common cause are so-called "anti-vaxxers," casuistically accused of crimes against humanity by the same enlightened parties who feel perfectly entitled to turn a blind eye to all the real atrocities being committed in their name. Vilifying those who do nothing more than refuse an injection of an experimental drug of, at best, dubious safety and efficacy, the purveyors of our public conscience (not stopping at the Pope himself[80]) nonetheless:

- Blithely ignore the sabotage of effective treatment options that has caused incalculable suffering and, by some estimates, killed upwards of half a million people[81] (with the toll mounting every day);
- Callously deny or neglect the evidence of vaccine injury irrefutably inscribed in the tortured bodies and anguished minds of untold persons;
- Tolerate the Big Pharma-sponsored bastardization of science and siege of the art of medicine, including the punitive persecution of independently-minded physicians dedicated to upholding the Hippocratic oath and the sanctity of the doctor-patient relation;
- Stare glassy-eyed away from the pleas of anguished parents speaking up for the rights of their children to grow up unmuzzled and unmarred by face-covering that immolates innocence and disfigures the human being;

- Stand complacently by or cheerlead as the civil rights and liberties (the right to freedom of speech, above all) basic to free society are mercilessly shredded in the machine of state, news rooms, Big Tech platforms, and the Cuisinart of public opinion.
- Collude in harsh and arbitrary (cf. the irrefutable evidence that vaccinees also readily spread Covid) discrimination against unvaccinated persons, which measures already threaten (e.g., in Austria) to lead to their criminalization and arrest;
- Participate in other corrosive offshoots of Matrix influence, thus falling (knowingly or not) in line with the Great Reset agenda.

In an early essay aptly named "Mob Morality and Unvaxxed" Charles Eisenstein builds upon Rene Girard's classic articulation of scapegoating to criticize the groupthink and destructive social dynamics so prevalent in Covid World today. After evoking how condemnation of the tainted "other" tends to snowball, so that those who play along gain confirmation and solidarity at the expense of the dehumanized other, Eisenstein (in a subsection titled "Hijacking Morality") gives an apt *précis* of how Matrix power can so easily gain a stranglehold on whole societies:

> The same kind of positive reinforcement cycle is what generates a mob. All it takes is a few loud people to incite it by declaring someone or something a target. A portion of the crowd goes along enthusiastically. The rest keep silent and conform in outward behavior even as they are troubled within; to each, it looks like he or she is the only one who disagrees. Writ large to the totalitarian state, the support of a majority of the population is unnecessary. The appearance of support will suffice.
>
> The mechanisms that generate the illusion of unanimity operate within science, medicine, and journalism as well as among the general public. Some conform enthusiastically to the orthodoxy; others complain in whispers to sympathetic colleagues. Those who voice dissent publicly become radioactive. The consequences of their apostasy (excommunication from funding, ridicule in the media, shunning by colleagues who must "distance themselves," etc.) serve to silence other potential dissidents, who prudently keep their views to themselves.[82]

What is the antidote to this social dynamic that traps our collective psyche in a vicious circle of ritual sacrifice and false communion, even as the Vaccine-Distance system of response traps our biology in mounting dysfunction? The question is as deep and wide as the river of human nature, but here are a few buoys: 1) Staunch and vigilant defense of the *principles* that underlie free society, especially in face of expedient emergencies that would appear to justify their abrogation; 2) An inward stance of self-reliance, and acknowledgment that the sovereignty of the free individual functions as the indispensable basis of truly democratic society; 3) Toleration of difference and encouragement of free debate along with a striving for, not uniformity, but participation in the essential unity underlying our shared spiritual humanity; 4) The exercise of critical reason that tears the Matrix-manufactured veil of illusion, making visible all that the Great Reset holds in store; 5) Action commensurate with, and practically responsive to, that critical insight; 6) Deliberate formulation and choosing of a different version of human destiny, a revisioning of history that begins with rediscovering America and its own past and future Renaissance.

CHAPTER 3

THE (BIO) INSECURITY STATE

I have presented Event 201 as evidence that our world-wide Covid response represents, *not* the spontaneous good faith effort of responsible authorities (international, national, and local) to serve public health by whatever salutary means possible, but a technocratic elite's deliberately planned strategy: one dictated, moreover, by ulterior economic, political, and ideological motives. One could, of course, reasonably claim that Event 201 seems insufficient evidence for such a damning claim. How could such a massive program of social and political control be effectively organized in so short a period of time, after so little practice? How could one simulation possibly succeed in training and coordinating so many parties at so many levels of complex operation, even if the few persons present were already highly accomplished in their own diverse domains?

Event 201 could not and did not accomplish that political miracle in and of itself. The Event, the pandemic, and the worldwide response to it represent the culmination of not months, or years, but *decades* of kindred forms of preparation: human words and deeds, plots and sub-plots, tending towards the end we see manifest as Covid World today. Indeed, as far as *event planning* is concerned (and here I refer specifically to high-level war game-like exercises), we will see that Event 201 represents but the tip of the iceberg: only the most recent of an impressively long series of kindred simulations.

As leading remarks by the likes of Fauci and Gates imply,[83] Covid-19 did not burst upon the world unexpectedly or even unannounced. Covid-19 has a backstory, a rich one, the comprehension of which requires the construing of a devilishly complex picture, a tapestry of many intertwining skeins of thought and action. Robert F. Kennedy, Jr. spins the material yarns in the *The Real Anthony Fauci,* the last two chapters of which concentrate primarily (although not exclusively) upon critical developments over the course of the last two decades. While I can hardly do justice to all the disturbing patterns traced in his last eighty pages, I will seek to offer my own condensed version of salient facts, figures, and off-color angles. I do so because understanding something of Covid World's troubling past is necessary if we are to turn the page on the confusion and strife that still characterizes life at present.

~

Fauci's Fakery

One red thread in the intricate tapestry of Covid history follows Dr. Anthony Fauci's own long career, particularly his penchant for wildly exaggerating, or even inventing, the dangers associated with one or another infectious disease. The title of Kennedy's penultimate chapter, "Hyping Phony Epidemics: 'Crying Wolf'" expresses the gist of this matter. Its first paragraph provides crucial historical perspective:

> In 1906, infectious disease caused a third of all annual deaths in the United States, and 800-1000 of every 100,000 Americans died of infectious disease. By 1976, fewer than fifty Americans per hundred thousand died of infectious diseases, and CDC and NIAID were under extreme pressure to justify their budgets. Hyping pandemics became an institutional strategy in both agencies. Pharmaceutical companies and international health agencies, banking and military contractors soon found purchase in the ecosystem, and random pandemics discovered their own self-perpetuating rationale. Dr. Fauci's critics chide him for routinely exaggerating—and even concocting—global disease outbreaks to hype pandemic panic, elevate the biosecurity agenda, boost agency funding, promote profitable vaccines for his pharma partners, and magnify his own power. The historical record supports these charges.[84]

Kennedy's reference to 1976 is not arbitrary. The date marks the year of the first of the relevant series of "global disease outbreaks," the 1976 swine flu.

At that time, Tony Fauci's long public health career was just budding. He was then acting chief of NIAID's Clinical Physiology Section of the Laboratory of Clinical Investigation, and so a first-hand witness, if not an active participant, in NIAID's handling of the swine flu affair. It is worthwhile to elaborate signal facets of that episode because many represent prototypes of patterns that recur in subsequent phony pandemics; later outbreaks materialized under Dr. Fauci's leadership after his accession to the top NIAID post in 1984.

Here, then, are the bare bones of the swine flu story.

The death of a single soldier after a drill at Fort Dix triggered the 1976 swine flu scare. After CDC scientists identified swine flu as the cause of the lung ailment that killed the soldier, the CDC and NIAID chiefs sounded the alarm, alerting the world to the incipience of a disastrous pandemic and triggering public demand for a saving vaccine. Agency officials met confidentially with Big Pharma vaccine developers and executives to plot strategy. After a lurid fear-mongering public relations campaign and a rushed rollout of inadequately tested vaccines, almost 50 million Americans were injected. In the end, though, it was not the dread disease but the vaccine itself that proved catastrophic.

The chief take-aways from 1976 fiasco? Below, I enumerate five features of the swine flu debacle that find all-too-resonant echoes in later repetitions of its typical pandemic plot.

Firstly, facts reveal a pattern of blatant deception, including outright lies. Kennedy:

> Pharma and NIAID told Congress, the White House, and the public that the Fort Dix swine flu was the same strain responsible for the 1918 Spanish flu pandemic which, they warned, had killed 50 million people worldwide. They were lying: scientists at Fort Dix, the CDC, and HHS knew that H1N1 was an ordinary pig virus posing no risk for humans.[85]

Secondly, and correlatively, the record displays a fantastical exaggeration of danger combined with the creation of a scenario that deployed the imprimatur of scientific authority to coerce government into initiating a mass vaccination program:

> In the end, the actual number of pandemic swine flu casualties in 1976 was not 1 million, but one. Dr. Harvey Fineberg, who authored the government's 1978 comprehensive post-mortem of NIAID's response to that fake pandemic, told the *WHO Bulletin*: "In '76, the virus was detected in a single military installation, at Fort Dix, New Jersey. In the ensuing weeks and months, not one related swine flue case was reported elsewhere in New Jersey, the USA or anywhere in the world.... At the same time, political decision-makers consistently thought that the scientists were giving them no choice but to go ahead with a mass immunization program."[86]

Thirdly, flawed science and inadequate government oversight resulted in implementation of a mass vaccination program that did far more harm than good:

The 1976 swine flu vaccine was so fraught with problems that HHS discontinued the jab after vaccinating 49 million Americans. According to news accounts, the incidence of flu was seven times greater among the vaccinated than the unvaccinated. Furthermore, the vaccine caused some 500 cases of the degenerative nerve disease Guillain-Barré Syndrome, 32 deaths, more than 400 paralyzations, and as many as 4,000 other injuries.[87]

Fourthly, government corruption led to company-friendly pharma deals dictating that the public (either directly or through government expenditure) bear the cost of, not only vaccine injury and death, but any and all financial liability.

Kennedy notes that congressional investigations ultimately discovered notes of in-house meetings between top public health officials (arranged, notably enough, by Fauci's boss, NIAID chief Richard Krause) and pharmaceutical company brass and vaccine developers. These notes record Dr Maurice Hilleman, Merck's renowned vaccine scientist, confessing that, in the case of the swine flu, the push for vaccine development "had nothing to do with science and everything to do with politics." Moreover:

> Merck and other manufacturers utilized their secret meeting with the regulators to hatch a scheme that would guarantee industry profits while shielding Pharma from liability. This innovation—now a persistent feature of Big Pharma's business model—turned out to be carte blanche for negligent and even criminal behavior....
>
> American taxpayers ended up paying for the swine flu vaccine coming and going, through guaranteed profits for Merck at the front end and outlays for piles of lawsuits from vaccine injury victims on the other side.[88]

The government in fact paid *$134 million* for the swine flu vaccine program while laying out over *$83* million to settle 1,604 liability claims. Processing those claims cost tens of millions of dollars more.[89]

This general situation has not changed, *except* insofar as complete legal protection for Big Pharma has been written into law by the PREP act, and insofar as the government itself is proving ever more recalcitrant in taking financial as well as ethical responsibility for vaccine adverse events.

Fifth, there transpired forceful and even unlawful and/or violent suppression of dissent within as well as without the ranks of science, industry, and government. Chief targets of that campaign included some of the most highly credentialed scientists and public health officials, persons whose viewpoints should most command conscientious attention and fair review, not only on account of their proven expertise, but also because of the ethical integrity evident in their willingness to undergo substantial personal risk for the sake of truth and courageous guardianship of the public interest.

> NIH's influenza and flu vaccine expert senior bacteriologist and virologist Dr. John Anthony Morris informed HHS bosses that the flu scare was a farce and that NIAID's campaign was a boondoggle to promote a dangerous and ineffective flu vaccine for a greedy industry.... When Dr. Morris protested the fraud, his direct superior ordered him to stand down, advising Morris "not to talk about this." When vaccine recipients began reporting adverse reactions...Dr. Morris disobeyed orders.... In response, HHS officials confiscated Dr. Morris's research materials, changed the laboratory locks, moved him to a small room with no telephone, reassigned his laboratory staff, and forbade him to see visitors except with permission, and blocked his efforts to publish his findings. Finally...HHS fired Morris for insubordination, citing a long list of drummed up charges, including failure to return library books on time.[90]

Once more, judging from the course of current affairs, it does not appear that matters have improved in this respect. On the contrary: today we witness like campaigns against physicians such as doctors Peter McCullough and Robert Malone.

In 1977, Dr. Morris instigated—and won—a wrongful dismissal suit against the NIH and HHS and gained widespread support for his grievances amongst others in the scientific community. Kennedy:

> The *New York Times* quoted a fellow scientist, B. G. Young, who characterized NIH's reprisal against honest scientists as "suppression, harassment, and censorship of individual investigators.... I finally came to realize that you either had to compromise yourself or leave."[91]

Unfortunately, one hardly need wonder if the *Times* would publish any like quotation, no matter how credible the source, today. As difference of opinion—scientific or otherwise—no longer appears to be valued with respect to Covid-19 vaccination and treatment, one can be virtually certain that anything Dr. Morris's contemporary heirs have to say is either ignored by the *Times* or condemned as misinformation.

The story of 1976 swine flu reveals that Anthony Fauci can hardly be reckoned the root of all NIH/U.S. public health evil. Rampant corruption and government and pharmaceutical company malfeasance preceded his tenure as NIH chief. Judging from subsequent history, however, young Fauci hardly took the 1976 swine flu scenario as an example of how *not* to conduct government business. On the contrary: if Fauci did not invent the (rather poorly executed) game plan, he ultimately became its master impresario, the Bill Belichik of the pandemic playbook so spectacularly showcased, ironically enough, in the year of America's Bicentennial.

It was in captaining his agency's response to HIV, the emergence of which roughly coincided with his assumption of NIAID directorship in 1984, that Tony Fauci pioneered the managerial style that characterizes his almost forty-year reign. Kennedy observes of that early phase of Fauci's rule:

> Even all those years ago, Anthony Fauci had already perfected his special style of *ad-fear-tising,* using remote, unlikely, farfetched and improbable possibilities to frighten people. Fauci helped terrify millions into wrongly believing they were at risk of getting AIDS when they were not.[92]

One can read about Fauci and his accomplices' politically masterful and medically catastrophic mismanagement of HIV in Kennedy's book. That story teaches many lessons applicable to Covid World, including the manner in which Fauci's championing of remdesivir mirrors, with almost uncanny exactitude, his earlier promotion of the equally ineffective and dangerous AZT.

Fauci's (mis)management of HIV occupied the lion's share of his attention for the first decade or so of his NIAID reign. Yet his handling of AIDS was only the beginning of Fauci's patented brand of pandemic politics; nor did his genius necessarily require a genuinely serious threat to kick into motion. The 21st century saw Fauci hype a whole string of phony pandemics in the long run-up to Covid-19: the 2005 bird flu, the 2009 Hong Kong swine flu, Zika in 2016, and Dengue shortly thereafter.

In all of these instances, as well as that of the 2020 coronavirus pandemic, the chief plot elements exhibited already in 1976 reliably recur. Fauci's policy and PR campaigns consistently repeat the same themes with only minor variations.

Kennedy's words introducing the 2005 bird flu are particularly choice:

> In 2005, Dr. Fauci revived NIAID's script from the 1976 debacle. This time the villain was an avian flu, H5N1. Like an agitated Chicken Little, Dr. Fauci had been warning the world about the imminent bird flu pandemic since 2001.[93]

For people today, two of the most notable features of the 2005 episode must be the role played by the British scientist and Wellcome Trust researcher,

Jeremy Farrar, and that performed by the epidemiological modeler Neil Ferguson. It was Farrar who provided the "scientific" basis for the supposed bird flu, identifying the reemergence of a virulent bird flu (H5N1) in humans, citing the case of a little girl who supposedly caught it from a pet duck.[94] Farrar later (in 2013) acceded to directorship of the hugely powerful Wellcome Trust, one of the world's largest foundations and the foremost funder of biomedical research. Unsurprisingly, fifteen years after his fateful bird-flu faux pas, Farrar's name pops up in connection with Fauci's coronavirus cover-up. I will return to that subject in the next section, but here need to share a few facts about the perhaps somewhat better-known pandemic manufacturer, Neil Ferguson.

In 2020, Ferguson famously predicted that Covid-19 would kill up to 2.2 million persons in the United States alone, triggering the wave of fear that swept, tsunami-like, over the whole nation. Ferguson, though, must have learned from his mistakes. In 2005 his margin of error had been even greater. In that year, he predicted the bird flu might take as many as 150 million lives. In fact, 282 people in the whole world died of the flu between 2003 and 2009. For the record, Ferguson's 2001 foot-and-mouth, 2002 mad cow disease, and 2009 swine flu estimates were hardly more accurate.[95]

The story of the 2009 Hong Kong swine flu, however, includes a few notable variations on the standard pandemic plot.

First, Bill Gates is by this time chief funder of the WHO (which declares the phony pandemic), as well a main financial sponsor of Neil Ferguson's outfit, the Imperial College of London, which predicted that the Hong Kong swine flu would take the lives of 65,000 persons in Britain alone. In fact, only 457 people in the UK died.[96]

Second, 2009 saw the debut of an important novel tactic: the timely changing of critical scientific terms in order to willfully reshape reality to conform to the Big Pharma agenda, now aligned with Gates's own. To understand the full import of the passage below, it's important to know that Gates entertains close financial and administrative ties with GlaxoSmithKline.

> WHO'S declaration [of a global pandemic] activated $18 billion worth of sleeper contracts that WHO—and Gates's other organizations—had pressured various African and European countries to sign with GlaxoSmithKline and other pharmaceutical companies. These secretive agreements obliged signatory nations including Germany, Great Britain, Italy, and France to purchase 18 billion dollars of various experimental, untested fast-tracked zero-liability H1N1 flu vaccines, most notably Glaxo's product, Pandemrix, in the event that the WHO declared a Class 6 pandemic.

> Then, just in time to trigger the sleeper contracts, WHO...changed the definition of Class 6 "pandemic," deleting the words and the requirement for "mass deaths around the globe." "You could now have a pandemic with zero deaths," explained Michael Fumento in *Forbes* magazine.[97]

This egregious, politically and economically motivated bastardization of science adumbrates the multiple crucial redefinitions (e.g., the meaning of *vaccine* or *herd immunity*) that have helped give us Covid World today.

I will spare you other gory 2009 details, including the lies scaring pregnant women into taking the vaccine and the (CDC verified) resultant steep rise in miscarriages.[98] History judged the 2009 pandemic a hoax and, in the words one leading European health authority, "one of the greatest medicine scandals of the century."

The Zika and Dengue episodes featured minor variations on the same script, the one staged yet again in our day and starring Covid-19.

Biosecurity Background

The history of technology plays a critical role in the Covid World backstory, yet does so less in its purely technical dimensions than by way of its intersection with political history. The Great Reset agenda that Schwab, Malleret, and their brethren now link so closely to Covid-19 took shape as the natural complement of a nexus of political developments that led to the rise of what Kennedy and others call "the biosecurity state."

Writers today speak of "the national security state" to denote government excessively focused, psychologically as well as practically, upon security concerns. To speak of "the biosecurity state" implies that not only is the state so oriented, but also that a great deal (even the lion's share) of attention lavished on security involves infectious disease, biowarfare, bioterrorism, as well as other matters that directly implicate human biology,

Combatting naturally occurring infectious disease, while clearly a public health issue, would not ordinarily be categorized as a prime national security concern of the type requiring major strategic involvement on the part of the Pentagon or CIA. Naturally occurring infectious diseases are not naturally part of any national security agenda. Yet biowarfare or terrorism (the deliberate use of biological agents, including pathogens that spread infectious disease) for military or terrorist purposes *does* bring public health concerns associated with infectious disease under the national security umbrella. If the United

States were to become the target of biological warfare, national security would dovetail with public health expertise, as in the capacity to produce and distribute a vaccine that would defend against bioterrorism. On the offense side, the ability to pose a mortal threat to other nations by virtue of bioweapon development and deployment may also figure prominently in national security planning.

For the last half century or so, but most especially since September 11, 2001, and the anthrax attacks that followed shortly thereafter, the chronicle of public health in the U.S.A. has been distinguished by the extraordinary degree to which public health policy pertaining to infectious diseases has been detached from its natural, non-military context, while being *increasingly and tightly linked to national security concerns associated with bioterrorism and biowarfare.* Since concern with infectious disease—the special province, for almost forty years, of the Fauci-led NIAID—has correlatively garnered more and more of the attention and resources allocated to public health as a whole, public health policy in general may be said to be likewise affected.

The flip side of that same coin: biowarfare, in the guise of either bioweapon development or biodefense or both, has become (especially since the 2001 anthrax incident) an increasingly central component of our national security agenda. Add to all this one more corresponding iteration—namely that, since 2001, national security concerns have become more and more pervasively woven into the fabric of American life—and we arrive, finally, at the concept of the *Biosecurity State:* a government in which biosecurity concerns play a disproportionate and even dominant role, shaping the very warp and woof of everyday existence, as has indubitably been the case since the onset of Covid-19 pandemic in early 2020.

Kennedy's last chapter, "War Games: Genesis of the Biosecurity State" begins by citing a distant but critical historical landmark:

> The United States began its first large-scale offensive bioweapons research during World War II in the spring of 1943 on orders from President Franklin Roosevelt, as a collaboration between the US military and its pharmaceutical industry partners. Pharma titan George W. Merck ran the Pentagon's offensive bioweapon program while simultaneously directing his drug manufacturing behemoth. Merck boasted that his team could deliver biowarfare agents without vast expenditures or constructing huge facilities. Another advantage of bioweapons, he remarked, was that their development could proceed under the guise of legitimate medical research.[99]

There is critical information here; more, perhaps, than first meets the eye. Not only does the passage give us a point of departure for construing the history of biowarfare in the US, it sets in stark relief a fact at once obvious and yet all too commonly overlooked: before biowarfare can be any kind of military business, it is first pharmaceutical business. Military operations involving bioweapon development (and, in most scenarios, biodefense) depend upon pharmaceutical research and development. This in turn means that *the more closely public health supervision of the field of infectious disease* (Tony Fauci's chief mission as head of the NIAID) *is associated with biowarfare and biosecurity concerns, the more it is indissolubly linked to pharmaceutical company activities and interests.* Biosecurity concerns thus may be seen as the seed of a close and lasting liaison between federally (including DOD) sponsored funding, research, and development pertaining to pathogens and infectious diseases, and the pharmaceutical industry.

That seed, however, took a while to sprout. While there is a clear and necessary connection between biowarfare (and so the military) and pharmaceutical company expertise, the connection between *public health* and military operations is not similarly inherent. Nor is, moreover, the link between public health and Big Pharma absolute because public health—unlike bioweapon development—does not begin and end with pharmaceutically engineered substances and treatments. It is only, in fact, the peculiar historic development of public health in the United States that makes it appear so, a history in which Tony Fauci plays a pivotal role. While biosecurity and Big Pharma were linked from the outset, public health agency did not routinely mediate and coordinate military and pharmaceutical operations until the post-9/11 era when—for reasons I will soon explain— Fauci's NIAID became the regular institutional organ of federal defense and private pharmaceutical company cooperation.

If public health agencies were not initially central to the covert bioweapon program inaugurated by Franklin Roosevelt in 1943, another, more independent arm of the government was. "The intelligence agencies," writes Kennedy, "were involved in the top secret program from the outset." In this connection, Kennedy cites the tragic figure of Frank Olson, an American bacteriologist, biowarfare researcher, CIA officer, and Merck employee. Tragic, because Olson eventually (in 1952) quit the bioweapon program because of moral qualms. Not long thereafter, he was—as the federal government itself finally admitted—murdered by CIA operatives.[100]

While Olson's resignation ended his involvement with biosecurity-related programs, it did not end the CIA's. As we will see, the CIA, and methods associated with its characteristic means of achieving control over persons and populations, continued to play a major role in the long and complex developments contributing to the rise of the Biosecurity State over three-quarters of a century. Former CIA deputy director Avril Haine's active participation in Event 201 represents just one visible sign that this influence remains very much operative today.

By 1969, the US bioweapons program had attained a high level of sophistication. According to the commander of the US Army Medical Research Institute of Infectious Disease, that program had the capability of producing weapons of "nuclear equivalence." That same director, however, acknowledged at least one clear and present danger bedeviling any such program: the difficulty of precluding the disastrous possibility of accidental release.[101]

The moral as well as practical abyss that yawns below any bioweapon program was not indefinitely ignored. In 1969, President Nixon officially closed the program. In 1972, America signed the Biological Weapons Convention prohibiting "development, use, and stockpiling of biological weapons" and shut most of its relevant laboratory facilities.

This, however, did not constitute the effective end of biosecurity operations in the United States. It did not do so for two major reasons. First, influential personnel in science, industry, and government long associated with the program continued to be invested in the continuation or revivification of biosecurity operations. Second, one means of so doing found historic inscription in the text of the Convention itself, the central clause of which contained a fateful exception. While the Convention outlawed manufacture of biowarfare agents in general, it nonetheless permitted it *for the purposes of vaccine production.* As long as it could be claimed that development and use of a given agent were linked, directly or indirectly, to vaccinological research and development, relevant R + D could legally march on through the corridors of history.

Past and future standard-bearers of America's biosecurity agenda—military contractors, Big Pharma brass, and public health heads like Anthony Fauci—have since strolled through that barn-door-sized loophole in the Convention's otherwise stringent guidelines. We can (amongst a long list of mostly tragic eventualities) thank that gaping loophole for the travail of Covid-19.

Bioweapon research never ceased. The current of government and pharmaceutical company cooperation ran on, strong but unseen, like a river under ice. On occasion, extenuating circumstances might force it to surface, even if invisibly. Note the Merck-like coincidence of Big Pharma and government in the person of Donald Rumsfeld in this Kennedy quote:

> [After the Biological Weapons Convention] the Pentagon and CIA spooks continued to cultivate bioweapon seed stock. Between 1983 and 1988, Searle Pharmaceuticals CEO Donald Rumsfeld, acting as Ronald Reagan's envoy in Iraq, arranged for the top-secret shipment of tons of chemical and biological armaments, including anthrax and bubonic plague to Iraqi President Saddam Hussein, hoping to reverse his looming defeat.[102]

After the end of the Soviet regime in 1988–1991, the American military-industrial complex looked around for another antagonist, a viable substitute for the enemy superpower whose existence justified its monstrous budget. The World Trade Center bombing in 1993 nominated Islamic terrorism for that role, but this cast had marked disadvantages. For years, no genuine threat materialized, and it was difficult to maintain the fear level at an acceptable public relations threshold. The second, more consequential, World Trade Center attack naturally boosted the profile of the War on Terror, but the delivery of anthrax-laden letters a scant week later provided another complementary—and in many ways more promising—window of opportunity.

The public could, after all, largely see for themselves whether Islamists were or were not stirring real trouble in their own backyard, and mostly the answer was . . . *not.* Germs, on the other hand, are another matter. No one *sees* germs, or can tell whether or not they are present to contaminate and kill. They can, moreover, spread far more quickly, and with far more deadly effect, than terrorist bombs or bullets.

September 11 and the resultant Patriot Act catapulted security concerns into the limelight in the U.S.A. That said, it was the anthrax letters, and the opportunistic genius of a few key figures, that ensured that germs, not guns, became the core of the national *Bio*security State that emerged from under the rubble of the WTC.

First and foremost amongst those figures was Robert P. Kadlec. If Fauci may be regarded as the prince of bioterror alarmism, Kadlec qualifies as its godfather, the career physician/retired Air Force colonel/bioweapons expert whose decades-long obsession with biowarfare paved the new century's way for Event 201, Faucigate, and our ongoing Corona Chronicles.

Kadlec Kountry

Kennedy introduces Robert P. Kadlec in cinematic terms:

> Kadlec is a Dr. Strangelove knockoff with deep ties to spy agencies, Big Pharma, the Pentagon, and military contractors who profiteer from the spread of bioweapon alarmism.... Kadlec played an historic leadership role in fomenting the contagious logic that infectious disease posed a national security threat requiring a militarized response.[103]

The decade or so running from the first WTC bombings in 1993 and September 11, 2001, the subsequent anthrax attacks, and the aftermath of those world-shaking events may be seen as the pregnancy and explosive birth of the Biosecurity State. Here are some telling signposts[104] of Kadlec's own bioterror career during that formative time:

- Using the 1993 WTC bomb attack as a prompt, Kadlec persistently stirred fears that an impending anthrax attack would end American life as we know it.
- In the mid-ninety-nineties and the aftermath of the Gulf War, Kadlec joined elite Air Force personnel with whom, under the auspices of UN weapons inspection, he vainly scoured the Iraqi desert searching for hidden caches of bioweapons (chiefly anthrax and botulism) thought to be in Saddam's possession.
- In 1999, Kadlec scripted a number of "illustrative scenarios" (a Chinese-sponsored "Corn Terror," for instance) vividly exhibiting what he believed to be America's marked vulnerability to biowarfare. These scenarios were the forerunners of the series of simulations that soon followed.
- In 1999, Kadlec organized the first full-scale bioterror simulation: a smallpox terrorist attack in the US.
- In spring of 2001, Kadlec penned a study for the National Defense University National War College promoting the idea of the creation of a Strategic National Stockpile (SNS) "to warehouse countermeasures including vaccines and antibiotics" and urged "regulatory changes to provide for mandatory vaccinations and coercive quarantines in the event of a pandemic."[105]
- In June of 2001, Kadlec, in cooperation with the Pentagon, organized a still more consequential smallpox simulation which he himself personally code-named "Dark Winter."

- That same summer, Kadlec, acting in concert with the DOD, authored a report arguing that the military lacks sufficient capacity to generate the vaccines necessary to protect troops from biological warfare. In sending the report to congress, the Department of Defense "officially launched its drive to revive bioweapons research."
- After the twin tower and anthrax attacks, in fall 2001, Kadlec secured a post as Special Assistant for Biodefense Planning under President George W. Bush.
- In 2004, Kadlec, working under ex-pharmaceutical executive Secretary of Defense Donald Rumsfeld, drafted the Public Health Security and Bioterrorism Preparedness Act and the Project BioShield Act, both of which Congress passed. The former, directing the secretary of HHS to maintain a Strategic National Stockpile, turned Kadlec's SNS dream into reality. The latter launched the Biomedical Advanced Research and Development Authority (BARDA).

The two Kadlec-inspired congressional acts represent one crest of the historic wave propelled by 9/11:

> Beginning with the 9/11 attack, the War on Terror triggered a tectonic shift in global security priorities and elephantine ripples in defense spending patterns across the globe as open democracies began shifting to a security state footing. The revival of US government interest in germ warfare opened new opportunities. The US biodefense budget went from $137 million in 1997 to $14.5 billion for 2001–2004.... Between 2001 and 2014, the United States spent around $80 billion on biodefense. *Since germ weaponry was still illegal, vaccines became a critical euphemism for the revival of the multibillion-dollar bioweapons industry* [emphasis added].[106]

The Kadlec-inspired acts creating the SNS and BARDA solidified the foundation of the Biosecurity State. Originally invested with $5 billion worth of purchasing power, the Strategic National Stockpile today contains $7 billion worth of biodefense and bioweapon-related material while BARDA funds research capable of making novel contributions to it.[107] Since inception of the SNS, the man responsible for its existence has exercised significant control over the stockpile and purchase of its contents, ensuring Kadlec's continuing clout in the new Biosecurity State.

Tony Fauci, Doctor at Arms

So much for the basis of Robert Kadlec's lasting influence, but what of the man who today doubtless represents the public face of Biosecurity State, Dr. Anthony Fauci?

During the critical 2001–2004 period, hawkish Dick Cheney acted as one of the most influential vice-presidents in history. Cheney and others in his circle (notably members of the conservative think tank the PNAC, or Project for a New American Century, including then Secretary of Defense and ex-pharma executive Donald Rumsfeld) supported expansion of the revived bio-weapons research program, but the Biological Weapons Convention presented real obstacles. The answer? Tony Fauci's NIAID:

> The Department of Defense had strict systems in place to ensure compliance with the Biological Weapons Convention. Those restrictions limited the Pentagon's freedom to undertake new research programs, particularly those referred to as "the leading edge of biodefense." Cheney's response... "was to transfer this research from the Department of Defense to the National Institutes of Health, specifically to the National Institute of Allergy and Infectious Diseases (NIAID). By about 2004, this transfer was complete, and NIAID had been transformed into an arm of the defense sector." This made the NIAID Director Anthony Fauci a major player in biodefense and germ warfare.[108]

How did Dr. Fauci play the game?

> Dr. Fauci...began maneuvering for a leading role for NIAID in milking the BARDA/Homeland Security cash cows. *NIAID's biosecurity budget went from zero dollars in 2000 to $1.7 billion after the 2001 anthrax letters, much of that for bioweapon vaccines* [emphasis added].
>
> Within five months following the anthrax postal incidents, Dr. Fauci had created two new sub-agencies to capture his share of the cheese: the NIAID Strategic Plan for Biodefense Research and the NIAID Biodefense Research Agenda for CDC Category A agents, which were those microorganisms designated by the CDC to be potential pathogens. To populate the sub-agencies, he assembled a cadre of his loyal deputies.... Their mission was to brand contagions as pressing terror threats, drum up pandemic panic, and lobby for government support for NIAID's new battery of biodefense vaccinations.[109]

The administration of public health should ideally function *independently* of military interests, on the one hand, and the pharmaceutical company interests, on the other. Good public health management could, of course, draw upon pharmaceutical expertise and serve national security interests when and where that might be appropriate, but should not be indentured to either, or squeezed into position as little but a structural link, a functional bridge between military and Big Pharma-inspired operations.

Since the first years of the new millennium, however, that is precisely the position occupied by Fauci and his NIAID, and his terrible performance reflects the tragic truth that, under Fauci, *America's public health agencies have not been operating with public health interests—independently, openly, and objectively construed—foremost in mind. Instead, other (primarily military and industrial) interests committed to means and ends often foreign and even antithetical to public health and welfare set the agenda.*

Covid-19 is one dreadful consequence of this dysfunction. It is so in each of two fundamental respects: the origin of Sars-CoV-2 virus and so Covid-19 itself; and the systematic response to the Covid-19 "pandemic." Let me look briefly at the first of these to end this section before turning to the second in the next.

Good governmental initiatives—the Biological Weapons Convention in 1972; the moratorium on "gain-of-function" experiments imposed in 2014 by the Obama administration to further blunt "the leading edge of biodefense"—admirably seek to safeguard the world from the Frankensteinian fancies of half-mad scientists and politicians whose lust for knowledge, power, and money incautiously puts the world at risk. Yet the system (the Matrix) consistently works to circumvent such hindrances.

> With Kadlec's guidance, BARDA would become a federal ATM machine for BigPharma, biodefense contractors, and gain-of-function researchers. Along with *Fauci's NIAID* and the Pentagon's DARPA, BARDA would be the other big-league funder for experiments to create pandemic superbugs in Wuhan and elsewhere.[110]

How could no-longer-legal gain-of-function experiments continue after 2014? I cannot here go into the complex combination of administrative deceit and regulatory negligence that allowed the experiments to go forward. I will, however, observe that if the system finds itself in danger of getting caught in the act, it naturally covers its tracks. Or tries to.

Historic threads link Kadlec, Fauci, Jeremy Farrar (Farrar, remember, was the British Wellcome Trust researcher who provided the phony scientific rationale for the 2005 bird flu), NIH chief Francis Collins, and others in what recent evidence more and more clearly reveals to have been a concerted effort to discredit the eminently plausible lab leak hypothesis.

Kennedy:

> At 2:47 in the early morning of February 1, 2020, four hours after his loyal grantee, virologist Kristian Andersen, informed Dr. Fauci that he and other leading biologists believed that the genetic sequence responsible for the "furin cleave" on the virus's spike protein...was highly unlikely to be the product of natural selection,[111] Dr. Anthony Fauci fired a carefully worded e-mail to Kadlec.... If Dr. Fauci's gain-of-function research had indeed minted Covid-19, then Kadlec would also be implicated. Kadlec served on the small so-called P3CO Committee charged with approving NIH's gain-of-function experiments.[112]

The first of February was indeed a busy one for Tony Fauci, as phone call and e-mail trails (although heavily redacted) attest. All evidence points to a no-holds-barred campaign by Fauci and his circle to head off any hint of suspicion. The first and chief objective: to change the tune, if not the minds, of scientists, such as Andersen, who were leaning towards challenging Covid's zoonotic origin, and could conceivably spill some *highly* inconvenient beans.

It must have helped, of course, that Andersen was financially and professionally beholden to Fauci. The record shows that that very afternoon, Fauci held a "top-secret" call with Andersen and several other scientists. The meeting and many intricately maneuvered follow-ups produced the desired (one would not want to say the inevitable) result. When a paper co-authored by Andersen appeared in *Nature Med* on March 17, it asserted:

> Our analyses clearly show that SARS-CoV-2 is not a laboratory construct or a purposefully manipulated virus.... It is improbable that SARS-CoV-2 emerged through laboratory manipulation of a related SARS-CoV-like virus.[113]

One of the few scientists on that mind-bending February 1 call was none other than Jeremy Farrar. If there is any doubt that Fauci and his accomplices did not have their hand on the wheel of the car, a March 6 email from Andersen should set the record straight. As reported in *The Washington Examiner*:

> Andersen had sent Fauci, NIH Director Dr. Francis Collins, and British researcher and Wellcome Trust director Jeremy Farrar an email on March 6, 2020, to "thank you again for your advice and leadership as we have been working through the SARS-CoV-2 'origins' paper" for *Nature* and to give them the chance to provide "any comments, suggestions, or questions about the paper or the press release."[114]

A day before Andersen sent this email, a now notorious paper appeared in *The Lancet* defending the integrity of the scientific work at Wuhan and condemning all those promoting any kind of lab leak theory as proponents of "conspiracy theory."[115] One hardly expects to find that phrase in a prestigious science journal supposedly dedicated to open inquiry and objective truth. The irony, of course, is that key signatories of the paper, including Jeremy Farrar and Peter Daszak, were soon accused of flagrant conflicts of interest. Accumulating evidence indeed shows, beyond a reasonable doubt, that Daszak, Farrar, and many others participated in a carefully orchestrated Fauci-led conspiracy to disguise (for all too obvious reasons) what now appears to be the true origin of Covid-19.[116]

The Lancet and (the more scientifically respectable, at least on the surface) *Nature* papers sufficed to put lab leak suspicions to rest for a good long while, though not, as we now know, indefinitely. The Biosecurity State is indeed formidable, but not invincible.

21st-Century America: A Case of "Long Covid"?

One of the most remarkable and revealing features of the whole Covid-19 story is the number of key parties (individuals, think tanks, foundations) who are not only largely responsible for the prevailing system of Covid response, but have likewise been integrally involved in the modern Biosecurity State ever since its inception twenty-odd years ago. Kadlec (who, recall, directed the Covid-19 response under President Trump) and Fauci are perhaps the most prominent cases in point, but this holds true for many others as well. An impressively long resumé of biosecurity service appears the rule amongst the core of four-star Covid generals and their faithful divisions. Correlatively, Event 201 is only one of many similar simulations that have trained players over a span of two decades, rehearsing the same basic text over and over—a playscript written, not by any humane Shakespeare of Public Health, but by military-medical-industrial-complex Iagos like Kadlec himself.

Take the very first Kadlec-inspired smallpox simulation in 1999, a joint exercise by the US Department of Health and Human Services and the just-formed Johns Hopkins Center for Civilian Biodefense Strategies, the first academic center devoted to biodefense.[117] The Johns Hopkins Center has indeed (like Kadlec and Fauci) been on set from beginning to end; for it is the very outfit—later renamed the Center for Health Security—that cosponsored Event 201 with the Bill and Melinda Gates Foundation and the World Economic Forum.

Characteristically, individual persons instrumental in the formation of critical organizations (such as The Hopkins Center) themselves have remained on stage for the whole of our ongoing biosecurity drama. Event 201 participant Tom Inglesby furnishes a case in point. Inglesby counts as a player of special note insofar as he is *both* current director of the Johns Hopkins Center for Health Security (and so effectively a sponsor of the Event itself) and, too, presently "on temporary assignment at the White House working on the Covid-19 response team."[118]

Very well, but what is Inglesby's connection to the inaugural smallpox simulation two decades prior? At that time, Inglesby, who had completed his residency and fellowship in infectious diseases at John Hopkins, held the post of assistant professor there, and—along with D. A. Henderson and Tara O'Toole, its first two directors—helped establish the center, which he himself has led since assuming directorship in 2009.

Nor are Inglesby and Johns Hopkins the only other actors playing starring roles in *both* the 1999 smallpox simulation *and* Event 201. Connection between at least two of the Event 201 co-sponsors date back the full twenty years. Kennedy:

> In 1999, the Bill and Melinda Gates Foundation committed $20 million to Johns Hopkins to establish the Bill and Melinda Gates Institute for Population and Reproductive Health. For the next two decades, Gates would direct a vast stream of funding to the enterprise of elevating biosecurity as the national priority. Some of his most visible investments funded a series of simulations presided over by Inglesby at his Johns Hopkins Center.
>
> Those simulations would make Inglesby the congenial face of biosecurity paranoia, feed the burgeoning biodefense industry, and help lay the foundation for the modern security state.[119]

Of course, Inglesby himself would hardly phrase it that way. In his "Letter from the Director" in the Center's 2010–2011 Annual Report, one can discern both the congeniality *and* the paranoia. Inglesby begins by citing the National Director of Intelligence's own words:

> The threat and destabilizing effect of nuclear proliferation, as well as the threat from the proliferation of materials and technologies that could contribute to existing and prospective chemical and biological weapons programs, are among our top concerns.[120]

Writing in the aftermath of Osama bin Laden's death, Inglesby accents the magnitude of the continuing threat:

> Without question, biological and nuclear threats persist and, along with the threats of natural disasters and pandemics, may even increase over time.

At that point, he proceeds to highlight, with admiral clarity, the manner in which public health concerns have been merged with national and international security concerns:

> As we've worked to address biological and nuclear threats over time, we have seen the traditional lines between many disciplines blur and even disappear. This is true, for instance, with regard to perceptions of disease outbreaks outside of the U.S. *Once considered purely public health problems, disease outbreaks are now recognized as potential threats to national and international security* [emphasis added].[121]

While Inglesby emphasizes the intersection of public health and national (as well international) security concerns, his letter exemplifies the contagious kind of thinking that can readily lead to the latter *encroaching upon* and indeed *usurping* the domain of the former. Judging from the character of the ensuing simulations, such usurpation not only indeed transpired, but constituted an emergent mind-set drilled into "Germ Game" participants with positively military rigor.

The following passage, characterizing these germ games, speaks of "Kadlec's simulations." The events indubitably bear the signature of the "Dr. Strangelove knockoff with deep ties to spy agencies, Big Pharma, the Pentagon, and military contractors," but they are *also* Inglesby's, whose Center hosted most of them, and Gates's who—along with Fauci's NIAID—funded and guided them.

Whatever their patronage, the playscript is frighteningly familiar (or familiarly frightening):

> Kadlec's simulations, and over a dozen that would succeed it over the next twenty plus years—many under Bill Gates's direction—shared common features. None of them emphasized protecting public health by showing Americans how to bolster their immune systems, to eat well, to lose weight, to exercise, to maintain vitamin D levels, and to avoid chemical exposure. None of these focused on devising the vital communications infrastructures to link frontline doctors during a pandemic or to facilitate the development and refinement of optimal treatment protocols. None of these dealt seriously with the need to identify off-the-shelf (now known as "repurposed") therapeutic drugs to mitigate fatalities and to shorten a pandemic's duration. None of them considered ways to isolate the sick and protect the vulnerable—or how to shield people in nursing homes and other institutions from infection. None of them questioned the efficacy of masks, lockdowns, and social distancing in reducing casualties. None of them engaged in soul-searching about how to preserve constitutional rights during a global pandemic.[122]

Thus the long list of negatives—what the simulations did *not* do—belies a blanket disregard of both public health and democratic considerations. The list of "positives" is correspondingly grim:

> Instead, the simulations war-gamed how to use police powers to detain and quarantine citizens, how to impose martial law, how to control messaging by deploying propaganda, how to employ censorship to silence dissent, and how to mandate masks, lockdowns, and coercive vaccinations and conduct track-and-trace surveillance among potentially reluctant populations.[123]

The simulation succeeding the 1999 smallpox game, "Dark Winter," unfolded over the course of two days in June 2001, a few months before 9/11. Its chief sponsor (the Pentagon) and its site (Andrews Air Force Base) set the militaristic premises of the exercise in high relief. The event war-gamed a smallpox attack commencing in Oklahoma City. True to scripted form, participants trained in all the strong-arm strategies and tactics cited above, the whole grotesquely misshapen ensemble of which was presented (at least in Kennedy's critical view) "as the only rational responses to the pandemic."[124]

Perhaps of even greater historical consequence, the script of the influential exercise (which gained great and laudatory attention after 9/11 and the ensuing anthrax attack) ended, not in success but in catastrophe. Why?

After reciting the whole inventory of coercive measures, Kennedy rehearses the end of the Dark Winter scenario and the chief conclusions drawn therefrom:

> The failure, in the Dark Winter case, to quickly implement such countermeasures allowed the galloping spread of the Pentagon's imaginary smallpox epidemic to overwhelm America's response capabilities, precipitating massive civilian casualties, widespread panic, societal breakdown, and mob violence. The Pentagon summary of the exercise concluded that *scarcity of vaccines to curtail the contagion's spread proved the most severe limitation on management options* [emphasis added].[125]

Anyone who refuses to see the outlines of the worldwide Vaccine-Distance System of Covid response adumbrated here is turning a blind eye to the historical record.

Dark Winter, though, counts as a very early exercise. There followed Atlantic Storm and Global Mercury in 2003, another iteration of Atlantic Storm in 2005, and many, many others.

> Dark Winter, Atlantic Storm, and Global Mercury were only three of over a dozen Germ Games staged by military, medical, and intelligence planners leading up to COVID-19. Each of these Kafkaesque exercises became uncanny predictors of a dystopian age that pandemic planners dubbed the "New Normal." The consistent feature is an affinity among their simulation designers for militarizing medicine and introducing autocratic governance. Each rehearsal ends with the same grim punchline: the global pandemic is an excuse to justify the imposition of tyranny and coerced vaccination.[126]

Providing us with further relevant background, Kennedy informs us that military intelligence planners first essayed "scenario planning as a strategic device" during World War II. The practice migrated into the corporate world in the latter half of the century by way of Peter Schwartz and his Global Business Network (GBN). Consequently, even before the turn of the millennium and the critical events that followed:

> Simulations had evolved into an indispensable vehicle for military policy makers, intelligence agency planners, public health technocrats, and the petroleum and pharmaceutical multinationals for reinforcing prescribed responses that allow predictable and rigid control of the outcomes of future crises.[127]

It was thus virtually inevitable that, as the Biosecurity State rose to prominence, its executors would adopt the tried-and-true technique for their own kindred purposes:

> After 9/11, the rising biosecurity cartel adopted simulations as signaling mechanisms for choreographing lockstep response among corporate, political, and military technocrats charged with managing global exigencies. Scenario planning became an indispensable device for multiple power centers to coordinate complex strategies for simultaneously imposing coercive controls upon democratic societies across the globe.[128]

We find ourselves here in the veritable nerve center of the Matrix. As Neo[129] knows, it's not a comfortable place to be.

2010: Lockstep and The Decade of Vaccines

Like Inglesby's letter, the "Lockstep" scenario was scripted in 2010, midpoint between the inaugural simulations at the turn of the millennium and Event 201 and Covid-19. As Inglesby's letter suggests, biosecurity issues had quickly risen to the top of the Obama administration's foreign policy agenda, and the President directed all government agencies to include a biosecurity angle in their ongoing operation. By this time, that was nothing novel for intelligence agencies; but the new decade nonetheless marked a heavier accent in one critical regard, at least according to Kennedy's version of the development:

> By 2010, US spy agencies were demonstrating a growing interest in vaccines as a foreign policy instrument.... Vaccination programs could justify intervention in developing countries with high disease burdens as a tool for social and political control.[130]

Whether or not one accepts Kennedy's characteristically critical perspective, 2010 represents a significant year in the history of, if not vaccine *science*, then vaccine *promotion*. In January 2010 Bill Gates delivered his "Decade of Vaccines" speech, as reported in this excerpt from the Bill and Melinda Gates Foundation's own website:

> DAVOS, Switzerland—Bill and Melinda Gates announced today that their foundation will commit $10 billion over the next 10 years to help research, develop and deliver vaccines for the world's poorest countries....
>
> "We must make this the decade of vaccines," said Bill Gates. "Vaccines already save and improve millions of lives in developing countries. Innovation will make it possible to save more children than ever before."
>
> Bill and Melinda Gates made their announcement at the World Economic Forum's Annual Meeting....

"Vaccines are a miracle—with just a few doses, they can prevent deadly diseases for a lifetime," said Melinda Gates. "We've made vaccines our number-one priority at the Gates Foundation...."

The foundation used a model developed by a consortium led by the Institute of International Programs at the Johns Hopkins Bloomberg School of Public Health to project the potential impact of vaccines on childhood deaths over the next 10 years.[131]

We have here the same cast of suspects: The Gates Foundation, the WEF, and Johns Hopkins (the Center for Health Security is likewise under the aegis of the Bloomberg School) were, of course, the co-sponsors of Event 201.

As usual, moreover, Dr. Fauci (who first teamed up with Gates all the way back in 1998) is right around the corner. Shortly after Gates's Decade of Vaccines speech, Gates's foundation teamed with WHO, UNICEF, and the NIAID to initiate a Global Vaccine Action Plan to turn Gates's money into practical action. Fauci himself and just four others (including the heads of WHO and UNICEF) manned the Plan's Leadership Council.

One should, though, not make *too* much of the novelty of the Gates pledge: Fauci and Gates had been pushing vaccine projects for years. As noble as Bill and Melinda's pledge may seem to some, many regard Gates's globalist vaccine-centric heroism as an unmitigated disaster for world health and, more broadly, international as well as national governance structures.

Vandana Shiva excoriates Gates as the individual who "hijacked the WHO and transformed it into an instrument of personal power that he wields for the cynical purpose of increasing pharmaceutical profits."[132] Jeremy Loffredo and Michele Greenstein strike a similar chord:

> The Gates Foundation has already effectively privatized the international body charged with creating public health policy, transforming it into a vehicle for corporate dominance. It has facilitated the dumping of toxic products onto the people of the Global South, and even used the world's poor as guinea pigs for drug experiments.... The Gates Foundation's influence over public health policy is practically contingent on ensuring that safety regulations and other government functions are weak enough to be circumvented. It therefore operates against the independence of nation states and as a vehicle for Western capital.[133]

Journalist Celia Farber, meanwhile, highlights the racial and neo-colonial dimensions of Gates's empire building:

> The racism is cloaked inside carefully crafted philanthropic manipulations such as "access" to drugs. It's never access to clean drinking water, education, sanitation, nutrition. It's a very blighting message for the US to constantly be browbeating Africans with our self-serving messaging that they are so sick, and we have just the drugs to "save" their lives. When the opposite happens, it's swept away and hidden behind the false front of charity. I call it Pharma-Colonialism.[134]

This criticism should hit all American denizens of our current Fauci/Gates-inspired Covid World with a gut-punching wallop. *The Covid mortality rates in the US exceeded those in virtually all African countries by orders of magnitude even though the African vaccination rate is a fraction of ours.* That one nonetheless *still* regularly hears propaganda about how we desperately need to increase the vaccination rate of developing nations in the interest of global health spotlights the profoundly illogical perversity of the prevailing Covid agenda.

One could add, too, that these critiques should reveal the terrible hypocrisy inherent in the stance of so many left-leaning persons who make a religion of decrying all traces of racism and colonialism in the United States, yet are utterly blind to how their unthinking support of the controlling Covid narrative unmasks them as unwitting cheerleaders of Pharma-Colonialism come home to roost. American citizens have been systematically subjected to the same willful ignorance of *real comprehensive public health concerns* that the Gates/Fauci/Big Pharma conglomerate has so destructively foisted upon too many "poorer" (most frequently African) nations in the past.

The 2010 Lockstep scenario excluded attention to genuine public health concerns as systematically as all prior and following simulations. The level and duration of the coercion endorsed, however, was novel. Correlatively, the Lockstep scenario offers a window that provides a clear view of a deeply disturbing phenomenon—namely, the degree to which the primary texts underwriting the Biosecurity State (and the scenario reports and simulations certainly qualify as such) are scripted by persons deeply influenced by thinking sourced in US Intelligence and the mind-frame of its spying agents.

As I have mentioned, CIA involvement in biosecurity affairs in general and simulations in particular harkens back—at least—to the very first simulations organized by Kadlec. Speaking of Dark Winter, Kennedy notes that the participation of Senator Sam Nunn in the role of POTUS lent peculiar prestige to the simulation before observing: "Most of the other key participants shared

Kadlec's intelligence agency pedigrees. CIA involvement was a consistent feature of this and all the subsequent simulations."[135] Event 201 proves no exception to this rule, as evidenced by Avril Haine's active participation.

Linking (in accord with the historical record) pandemic politics and vaccine promotion, Kennedy provides telling perspective as to why the constant CIA presence at events intended to model suitable pandemic response should so trouble us:

> The pervasive CIA involvement in the global vaccine putsch should give us pause. There is nothing in the CIA's history, in its charter, in its composition, or in its institutional culture that betrays an interest in promoting either public health or democracy. The CIA's historic preoccupations have been power and control.... The CIA does not do public health. It does not do democracy. The CIA does *coups d'état.*[136]

Later, Kennedy fleshes out this dire declaration in specific connection to the techniques taught at the simulations:

> Virtually all of the scenario-planning for pandemics employs technical assumptions and strategies familiar to anyone who has read the CIA's notorious psychological warfare manuals for shattering indigenous societies, obliterating traditional economies and social bonds, for using imposed isolation and the demolition of traditional economies to crush resistance, to foster chaos, demoralization, dependence and fear, and for imposing centralized and autocratic governance.[137]

Lockstep represents a signature case in point. First of all, Peter Schwartz, the author of the scenario, sports a resumé steeped in intelligence agency influence, including directing Stanford's Strategic Environment Center when the CIA was running its MK-Ultra program (which involved investigating psychological warfare) out of the Center. Nor, given Kennedy's mention of indigenous societies, is Schwartz's tenure as head of Royal Dutch/Shell irrelevant, especially perhaps when we recognize that Lockstep was not (like Event 201) written for live simulation, but the name of the crucial section in a Rockefeller Foundation scenario report titled "Scenarios for the Future of Technology and International Development."[138]

The proof, however, is in the pudding, so here is a sample passage from Schwartz's 2010 Lockstep script:

> In 2012, the pandemic that the world had been anticipating for years finally hit. Unlike 2009's H1N1, this new influenza strain—originating from wild

> geese—was extremely virulent and deadly. Even the most pandemic-prepared nations were quickly overwhelmed when the virus streaked around the world, infecting nearly 20 percent of the global population and killing 8 million in just seven months....
>
> The pandemic also had a deadly effect on economies: international mobility of both people and goods screeched to a halt, debilitating industries like tourism and breaking global supply chains. Even locally, normally bustling shops and office buildings sat empty for months, devoid of both employees and customers.
>
> During the pandemic, national leaders around the world flexed their authority and imposed airtight rules and restrictions, from the mandatory wearing of face masks to body-temperature checks at the entries to communal spaces like train stations and supermarkets. *Even after the pandemic faded, this more authoritarian control and oversight of citizens and their activities stuck and even intensified. In order to protect themselves from the spread of increasingly global problems—from pandemics and transnational terrorism to environmental crisis and rising poverty—leaders around the world took a firmer grip on power* [emphasis added].[139]

This sounds hauntingly familiar, doesn't it?

Notice, too, the clause: *Even after the pandemic faded....* That puts us right back in the lap of the Great Reset, the groundwork for which the Matrix has been steadily preparing for some twenty-odd years.

Chapter 4

TRANSHUMANISM 2020: THE CROSS AND THE MACHINE

To anyone acquainted with the history rehearsed in the prior chapter, it will likely appear that persons who condemn critique of the mainstream Covid narrative as "conspiracy theory" do so out of deficient knowledge, political naïveté, or a willful combination of both. No one who has studied and absorbed the relevant facts can fail to see that the controlling Covid-19 narrative represents the latest iteration of a pandemic playbook scripted and rehearsed, again and again, over the last two decades. The parties who authored that playbook have, moreover, not had public health concerns foremost in mind. Rather, commercial, political and military interests have co-opted public health agency and effectively dictate policy that revolves, more and more, around the peculiar brand of paranoia characterizing the Biosecurity State.

Those who discard such allegations as mere "conspiracy theory" seem to me kin to a farmer who, suffering nightly loss of his chickens and finding the yard pocked by foxy footprints, catches the dapper creature strolling into the yard one evening, and—fancying him an honorable and upstanding citizen—blithely believes the smooth-talking fellow's aggrieved disclaimer of any and all responsibility.

It may be evident, too, that to credit the truths I have sought to convey does not require one to buy into an overly simplistic construction of the vortex of power I have called the Matrix or to conjure the image of a small cabal of villainous evil-doers deliberately plotting to take over the world. Even if such a notion may hold a grain of truth, it does not tell the whole story. Is, for instance, Tom Inglesby, longtime director of the Johns Hopkins Health Security Center and the "congenial" face of U.S. biosecurity, an evildoer intent on magnifying his own power and subjecting the citizenry of the world to a regime of quasi-totalitarian control?

Perhaps; perhaps not. The point is that Inglesby and his ilk can play a crucial role at the upper echelons of the Matrix hierarchy even if not wicked or ill-intentioned. All that is necessary is buy-in to a mind-set and operating manual native to certain sectors (most notably, military, intelligence, and corporate-industrial) that mold the technocratic agenda. Outstanding features of the typical *modus operandi* characteristic of those sectors include: centralized command and control; a hierarchical power structure; a technocratic form of rationality that perceives individual units as, not autonomous agents, but functional parts of larger system; rigid discipline and regimentation; compulsion and the use of force; destruction of competition and dissent; and, in general, an end-justifies-the-means war mentality. To the degree that said sectors have invaded public health agency, it is only to be expected that government response to Covid would reflect such largely top-down autocratic patterns of thought and behavior.

Technocrats in public health and like-minded accomplices in the military, in intelligence, in industry, in academia and science, in international organization, in media and Big Tech *might* believe that the Matrix agenda they support and promote serves not only their company's or agency's bottom line, but the best interests of humanity, as well. It may be that Tom Inglesby of the Johns Hopkins Center (and, for his part, Klaus Schwab at the WEF) do indeed think so.

That, however, does not mean that such is the case.

As well-intentioned as some of its executors may or may not be, I regard the technocratic agenda as essentially evil because it is constructed upon premises inherently antithetical to democracy, civil rights and liberties, and the betterment of humanity. That is in good measure on account of ideological pollution deriving from the various vested interests feeding into Matrix power as well as historic residues of colonial/imperialist political economies and salvational religious ideologies that inform the deeper levels of the collective mind of the power elite.

In her critique of Bill Gates's so-called philanthropy, Celia Farber calls it out as "Pharma-Colonialism." In characterizing the Matrix agenda, one could borrow and build upon that provocative coinage. Integrating other important sources of influence, we could speak of the modern technocracy evident in Covid management as a *Global Pharma-Colonial Para-Military Evangelical Psychops.* The official Covid system of response has been promoted as *The (Only) Way to Save the World* from a deadly and intractable enemy (Russians, Islamic extremists, the devil, and deadly pathogens all fit that bill). Its proponents adhere to it with positively religious zeal, blind or indifferent to the manner in which the technocratic Great Reset agenda undermines impartial science as well as due respect for the organic integrity of the body. Medical freedom and other basic civil rights and liberties are subverted, along with the physician-patient relationship, local prerogative, citizen advocacy, and much else basic to a free society and humane existence.

The attentive reader may well have noticed that the upbeat tenor of Schwab and Malleret's annunciation of the Great Reset contrasts sharply with the dark, spooky, macabre alarmism that colors the complexion of the Biosecurity State. While both are distinctly apocalyptic in tone, the former tends towards *utopian* prospects while the latter inclines steeply toward *dystopian* visions of the end of life as we know it. The difference, however, may ultimately be more cosmetic than substantive, for—as the spirit as well as the letter of Schwab's book reveals—*the ideological and practical agendas of the dystopian and utopian strains of the technocratic imagination converge and merge in the phenomena of Covid-19 and the global response to it.* Nor is it sheer accident that the dawn of the biosecurity era and the Fourth Industrial Revolution are, historically speaking, essentially one and the same.

Klaus Schwab published his *Fourth Industrial Revolution* in 2016, but the technological developments heralded by the book date back to the turn of the millennium. It was around that time that the computer and digital capacities characteristic of the Third Industrial Revolution (which runs roughly from 1960 forward, and includes semiconductors, mainframe and personal computing and the internet) spawned novel developments ("a much more ubiquitous and mobile internet, smaller and more powerful sensors...artificial intelligence and machine learning"[140]) that comprise—in Schwab's mind at least—yet another quantum leap in human culture.

As the anthrax letters in 2001 are often hailed as "the nativity of the modern 'Biosecurity Agenda'" its watershed years match those marking the advent of the Fourth Industrial Revolution.

This coincidence suggests what could (if it were not duly rectified) be reckoned a glaring deficiency in the last chapter's treatment of the Biosecurity State. Following Robert F. Kennedy, Jr.'s account, I sought to delineate the chief constituents of that State by tracing the intersection of military, intelligence, pharmaceutical, and governmental public health agency. I omitted, however, any concerted attention to another crucial constituent, Big Tech. I did so *not* because technology may be considered less important than any of the other aforementioned sectors, but rather the contrary. As the very term "technocracy" suggests, it is by looking more closely into the essence of technology, especially the peculiar forms of it unique to the Fourth Industrial Revolution, that we may approach the philosophical gist of the Great Reset agenda and finally begin to probe, in a more deliberate and consequential way, the spiritual dimensions of the momentous historical questions posed to us by Covid-19.

It is important to pay due attention to the historical origins of the Biosecurity State. As with the CIA and Intelligence community, Big Tech was on the scene from the first and proved a formative influence on biosecurity-related policy. In fact, close bonds between Tech and Intelligence predate the Fourth Industrial Revolution by at least three decades, featuring as one (sometimes overlooked) element of the Third.

> It's worth recalling here that the defense and intelligence agencies had a beachhead in the tech industry from its birth: the Defense Advanced Research Project Agency, DARPA, created the Internet by building the ARPANET grid in 1969.[141]

The historic defense-intelligence-tech liaison endures today and, in the guise of DARPA, helped fuel developments responsible for Covid World:

> DARPA was perhaps the largest funder of gain-of-function research, outstripping even Dr. Fauci's NIH in some years. In 2017 alone, DARPA laundered at least $6.5 million through Peter Daszak's EcoHealth Alliance to fund experiments at the Wuhan lab.[142]

Another Kennedy paragraph conveys a sense of both the ongoing bond between the tech, military, and intelligence communities as well as the insertion of these into the larger Matrix super-structure:

> In 2010, DARPA's visionary director, Dr. Regina Dugan, moved to Google as an executive, and in 2016, she transferred to Google's competitor, Facebook.... In 2018, she moved again, to run Wellcome Leap, a health technology breakthrough innovation project of Wellcome Trust. Her peregrinations offer another example of the incestuous links between Big Tech, Big Pharma, and the military and intelligence agencies.[143]

So much, for the moment, for relevant history. Let us turn now to other facets of the unique role played by technology in producing Covid World, past, present, and future.

The reasons technology is so central to the Matrix agenda are, on one level, obvious and, on another, so deep as to be largely hidden. I will briefly address the former before exploring the more profound levels of the question.

The Great Reset envisions a dramatic transformation of human life and culture, and anyone with eyes to see and ears to hear today experiences the manifold ways by which technology supplies potent (some might say, irresistible) means to that end. The transformations effected are especially all-pervasive in the case of the Fourth Industrial Revolution and its *characteristic merging of physical, digital, and biological realities.* Ramsbotham notes that, even before Covid-19, Schwab and his WEF promoted the Fourth Industrial as

> a new chapter in human development, enabled by extraordinary technological advances...merging the physical, digital and biological in ways that create both huge promise and great peril. The speed, breadth and depth of this revolution is forcing us to rethink how countries develop, how organizations create value and *even what it means to be human* [emphasis added].[144]

One might well consider Schwab's 2020 book *Covid-19: The Great Reset* a kind of rewrite of *The Fourth Industrial Revolution.* In the more recent text, Schwab enumerates recent developments that bear out his earlier prophecy:

> When it was published in 2016, *The Fourth Industrial Revolution* made the case that "Technology and digitization will revolutionize everything, making the overused and often ill-used adage 'this time is different' apt. Simply put, major technological innovations are on the brink of fueling momentous change throughout the world." In the four short years since, technological progress has moved impressively fast. AI is now all around us, from drones and voice recognition to virtual assistants and translation software. Our mobile devices have become a permanent and integral part of our personal and professional lives, helping us on many different fronts, anticipating our needs, listening to us and locating us, even when not asked to do so.... Automation and robots are reconfiguring the way businesses operate with staggering speed and returns on scale inconceivable just a few years ago.[145]

One may well debate the pros and cons of all this "progress," but the fact of change can hardly be denied. That truth remains in force with respect to advances in biotechnology, even if—Schwab's questionable optimism notwithstanding—debate evaluating comparative risks and benefits here should be all the more imperative:

> Innovation in genetics, with synthetic biology now on the horizon, is also exciting, paving the way for developments in healthcare that are

> groundbreaking. Biotechnology still falls short of stopping, let alone preventing, a disease outbreak, but recent innovations have allowed the identification and sequencing of the coronavirus's genome much faster than in the past, as well as the elaboration of more effective diagnostics. In addition, the most recent biotechnology techniques using mRNA and DNA platforms make it possible to develop vaccines faster than ever. They might even help with the development of new bioengineered treatments.[146]

So much for the manifest power of technology to change the very tone and texture of human existence. The critical question (so pressing with respect to biotechnology, including Covid-19 vaccines, but relevant across the board) remains: *To what effect?* Are the resultant transformations for the better, or for the worse? Are these ever more powerful technological tools by means of which humanity is progressively wrenched into new cultural and even biological forms instruments of good or evil?

I have argued that the technocratic Matrix agenda should be judged evil at root insofar as it builds upon premises contrary to those freedoms essential to human dignity. I have also recognized technology as the very backbone of technocracy. Does technology itself then need be regarded as inherently evil, a devilish instrument put into human hands so we may better wreck all that is sacred in the creation and ruin what some may regard as God's own design? More concretely: if technocracy must be regarded as inherently authoritarian and thereby contrary to human love and freedom, *does technology*— particularly the acceleration of technological advance associated with the Third and Fourth Industrial Revolutions—necessarily lead to technocracy? Is the equation *Technology = Technocracy* written indelibly into the law of the land; inscribed, like Mosaic Law, in some Google-given tablet?

My own answer to that question is double-edged.

I write these very words on a computer that, while producing script far less picturesque than Rilke's or my own curlicued hand, is now, for me, far more enabling and efficient: a tool without which I do not know if this text would ever have been composed. Most of the sources of the information I have drawn upon in its writing derive from web-based sites and platforms which, today, provide the chief means of contesting a legacy media too often bought and sold by pharmaceutical and other vested interests. The Canadian truckers that encircled Ottawa organized and fund-raised via the internet. Tech *can* be a tool that promotes, rather than degrades, democracy, human creativity, and individual initiative. I imagine it might be claimed that the tech we are discussing here itself arose, like some exotic tree of digital filigree, from just that kind of very American soil.

Technology thus may be a *necessary,* but is not a *sufficient,* condition of technocracy. No simple equation holds.

So much for the one hand.

On the other hand, however, it should be openly acknowledged: something abides in the very nature of technology that makes it not only conducive to technocratic ends, but molds it as a kind of independent force that pushes humankind in precisely that direction. The more powerful and pervasive the technological means, the more potent this force, which consequently rises to peculiarly elevated intensity in both the Third and (still more) the Fourth Industrial Revolution.

Schwab himself repeatedly declares that the alterations catalyzed by Fourth Industrial Revolution technology are so fundamental as to alter the very nature of, not only what human beings can or cannot *do*, but what a human being *is* or *is not*. His Fourth Revolution is consequently no purely industrial matter, but portends a kind of philosophical upheaval as well; a change in the very idea of what, in the Western philosophic and religious traditions, used to be called "man," when that term could be understood to imply not one or another sex, but the metaphysical essence of man and woman as one original being. That idea is registered in the title of Teilhard de Chardin's classic *The Phenomenon of Man*,[147] and, perhaps most famously, in Genesis: "So God created man in his own image, in the image of God created he him; male and female created he them."[148]

What, then, is the nature of the proposed change in our very idea of who and what we are? Salient details of FIR (Fourth Industrial Revolution) technology offer pregnant hints. Schwab speaks, for instance, of the capacity to manufacture vital organs by means of 3-D printer technology; of the unique and indeed potentially superhuman potentials implicit in AI; and of the capacity of biotechnology to seize control of the human genome, deliberately manipulating our mRNA/DNA programming to produce desired results, including "designer babies." These and multiple other instances of "the merging of the physical, digital and biological" point towards the crux of a new idea: namely, *the re-creation of the human being as a product or offspring of man's own technological innovation; a merging of the very idea of man and machine.*

Schwab, an economist, does not really style himself a philosopher. While certainly aware of some of the broader implications of his agenda, he does not set his sail towards deep metaphysical waters. Others, however, are less shy, and willingly furnish the term that aptly describes the intellectual predicates that underwrite the more visible practical and sociopolitical dimensions of Schwab's Great Reset agenda. That agenda rests—whether such be consciously acknowledged or not—upon *transhumanist* premises.

The pedigree of philosophical transhumanism is long and complex. I can hardly here offer any adequate historical review (that would require a book in itself) but can point out some instructive landmarks.

Many date general use of the term to an influential 1957 article by Aldous Huxley titled, simply, "Transhumanism." Huxley opines:

> Up till now, human life has generally been, as Hobbes described it, "nasty, brutish and short": the great majority of human beings (if they have not already died young) have been afflicted with misery.... We can justifiably hold the belief that these lands of possibility exist, and that the present limitations and miserable frustrations of our existence could be in large measure surmounted.... The human species can, if it wishes, transcend itself—not just sporadically, an individual here in one way, an individual there in another, but in its entirety, as humanity.[149]

Huxley's words well convey two leading features common to many (though not all) of the diverse varieties of transhumanism: the utopian strain that sees the human being as the agent of its own transcendence; and the collective, rather than individual, emphasis inscribed in this quasi-religious, salvific form of belief.

An aspect that Huxley does not highlight has, however, emerged as increasingly central to the school of thought: namely, the notion that it is an ever more sophisticated material technology that provides the means by which the human race may fulfill its inveterate desire for redemptive self-transcendence. In 1990, thirty-three years after Huxley, Max More penned an article "Transhumanism: Towards a Futurist Philosophy,"[150] updating Huxley's working definition. Recognizing the humanist roots of the philosophy, More nonetheless sounds the chord that was to become ever more dominant over the next three-plus decades: "Transhumanism," writes More, "differs from humanism in recognizing and anticipating the radical alterations in the nature and possibilities of our lives resulting from various sciences and technologies."[151]

Eight years later, in 1998, Nick Bostrom and David Pearce founded the World Transhumanist Association. Four years after that, smack dab in the midst of the seminal years of the Fourth Industrial Revolution and Biosecurity

State, the WTA (by now rechristened as Humanity+) issued The Transhumanist Declaration, and formally defined Transhumanism as:

> 1. The intellectual and cultural movement that affirms the possibility and desirability of fundamentally improving the human condition through applied reason, especially by developing and making widely available technologies to eliminate aging and to greatly enhance human intellectual, physical, and psychological capacities.
>
> 2. The study of the ramifications, promises, and potential dangers of technologies that will enable us to overcome fundamental human limitations, and the related study of the ethical matters involved in developing and using such technologies.[152]

Following the trail of these historical sources, one can gain a sense of contemporary transhumanism's philosophical ancestry. Some current versions, however, including streams that feed Matrix ideology, take a disturbing turn, exposing the dark shadows cast by the sunny aspiration of what has from the first been a distinctly Icarian adventure.

Robert F. Kennedy, Jr., proves keenly aware of the transhumanist ground of the Great Reset and the Biosecurity State agendas, and his book provides evidence of relevant historical connections. In 1993, Peter Schwartz, Lockstep's author, cofounded *Wired* magazine, which served as a chief vehicle of mainstream reporting on the fast-growing online culture. Recalling Schwartz's own military and CIA background, as well as his Big Tech affiliations, may prepare us for Kennedy's grim characterization of the magazine's bent:

> *Wired* is also the fountainhead of the equally sinister movement transhumanism, which advocates for the integration of human beings and machines. The movement's ancillary aims include extending the lifespans of key Silicon Valley billionaires indefinitely and "liberating humanity from biological restraints"—using AI, novel therapies like stem cells and nanobots, vaccination, and subdermal chips.

Kennedy continues to note the terms in which Jacques Ellul—an early critic of transhumanist ideology—describes the methods and ends commensurate with the transhumanism's "elegant capacity for top-down control of humanity":

> For the psychocivilized society, the complete joining of man and machine will be calculated according to a strict system, the so-called "biocracy." It will be impossible to escape this system of adaption because it will be

> articulated with so much scientific understanding of the human being. The individual will have no more need of conscience and virtues. His moral and mental furnishing will be a matter of the biocrat's decisions.[153]

As outrageous as the above-mentioned transhumanist fantasies may sound, they may not be so very far-fetched. Contemporary transhumanism can hardly be considered a fringe phenomenon; on the contrary, it runs as a constant undercurrent in the thought-stream of Big Tech, and powerful Matrix personalities count as devoted adherents:

> Transhumanism, in its various doctrinal approaches, has fervent acolytes among the Silicon Valley elites, including C-suite titans at Microsoft, Facebook, Tesla's Elon Musk, Google Engineering Director Raymond Kurtzweil, PayPal founder Peter Thiel, satellite and biotechnology titan Martine Rothblatt, and Bill Gates.[154]

This information should snap us back to the still-pending and ever more urgent question: what is it about Fourth Industrial Revolution technology, and its ever-increasing sway, that lends itself to technocratic autocracy? What is it about FIR tech that tends to blend utopian visions of an existence liberated from humanity's chronic ills into dystopian visions of a system of total social control and the extinction of the morally conscious, free human being?

The question, I think, directs us toward the heart of the matter at hand: the religio-mythical[155] foundation of Covid World itself. To begin seeking an answer, I would refer to the Huxley and WTA excerpts cited above and juxtapose the celebration of the transcendence of human limits inscribed there with the contrasting perspective expressed by contemporary writer Paul Kingsnorth. While ecological crisis counts as Kingsnorth's immediate concern in the passage below, his words possess more universal relevance:

> A crisis of limits is a crisis of culture, and a crisis of culture is a crisis of spirit. Every living culture in history, from the smallest tribe to the largest civilization, has been built around a spiritual core: a central claim about the relationship between human culture, nonhuman nature, and divinity. Every culture that lasts, I suspect, understands that living within limits—limits set by natural law, by cultural tradition, by ecological boundaries—is a cultural necessity and a spiritual imperative. There seems to be only one culture in history that has held none of this to be true, and it happens to be the one we're living in.[156]

If what Kingsnorth asserts in the last sentence here is true (and I believe it is), I would suggest it is so because not only Matrix titans qualify as transhumanists. In fact, transhumanism functions as the religio-mythical correlate of contemporary mainstream culture in general, and has done so with increasing strength since Bacon, Descartes, Galileo, Newton, and the scientific materialism that followed in their wake paved the way for the series of industrial revolutions that commenced in the 18th century. The more extreme and radical forms of transhumanism current today (and which underwrite the Matrix/Great Reset agenda) represent no aberrant digression from the dominant trend of Western intellectual history over the past 500 years. On the contrary, these ideologies represent the logical culmination of that history, the apocalyptic climax of the modern mind.

The trio of terms central to Kingsnorth's argument provides one key to exploring this terrain. Every philosophy, religion, or worldview depends upon its interpretation of the essence of, and relations between, "human culture, non-human nature, and divinity" (the same trinity of terms one author, employing a traditional vocabulary, calls *Man, God, and the Universe* in a classic work by that name[157]). An understanding of major eras of cultural history can accordingly be approached by way of inquiry into the peculiar construction of this triad characteristic of a given age, while transitions of one to another manifest in and through radical permutations of the same. As the transhumanist philosophy grounding the Great Reset agenda can be comprehended as a signal development within the wider horizon of the modern era, its understanding requires gaining at least a preliminary grasp of the most fundamental lineaments of the modern mind.

Western intellectual history is traditionally divided into three main epochs: the classical, the medieval, and the modern. Certain limitations attend this convenient schema; most critically, perhaps, the manner in which it effectively marginalizes indigenous cultures as well as skeins of pagan culture radically distinct from the Greco-Roman roots of classical civilization. Nonetheless, it serves as a useful background and point of departure, especially because the scientific intellect that features as the indisputable core of modernity represents both an outgrowth of the project of knowledge (*episteme*) inaugurated in ancient Greece, and a virtual overthrow of the Christian universe of being characteristic of the medieval worldview.

Within the confines of this text, I can hardly do justice to the profound, indeed almost inexhaustible, complexities that unfold over millennia of cultural historical transformation. Nonetheless, falling back upon our founding trinity, some basic, readily recognizable postulates may be proposed that can serve to orient an understanding of the peculiar nature of the transhumanist philosophy so instrumental in the genesis of our contemporary Covid World.

Firstly, it does not require great erudition to recognize that *divinity* played a central if not sovereign role in the worldviews informing both the classical and medieval eras. True, the polytheism evident in the rich mythology of the former contrasts markedly with the monotheism central to Judeo-Christian tradition. Even so, be it the gods of the Olympian pantheon, or the one God of Abraham, Isaac, and Jacob, the *logos* inherent in the Platonic *Nous*, or the spiritual shining of a beloved Son, it is safe to say that one or another form (or forms) of supernatural intelligence and power commanded the reverence due to a being (or beings) transcending the sphere of mortal human existence.

It is also true that, despite the strong strain of otherworldliness implicit in certain aspects of both Greek philosophy and Judeo-Christian culture, nature, and the cosmic beauty and order inherent in it, has for much (if not most) of Western intellectual history been viewed as faithfully reflecting and manifesting divine intelligence and thus worthy of honor and reverence. This is especially true of the heavenly or celestial nature so manifestly sublime in radiance and in the orderly movement that suits it to represent, in Emerson's words, "the type of Reason."[158] In Old European pagan streams as well as diverse indigenous cultures, Nature herself earns still more devoted attention, worshipped as no mere mirror of transcendental intelligence, but divinity itself immanent in the creation as a whole and all its multiplex forms. One or another form of the Great Mother (the Celtic Brigit, for instance), more or less coincident with (Mother) Nature herself, may be revered as the very source and origin of the creation and all life dwelling therein.

What, then, of the human being or (to employ, for the moment, the traditional term) Man? The diversity of visions here can, once again, hardly be plumbed; but, following Kingsnorth, this much can be unequivocally stated: Before the modern era, the human being did *not* regard himself as sovereign in the cosmos. He did not view himself as the primary and even sole source of conscious intelligence, and so, in his own being, arbiter of meaning and purpose and framer of his own destiny. As Kingsnorth aptly states, the rightful province and prerogative of the human self had always been constrained within limits—limits imposed by reverence for sources of order and intelligence superior to the mortal self, be these regarded as divine, natural, or (most frequently) a confluence of both. In kindred fashion, spiritual responsibilities flowing from cultural heritage—the counsel of ancestors bearing wisdom passed down through generations—has both shaped and constrained ambition.

This ground of culture, however, began to shift with the advent of modernity, the nexus of complex, interrelated developments associated with the three-pronged siege of the medieval world represented by the Renaissance, the Protestant Reformation, and (last, but far from least) the Scientific Revolution.

Even in the domain of nascent science, however, the transformations that founded the modern era were slow in coming. God did not lightly or readily surrender the uncontested reign so long enjoyed. When the first great astronomical pioneers of what would, in due time, become modern natural science combined imaginative genius, mathematical reason, patient empirical observation, and novel technology (such as Galileo's telescope) to unlock the keys of the cosmos, they did so in the spirit not of denying the sovereignty of the divine ruler of the universe, but of revealing and sharing in the glory that shone forth in their discoveries. Copernicus and Kepler, Galileo and Newton were not then "scientists"—the word did not come into use until the 19th century—but *natural philosophers*, revealing and participating in the *logos* or reason bodied forth in the creation. Far from denying the idea of divinity, they strove to bear original witness to the supreme intelligence from which their own human minds drew as candles of flame from the fiery source of heat and light itself.

In that form of participation, moreover, lay the essence of the traditional conception of (the being of) man himself. By "traditional," I here mean consonant with both classical and Judeo-Christian streams of culture. Just as the devoutly Christian early astronomers' vision of deity would have been inconceivable without the Neoplatonic underpinnings of their speculative genius, *theological* topoi, on the one hand, and *philosophical* ideas of mimesis and participation, on the other, often blent more or less seamlessly in the understanding of the archetype, the primal origin and image, of human being. Here, for instance, is a passage from Kepler's *Harmonia Mundi* (1619) wherein he announced his third and last law of planetary motion:

> The whole of creation forms a marvelous symphony, in the order of ideas and of spirit, as well as in that of material beings. All is held and linked together by mutual indissoluble affinities: all forms a harmonious whole. In God, there is the same harmony, a harmony supreme; for God has created us in His image, and has given us the idea and feeling of harmony.[159]

Kepler's frame of mind will appear profoundly alien to modern scientific sensibilities. Yet Kepler may be considered a scientific genius, one instrumental in uniting, in what he christened "celestial physics," the disciplines of astronomy and physics.[160] His laws of planetary motion hold good today. Indispensable to Newton's gravitational theories, they remain essential elements of the foundation of modern science. How then can it be that Kepler's own description of the gist of his work sounds to us so thoroughly and irrevocably "unscientific"?

The continuation of the passage sets in still greater relief the ground of the contrast:

> All that exists is living and animated, because all is linked together; there is no star that is not "animal," that has not a soul. The souls of the stars are the cause of their movements and of the sympathy that unites them one to another; this explains the regularity of natural phenomena.[161]

Kepler's frank exposition clarifies the immeasurable gulf that yawns between his worldview and that of his modern scientific descendants. For Kepler, nature, the non-human universe, is not exclusively or even most fundamentally material in character. Rather, it is intrinsically living, animated, ensouled. Furthermore, it is the metaphysical nature of soul (*anima*) itself, its indwelling affinities, that proves the ultimate cause of and reason for the regularities that give rise to scientific laws.

Kepler's celestial physics is thus nested in an unabashedly metaphysical vision of the nature of things themselves. He does not seek to trace the cause of phenomena to purely material or mechanical sources and processes, but (reversing that logic) traces observable material phenomena to immaterial or supersensible sources and causes, the ultimate or (to employ Aristotelian terms) "final" cause of which is God: the Soul of souls and unified origin of the sympathies linking all the members of the cosmos in harmonic order. The mathematics so essential to his quest do not serve as a means of reducing reality to abstract measurable quantities, but—in keeping with the Pythagorean spirit that informs Kepler's vocation—serve as a formal language that enables apt symbolization of immaterial soul-spiritual agencies and principles at work in the cosmos.

Before scoffing at or blithely dismissing Kepler's views as hopelessly antiquated, it may be well to remember that his intellectual acumen and achievement, like that of the equally religious Isaac Newton after him, dwarfs that of most persons who call themselves scientists today. Nor did Kepler's metaphysically grounded cosmology prevent him from discovering so-called physical or scientific laws valid still today. On the contrary, it is more than probable that the religious and aesthetic dimension of Kepler's worldview provided the inspiration and will that enabled his discoveries. What I here wish to highlight, however, is the manner in which Kepler's vision may furnish a background against which the founding suppositions of the modern mind may be seen to stand out in starkly dramatic contrast.

Referring, once more, to the trinity of divinity, nature, and the human being, it is clear that, for Kepler, an underlying unity prevails, and that the latter two (nature and the human being) reflect and participate in the life and intelligence of the first. Worship is naturally due to the first and final cause of all; but both nature and the rational mind, as fit reflections of that first, are inherently ennobled and (at least in that ideal aspect) also worthy of honor, and even reverence, by virtue of that original likeness.

If, on the other hand, we turn our attention to the modern mind, the worldview born of the scientific intellect as such evolved in the wake of Bacon and Descartes, Galileo and Newton, Darwin and Mendel, we will read a long story that comes to a very different conclusion. With religion relegated to the margins of intellectual culture, science wields the scepter of sovereign truth; but the reason enthroned today bears little or no resemblance to that which inspired Kepler, for it recognizes no divine original. In the halls of science, God is not just dead (as Nietzsche proclaimed almost a century and a half ago), but dead as a doornail.

By "God" here I mean not merely the Judeo-Christian deity, but any and all species of divinity, as per the peroration of that rather notorious atheist, biologist Richard Dawkins:

> I know you don't believe in an old bearded man sitting on a cloud, so let's not waste any more time on that. I am not attacking any particular version of God or gods. I am attacking God, all gods, anything and everything supernatural, wherever and whenever they have been or will be invented.[162]

No divinity, then, for the modern mind, the profile of which we thus may begin to construct by crossing out, by *voiding,* the first of our three terms.

With God gone, and anything and everything "supernatural" erased from the equation, it might seem to stand to reason that nature might gain compensatory weight. After all, with everything supernatural banished entirely from the universe of thought, nature would have to expand to fill all available space, and its significance thus be correspondingly amplified.

So one might think; and yet—historically speaking—while nature does "fill in" for the absent God in a certain quantitative sense (occupying all available space, nature now is "all in all"[163]), it does *not* do so in any qualitative sense. Indeed, the case is quite to the contrary. If nature, in Kepler, is full of soul, expressive of and indeed essentially continuous with the living godhead, the modern mind construes nature (metaphysically if not emotionally) in an essentially negative guise. Nature is, instead, an ensemble of material forms and forces devoid of all the traditional attributes of deity: Intelligence, Consciousness, Purpose; indwelling Soul (anima) or Spirit.

All this is already there in René Descartes, one of modernity's philosophical godfathers. In historian Richard Tarnas's description of the Cartesian view of nature, we already begin to gain a glimpse of technocentric transhumanism on the far horizon:

> In contrast to the mind, all objects of the external world lack subjective awareness, purpose, or spirit. The physical universe is entirely devoid of human qualities. Rather, as purely material objects, all physical phenomena can in essence be comprehended as machines—much like the lifelike automata and ingenious machines, clocks, mills, and fountains being constructed and enjoyed by 17th-century Europeans. God created the universe and defined its mechanical laws, but after that the system moved on its own, the supreme machine constructed by the supreme intelligence.[164]

Descartes's deist divinity, essentially separate from the universe he created, would in due time become thoroughly dispensable. That separation, in dramatic contrast to Kepler's vision, manifests in the essential *inanimacy* of all matter and indeed nature as a whole. Nature became, not a vital body shaped and enlivened by a soul, but a collocation of atomic parts:

> The universe, therefore, was not a live organism...endowed with forms and motivated by teleological purpose. If such preconceptions were set aside and man's analytic reason alone employed to intuit the simplest, most self-evident description of nature, then it was apparent that the universe was composed of non-vital atomistic matter. Such a substance was best understood in mechanistic terms, reductively analyzed into its simplest parts, and exactly comprehended in terms of those parts' arrangements and movements: "The laws of Mechanics are identical with those of Nature."[165]

From Descartes in the early 17th century, it is, in many respects, just a hop, skip, and a jump to contemporary best-selling author Michael Pollan:

> My default perspective is that of the philosophical materialist, who believes that matter is the fundamental substance of the world and the physical laws it obeys should be able to explain everything that happens. I start from the assumption that nature is all that there is and gravitate toward scientific explanation of phenomena.[166]

Pollan, a non-scientist, speaks here as a fit representative of everyman—which does not mean every single person, but the exemplar of the prevailing view in today's world.

So much—or rather so little—for Nature and Divinity in the mind of the modern scientific materialist. In examining these two terms of our essential trinity, we have so far discovered, one might say, a whole lot of nothing. God or divinity is Not; and Nature is Not what God (and the World Soul) once Was: Intelligent, Conscious, Purposive, Alive.

There is, though, something to be said for Nature: it is (like) a Machine.

That leaves, naturally, the third and last term: Man.

Not unexpectedly, here, indeed, the account is paid for, the deficit made up; at least after a fashion. If the death of God and the mechanization of nature create a spiritual black hole, an abyss of meaningless unconsciousness, the modern human being—though profoundly challenged by these trying existential circumstances—tries mightily to fill the void. Tarnas offers cogent insight into the ground of the modern worldview towards the end of his own portrait of the Cartesian legacy:

> Whereas Luther's foundational certainty was his faith in God's saving grace as revealed in the Bible, Descartes's foundational certainty was his faith in the procedural clarities of mathematical reasoning applied to the indubitability of the thinking self. Moreover, by his assertion of the essential dichotomy between thinking substance and extended substance, Descartes helped emancipate the material world from its long association with religious belief, freeing science to develop its analysis of that world in terms uncontaminated by spiritual or human qualities and unconstrained by theological dogma. *Both the human mind and the natural world now stood autonomously as never before, separated from God and from each other* [emphasis added].[167]

Tarnas's next and conclusive Cartesian paragraph begins by oblique allusion to what is, perhaps, the most famous philosophical assertion of all time—"I think, therefore I am"—and everything those words imply:

> Here, then, was the prototypical declaration of the modern self, established as a fully separate, self-defining entity, for whom its own rational self-awareness was absolutely primary—doubting everything except itself, setting itself in opposition not only to traditional authorities but to the world, as subject against object, as a thinking observing measuring, manipulating being, fully distinct from an objective God and an external nature. The fruit of the dualism between rational subject and material world was science, including science's capacity for rendering certain knowledge of that world and for making man "master and possessor of nature." In Descartes's vision, science, progress, reason, epistemological certainty, and human identity were all inextricably connected with each other and with the conception of an objective, mechanistic universe; and upon this synthesis was founded the paradigmatic character of the modern mind.[168]

There is a quotient of grandeur in our modernity. Why, after all, should the aspiring human being, discovering anew the power of the mind and strength of the hand after centuries of medieval cloistering, be constrained by the dusty edicts of some imperious Father? Had not that titan of art, Michelangelo, already depicted the passing of the torch of creation from God to Man on the ceiling of the Sistine Chapel more than a century before Descartes, in his famous *Discourse*, replaced Yaweh's inscrutable "I am that I am" with the far more logical "*ego cogito, ergo sum*"? Had not Leonardo DaVinci, consummate artist, inventor, and exemplary Renaissance man, displayed the technological prowess that would assuredly crown man's scientific progress, foreshadowing the day he might do truly unheard of things, even don wings and fly into the abode of angels, birds, and God?

We owe, no doubt, an inestimable debt to the spiritual, intellectual, emotional, and practical emancipations that date back to the dawn of the modern era. There can hardly be a question of simply going back to an age before time could be counted on a mechanical clock, or an artist could paint the human figure in perspective, or an engineer employ calculus. The breakthroughs that inaugurated modernity are irrevocably a part of who we are in the present and who we may be in the future: an ineradicable aspect of what it means to be a human being or what any man or woman today may might mean when he or she says *I am.*

None of this, however, should obscure the glaring—indeed, fatal—deficiencies written into the modern worldview as such has been sketched here. The elevation of the modern scientific version of the "rational" human intellect to a position of sovereignty—sole sovereignty—in the cosmos, unlimited (as Kingsnorth says) by responsibility to any operative idea of divinity *or* sense of the sacred integrity of a (not dead, purely material, but) living nature of which we are a part, is a recipe—not for heaven on earth, as Francis Bacon and some of his modern heirs might imagine—but cataclysmic disaster: the wholesale catastrophe written all over the face of the world today.

I do not think I have to catalogue in detail all the ills afflicting our contemporary world: ecological demise; economic inequality and crushing poverty; warfare stoked by religious as well as ethnic and national divisions; mass migration resulting in a refugee crisis of historical magnitude; and much else, including... the Covid-19 pandemic and all the destruction wrought in its name.

I am not blaming science, all science, for the ravages of Covid. True, I do believe that science, insofar as it remains unequivocally committed to philosophically materialist premises, remains epistemologically and ethically crippled and crippling. So long as physics fantasizes that it can operate without metaphysics; so long as matter is viewed as mindless, and mind itself nought but airy nothingness that can only be understood once reduced to measurable neurophysiological function, science will be ill equipped to discover knowledge that breeds, not merely technical power, but the Wisdom that, by its very nature, serves the Good.

That said, there nonetheless remains a world of difference between Matrix technocrats and those doctors who pursue their vocation in a manner responsive to codes of ethics and professional integrity that have earned science and medicine the great repute they still hold (albeit ever less deservedly) today. It is these individuals who have heroically pushed back against the falsehoods and coercion that have sprouted like noxious weeds in the fields of their expertise. Most importantly, these scientists and doctors, all of whom display courage, intelligence, and compassion in the midst of the Covid crisis, are guided by truly *human*, rather than *transhumanist,* ends and means.

The philosophy of transhumanism, on the other hand, bends the arc of justice in the wrong direction because, like René Descartes, it leaves the heart out of the equation of who *I am* in my standing as a human being. Transhumanism *extends* modernism in a particular direction. That direction is *not* one which (while embracing the good inherent in the Renaissance and religious and scientific revolutions that inaugurated modernity) recognizes and seeks to redress the flagrant deficiencies inherent in the modern worldview.

Those deficiencies have unfortunately grown ever more dominant over the course of time, and, correlatively, ever more destructive, even exponentially so. It is thus absolutely requisite for humanity at large to recognize and address those deficiencies which—while certainly causing material (sociopolitical, economic, ecological) harm—are not originally or essentially practical, but intellectual, spiritual, and moral in nature.

Transhumanism, however—contrary to this urgent imperative—is the name of the philosophy that does not see anything wrong with modernity; does not recognize the corruptive influence of the ideology largely responsible for the world as we see it today. The transhumanist answer to the challenges currently confronting humanity does *not* entail reconsidering the modern construction of *human being, divinity, and nature* as such has been sketched here, but rather affirms the whole package: the absence of divinity, the materiality of nature, and the unquestioned sovereignty of the scientific intellect and the technical mastery over nature it affords.

Not only does transhumanism approve the modern model, it deliberately puts humanity's foot to the pedal, exhorting us to speed ever faster down the same highway, imagining the magical machine of technological culture will catapult us over the precipice visible just ahead. Deaf to the engine noise bespeaking underlying issues, we are thus loudly exhorted that the way to salvation entails doubling down on our deficiencies. We are thus encouraged to pretend that the same ideological and technical machinery that got us into this mess will, if driven hard and fast enough, somehow get us out of it; lift us up over.

I have spoken of transhumanism as an extension of modernism. This is true, but it is at the same time an extension radical enough to constitute, finally, a qualitative leap: a new, distinctly different worldview with its own peculiar ethos. This may have something to do with what some might call "postmodernism." Yet while it is not clear to me what that multivalent term connotes, the essential nature and character of transhumanism, as a permutation of modernism, can be lucidly and compactly articulated.

The modern premises hold: transhumanism recognizes no traditional divine or supersensible reality of any description, and conceives of nature as raw material for the sovereign scientific intellect's designs. Yet whereas the modern imagination idealizes control over nature, the transhumanist takes matters a decisive step further. By virtue of the ever greater technical power afforded by the ever greater breaking down of nature into ever smaller atomized pieces and its increasing conversion into digital, electronic, and bioengineered devices, transhumanism does not seek so much to *control* the power of the natural world as to *replace* it with realities of its own artificial make and design. The universe of sun, moon, and stars; of earth, air, fire and water: this is no longer to be our home, the place we inhabit. Universe is to become Metaverse: natural reality converted, wholesale, to a virtual reality that can better suit its maker's needs.

Yet that is not all: the machines that are the offspring of the scientific mind will allow us to do much more than recreate nature. By virtue of those same machines, we will reinvent, indeed *replace*, our own selves with "enhanced" models, thus literally changing, digitally-physically-biologically, as Schwab announced, "what it means to be human." Our brainchild, the artificial intelligence (AI) that we create, will, after all, surpass in all directions our mortal mental capacities. The process of merging human and artificial intelligence is, in many ways, already underway. Our bodies, now tragically subject to all "the thousand natural shocks that flesh is heir to" and so manifestly imperfect in their natural organic state, will likewise in time become replaceable, not only, as now, in part, but eventually, as a whole.

Indeed, this transformation of mind or intelligence and body will ultimately enable us to transcend the sphere of biology, of organic and evolutionary nature, altogether. Ray Kurzweil, Google executive and leading transhumanist, affirms that down the line human beings *per se* will no longer be biological organisms at all:

> This will be the next step in evolution, the next high-level paradigm shift.... Most of the intelligence of our civilization will ultimately be nonbiological. By the end of the century, it will be trillions of trillions of times more powerful than human intelligence.[169]

Psychologist and phenomenologist Robert Romanyshyn elaborates Kurzweil's transhumanist vision:

> Between the 2020s and the end of the century the quality of being embodied will increasingly no longer be a part of being human. On the contrary, the quality that will mark one as human will be intelligence. Biological, instinctual, embodied intelligence, which evolved in relation to nature, will be replaced by digital intelligence apart from nature.[170]

Romanyshyn is an astute critic, and the close ties between Kurzweil's transhumanism and the strict separation of mind and matter characteristic of Cartesian dualism do not escape him:

> Nearly four hundred years ago Descartes imagined this possibility. "I think, therefore, I am," was his philosophical expression of this vision. A pithy summary of the spectator mind in flight from the flesh, it anticipates Kurzweil's bold claim.[171]

Romanyshyn remarks as well, moreover, the multiple ways in which the radical transhumanist agenda *exceeds* its modernist ancestry:

> But [Kurtzweil's] claim goes far beyond Descartes in three significant ways.
>
> First, the philosophical idea has become a scientific fact, or at least the claim to be so with exponential advances in the areas of genetics and computers.
>
> Second, Kurzweil's claim extends well beyond the mind of an "I" who thinks to the "We" of a collective world-wide-web computer mind and its trove of all human intelligence.
>
> And third, Kurzweil's claim is a radical shift from thinking as an activity of a philosophical mind to thinking as a matter of the bits and bytes of data of a computational mind. It is a change from thinking as a meditative act to thinking as a calculative act.[172]

So the transhumanist agenda literally remakes two terms of our holy trinity (nature, and the human being) in its own technocratic image. Yet what of the third? Is divinity and the realm of spirit left out altogether?

By no means. The acme of the transhumanist project entails (contra Kingsnorth) a transcendence of all natural limits by means of technology, and, correlatively, transcendence of the limits imposed upon the human being on account of his or her embodiment as a part of organic evolutionary process. Such transcendence has always been inherent in the very nature of spirit *per se* and a chief prerogative, too, of an all-knowing and omnipotent God. Is it not clear that constructing the kinds of systems (already largely in place) that record and process virtually illimitable amount of data, affording the power to see, know and, ultimately, control all, is a simulacrum of the kind of capacity traditionally reserved for God?

This paints technological ubiquity in a singularly dark light, but Kurzweil—who employs the term *Singularity* to denote a kind of transhumanist apocalypse that results in the redemption of existence—offers a positively transfiguring version of the same:

> This is the ultimate destiny of the Singularity and of the universe.... Our civilization will...expand outward, turning all the dumb matter and energy we encounter into sublime intelligence—transcendent—matter and energy. So, in a sense, we can say that the Singularity will ultimately infuse the universe with spirit.[173]

This is the technocrat's dream of salvation: the transhumanist's vision of the resurrection, not of the body of Jesus Christ, but of the universe as a whole. It is resurrection accomplished, not by realization of the divinity inherent in the human being, but by the deification of technology, the apotheosis of the Machine.

The Paul Kingsnorth essay I have cited ("The Cross and the Machine") tells the story of that author's own spiritual career and, in particular, the former ecological-activist-Zen-witch-atheist's recent (2021) conversion to Christianity. Critical to that story is Kingsnorth's ingestion of the Irish philosopher John Moriarty's insight that "The story of Christianity is the story of humanity's rebellion against God."[174]

What that sentence means is a conundrum worth contemplating. The ground covered in this chapter can, perhaps, help toward a preliminary understanding.

If, for the purposes of argument, we accept for the moment the ground of Christian belief—that Jesus Christ represented divinity embodied in human form—then Pilate, Caiaphas, and the rest of the crew's crucifixion of Jesus can logically be comprehended as "a rebellion against God"; a willful refusal to accept the divine grace, mercy, and love incarnate in the person of the Son. What could conceivably motivate such an act? Obviously, disbelief in the truth of the premise; denial, for any one of innumerable very plausible reasons, of Jesus's divine mission and salvific power.

One of those reasons may be that man does not like to be dependent, or recognize a power greater than his own, even when it comes to no less a matter than the "saving" of his soul and that of the world. Rather than recognize a higher power, he—naturally distrustful of any higher authority—would rather do it on his own (if, that is, he so much as believes he has a soul that need be "saved," however that may be understood).

Ray Kurzweil follows in a long line of individuals, dating back at least to Francis Bacon, who believe the scientific intellect and the technological capacity it enables supplies the key to salvation. That salvation lies in our capacity to overcome the ills "flesh is heir to": the travail of earthly toil; the suffering born of childbirth; debilitating illness; even the tragedy of death. These are the primal curses laid upon Adam and Eve upon their exile from the Garden, which—in the Christian vision—can only be redeemed, and transformed into blessings, by way of whoever and whatever force bears the name of Christ, a power at once mysteriously wholly human and divine. If that force is not necessarily outside the soul, it is nonetheless certainly superior to anything born of calculation; the *ego cogito* as such has morphed into the scientific intellect, modern technology's superhuman will to power, and modern man's ill-fated attempt to rebel against God, and go it alone.

Paul Kingsnorth is no soft-minded religionist, and is as keenly aware as any good liberal of the monumental sins of the church into which he was (nominally) born. Speaking of his own upbringing in urban England in the 1980s, he writes:

> The age taught another faith: Religion was irrelevant. It was authoritarian, it was superstitious, it was feeble proto-science. It was the theft of our precious free will by authorities who wanted to control us by telling us fairy tales. It repressed women, gay people, atheists, anyone who disobeyed its irrational edicts. It hated science, denied reason, burned witches and heretics by the million. Post-enlightenment liberal societies had thrown off its shackles.... Religion was dying a much-needed death at the hands of progress and reason.[175]

Still, atheist that he was, the nature-loving Kingsnorth, like most of the rest of us, can see all too well what modern man, led by a scientific intellect freed from all traditional bounds, has accomplished in the name of its version of "progress and reason":

> Nobody with eyes to see can deny what humanity has done to the living tissue of the planet, though plenty still try. There were big systemic reasons for it, I discovered: capitalism, industrialism, maybe civilization itself. Whatever had got us here, it was clear where we were going: into a world in which industrial humanity has ravaged much of the wild earth, tamed the rest, and shaped all nature to its end.[176]

Thus bearing witness to the disastrous effects of modern man's *hubris,* Kingsnorth's hard-won religious insight finally kicks in:

> The rebellion against God manifested itself in a rebellion against creation, against all nature, human and wild. We would remake Earth, down to the last nanoparticle, to suit our desires, which we now called "needs" Our new world would be globalized, uniform, interconnected, digitized, hyperreal, monitored, always-on. We were building a machine to replace God.[177]

Welcome to our brave new *transhumanist* world, long well underway.

Welcome to the *Great Reset*, proudly sponsored by the makers of *Covid-19*.

Red or blue, veteran or youthful neophyte, welcome, fellow citizen, to...*the Matrix*.

Chapter 5

LEVIATHAN: ENLIGHTENMENT'S SHADOW

Klaus Schwab and Thierry Malleret imagine Covid-19 as a turning point in time, a critical watershed in the history of humanity. In their vision of the Great Reset, every aspect of human life will undergo profound change; not only our science and technology and the material world transformed, but our economy and forms of social, cultural, and political existence, and even the human body itself. All is destined to undergo fundamental metamorphosis; so much so, indeed, that the human being of today may be hard put to imagine what life holds in store for her tomorrow.

There is a degree of truth in this prophecy. Few persons would contend that Covid, and the global response to it, has not in fact already transfigured our world in countless ways. It has done so not only materially, but socially, psychologically, and even spiritually. In all these respects, we are changed—and changing.

It is not, however, the simple past, but the present participle that is the operative tense here. The process of change is by no means concluded; nor are the chief results yet fixed in law or in stone. Crucial Covid-related questions are still debated by doctors and law-makers, by citizens, school-boards, and government councils. The cauldron of consciousness remains heated, the transformative alchemy still very much under way, and the distinct forms that will emerge from the complex interactions are as yet very much in doubt.

The entire process holds both great promise and still greater peril. Covid-19 has thrown down a gauntlet at the foot of humankind; and a great deal depends upon how We, the People—individually, and collectively—meet that challenge. In crafting our response to Covid-19, and our response to the official response to Covid-19, we are reframing the lineaments of our future, both as Americans engaged in the vital process of reinterpreting the meaning and force of our Constitution, and as world-citizens standing up for the essential rights accorded (or denied) every person by virtue of their membership in what Voltaire, torchbearer of the Enlightenment, might have called the Party of Humanity.

Schwab, the WEF, the WHO, and the whole global machine responsible for the official worldwide Covid response[178] propose one sort of answer to that challenge, the only one—or so reigning authorities would have us believe—representing a rational, science-based, humane, effective response to the Covid scourge. From another perspective, however, the whole affair looks suspiciously like a false flag operation, and Covid-19 a convenient if not deliberately planned excuse to promote, not public health and human welfare, but pharmaceutical profits and the political, economic, and social agenda of the Great Reset. Correlatively, the official measures actually instituted in response to Covid-19 are not only disastrous for public health, but corrosive of the legal, political, social, intellectual, moral, and spiritual foundations of American society in particular, and the free world in general.

The story I have told so far, in all its many subplots and chapters, bears this out. Events over the last three or four months[179] confirm the dynamics I have explored, showcasing the gigantic machinery of Matrix power all the more clearly and dramatically. Even as resistance to the controlling narrative has gained powerful momentum, the strategy and tactics of oppression (government overreach and a dictatorial exercise of power; proposals of new laws corrosive of basic human and parental rights; blanket media censorship and curtailments of freedom of speech; popular demonization of dissent; scientific fraud; governmental and corporate cover-up of inconvenient truths; crackdowns on dissident doctors and criminalization of medical dissent; ongoing denial of vaccine-injury and death; proposal of broad international edicts; the introduction of technologies conducive to the centralization of power and surveillance capabilities; and more) remain powerfully in force and on display.

At this juncture, rather than immediately highlighting particular events, I wish to initiate a concerted attempt at comprehending the entire complex of the dynamics I have elaborated within a broader intellectual-historical context. I wish, that is, to take further the exploration, commenced in the last chapter, of all that is spiritually and philosophically at stake in our construction of Covid World; in what we ultimately choose to make of the chapter of history we all are writing at this pivotal moment in time.

Why, when immersed in the urgent conundrums of our contemporary scientific and sociopolitical dilemmas, is such broad overview critical or, indeed, relevant at all? If we are to direct human destiny away from destructive ends and towards a constructive rejuvenation of life and culture, it is essential that we avail ourselves of the lever of historical understanding. Sound forward-looking vision requires perspective on the past so that we may more consciously shape the future rushing towards us with frightening speed.

I concluded the last chapter by citing Paul Kingsnorth's pithy critique of the transhumanist project that underwrites the Great Reset agenda. Kingsnorth first evokes the image of our emerging technocratic reality ("Our new world would be globalized, uniform, interconnected, digitized, hyper-real, monitored, always on") before landing his counterpunch: "*We were [are] building a machine to replace God.*" Kingsnorth implicitly endorses a religious perspective that, constraining the ambitions of purely human intelligence within spiritually salutary limits, presumably offers some kind of alternative to the technocratic dystopia he fears may overwhelm the world.

I noted too, however, that (the only recently converted) Kingsnorth proves keenly aware of some of the very good reasons why religion no longer rules the world as it did in the Middle Ages. Modernity, indeed, is all about the transfer of cultural power from what we call "religion" to what we call "science," an epochal transition largely effected by the combined forces of the Renaissance, the Reformation, and the Scientific Revolution. Yet Kingsnorth references none of these by name as he concludes this passage, but instead names the historic movement that sums and caps them all: "Post-enlightenment liberal societies had thrown off its shackles.... Religion was dying a much-needed death at the hands of progress and reason."[180]

Kingsnorth here alludes to the Enlightenment—that period that some construe as beginning as early as (cf. Descartes) the first part of the 17th century, but the heyday of which runs through the 18th, culminating in the American and French Revolutions and (in the philosophic arena) the great late works of Kant. It is the Enlightenment, often called the Age of Reason, that is not so much the *dawn* as the common *day* of Modernity, both the spirit and letter of which still reign supreme in our world. Diverse contemporary "isms"—modernism, postmodernism, secular humanism, and transhumanism, to name a few—are offshoots. As Kingsnorth implies, now, some 275 years or so after Diderot and d'Alembert began publishing the *Encyclopédie*, it is still the ideology bred of the Enlightenment ideals of Science, Reason, and Progress that conditions every aspect of our lives.

This remains patently, undeniably true with regard to Covid World today, which is, from start to (as yet unconcluded) finish—from gain-of-function lab leaks to operation WARP speed, to the endless edicts of our scientifically-minded public health authorities—a product of Enlightenment. In the Muslim world an Ayatollah may still be regarded as supreme ruler; here, however, it is Dr. Anthony Fauci, in his personification of "the science" itself, who wields the power to close down the church with a casual wave of his executive arm.

Writers such as Kingsnorth, however, are appalled by what they perceive to be the ideological legacy of the Enlightenment and all the flaws he and others (Patrick Deneen, for instance[181]) see as endemic to the "liberal" society that qualifies as its modern-day progeny. With good reason, to be sure: in addition to all the egregious failings such critics attribute to "liberal" ideology in its pre-Covid political and socioeconomic manifestations (social atomization and the disorientation bred of a spiritually impoverished consumerism, for instance), the nominally liberal faction of the American polity today has lent staunch and largely unwavering support to the controlling Covid narrative. A cogent argument can be made, in fact, that the totalitarian nightmare represented by the Matrix and the whole Great Reset agenda represents the logical culmination of Enlightenment thinking and the "liberal" ideology associated with it. In this view, the "liberal" ideology that champions freedom and equality is construed as transforming, by virtue of its own internal logic, into brands of authoritarianism that dramatically subvert its supposed values. Renowned social critics Theodor Adorno and Max Horkheimer make just this argument in the classic work commenced in the shadow of the Third Reich, *Dialectic of Enlightenment*,[182] the gist of which I shall try succinctly to review here.

In the previous chapter, I elaborated certain premises basic to modern philosophy by way of reference to Descartes. While the foundational logic of the *ego cogito* inevitably remains fundamental to the Enlightenment thinking Adorno and Horkheimer so probingly analyze, it is not Descartes, but the more pragmatically oriented co-founder of modernity that features prominently at the very beginning of *Dialectic of Enlightenment.*

Lord Francis Bacon, Descartes's early 17th-century contemporary, worked out of philosophical premises both congruent to and in tension with those of Descartes. Like Descartes, Bacon more or less marginalized God and thoroughly objectified nature, which he construed as material resource. Also like Descartes, Bacon understood knowledge as a process of understanding the world in a manner that allowed man to attain mastery over it. Descartes, however, superb mathematician that he was, placed chief emphasis on the mind's rational capacities as the beginning and end of the project of knowledge. On the other hand, the more practical Englishman ("the father of experimental philosophy" according to Voltaire), championed empirical observation and practical experiment as the principal means of acquiring knowledge. Correlatively, and most crucially, the measure of success, for Bacon—and indeed, the motive and end of knowledge itself—was not contemplative insight (no "*ego cogito, ergo sum*") but utility or practical power. To know something was to know how it worked and—critically—the *use* that could thereby be made of it. The end of science was, in a word, technology: man's means of utilizing nature, the things of the world, to create other things that fulfill his needs and desires.

Modern science, caring little for philosophical distinction between its French and English forefathers, owes its unparalleled accomplishments to its masterful blending of Cartesian rationalism and Baconian empiricism. Yet is it not, in fact, the temper of the latter that holds chief sway? Is it not technological aims which currently command and direct science, the project of knowledge, more than the other way around?

The notion of mastery over, and, indeed, domination of, nature, inheres in the very concept of technology as such has developed in conjunction with modern natural science. As it is precisely the dynamic of domination, as it extends from man's relation to nature to man's domination of other men and women in society, that is Adorno and Horkheimer's principal theme, it is no surprise that the twin characters of Lord Bacon and technology virtually leap onto the stage in the first act of *Dialectic of Enlightenment*.

On page one, Adorno and Horkheimer cite a choice Baconian passage transparently equating knowledge with power:

> Therefore, no doubt, the sovereignty of man lieth hid in knowledge; wherein many things are reserved, which kings with their treasure cannot buy, nor with their force command.... Now we govern nature in opinions, but we are thrall unto her in necessity: but if we would be led by her in invention, we should command her in action.[183]

Covid World translation: if we learn from nature herself the secrets of molecular biology, we can mime and game her operations (with mRNA biotechnology, for instance) so as to control the threat of infectious disease she poses, and—if we so choose—ourselves employ biological weapons to defend ourselves or threaten other human beings. By extension, our growing command of genetic engineering may allow us to commandeer the very design of life itself.

Adorno and Horkheimer's own commentary on this citation first links the Baconian theme of knowledge as power to economic and political developments associated with the democratic systems of governance that emerged out of the Enlightenment era:

> Although not a mathematician, Bacon well understood the scientific temper which was to come after him.... Knowledge, which is power, knows no limits, either in its exploitation of creation or in its deference to worldly masters. Just as it serves all the purposes of the bourgeois economy both in factories and on the battlefield, it is at the disposal of entrepreneurs regardless of their origins. Kings control technology no more directly than do merchants.[184]

Thus, in the new age, it is no longer traditional (or appointed, or elected) rulers that wield ultimate authority, but whoever it is that is in control of the scientific and technological know-how that confers true power.[185] As the passage implies, this dynamic possesses explosive *liberatory* potential, one central to the transformative character of Enlightenment thought. Yet Adorno and Horkheimer nonetheless see the conditions for destructive imbalances in power, a logic of domination, inscribed in the philosophical ground of the political economy characteristic of liberal democracy and the modern nation state:

> Technology is the essence of this knowledge. It aims to produce neither concepts nor images, nor the joy of understanding, but method, exploitation of the labor of others, capital.... *What human beings seek to learn from nature is how to use it to dominate wholly both it and human beings. Nothing else counts* [emphasis added] .[186]

This is a damning indictment, to be sure, and one that raises a critical, as yet unanswered question: how, precisely, does technology—knowledge as power—serve such unholy ends?

In its worldly enterprise, technology remains allied to and dependent upon scientific methods of analyses that reduce the *multiplicity of things and qualities* inherent in nature to *a uniform system of measurable quantities:*

> Bourgeois society is ruled by equivalence. It makes dissimilar things comparable by reducing them to abstract quantities. For the Enlightenment, anything which cannot be resolved into numbers, and ultimately into one, is illusion; modern positivism consigns it to poetry. Unity remains the watchword from Parmenides to Russell.[187]

Horkheimer and Adorno elaborate this argument by contrasting the methods of modern science with shamanistic forms of magic characteristic of premodern cultures. In magical rites, the sacrificial animal (the lamb or hind), while not ascribed a peculiar individuality, does maintain a *special representative* quality. In fulfilling its function, it links to *another, higher order* of existence. Science, however

> puts an end to this. In it there is no specific representation: something which is a sacrificial animal cannot be a god. Representation gives way to universal fungibility. An atom is smashed not as a representative but as a specimen of matter, and the rabbit suffering the torment of the laboratory is seen not as a representative but, mistakenly, as a mere exemplar.... In functional science the differences are so fluid that everything is submerged in one and the same matter.[188]

We are confronting here not only the objectification of nature mentioned already, but a correlative *quantification* that makes the objects of scientific analysis—including human beings, themselves today routinely transformed into numbers or statistics—subject to the mind that erects and commands the system:

> The manifold affinities between existing things are supplanted by the single relationship between the subject who confers meaning and the meaningless object, between rational significance and its accidental bearer.[189]

Think, here, of the vaccine-injured: as their number is regarded as small, indeed insignificant by our reigning health authorities ("the subject who confers meaning"), Brianna Dresser, Kyle Warner, Maddie de Garay and others[190] are indeed *meaningless objects*. Theirs, however, is only an extreme case of a more general point. In the system of science, it is not the person, but the statistic—*and* its interpretation—that counts.

Unfolding their argument still further, Adorno and Horkheimer rehearse the genesis of the scientific mind as they move seamlessly from Descartes to Bacon,[191] from the epistemological sovereignty of the human subject to the agent of practical power:

> The awakening of the subject is bought with the recognition of power as the principle of all relationships. In face of the unity of such reason the distinction between God and man is reduced to an irrelevance, as reason has steadfastly indicated since the earliest critique of Homer.[192]

Here, as per our prior triadic analysis in the last chapter, we see man as sovereign intellect effectively usurping the place of divinity, surpassing (contra Kingsnorth) all reasonable limit; all constraint, that is, upon the power of human reason:

> In their mastery of nature, the creative God and the ordering mind are alike. Man's likeness to God consists in sovereignty over existence, in the lordly gaze, in the command.[193]

The culmination of Horkheimer and Adorno's general argument finally *extends rational man's God-like dominion over nature into the political realm,* wherein application of the same ruling principle results in "the man of science," or those leagued with him, wielding dominion over others:

> Myth becomes enlightenment and nature mere objectivity. Human beings purchase the increase in their power with estrangement from that over which it is exerted. *Enlightenment stands in the same relationship to things as the dictator to human beings* [emphasis added]. He knows them to the extent that he can manipulate them. The man of science knows things to the extent that he can make them. Their "in-itself" becomes "for him." In their transformation the essence of things is revealed as always the same, a substrate of domination.[194]

Horkheimer and Adorno draw out the logic of the argument to its socio-political conclusion in a manner that predicts, with all too resonant relevance, leading features of Covid World today:

> Not only is domination paid for with the estrangement of human beings from the dominated objects, but the relationships of human beings, including the relationships of individuals to themselves, have themselves been bewitched by the objectification of mind. Individuals shrink to the nodal points of conventional reactions and modes of operation objectively expected of them. Animism had endowed things with souls; *industrialism makes souls into things* [emphasis added].[195]

This oppressive deadening may originate in the commercial sphere but, hardly stopping there, eats its way into the internal organs of culture and government as well. Dance numbers featuring contemporary Rockettes dressed as vaccine needles celebrating the "safe and effective" message, anyone? —

> The countless agencies of mass production and its culture impress standardized behavior on the individual as the only natural, decent, and rational one. Individuals define themselves now only as things, statistical elements, successes or failures.[196]

What (so the Machine asks of us) percent of persons are vaccinated in *your* region? Why, moreover, is this so important?

> Their criterion is self-preservation, successful or unsuccessful adaptation to the objectivity of their function and the schemata assigned to it. Everything which is different, from the idea to criminality, is exposed to the force of the collective, which keeps watch from the classroom to the trade union. Yet even the threatening collective is merely a part of the deceptive surface, beneath which are concealed the powers which manipulate the collective as an agent of violence.[197]

Those "powers" call to mind the Matrix (or Machine). The political terminus of this whole train of thought is both awful and predictable: "Enlightenment," Adorno and Horkheimer tell us, "is totalitarian."[198]

Horkheimer and Adorno's philosophically dense analysis (no easy read, surely, especially for persons that may be unaccustomed to continental philosophy) sheds bright cold light on the whole Covid phenomenon. It helps furnish an answer to the crucial question raised in the last chapter: what is it about the nature of technology that—even while technology certainly *can* serve egalitarian ends—tends to bend the arc of its use in the opposite direction, so that it all too often leads to power imbalances that constrain rather than enhance human freedom?

That dynamic inheres in technology's dependence on intellectual processes that turn qualitative matter and substance into measurable and manipulable quantities—autonomous consciousness into forms of objectivity subject to manipulation and control. That transformation is not necessarily odious; it may operate in enterprises as basic and necessary as the building of a house. However, it inevitably becomes nefarious—transforms into a source of oppression—when nature as a whole is thus treated, and when the "subjects" operated upon happen to be sentient beings, especially human ones. People are thereby robbed of their status as free agents, and instead come to serve as mere data points, statistics that function as "a substrate of domination."

This dynamic can often operate even in situations in which use of a technological device may, in one dimension, provide the human subject with opportunities for kinds of agency and choice it would otherwise not possess, as is most certainly the case with much contemporary information-based technology. Who would seriously contest, for instance, that as cell-phone and internet users, our lives, and indeed our public institutions themselves, are not increasingly under threat of increasing Big Tech control? This dynamic is, too, at work in the push for vaccine passports and digital IDs, the ultimate effect of which is to transform sovereign citizens into objects that can be monitored and regulated by the One Power that controls and commands the system.

> The self, entirely encompassed by civilization, is dissolved in an element composed of the very inhumanity which civilization has sought from the first to escape. The oldest fear, *that of losing one's name*, is being fulfilled.[199]

Even the few passages of *The Dialectic of Enlightenment* so far cited suffice to produce a sense of how and why that ideology can culminate in the kind of authoritarianism that Adorno and Horkheimer witnessed in their time; and we—in admittedly a different, yet nonetheless deeply kindred guise—even now are experiencing in our own Covid-coded world, courtesy of the brutal power of the Machine-like Matrix that hides behind the veneer of public health.

As I have stated before, it is by no means necessary for individuals who function as part of the system deliberately to wish to act as agents of control and even domination. Indeed, *the moral authority and practical efficiency of the system depends precisely on most persons and parties remaining largely unconscious of how they are indeed doing just that.* The company, school, or athletic league—at whatever level— that requires vaccination; the theatre or club that excludes those who cannot verify their status as vaccinees: all participate in the ultimately totalizing dialectic of enlightenment analyzed by Adorno and Horkheimer as they sought to understand the logic that enabled the rise of a fascist regime. That regime endangered their lives, forced their exile, and threatened the very existence of the free world—the world of liberal democracy—that Enlightenment-era philosophy originally sanctioned and birthed.

A profound contradiction clearly surfaces here. *How is it that the same ideas that played so vital a role in catalyzing the revolutionary movements that gave rise to liberal democracy simultaneously function as the ideological ground of that same political, economic and cultural initiative's internal rupture and disintegration?* In the wake of Horkheimer and Adorno, Paul Kingsnorth may well decry the world that has emerged under the aegis of Enlightenment-inspired ideals of science, reason, and progress. He may justifiably lament the decay of religious sensibility historically associated with their ascendancy. Even so, without depreciating Kingsnorth's devotion to the Romanian Orthodox church he joined in Ireland, I do not believe he imagines theocracy the answer to our contemporary ills.

Enlightenment thought, after all, did not arise in a cultural vacuum, but originally surfaced in concerted and passionate opposition to the forms of sectarian intolerance exhibited in the religious wars that, after the Reformation, turned much of Europe into a battlefield of bloody religious strife well on into the 18th century. The infamous St. Bartholomew Day Massacre, a sordid betrayal of trust that resulted in the murder, by French Catholics, of thousands of French Huguenots in 1572, counts as one low point. Almost two hundred years thereafter, in 1761, the flames of religious hatred still burned brightly, and it was the monstrously unjust yet publicly sanctioned torture and execution of the Huguenot Jean Calas in 1762 that prompted Voltaire to do his utmost to stem the still churning tide of religious violence by writing his classic *Treatise on Toleration.*[200]

Religious intolerance was hardly the only form of irrational dogma and political oppression that Enlightenment thinkers from Locke in England[201] to Montesquieu and Condorcet in 18th-century France (cf. the former's *The Spirit of Law*,[202] which formulated the doctrine of the separation of powers; and the latter's critique of slavery and defense of women's rights) and Kant in Germany[203] reasonably, and often passionately, resisted. True, with respect to religion, most (though not all) Enlightenment thinkers did not wish to do away with God altogether: Locke remained a Calvinist, and most of the Frenchmen held deist rather than atheist views. Correlatively, few could be considered avowed democrats; on the whole, Enlightenment philosophy could be considered a largely aristocratic movement.

Even so, Enlightenment thinking, in the name of the fair Goddess of Reason and her more plain but equally powerful sister, Common Sense (recall Tom Paine, whose tract by that title helped kindle the American Revolution[204]) aggressively pushed back against the arbitrary authority of despotic monarchs and their not-so noble nobles as well as that of the unduly privileged and often corrupt clergy. In so doing, the adherents of enlightenment paved the way for one of the most politically revolutionary concepts of all time: namely, the idea that common persons (and, collectively speaking, We, the People) do not exist to serve the King, or the power of the state, but vice versa. Correlative is the idea that—by virtue of nothing more and nothing less than their humanity—the individual citizen is possessed of certain unalienable rights, given by God, which rights it is a chief duty of civil government, duly formed by *consent of* the People, to protect. Such a political philosophy aims to ensure that government's administration of the affairs of the *polis* will advance, rather than obstruct, the general welfare. That end cannot be attained if it passes laws, issues executive orders, or otherwise acts in such a manner as to contravene those basic liberties reflective of the sovereignty of the human person.

Enlightenment is no simple matter, but a highly complex one, and its historic legacy is both dual and duplicitous. In one logical extension of the ideological tendencies inherent in Enlightenment thought, we arrive at the grim reality of totalitarian dystopia which, in its early phases, often disguises itself as one or another form of state-sanctioned ideal (the eugenics of Aryan supremacy, or that of the biotech and social engineering-enabled efficiency of the technocratic machine). In another, alternative reception of Enlightenment tradition—one that must include not only preservation of its real ideals, but, as well, critical recognition and transformation of the shadows that darken its light—we arrive at a very different destination: a cathartic recommitment to the principles that founded the free world.

The crucial question thus emerges: how do we distinguish between the two interpretive paths? How do we rightly discern, on the one hand, the salient core concepts of enlightenment, the enduring ideals that still provide indispensable inspiration and principled guidance, and, on the other, the philosophical flaws that invite injustice and oppression? How do we discriminate between means that realize authentic ideals and the distorted forms and twisted applications of ideological tendencies that lead down the road of violent misrule?

This critical task is a challenging, yet urgent one, because it is just this pitched conflict between these two alternative receptions of Enlightenment thought that characterizes our present moment in time and furnishes its apocalyptic intensity. Covid World is the historic site of a legendary battle between, on the one hand, the power of true enlightenment that may move the citizens of the world towards greater responsiveness to the prerogatives of freedom and the commands of love, and, on the other hand, the forces of "rational" efficiency and an unbridled will to power, which—though gilded by promises of safety, security, and brilliant technological enhancements of life—lead to material and spiritual degradation, a regime of ever increasing constraint and control of the many by the few, and ongoing strife: the demoralization and dehumanization of the race.

I wish initially to pursue this critical task by taking up some of the chief arguments advanced in Patrick J. Deneen's notable book *Why Liberalism Failed.*[205] Although its reading will first serve primarily to deepen understanding of the ground of global dysfunction, that sobering exercise may, like

Adorno and Horkheimer's critical project, prove a necessary prelude to more forward-looking vision.

Deneen's book appeared some seventy-five years after *Dialectic of Enlightenment* and takes liberalism rather than Enlightenment as its nominal subject. These two, however, are deeply kindred (in many respects, synonymous) topics; and while Deneen writes in a very different idiom from our more theoretical continental critics, his thesis echoes Adorno and Horkheimer's with almost uncanny precision. That it does so should not be too surprising; for while the outward circumstances of Adorno and Horkheimer's Germany and that of 21st-century America may differ dramatically in many respects, the ideological lines of force so presciently analyzed by the German duo have hardly been overturned or even meaningfully amended. On the contrary, in the seven-odd decades since the close of World War II, the Third and Fourth Industrial Revolutions have only accelerated the ideological, sociocultural, and political dynamics Adorno and Horkheimer elaborated, and granted them a global momentum.

Horkheimer and Adorno contend that enlightenment contains the seeds of its own destruction, and that (failing the self-reflection that is impeded by its inherent blindness to its own shadow) this destruction proceeds in accordance with a logic *internal* to Enlightenment thought itself. Deneen repeatedly declares the same of liberalism. His conclusion begins: "*Liberalism has failed because liberalism has succeeded.*" After alluding to the "endemic pathologies" generated by liberalism, Deneen expands upon the challenge facing all of us afflicted by that dysfunction:

> The narrowing of our political horizons has rendered us incapable of considering that what we face today is not a set of discrete problems solvable by liberal tools but a systemic challenge arising from pervasive invisible ideology. The problem is not in just one program or application but in the operating system itself.[206]

What is the mark of that failure? For Deneen, as well as for Adorno and Horkheimer, it is undue constraint and even wholesale loss of the genuine liberty which liberal or Enlightenment thought originally intended to provide and protect.

Adorno and Horkheimer characteristically provide a theoretically dense yet practically pointed formulation of the extinction of self-determination: one that—explicitly equating enlightenment with liberalism—almost could serve as a kind of abstract of Deneen's book:

> [Enlightenment] amputates the incommensurable. Not merely are qualities dissolved in thought, but human beings are forced into real conformity. The blessing that the market does not ask about birth is paid for in the exchange society by the fact that the possibilities conferred by birth are molded to fit the production of goods that can be bought on the market. Each human being has been endowed with a self of his or her own, different from all others, so that it could all the more surely be made the same. But because that self never quite fitted the mold, *enlightenment throughout the liberalistic period has always sympathized with social coercion. The unity of the manipulated collective consists in the negation of each individual* [emphasis added].[207]

Deneen supplies an analogous, but politically more concrete and detailed, version of liberalism's self-destruction:

> One can envision the perpetuation of a political system called "liberalism" that, becoming fully itself, operates in forms opposite to its purported claims about liberty, equality, justice, and opportunity. Contemporary liberalism will increasingly resort to imposing the liberal order by fiat—especially in the form of the administrative state run by a small minority who increasingly disdain democracy. End runs around democratic and populist discontent have become the norm, and backstopping the liberal order is the ever more visible power of a massive "deep state," with extensive powers of surveillance, legal mandate, police power, and administrative control. These methods will continue to be deployed despite liberalism's claim to rest on consent and popular support. Such a conclusion is paradoxical, not unlike Tocqueville's conclusion in *Democracy in America*, in which he envisions democracy culminating in a new form of despotism.[208]

Deneen's book gained wide attention in part because, appearing in the aftermath of Trump's election in 2016, many liberals looked to it for explanations of how the unthinkable could have in fact transpired. Deneen's analysis, however, proves still more prescient in prospect than in retrospect. Appearing shortly before Covid-19 brought a hammer down on the world we thought we knew, Deneen here envisions, with almost eerie accuracy, the political situation we find ourselves in today, even if many so-called "liberals" remain both stubbornly and dangerously blind to its frightening reality.[209]

That said, Deneen, no less than Adorno and Horkeimer, does acknowledge that—despite the drastic dysfunction he ascribes to enlightenment-cum-liberalism—it remains an essential point of departure for any more viable future.

> The achievements of liberalism must be acknowledged, and the desire to "return" to a preliberal age must be eschewed. We must build upon those achievements while abandoning the foundational reasons for its failures. There can be no going back, only forward.[210]

What path, then, does Deneen offer that may point us in the right direction? We can best begin exploring that question by understanding the history and rationale of the "liberal" ideology dominant in the West today.

First, it should be made clear that, as Deneen repeatedly emphasizes, he understands "liberalism" much more broadly than most people do. "Liberalism," for Deneen, represents no narrowly political perspective conveniently set off against a familiar alternative, but an entire worldview upheld, in principle, by both political "conservatives" and "liberals" and, thus, in an American context, most Republicans as well as Democrats. To lay the foundation for an understanding of that worldview, Deneen introduces his reader to relevant aspects of the intellectual and political history that clarify the terms of its advent in the modern era. Following Deneen, we discover that the emergence of the liberal worldview revolves around the redefinition of the key idea that lends "liberalism" its name: liberty itself.

Chapter One begins:

> The deepest commitment of liberalism is expressed by the name itself: liberty. Liberalism has proven both attractive and resilient because of this core commitment to the longing for human freedom so deeply embedded in the human soul. Liberalism's historical rise and global attraction are hardly accidental; it has appealed especially to people subject to arbitrary rule, unjust inequality and pervasive poverty.[211]

That appeal, while spectacularly evident in the political revolutions sparked by Enlightenment thought, is hardly of recent vintage. Deneen proceeds to sketch some of the background we need if we are to begin to understand the modern *redefinition* of liberty constitutive of contemporary "liberalism" itself:

> The word *libertas* is of ancient origin, and its defense and realization have been a primary goal from the first forays into political philosophy in ancient Greece and Rome. The foundational texts of the Western political tradition focused especially on the question how to constrain the impulse to and assertions of tyranny, and characteristically settled upon the cultivation of virtue and self-rule as the key correctives to the tyrannical temptation.[212]

Here already we strike upon a chord that sounds rather foreign to the modern ear. Deneen elaborates the manner in which moral concerns proper to *individual* conscience coordinate with salutary modes of political governance, a teaching most strongly rooted in classical Greece:

> The Greeks especially regarded self-government as a continuity from the individual to the polity, with the realization of either only possible if the virtues of temperance, wisdom, moderation, and justice were to be mutually sustained and fostered. Self-governance in the city was possible only if the virtue of self-governance governed the souls of citizens; and self-governance of individuals could be realized only in a city that understood that citizenship itself was a kind of ongoing habituation in virtue, through both law and custom.[213]

In Deneen's account, Roman and, consequently, medieval Christian traditions, while retaining the Greek accent upon virtue, further developed a variety of legal and political forms that functioned to constrain authoritarian tendencies and, to some degree, opened avenues of popular representation. In so doing, both classical and Christian influences prepared the way for modern liberalism. Deneen distills the essential tenets of the tradition of political thought sourced in classical and Christian precedent:

> Liberty had long been believed to be the condition of self-rule that forestalled tyranny within both the polity and the individual soul. Liberty was thus thought to involve discipline and training in self-limitation of desires, and corresponding social and political arrangements that sought to inculcate corresponding virtues that fostered the arts of self-government.[214]

Even while drawing upon this cultural inheritance, the liberal ideology birthed by Enlightenment thought dramatically transformed it. In fact, the advent of modernity, in Deneen's view, ultimately hinged upon *repudiation* of these time-honored precepts. Many traditional social and political forms increasingly came to be regarded, not as reliable partners in the joint project of securing liberty, but as the primary obstacles to its attainment. "The foundations of liberalism," writes Deneen

> were laid by a series of thinkers whose central aim was to disassemble what they concluded were irrational religious and social norms in the pursuit of civil peace that might in turn foster stability and prosperity, and eventually individual liberty of conscience and action.[215]

At the root of the profound transformation thus effected lay a sea-change in fundamental "anthropological assumptions": the reigning understanding of the nature of human being.

It should be no surprise that the names of Descartes and Bacon feature prominently in Deneen's account of the revolutionary currents of thought that accompanied—and indeed ushered in—the advent of modernity and the liberal ideology associated with it. Neither Descartes nor Bacon are renowned as political philosophers;[216] even so, they were instrumental in redefining the human being's vision of itself and its relationship to (newly modified concepts of) nature and divinity. While the modern intellect has become accustomed to forms of specialization that mercilessly fragment the field of knowledge, an underlying unity perpetually attends thought itself. As a result, it was inevitable that Descartes's radical initiatives in the domain of epistemology and mathematics, and Lord Bacon's in the related departments of science and its practical application, were deeply interwoven with the sociopolitical visions that emerged at the dawn of modernity.

Descartes, we may recall, conceived of the human self as such existing in a state of radical autonomy, essentially disconnected from any constitutive relationship to either nature or God. Tarnas again:

> Descartes helped emancipate the material world from its long association with religious belief, freeing science to develop its analysis of that world in terms uncontaminated by spiritual or human qualities and unconstrained by theological dogma. Both the human mind and the natural world now stood autonomously as never before, separated from God and from each other.[217]

That autonomous self whose rational thought grounds its own identity, and (following Bacon) whose prospective mastery of nature provides fertile pasture for the free exercise of will, does not, however, finally live alone in solitary contemplation or occupy all its energies in feats of technical prowess. That self must, as well, live in relation to other human beings, and find fit means of governing itself in the state of civil society. In examining the political philosophy that founds modern liberalism, we find, consistently enough, that *the same anthropological assumptions that underly both Descartes's and Bacon's thinking function as the philosophical foundations of political liberalism and its radical redefinition of liberty itself.*

Deneen identifies three initiatives that fueled the "revolution in thought and practice" constituting the rise of political liberalism. I will here quickly review all three, albeit in an order different from Deneen's.

The first may be the most familiar: it involves reliance upon *individual reason* as the principle means of, not only theoretical, but practical judgment: the discernment of what is just and good. This principle cuts decisively against the grain of traditional norms linked to the classical and Christian ideas of liberty as self-rule insofar as these were closely associated with

> norms and social structures arrayed extensively throughout political, social, religious, economic and familial life. What were viewed as the essential supports for a training in virtue—and hence, preconditions for liberty from tyranny—came to be viewed as sources of oppression, arbitrariness, and limitation.[218]

In this connection, Deneen mentions both Descartes and Thomas Hobbes as champions of an "individualistic rationality" that might mend the "rule of irrational custom and unexamined tradition—especially religious belief and practice"[219] that so readily leads to illegitimate abuse of power and ongoing conflict in society. Notably, both these thinkers (though especially Hobbes) emphasized a centralized state, operating as an extension of the reasoning self, as the chief means by which rational government might be effectively implemented and enforced so as to ensure greater peace and prosperity for all.

The second initiative harps on a theme we have already discussed at length: man's dominion over an objectified nature. In the context of *political* philosophy, Deneen emphasizes that man's mastery over nature enables him to exercise freedom in the form of practical action (including technological and economic enterprise) unlimited by any natural constraints. This, too, in Deneen's mind, clashes with a crucial dimension of inherited notions of true "liberty":

> A revolution in modern science thus called as well for overturning such philosophical traditions as Stoicism and Christian emphasis upon "acceptance" in favor of belief in an expanding and potentially limitless human capacity to control circumstance and effect human desires upon the world.[220]

The third point Deneen mentions pertains most directly to the heart of the matter of the nature of human being. Traditional ideas of liberty, in both classical and Christian contexts, revolved around an ideal of virtue. The new political initiative underlying liberalism, however, throws virtue overboard, considering it an albatross around the neck of human ambition, or a dead weight that can only serve to sink the ship of our human state. "Politics," writes Deneen, would be based upon reliability of "the low" rather than aspiration to "the high."

Machiavelli emerges as a trailblazer in this department, a philosopher who, in his classic work *The Prince,* repudiates ancient philosophic and religious ideals because:

> the gap between how people actually behave and how they ought to behave is so great that anyone who ignores everyday reality in order to live up to an ideal will soon discover that he has been taught how to destroy himself, not how to preserve himself.[221]

Deneen expands upon Machiavelli's argument:

> Machiavelli proposed grounding a political philosophy upon readily observable human behaviors of pride, selfishness, greed, and the quest for glory. He argued further that liberty and political security were better achieved by pitting different domestic classes against one another, encouraging each to limit the others through "ferocious conflict" in the protection of their particular interests rather than by lofty appeals to a "common good" and political concord. By acknowledging ineradicable human selfishness and the desire for material goods, one might conceive of ways to harness those motivations rather than seeking to moderate or limit those desires.[222]

Machiavelli's opinions hardly strike one as "liberal." It is, however, not difficult to discern in them the outlines of the principles underlying the free market economy so central to liberal ideology. Commensurately, Deneen, while openly recognizing that none of the thinkers cited (neither Descartes nor Bacon nor Hobbes nor Machiavelli) could readily be classified as "liberals," maintains that their "revolutionary reconception of politics, society, science and nature…laid the foundation of modern liberalism."[223] Deneen elaborates:

> A succession of thinkers in subsequent decades and centuries were to build upon these three basic revolutions of thought, redefining liberty as the liberation of humans from established authority, emancipation from arbitrary culture and tradition, and the expansion of human power and dominion over nature through advancing scientific discovery and economic prosperity.[224]

In this summary, Deneen somewhat slights the influence of the last chief, Machiavellian point. This is actually his first and most basic premise, the presumed ground upon which all else rests: namely, that *the new definition of "liberty" entails release from the burden of undue self-constraint, the moral scruples and spiritual aspiration inherent in the idea of virtue.*

As may be surmised from the title of his book, Deneen does not believe that the results of the liberal revolution in thought and politics have been predominantly salutary. More pointedly, he does not (like Frances Fukuyama) believe that the widespread calamity so visible in the so-called "free world" today can be chalked up to defective application of what remains a sound and noble framework rather than serious fault lines inherent in the foundation of liberal thought.

With certain crucial reservations, I agree, and moreover, view the current political catastrophe of Covid World as a logical culmination of, not only Enlightenment thought, but the liberal ideology so closely allied with it: a betrayal of genuinely liberal values by virtue of a dynamic internal to the system of thought that comprises liberalism's intellectual, moral, and spiritual foundation. As such, Covid World itself may be regarded as a kind of apocalypse of the liberal mind: at one and the same time, an abysmal catastrophe and a blinding revelation of much that has long been wrong. So, too, it represents a unique opportunity for urgently needed transformation.

As I have stated, the gist of Deneen's argument echoes that of Adorno and Horkheimer; yet Deneen's analysis, while less metaphysically elaborate, provides a more concrete and practically detailed account of the logic of coercion and erasure of differentiated individuality both the German theorists and Deneen criticize. In particular, Deneen delineates how *the reduction of souls to things* which Adorno and Horkheimer ascribe to Enlightenment thought translates into a particular brand of polity, one defined by the *mutually reinforcing relationship* between two terms often placed in a contestatory relationship: namely, *the state* and the *autonomous individual.* Deneen construes the resultant (seemingly paradoxical) coincidence of "individualism" and "statism" as the basis of political liberalism.

The distinctive character of that ideology hinges upon the peculiar fashion in which the "autonomous" individual creates and defines the state, and vice versa. In every which way, the philosophical and anthropological assumptions that authorize the modern redefinition of liberty remain the crux of the matter. That critical redefinition, in turn, catalyzes and coincides with both the emergence of the modern nation state—a form of governance ostensibly designed to secure and protect the liberty of its citizens—and the dynamic by which that state tends to accrue forms of power that finally suppress and even extinguish real individual liberty. To understand the relevant sociopolitical dynamics, we, following Deneen, need pay further attention to two 17th-century philosophic giants: Thomas Hobbes and John Locke.

Like his 17th-century contemporaries,[225] Descartes and Bacon, Hobbes looks at human nature itself through the lens of a self or subject imagined to be essentially separate from anything and anyone else. "According to Hobbes," writes Deneen, "human beings exist by nature in a state of radical independence and autonomy"[226]—a human condition unconstrained by any constitutive relationship to divinity, moral obligations responsive to limits inherent in the natural order of things, or relations of mutual affection and concern for other human beings. This premise gives rise to the new interpretation of liberty Deneen construes as fundamental to modern liberalism, one premised not upon self-governance, but rather *the freedom to pursue self-interested activity in the absence of undue external constraint.* For Hobbes (like Spinoza), *self-preservation* qualifies as the principal form of self-interest, and the natural right to act so as to achieve that end is virtually definitive of liberty itself:

> THE RIGHT OF NATURE, which Writers commonly call *Jus Naturale*, is the Liberty each man hath, to use his own power, as he will himselfe, for the preservation of his own Nature; that is say, of his own Life; and consequently, of doing any thing, which in his own Judgment, and Reason, he shall conceive to be the aptest means thereunto.
>
> By LIBERTY, is understood, according to the proper signification of the word, the absence of external Impediment...[227]

The isolated individual, however, even though at liberty to do whatever he wishes, cannot very well secure his own well-being in the face of nature's hostility. Moreover, if he enters into relationship with others to obtain the advantages gained through cooperation, competing self-interest fueled by unruly "natural passions" inevitably lead to destructive antagonisms. Thus the paramount need for some sovereign body (whether this be a monarch or some governing assembly matters little to Hobbes) as a means of preserving each individual's liberty in the social state:

> The final Cause, End, or Designe of men (who naturally love Liberty, and Dominion over others) in the introduction of that restraint upon themselves, (in which we see them live in Common-wealths) is the foresight of their own preservation, and of a more contented life thereby; that is to say,

> of getting themselves out from that miserable condition of Warre, which is necessarily consequent (as has been shewn) to the natural Passions of men, when there is no visible Power to keep them in awe, and tye them by feare of punishment to the performance of their covenants.[228]

The governing body, which I will here refer to in its modern form as the state, thus emerges at the behest of a collection of self-interested individuals who enter into certain agreements presumed to advance the liberty of all, and who empower the state to be the organ that both codifies those agreements in the form of law and possesses the power to enforce the same. Key to Hobbes's vision, moreover, is the paramount truth that the system only functions if—once the state is legitimated by collective consent—individual citizens pledge unqualified allegiance to it. Once duly constituted, the power of the state approaches the absolute.

John Locke, Hobbes's philosophic heir, extends Hobbes's argument, lending greater weight to an expanded field of individual self-interest dependent upon state sanction. Deneen:

> For both Hobbes and Locke, we enter into a social contract not only to secure our survival but to make the exercise of our liberty more secure. Both Hobbes and Locke—but especially Locke—understand that liberty in our prepolitical condition is limited not only by the lawless competition of other individuals but by our recalcitrant and hostile natures. A main goal of Locke's philosophy is to expand the prospects for our liberty—defined as the capacity to satisfy our appetites—through the auspices of the state. Law is not a discipline for self-government but the means for expanding personal freedom: "The end of law is not to abolish or restrain, but to preserve and enlarge freedom."[229]

The positive power of the state and that of the individual attached to it is, however, purchased at the cost of norms and traditions deriving from alternative, competing forms of authority:

> We accept the terms of the social contract because it will actually increase our personal liberty by eliminating customs and even laws that can be thought to limit individual freedom, even while expanding the prospects for human control over the natural world.[230]

This constitutive dynamic creates synergy between state power and individual liberty, effecting a paradoxical unity of individual and state interest that Deneen calls "statist individualism":

> Thus, for liberal theory, while the individual "creates" the state through the social contract, in a practical sense, the liberal state "creates" the individual by providing the conditions for the expansion of liberty, increasingly defined as the capacity of humans to expand their mastery over circumstances. Far from there being an inherent conflict between the individual and the state—as so much of modern political reporting would suggest—liberalism establishes a deep and profound connection: its ideal of liberty can be realized only through a powerful state.[231]

Deneen repeatedly emphasizes that a principal means by which the state enables and expands individual freedom involves its capacity to empower human control over nature and promote the free economic activity thus made possible. That might include, for instance, laws legalizing fracking; drilling for oil in the ocean, desert, or tundra; or licensing the use of pesticides or pharmaceutical products conjoined with the allocation of funds for the research and development that makes such enterprises possible and policies that may protect and incentivize such activity. Deneen stresses, as well, that the individual functioning "as a disembedded, self-interested actor" does *not* arise spontaneously in any (fictitious) state of nature, but represents a deliberate invention by way of "elaborate intervention by the incipient state in early modernity, at the beginning of the liberal order."[232]

That intervention consists in large measure of weakening and even nullifying the individual's commitment to "traditional ties and relationships" embedded in non-state communities of concern—religious affiliations, professional guilds, community groups of all sorts, even the family—because such attachments generally promote values (compassionate concern for others, for instance, and the cultivation of virtues and excellencies of a spiritual rather than utilitarian kind) essentially at odds with the motive of *independent self-interest* that fuels the machine of state. While, on one level, such commitments and values may appear quite congruent with those underlying the state (a Boy Scout's code of honor *may* not hinder his future success as an entrepreneur or statesman), privileging those commitments ultimately binds the individual in a manner incommensurate with the kind of enterprise liberal ideology most values and legitimates: his power to act as autonomous agent, governed by his own interest, in the free market of worldly opportunity. Reciprocally, the rewards reaped by way of such an enterprise typically serve, not only to enrich the successful individual, but to profit the state as well. A thriving economy supplies a solid tax base; productivity resulting from various forms of activity (including, of course, technological and entrepreneurial invention) provides the material and human resources necessary for state power.

It is, however, not overly difficult to see how this liberal "uniting of statism and individualism" naturally leads, by a logic internal to the system itself, to a *magnification* of state authority that can ultimately result in undue constraint of individual prerogatives; even, indeed, to tyranny. *The liberal individual, after all, has defined herself (or rather allowed herself to be defined) in such a manner that her fundamental freedoms and indeed very identity depend largely or entirely upon conditions created and protected by the state.* She has, moreover, accorded that governing state the authority to make law, and the (material) power to enforce it; whereas she herself can neither make law nor marshal any remotely comparable physical force. From the outset, the deck is stacked in favor of the state; but its hegemony rests upon one further, decisive feature. The very definition of liberty upon which the whole ideological system builds establishes norms that put the state in a convincing position frequently to claim—not only the superior force of law—but *higher moral authority* deriving from its status as the representative organ of collective will and guardian of the general welfare.

According to the modern definition of liberty, the individual's legitimate and legally recognized ends are chiefly confined to self-interest—first and foremost, self-preservation, and secondarily, the freedom to engage in activity (including economic enterprise) that can satisfy sense-based needs and desires. These freedoms, however, all pertain to existence and action in the field of worldly enterprise opened by the state, within which purely objective and objectified sphere value remains subject to quantification and rational calculation. This holds true even, and perhaps most especially, for the principle of self-preservation which—when viewed from the higher perspective of the state—translates readily into sheer number of lives lost or saved. Because the liberal definition of liberty does *not* intrinsically include reference to any immaterial principle or spiritual value (reference to an ideal of virtue stemming from God or the Good for instance), the individual person's very identity has no recognized standing in any world other than that controlled and ordered by state, which is thus licensed to (de)value her person in accord with its own "rational" system of accounting.

The newly operative definition of liberty thus, in the name of the radical autonomy of the subject, actually empties the human individual of any qualitative or transcendent value—any value exceeding that of sheer existence and satisfaction of worldly desires, which terms the state, by way of science and technology, readily translates into the statistics that provide a basis for "moral" judgment and policy decision. Moreover, as soon as morality is reduced to the sphere of number or quantity, the state, because it represents the collective, and so the Many rather than One, always wins. In any state system that reduces all differences to a single, horizontal level of meaning—the laboratory rabbit rather than the sacrificial lamb—the greatest number always defines the greater good, and what can be claimed in the name of the public always trumps the private interest.

An example relevant to Covid World can concretize these ruminations. If the law precludes me from claiming a natural or religious right to bodily autonomy as a reason for refusing a prescribed vaccine (which is indeed the case in California with respect to *all* mandated childhood vaccines), and the state maintains that vaccination saves X number of lives or prevents X number of serious illnesses and so represents a net positive for public health, I have no moral ground upon which to stand to oppose its dictate; at least, so long as it can plausibly *claim* that science verifies its calculation. My personal self-interest, including my judgment as to what may best preserve my life and health, is of no account[233] in comparison with the state's guardianship of an incomparably greater number of persons. Appeal to any other, higher moral ground (my relation to an intelligence superior to that of the human intellect, creative of my body, which thus accrues an *incalculable* value) is automatically precluded and summarily discarded as entirely irrelevant to the only measure that counts: the state's own "rational" calculation of public good.

Correlatively, and in a manner that corroborates Deneen's analysis, it is very obvious today how the state indeed seeks to erase all cultural forms that might interfere with the power of its edicts to regulate the agency of individual persons. Covid World has triggered an unprecedented attempt on the part of federal governments to control *all* levels of health management, so neither hospitals nor individual physicians, nor even, in many instances, individual patients themselves possess independent power of deliberation and decision. In particular, the traditionally sacrosanct doctor-patient relationship has been unceremoniously cast aside as a relic of less enlightened era of health care. Insofar as that relationship enshrines individual difference and concrete human relationship as the basis of ethical and effective medical practice, it qualifies as anathema to the burgeoning power of the contemporary state apparatus.[234]

In marked contrast to the type of morality written into the liberal ideology dominant today, any genuine ethics intrinsically depends upon a degree of *selflessness* that extends my sphere of interest beyond my own person so as to include vital reference to divinity, natural limits, the bodies and souls of other human beings, universal principles held as worthy of observance in their own right, or (ideally) all of the above. It is thus folly to try to frame a morally sound system of governance upon the principle of self-interest as such derives from its essentially utilitarian Hobbesian and Lockean formulations.[235]

At one level, the contemporary liberal conscience naturally recognizes this very clearly; so much so, that this conscience imagines itself as *founded upon* and *pervaded by* compassionate regard for the Other. Yet genuinely selfless activity depends upon an authentically and irreducibly *spiritual* (not political or economic) concept of the self; one ultimately and essentially independent of the type of (self-)identity created by and responsible to the state. Lack of such a concept inevitably cripples the human capacity to attain to authentic regard for the Other, who, after all, cannot be conceived or related to as anything other than another *Self*, identical in *type* (though not in individual character) to one's own.

Stuck, as it is, in the philosophical quicksand prepared by the likes of Hobbes and Locke, liberal ethics too often looks, in practice if not theory, *not* to the *incalculable* value of *real* individual selves, the distinct worth of *singular* human beings, but to abstract rationalistic concepts of the general good or vaguely collectivist notions of "the welfare of humanity" (or a given, usually oppressed, subgroup thereof) which compensate (albeit inappropriately and inadequately) for the spiritual deficiency inherent in its intellectual underpinnings. Nothing exemplifies this more clearly than the ruthless indifference with which the leftward-leaning ranks of the American polity has, in cooperation with government and medical authorities, uniformly denied the very *existence* of vaccine-injured and killed individuals, effectively erasing, so far as is possible, the names of such persons from the public record and the secular Book of Life. Any consequential recognition of the actual facts of these persons' life stories threatens the concept, the *idée fixe*, that vaccines are a boon to humanity at large, functioning as a kind of saving grace capable of rescuing humankind as a whole from unnecessary suffering and death.[236]

It is this species of ideological formation which allows the liberal mindset to be so readily captured and co-opted by a technocratic Great Reset agenda that employs the *vocabulary* of liberal humanitarian values even while assiduously working to impose authoritarian forms of rule *antithetical* to real equality, mutuality, and liberty in society. As a citizen of the modern liberal state, I am in fact (whether I will or no) made hostage to a system of value authorized—in fact charged—to treat me as nothing but one of any number of *indistinguishable* selves, a statistic to be entered into the state's own rational calculus of the public good, the validity of which too often finds uncritical sanction in a likewise "liberally-minded" populace.

The hollowing of individual rights, and the moral impotence of the private person in face of the massive authority of the state, flows directly from the philosophical and anthropological assumptions underlying liberal ideology. "Enlightenment thought," say Adorno and Horkheimer, "stands in the same relationship to things, as the dictator to human beings." Having defined herself as an all-powerful subject over against an objectified nature, one constrained by no higher power flowing from reverence for divinity or membership in a sacrosanct natural order, the autonomous individual of the liberal regime sets herself up to be treated as just such a "thing," a pawn in the greater game of the calculation of self-interest played by the infinitely greater power of the state. The individual human subject that imagined itself sovereign in intellect and master of an objectified nature becomes the meaningless object of the sovereign mind of the state, which qualifies as the new god-like power that far outstrips the individual with respect to scientific and technical resources, legislative power, economic as well as military might, and even (because of its claim to concentrate the manifold public interest in its own singular master agency) moral authority.

Horkheimer and Adorno provide a characteristically profound but dense discussion of this theme. The Spinoza citation they take as a point of departure puts the modern redefinition of liberty in a nutshell, revealing, with admirable precision, the perversion inherent in its moral logic. After the ethical horizon of human being is contracted to self-interest, the self (indifferently one's own, or another's) is abstracted from lived reality and, finally, in the form of a purely rational function, awarded illimitable agent power:

> Spinoza's proposition "the endeavor of preserving oneself is the first and only basis of virtue" contains the true maxim of all Western civilization.... The self which...was no longer supposed to be either a body or blood or a soul or even a natural ego but was sublimated into a transcendental or logical subject formed the reference point of reason, the legislating authority of action.[237]

After thus moving from Spinoza to Descartes, we advance to critique of the liberal system of political economy and its inevitable metamorphosis into *technocratic regimes of state control.*

> In the bourgeois economy the social work of each individual is mediated by the principle of the self; for some this labor is supposed to yield increased capital, for others the strength for extra work. But the more heavily the process of self-preservation is based on the bourgeois division of labor, the more it enforces *the self-alienation of individuals, who must mold themselves to the technical apparatus body and soul* [emphasis added].[238]

Are not the quality of life of a Lyft driver, or warehouse worker hired by Amazon, or even an Apple employee in his cubicle, profoundly conditioned by the political economy that everyone is plugged into, whether they will or no? While individuals theoretically possess the opportunity for economic self-determination and advancement, does the system encourage or even allow for creative contribution or spiritually as well as materially rewarding labor? Do not the liberal ideology and its associated political economy mercilessly push us to "mold [ourselves] to the technical apparatus body and soul"?

For Adorno and Horkheimer, the prevailing ideological, political, and economic system portends both the progressive disintegration of the autonomous self and its sublation into the masterful machine of state...

> Enlightened thinking has an answer for this, too: finally, the transcendental subject of knowledge, as the last reminder of subjectivity, is itself seemingly abolished and replaced by the operations of the automatic mechanisms of order, which therefore run all the more smoothly.[239]

...before circling back to the self-interested economics that fuel the whole system:

> The technical process, to which the subject has been reified after the eradication of that process from consciousness, is...free from meaning altogether, since *reason itself has become merely an aid to the all-encompassing economic apparatus* [emphasis added].[240]

The next sentences exhibit an almost uncanny prescience when viewed from the perspective of the Covid World produced and staged by the medical-industrial complex. Science and (Bio)Technology, instruments of reason, intend to bring nature under control, but, (as history, including that of Covid) so amply demonstrates, the fated consequences are always drastically unpredictable:

> Reason serves as a universal tool for the fabrication of all other tools, rigidly purpose-directed and as calamitous as the precisely calculated operations of material production, the results of which for human beings escape all calculation.[241]

Did the government "calculate" the effect of lockdowns and other technocratic measures *reasonably?* Whatever your opinion about that may be, our "progress" towards ever greater technocratic control and efficiency is, Adorno and Horkheimer remind us, perfectly "rational"—at least, according to the definitions of "reason" and "liberty" written into the philosophic charter of Enlightenment thought.[242]

Adorno and Horkheimer's analysis of the dialectic of enlightenment, in fact, diagnoses and challenges the most treasured premises of the Age of Reason:

> Reason's old ambition to be purely an instrument of purposes has finally been fulfilled. The exclusivity of logical laws stems from this obdurate adherence to function and ultimately from the compulsive character of self-preservation. The latter is constantly magnified into the choice between survival and doom, a choice which is reflected even in the principle that, of two contradictory propositions, only one can be true and the other false.[243]

Adorno and Horkheimer's intensely theoretical idiom can both excite and frustrate understanding, but anyone who experienced the early days of Covid can grasp what they are saying here. How else could devastating months-long lockdowns and indeed the whole Covid package be sold except on the basis of the stark dualism implicit in the principle of self-preservation, which can all too easily be translated into the byline that underwrites the whole of our official Covid Response: Not "*Live Free...*" but "*Lock Down* (or vaccinate or mask...) *or Die.*" Survival or Doom. Individually and *en masse.*

Montesquieu, one of the Enlightenment luminaries to whom we will soon turn in order to understand the real contribution of that era, associated each of three chief forms of governance with a single ruling principle. *Monarchy,* he asserted, depends upon the wisdom and ethical integrity of the sovereign, and so banks on *Honor. Democracy,* in accord with the classical and Christian traditions of self-governance to which Deneen refers us, relies on *Virtue. Despotism,* on the other hand, runs on the psychological correlate of the cardinal principle of Self-Preservation: *Fear.*

Adorno and Horkheimer recognize, along with Montesquieu, that a political philosophy that takes the principle of self-preservation as ultimate end rather than provisional point of departure cannot truly be "rational" at all, *whatever* claims may be made in the name of science and reason. True, despotic master-minds can and do manipulate fear for their own ends; but whether intentions be good or ill, the technocratic administration of public health and welfare never increases health, harmony, and peace because the "natural passions" (Hobbes) cannot thus be ruled, or ruled out. Consequently:

> Nature as true self-preservation is thereby unleashed, in the individual as in the collective fate of crisis and war, by the process which promised to extirpate it.... *The self, entirely encompassed by civilization, is dissolved in an element composed of the very inhumanity which civilization has sought from the first to escape* [emphasis added].[244]

Think, first of all, of the gross contradiction between the purportedly humanitarian and community-minded ethics of those promoting mass vaccination and the violently *inhumane* persecution of the unvaccinated—and even vaccine-injured!—triggered by government posturing and policy, and the "mob morality" (Eisenstein) it both instigated and abetted.

More generally speaking, do not Adorno and Horkheimer speak eloquently of the state of the human being in today's globalist reality? The rule of science and technology, which, in modern technocracy, swallows government whole, promises to rescue humanity from its fallen state and the endemic afflictions of toil, strife, suffering, and death—or, at the very least, to help heal and improve our lot. Yet insofar as the principle of the autonomous self's own preservation and egotistical interest serve as the (im)moral core of the whole philosophy, Enlightenment ideology, in the form of the modern liberal democratic state and (even more) its global extension, has actually delivered just the opposite: a human world at ever greater odds with itself and nature and consequently riven by constant crisis and outright war. Meanwhile, authoritarian forms of control at the state, national, and international level increasingly compromise or destroy the liberty, agency, and dignity of individual human beings.

As both Adorno and Horkheimer and Deneen reveal, the root of the problem inheres in the faulty philosophical premises that underwrite contemporary political culture and its flawed concept of liberal democracy. The two most basic assumptions, as already detailed in the prior chapter, entail the objectification of nature inherent in a materialist/mechanist cosmology and the sovereignty of the autonomous "rational" human subject, the *cogito* that claims a positively god-like power of knowledge.

These twinned ideas are both explicitly inscribed in the very first paragraph of Hobbes's *Leviathan,* which builds political philosophy upon these very premises. Hobbes:

> NATURE (the Art whereby God hath made and governes the World) is by the *Art* of man, as in many other things, so in this also imitated, that it can make an Artificial Animal. For seeing Life is but a motion of Limbs, the beginning whereof is some principall part within: why may we not say, that all *Automata* (Engines that move themselves by springs and wheels as doth a watch) have artificial life? For what is the *Heart,* but a *Spring;* and the *Nerves,* but so many *Strings;* and the *Joynts*, but so many *Wheeles,* giving motion to the whole Body, such as was intended by the Artificer?[245]

What better license could a contemporary transhumanist wish for his project of recreating human being (body and all) by way of the art of modern technology?

Hobbes continues to expand his metaphor so as to apply it, not now to the individual body, but to "the Body Politique":

> *Art* goes yet further, imitating that Rationall and most excellent worke of Nature, *Man.* For by Art is created that great LEVIATHAN called a COMMON-WEALTH, or STATE, (in latine CIVITAS) which is but an Artificiall Man, though of greater stature and strength than the Naturall, for whose protection and defense it was intended; and in which, the Soveraignty is an Artificiall *Soul,* as giving life and motion to the whole body.[246]

Hobbes proceeds to correlate the multiple features of the Commonwealth with parts of the body or faculties of mind, concluding with reference to the social covenant that originally generates the state, to which almighty organ the individual owes, in his system, unconditional allegiance:

> Lastly, the Pacts and Covenants, by which the parts of this Body Politique were at first made, set together, and united, resemble that *Fiat,* or the *Let us make man,* pronounced by God in the Creation.[247]

We thus return here, at the end, to the Tower of Babel motif lent concise modern articulation by Paul Kingsnorth: *We are building a machine to replace God.* Hobbes, though, makes explicit that it is a *political* machine we are building. Moreover, he—along with the other thinkers discussed in this chapter—lets us in on some of the inside secrets of the *philosophic anatomy* of the gigantic mechanism we have already awarded diverse monikers: Matrix, Technocracy, Deep State. We can now add another to the list; one that boasts a peculiarly biblical ring: *LEVIATHAN.*

PART II

MODERNITY DAWNS

Chapter 6

THE ROOTS OF MODERN LIBERALISM I: DEPRAVITY TO DIGNITY

One would naturally expect the author of *Why Liberalism Failed* to envision some form of remedy for the terminal illness afflicting liberal democracy, and Deneen offers a provisional response to that imperative in his conclusion. His deliberations kick off by reiterating that any effort to improve upon liberalism need begin by recognizing the genuine value it bears. Any path forward, he observes,

> must eschew liberalism's ideological dimensions yet be cognizant of its achievement and the rightful demands it makes—particularly for justice and dignity.... If we hope to create a humane postliberal future, we cannot pretend that the age of liberalism did not happen or that its basic contours can simply be jettisoned in some sort of restoration of an idyllic preliberal age. That age never existed.[248]

In the wake of this acknowledgment, Deneen foregoes any grand attempt at what he calls "epic theory," any comprehensive intellectual revisioning of the grounds of our political culture. Instead, he counsels that the first arena of redress need be revivification of those traditional forms of culture devalued and even destroyed by liberalism:

> Instead of trying to conceive a replacement ideology (or returning to some updated version of an alternative, such as a renascent Marxism), we should focus on developing practices that foster new forms of culture, household economics and polis life.[249]

Deneen, however, does not quite stop there, for he recognizes the necessity of radically transformative intellectual vision. "From the cauldron of such [cultural] experience and practice," he opines, "a better theory of politics and society might ultimately emerge."[250] Moreover, in the preface to the later edition of his book—written (unlike the body of the text) after the political convulsions of Trump's election in 2016 and Brexit— Deneen acknowledges that history has lately hurtled forward with unexpected speed so that the pressing need for epic theory may be already hard upon us.

In the wake of the cataclysmic disruptions of the pandemic, globalist calls for the Great Reset, and the Covid-fueled growth spurt of the leviathan World Order, it would appear that the time for epic theory may indeed be near at hand. In the absence of any creative rethinking of our political philosophical heritage, technocracy and transhumanism, those influential legatees of liberal ideology, threaten to continue greasing the wheels of humanity's car as it races headlong down the track of disaster.

Deneen provides a fertile point of departure for such intellectual adventure in both a deficient and efficient guise. With respect to the former, Deneen's critical premises display a visible crack. How, after all, can it truly be the case that liberalism holds such great and genuine value that no viable political future can retract its initiatory promise, and yet, at the same time, count as so fundamentally flawed as to lead inevitably to its own betrayal and destruction? Can one and the same idea simultaneously be considered the origin and source of indispensable good and manifest evil? The question is especially pertinent when that evil is insistently chalked up to no extraneous deformation or failure in application, but the essence of the thing itself.

It is no sterile logic that inclines one to be skeptical of such flagrant philosophical contradiction. True, all powerful ideas create not only light, but dark shadow; yet even while possessing a common source, these are not one and the same. May it not then rather be that what Deneen calls "liberalism" contains a core of pristine truth and goodness that constitutes its undying appeal, but that this radiant center undergoes disfiguring corruption in the course of its translation to the stage of (post-)modern history?

Deneen adopts a version of this argument. The corruption, he maintains, inheres in the redefinition of the very idea of liberty that inaugurates modern political theory and practice. That is well and good as far as it goes, and—as we have seen—it goes quite far; but it does not solve the problem altogether. History bears witness to the truth that the radical autonomy of self that Deneen so reviles, and which constitutes the crux of the modern redefinition of liberty, carries within its husk the seed of a novel brand of liberation, the inspiring force of which had not manifested in like kind or degree in prior ages. Do not the clarion calls for liberty, equality, justice, and fraternity that kindled the revolutionary era and the birth of our nation still resonate in the hearts and minds of true Republicans and Democrats the world over? If freedom has ever and always been a chief concern of humankind, had its call ever sounded with quite the same resonance before? The political upheavals of the American and the French revolutions: was there scarce more kindling these revolutionary fires than the injustice of taxation without representation or demeaning shortages of bread? The causes of rebellion included material oppression, to be sure; but did not the sights of many who rebelled aim higher than redress of economic imbalance, or the exchange of an oppressor's abusive Will to Power for an oppressed people's own version of the same? Had no new star appeared in the firmament of the mind inspiring—not the cruder instincts of self-preservation and material fortune—but a more sublime octave of human hope and aspiration?

The young poet Wordsworth, landing (as fate would have it) in Calais on the first anniversary of the Fall of the Bastille in 1790, remembered the unforgettable tenor of the hour:

> 'Twas a time when Europe was rejoiced,
> France standing on the top of golden hours,
> And human nature seeming born again.[251]

Another passage in the poet's epic autobiography gives fuller account of how even the dull forms of political administration caught the brilliant light of Reason and millennial aspiration in his youthful mind:

> Bliss was it in that dawn to be alive,
> But to be young was very heaven: O times
> In which the meagre, stale, forbidding ways
> Of custom, law, and statute took at once
> The attraction of a Country in Romance;
> When Reason seemed the most to assert her rights
> When most intent on making of herself
> A prime Enchanter to assist the work
> Which then was going forwards in her name.
> Not favoured spots alone, but the whole earth
> The beauty wore of promise...[252]

Meanwhile, a decade and a half before, Tom Paine penned these famous words agitating for America's break from Britain:

> These are the times that try men's souls. The summer soldier and the sunshine patriot will, in this crisis, shrink from the service of their country; but he that stands by it now, deserves the love and thanks of man and

> woman. Tyranny, like hell, is not easily conquered; yet we have this consolation with us, that the harder the conflict, the more glorious the triumph. What we obtain too cheap, we esteem too lightly; it is dearness only that gives every thing its value. Heaven knows how to put a proper price upon its goods; and it would be strange indeed if so celestial an article as FREEDOM should not be highly rated.[253]

Despite the soaring rhetoric of these famous sentences, some might still wish to drag that celestial article down to earth. The casting off of the cloak of tyranny may well be bracing for the soul, but is the revolutionary sentiment, at root, not itself yet another form of self-interest, one as soon ready to lord it over others as the erstwhile oppressors?

The brutal aftermath of the French Revolution, and no few twists and turns of America's own revolutionary era politicking, may appear to confirm such cynical opinion; in the former case, spectacularly and horribly. Even so, violent perversion of the noblest ideas cannot entirely belie the purity of the original impulse, the novel species of hope for the whole of humankind that fueled the young Wordsworth's enthusiasms and Paine's resolute determination. We need reckon here, as well, Voltaire and other Enlightenment intellectuals' campaigns on behalf of undogmatic truth, tolerance and justice, crusades that frequently landed this or that *philosophe* in prison, or condemned him to exile, or even (as in the case of Condorcet) to martyrdom.

Is the radical autonomy displayed by such figures suggestive of self-interested forms of liberty? I do not think Patrick Deneen would allege so. Yet neither are the words and deeds of Enlightenment *philosophes,* American revolutionaries, or youthful British bards readily compatible with the conservative tenor of Deneen's championing of traditional forms of culture, custom, and authority.

It cannot, after all, be forgotten that tradition and custom, including that based in local community, does not in and of itself guarantee sound morality, spiritually sustaining forms of religious observance, or regular cultivation of the forms of self-governance. While such forms may indeed, at their best, be *necessary* conditions for the cultivation of the genuine liberty Deneen prizes, the forms in and of themselves are not *sufficient* to ensure these ends. Tradition and custom can be, and all too commonly have been, seedbeds of dogma, prejudice, and man's inhumanity to man as well as salutary molds of culture. It was against just such degraded kinds of culture, especially that perpetrated under the aegis of religion and in the name of God, that so many

Enlightenment era luminaries resisted and rebelled. As a rule, they did so, not out of professed self-interest, but in the name of what to them appeared a more just and inclusive idea of humanity. In so doing, it was these figures, more than Thomas Hobbes, who founded the liberal order, and did so in a manner worthy of the name.

To be sure, the likes of Voltaire, Paine, and Wordsworth were steeped in certain philosophical and literary traditions. We are hardly speaking here of culture destroyers or unmoored economic opportunists. It is also true that the youthfully radical Wordsworth fell back in bitter recoil from the failed French Revolution, and sought solace and restoration in precisely the kind of domestic, local, and inward-directed self-culture Deneen rightly treasures. Nonetheless, the paramount truth remains: one cannot well compass the revolutionary impetus of the Enlightenment era and its unprecedented championing of the universal ideals of liberty, equality, and fraternity within a conservative frame that bridles at the impulse to reject the old and create the world anew. Whatever the positive contribution of various streams of custom and tradition may have been to the temper of the times, an incisive refusal to obey socially prescribed norms and established authority stands out as its chief if not defining feature. Such transgression was, however, for the most part in the name of, not self-preservation or emancipation from all other-regarding attachments, but principles of a higher order, whether under the aegis of God, the Law of Nature, or the Party of Humanity.

Adorno and Horkheimer, writing in the dark shadow of Nazi Germany, present a very jaundiced view of the Enlightenment. They, like Deneen, acknowledge its watershed value, but do not expand at any length upon the benefits conferred. This is a dangerous tendency, because it all too readily leads to the neglect, decay, and even deliberate disregard of the values and ideals that founded liberal democracy. If we are to tell the true story of liberalism, we need clarify, too, the *salutary* essence at the core of that mind-set that helped inaugurate the present era of Western civilization and isolate that aspect of liberty unique to Enlightenment thought and the modern era. That aspect will not be reducible to the kind of radical autonomy previously elucidated; rather, it represents *a distinct and fundamentally different archetypal idea* that must be clearly distinguished from the inferior form, even if, from a certain low vantage, the two may look very much alike.

Just this project of critical discernment may well be the springboard of a novel adventure in epic theory, and Deneen (and herein lies the theoretical *efficiency* of his discourse) may perhaps indicate a point of departure for the same. Deneen clearly recognizes that the political ideology he identifies as liberal derives from certain philosophical or anthropological premises, which he delineates in connection with references to Descartes, Bacon, Hobbes, Locke and the ascendancy of natural science. I have also sketched these premises, and sought to set them within the framework of shifting understandings of the three terms that ground all worldviews: Divinity, Nature, and Humanity. If we are to discover the character of the new idea of liberty that entered the stream of history in the Enlightenment and Revolutionary era, we may well imagine that this would be premised on *an essentially different interpretation of this trio of terms than that operative in the philosophy and anthropology I have so far described*, because that lends itself all too readily to the "dialectic of enlightenment" and the authoritarian tendencies emerging, with "liberal" support, in Covid World today.

That critical project, however, can only be accomplished by reference to a more generous historical frame than that considered by either Deneen or Horkheimer and Adorno. These writers focus on a distinct, admittedly crucial strain of modern thought, but the radical originality and enduring value inherent in our modern liberal heritage can only be comprehended when viewed in the context of a broader understanding of modernity in general and the earth-shaking world-historical transformations that inaugurated it. The Renaissance, the Reformation, and the Scientific Revolution all undergird the Enlightenment and the revolutionary era. To grasp the impetus that birthed the modern world, it is necessary to gain some sense of the chief currents of thought that led humankind *out* of medievalism. Construing that transition—one that may be articulated, again, by reference to changing ideas of God, Nature, and Humanity itself—naturally requires a measure of understanding of the Middle Ages. Without some background as to the nature of the era preceding the modern, any attempt to comprehend the latter's essential nature tilts at windmills.

While I can hardly do justice to the complex and multifaceted character of thought in the Middle Ages, I will nonetheless endeavor to paint some of the defining features of the era. Even broad brushstrokes, however, do not license elision of the most significant differences internal to the medieval age. Explicit recognition of these will, moreover, ultimately aid in distinguishing salient features of the modern. Consequently, I present my summary version of currents of medieval thought in the form of three sequent phases (early, middle or high, and late). Throughout the exposition, the reader should bear in mind that I describe fluid and transmissible currents that (despite the heuristic division) do not admit of fixed boundary.

Throughout the Middle Ages, God stood as the supreme and sovereign term in all forms of thought so that conceptions of human and non-human nature derived from, and were defined in relation to, (the idea of) God. Neither man nor nature were regarded as significant or worthy of notice in and of themselves. To think about the nature of things (including man) in any fashion entirely separate from consideration of God would have been virtually inconceivable. The constitutive relation between both man and nature, on the one hand, and God, on the other, was, moreover, understood to be fundamentally conditioned by *the event of the Fall.* The consequences of that fateful occasion were more or less all-encompassing, determining, in their essential lineaments, the character of human nature; the tenor of human existence on earth and our (other)worldly destiny; and the prevailing view of the created world itself. As is commensurate with the air of tragic misfortune implicit in the very notion of the Fall, while all is perfectly good in the realm of God, early medieval thought did not cast either humanity or nature in a very favorable light.

The life and thought of one man shaped, more than any other, the temper of the medieval mind and, as well, the character of the Catholic Church, the institutional form that reflected and embodied that mind's character. By virtue of the power of his thought, will, and verbal acumen, Augustine of Hippo (354–430) transformed the drama of his own spiritual life into the mold of Christian religion after a fashion that set the tone of European culture for a thousand years. Augustine's struggle with his own passionate nature and climactic conversion formed the ground of the doctrine he eventually formulated and espoused. That doctrine revolved around the primal act of disobedience that marked man and woman with the stain of *original sin*—an indelible blemish that estranged humankind from the felicity of spiritual union with God, and which could only be expunged by virtue of the redemptive power of Jesus Christ. Medieval man or woman could not hope to earn salvation by virtue of their own merit or strength; the weight of sin was far too great and irremovable for such weak effort. It was only the sacramental ministry of the Catholic Church, founded upon the Rock of Peter and the lineage of apostolic succession, that could offer the medieval person true hope of salvation.[254]

For the bulk of the populace, living conditions in much of what Petrarch called "the dark ages"[255] were relatively poor and grim. Commensurately, and in accord with the Christian teaching, nothing in the world mattered so much (indeed, nothing really mattered at all) outside of attainment of that salvation that might release the human soul from the sinful affliction native to its existence in this world. Earthly life, after all, unfolds within the confines of a natural world that fell from grace along with Adam and Eve at the beginning of time. The worldly pleasures that remain available to us persistently tempt the soul to indulge, again and again, in the carnal nature and wayward desires responsible for original sin. Life in this world is therefore nought but a staging ground for life in the next. The faithful may look forward to eternal beatitude in the heavenly city of God above, but endless affliction in a darkened and hellish void await those who fail to resist the lure of vice and earthly pleasure, and eschew the saving power of the Son of God administered by the Church and its sacraments.

The chief concerns of the medieval man and woman may well appear profoundly foreign to the sensibility of most modern persons, including, perhaps, many who count themselves Christian. The human being's own capacities of thought and volition feature as the indisputable center of contemporary existence, yet count for *relatively* little within the frame of a mentality intensively focused upon the salvation of the soul and its reunion with God in another life. Historian Carl Becker writes of how the principal intellectual preoccupations of any given century may well be captured by a few key words. Becker cites "matter, fact, matter-of-fact, evolution and progress" as catch-words expressive of the soul of the 19th century, and "relativity, process, adjustment, function and complex" as those characteristic of the twentieth. "In the 13th century," writes Becker, "the key words would no doubt be God, sin, grace, salvation, heaven and the like."[256]

In this spirit, Richard Tarnas gives apt expression to the uniquely Augustinian flavor of the medieval view of nature and life in this world, accenting, too, the human being's rightful *disinterest* in it:

> Augustine gave up the field of this world, whose fallen tendency was naturally negative. In Augustine's vision, Christ had indeed already defeated Satan, but in the transcendent spiritual realm, the only realm that genuinely mattered. The true religious reality was not subject to the vagaries of this world and its history, and that reality could be known only through

> the individual's experience of God as mediated by the Church and its sacraments.[257]

More pointedly, Tarnas emphasizes how the Augustinian view of human nature not only characterizes the medieval temperament, but exerts an enduring influence on the Western psyche:

> The man who so decisively declared God's love and liberating presence in his own life also recognized, with a potency that never ceased to permeate the Western Christian tradition, the innate bondage and powerlessness of the human soul as perverted by Original Sin. From this antithesis arose the necessity for Augustine of a divinely provided means of grace in this world: an authoritative Church structure, within which haven man could satisfy his overriding needs for spiritual guidance, moral discipline, and sacramental grace.[258]

What I have so far articulated represents the chief tenor of what I class as the first phase of medieval thought. Its import, however, is by no means confined to a strictly delimited period of time, and remains deeply relevant to the latter phases as well. The cardinal fact of God's undisputed supremacy and the centrality of faith and quest for saving grace remain constants throughout the Middle Ages.

Even so, by the time Thomas Aquinas (1225–1274) lived and wrote his famous *Summa Theologica*, some of the harshest conditions of life in the dark ages had somewhat ameliorated, and fresh currents of thought were afoot, including new initiatives in the field of scholastic learning. Aquinas, in particular, built upon the enormous wealth of intellectual resource made available in the form of texts of Aristotle that had migrated from Islamic centers of learning into the European world. Marrying Aristotle's philosophical genius and scrupulous logical method to his devoutly Christian belief, St. Thomas methodically built one of the most imposing theological edifices ever constructed by a human mind; a fitting complement to the great medieval cathedrals likewise painstakingly built, stone upon stone, over the course of decades.

The very extent of St. Thomas's theological project—a work endeavoring systematically, in the spirit of Aristotle (often referred to as simply "the Philosopher"), to address many if not all of the most pressing questions pertaining to theology, ontology, cosmology, ethics, politics, aesthetics, and more—clearly indicated a somewhat altered estimation of the capacity of the human mind and the *rational faculty* that defines our uniquely human nature and licenses the pursuit of knowledge. Augustine, too, had been a deeply learned man, but his own turbulent personal struggles with his passionate nature had led to the strong accent placed on his doctrine of original sin[259] and, too, his paramount faith in the redemptive power of traditional ecclesiastical authority, doctrine, and prescribed sacramental ritual. Without formally contradicting Augustine, St. Thomas—less fixated upon stark dualisms of flesh and spirit—was more favorably disposed towards both nature and human reason. Indeed, Aquinas's reevaluation of both nature and reason (the latter inspired in part by the supreme dignity accorded contemplative thought by "the Philosopher") marked a historic pivot in the relations between God, Nature, and Humanity.

Aquinas's theology presents Christianity as an eminently rational religion, one grounded in reason as well as revelation. Not only did he seek rational proof for the existence of God, Aquinas lifted reason itself up to virtual parity with faith in revelation and observance of sacramental ritual as effective means of communion with, or participation in, the godhead. Correlatively, as he found in the nature of God's creation more evidence of rational design and less of evil aberration than did Augustine (who, while he could hymn the beauty of the cosmos as well as any, nonetheless more regularly fell back upon the urgent necessity of aversion to all natural appetites), *the idea of nature* acceded to a more honorable place in the frame of Aquinas's philosophy.

Historian Anthony Pagden parses the essential difference between Augustine and Aquinas as follows:

> For St. Augustine, by far the most powerful and most influential of Aquinas' predecessors, life on earth...had been a mere way station, a place of passage for the human soul on its journey to the afterlife. All that was redemptive in man—all that really mattered—came not from his or her own nature but from God's grace. For Aquinas, by contrast, the basic character of humanity was determined by nature. For Augustine, grace erased human nature. For Aquinas, it perfected it. And the phrase *Gratia naturam non tollit, sed perficit* ("Grace does not erase nature, but it perfects it") became, as Descartes' *ego cogito ergo sum* was to be for later generations, the summation of an entire system of thought.[260]

For Aquinas, nature stood for the God-given order of things as reflected in the underlying—and ultimately intelligible—lawful patterning of creation. Nature thus should not elicit aversion from the religious individual; on the contrary, its inherent order could act as an effective mediation between the human and divine intelligence. Coordinately, the faculty by which the human mind might perceive that natural order—*the light of reason*—functions as a means of the human being's own willed and active participation in the godhead.

It is this general conception that gave rise to Aquinas's own definition of *natural law*, a concept—not invented, but reformulated by Aquinas—that exercised tremendous influence on moral and political philosophy down through the centuries on into the Enlightenment and even the present day and its Covid World controversies. The concept finds indelible inscription, too, in the American Declaration of Independence, wherein Thomas Jefferson memorably alludes to "the laws of Nature and of Nature's God."

To understand Aquinas's formulation of natural law, it is helpful to know that Christian scholasticism formally recognized three hierarchically ordered classes of law. The first and highest consisted of *divine or eternal law*, connate with the divine mind or intelligence of God, and available to the human mind, if at all, through the medium of revelation. The lowest class consisted of *positive or human law.* These are conventional edicts issued in the name of the orderly regulation of society, and may be as trivial yet necessary as legislation governing which side of the road one drives on.[261] In between divine or eternal and positive stands *natural law.* Aquinas's own authoritative definition of *ius naturale*—a crucial passage which simultaneously describes that *rational* capacity that qualifies as the distinguishing characteristic of our human being—reads as follows:

> Since all things subject to Divine providence are ruled and measured by the eternal law...; it is evident that all things partake somewhat of the eternal law, in so far as, namely, from its being imprinted on them, they derive their respective inclinations to their proper acts and ends. Now among all others, the rational creature is subject to Divine providence in the most excellent way, in so far as it partakes of a share of providence, by being provident both for itself and for others. Wherefore it has a share of the Eternal Reason, whereby it has a natural inclination to its proper act and end: and this participation of the eternal law in the rational creature is called the natural law.[262]

Historian Anthony Pagden parses Aquinas's medieval complexities in these terms:

> It was Aquinas who provided the account of the natural law that was to become authoritative—doctrinal, indeed—until the 17th century. Law is one of the means (the other is Grace) by which God moves us to our ends or good. Animals also act toward their ends, but only by means of the

> instincts that God has implanted in them. At some level, humans also have a purely instinctual understanding of the natural law. (Their response to hunger, thirst, and the fear of death is not very different from that of other animals.) But they also "participate" in the Eternal Law through the rational comprehension of God's laws, and this is unique to them alone. This is what Aquinas understood by the natural law. It allows human beings to direct themselves, by their own understanding and volition, towards their ends.[263]

To this lucid exposition may be added that the vehicle of the human being's understanding, and so perception of natural law (which perception in turn guides willed action in pursuit of rightful ends), is *reason* ("the rational comprehension of God's laws"). Pagden continues to note that Aquinas's treatment of natural law does indeed make this law, and the rational faculty that perceives it, central to any consideration of the essential nature of *human being:*

> This [definition of natural law] raised the natural law from a basic instinct to the level of something that served as a bridge between the purely human and the divine. Natural Law was nothing less than "the impression of the Divine Light within us." By defining it in this way, Aquinas had made it the basis of all further discussion of what was to be "human."[264]

In reading this chapter, my modern reader may be wondering: *Why in the world, in this book about Covid, am I mucking about in abstruse medieval theology?* Such a sentiment is, of course, a reflection of the tenor of our times, when learning in general, and learning of European intellectual history in particular, is considered—at best—*passé,* and, in any event, hardly integral to due consideration of the pressing issues of the day. I beg to differ, and would opine that St. Thomas, for all his seemingly abstruse language, not only may help us understand the ideas instrumental to the founding of this nation and seminal to the very conception of the American republic, but, correlatively, may have more to say to us about *what it means to be a human being* than does Klaus Schwab. Moreover, willfully refusing to learn of and reflect upon contrasting systems of ideas consigns us, willy-nilly, to a course of intellectually impoverished default to the *illiberal* agenda of the technocratic powers-that-be as well as to our contemporary Covid World's crash course in—not history—but transhumanist futurity.

The third and last phase of medieval thought stands in a relation of dialectic negation to the preceding phase, even as the second phase did so to the first. If the Augustinian worldview posits a sharply dualistic distinction between a host of paired terms (God and human as well as non-human nature; heaven and earth; spirit and matter; revelation and reason) Thomas Aquinas worked—not, to be sure, to *dissolve*—but rather to *bridge* these differences. The doctrine of natural law presents it as a medium between eternal or divine and positive human law. Correlatively man's rational faculty (alternatively described as the light of God and of Nature within him) gives human reason, as exercised in and upon the things of this world, at least indirect access to divine intelligence.

The last, late phase of medieval philosophy carried the momentum of St. Thomas's scholastic momentum forward. The outcome, however, was not confirmation of the conciliatory synthesis of reason and revelation or the realms of God and nature Aquinas had striven so long and hard to achieve, but—by way of intensifying the very Aristotelian logical rigor Aquinas had employed, and combining it with new forms of empirical investigation—another fateful *falling* apart of the two halves of the universe. The signal development in this regard goes under the aegis of *nominalism,* and a British priest and philosopher born not long after Aquinas died figures as its leading proponent.

William of Ockham did not set out to challenge traditional ecclesiastical authority; on the contrary. Ockham, though, was anything but a sentimental or fuzzy-minded religionist. As indicated by the acuity memorialized in the phrase by which he remains known today ("Ockham's Razor"), Ockham expertly wielded a keen analytic intellect. Even so, his critical efforts were spurred on in part by the Church's condemnation of certain French scholastics who had taken the Aristotelian spirit of rational and empirical exploration in what the authorities thought was a questionable direction and were developing ideas of physics and cosmology (including a moving earth) that contradicted established dogma. Ockham employed his mind in a counterattack designed to preserve the unique sanctity and truth of traditional doctrine and scripture. Tarnas:

> In the wake of the Church's condemnation of the Parisian secularists, Ockham strove above all to limit the presumed competence of the natural human reason to grasp universal truths. Although his intentions were entirely to the contrary, Ockham proved to be the pivotal thinker in the late medieval movement toward the modern outlook.[265]

Tarnas continues to give a concise explication of the nominalist philosophy that ultimately proved so deeply influential:

> The central principle of Ockham's thought, and the most consequential, was his denial of the reality of universals outside of the human mind and human language. Driving Aristotle's stress on the ontological primacy of concrete particulars over Platonic Forms to its logical extreme, Ockham argued that nothing existed except individual beings, that only concrete experience could serve as a basis for knowledge, and that universals existed not as entities external to the mind but only as mental concepts. In the last analysis, what was real was the particular thing outside the mind, not the mind's concept of that thing. Since all knowledge had to be based on the real, and since all real existence was of individual beings, then knowledge must be of particulars. Human concepts possessed no metaphysical foundation beyond concrete particulars, and there existed no necessary correspondence between words and things.[266]

Intellectual history is an ever-evolving drama, one dynamic of thought always transforming another. At the same time, it consists of a core set of key ideas that remain constant throughout time. I remember when, as an undergraduate at Cornell University in the mid-1970s, I took a course in Intellectual History that had the Arts Quad buzzing. We were introduced, in that class, to the latest in French critical, structuralist, and post-structuralist theory: Jacques Derrida, of course—but also Ferdinand de Saussere. The nucleus of de Saussere's linguistic theory? The "arbitrariness of the signifier," or (as in Ockham's doctrine) the lack of any intrinsic relationship between words and the things that they signified.

The more things change, the more they stay the same, and Ockham's nominalism can well be regarded as the basis of the various forms of materialism—philosophical, scientific, sociopolitical—that remain dominant today. "False universals," after all, have been the *bettes noirs* of academic thinking in most departments now for half-a-century. Unfortunately, this leaves progressive liberals, our modern-day nominalists, in something of an intellectual pickle when it comes to grounding the ideals of equality, justice, and universal humanity they so passionately espouse. No matter: philosophical justification and consequential intellectual debate have long ceased to figure as modern liberalism's strong suit. For some time, such deliberative methods have been decisively trumped by other more easily learned forms of persuasion.

Premises basic to the modern materialistic vision of the universe find clear articulation in Ockham, even if outright materialism lay still in the distant future. More immediately historically consequential, perhaps, was the wedge driven, once more, between reason and revelation; between, on the one hand, knowledge pursued by way of logic and study of nature, and, on the other, faith in Holy Scripture as the principal (if not sole) record of God's infinite wisdom.

This fateful split persists today, in the crippling schism between what passes for science, on the one hand, and religion, on the other. When a popular science writer such as Stephen Jay Gould endorses the notion that science and religion occupy equally legitimate but *completely separate spheres of knowledge* (what Gould calls "Non-Overlapping *Magisteria*" in accordance with the doctrine of "NOMA" he expounds in his book *Rocks of Ages*[267]), he writes as an heir of Ockham's radical dualism.

For Ockham, though, there was little doubt as to which sphere, which *magisterium*, deserved preeminence: namely, the religious sphere accessible solely via revelation. The conclusion, however, evidently reached by those beholden to today's coterie of "health experts" clashes—and dramatically so—with William of Ockham's. Science, and the reason that provides knowledge of this material world, rules the roost. Religious revelation as recorded in scripture? That (as the likes of Richard Dawkins will tell you) is a figment of a diseased imagination.

Centuries lie between Ockham's time and ours; and the saga of God, Man, and Nature scripted by the human mind includes many crucial chapters between then and now, chapters narrating critical developments preparing the advent of the modern mind and the Enlightenment ethos. We have already discussed, in some detail, the seminal views of the 17th-century philosophers Bacon, Descartes, and Hobbes. Before, however, returning to these figures, and revisiting the philosophical principles underlying both the scientific and the liberal worldview that figure so centrally in our Covid controversy, we need explore the intervening period and gain some sense of how the human mind changed over the course of the 15th, 16th and 17th centuries. We need explore, that is, how the Renaissance and the Reformation, ringing dramatic changes on reigning concepts of God, man, and nature, played their colorful and crucial parts in leaving the Middle Ages behind, and ushering in the modern world.

In 1341, even as William of Ockham's philosophical nominalism was taking Oxford and Paris by storm, Francesco Petrarcha was crowned poet laureate at the Capitoline in Rome. As indicated by the ceremony staged in the heart of Western Christendom, Petrarch was an observant Christian, yet one who owes his renown not (like Aquinas) to any theological innovation, but rather to the seminal role he played in the revival of interest in classical learning, the great heritage bequeathed by Greek and Roman philosophers, poets, dramatists, orators, and statesmen.

We have already seen how it was rediscovery of the texts of Aristotle that enabled Aquinas's magisterial reformulation of Christian theology, but the poet's reception of the classical heritage took a dramatically different turn than did the saint's. Whereas Aquinas Christianized Aristotle's philosophy—and did so religiously—Petrarch, following the footsteps of revered ancient writers, exhibited a burning interest in the life of letters for its own sake. That interest coincided with a new appreciation of the full range of human intellectual and imaginative capacities as such find expression in a wide variety of genres of speech and of writing.

Reverence for the classical tradition—not in place of, but alongside, and on equal footing with the Judeo-Christian—inevitably implied a dramatic shift in the center of intellectual and spiritual attention. The biblical heritage that nourished Augustine and Aquinas revolves around a specific historical plot: a narrative that hinges upon the relation of humankind (as initially represented by the Hebrew people) to one God; to the terms of the keeping (or betrayal) of the covenant; and to the drama of sin and redemption through Christ inscribed in the plot of personal as well as collective human history.

Classical writings represent an altogether different story. They do not revolve around the figure of Yahweh, or God the Father. If they happen to address the destiny of the soul, they do so (as in Plato's famous parable of the cave) in very different terms than those set out in scripture. Many of the classic texts featured different forms of divinity (the gods of the Greek and Roman pantheon), and their principal interest typically lay as much in human beings' relationships to one another and in all the multifaceted aspects of life in this world, as it did in relation to the (equally multifarious) forms of the divine.

The ancient tradition resuscitated and celebrated by Petrarch was thus not a revealed religion dedicated to the Word of the One God, but rather an essentially *humanist* one, focused as much upon man as upon divinity, and entertaining distinct (if not necessarily wholly incommensurate) forms of relation between man, nature, and divinity than the Judeo-Christian.

Petrarch's most original and enduring contribution to this tradition of *classical humanism* consists of his famous *Canzoniere,* the 366 poems (most of them in the peculiar form of the sonnet Petrarch himself invented) immortalizing the poet's love for Laura: a work that set the standard for lyrical love poetry for centuries.

Canzoniere XXXV

Alone and thoughtful, through deserted field
I go with lowered head and measured pace,
my eyes intent that I might flee in haste
should any human footprint be revealed.
I find no other shelter to conceal
my burning heart than some secluded place,
for once among the crowd my wretched face
betrays the very flames it hoped to shield;
so that by now I think the hills and stones,
the rivers and the forests are aware
of the life I lead, to others dim;
and yet I find no path so overgrown
that Love does not come with me everywhere,
speaking with me the while, and I with him.[268]

In spearheading the revival of the classical humanist tradition, Petrarch proved an augury of things to come; the first precocious representative of a brilliant new age, one that would not truly begin to flower until a century or so after his crowning in Rome. Tarnas puts the matter thus:

> What was new in the late Middle Ages was not any lack of spirituality in Petrarch but rather the overall character of his approach to human life. The demands of his religious temperament were in continuous creative battle with his desire for romantic and sensuous love, for secular activity in diplomatic and courtly circles, for literary greatness and personal glory. It was this new self-reflective awareness of human life's richness and multidimensionality, and his recognition of a kindred spirit in the great writers of antiquity, that made Petrarch the first man of the Renaissance.[269]

Petrarch's access to the ancient texts he admired was, though, far more limited than he would have liked. While the writings of Aristotle had made their way into Europe via Arabic centers of learning, the same could not be said of the vast majority of the works of Aristotle's revered teacher, Plato. That changed, however, in the 15th century. Responding, in part, to Petrarch's contagious enthusiasms, scholars sought—and found—many ancient (especially ancient Greek) texts, the influx of which invigorated a modern wave of humanist learning and creative genius.

Under the benevolent and learned patronage of the Medici (first, Cosimo, and later, Lorenzo the Magnificent) in Florence, Marsilio Ficino assumed leadership of the Platonic Academy in 1462. Ficino completed the first Latin translation of Plato's dialogues in 1470, and his related commentary *(Theologica Platonica)* in 1482. The infusion of Platonic and Neoplatonic genius, as well as that of other esoteric ancient texts, into the intellectual bloodstream of the West inspired a profound transformation of philosophic, aesthetic, and religious sensibilities, one that took Petrarch's inspiring vision of the possibilities of the human mind and imagination to newly exalted heights. No single work exemplifies this expansion of human prospect more consummately than *Oration on the Dignity of Man,* a text composed in 1486 by Pico della Mirandola as an introduction to the 900 theses the young Italian scholar hoped to defend, in public dialogue, in Rome that same year.

Pico's thinking was syncretist in character. He absorbed the canonical biblical account of the creation of man, but—eschewing literalism—combined this with wisdom gleaned from other spiritual traditions and his own inspired imagination to conjure a complex yet supremely exalted image of the nature of man. According to Pico's version of creation, after fashioning the cosmos, God engendered, too, its creatures, fixing each of their respective natures within the bounds appropriate to the kind. In the unique case of man, however, God declined to set prescribed limits; to humankind alone was granted the sublime gift of freedom of self-determination. The human being might sink in stature to the level of the lowest natures; yet she also possessed the capacity to ascend to higher forms of consciousness and indeed, if she so willed, might even attain to the rarefied region of divinity itself:

> Neither an established place, nor a form belonging to you alone, nor any special function have We given to you, O Adam, and for this reason, that you have and possess, according to your desire and judgment, whatever place, whatever form, and whatever functions you shall desire. The nature of other creatures, which has been determined, is confined within the bounds prescribed by Us. You, who are confined by no limits, shall determine for yourself your own nature, in accordance with your own free will, in whose hand I have placed you. I have set you at the center of the world, so that from there you may more easily survey whatever is in the world. We have made you neither heavenly nor earthly, neither mortal nor immortal, so that, more freely and more honorably the molder and maker of yourself, you may fashion yourself in whatever form you shall prefer. You shall be able to descend among the lower forms of being, which are brute beasts; you shall be able to be reborn out of the judgment of your own soul into the higher beings, which are divine.[270]

What a difference from the Augustinian universe of being! For him, man's nature bore the indelible stamp of original sin, of the primal transgression that circumscribed his nature on all sides. This condemned him to live his life in this world as if in exile from his true and only home; to dwell and languish in the dark half of a universe cut in two. Man's whole concern orbits around God and the (infinite, albeit uncertain) grace that might release him from his earthly travail. Not so for Pico, who avails himself of God's own authority in setting the human being herself at the center of the world, and ascribes to man's own nature the capacity to traverse the space between heaven and earth, the mortal and the immortal realms, and even (like Christ himself) divine and human being. In the beginning, therefore, man and woman are tinged with more than a blush of divinity. Nor does any infamous Fall deprive them of the divine right they may reclaim, not only or primarily by way of grace, but by exercise of their own free will in fulfillment of the higher octave of their nature.

Pico della Mirandola writes as a humanist, centuries before the advent of any transhumanist ideas. For him, man's rightful striving aims toward lofty spiritual ideals, and need be guided by the morality inherent in "the judgment of...[the] soul." Even so, if writers such as Kingsnorth and Deneen criticize contemporary liberalism on accounts of its refusal to place *any* limit on human prerogative, the seed of that boundless aspiration (an ambition unthinkable within the context of a medieval frame of mind) may be found in Pico's *Oration*, the unofficial manifesto of Renaissance man.

If man thus acceded to a new and unparalleled importance in Pico's exemplary Renaissance vision, nature, too, basks in the glow of a new dawn. The Platonic and Neoplatonic tradition that played so prominent a part in Renaissance humanism retained, to be sure, a degree of other-worldly idealism. Even so, the Neoplatonic teaching that envisions nature, in the guise of the World Soul, as an emanation of the One or One Mind (*Nous*) that governs all, ascribes to nature its own nobility and grandeur, its own form, one could surely say, of divinity. We have already seen how the sublime Pythagorean order of the cosmos figured into Kepler's astronomical contemplations. The harmonious beauty of the universe—especially that of the heavens—remained a potent force in the thinking of countless intellectual luminaries, not excluding Sir Isaac Newton himself, so chronically and poorly misunderstood only as the chief architect of a mechanical philosophy.

The Renaissance may thus be seen as representing a kind of reversal in the reigning order of things. Whereas in the Middle Ages the very idea of man and of nature were prescribed by a prior idea of God, who in turn qualified as the undisputed sovereign and source of all, now man and nature, while not usurping the sovereignty of the divine, nonetheless are placed (as in Pico's legendary account) at the center. Ideas of God emerge in relation to *relatively* autonomous ideas of man and nature as much as the other way around. In effecting this epochal transformation, the Renaissance—that revival of the tradition of ancient classical learning that birthed what we know as philosophy, art, and science—may rightfully be regarded as the morning of modernity.

> With the Renaissance, human life in this world seemed to hold an immediate inherent value, an excitement and existential significance, that balanced or even displaced the medieval focus on an afterworldly spiritual destiny. Man no longer appeared so inconsequential relative to God, the Church, or nature. On many fronts, in diverse realms of human activity, Pico's proclamation of man's dignity seemed fulfilled. From its beginnings with Petrarch, Boccaccio, Brunni, and Alberti, through Erasmus, More, Machiavelli, and Montaigne, to its final expressions in Shakespeare, Cervantes, Bacon, and Galileo, the Renaissance did not cease producing new paragons of human achievement. Such a prodigious development of human consciousness and culture had not been seen since the ancient Greek miracle at the very birth of Western civilization. Western man was indeed reborn.[271]

So the *mold* (Pico) of modern man was made, the die of the future cast—by his own hand. Even so, many momentous events needed to unfold over the course of the next several centuries before Renaissance man's Promethean impulse—leavened by enlightened liberal ideals—exploded in the form of political as well as intellectual revolution, birthing a nation named (by the Renaissance explorer who "discovered" its land mass in 1492[272]) "America."

Chapter 7

THE ROOTS OF MODERN LIBERALISM II: HERE I STAND

I am not alone in attempting to comprehend the significance of Covid-19 by reference to seemingly distant historical phenomena. As we have seen, Schwab and Malleret pursue a similar tack in *Covid-19: The Great Reset.* Addressing the pivotal role of pandemics in instigating historic change, Schwab and Malleret cite the plague that ravaged Europe in the second half of the 14th century, invoking no less an authority than medieval historian Barbara Tuchman, who declares: "The Black Death may have been the unrecognized beginning of modern man."[273]

Insofar as Schwab and Malleret suggest that Covid-19 may mark a like watershed, these authors, no less than myself, endeavor to connect the significance of the present moment to the onset of the Renaissance and dawn of modernity. Like Schwab and Malleret, I too believe Covid World can and should provoke far-reaching, indeed revolutionary change in human society and culture. The similarity between our parties ends there, however, for while Schwab and Malleret embrace a technocratic transhumanist vision that would leave all traces of classical humanism behind, I would endorse a very different model of rebirth, one that indeed harkens back to the intellectual and artistic brilliance of the European Renaissance. While the Black Death wrought havoc on the continent, it is to the likes of Petrarch, Ficino, Pico, Leonardo, Michelangelo, and Shakespeare *et al* that we should look for the wellsprings of modernity more than the manifold perturbations—as dramatic as these may have been—precipitated by a cursed plague.

In view of the nightmarish temper of our time, it may be well to remember, too, that the luminous genius of the Renaissance shone against a dark and disastrous background. Not only did the Black Death devastate Europe, but all kinds of other horrible mischief was afoot at the dawn of modernity. Tarnas cites a litany of terrors that tarnished the times: the ravages of the Hundred Years' War between England and France; religious conflict that spilled over national boundaries to infect and afflict much of Christendom; crushing economic depression oppressing virtually the whole population for decades; the Inquisition and rampant ecclesiastical corruption; the ever-present threat of invasion by Turkish infidels, and more.

If the violence that backgrounded the Renaissance genius was very real, so was the quotient of cultural and spiritual unity that enabled, materially as well as spiritually, its great achievements. Much of the most magnificent Renaissance art was commissioned and funded by the Church, which, during this period, acted (in its creative rather than corrupt aspect) as a truly catholic institution that included within its capacious embrace many of the pagan and esoteric currents evident in Renaissance art and philosophy. If St. Thomas Aquinas had attained a vision that brought God, Man (in his rational part), and a Nature completed by grace together in a kind of cooperative communion, the Renaissance—pushing aside, for now, the sterile formalities of nominalism—did so as well. It did so, however, in a distinct guise; one that put not God, but Promethean man at the center of a world reillumined and reborn.

In the glories of the great Renaissance masterpieces of art, architecture, and philosophy, divinity, humanity, and nature coexist in a state of imaginative exaltation. That elevated niveau of culture could hardly endure indefinitely, especially since—even as Michelangelo was painting the divine spark passing between God and man on the Sistine Chapel ceiling—the institutional ground beneath his feet was shifting. The cracks in the foundation of the Church—still now, and for the last time, the organizing structure and indispensable scaffold of Western culture—were widening ominously. The spreading fissures would soon issue in a quake that would shake the church to its core, and bring to an end its thousand-year-long reign as the premier arbiter of Truth and Goodness in the province of the Western mind.

A span of five short years near the beginning of the 16th century provides a window on the past, present, and future hue of human culture; one that contains, as if in stained glass, images representative of the seminal initiatives characterizing the 15th through 17th centuries: the Renaissance, Protestant Reformation, and Scientific Revolution. Singularly as well as collectively (these movements are not discrete but overlap), these initiatives transformed the concepts of divinity, humanity, and nature that build the world in which humankind dwells.

The relevant events are these:

In 1512, Michelangelo finished painting the Sistine Chapel ceiling, completing this iconic representation of the Renaissance spirit.

Between 1512 and 1514, Copernicus works on his *Commentariolus*, the first sketch of the heliocentric theory central to the forthcoming Scientific Revolution.

In 1513, Machiavelli's *The Prince* appears, another work of Renaissance genius that reveals something of its darker side and looks forward to the political-philosophical deliberations pursued by Hobbes, Locke, and later Enlightenment thinkers.

In 1517, Martin Luther nails his ninety-five theses to the door of the church in Wittenburg, triggering the Protestant Reformation that would convulse Europe and alter its cultural landscape forever.

As we have already paid some heed to the Renaissance, let us turn to this last-named occasion first: Luther and the Reformation.

The pivot from the medieval to the modern era cannot be identified with any single individual. Even so, none—not Copernicus, not Descartes, not Newton—plays a more prominent role therein than Martin Luther. In itself, this is paradoxical, for in many key respects Luther represents a throwback to not only the early, Augustinian phase of medievalism, but also the juridical morality associated with the ancient Judaic taproot of Christian culture.

The ramifications of the Reformation are multiple and themselves steeped in paradox. Before endeavoring to sketch the outline of some of its most prominent effects, it is necessary to grasp the gist of Luther's religious inspiration. The reference to Augustine is hardly incidental in this connection. Not only did Luther first take orders in the Augustinian Monastery in Erfurt, his belief and teaching, like Augustine's, revolved around his inner spiritual travail and revelatory discovery of the power of faith.

As a young monk of singularly melancholy temperament, Luther felt oppressed by the wages of sin and his own helpless inability to lift a burden that threatened eternal damnation. His mental affliction was so severe as to endanger his very life. At a crucial moment, however, Luther's consciousness flooded with the cathartic realization that, if it was indeed not within his power—by means of reason, good works, or any other form of human competence—to redeem himself, *the free bestowal of such saving grace was precisely the essence and power of God.* Correlatively, unwavering belief in the power of grace constituted the unshakable ground of true faith and the core of authentic religious sensibility. In his lecture on Luther, Emerson writes:

> A venerable monk of his order succeeded in impressing him with the conviction that "*justification was of grace by faith*" This doctrine, which was

to him not a theological formula but an expression for all his belief in God's Government, proved the seed of the Reformation.[274]

Circumstances conspired to grow that seed. The Catholic Church, accustomed to immense power, had long suffered from widespread internal corruption. The popular practice of granting indulgences, which allowed persons to purchase readier access to heaven[275] by monetary contribution, represented one conspicuously visible sign of spiritual decay. In Luther's eyes, it made a mockery of faith, and his public opposition to it led by way of a series of altercations to Luther nailing his *Ninety-five Propositions against Indulgences* to the door of the Church of Wittenberg.

Thus the Protestant Reformation—ignited by Luther's righteous faith, sustained by his indomitable will, and facilitated by the north German states' geopolitical distance from Rome—launched on the last day of October 1517.

Luther's repudiation of indulgences soon grew into a rejection of the institution of the Roman Catholic Church as a whole. The complex theological doctrine built up over centuries; the hierarchal power structure crowned by the absolute authority of the pope; the practice of sacramental ritual centered upon (though not limited to[276]) the celebration of mass; the reverence accorded iconic images: all this and more Luther cast aside as corrosive of the true faith that concentrated directly and exclusively upon the power and mercy of God as revealed in scripture and realized in the heart and mind of the adherent of Christian liberty.

Luther (or rather, the many who took up the master's teaching and applied its force to ecclesiastic institution) accordingly built his own church upon the rock of personal faith and its indispensable origin and anchor: the revealed Word of God, recorded, indelibly and unchangeably, in holy writ. The Protestant doctrine of *sola scriptura* ("by scripture alone") views the Bible as the only infallible source of religious truth, making all other forms of authority subject to review in light of the timeless wisdom therein revealed.

One might imagine such premises might give rise to a simple form of faith, but Luther's seemingly straightforward teaching contains hidden complexities.

Within the domain of strict religious observance alone, Protestantism consists of two, potentially divergent impulses. On the one hand, the priority accorded individual faith and one's personal relationship to God emancipates Luther's followers from the shackles of traditional authority, setting him or her on a path of spiritual autonomy, empowerment and freedom. On the other, the belief that the Bible alone tells the whole (and nothing but) the truth can—if not tempered by other broadening influences—narrow the purview of the mind and incline the faithful Protestant toward literalism and dogmatic species of fundamentalism. The legacy of the Reformation and its role in the formation of the modern mind involves a complex interplay of these two contrary impulses and their multiple effects.

In fact, when inquiring into the subject of Luther and his orb of influence, one finds oneself confronting paradox again and again. Perhaps the most consequential of all such contradictions centers upon the status of religion itself in human life and culture. It would be difficult to imagine a man more committed to his faith, or deferential to his God, than Martin Luther. The irony here lies in the manner in which the very intensity of Luther's religious conviction culminated in a spiritual revolt that fractured the unity of the Church and, in so doing, contributed decisive momentum to the *secularization* of society that plays so central a role in the development of modern consciousness.

I spoke previously of how the vast umbrella of the Church, for centuries the dominant spiritual and even political force in the West, provided the relatively stable cultural framework that facilitated creative accomplishments in the arts and sciences. The Protestant Reformation, however, spreading from its humble origins in northern Germany with alarming alacrity, stirred disruptive controversy and decades if not centuries of often violent strife. In particular, the Thirty Years' War (1618–1648) plunged Europe into bloody conflict driven by religious differences. In its aftermath, the Church no longer stood as a unified institution widely recognized as the sovereign authority on any and all questions of spiritual concern. For better or worse, Europe lost a kind of spiritual cohesion that it would never again achieve.

This simple fact bore tremendous, and tremendously varied, repercussions. On the one hand, Luther's empowerment of individual judgment and prerogative dealt a severe blow to traditional authority in general, *all* species of which his actions exposed as potentially arbitrary. Called before the Diet at Worms and commanded to recant his theses, Luther declared:

> Unless I am convinced by Scripture and plain reason—I do not accept the authority of popes and councils, for they have contradicted each other—my conscience is captive to the Word of God. I cannot and I will not recant anything, for to go against conscience is neither right nor safe. God help me. Amen.[277]

While the record does not seem to be clear on the matter, tradition has it that before "*Gott helfe mir*" ("God help me"), Luther added the famous words, "*Hier stehe ich. I kann nicht anders.*" "Here I stand. I cannot do otherwise."

Once Luther, at risk of his life, thus stood on his own cognizance (and that of his God) alone against the massive edifice of the Church, no temporal authority—be it Church, King, State, National or International Assembly—could ever again be surely regarded as sacrosanct and invulnerable to criticism levied by the conscientious individual in the name of higher law.

Even while thus empowering the *individual's* own religious convictions, Luther nonetheless splintered and brought low the power of the Church establishment. Fractious theological dispute ultimately precipitated the Thirty Years War and innumerable subsequent (if lesser) conflicts, the force of which shattered the foundations of Church authority and occasioned a general decline in the prestige of religious institutions in human life and culture.

The peculiar nature of Luther's religious beliefs, even while reinvigorating religious sensibilities across much of Europe, contributed—and dramatically so—to that decline. In another of the paradoxes seemingly endemic to Protestantism, Luther's valorization of faith in God's grace as the preeminent principle of the religious life—a privileging that contained a sometimes implicit, sometimes explicit repudiation of Renaissance-inspired Christian humanism such as that of his illustrious contemporary Erasmus—ultimately resulted in a severe constriction of God's domain of direct influence. The range of concerns subject to theological deliberation shrank, resulting in a greater, rather than lesser, degree of human autonomy.

The key issue in this connection involves man's relation to God, on the one hand, and nature on the other, and the human faculties proper to each according to Protestant precept.

The doctrine of *sola scriptura* can, after all, quite clearly lead to a religious *disinterest* in nature. If all that really matters is the individual's personal faith in God's grace as such can be learned—and *only* be learned—from scripture read in the light of faith, why pay nature or the world much real heed at all?[278]

The starkly dualistic Augustinian background of Luther's Protestantism emerges strongly here. Correlatively, for Luther (and contrary to the teachings of both Aquinas and the Renaissance humanists), human reason, imagination, and work in no wise suffice to bridge the gulf between spirit and matter, and so suffer a corresponding devaluation. The fundamental split between God and nature inevitably brings related schisms in train: reason no longer (as in Aquinas) holds with faith; nor can any science of this world inform a religion so exclusively devoted to God in heaven (even if He does speak to the human conscience), *or vice versa.*

Although this whole set of dualities—God/nature, faith/reason, religion/science— did not become cemented into fixed contraries until much later, Luther's refurbished Augustinianism clearly lays the groundwork for the radical dualism etched so sharply in the contemporary mind. The schism naturally rears its head in the Covid wars today. Many who oppose Covid dictates do so (as Luther did in Worms) in the name of God, faith, freedom, and conscience. Not that Covid dissidents all eschew science or the force of reason and of evidence; on the contrary. Even so, invocations of deity and the rights afforded by God are prevalent in the discourse of dissent, while defense of the mainstream position, staked out on the turf of science and reason, seldom entails appeal to natural rights or higher powers.[279]

The rifts that divide us still were thus drawn five hundred years ago. May it not be time to reexamine these habitual demarcations and query the underlying philosophical justification for these lines drawn in sand?

Pursuing such an inquiry requires additional historical reflection, which may be furthered by posing this pressing question: how is that Luther—no Pico intent upon celebration of the dignity of man, but a 16th-century Old Testament-style prophet who would have man bend low in abject humility before God—unwittingly contributed to the privilege accorded, *not* to the *first,* but to the *second* of each of the above mentioned pairs; that is, to the superiority of man, reason and science as opposed to God, faith, and religion?

On a sociopolitical level, the ravages effected by the seemingly unending wars of religion did inestimable damage to the prestige of religious authority. On a more purely intellectual level, however, the tenets of nominalism, which formed an important part of Luther's own training, come prominently into play.

Nominalism, as we have seen, pushed back against certain Thomist initiatives, reasserting Augustinian-style dualisms of God and nature, *but with a difference.* Augustine's strongly other-worldly dualism harkened back to forms of Platonic idealism, but the nominalists were heirs of Aristotle's rigorous formal logic. While indeed denying that reason could supply insight into God and so be pertinent to the kind of theological questions that mattered most, the followers of keen-minded Ockham willingly saw reason as the chief if not sovereign tool in the careful analysis of natural and material phenomena, knowledge of which retained, after all, its own distinct (if, in their minds, inestimably inferior) value and utility.

Having gone thus far, it is not difficult to discern the long-term consequences of the dynamics I am sketching. Luther's doctrine of *sola scriptura* and justification by faith ultimately denied both human reason and observant engagement with nature—the world around us—any meaningful role in the exploration of man's relation to God and so to all pressing theological questions. Predictably, this split ultimately acted not so much to preserve or increase the glory of God but rather worked to His decided detriment.

The split was by no means absolute, nor did Protestantism incline all who followed Luther to look away from nature. The study of nature found its way back to God in influential streams such as Böhmist theosophy and the natural theology so important—in Protestant circles as much or more than Catholic ones—well into the 19th century. Even so, the underlying dualism prompted by nominalism did drive a wedge between science and religion, and the force of the impact worked, over time, to the decided favor of the former.

Humanity's quest for knowledge— for adequate understanding of itself and its world—remains irrepressible; and in times when material deprivation does not unduly restrict range of mind, man's own powers of cognition and active volition will not, finally, suffer diminution. If they cannot be duly exercised in direct relation to God, humankind is liable to forsake religious contemplation for occupations more suited to fit the exercise of human agency: science, art, commerce, technology. The splitting of God, faith, grace and scripture from the world of man in nature, combined with the proto-scientific methodology of nominalism, freed the human being to live, think, and act in nature in accordance with the laws and functions proper to this realm, relatively *unconcerned* with religious matters. These were increasingly regarded as proper to another, separate sphere.

So was the stage set for what we today call science to largely eclipse religion as the chief arbiter of truth in the world. The story, as I tell it, suggests that religion itself played a major role in this transfer of power, more or less voluntarily handing over the reins of reason to what would ultimately emerge as a kind of adversarial power.

Historically speaking, natural philosophy had largely figured as a form of study consistent with and supportive of theology. The Ptolemaic universe, for instance, had been understood to be congruent with the cosmology inscribed in the Bible. For early modern man, however, this was about to change—and with momentous consequences.

Neither the Copernican nor the broader Scientific Revolution happened overnight. Copernicus first sketched his ideas of a heliocentric universe in 1514, but the Polish astronomer, while sharing his speculations with a small circle of associates, did not relish public exposure. *De Revolutionibus,*[280] the first Copernican essay of heliocentrism to be published, did not appear until 1543, the year of the astronomer's death. Nor did Copernicus's ideas, when first introduced, elicit an antagonistic response from the Church. Copernicus was an observant Catholic and trusted consultant to the Church in Rome. The pope himself heard and approved a lecture by Copernicus almost a decade before *De Revolutionibus*—a work dedicated to the pope—appeared in print.

The initially welcoming posture of the Church may be regarded as consonant with the capacious intellectuality (one peculiarly open, as we have seen, to Hellenistic currents) characteristic of the Renaissance-inspired Christian-humanist brand of Catholicism traceable back to Petrarch and the doctrine of "learned piety" *(docta pietas).* Yet as the Protestant Reformation caught fire in Europe, the climate of official Christian opinion towards the new scientific developments underwent a decided sea-change. The Copernican theory appeared to conflict with a number of biblical passages that had long been understood to affirm a geocentric cosmology, a universe that revolves around the center of an immovably fixed earth. Given Luther's uncompromising dedication to the doctrine of *sola scriptura*, Copernicanism could not but incite concerted resistance from leading Protestants reformers.

Tarnas provides a sense of the color of the conflict, one that catalyzed the radical divergence of scientific and religious authority familiar to this day:

> To have biblical revelation questioned by human science was just the kind of Hellenizing intellectual arrogance and interpretive sophistry the reformers most abhorred in Catholic culture. Protestants were therefore quick to recognize the threat of Copernican astronomy and condemn the impiety.... Luther called Copernicus an "upstart astrologer" who foolishly wished to reverse the entire science of astronomy while flagrantly contradicting the Holy Bible. Luther was soon joined by other reformers like Melanchthon and Calvin, some of whom recommended

> that stringent measures be taken to suppress the pernicious heresy. Quoting a passage from the Psalms, "the world also is established, that it cannot be moved," Calvin asked: "Who will dare to place the authority of Copernicus above that of the Holy Spirit?"[281]

The conflict, though, did not come to a real head until a century or more after Copernicus first entertained serious consideration of the heliocentric theory.

By the turn of the 17th century, much had changed in ecclesiastical as well as scientific circles. Mortally threatened by the startling success of the Protestant revolt, the Catholic Church responded, not by upholding the more truly catholic attitude or liberal forms of Christian humanism characteristic of its Renaissance-style profile, but by attempting to outdo Protestantism on the ground of its own unswerving devotion to Christian fundamentals. In contrast to the Protestantism doctrine of *sola scriptura*, the Catholic Church understood these to include, not only holy scripture, but the traditional Church apparatus meant to interpret and apply it: formal Church doctrine, the hierarchal organization culminating in the office of the pope, and sacramental ritual practice.

The stance thus taken by the Roman Catholic Church was not one naturally congruent with any unorthodox or more eclectic outlook. Accordingly, the Counter-Reformation, initiated as an antidote to Protestantism in the mid-16th century, proved a largely reactionary force; one especially prone to the kind of violent persecution notoriously represented by the offices of the Inquisition. Consequently, the manner in which Protestant theology, despite—or precisely because of—its peculiarly faith-based theocentric perspective, could work to narrow the range of concerns constructively engaged by religious considerations was by no means limited to Protestant circles. Under the auspices of the Counter-Reformation, that restriction spread to the Christian West as a whole.

Meanwhile, Copernicus's ideas slowly gained traction, especially amongst unorthodox thinkers still under the influence of Renaissance-inspired Neoplatonic and esoteric currents of thought. The first tragic consequence of the impending clash of worldviews revolved around Giordano Bruno, an Italian friar and polymath known for his unorthodox and (by the standards of the Church) highly questionable beliefs. In the wake of intellectual and political tensions that evolved over the course of many years, Bruno found himself, by order of the Inquisition, extradited to and imprisoned in Rome in 1593.

There he was tried for a host of allegedly heretical positions—including his Copernican cosmology.

Bruno defended himself ably at his trial, which lasted seven years. Hardly jealous of martyrdom, Bruno made any number of concessions to the authority of the Church. Like Luther before him, however, Bruno would not repudiate his core beliefs, or tender the full recantation demanded by the Church. Once the tribunal found him guilty, Bruno was given a further eight days to contemplate what lay in store for him. Scorning accommodation, Bruno remained stubborn in his refusal to recant, and finally was hung naked upside down and burned at the stake in a Roman public square on February 17, 1600.

An inauspicious beginning, to be sure, to the new century that would—fittingly enough—see the rising star of the science eclipse the waning influence of an increasingly divided, dogmatic, irrational, and intolerant Church. In the aftermath of Bruno's execution and all that followed in its wake, religion in the West would never again enjoy the same kind of intellectual, moral and spiritual authority it had long possessed.

Given the range of accusations against Bruno, it may not be accurate to represent his lengthy trial as a pitched battle between scientific reason and religious tradition. That said, it is nonetheless surely justified to cast the equally, if not still more famous, trial of Galileo in just that light. In 1633, a third of a century after Bruno burned at the stake, Galileo Galilei appeared before the same Inquisitorial Office to answer to the charge of subscribing to heretical (a.k.a. heliocentric) cosmological views in blatant contradiction of Holy Scripture. Less heroically minded than Luther, or Bruno, Galileo officially denied his adherence to ideas which he had clearly championed, thus escaping possible corporal punishment or death. Found guilty, even so, of a suspicious harboring of heresy, Galileo was ordered to issue formal recantations and placed under house arrest, under which restriction he lived and worked for the duration of his life.

In retrospect, it is clear that in judging Galileo the Church condemned itself to a crippling species of intellectual irrelevance, and did so in a manner it has never been able to rectify. For what the Church did on this occasion amounted to forfeiture of the recognized authority of organized religion meaningfully to inform the human mind in its effort to understand the nature of the universe, and to employ the faculties of reason, imagination and sense in progressive and undogmatic revision of ideas pertaining to the Creation. The abdication of intellectual responsibility exercised in this case thus prepared the ground for a world in which religion can presume to speak authoritatively about God and, too, the human being's *subjective* relation to divinity, but has very little significant say as to what the human being makes of nature and, indeed, the whole riddling phenomena of the world in which she moves and lives. In the long wake of the epochal trial of Galileo, religion thus becomes *primarily* a matter of faith, anchored in the revealed truth of Scripture, whereas the newly emerging natural philosophy (what we call science) assumes, over the course of time, more or less of a monopoly over the exercise of reason and of sense as these apply to, and generates concepts of, not only nature, but man himself in his objective interactions with the created world.

In this connection, it is helpful to call attention to the unique development of the capacities of both empirical observation and scientific reasoning that prepared and grounded Galileo's belief in a heliocentric universe.

In the late 16th century, Tycho Brahe, financially supported by a set of unusually liberal-minded patrons in positions of political power, was able to build observatories fitted with appropriate instruments on an island dedicated to the purpose of astronomical research. Thus equipped, Brahe spent the better part of two decades compiling astronomical data of unparalleled accuracy and scope. Upon his departure from the island, Brahe knew he needed the aid of another stellar mind to help make sense of the data he had so painstakingly collected. He sought and found Johannes Kepler, whose dedication to the Pythagorean and Neoplatonic harmony of the cosmos we have already encountered. The potent combination of the unprecedented quality of Brahe's empirical observations—and so of evidence supplied by the human senses enhanced by appropriate technology—combined with the genius of Kepler's mathematical reasoning, enabled the latter to achieve his brilliant formulation of the three fundamental laws of planetary motion. In 1609, Kepler published *Astronomia Nova,* wherein he propounds the first two laws of planetary motion. In 1619, he published *Harmonia Mundi* (the text cited earlier), which contains his explication of the third.

It was the virtually unprecedented scientific firepower provided by Brahe and Kepler that paved the way for Galileo's conversion to the heliocentric model of the universe. Consequently, when the Church condemned Galileo, it was not only a particular cosmological vision that it rejected (this would have been momentous enough), but the most original and powerful means of the scientific investigation of nature humankind had ever known.

Galileo added substantially to what was emerging as modern scientific method, a quantitative and evidenced-based means of inquiry that finally replaced, even as it transformed, the ancient Aristotelian system of natural philosophy and the medieval scholasticism cast in its mold. We find the essentials of modern scientific method sketched in Tarnas's description of all the various yet related means by which Galileo pioneered the metamorphosis of natural philosophy into what we today recognize as science:

> To combat the Aristotelians, Galileo developed both a new procedure for analyzing phenomena and a new basis for testing theories. He argued that to make accurate judgments concerning nature, scientists should consider only precisely measurable "objective" qualities (size, shape, number, weight, motion), while merely perceptible qualities (color, sound, taste, touch, smell) should be ignored as subjective and ephemeral. Only by means of an exclusively quantitative analysis could science attain certain knowledge of the world. In addition, while Aristotle's empiricism had been a predominantly descriptive and, especially as exaggerated by later Aristotelians, logico-verbal approach, Galileo now established the quantitative experiment as the final test of hypotheses. Finally, to further penetrate nature's mathematical regularities and true character, Galileo employed, developed, or invented a host of technical instruments—lens, telescope, microscope, geometric compass, magnet, air thermometer, hydrostatic balance. The use of such instruments gave a new dimension to empiricism unknown to the Greeks.[282]

The Galileo-inspired overthrow of the Aristotelian system forms a kind of analogue to Luther's repudiation of the hallowed institution of the Catholic Church. The latter was more visibly dramatic, but the former may have been equally important and was, in a way, far more decisive. The Catholic Church endures, revered as the hearth of true religion by millions, but today, modern science holds largely undisputed say over what does or does not pass for the truth of nature, and any "natural philosophy" (the term itself smacks of anachronism) incommensurate with the prescribed quantitative/experimental method is hardly considered worthy of serious consideration.

Both the Protestant and the Scientific fully deserve to be called Revolutions, insofar as both represent successful revolts against one or another traditional system that had become mired in habit, dogma, and prejudice. Both might be said to manifest, each in its own markedly different way, an uprising of the human spirit in its undying quest for truth and freedom. Both, unquestionably, contributed profoundly to the advent of modernity.

Even so, unlike the Scientific Revolution, the Protestant Reformation hinged upon a profoundly conservative element: a call for renewed fidelity to *truth already revealed*. The horizon line of science bent toward the future, while Luther, for all the keen power of his vision, had eyes in the back of his head. It was therefore natural that Protestantism should spark the reactionary Counter-Reformation. Consequently, when the tormented Old Church and the aspiring New Science came into conflict in the trial of Galileo, and the vanguard of humankind's pursuit of knowledge collided with its inveterate desire for the time-honored certainties of faith, the latter—still clutching the reins of worldly power—won the battle, only to lose, disastrously and nigh completely, the war of ages.

Given the inexorable flow of history, it could hardly have been otherwise; at least once the Church settled on its verdict. Once the case was convened, it was not simply Galileo Galilei, in his private person, that was on trial. In sharp contrast to Dr. Anthony Fauci, Galileo could rightly be regarded as representative of science itself. Consequently, the Church's condemnation amounted to little less than a repudiation of the human project of knowledge as such harkens back to the origins of the episteme in ancient Greece; and so, too, a renewed splitting of the Judeo-Christian and classical roots of Western culture. From that point on, *faith* in the former no longer readily cooperated (as it did much more seamlessly for certain Renaissance figures) with reason; the *rationality* stemming from the latter.

Man's heart and mind were cleft in two, and today it looks as if the still festering wound may—if no healing medicine is found—prove fatal.

Correspondent to the nature of the affliction, that medicine *cannot* take the form of a reassertion of the primacy of God, or religion, or faith in a manner that marginalizes the initiatives that constitute the ground of the modern era. What are these? Broadly stated, pursuit of the project of knowledge and discovery of the laws of nature by means of the sciences and arts, and concomitant cultivation of the human being's own capacities of reason, sense, and imagination.

Cosmological and ethical correlatives follow these accents. The modern, unlike the medieval mind, does not interest itself primarily in the human being's otherworldly destination. Instead, our preoccupation is with man in nature: who, and what (s)he is, can and will do, in *this* world, by virtue of those natural capacities Lord Bacon (for one) would affirm to be themselves the gift of God. Fulfillment of God's commission lies not in the neglect or depreciation of those faculties, but their full employment.

I return, once more, to what was previously stated: with the dawn of the modern era, it is not so much man's understanding of God that determines his idea of nature as well as that of his own being; rather, it is his idea of nature, as arrived at by his own powers of reason and observation, that more and more determines both his idea of divinity (including whether or not it is credited with existence at all) and of himself, as he views himself reflected in nature's mirror.

The eminence, even preeminence, of the idea of nature here is truly foundational. For the medieval person, the *other* (heavenly or spiritual) world featured as the principal locus of reality. Religious doctrine determined worldview, and described our earthly domain as ephemeral and of only passing importance. The same cannot be said for the modern individual, who, by nature of her more scientifically minded constitution, regards life on earth as of supreme value, and—even if she believes in one or another form of life after death—refuses to regard it as an insignificant staging ground. Instead, life *here* represents the scene in which she most fully succeeds—or fails—in realizing her being, the essential nature of her humanity.

Yet even this description, this identification of nature with the human experience of the world, does not do justice to the purview and influence of the idea of nature in the formative, early phase of modernity. I previously cited historian Carl Becker (*The Heavenly City of the Eighteenth-Century Philosophers*) on the key words that define the climate of opinion characteristic of one or another century. Becker provides lists of such for the 13th, 18th, 19th, and 20th centuries. The gap is provocative, and surely the first words Becker cites for the eighteenth were already gaining prominence prior to its dawn:

> In the 18th century the words without which no enlightened person could reach a restful conclusion were nature, natural law, first cause, reason, sentiment, humanity, perfectibility.[283]

Becker's words imply that, for the modern individual, nature and its laws provide the key to attaining a more enlightened state of humanity, and even (in accord with the chief thesis and title of Becker's book) of achieving the Augustinian vision of "the heavenly city," but relocated to this world—to human life, here, on earth.

In light of the state of the world today, this vision appears nought but a fantastic utopia. Fair enough; but we should not imagine we are beyond such dreaming. Just watch the famous video advertising the WEF's imagination of the future,[284] one in which, absolved of personal responsibility by the wise and beneficent technocratic powers-that-be, the mass of the human population will nonetheless enjoy unblemished felicity. As we look at a handsome young man with perfect teeth break into an infectious grin, we are told: "You will own nothing, and you will be happy."

Bitter experience teaches us something of how today's Matrix proposes to move us towards that happy ending. But what of those early moderns, our forefathers and godmothers? What promise did nature, and nature's laws hold for them, those intellectual adventurers who (as Becker implies) never tired of invoking these magic words? What, after all, was *nature* to them?

While a satisfactory answer to that question would require at least a book in itself, we may highlight key points here. First and foremost, if Luther put complete faith in scripture, the early modern philosophers, of whatever religious or non-religious stripe, had their own sacred text. Nature itself was often regarded as the holy book which, if one learned (by way of the "natural" light of reason) to read aright, would discover unto you the Law, the true Word of God.

This is as much as saying: *Nature itself was Revelation.*

Indeed, by the 18th century, no few enlightened philosophers considered biblical scripture corrupt. "Holy writ" consisted of words written by the all-too fallible-hand of man, for his own all too selfish purposes. God himself—if he was held to exist at all—was increasingly construed as the impersonal deistic "First Cause" rather than a passionately interested Personality. To the rational minds of writers such as Voltaire and Tom Paine, it was clear that the fantastic biblical tales, full of miraculous unnatural causes, were just that, and stood in stark contrast to the incorruptible truth recorded in the Creation itself, the great Book of Nature. So opined Tom Paine in his aptly titled book *The Age of Reason.*

> That which is now called natural philosophy, embracing the whole circle of science, of which astronomy occupies the chief place, is the study of the works of God, and of the power and wisdom of God in his works, and is the true theology.
>
> As to the theology that is now studied in its place, it is the study of human opinions and of human fancies concerning God. It is not the study of God himself in the works that he has made, but in the works or writings that man has made; and it is not among the least of the mischiefs that the Christian system has done to the world, that it has abandoned the original

> and beautiful system of theology, like a beautiful innocent, to distress and reproach, to make room for the hag of superstition.[285]

Paine published these words in 1796, almost two-hundred years after Bruno was burned at the stake. In between, the Scientific Revolution had proceeded apace. Brahe, Kepler, Galileo all made their seminal contributions. Bacon played his role as "the Father of experimental philosophy." Descartes contributed not only the radical philosophical revolution expressed in the *ego cogito,* but the coordinate geometry and corpuscular atomic theory of matter that furnished both the conceptual and material basis of a mechanistic world-view. Harvey, Boyle and Hook added their significant two cents. Above all, tying this whole universe of thought together with gravity's rainbow, was the man who, more than any other, represented the passing of the divine torch of creation to (not, now, the great artist Michelangelo and his Adam but) the Man of Science; the English genius whom the Frenchman Voltaire called the greatest man that ever lived, and whom Alexander Pope immortalized (along with the reigning Spirit of the Age) in one famous couplet:

> *Nature, and Nature's laws lay hid in night.*
> *God said, Let Newton be! And all was light.*[286]

What is the poet saying? On some level, we all know, because—quantum physics notwithstanding—Newton, more than any other individual (with the possible exception of Charles Darwin) has indeed created the world in which we live: the idea of the nature of Nature, the Reality of the Universe, that we all, knowingly or not, drink in with our mother's milk. Tarnas gives a thumbnail sketch of the substance of the Newtonian vision, and the staggering genius of the achievement that brought the Copernican revolution full circle a little more than a century-and-a-half after the Polish astronomer drafted his *Commentariolus*:

> It finally fell to Isaac Newton, born on Christmas Day the year of Galileo's death, to complete the Copernican revolution by quantitatively establishing gravity as a universal force—a force that could simultaneously cause both the fall of stones to the Earth and the closed orbits of the planets around the Sun. Indeed, it was Newton's astounding achievement to synthesize Descartes's mechanistic philosophy, Kepler's laws of planetary motion, and Galileo's laws of terrestrial motion in one comprehensive theory. In an unprecedented series of mathematical discoveries and intuitions, Newton established that to maintain their stable orbits at the relative speeds and distances specified by Kepler's third law, the planets must be pulled toward

> the Sun with an attractive force that decreased inversely as the square of the distance from the Sun, and that bodies falling toward the Earth—not only a nearby stone but also the distant Moon—conformed to the same law. Moreover, he mathematically derived from this inverse-square law both the elliptical shapes of the planetary orbits and their speed variation (equal areas in equal times) as defined by Kepler's first and second laws. Thus all the major cosmological problems confronting the Copernicans were at last solved—what moved the planets, how they remained in their orbits, why heavy objects fall toward the Earth, the basic structure of the universe, the issue of the celestial-terrestrial dichotomy. The Copernican hypothesis had provoked the need for, and now found, a new comprehensive, and self-consistent cosmology.[287]

How could a dusty book and its tale of seven days and nights (no matter that Newton himself put great stock in it) compete with such persuasive brilliance? Such superhuman reason, and incontrovertible coherence of argument? No wonder the modern world worships at the altar of science rather than religion, and looks to lab coats rather than frocks for answers to the problem of existence. Evidently, no one nailed it like Newton.

Unfortunately, Sir Isaac, ply his role as light-bearer as he might, could not solve all the world's problems. We now know well that there are limitations—severe limitations—even to his thought-model, which cannot, after all, finally be regarded as the absolute truth of the universe. By now, we know that any sort of Newtonian fundamentalism ultimately serves the cause of truth little better than the biblical brand, even if it may appear to be materially of more use.

The question, however, of the *limitations* of the modern scientific worldview and its attendant revolutionary transformation of the character of thought and constitution of knowledge need be revisited in later chapters. The task of this one is to identify what the Scientific Revolution, along with the Reformation, have to tell us about the core values of the modern era; that radiant gist that features, too, as the seed of *liberty* without culture of which the tree of human freedom cannot grow.

I have highlighted the central role played by nature in both its *empirical* dimension—the reality of the world available to the senses (aided, perhaps, by scientific instrument)—and its more *ideal* register. In the latter capacity, nature stands for the ostensible *source* of the law and order of things, which in turn reveals (to the deist, at least), the supervenient hand of the First Cause or God. Knowledge of the informing divine intelligence, or the true nature of things themselves, is, moreover, accessible to human reason[288]—at least, is so upon application of suitable method.

This last caveat can serve to direct our attention to the individual who, perhaps more than any other, makes spectacularly conspicuous the truth that the early modern worship of nature is only matched—indeed, perhaps overmatched—by its preoccupation with and illimitable faith in the capacity of the human mind. Indeed, if the dawn of modernity and Enlightenment cannot be understood without reference to the immense privilege accorded the idea of nature, it may nonetheless be declared that its philosophical ground was prepared by calling into question the certainty of our knowledge of its very existence.

No one in the formative years of modernity exemplifies radical doubt as consummately as René Descartes, who began his own unique quest for certain knowledge by calling everything into question—everything, that is, but the *agency of the consciousness capable of doubting.* If nature and the discoverable objective laws of her governance serve as the keys to the kingdom (be that construed as a heavenly or earthly one, or a combination of the two), Descartes, in the flush of his own hot pursuit of truth, had the audacity to bracket all but the activity of thought itself, the center of which he located—not in any concept of God external to his own reasoning process—but in that very process itself and its ontological source in his own human being. *Ego cogito, ergo sum*: No one (not Michelangelo adorning the Sistine ceiling, not Newton comparing the fall of an apple to the orbit of the moon) ever painted a bolder, more daring picture of the autonomy of mind, or placed the Self more firmly and immovably in the center of the universe, pushing—not only Earth and Sun—but God himself respectfully, but firmly, aside.

Pagden provides a tangible sense of how the Cartesian initiative, so basic to scientific method, not only transformed the mold of human thought, but (as an inevitable consequence thereof) the human universe in its entirety:

> Above all, what the moderns had achieved was to have severed scientific inquiry forever from any reliance upon any prior condition, belief, custom, or authoritative text. They had made the "I" the center of all inquiries into the human condition. Starting from these premises, the writers of the Enlightenment set out to construct an entire program for social, intellectual, and moral reform, one that would ultimately transform not only those countries where it took effect but gradually the whole of Europe and finally the entire world.[289]

A passage such as this brings us to the verge of understanding something of that deeper, authentic sense of liberty connate with the genesis of what ultimately becomes the modern liberal worldview. We are speaking here, to be sure, of an *autonomy of self*, but Pagden's paragraph, and Descartes's *cogito*, and indeed most of what has been discussed in this chapter, serves to give notice that what we are speaking of here is, first and foremost, *not* the liberty to participate on equal terms with all others in the affairs of the world, as that world has already been fixed in form, but *freedom of thought.* This freedom resides in the liberty *not* to consent to the world as is and play by the established rules of the game, but to question and criticize it—and any and all forms of putative authority—because all such are, ultimately, themselves products of human thought and so fallible.

This is not to say that all authority is wrong or corrupt or irrational or arbitrary or simply out-of-date, but to declare that it—and any interpreted truth it upholds (and all truth is interpreted)—*may* be and, indeed, *must* be all the more subject to criticism the higher and more absolute its claims upon truth. That is because history teaches that it is all too often deeds done in the name of one or another sovereign Power—be that God, or King, or indeed (as in the French Revolution) Reason itself—that most violently abuse the name of God, or royal prerogative, or rational judgment. The enlightened mind thus may not necessarily insist that there is no God, but *does* insist that citizens have a natural and unalienable right to question whether or not reigning authorities have forged his name in the signing of the law people are commanded to obey. It regards the individual mind as capable of passing the objective test by which knowledge is separated from illusion, fact from supposition, and science itself from "the hag of superstition."

This *freedom of thought* which, in its public and social expression assumes the form of *freedom of speech*, constitutes the heart of that *intellectual liberty* that lays the foundation of all real political freedom. Tyrants know that the props of power are sunk, not in the firm ground of incontrovertible fact, but in the fluid stuff of thought and opinion, which must be fixed in place if the whole edifice is not to collapse like a flimsy house of cards. So do the guns of power aim at the mouths of poets and protestors; so are the deadliest bullets nought but silencers.

Intellectual freedom is thus the very element of democracy, the air without which it cannot breathe. It is the vivifying atmosphere that so intoxicated Wordsworth in Calais at the onset of the French Revolution, and that inspired Tom Paine to pen the tract of *Common Sense* that helped loose the New World free from the chains of the Old. While Romantic poets might argue with Sir Isaac Newton and his *Opticks* (William Blake declared that Newton "destroyed the poetry of the rainbow"), humankind nonetheless rode the steed of science into the modern era because it was science more than religion that respected the intellectual liberty that constitutes the first and cardinal law of the mind, and so (whether or not so-and-so did or did not profess belief in God) honored *Logos*, Reason, the creative life of the divine Word, the force and truth of which can never be limited to books already writ or lines already spoken.

It is this unceasingly self-questioning spirit that forms, in truth, the kernel of the scientific method that Ernest Gellner identifies as the crux of what he calls "Enlightenment rationalism," the worldview that displaced medieval religiosity and inaugurated modernity. Gellner:

> Enlightenment Rationalist Fundamentalism, of which I am a humble adherent, repudiates any substantive revelations. It repudiates that substantive absolutization so characteristic of some post-Axial world religions which attribute an extra-mundane and transcultural authority to given substantive affirmations and values....
>
> The precise details of scientific method, of the cognitive procedure discovered in the course of the Scientific Revolution and codified by the Enlightenment, continues to be contentious.[290]

Fair enough. But we do, Gellner suggests, know the essentials:

> There are no privileged or a priori substantive truths.... All facts and all observers are equal. There are no privileged Sources or Affirmations, and all of them can be queried.[291]

This openness to question, this perfect impartiality, this recipe for unending creative intellectual agency, makes up the magic of science, rightly construed and practiced. Nor can the essence of the Enlightenment sensibility be understood without comprehending, and embracing, the ethic here suggested: an intellectual code of honor that spread to inform not merely natural science but the whole texture of Enlightenment culture, including what came to be called "the sciences of man."

For the method of studying and coming to know nature doubled as a means of humanity studying and coming to know itself. The enlightened 18th -century *philosophe* (Montesquieu, Voltaire, Condorcet) may have lost some of the sublimely exalted genius of the true Renaissance man, but nonetheless counts as an updated version of the same; one who, perhaps, gains in capacities of critical reason and sociopolitical acuity what may have been lost in sublimity and proximity to the divine. One could say of (for instance) Voltaire, that, above all, he dedicated himself to the cause of intellectual freedom on behalf of the nascent universalism that underwrites the "Party of Humanity."[292]

Pagden provides a succinct synopsis of the Enlightenment, and so the seed of the modern liberal spirit:

> Enlightenment has been identified with an exalted view of human rationality and of human benevolence, and with a belief, measured and at times skeptical, in progress and in the general human capacity for self-improvement. It has been broadly understood to stand for the claim that all individuals have the right to shape their own ends for themselves rather than let others do it for them and—what comes to much the same thing—to live their lives as best they can without help or hindrance from divine decrees. It has been seen as the source of most modern liberal, tolerant, undogmatic, and secular understandings of politics and as the intellectual origins of all modern forms of universalism, from a recognition of the essential unity of the human race and the evils of slavery and racism right through to the humanistic sentiments behind *Médicins sans frontiéres*. It is widely regarded as having been the intellectual origin of our still slowly emerging conviction that all human beings share the same basic rights and that women think and feel no differently from men or Africans from Asians.[293]

Such a perspective helps clarify why Patrick Deneen, despite the "failure" of liberalism, recognizes there is no path forward that does not incorporate its contributions, and what Horkheimer and Adorno mean when they state that there is no freedom without Enlightenment. Correlatively, if we would preserve our liberty by opposing the Leviathan Machine of International (Dis) Order that I have called the Matrix, perhaps we would do well to resist the temptation prematurely to imagine that God alone can answer our prayers, and rather take a page from the Age of Reason, renewing, in the Cartesian spirit of radical doubt, the endless effort to better study and to know not only the true laws of nature, but—reflected in that august light—our own deeply inscrutable human selves.

Chapter 8

ROOTS OF MODERN LIBERALISM III: DOWN WITH LOCKE

Michelangelo. Luther. Copernicus. I have addressed all the luminaries listed in the aforementioned 16th-century (1512–1517) window of time with the exception of Machiavelli.

All of these figures owe a measure of added significance to their close association with one or another major historical movement (the Renaissance, Reformation, or Scientific Revolution). The Renaissance statesman Machiavelli stands out most as the first in a line of eminent thinkers[294] to lend original—and distinctly modern—attention to the subject of *political science.*

It is not without meaning that Machiavelli's *The Prince* was composed and first distributed in 1513, in close temporal proximity to Martin Luther's nailing of the ninety-nine theses to the Wittenberg church door. An elevation of the historic importance of *the state* must be reckoned yet another consequential—and distinctly secularizing—effect of the violent fracture suffered by the Church. Tarnas:

> The Roman Catholic Church had maintained the general, if sometimes controversial, allegiance of virtually all Europeans.... With the Reformation, the universal ambition and dream of the Catholic imperium was finally defeated. The resulting empowerment of the various separate nations and states of Europe now displaced the old ideal unity of Western Christendom.... There was now no higher power, international and spiritual, to which all individual states were responsive.... The individual secular state now became the defining unit of cultural, as well as political authority. The medieval Catholic matrix unifying Europe had disintegrated. [295]

Tarnas here points to a development integral to the advent of modernity. If, in the course of the 17th and 18th centuries, science gradually replaced religion as the privileged means of coming to know and describe the nature of reality, the *polis* (either in the form of the nation or related species of state organizations) accedes to a new order of prominence. As humankind's goals assume more worldly and outward (rather than inward and immaterial) form, the power relations underlying the sociopolitical organization of society earn new regard in the mind of leading thinkers, and, too, added moral and spiritual as well as practical weight. Rather than the questions of sin and salvation that preoccupied the medieval mind, the modern individual's spiritual interest comes, more and more, to revolve around issues of *human freedom,* thus making politics an increasingly self-conscious and central dimension of moral culture.

Tarnas explains how the Protestant Reformation, and the resistance to authority intrinsic to it, spearheads this development:

> With secular rulers now defining the religion of their territories, the Reformation unintentionally moved power from church to state.... And because many of the principal monarchs chose to remain Catholic, their continuing attempts to centralize and absolutize political power caused Protestantism to be allied with resisting bodies—aristocrats, clergy, universities, provinces, cities—that sought to maintain or increase their separate liberties. Hence the cause of Protestantism became associated with the cause of political freedom.[296]

In view of our preoccupation with the roots of liberalism, Tarnas's concluding thoughts on this matter should hold special interest even while accenting the Reformation's profoundly paradoxical consequence:

> The Reformation's new sense of personal religious self-responsibility and the priesthood of all believers also abetted the growth of political liberalism and individual rights. At the same time, the religious fragmentation of Europe necessarily promoted a new intellectual and religious diversity. From all these factors ensued a succession of increasingly secularizing political and social consequences: first, the establishment of individual state-identified churches, then division of church and state, religious toleration, and finally the predominance of secular society. *Out of the exceedingly illiberal dogmatic religiosity of the Reformation eventually emerged the pluralistic tolerant liberalism of the modern era* [emphasis added].[297]

The Englishman John Locke played an especially key role in formulating the political philosophy that accompanied and, to a considerable degree, fostered these developments.

Locke's ethical and political philosophy, which deeply influenced Montesquieu, Hume, Rousseau, Kant and other important European philosophers, proved foundational to Enlightenment-era thinking pertaining to questions of liberty, equality, natural law, human rights, and related ethical and political concerns. Correlatively, Locke's systematic deliberations (laid out primarily in *A Letter on Toleration*; *Two Treatises of Government*; and *An Essay Concerning Human Understanding*)[298] prepared the intellectual ground for the American and subsequent French revolutions.[299] If we wish truly to understand the intellectual premises underlying modern democratic systems of governance, and so the ideas that inspired the founding of our nation, we would do well to spend a little time with Locke, regarded by some as the "father of liberalism."

We have previously encountered Locke in the context of Deneen's critique of liberalism, and in loose association with Deneen's treatment of Thomas Hobbes. Now, however, it need be emphasized that, while Hobbes and Locke share certain premises (both take the "state of nature" initially postulated by Hobbes as a premise for the social contract theory that underwrites their political philosophy), Locke and Hobbes differ more than they concur, and do so in a manner commensurate with the distinct political circumstances experienced by each during their respective lives.

Thomas Hobbes was born in 1588, and spent the better part of his maturity living through the violent Thirty Years' War (1618–1648) and English Civil Wars (1642–1651). Given the upheaval occasioned by these conflicts, it is hardly surprising that Hobbes should put a premium on stability; and the religious fractiousness entailed in the wars inclined him toward a political philosophy that invests near absolute power in the state apparatus. Locke, on the other hand, was born in 1632. By the time he was sixteen, the Peace of Westphalia had ended the Thirty Years' War; by the time he was twenty, the Civil Wars appeared in the rear-view mirror.

Rather than idealizing state power, Locke was far more concerned about its potential abuse, especially when such was perpetrated under the aegis of the doctrine of the divine right of kings.[300] Despite the diminishment of monarchical power that followed upon the mid-century civil wars, the question of the relative authority of royalty and Parliament remained of pressing concern in England in the latter half of the 17th century. The issue came to a head after the accession of a Catholic, King James II, to the throne in 1685 and the birth of a potential heir (and so the prospect of a Catholic dynasty) in 1688. As a Protestant (a devout Calvinist) long engaged in the ongoing power struggles between Protestant and Catholic factions, Locke had significant personal stake in the machinations that ultimately led to the 1688 Glorious Revolution that deposed King James II and finally cemented the principle of the supremacy of the Parliament over the Crown in England. His first-hand experience of the divisive character of religious difference as well as the threat to personal liberty posed by monarchical government (Locke felt compelled to remove himself to the Netherlands for some years) naturally influenced Locke's highly original and even revolutionary political deliberations.

As previously discussed, theology *per se* as well as dogmatic species of religious authority lost considerable power and prestige in the early modern period even as forms of science identified with the exercise of human reason gained the same. Even so, few major Enlightenment-era thinkers espoused atheism.[301] On the contrary, firm belief in a divine intelligence (often, but not always, called God) construed as the sovereign source of law and order in the universe continued to serve as an indispensable foundation for scientific exploration in domains as superficially diverse as cosmology, ethics, and politics.

I say "superficially" because many thinkers of this era understood (generally speaking, far better than we) the deep connections that make one whole of the natural and human universe, weaving together in a single cloth the style in which human beings think about the universe and the manner in which we conceive of, and order our relationships to, one another. Here is a prose passage that, upon discovery of its author, may prove revealing in this regard:

> This most beautiful system of the sun, planets, and comets could only proceed from the counsel and dominion of an intelligent and powerful Being. He is eternal and infinite, omnipotent and omniscient.... He governs all things and knows all things that are or can be done. We know him only by his most wise and excellent contrivance of things, and final causes; we admire him for his perfections, but we reverence him as his servants; and a god without dominion, providence, and final causes, is nothing else but Fate and Nature.[302]

Are these the pieties of some forgettable theologian? No, these words are authored by Sir Isaac Newton in his famous *Principia.* Nor did Newton and his staunch Anglican followers imagine science, religion, and politics as separable fields. Rather, they opined that the lawful arrangement Newton discovered in the universe, one created and sustained by divine intelligence, should serve as a model of sociopolitical order. As one historian of science phrased the political mission of an influential group of intellectuals gathered around Newton:

> The same providence that generates the mechanical laws at work in the universe oversees the workings of society and government, and men must see to it that their political and economic actions conform to the stability and harmony decreed by supernal authority.[303]

Montesquieu's *The Spirit of the Laws* (1748) is undoubtedly one of the most influential books of political philosophy ever scribed. The work that first elaborated (if it did not introduce) the theory of the separation of executive, legislative, and judicial powers, it informed the thinking of Adams, Jefferson, and other American founders, most all of whom were deeply versed in Enlightenment-era philosophy.

Montesquieu, born into a Huguenot family but educated in a Catholic school, was not known as a particularly religious man. Like Locke and most of the French *philosophes,* he regarded himself as a man of reason and of science and disapproved of the sectarian intolerance that so often proved a powder keg of violence. Even so, Montesquieu begins his renowned work by grounding his idea of law—the title and subject of his text—in a divine intelligence that creates and preserves the nature of things. Montesquieu clearly sees this postulate as required by the dictates not of faith, but of reason:

> Laws, in their most general signification, are the necessary relations arising from the nature of things....
>
> They who assert that a blind fatality produced the various effects we behold in this world talk very absurdly; for can any thing be more unreasonable than to pretend that a blind fatality could be productive of intelligent beings?
>
> There is, then, a prime reason; and laws are the relations subsisting between it and different beings, and the relations of these to one another.
>
> God is related to the universe, as Creator and Preserver: the laws by which He created all things are those by which He preserves them. He acts according to these rules, because He knows them; He knows them, because He made them; and He made them, because they are in relation of His Wisdom and Power.
>
> Since we observe that the world, though formed by the motion of matter, and void of understanding, subsists through so long a succession of ages, its motions must certainly be directed by invariable laws; and could we imagine another world, it must also have constant rules, or it would inevitably perish.
>
> Thus the creation, which seems an arbitrary act, supposes laws as invariable as those of the fatality of the Atheists.[304]

While *law* as such does not appear in the title of Locke's relevant books (as it does in Montesquieu's) the *principle* of law in its distinct varieties plays a central role in the Englishman's political philosophy. Locke's concepts of divine and of natural law, moreover, ultimately furnish the basis of his decisive difference from Hobbes, who in many respects counts as Machiavelli's heir and Locke's most important predecessor.

As we have already seen, the nature of *liberty* proves the pivot of many of the most critical deliberations of political philosophy.

Both Hobbes and Locke recognize liberty as a natural right deriving from the law of nature, whereby every person seeks to preserve his or her own being. Both recognize, too, that— solitary existence proving, as a rule, untenable— human beings inevitably seek society and will devise and willingly consent to forms of governance designed to regulate their interactions and ameliorate the potential for conflict inherent in social existence. The chief difference between the two Englishmen arises in connection with the important matter of *sovereignty*: whether sovereign power is invested in the *state* (as represented by that body charged with the task of governance) or in the *individual.* Relevant, too, is the correlative question as to the ultimate source from which that sovereign power is supposed to derive.

For Hobbes, the efficacy of government depends upon its nigh absolute authority, even if the basis of the state's legitimacy inheres in the initial condition of the people's consent. That consent is granted insofar as the persons comprising the society agree that submission to the rule of the governing body best serves the preservation of all. The state fulfills that all-important function primarily by ensuring the maintenance of law and order, in the absence of which chaos born of strife and even violence would inevitably ensue. Fidelity to its charge is, moreover, supposed effectively *ingrained* in the nature and constitution of the sovereign state itself in the same way that infallible judgment is supposedly invested in the office of the papacy (and so the person of any given pope). The state comes thus irrefutably to stand, symbolically as well as practically, for *the collective interest of the people as a whole.*

Once having consented[305] to the formation of the state and submitting to its governance, the individual has *no* legitimate grounds for revoking that consent. She has handed over her right of independent judgment in her initial act and consequent enjoyment of the benefits of society. Dissent can thus always legitimately be regarded as an act of rebellion against the just authority of a state, the governing body permanently representative of the welfare of all.

Thus, while *right*, by virtue of consent, originally contributes to the *might* of the state, once that state is duly constituted, the might or *power* proper to its superiority becomes the effective measure of right. There is no recognized court of moral judgment independent of state authority; nor does the citizen possess recourse to any higher law that could justify opposition to or dissolution of the state.

This is the political philosophy underlying *The Leviathan.* If you find yourself tempted to believe it antiquated, the fanciful product of a 16th-century Englishmen scared out of his wits by religious and civil strife, just take a look around.

In this Hobbesian world, the citizen's natural rights are limited more or less exclusively to that of self-preservation. For John Locke—a man all too familiar with the vagaries of royal power—the natural *rights* devolving from natural *law* have a significantly broader purview. These rights guarantee protection, both moral and legal, against all measures infringing upon a wide orbit of prerogatives included under the aegis of "Lives, Liberties, and Estates" or, in another formulation, "Life, Health, Liberty or Possessions."[306] These rights include, too, provision for equal treatment, so that laws unjustly favoring one or another party could be opposed on the basis of the rights deriving from natural law, which in turn, derives legitimacy from the highest source of authority: namely, *divine law.*

How, one might inquire, is that law to be known or recognized? By virtue, naturally, of the faculty of reason, the "light of nature" shining within the conscience of the human being, given and available to all whose sight is not artificially obscured by prejudice or vice. Natural law is thus for Locke "a universally obligatory moral law promulgated by the human reason as it reflects on God and His rights, on man's relation to God and on the fundamental equality of all men as rational creatures."[307] Alternatively (but similarly) phrased, "Reason, which is that Law, teaches all Mankind, who would but consult it, that being all equal and independent, no one ought to harm another in his Life, Health, Liberty, or Possessions."[308]

In addition to divine and natural law, Locke recognized two lower varieties. Both *civil law* and *the law or reputation or opinion* are all-too-human in origin, and thus permanently open to question. Neither can, by right, command the species of authority reserved for natural law and the divine law it reflects.

The overall design of Locke's ethics and its scaffold of various, hierarchically conceived orders of law is distinctly reminiscent of Aquinas.[309] In Locke, however, the doctrine of natural law takes on political overtones largely absent from the theological context of the idea in Aquinas's *Summa.* If reason judges a civil law to be considered contrary to natural law, and so violative of the unalienable rights accorded (by God, not man) to the individual, Locke's political philosophy justifies resistance to, and even rebellion against, the king or state that persists in enforcing such morally indefensible legislation. Historian James MacGregor Burns:

> By denying that kings were divinely authorized or were sovereign, that government was their property, or that people's rights depended on their grace and favor, Locke struck blows at the pillars of absolutism. In their place he envisioned a civic order founded on the consent of the governed, in which the people, possessed of inalienable natural rights to "Lives, Liberties, and Estates," were sovereign and government was responsible to them for action or inaction. That meant, contrary to Hobbes, that the people retained the right and power to dissolve their government and create a new one.[310]

As noted in the Preface to his *Treatises of Civil Government*, Locke wrote that tract with a tangible political aim. He wished to justify the replacement of one (Catholic) king with another (Protestant) one: "To establish the throne of our great restorer, our present king [William] and to make good his title in the consent of the people."[311]

Whether or not Locke's political theory was sufficient to that end (David Hume thought not [312]) may be debated. What we do know, however, is that the revolutionary import of Locke's ideas *was* amply realized a little less than a century later. Thomas Jefferson borrowed extensively from Locke and the natural law tradition in penning the Declaration that asserted America's independence from the irrational tyranny exercised by yet another English King:

> When in the Course of human events, it becomes necessary for one people to dissolve the political bands which have connected them with another, and to assume among the powers of the earth, the separate and equal station to which the Laws of nature and of Nature's God entitle them, a decent respect to the opinions of mankind requires that they should declare the causes which impel them to the separation.
>
> We hold these truths to be self-evident, that all men are created equal, that they are endowed by their Creator with certain unalienable Rights, that among these are Life, Liberty and the pursuit of Happiness.—That to secure these rights, Governments are instituted among Men, deriving their just powers from the consent of the governed,—That whenever any Form of Government becomes destructive of these ends, it is the Right of the People to alter or to abolish it, and to institute new Government, laying its foundation on such principles and organizing its powers in such form, as to them shall seem most likely to effect their Safety and Happiness.[313]

Thus was America born; thus were the embers of revolution stirred and kindled into flame on the hearth of philosophy.

We return, then, to still pending and ever-more pressing questions:

What is enlightenment?

How is it so constituted and composed that it may lead *both* to the birth of a New World graced by the Statue of Liberty, *and* to the destructive dialectic that threatens to restore the very sort of despotic rule it once so famously deposed?

What is the real gist of the idea of liberty itself? What is the spiritual source of that idea? How may this be distinguished from interpretations that represent degradations or corruptions of the ideal of human freedom in modern times?

That first question proves the ground of the other. Drawing upon the explorations so far pursued, we can endeavor to draw together key motifs and sketch the rough outline of an answer.

The question itself is an historic one, as Anthony Pagden informs us:

> In December 1783 the *Berlinische Monatsschrift*, a widely read and generally progressive journal, published an article by a theologian and educational reformer named Johann Friedrich Zöllner. The article...might have passed unnoticed...if it had not been for a single footnote. "What is enlightenment?" Zöllner asked. "This question, which is almost as important as what is truth, should indeed be answered before one begins enlightening. And still I have never found it answered!" It was perhaps the most significant footnote in the entire history of western thought—it was certainly the most widely discussed. Six years later, shortly before the outbreak of the French Revolution, the German poet and philosopher Christoph Martin Wieland—once described as the German Voltaire—while seated on the toilet and reaching for what he coyly calls a "maculature" (in other words, a piece of toilet paper), found, "not without a slight shudder of astonishment," that the sheet of "good white soft paper" he held in his hand had printed on it six questions, the first of which was: "What is enlightenment?"[314]

Pagden's book comprises one well-informed attempt to answer the question, and its four-hundred-plus pages provide a more comprehensive response than any I can offer here. The passage cited at the close of the prior chapter of this book represents a cogent prefatory distillation, but my quotation truncates Pagden's answer. The relevant section continues:

> As an intellectual movement, it [the Enlightenment] also saw the beginning of those disciplines—economics, sociology, anthropology, political science,

> and certain kinds of moral philosophy—that dictate much of how we view, and attempt to control our lives today. Modernity was the creature of a great many intellectual and scientific configurations, from the invention of the steam engine to the Internet, very little of which can be attributed to the Enlightenment (even if it was the 18th-century German philosopher Gottfried Wilhelm Leibniz who first devised the binary system on which the modern digital computer is based).
>
> What can be attributed to it, however, is the broadly secular, experimental, individualistic, and progressive intellectual world that ultimately made those innovations possible—a world in which the old and apparently unassailable forms of association, of belief and tradition, that had for centuries divided human beings into mutually suspicious and often brutally homicidal groups were slowly and painfully, but irreversibly abandoned.[315]

Pagden furnishes a window of insight. Even so, a somewhat more systematic synopsis, one drawing together in one place the chief points elaborated over the last few chapters, may bring us closer to a somewhat fuller answer. In memory of Wieland's maculature, I present my own summary response to the *first* question printed upon it in the form of *six* integrally interrelated thematic points. The first echoes Pagden's emphatic conclusion:

1. *Sapere aude!* (Corollary: Radical Doubt, or Question Authority!)

The first and foundational principle of Enlightenment cracks open the heavy door of the medieval mind, letting in the rays that augur the morning of modernity. Enlightenment engages the original force of the human intellect, and begins by laying aside the book of truth *already* revealed, upon which stands any and all forms of traditional and customary authority.

Ernest Gellner, self-professed adherent of "Enlightenment Rationalist Fundamentalism," delivers the gist of the matter with admirable punch in the lines already cited:

> There are no privileged or a priori substantive truths.... All facts and all observers are equal. There are no privileged Sources or Affirmations, and all of them can be queried.[316]

Historically speaking, the reigning systems of authority naturally feature as the principal objects of enlightened critique. That meant, first of all, the Church and its dogmas as well as the time-honored system of scholastic philosophy. Yet this first, cardinal principle obviously has wide sociopolitical as well as scientific and spiritual implications. It cuts at the root of the poison tree of prejudice wherever and whenever it grows.

In and of itself, the impulse that initiates Enlightenment does not necessarily involve repudiation of all traditional or customary authority, but *does* demand that these be subject to review in order to examine whether they reflect true wisdom or arbitrary edict, intolerance, and abusive privilege.

The term "radical doubt" stems from Descartes, whose philosophical method entailed discarding any position the validity of which one could not certify with absolute certainty. Later thinkers perhaps still more closely allied with the spirit of Enlightenment (such as Jean le Rond d'Alembert in his *Preliminary Discourse to the Encyclopedia of Diderot*[317]) doubted Descartes's certainties and criticized a method intent upon arriving at a system of definitive conclusions. It was a closed rather than open book.

In the first paragraph of his 1784 essay "What is Enlightenment?" Immanuel Kant gives classic formulation to this first and most important principle:

> Enlightenment is the human being's emancipation from its self-incurred immaturity. *Immaturity* is the inability to make use of one's intellect without the direction of another. This immaturity is self-incurred when its cause does not lie in a lack of intellect, but rather in a lack of resolve and courage to make use of one's intellect without the direction of another. "*Sapere aude!* Have the courage to make use of your own intellect" is hence the motto of Enlightenment.[318]

This first principle opens onto all the others.

2. *Study Nature*

Gellner pronounced the sentences cited above in an effort to explain scientific method. Paradoxically, the *open mind* thus required legitimates the *authority* accorded science that—largely displacing that of religion—stands as a central pillar of the modern mentality.

Correlatively, the prestige of science depends upon the impersonality and *objectivity* of the truth it confers, the ground of which is *nature* herself.

The law and order evident in nature were considered by most Enlightenment thinkers as reflective of divine intelligence; others considered non-human and even human nature as the effect of purely material forces and laws. Either way, the study of nature served as the royal road to knowledge: of the world, of the human being, and (for some) even divinity itself.

If Scripture is no longer to function as the privileged source of revealed truth, the human subject in search of answers to the riddles of existence nevertheless requires an alternative authoritative (some would, some would not say, "sacred") *text*, one not originally subject (like all man-made things) to the human will. Nature, in its diverse guises—as the created universe or simply the objective world in all its myriad aspects (including the human creature)—fit the bill.

Nature served as *standard of proof* as well as object of study. Any posited truth need pass the test of *factual evidence*. Neither theological dogma nor forms of logical tautology pass muster. The human being asks questions and proposes answers. It is Nature herself who answers true or false.

Finally, for the Enlightenment mentality, nature and human life in it serve as a (if not the) principal locus of value. Any other, supernatural world (including any heavenly one entered after death) no longer serves as the exclusive or privileged spiritual destination of the striving human soul.

3. Humanism in the Age of Reason

The chief point here is largely implicit in the first two, and has been elaborated fairly extensively in the prior chapters. If the enlightened person is a student of nature, she is so most importantly to know her own human nature—to know, that is, herself. As the first lines of Epistle II of Alexander Pope's "An Essay on Man" tell us:

> *Know then thyself, presume not God to scan;*
> *The proper study of mankind is Man.*

The first word here, too, possesses special relevance: the Enlightenment project is a project of right cognition *(cogito)*, of *knowledge*, the principle vehicle of which is reason, which vaunted faculty features as the most essential attribute of the human being. Faith, pure and simple, blind or seeing, does not cut it for the modern; nor is it sufficient to worship *Logos* in the person of Jesus of Nazareth. The Word and the Spirit of the Law must be *recognized* in and through the agency of the human being's own rational intelligence, as such is exercised in its study of the universe of things, of which the human being is part. Reason, in fit combination with the information gained through sensible experience and systematically pursued in the form of science in all its encyclopedic reach, can stead the human being well in the quest for Truth—and Freedom.

4. Progress

Speaking of the nature of the human being, such is not to be understood as originally and indelibly flawed and fallen. The present, and still more the future, is more important than the past, which surely should be studied, but principally because the knowledge thereby gained enables the fashioning of a more perfect future. If human life is mean or low, that is a betrayal or corruption rather than illustration of our rightful estate. Knowledge is, too, as Bacon said, practical power: the means of transforming the world so as to improve the human condition. It is primarily such self-willed striving and effort, with or without the assistance of God's grace, that can lead the human being towards felicity—in this world.

5. The Statute of Liberty: The Individual and the State

The fifth point is implicit in the first: the *agent* of radical doubt, of the one who initiates critical questioning, can be none other than the *individual. Cogito, ergo sum*: It is always the "I" that thinks, the Self that is the subject of knowledge—and of freedom. Institutions such as the Church are conservative in nature and protective of the status quo. Luther stood in the singularity of his person and individual conscience against the monumental edifice of Rome; as did (with admittedly different results) Bruno and Galileo.

These last two were persecuted by the Church, but it was the power of independent German states that helped shield Luther from its wrath. In the aftermath of the Wars of Religion, the secular state emerged as the body possessed of both the might and authority to protect the individual in her natural rights. If the state can persecute—which it could and did—it did so (in Locke's mind, at least) in violation of its charter. The *good* government is the servant of the individual, by whose consent it rules; and is armor against the *bad*: the tyrannical despot, and (just as importantly) the intolerant neighbor. Jefferson (if I may re-cite lines that cannot be too often rehearsed) states the gist of the matter with admirable lucidity:

> All men are created equal, and possessed of certain unalienable Rights, That among these are Life, Liberty, and the pursuit of Happiness. *To secure these rights, Governments are instituted among Men, deriving their just powers from the consent of the governed...*

As Deneen so well explains, the sovereign individual is, sociopolitically speaking, a child of the modern state, *and* vice versa.

In 1791, with the passage of The Bill of Rights, those unalienable Rights were expanded, in the United States, to include, *first* of all, freedom of speech, religion, press, and peaceable assembly.

The statute stands. Let the Liberty Bell ring.

6. The Party of Humanity

The individual's unalienable rights of freedom and equality derive from the idea of a universal humanity shared by *all* persons by virtue of their participation in the race. Philosophically speaking (which, I realize, is not the current idiom) this is the human archetype. Traditionally (or religiously) this might be called the divine image (the human being, male/ female, made in the image of God); Platonically or Neoplatonically, it might be called "the inner man" or "the authentic human principle."[319] Moderns tend to eschew any metaphysical construction of the notion of universal humanity, the moral and emotional currency of which they nonetheless spend most liberally.

How this idea is in fact to be understood is a matter of great, even decisive import, and I will turn attention to it later in this and in subsequent volumes. For now, however, it is sufficient to note that Enlightenment, in addition to empowering, reciprocally, the free individual and sovereign state, further imagines every human being as a citizen of the world, a member of the Party of Humanity. The universalism thus endorsed is the antecedent of international organization.

As we have seen in discussion of the dialectic of enlightenment, if interpreted superficially or materialistically, this idea can morph into problematic forms of globalism. Rather than universalism, Kant preferred the idea of *cosmopolitanism.* He imagined such cosmopolitanism as the spiritual ground of what could, perhaps, manifest as the antithesis of the constant state of war that tore at Europe for centuries: *perpetual peace*. That ideal is the subject of one of the great German thinker's latest and most influential works, *Toward Perpetual Peace: A Philosophical Project*, [320] the mention of which can serve as a kind of fitting capstone of Enlightenment thought, and this brief summary.

~

Perhaps this synopsis highlights a truth clearly enough suggested by chronology alone: while everyone would do well to possess a basic understanding of enlightenment, the topic possesses unique relevance to one nation in particular. As can be said of no other country, America is a child of the Enlightenment, born in the wake of powerful currents spreading from Europe and swirling for a century (or two or three) around her shores. While not every idea listed in my abstract fits this country like a glove, most do. America, after all, is the New World, and where else could one better hope to realize the future dreams of humankind?

Thus the soul of the nation bears the stamp of the period of its birth, and in no respect is that more material and visible than in the democratic impulse—the ideal of liberty and justice for all—that distinguishes America's unique political character and mission. The statue at Ellis Island (a gift, appropriately enough, from France) holds high a legacy as well as a promise. It is the mind of Enlightenment that lights the torch of liberty.

Yet we all know, too, what terrible darkness shadowed that light from before the beginning, and continues to do so. The original sins of the genocide of native peoples, the importation and enslavement of Africans, and the disenfranchisement of women have transformed into present day versions of the same: endemic and occasionally lethal racial discrimination; a culture of runaway incarceration; persistent gender inequality; gross and growing economic injustice. Our initial promise and national pledge ("with liberty and justice for all") has thus been broken and betrayed. Indeed, the very ideals so sanguinely trumpeted as the honor badge of our national character have too often propped up a facade of righteousness masking gross transgression. The shining city on the hill has always cast a long black shadow, one that today increasingly threatens to engulf us in darkness and transmute the mythic American dream into a waking nightmare.

Yet just as the United States may stand as an iconic beacon of an idea of freedom which belongs to all the world, such corruptions, while perhaps peculiarly poignant in an American context, are hardly our problem alone. Pagden rehearses the serious charges directed at the heritage of Enlightenment thought by disaffected critics of the Euro-American way:

> Today, many have grown suspicious of precisely those values and aspirations that are now closely identified with the "West"—itself an 18th-century coinage—of which the Enlightenment is seen as the most heinous representative. The past century and a half of Euro-American history has come to be regarded—and not without reason—as little more than a litany of war and oppression, colonization and exploitation. In the light of such a history, the airy, optimistic, ecumenical claims of the Enlightenment—or what is widely taken to be the Enlightenment—have come to look threadbare, if not hypocritical and presumptuous. It is the Enlightenment that is

> now accused of being responsible for a "Eurocentrism" that led inexorably to an implacable intolerance of everyone, and everything, that rose to challenge its rationalistic, reductive objectives, thus making it the midwife to modern imperialism and modern racism.[321]

Pagden proceeds to observe that "these accusations are not entirely groundless." Certainly not. Yet it is of the utmost importance to investigate, with care and conscience, what can be educed as valid and substantive ground for critique of Enlightenment ideology, and what cannot. The basis for legitimate critique seems to me to fall into three broad types:

1) The first avenue of approach does not so much criticize Enlightenment thinking *per se* as condemn actions that fall short of or betray its professed ideals. Jefferson, the author of the Declaration so resonantly affirming that "*all men are created equal,*" may be faulted for owning slaves, or for consenting to laws denying women the right to vote. More generally, the Founding Fathers may legitimately be upbraided for designing and defending government that denied equality to all but propertied white males. Innumerable other instances from home and abroad could readily be cited.

It should be relatively obvious that such criticism does not in fact impugn the Enlightenment ideas or ideals in question, but rather relies and stands upon them in order to condemn their corruption. The distinction between the integrity of the ideals themselves and the character and conduct of historical persons or parties should be evident enough. If it is so, however, in *theory*, in *practice* that distinction is not always clearly maintained, but, on the contrary, often confused and conflated. That is no doubt in part because high ideals, which are intrinsically universalist in nature, can and do often function as moral cover for actions that—in concrete, particular fact—betray those ideals. This dynamic can, *á la* nominalist and materialist traditions, lead to a suspicion of the objective reality of the universal or archetypal register of being intrinsic to the ideals themselves. It ultimately fosters a view of politics that (consciously or not) tends towards the Machiavellian or Hobbesian (and finally Nietzschean) vision of the will to power as the controlling principle of sociopolitical existence.

2) Enlightenment ideals may themselves be deemed sound and admirable, but recognized as partial and (to a greater or lesser degree) exclusive of other, complementary ideals. If the latter are not in some wise incorporated in praxis, valid ideals, by dint of one-sidedness, inevitably transform into deficient and even destructive modes of social praxis.

The Enlightenment era distrust of traditional authority, for instance, while clearly possessing justification in its own right, can devolve into an unreasoned repudiation of worthwhile ideas and initiatives simply because such may be associated with one or another tradition (religious, or philosophical, or political) disfavored by a given individual. Correlatively, I do think it fair to say that modern Enlightenment-influenced thought *tends* to value a particular set of archetypal ideas revolving around individuality, illimitability, progressive change and innovation, and universality in preference to a complementary set revolving around tradition, roots, community, limits, and stability. This archetypal difference clearly plays a part in Deneen's critique of liberalism, which political predilection likewise favors the first constellation of ideas (historically, at least) even while conservatism lists towards the second.

Those familiar with the field of archetypal studies may recognize here the senex-puer polarity (the senex is the archetype of the *wise old man*; the puer that of *eternal youth*) James Hillman and others examine in a book of essays dedicated to the topic.[322] As Hillman teaches, any truly constructive initiative, even if it may favor one or the other pole of the senex-puer duality, must find a constructive way of integrating the opposite. New Jersey bard William Carlos Williams, afficionado of his friend Ezra Pound's dictum "*Make it new,*" charged London-based American expatriate T. S. Eliot with indenture to an exhausted Old World culture. Eliot, for his part, discussed how every artist must strike a *balance* between "Tradition and Individual Talent" in a famous essay so named.[323]

Failing to achieve some such balance, any intellectual or cultural initiative will inevitably be ghosted (if not wholly overtaken) by the dark shadow of the repressed opposite, yielding results that are, at best, innocuous or sterile, and at worst, terrifying. Thus the Jacobins, radical champions of liberty in revolutionary France, failed to incorporate moderate elements that might lend a modicum of structural stability and order to their rule, which consequently degenerated into the Reign of Terror that violently cut off the freedom (and too often the heads) of innumerable citizens.

On the other hand, Enlightenment-era annals include diverse instances of one or another figure blending freethinking originality *and* wisdom deeply informed by tradition, or radical *and* conservative elements in the texture of their life and thought. Montesquieu's, and aspects of Locke's political philosophy can serve as relevant examples.

3) As the first line of criticism actually upholds rather than condemns the Enlightenment worldview, and the second can be construed as essentially monitory and corrective, it is this last, "third rail" that offers a more fundamental critique, and likely functions as the ultimate ground of many of the truly malign effects that can rightfully be attributed to Enlightenment ideology. The critical impetus here derives from the variability inherent in the very terms so basic to Enlightenment thinking. *Nature, Reason, Knowledge, Liberty, Individuality, Humanity.* These are big words and concepts, and everything depends upon how they are (consciously or unconsciously) construed or interpreted: separately, and as a whole complex constellation of interrelated ideas.

Any and every worldview implies a certain interpretation of nature, humanity, and divinity. The understanding of these terms characteristic of a given period depends, in turn, upon ancillary key concepts, the relevant set of which—as Carl Becker so aptly notes—changes over time. *Natural law, reason, first cause*...these and kindred terms, as we have seen, prove fundamental to Enlightenment thinking; but how exactly they are understood remains open to question and radically variable interpretation. Does "reason" mean the same thing for John Locke, or Montesquieu, or Tom Paine, as it does for Horkheimer and Adorno as they critique the dialectic of enlightenment? Is the *ego* that is the subject of the Cartesian *cogito* the same human *subject* to whom Kant addresses his categorical command *Sapere aude*! (Dare to know)? If so, are these identical with the autonomous self Patrick Deneen so forcefully critiques?

Both Horkheimer and Adorno and Deneen trace profound cultural and political dysfunction to certain intellectual premises underlying Enlightenment or liberal ideology. Are these the *same* premises I outlined in my synopsis and sketched over the course of the last several chapters? The *same* intellectual initiative that led to the birth of the United States of America, and, more generally, to the cherished values many persons all over the globe would recognize as their own?

Such questions call for redoubling our pending effort to comprehend the underlying basis of *the dual legacy of the Enlightenment*. We need resume, that is, the effort to distinguish those aspects of Enlightenment thought and ideals that are irreducibly positive, and which remain the indispensable core of any viable future, from those elements that are intrinsically problematical and flawed. It is the latter that invite distortion, corruption, and the calamity so visible in the modern world that remains—spiritually as well as materially—progeny and product of the Enlightenment.

We have already delved in some detail into Adorno and Horkheimer's and Deneen's critique of the heritage of the Enlightenment. Now, however, we are in a position to revisit the terms of these critiques against the background of the intellectual and cultural history sketched over the last few chapters, much of which highlights the *creative contributions* of that heritage and provides a more comprehensive framework of understanding.

The last, third line of criticism thus aims at pursuing a critique of enlightenment on, so to speak, its own terms—terms consistent with a peculiarly Western tradition of critical philosophy. Such an approach recognizes that the prevailing mold of the modern mind can only truly be transformed by working from *within* the storied depths of its extensive catacombs. Despite certain contemporary trends that imagine otherwise, it is impossible effectively to address the problems that confront us by jumping ship or throwing the whole cargo of Western thought overboard, as if it were nothing more valuable than so many chests of East India Company tea.

I refer to the current tendency, ever more prominent since the heady dawn of Derridean deconstruction half-a-century ago, to pretend that metaphysics is thoroughly outmoded so that we had best confront the pressing problems of contemporary life by eschewing philosophically oriented discourse altogether and sticking, with dogged ferocity, to reading and rewriting a social text scripted more or less exclusively in the language of race, gender, and class. The fallacy of such an attitude—one so pervasively dominant today as not to require or even admit of representative example—derives from the singularly uncritical illusion that we can somehow escape the bondage and biases of inherited forms of thought by simply dismissing the episteme, the project of knowledge, altogether, and declining to read the books that supposedly have infected Western culture with hurtful prejudice. Unfortunately, the most signal result of this intellectual malaise is a persistent unconsciousness of the most basic premises of one's own thought forms, which then perforce continue to manifest untransformed varieties of the very ideology one has supposedly rejected and magically transcended. Consequently, the very class of persons most anxious to repudiate the dominant forms of Western consciousness themselves end up as perpetrators of the sins of the fathers; simultaneously vehicles and victims of the dialectic of enlightenment.

No issue showcases this profoundly destructive dynamic more vividly than Covid World.

First of all, it should be frankly acknowledged that—*despite* ubiquitous critiques of racist and colonialist Eurocentrisms—the liberal ideology current today (and I employ the term "liberal" in the deeper and broader sense articulated by Deneen, and so to include most "conservative" as well as "liberal" politics) still buys lock, stock, and barrel into the Enlightenment worldview and the values it promotes.

The prevailing faith today, especially in international circles, remains no religious tradition, but a secular "religion of humanity" (cf. point #6 in the above synopsis) which (especially in its newer transhumanist permutation) trusts implicitly in the Truth of Science and looks to it and technology for the "progress" that can save civilization and create a better future. As in the 18th century, this rationalist/empiricist epistemology cooperates with the reigning political philosophy. While the corrosive dialectic of enlightenment has proceeded so far that our once sacrosanct individual rights have come increasingly under severe threat even in the so-called free world, the ideals of liberty, equality, and (the now dominant buzzword) justice remain the key words of the liberal creed, providing moral substance and commanding fervent and often highly charged devotion. Those championing these ideals typically look (as per the linkage of statism and individualism) to the administrative power of the nation state to secure and protect these rights.

Indeed, all in all, while not every single nuance of the worldview distilled in my six-point synopsis finds ready reflection today (many progressives take a less than sunny view of human nature and, in a kind of self-flagellating throwback to Puritanism, regard congenital racism as the new form of original sin), the overall framework holds largely and powerfully intact, though this truth generally goes largely unrecognized in our progressive, forward-looking culture.

This, however is no benign or harmless oversight; on the contrary, refusing consciously to acknowledge the historic origin of the values one espouses precludes self-conscious grasp of the *principles* that underwrite moral judgment. This not only weakens the capacity to promote those values; it renders one vulnerable to shadow forces (the negative, flip-side of archetypal ideas that emerge when these are enacted in an extreme and imbalanced fashion), and thus positively invites the corruption of those same values.

Progressive "social justice" movements today illustrate this all too vividly. Instead of championing liberty, equality, and fraternity, we hear today of "diversity, equity, and inclusion." The difference between these sets of terms would be worth an in-depth exploration. I will not undertake such here, but merely suggest that the transition from the first to the second set of terms can be read as, not only a dilution, but a degradation of authentic ideals.

Liberty, equality, and fraternity represent real spiritual ideals that cannot readily be translated into external or material form. Diversity, equity, and inclusion are much more immediately referable to external markers, and invite material and quantitative rather than spiritual and qualitative construction of social and ethical issues. (How many persons of color in this school? How many ethnicities are represented in this class? What dollar amount should we assign for reparations to restore a modicum of equity to that class of persons historically disadvantaged by slavery?) Correlatively, the ideological rigidity and proselytizing fervor that too often characterizes "social justice" initiatives today (initiatives very anxious to employ state power to achieve perceived goals) can well be construed as part and parcel of the "reign of quantity" and "dialectic of enlightenment."

The relevant mindset is, moreover, deeply congruent with the liberal community's uncritical embrace of the official Covid response, which enacts a systemic *betrayal* of the ideas that comprise the salutary spiritual core of the Enlightenment ethos.

Paradoxically enough, this angle of vision may prove one means of identifying and isolating the irreducibly *positive* values that underlie modernity. By holding Covid World up to the mirror of history, and comparing the actions comprising the official Covid response with many of the ideas articulated in my synopsis, we may perhaps begin to bring more clearly into view the core principles representing the philosophical and moral foundation of free society, and the destructive consequences of their sore neglect.

Glancing over the six principles with this end in mind, the very first stands out. In discussing it, we will, per force, engage the others (most immediately, the second and third) as well.

The tenet of radical doubt, the fundamental obligation—simultaneously intellectual, ethical, and spiritual— to submit any and all authoritative truth claims to critical examination, represents the first spectacular casualty of the pandemic and the campaign of fear that marked its official promotion.

Originally applying most powerfully to Church dogma (including the supposition of a geocentric universe), it points to—not only the license, but the obligation—to put "apparently unassailable forms of association, of belief and tradition" (Pagden) to the test of individual reason, conscience, and empirical evidence (nature). As such, it serves as the foundation of scientific method. Consequently, it is the rigorous observance of this principle—which naturally applies to scientific as well as religious and other forms of belief—that duly *legitimates* professions of knowledge and of truth in the modern world.

Covid World begins, however, with a dramatic and nigh complete abrogation of this principle in scientific, governmental, and civic circles. That beginning, moreover, never seems to end.

From the first, the Covid party line was promulgated in the scientific and medical as well as political sphere. Active, lively debate in the councils of science, and on the streets of cities, was not encouraged as an indispensable component of both scientific and democratic process. Instead, dissent from the officially authorized version of the truth was represented as ignorant, deluded, and dangerous: in short, a threat that should not be tolerated, but rather stamped out by any means necessary.

That is why Cait Corrigan, who stands for millions like her, was officially disinvited to her own graduation.[324]

That is why, in June of 2020, Canadian physiologist Dr. Donald Welsh, anguish palpable in his voice, declared: "Science has not been functioning properly for the last fifteen months as we address Covid-19."

That is why the mainstream medical career of renowned veteran physicians, like Dr. Paul Marik, have been destroyed.

On the medical front, this betrayal of scientific method, while evident in most every aspect of the Covid response, crystallized most transparently around the vaccine issue and the official dictum that vaccines are "Safe and Effective." From the first, this assertion was presented—not as a scientific hypothesis subject to critical question and inquiry—but as irrefutable truth; a form of quasi-religious dogma.

I say "quasi-religious" because, as the means of its *supposed* verification violated the most basic precepts of scientific method, it is not and never was scientific position, but always already a kind of myth, one designed to serve specific economic and political ends.

Let me further explain.

As the basis of scientific method, the tenet of radical doubt possesses a critical correlate, lucidly articulated by Karl Popper. In order for the truth of any scientific hypothesis to be even tentatively "verified," it must be subjected to *falsification.*[325] That means, it must be possible to imagine and formulate scenarios that definitely disprove the truth of a hypothesis. Newton's theory of gravitation would, for instance, be falsified if one dropped a baseball and, rather than falling to the earth, it floated upwards. Consequently, experiments should be designed and conducted in such a way that, if certain, unambiguously defined results are obtained, the proposed theory must be regarded as failing nature's test of evidence, and thus rejected as representative of scientific truth.

It is very clear that, from the first, the claim that the Covid vaccines are "safe and effective" was never thus tested. Certain inadequate and improperly conducted trials were run, but reasonable criteria for falsification were *never* clearly established. Moreover, in terms of the evidence supplied by observation of real time results after the roll out of the vaccines, the goal posts for what did or did not constitute "success" or efficacy were, as everyone knows, *ex post facto,* constantly moved.

Historically, an effective "vaccine" has been popularly understood to prevent infection and transmission, a standard that Covid mRNA gene therapies obviously woefully failed to meet. By now, moreover, a huge body of evidence is available that should rationally falsify claims that the vaccines are "effective," *if* standards of falsification (and thus scientific proof) had *ever* truly been on the table.

If falsification procedures have been lacking with respect to the matter of vaccine efficacy, the situation is even more egregious with respect to safety, in which context any pretense of real falsification was summarily abandoned from the first. By any reasonable measure, it is tragically clear from official data that the incidence of injury and death dramatically exceeds historic standards many, many times over. If the statement "the Covid vaccines are safe" is regarded as a scientific hypothesis, the evidence unambiguously indicates that empirical evidence, *the test of nature,* clearly *falsifies* that hypothesis, which must then, scientifically speaking, be regarded not as a (tentative) truth, but as a confirmed lie.

It should, moreover, be perfectly evident that within the canons of science, properly understood, there is no possible or reasonable justification for the active suppression of dissenting views, especially when these represent the conscientiously considered opinions of eminent scientists. The encouraging of such suppression and its explicit or tacit sanction by the community of scientists and the public at large is not (as the machine of state would have us believe) in the public interest. It is, however, the end of science, and the sure means of eroding the prestige and public trust it has won over the ages.

If the government and its health experts (headed by Dr. Anthony Fauci) were genuinely interested in scientific truth, and the public good that could flow from legitimate scientific inquiry, the highly qualified proponents of dissenting views should have been welcomed and their input incorporated into relevant decision-making processes from the first. Censoring their opinions might be defensible *if* these scientists were clearly impugning the integrity of science: promoting arguments not substantiated by reason or evidence; fraudulently manipulating data; arbitrarily dismissing contrary views and evidence; breaking codes of professional conduct and collegial respect; and, on that basis, encouraging—or even daring to try to compel—a course of action that could endanger the lives of untold persons.

Yet it is not the likes of Peter McCullough, Pierre Kory, George Fahreed, Harvey Risch, Robert Malone *et al* who can rightfully be so charged, but Fauci and his minions here and abroad.

The very fact that the health authorities have felt it necessary forcibly to silence respected critics from within the medical and scientific community, should—no matter what one's personal and professional views respecting vaccination and the like—be a sign of clear and present danger that the government's scientific business is not being conducted with the interests of truth and the public good foremost in mind. Indeed, within the circle of reputable and responsible scientific and medical practitioners (and here I am not speaking of anything else) the notion of "*misinformation*" should have no place whatsoever. If debate is open and free, truth will out; *that* is the scientific method. The only real danger lies, not in difference and dialogue, but in political and corporate control of the community of science.

Does not our Western heritage teach this truth? Perhaps the most famous bit of "misinformation" ever: that the earth revolves around the sun. We have seen what price the Church itself paid for the suppression of this once blasphemous truth.

So much for the repeated claim that our official Covid Response is "following the science" and thus living up to the rule of reason characteristic of our Enlightenment heritage.

So much for our pretense to be governing—and agreeing to be governed—as *rational* human beings.

This last remark pushes us from the domain of science into that of politics. As observed in our prior rehearsal of relevant cultural and intellectual history, epistemological and political currents run, like the waves of a single stream, concurrently; and the profound and systematic corruption of the integrity of science—which we look to for truth—is accompanied by an equally disastrous corruption of the politics and the practice of governance, which we look to as the principal executor of goodness, the administration of moral and material justice in the public realm (cf. Point #5). The corruption of the very foundation of the project of knowledge is accompanied by a like betrayal of the first principles of liberal democratic governance as articulated by the likes of Locke and Montesquieu and inscribed in the founding documents of the United States of America.

The official Covid agenda, falsely tricked out in the royal robes of science but without sound empirical or rational basis for its claims, consequently depends on the gross and systematic violation of politically guaranteed freedoms to enforce its program. I have already documented the comprehensive abrogation of constitutionally guaranteed rights—first and foremost, the first amendment rights of freedom of speech, religion, assembly, and the press—characteristic of the official Covid response, which governmental overreach manifestly flies in the face of the enlightened political philosophy instrumental to the founding of this nation and (subsequently) democratic forms of governance across the face of the globe.

All this is driven forward, of course, in the name of that crown jewel of Enlightenment philosophy: that religious reverence for the Party of Humanity (Point #6) that moved so many to believe that, by obeying government edicts and disdaining, excluding and even violently ostracizing those who declined to do so, they were "doing their part" and placing the value of the Other, the human community at large, above and beyond their own self-interest. Yet *"the welfare of humanity is always the alibi of tyrants,"* and #6 is last on my list for a reason. If a given regime governs in a manner that betrays the prior principles upon which any grounded and genuine relation to the idea of humanity depends, one can be sure that the vision of humanity and its welfare *actually* operative is partial, corrupt, partisan, and based on illusion rather than truth.

Refer, for instance, to Point #5, and the protection of individual rights and liberties integral to it: the government's own preeminent duty to guarantee and preserve the essential freedoms basic to democratic society. Why has the official Covid response met with such impassioned resistance both here and abroad? Because people intuit that compelling any citizen to submit to an injection that has not been proven either safe or effective violates the natural rights—indeed, the most basic such right of self-preservation—of the individual, and so the foundation of both human morality and legitimate governance in a democratic society. Citizens around the world recognize that it is the responsibility of persons of conscience to resist the imposition of a civil law which so clearly contradicts the just order of things and contravenes people's unalienable rights. Those rights are grounded in an intelligence the authority of which transcends that of any government or particular person; a *logos* that functions as the source of all universal ideals (including liberty and equality), and which the likes of Locke, Montesquieu and Jefferson (none of whom were religious enthusiasts, and all of whom were eminently rational persons) recognize as a species of divinity.

It is true, of course, that many persons who oppose the official Covid response do so in the name of both God and freedom. The name of God, however, does not carry much legal weight in the western world today, although—for better or for worse—that has been changing. I would in any event suggest that (although religiously inclined, after my own fashion) we can hardly solve our problems by reverting to a medieval order wherein God was all in all, and biblical scripture the one privileged source of revealed truth.

In the wake of the Renaissance, Reformation, Scientific Revolution, and Enlightenment, it seems right and proper that any claims made in the name of God need comport with claims made in the name of the nature of things as revealed by reason and by science, and so, too, the peculiar genius of our species, the Spirit of Humanity.[326] Because ultimately, as in Pico's Renaissance vision, and the most enlightened writings of the French *philosophes,* and even, in his way, St. Thomas, we must come to recognize and hold sacred, not simply God, or Man, or virgin Nature, but that *Logos,* that law—at once divine and natural—that holds (like a grail) the mystery of the *convergence* of these three. It is in striving to do so—not parroting old tropes, be these "liberal" or "conservative" in tenor—that we might make ancient Wisdom new, and begin to find a better way forwards towards the future.

The path toward such vision, however, is prepared by clear sight of the world before us: the still dark Covid World that persistently threatens—in the never-resting guise of the leviathan Machine—to overwhelm us. That dark

Power pretends to hold high the torch of enlightenment, but the muse of history reveals all too clearly that it really seeks to extinguish that bright source. The powers-that-be today (name them how you will) do not honorably represent the true value of our Western heritage. Instead, we are governed from powers on high that rule irrationally in the name of reason, unscientifically in the name of science, and inhumanely in the name of humanity.

For what we face today is nought but a form of medievalism in a modern guise. Science itself has acceded to the throne of culture, but—like the Church before it—its institutions have been infected by greed, power, and politics. It rules with an arrogant swagger, sure of its by now centuries-old reign; but more and more, its offices are corrupt, and—in the highest circles—it no longer even pretends to have to live up to its name, to justify its power by chaste observance of the rites that ushered in its ascendancy, or any true devotion to the cause of truth and reason.

"*Vaccines are Safe and Effective.*" This, as stated, is no scientific truth, but religious dogma authorized—not by reason—but the "hag of superstition." Indeed, is it not obvious that vaccines are the new Indulgences of the modern all-powerful Church of Scientism and Technology, whose board and clergy consists of Big Pharma and Big Tech CEOs, the WHO and WEF global elite?

There is, we are constantly told, much of which to be horribly afraid. Devilish Nature always has another nasty trick (a.k.a, *the next pandemic*) up her sleeve, and if we are not prepared, there will be hell to pay. So: trust us. No need for you to take responsibility for your own health, body and soul. We health experts, we alchemical magicians, we will mix and we will administer the elixir that will save you from sickness and death, now and forever more.

Of course, it comes at a price: human freedom.

In 1411, one-hundred years before Luther, Prague university professor and theologian Jan Hus began speaking out, persistently and powerfully, against Indulgences and other abuses of Church authority. Dispute followed dispute. Many times, Hus was ordered to recant. He would not.

In 1415, Jan Hus, the Luther before Luther, was burnt at the stake.

Remember Ernest Gellner's description of the first rule of Enlightenment Rationalism?

> *There are no privileged or a priori substantive truths.... All facts and all observers are equal. There are no privileged Sources or Affirmations, and all of them can be queried.*

Who would dare maintain that such holds in the domain of vaccine science—in the domain of medicine—today? No unsettling queries, no inconvenient truths are tolerated. Disagreement is not regarded as the engine of true science, but as *heresy*— increasingly punishable, not only by professional discipline and exile, but by criminal law.

And if your dissident doctors and scientists are the disobedient clergy who must be silenced, your everyday anti-vaxxers—the defenders of health freedom who stand on the unalienable rights of bodily autonomy—are the new Huguenots, to be shunned, exiled, or tortured on the rack of public opinion in front of cheering crowds. Likewise, and still more tragically, are the vaccine-injured, who—for the sin of wishing to testify to the terrible natural facts, the empirical evidence scribed in the visible form of their afflicted bodies—are silenced, denied, and indeed, in far too many instances, driven to the terrible extreme of self-slaughter.

Science? Reason? Tolerance? Benevolence? Liberty? Love of your fellow human being? These are indeed Enlightened values, but one may as well attribute them to the Spanish Inquisitor as to our governing regime, the Leviathan Machine today, which is—alas—equipped with *far* more powerful tools of surveillance, and more far-reaching and subtle tools of torture.

Indeed, the ruling regime today is likely far more powerful and dangerous than its medieval and early modern counterparts; more powerful and dangerous than the Roman Catholic Church, or any tyrannical King. Because today, the Leviathan state is so much more than one readily identified central power or body. It is, as we have seen, an integrated Matrix of elite persons, corporations, institutions, and international as well as national organizations. As far as Covid is concerned, the Church itself has been, to some degree, taken in (the pope encourages vaccination), though it remains a relatively poor brother amongst the more relevant titans of power.

This, then, is the profound irony we confront today. The modern world professes (even if unconsciously) enlightened values of rationality, progress, liberty, and humanity. Yet the very sectors of society that rose to displace the reigning power of the Church have themselves been melded into a frightful organ of power as dogmatic, intolerant, tyrannical, and corrupt as the Church at its Inquisitorial worst. Today, in Covid world, science is not science; medicine does not aim to heal; government is not democratic; the press (including Big Tech sponsored social media) is not free; and commerce does not serve to equalize opportunity. Just as the authority of the Church was destroyed from within because it no longer served God and betrayed Christian values in the name of Christ; so do the "enlightened" elites of today, from Schwab to Fauci to Tedros and indeed the Matrix as a whole, betray the very heritage they purport to represent.

Blinded by fear and by ignorance to the systematic corruption of our own ideals, we find ourselves far down the road of the diabolical dialectic that turns true enlightenment into its opposite, and democracy into despotism. More and more Americans—and more and more truly cosmopolitan citizens of the world—are waking up to the bitter truth that the people can trust no one but themselves and the Spirit that speaks, in freedom and love, in the sacred precincts of the conscience.

Superavit

Never does the heroic deed
go up in smoke. The funeral pyre
taught this to Constance—
from the hot baptismal fire
a noble spirit rose yet higher.

There looms yet large in our own day
the Reformer Hus.
Awed by fiery intellect,
we bow still in deep respect
before his genius.

He, whom the Council condemned,
was, at heart, deep and pure,
persuaded of his office.
The glowing stake wrote his name
in the illumined book of fame.

—Rainer Maria Rilke [327]

Chapter 9

UNNECESSARY HYPOTHESIS: THE ECLIPSE OF THE LOGOS

Paul Kingsnorth, author of *Real England*,[328] can hardly be accused of carelessly dispraising the roots of his culture. It is, however, true that the ex-ecoactivist, one of today's most consistently insightful critics of the Matrix/Machine, can speak as convincingly as anyone of the ravages wrought by the Western mind-set, especially in its modern guise. Alluding to the civilizational structures responsible for his middle-class upbringing, Kingsnorth writes:

> Today's left is correct to point out that these structures were built on empire and slavery and the razing of forest and the stripping bare of the wealth of nations we overpowered. But there was something else too that made me pucker my lips when I heard the phrase "Western civilization."
>
> It was, I think now, an instinctive feeling for the arrogance of modernity. Our etiolated rationalism, the desire to impose our will on the world, the assumption that *we know best* which survived the collapse of our empires and flowed effortlessly into the age of "development." The insistence that African children should attend Western-style schools and be issued laptops; that Pacific islanders should become Protestant Christians in suits and ties; that all nations everywhere should "trade freely" with our Black Ships (as if they had the choice) and set themselves up as "liberal democracies" just like ours; that our wars are good wars and their wars are bad wars; that all the world will be progressing together when They have all agreed to become like Us.[329]

Despite such sentiments, Kingsnorth refuses to indulge in any kind of one-sided repudiation of the West. In fact, in a series of essays themed "The Culture of Inversion," Kingsnorth excoriates the woke ideology that can find little or no good in it. Caught between abhorrence of the worst consequences of Western civilization and tempered appreciation of a tradition he can and will not disown, Kingsnorth finds himself somewhat at a loss as to the ground upon which he might stand to defend the West, if indeed he should feel moved to do so:

> This is why, though I will never condemn those "dead white men," neither can I stand up and "defend the West" in some uncomplicated fashion. The West is my home—but the West has also eaten my home. Should I stand up to save it from itself? How would that happen? What would I be fighting for?[330]

These are vexing questions, and the writer's words bespeak an inner anguish. Seeking further to clarify the issue for himself and his readers, Kingsnorth—distancing himself from the culture wars that so often dominate today's politics—aims to shift the ground of discussion:

> No, when we are talking about fighting for "the culture," or fighting against it, I think we are missing the mark. Culture is, after all...a spiritual byproduct. Cultures are built around claims and beliefs about the otherworld: about God or gods, about correct worship, about the nature of reality and the meaning of virtue. Knock out the spiritual core of any culture, and however hard people fight, its fate is sealed.[331]

These are wise words, and the perspective expressed here resonates with the angle Kingsnorth explores in both "The Cross and the Machine" and "What Progress Wants."[332]

"Progress," of course, represents one of the chief ends of Enlightenment, the fourth point of my six-point synopsis of Enlightenment ideals. In his essay, however, Kingsnorth construes progress as the common name of an all-consuming dark force, essentially the same mythically-charged monster poet Alan Ginsberg hails as Moloch,[333] and other biblically-minded critics, the Adversary or Anti-Christ.

Why such heavy and sinister weight placed upon the shoulders of what appears a relatively benign concept? Who, after all, wants to stand in the way of the inventive momentum that has given us everything from flush toilets to electric light bulbs and now—in the brightening dawn of the Fourth Industrial Revolution—continues to promise so much more?

Today many recognize that the God of Progress deals as generously in curse as in blessing; and it can be difficult to tell which is which. Kingsnorth gives philosophical reasons for questioning the benevolence of this powerful deity, one whom the human being, in an inversion of the biblical *topos*, creates in its own image:

> The modern epoch, guided by science, reason, and the self, rejects the notion of anything "unseen" or "beyond." From the 18th century onwards, philosophy sweeps away religion: the world is now understood in purely

> human terms, and managed with purely human notions. Everything becomes immanent: literally down-to-Earth. There are no principalities or powers, and so everything is potentially transformable and explicable through human might. This is another way of framing Guénon's "Western deviation": a "progressive materialisation" that leads us into a "reign of quantity," in which we take on the role of the Creator for ourselves.[334]

René Guénon's book *The Reign of Quantity and the Signs of the Times*[335] appeared in 1945, and so at virtually the same time as Adorno and Horkheimer's *Dialectic of Enlightenment*. As the cited material suggests, the coincidence is not accidental: the two books, both published near the end of the Third Reich, harp on similar themes. Kingsnorth sums the gist of Guénon's argument with the punch line: "What Progress wants is the end of transcendence."

Thinking in concert with another writer, the Italian philosopher Augusto Del Noce, Kingsnorth laments the break with tradition and consequent sanction of a philosophy of radical immanence:

> Both the followers of Plato and the followers of Christ (not to mention every other culture on Earth, in their own particular way) believed that truth was transcendent, eternal and uncreated, and could be known through some combination of faith, practice and reason. No longer.[336]

In Kingsnorth's mind, this loss of transcendence marks the end of religion and the beginning of a modern era that has bequeathed us our hopelessly broken world. Asking, with Del Noce, *what is it that the modern mindset renders no longer possible?*, Kingsnorth summarizes the Italian's response:

> The answer...is simple: what is excluded is the "supernatural," religious transcendence.... For rationalists, certainty about an irreversible historical process towards radical immanentism has replaced what for medieval thinkers was faith in revelation.[337]

In accord with this orientation, Kingsnorth's Covid World essays suggest that humanity's path forward need involve a recovery, a reclamation of the religious sensibility that countenances a quest for transcendence, and so some form of reconnection with what he here unabashedly names "eternal and uncreated" truth.

I approve the transcendental drift of Kingsnorth's thought as well as Del Noce's, but not without caveat. Despite his sensitivity to cultural roots, I am not sure Kingsnorth—who openly confesses his confusion as to the salient core of Western culture—sufficiently acknowledges what both Adorno and

Horkheimer (whom he does not discuss) and Patrick Deneen (whom he does) clearly recognize: that we cannot move beyond the dire deficiencies of our modern Western Enlightenment-influenced worldview by turning back the clock to some pre-18th-century mentality and pretending that everything after St. Francis represents a giant mistake. On the contrary, any viable future vision need integrate Enlightenment-era ideals and values—not partially or fragmentarily, but integrally and completely. Such a vision need account for the revolutionary necessity that marked the advent of these ideals in world history and so, too, the dawn of modernity.

Correlatively, does not any warm embrace of a search for transcendence need be approached with caution? Did not a decidedly otherwordly orientation qualify as a defining feature of the Augustine-influenced medieval era that modernity sought—for good reason—to leave behind? Is it conceivable that a reversion to religion, as such has traditionally been construed and practiced in the mainstream of Western culture, can offer a novel account of the nature of reality so as to push science aside, reclaim the throne of cultural sovereignty, and guide us towards a new and better tomorrow?

This is unlikely in the extreme. Nor do I believe revival of traditional forms of worship or adoration of God (Father *or* Son) can license *circumventing* the tasks prescribed by our modernity. That requires honoring the inherent value of our existence as embodied human beings living in space and time, engaged with a world we are given to know—or at least *experience*—through our senses.

Indeed, this truth of which Kingsnorth speaks; this truth that is, and always has been, "transcendental, eternal and uncreated"—even presuming we could attain knowledge of it, what good might that do, if we did not further understand how such *supernatural* verity relates to nature, and human life in it, here and now? Any attempt to reinstate a medieval or Protestant insistence on the supremacy of biblical revelation (*sola scriptura*) revisits the same ground that so failed the Church in the 16th and 17th centuries.

Moreover, if anything can be stated with absolute certainty, it is not the debatable meaning of any scriptural revelation, but this: *nature*—at least in her earthly aspect—is *not* eternal or uncreated, but *changes*.

The same can be said of the mortal human being, body and soul. Our psychological as well as our physical existence is marked by processes of growth, decay, and metamorphosis. No ontology that identifies truth more or less exclusively with a transcendent, eternal, uncreated realm of being—be it called "the heavenly city of God" as in Augustine, or simply *nous* (the intelligible realm of ideal form) as in Plato—can in and of itself quench our modern thirst to know the nature of things in themselves. That nature—whatever its ultimate essence—includes existence in a sensible world that is, visibly and indubitably, a realm—not of everlasting being—but of becoming, and thus a world of *progress*. Or *regress*. Or both.

Even so, it *is* true that early modern thinkers from the Renaissance to the Enlightenment were by no means postmoderns enamored of transience and probabilistic happenstance, or even Romantics infatuated (like Goethe) with processes of organic unfolding. Philosophers such as Descartes or Newton or Montesquieu sought to arrive at the *laws* that explained diverse phenomena in terms of invariable patterns and so that degree of *regularity* that render them *intelligible* (as *principles* of reason or ideal *types*) to the mind.

In fact, the episteme, the project of knowledge, has always entailed one or another method of construing the *ratio* relating sensible and intelligible forms, as in Plato's Divided Line. Such *ratio* is the root of *reason*, which is intimately related to the Greek notion of *logos*, and, by extension, our concept of *law*. All of these interrelated terms are integral not only to the more metaphysical dimensions of the project of knowledge but, as we have seen, to the extension of the episteme into the related domains of morality and political (as well as natural) science. The Parable of the Cave that introduces Plato's elaboration of the Divided Line (the clearest and most famous exposition of the foundation of Platonic ontology and epistemology) appears in Book VI of his *Republic*, in which context it spearheads the philosopher's attempt to sketch the political philosophy and forms of governance conducive to the establishment of an ideal state.

I pursue these peregrinations with this point in mind: if we are, *á la* Kingsnorth and his fellow critics of the Machine (from Mumford and Guénon to Deneen and Del Noce) to frame a more viable vision of the future, we need confront what has, since Luther and Galileo, most egregiously crippled the *spiritual* progress of Western culture: what Emerson called "the adulterous divorce...between the intellect and holiness."[338] I understand Emerson as highlighting the division between the study of the nature of the universe and of man contributed by reason, philosophy and all the branches of science (which intellectual endeavor we may call the episteme, or project, of knowledge); and that lived (*felt* and *willed*) relation to the divine source of all which in the Judeo-Christian tradition finds expression in theology and religious practice.

As a consequence of developments in the early modern period already discussed, the modern worldview looks to science for knowledge of nature, and (if not moved to atheism) to religion for relationship with God. The laws of nature are thought to be essentially unrelated to the spiritual laws ordering the relation between divinity and humanity; the *logos* of one (the basis of scientific laws, and our perception of them) is entirely distinct from the *logos* of the other (the divine Word). Correlatively, the sensible world of material nature is imagined as fundamentally and essentially separable from any moral or spiritual truth.

Unlike Newton, the typical science-minded person of today does not think the law of gravity has anything to do with divine intelligence or the moral ordering of human affairs. On the contrary, mainstream scientific culture encourages us to believe that the causal agency invested in scientific law *replaces* that traditionally attributed to divine law, rendering belief in the latter—at least with reference to natural history—extraneous, irrational and (to speak bluntly) little more than anachronistic, ignorant nonsense.

This fateful schism—between God and Nature, religion and science, spirit and matter, reason and revelation, the mind and the heart—is by now deeply ingrained in our culture. It is so entrenched that an astute nature-loving writer like Paul Kingsnorth can—upon overview of the crises of our times—seek for answers under the aegis of religion or a quest for transcendence *without* explicitly questioning the epistemological premises that underlie the science that frames our understanding of nature. Kingsnorth does not (in his Covid-era Substack essays, at least) presume to ask whether the spiritual deficiency in our culture does not stem in good measure from the way we presume to *know* the sensible sphere, the multiplicitous phenomena that comprise our experience of *this* created world.

To put the gist of the matter another way: I would contend that Kingsnorth is wrong, and on the wrong track, when he says "From the 18th century onward, philosophy sweeps away religion," implying that we owe our present, desperate plight to this rude displacement. While it is undoubtedly true that modern science rests upon philosophical premises introduced and elaborated in the early modern period, and would have been inconceivable without the intellectual revolution engineered by the likes of Descartes and Bacon, if philosophy enjoyed a relatively brief period of ascendancy (the eighteenth is sometimes called "the philosophic century"), its cultural clout was superseded in relatively short order by the brainchild we call science. The central and defining story of modernity features not only the early rationalist critique of religion spurred by dogmatic intolerance, but, as well, the subsequent chapter that features *science sweeping away philosophy,* and acceding to the throne of culture it still occupies today.

We are not, after all, ruled by philosopher-kings, as Plato recommended. Far from it. We are—as Covid World demonstrates— governed by scientists, or rather, by the techno- and bureaucratic derivatives thereof: Dr. Anthony Fauci, a host of world "health experts," and the computer scientists who make the models and algorithms that run our lives.

That accession, moreover, assumes the form of a usurpation, even a matricidal coup. Once Science took the throne, it willfully forgot and abused its parentage, and put Philosophy, the love of Wisdom, away in a closet—or a dungeon. Science has subsequently pretended it can rule wisely *without* the antiquated guidance of any sort of deep metaphysical reflection, any contemplative reconsideration of the ground of its knowledge and its power, forgetting all the while that it owes its very birthright to the same.

The success of that experiment? The state of the world speaks volumes on that score.

I do not intend to suggest that Kingsnorth's call for contemplation of a transcendental dimension of an "eternal, uncreated" being is out of place or misguided. On the contrary, I wish merely to suggest that such can only be truly transformative if cast in *an undogmatic, distinctly modern, and philosophically self-conscious mold*: one that deliberately confronts and contests the materialistic premises that ground the current scientific construction of the nature of nature. That means, too, a worldview that—breaking decisively with the ontological dualism that pervades so much of Western thought—recognizes that transcendental knowledge can only prove its validity and worth insofar as it truly reveals the value inherent in our earthly or material existence and affords a revelation of the meaning of nature and the embodied life of the human soul.

This insistence might be considered trivial if history did not confirm that an orientation towards the transcendent has often come at the cost of more down-to-earth commitments. That is indubitably the case, not only with diverse species of Eastern philosophy, but (more immediately relevant to Kingsnorth's argument) for Plato and medieval Christianity. Both of these streams accord a spiritual, ideal or heavenly "other" world an ontological and valuative superiority that derogates that of the sensible world in time. In the Parable of the Cave, Plato regards our phenomenal existence as a realm of shadows comprised of insubstantial and deceptive images that delude and blind us from appreciating the higher reason illumined by light of the sun. Christianity, in the wake of Augustine, has never cast off a kindred Platonically-influenced sense of the inherent fallenness of earthly existence; an aversion to nature that regards this world as, primarily, a realm of devious temptation.

The historical record reveals two closely related and convenient ways to avoid the effort involved in attaining to detailed and comprehensive knowledge of the nature of this (visible) world, the very aim characteristic of the encyclopedic endeavors of Enlightenment philosophers. First, one can declare this world purely phenomenal and so essentially illusory. Secondly and correlatively, one can decide—true being and meaning abiding elsewhere—the effort is, in any case, not worth the effort.

The poet Rilke, whose Catholic upbringing was marked by his mother's excessive piety, registers an eloquent complaint on this score. Insofar as Rilke here holds Christianity's otherworldly orientation directly responsible for the unconscionable ravages of this world, the passage offers a telling counterpoint to Kingsnorth's call for transcendence:

> They have made a *métier* out of Christian living.... In their zeal, they do not hesitate to make this life, which should be an object of desire and trust for us, bad and worthless—and so they hand over the earth more and more to those who are ready to gain at least temporary and quickly run profit from it, vain and suspect as it is, and no good for anything better. This increasing exploitation of life, is it not a result of the century-old denial of the worth of this world? What folly to direct our thoughts to a Beyond, when we are surrounded here by tasks and expectations and future prospects! What deceit to misappropriate pictures of present delight in order to sell them behind our backs to heaven! Oh! the impoverished earth ought long ago to have called in all these loans which have been drawn on its happiness so that the Hereafter might be adorned with them. Does death really become less opaque because these lightning devices have been dragged into place behind it? And, since a vacuum cannot persist, will not all that has been taken away from earth be replaced by sham? [339]

It is thus well and good to drop the names of Plato and Christ, and recognize the yearning for spiritual transcendence innate in the soul, but how are we to seek knowledge of the eternal in a fashion that does not repeat, in a new guise, the destructive ideological partialities and prejudices of our premodern past? How are we to do so in a manner commensurate with the impulse that precipitated the Renaissance, Reformation, Scientific Revolution, and Enlightenment, and all the authentic soul-spiritual aims inherent in the evolution of consciousness that birthed our modernity?

I am suggesting the necessity of seeking a teaching that reconciles the project of knowledge—the episteme sourced in ancient Greece—with the religious inspiration associated with the Hebrew and Christian tradition, annulling "the adulterous divorce…between intellect and holiness."[340] Following this Emersonian theme, this may well require attaining an "*original* relation to the universe,"[341] one that takes no traditional doctrine (scientific or religious) as endpoint. Where might we find a teaching that delivers knowledge of not a purely mystical or religious reality, but the entirety of our experience of nature and culture—the whole of the created world in a manner that values rather than denigrates the same? How may we cultivate a frame of mind that supplies knowledge of a sort that promotes progress, spiritually *as well as* materially construed? A teaching, moreover, that achieves that goal in a manner commensurate with the cardinal value of that *liberty* that serves, by virtue of natural law, as the proud birthright of the individual soul, and does so after a fashion responsive to the *universal spirit of humanity* that bonds all citizens in freedom and in love?

Yes, by all means, let us have Plato, and Christ, and transcendent truth once again, but not in any old form that does not transmute the very ground—ontological, cosmological, epistemological, moral, religious, political, and economic—of our modernity.

The first words of Emerson's first book—notably titled, simply *Nature*—speak to this aim:

> Our age is retrospective. It builds the sepulchres of the fathers. It writes biographies, histories, and criticism. The foregoing generations beheld God and nature face to face; we, through their eyes. Why should not we also enjoy an original relation to the universe? Why should not we have a poetry and philosophy of insight and not of tradition, and a religion by revelation to us, and not the history of theirs?[342]

This, of course, is a tall—a toweringly tall—order. How might we so much as begin so daunting an enterprise? We have, as a point of departure, the still pending question: how and why is it that genuine Enlightenment ideals have metamorphosed into the catastrophe of our modern Machine-driven dialectic of enlightenment, the soul-numbing reign of quantity that licks the boots of a Moloch-like God of Progress? If the aforementioned values and impulses reflect constructive evolutionary currents, what is it in the historic articulation of the modern worldview—one definitively shaped by the "new faith" in modern science—that has proved conducive to imperialism, racism, sexism, colonialism, ecological destruction, social and economic inequity, political despotism, even totalitarianism, and all the disasters afflicting humanity today?

In responding to the provocation provided by Paul Kingsnorth, we have found a path for inquiry into this issue. Is it not probable that the root of the problem inheres in precisely the systematic schism that has cleft modern consciousness in two? As we have seen, *logos*—reason—figures as the vital center of the modern worldview. In light of this, how are we to construe our nature and destiny if our sense of the material and spiritual worlds is hopelessly split, so that we imagine the physical laws discoverable by science to have nothing whatsoever to do with the moral universe wherein we move and live as human souls? Today, imagination of the *amoral* character of scientific law delimits our vision of reality so that we have no intellectually coherent sense of any soul-spiritual dimension of existence at all. A materialistically construed nature has swallowed humanity and divinity whole.

Who, after all, can gainsay the truth that, as it stands with humanity at present, our forms of material knowledge offer no spiritual enlightenment, while our forms of spiritual knowing bear all too little material force?

In view of this predicament, we must look to the very ground of our modern science—the bearer of modern culture's sovereign crown, and arbiter of its truth—for the cause of our afflictions. Nor should we, after all, be so clueless in this regard. We have already identified ample cause for concern and pressing questions which harken back, once more, to the philosophical and anthropological assumptions underlying modernity's prevailing view of nature, divinity, and humanity. In fact, we have covered much of the relevant ground already; identified specifically modern constructions of nature, man, and divinity that invite the diverse kinds of catastrophe marring the face of the globe today. Now, after the history recounted in the present part of the book, it remains for us to elaborate those problematical premises more fully and clarify the critical difference between those molds of Enlightenment thought conducive to true human dignity and freedom, and those that tend towards annihilation of the same.

We can start, once more, with Descartes, for the ontological, cosmological, and epistemological assumptions inscribed in the *cogito, ergo sum* establish the central type of the modern self and, coincidently, constellate the ground of its native deficiencies. While I have praised the spirit of radical doubt exemplified by Descartes and lauded his effort to discover truth, not by reference or deference to any external source but in and through the action of his own mind, it nonetheless remains imperative to look still more closely at the peculiar mode of thinking or reason characteristic of the *cogito* and the type of world the Cartesian subject effectively constructs.

A terrible thirst for *certainty* catalyzed Descartes's philosophic quest, and he could not find the well of truth outside the domain of his own mental agency. He could not interpret, with any degree of assurance, the testimony of his senses, and so averted his contemplative gaze from the body and from nature. Any dogmatic concept of God, too, was, for the sharp-minded Frenchman, a brand-product manufactured and delivered from elsewhere: from a source the veracity of which he could neither test nor trust. All that he could affirm with absolute certainty was the current of his own intellectual activity; a current, he discovered, that inevitably eddied back to its own center. As Descartes registered this fact, the resultant shock of surprised recognition prompted, as a kind of philosophic abreaction, the famous formula: *cogito, ergo sum.* Thus was the modern mind cast in a self-reflexive mold of thought; thus was the human being recreated in the image of a self-subsistent deity, center of the universe.

As history demonstrates, this revision conferred great power upon the human self, the *ego* become, suddenly, less a *subject* than a *sovereign*, or somehow, both at once: a being and a consciousness separate from an objective world outside it, and one that owed no real allegiance or tribute to any superior form of intelligence. Nor was this subject bound, by bonds of kinship or reverence, to any world—any nature—it did not itself create.

This description may seem not to square with certain facts pertaining to Descartes himself, insofar as he remained—for the record, at least—a faithful Catholic, and one always anxious to demonstrate how the forms of his thought confirmed rather than conflicted with Church doctrine. That dogma, of course, prescribed worship of no autonomous human agency, but adoration of the one Almighty All-knowing Creator God. Yet Descartes's very anxiety on this score invites the suspicion attached to one who protests too much. There is good reason why Descartes did not escape charges of atheism, and why, some years after his death, the Catholic Church banned his books. Neither the skeptical bent of his intellectual genius nor the premises of the philosophy generated by his method of thinking comported well with traditional theology. They did so much less, in fact, than in the case of Kepler prior to him, or Newton or Montesquieu after.

I have previously cited passages from Kepler, Newton, and Montesquieu (as well as Aquinas and Locke) that bear witness to the religious conviction that underwrites their philosophy, whether that philosophy be primarily natural or political in kind. To be sure, these various figures exhibit diverse and, in many respects, widely divergent types of thought. The ensemble represents quite a mix of Catholic and Protestant, theistic, Neoplatonic, and deistically inclined casts of mind. Even so, all pledge allegiance, not merely to God, but—in one form or another—to the law that, as the emanation of divine intelligence or reason, lends meaning, pattern, and order to the universe: the law that thus manifests in—and indeed as—nature.[343]

We could express this truth in a manner that respects both Greek and Judeo-Christian traditions (and indeed suggests the principal avenue of their confluence) by saying that all these figures recognize a *Logos*—a Reason or Word or creative intelligence that is the origin and ground of *all* law. That *Logos* is, in the words of the Gospel of John, one with God, and representative of the emanent power of the divine mind that creates and preserves the universe.

Descartes's oeuvre hardly lacks professions of allegiance to God as the Supreme Being and Intelligence. I would, however, contend that, whatever the letter of one or another Cartesian text may be, the spirit of his philosophy, as elaborated in his famous *Discourse*, does *not* exhibit a similar deference to any *Logos* emanating from the Godhead. That is, the very essence of the *cogito* involves what amounts to a *usurpation* of the sovereignty of the *Logos* by what is manifestly and explicitly no sort of divine, but a purely human reason. For Descartes, the agent source of all possible science or knowledge inheres *not* in a divine intelligence, or *Logos,* in which the aspiring human mind may *participate* and, in so doing, gain a degree of *enlightenment,* but in the peculiarly self-reflexive brand of "rational" cognitive process that finds formulaic expression in *cogito, ergo sum.*

The consequences of this epochal displacement are multiple and profound. In positing itself as the very fount of being and conscious intelligence, the ego practically denies divinity (godhead) that privilege, and *simultaneously,* deprives the sensible universe—nature, or the Creation—the status of an immanent or embodied expression of divine *Logos.*

The path towards this result had already been prepared by nominalism's exaggeration of the dualism latent in so much Western philosophy and theology, but Descartes radicalized the spirit/matter (or mind/body) split still more rigidly and starkly. The self-conscious human ego counts as *res cogitans*, a thinking substance or subject. Nature, on the other hand, stands opposite that conscious intelligence as *res extensa*—a substance or "thing" lacking consciousness, inherent intelligence, or any indwelling principle of life. Nature is rather essentially inert matter, the defining character of which is nothing but pure extension. This understanding naturally goes hand in glove with Galileo's reduction of nature's reality to those primary qualities (weight, volume, spatial extension, and the like) subject to exact measurement and quantification. It also invites the kind of corpuscular atomic theory (borrowed from Presocratic Greek philosophers such as Democritus and Leuccipus) that Descartes embraced, insofar as all those primary qualities could be plausibly understood as effects of collocations of particles that comprised the "substance" of matter, and so nature itself as *res extensa* writ large.

This construction of nature lends itself to the kind of mechanistic materialism that underwrites Descartes's natural philosophy and continues to condition mainstream thinking today. (This is so despite quantum physics, systems theory and other relevant 20th-century developments that, theoretically speaking, render the paradigm obsolete in the precincts of science itself.) If nature is nought but a giant billiard table populated by inanimate atomic units, then causality can naturally be explained on the model of all that results from the interplay of these atomic units and the purely physical "forces" evidently involved in their interactions. It seems perfectly rational that one billiard ball will be sent into a given pocket of the universe when another, traveling at a specific measurable speed, strikes it at a given angle, so that the laws of mechanics, once discovered, can provide perfectly "natural" and purely material explanation for anything and everything that transpires upon the uniform surface of the cosmos.

Michael Pollan again:

> My default perspective is that of the philosophical materialist, who believes that matter is the fundamental substance of the world and the physical laws it obeys should be able to explain everything that happens. I start from the assumption that nature is all that there is and gravitate toward scientific explanation of phenomena.[344]

The mechanical philosophy, however (and, it should be emphasized, its effective extension into diverse fields of human and social as well as natural science, most all of which remain governed by the rationalist spirit of mechanism), rests upon theoretical premises fundamentally *incommensurate* with traditionally received ideas of *logos* and of law. It is, moreover, the degradation, occultation, and even occlusion of the latter—perhaps more than any other single feature—that marks the horizon of the modern era.

What befalls the (idea of the) *Logos* in the course of the fateful transition to a world dominated by what today qualifies as science?

Even as the Cartesian subject or ego appropriates consciousness and intelligence to itself, it effectively *relocates* the putative source of law and pattern from godhead (divine *Logos*) to material nature itself. This is the basic premise of modern science: nature is governed by laws, discoverable by reason and experiment, the origin and cause of which is in no wise supernatural, spiritual, or immaterial. Modern science does not recognize these dimensions of being as "real." It is rather nature itself objectified as *res extensa*—and so not conscious or intelligent—that functions as the source and cause of the lawfulness observable in natural phenomena.

Canonical streams of both philosophy and religion in the West, however, understand law—and the observable regularities that derive from it—to be sourced in *logos* in such a way that *conscious intelligence and intention are inseparable from the causal agency and power manifested in the predictable patterning of phenomena indicative of lawfully regulated activity.*[345] When science shifts the source of law to a nature construed as essentially inanimate, a mind sensitive to the original idea of *logos* or *ratio* cannot but perceive a profound logical contradiction. In the modern view, the very source and origin of law is thus represented as a "substance" (matter), the defining feature of which is the total lack of any indwelling power or intelligence that would enable it effectively to constrain phenomena to conform to lawful patterns of action.[346]

In the billiard ball table analogy, the purely mechanical explanation of all that happens seems perfectly natural if not more or less self-evident. Even so, a first and final question remains entirely unanswered, one that belies the self-evidently "rational" construct of this world, and highlights the dark mystery hidden at its source. It is a question that the biologist Ursula Goodenough poses, even while confessing the feelings of awe, wonder, and even terror it excites. "Where," Goodenough asks, "do the laws of physics come from?"[347]

As Goodenough implies, the answer to that question, which cannot but take physics into the realm of metaphysics and science into the sphere of philosophy, remains entirely beyond the pale of what the mainstream mind recognizes as valid "knowledge" and normative "reality" today. This points to the hubris of the modern mentality, which—in the wake of Descartes and Galileo—restricts its conception of the nature of the universe to a conceptual form amenable to a very circumscribed sphere of what it believes it can, employing a specific "scientific" method, "know" and prove with *certainty*, defining all that falls outside the dim and flickering circle of light cast by that form of cognition as unreal and immaterial to human concern.

Such a worldview cannot but remind one of the persons shackled in the depths of Plato's cave, convinced that the shadows cast on the wall as figures pass in front of the light of the fire behind them represent the whole of reality. These cave-dwellers, too, are ignorant of the infinitely greater light of the sun, and so jealous of their own version of "truth" that they are prone to kill any who escape from their predicament, ascend to the daylight above, and return to tell them of the glory and infinitely greater light of the world there witnessed.

We have heard of Kepler's and Newton's answers to the question Goodenough at least has the courage and honesty to pose. Their answers are, at one and the same time, profoundly different and very much the same. One way or another, the lawful behavior of the cosmos derives from the *Reason* inherent in divine intelligence, the causal power innate in the *Logos* that, from the beginning, creates and preserves the world. It should go without saying that the *ratio* latent in such a *Logos* is of a fundamentally different type than the "rationality" which (as in the mechanical philosophy) derives from reasoning restricted to a world of sense construed as the only "real" world and regulated by chains of purely material and efficient causation.[348]

I alluded earlier to the ground of this difference. The ratio inherent in the *Logos*—Platonically or Christologically understood—bridges the gap between two distinct worlds, two ontologically and cosmologically distinct dimensions. Most explicitly, these are the *intelligible* and the *sensible* in Plato and the *divine* and the *human* in the Gospels; but other important dualities apply as well: the eternal and the temporal, being and becoming, the heavenly and earthly worlds.

When Kingsnorth and Del Noce complain—rightly—about "radical immanence" and "the end of transcendence," they are, in fact, lamenting not only the disappearance of any region of transcendence from the geography of consciousness, but—*perforce*—the occlusion of any idea of an effective, living *Logos*, any idea of the *ratio* between the terms of the above-named dualities. Such a *Logos* provides, too, for the underlying continuity and indeed unity—which is *not* to say "sameness"—subsisting between transcendent and immanent spheres of being. Philosophically speaking, one can say as well that it is that *logos* or *ratio* that creates and preserves the *relation* between sensible form and intelligible idea, and in so doing grounds the episteme, the project of knowledge itself. It does so by enabling the student of nature to trace diverse particular phenomena to universal principles, and so bring the multiplicity of phenomena under the aegis of a law intelligible to the mind.

Perhaps this discussion may suffice to make evident that the philosophical ground plan of scientific materialism—its epistemological foundation[349]—involves a logical aporia obscured by circular reasoning and a confusion of levels. The behavior of matter—which itself is imagined as unintelligent and void of any indwelling formative agency—is supposedly determined by scientific laws. These laws, however, are understood to be mere epiphenomenal expressions of the properties somehow "inherent" in matter.

This fatal epistemological flaw manifests as a consequence of the rigid mind/body or spirit/matter dualism underlying Cartesianism, which provides no viable mediation between the intelligible and sensible worlds. As a matter of historical fact, this *dualism* has actually devolved into *monism*. Mind, spirit, consciousness, invisible forms of intelligence: all are regarded (if acknowledged at all) as functional byproducts of matter and the patterns of energy associated with its swirling. Insofar as Platonism regards sensible phenomena as images and effects of archetypal ideas which alone are ascribed authentic (because enduring rather than ephemeral) being, the modern understanding may be construed as a kind of inversion of Platonic ontology.

Unlike modern consciousness, however, Plato, as his famous discussion of the Divided Line in Book VI of the Republic demonstrates, embraces an ontology and cosmology that recognizes distinct planes of reality, and attempts to provide an at least preliminary account of the *logos* that mediates the worlds of idea and sense. Chief advocate and connoisseur of the noetic ground of all true science, Plato pokes serious fun at those who believe they can acquire authentic knowledge of the cosmos by means of modes of cognition bound and tied to the logic of the senses:

> We establish, then, said I, astronomy as the fourth discipline...if any one contemplates the various bodies in the firmament, and, by earnestly looking up, apprehends every thing, you think that he has intelligence of these things; and does not merely see them with his eyes; and perhaps you judge right, and I foolishly. For I, on the other hand, am not able to conceive, that any other discipline can make the soul look upwards, but that which respects being, and that which is invisible; and if a man undertakes to learn any thing of sensible objects, whether he gape upwards or

> below downwards, never shall I say that he learns; *for I aver he had no science of these things;* nor shall I say that his soul looks upwards, but downwards, even though he should learn lying on his back, either at land or at sea.[350]

Plato continues to counsel that visible nature can serve as a path to knowledge of real being but *only* if the mind avails itself of "reason and the dianoetic power"—that is, participation in *Logos*—to bridge the difference between one and the other:

> But what was the proper way, said you, of learning astronomy...? In this manner, said I, that these variegated bodies in the heavens, as they are varied in a visible subject, be deemed the most beautiful and most accurate of the kind, but far inferior to real beings.... Which things truly are to be comprehended by reason and the dianoetic power, but not by sight.... That variety in the heavens [is] to be made use of as a paradigm for learning those real things.[351]

Not many thinkers today in any field take philosophical idealism seriously. Modern science, steeped in a stream of thought that long ago moved from Plato to Aristotle to nominalism to positivistic materialism, looks with disdain (if it indeed looks at all) upon the metaphysical imagination. After all, does not the technological prowess afforded by its methods confirm the authority of *its* version of universal truth?

One can, however, readily adduce good reason to dispute such self-assured intellectual complacency. Is it not the very premise of scientific inquiry, the project of knowledge, that particular material *facts* can be explained by general *principles*? And who would dare maintain that facts and principles are really one and the same thing?

American philosopher Anthony Damiani, an unapologetic Platonist, provides a cogent formulation of the gist of the intellectual confusion precipitated by a *Logos* absent without leave:

> We see a situation today where the *intelligibility* of scientific laws is subsumed under and reduced to the same level as the material phenomena that those laws are meant to explain.... Astronomers of today...fail to use their understanding as a springboard into the higher realms of being.[352]

Why do these philosophical conundrums matter to our theme? Because one effect of these maneuvers is to *divorce* the order evident in nature and indeed the very concept of "law" itself from any notion of divine reason (*Logos*), the godhead traditionally understood as the source of truth, beauty, goodness, being, consciousness, intelligence, light, life, and order in nature.

The sublime grandeur of the Creation has always spoken to humankind of a fount of intelligence and power that dwarfs its own comparatively puny capabilities. Humankind has often looked to the creation for inspiration and instruction in the higher laws by which it might seek to order its own conduct and so participate in a cosmic wisdom and beauty that endows individual existence with significance. Philosophy (and religion, as well, in its more intellectual aspects) understood that cosmic wisdom to be expressed in the *Logos*. The aspiration to elevate the mind in order to attain to insight into and participation in that *Logos* furnished the ground of natural philosophy which, by definition, could not but edify and ennoble. That spirit, that aspiration, breathes, as we have seen, through the works and words of some of the great pioneers of modern science.

Yet the separation of subject and object, God and nature had always been present as a more or less explicit tendency in both Judaism and Christianity. That tendency found new and potent expression in medieval nominalism and, too, in Luther. Meanwhile, the human self (like a child or youth rebelling against her parents) sought a new degree of autonomy and the dignity due a creature made in the image of God and christened as the veritable crown of Creation.

Almost insensibly at first, the human being's desire to *know* the mysteries of nature became more and more conditioned by a desire *to master and command*; a motive first—as with Lord Bacon—construed as fulfilling the covenant with a transcendent God who had deliberately put nature at man's service. "The sovereignty of man lieth hid in knowledge"[353]— such, indeed, became the creed of modern man. Thus directed to *command* nature, the human mind eventually grew more and more jealous of its rule, and so loathe to ascribe the source of law and order in the universe to any sort of marvelous intelligence. Increasingly, it declined to entertain the very idea of any form of Reason that might exceed the bounds of that brand of causality its own egocentric rationality could readily conceive and control.

Descartes represents the critical pivot. We have just read Plato's account of how best to view heavenly phenomena. Compare that passage to one from Descartes's essay "On Meteorology"—one of three appendices affixed to the *Discourse on Method* that contains the famous *cogito*.

Historian of science Richard Westfall introduces and comments on the relevant text for us. His first words are jarring:

> The sense of wonder repelled Descartes. One of the goals of his natural philosophy was the abolition of wonder by displaying the physical necessity of supposed marvels.
>
> > It is our nature to have more admiration for the things above us than for those that are on our level, or below. And although the clouds are hardly any higher than the summits of some mountains, and often we even see some that are lower than the pinnacles of our steeples, nevertheless, because we must turn our eyes toward the sky to look at them, we fancy them to be so high that poets and painters even fashion them into God's throne, and picture Him there, using His own hands to open and close the doors of the winds, to sprinkle the dew upon the flowers, and to hurl the lightning against the rocks. This leads me to hope that if I here explain the nature of clouds, in such a way that we will no longer have occasion to wonder at anything that can be seen of them, or anything that descends from them, we will easily believe that it is similarly possible to find the causes of everything that is most admirable above the earth.
>
> *Les Météores* then proceeded to explanation of all these things (clouds, winds, dew, lightning, and other things as well), explanations that invoked only physical necessity—all intended, as he said in conclusion, to remove "any reason to marvel" about phenomena in the skies.[354]

Plato views contemplation of the heavenly bodies as a means of elevating the human mind so that it may comprehend the Ideas that transcend (*and* invisibly order) even the most sublime appearances of the sensible world. Descartes, on the other hand, is most anxious not only, like Newton, to show that one law reigns supreme in the terrestrial and celestial spheres, but also to extinguish the aura of divine mystery that shrouds heavenly phenomena. Our supreme rationalist unapologetically drags the sublime scenery of sky down to the earth where, like an obedient cart horse, his mechanically inclined mind may ride and command it at will.

The comparison conveys the sense of the degradation and indeed occlusion of the *Logos*, the tragic darkening of the light of the mind, that transpires in the course of modernity, even in the encyclopedic cubicles of the Enlightenment itself. Cartesian dualism and atomistic materialism helped birth a science that, even while worshipping the Goddess of Reason, defines knowledge itself as inherently irreverent: not sacred, but profane. Concomitantly, it rebuilds the project of knowledge upon ground that is not merely intellectually shaky, but riven by the philosophic equivalent of the San Andreas fault: "a situation...where the *intelligibility* of scientific laws is subsumed under and reduced to the same level as the material phenomena that those laws are meant to explain."[355]

Thus, by a philosophical sleight-of-hand that has become second nature to the modern mentality (which means, too, its *unconscious* ideological ground), lawfulness and order in nature does not (as had historically been the case) reflect and bear witness to any sort of supernatural or supersensible intelligence. On the contrary, because such lawfulness is viewed as a property of nature, which itself is *a priori* construed as purely material and inherently unintelligent, lawful order in nature is seen, paradoxically enough, as a persuasive reason for *denying* the reality of any sort of divinity.

In the modern view of things, nature has thus, so to speak, *absorbed* the *Logos*—the source of lawfulness—into itself, while at the same time utterly nullifying or negating it. Materialism or naturalism replaces an idea (*Logos*) historically associated with Life, Light, Reason and the like emanations of divinity (the very source, one might say, of true *enlightenment* itself) with principles of blind, purely mechanistic causation, the iron rule of the twin gods of modern science: chance and necessity.

It should be recognized that the form of reality attributed to nature in the modern conception is a very particular, historically determined form. It is not, for instance, animistic, but specifically framed to be comprehended by just the type of rationality exemplified by the modern scientific intellect. Not only, moreover, can nature as *res extensa* be *comprehended* by human reason; stretched out upon the gurney of the Cartesian coordinate plane that provides the uniform ground necessary for all kinds of mathematical calculation, this inert, material nature is also subject to *mastery* and *possession* by the same intellect that constructs its essential form. Qua unintelligent, inert matter, nature as such cannot assert the kind of moral claim that would naturally accrue to it if it were regarded as the immanent expression or embodiment of a divine *Logos* responsible for the order of the creation as a whole; the manifestation of an all-encompassing intelligence of which the human mind itself were but a part and microcosmic expression.

We catch a glimpse here of a fateful and, indeed, tragic consequence of the modern construction of mind. Insofar as the ego posits its own cognitive process as source and center of certainty, the truth it attains (including, preeminently, its scientific knowledge of nature) loses any *intrinsic* connection with morality. It does so because this construction of "truth" deprives it of any inherent relation to the Good, insofar as that Good might be held to flow from action that participates in and conforms to the order of a larger whole or unity, an intelligence *superior* to that of the human ego and so qualified to lend the application of the human intellect ethical compass and spiritual direction.

The lawfulness expressive of the *Logos* having been reassigned to a purely material, essentially *dead* (comprised, finally, of atomic units of unintelligent, inanimate matter) nature, divinity itself loses, first of all, its being as reason, its defining *logos*. The name of God and the practice of religion consequently become the signs and insignia of patently *"irrational"* forms of belief: faith in a species of divinity the agency of which becomes identified with a brand of superstition viewed as the *antithesis* of rationality.

Correlative to this loss of *Being as Reason*, divinity likewise loses its *Reason for Being*. It is recast as a product of fantasy and desire unnecessary for—and indeed preclusive of—"scientific" explanation of the nature of the universe.

Richard Tarnas addresses the peculiarly scientistic mold of the modern mind and the philosophical consequences thereof:

> It is true that in the eyes of not a few scientists and philosophers, science itself contained a religious meaning, or was open to a religious interpretation, or could serve as an opening to a religious appreciation of the universe. The beauty of nature's forms, the splendor of its variety, the extraordinarily intricate functioning of the human body, the evolutionary development of the human eye or the human mind, the mathematical patterning of the cosmos, the unimaginable magnitude of the heavenly spaces—to some these seemed to require the existence of a divine intelligence and power of miraculous sophistication. But many others argued that such phenomena were the straightforward and relatively random results of the natural laws of physics, chemistry, and biology. The human psyche, longing for the security of a cosmic providence, and susceptible to personifying and projecting its own capacity for value and purpose, might wish to see more in nature's design, but the scientific understanding was deliberately beyond such wishful anthropomorphizing: the entire scenario of cosmic evolution seemed explicable as a direct consequence of chance and necessity, the random interplay of natural laws. In this light, any apparent religious implications had to be judged as poetic but scientifically unjustifiable extrapolations from the available evidence. God was "an unnecessary hypothesis."[356]

Thus consigned by edict of Enlightenment Rationalist Fundamentalism (Gellner) to the status of an *unnecessary hypothesis,* the very notion of divinity becomes subject to dismissal (and often marked disdain) by the now central and sovereign ego, the human self identified with its scientific genius. It is naturally this same intellectual power that confers upon the human being practical *power* over nature.[357] With God effectively out of the picture, and nature construed as purely material stuff operated on by amoral forces of "chance and necessity," the exercise of that technical power goes forward unconstrained by any limits imposed by respect for either (non-existent) deity or any sacralized natural law and order. Man himself, in this construct, is solely responsible for his own well-being and for conferring meaning and purpose upon an otherwise inherently meaningless cosmos. He is likewise solely responsible for any moral order that would regulate his relationships to both nature and others of his kind.

This, however, as history proves, represents a profoundly untenable situation, because the autonomous self's being and existence—originally constituted as essentially separate from any larger whole represented by God or Nature—has no compass by which to navigate life except that of satisfaction of its own needs and desires. Such include not only material exigencies, but as well (and very importantly) the psychological desire, inscribed in the very foundation of our modern ideology, to affirm, preserve, and exercise the dominion over all things: all that is not the "rational" human self that first established its identity by way of the god-like *cogito*.. That "not-self" includes, naturally, the whole of nature, *as well as other human souls.* We consequently circle back to Adorno and Horkheimer's elaboration of the dialectic of enlightenment, the logic of which determines that the "rational" self's dominion over "things"—nature and the world at large—translates into treatment of other human beings as, likewise, a "substrate of domination."

We can, at this juncture, understand how the inflationary aggrandizement of the human ego and of a certain kind of reasoning (or cognitive activity) rebounds upon its own head in a fashion that—in a classic enantiodromia—culminates in the effective *nullification* of the authenticity and autonomy of the human subject.

The ego—even if it construes the whole of nature to be of a material character—cannot help but envision the universe thus constructed as descriptive of the larger reality (the nature of the universe) of which it, as a finite organism, is only a part. Consequently, the putatively all-powerful human "I" comes to see *itself* in the mirror of the mechanistic nature it has projected as reality. This is all the more persuasive when, in the aftermath of Darwin, mechanistic nature comes to supply the scientific mind's own creation myth, the narrative account of its own origin. As a result, the modern human being comes increasingly to consider itself as a mere animal product of physical, chemical, and biological material forces and, at the transhumanist limit, little more than a form of pseudo-consciousness thoroughly conditioned and indeed determined in its *modus operandi* by certain specifiable "algorithms" that map biopsychic processes.[358]

Such an entity is no longer a subject possessed of the degree of freedom or the kind of autonomous consciousness proper to a human being. It is rather a kind of automaton. As Robert Romanyshyn and others observe, as science and technology advance along these lines, the contemplative *cogito*, the imaginative capacity of the human mind ineluctably transmogrifies into the calculative algorithmic power of the worldwide web and evolving versions of AI.

In the system of this brave new world, the human entity all too often possesses "value" only insofar as it may be manipulated and exploited by those in command of the operating system. Big Tech moguls today—acting as one arm of the Matrix—accordingly devise means of exerting ever tighter control over the behavior of those habituated to the use of their platforms.

That, however, is just one aspect of the fearsome power of the Matrix. Covid World and the Great Reset agenda reveal, with frightening clarity, how the historic process that effects eclipse of the *Logos* paves the way for a technocratic totalitarianism that annuls the freedom of the individual, *extinguishing* the very sovereign selfhood that set the machine of modernity running in the first place.

That, one could say (with Kingsnorth and a host of others) is "Progress."

PART III

ORIGINAL RELATION

Chapter 10

THREE BY THREE: LECTURE ON THE TIMES

I pen these words on July 4, 2022, one year and five days after writing the first words of this book,[359] and 246 years (one revolution of the planet Pluto) after the signing of the Declaration of Independence. Time is catching up to me; or rather, the *Times* are. Not the *New York* variety, which once-honored circular (like most so-called "liberal" news and media outlets) still has its head stuck in the sand of the controlling Covid narrative, but the Spirit of the Times, the *Zeitgeist,* the nature of which Ralph Waldo Emerson introduces in a lecture delivered in a Masonic Temple in Boston in 1841:

> The Times, as we say—or the present aspects of our social state, the Laws, Divinity, Natural Science, Agriculture, Art, Trade, Letters, have their root in an invisible spiritual reality. To appear in these aspects, they must first exist, or have some necessary foundation. Beside all the small reasons we assign, there is a great reason for the existence of every extant fact; a reason which lies grand and immovable, often unsuspected behind it in silence.[360]

Note the Platonic premises of the American Transcendentalist's overture: Emerson's avowal of the "invisible spiritual reality" that exists as the ontological ground underlying historical phenomena. Note, too, his reference to *reason*, and—especially—his distinction between its two kinds.

By those "small reasons," I take Emerson to mean readily comprehensible motives or forces and related chains of material cause and effect. By that "great...grand and immovable" reason, I understand him to invoke a higher order of intelligence, one that, rooted in "eternal and uncreated truth" (Kingsnorth) *manifests* the ideas or principles indwelling "invisible spiritual reality" in the form of current affairs. This may also implicate (for here it is necessary to supplement Emerson's incorrigible optimism) the impetus leading to the reform of laws, institutions, and other sociopolitical realities that represent distortions or betrayals of those same ideas. One could think, for instance, of the idea of human freedom that fueled the American revolution, and contemporary attempts to counteract the illegitimate government censorship that curtails liberty.

In enabling such agency, the faculty of Reason performs the holy offices of *Logos*, the divine Word that connects God and man, mind and matter, everlasting being and current events. "The Times," continues Emerson,

> are the masquerade of the eternities; trivial to the dull, tokens of noble and majestic agents to the wise; the receptacle in which the Past leaves its history; the quarry out of which the genius of tomorrow is building up the Future. The Times—the nations, manners, institutions, opinions, votes, are to be studied as omens, as sacred leaves, whereon a weighty sense is inscribed, if we have the wit and the love to search it out. Nature itself seems to propound to us this topic, and to invite us to explore the meaning of the conspicuous facts of the day.[361]

If, following in Emerson's footsteps, we aim to assess the tenor of these, our times, and, stepping for a moment out of the headlong rush of affairs, pause upon the Commons to look upon the prospect our day presents, we suffer a sinking if not a breaking of the heart. I cannot begin to inventory all the plagues that desecrate our national landscape, including the violence visited daily by one human being upon another, or (too, too often) upon many others.

How is it that on this, the anniversary of our country's origin, the joy of the celebration of birth is destroyed by an iron cold hand dealing out death in the Land of Lincoln; indeed, in my home town?[362] How is it that the stitches that hold us together as a people, frayed by lawlessness on all sides, threaten to unravel and undo us all? America, a nation born—not without defect—but nonetheless under the stars of liberty and of hope, where is your bright promise now? Divided and divided, the ship of state groans in conflict and splits in strife, and the people, hands limp upon helm or sail-rope, lose themselves at sea.

If we lack compass and direction, it must needs be because we have lost sight of our guiding star: that spiritual nature that (as Emerson teaches) constitutes the ground of our humanity. How can such tragic self-forgetfulness have overtaken our kind? The initial portion of this book, especially the immediately preceding part, provides—if not an explanation—a framework for understanding that urgent question. Let me here rehearse a deliberately streamlined version of salient developments.

Our conscious understanding of who and what we are as human beings depends upon correlative constructions of the nature of the universe and of divinity. In the course of the early modern period, the *Logos* that had traditionally been construed as *both* the divine image of man and the source of law and order in nature, the *ratio* between intelligible and sensible and the divine and human worlds, was appropriated by an autonomous human ego that conceived its own being and intelligence as both self-subsistent and essentially separate from divinity and nature. Concomitantly, that human subject construed nature as a whole to operate in accord with "laws" derivative of its own restricted form of "rational" cognition. Eventually, this human subject comes to understand the nature of reality as a whole—including its own being and consciousness—on the basis of the consequent mechanical philosophy, which gradually assumes the form of a dominant *ideology* that pervades and thoroughly conditions every aspect of human life and culture.

Insofar as the mechanistic worldview posits the essential unit of all reality (including the human) to be atomistic units of dead, unintelligent, and non-purposive matter, the ideology it sponsors inevitably undermines humankind's own conscious relation to the soul-spiritual foundation of being. As this fundamentally nihilistic and isolating frame of mind penetrates the human psyche ever more deeply, any explicit affirmation of transcendent ideals, lacking corroborating metaphysical conviction, appears ever more suspect. Truth, Beauty, and Goodness increasingly come to be seen as words signifying nothing, and a Machiavellian will to power governs academic as well as practical policy. This contaminates even the residual species of idealism evident in social justice movements that, while functioning as a persistent reminder of the inextinguishable character of the human spirit, are hamstrung by lack of any philosophical ground consistent with their sociopolitical initiatives and so often metamorphose into their own form of coercive ideology and divisive culture warfare.

Correlatively, in accord with the conditions prescribed by a materialist ideology, social and political life is increasingly guided—not by genuine humanistic aims or soul-spiritual values—but by the goal of establishing closed systems of control within which efficiency can (theoretically, at least) be optimized—often to the advantage of the already rich and powerful. Education, the economy, and government dance to the same lifeless tune. Technocracy, often guided by explicitly or implicitly transhumanist goals, becomes the norm; and its reach increasingly extends into the most intimate recesses of private life.

The fragmentation, demoralization, and dehumanization that inevitably ensue excites, too, a conservative backlash, which aggressively tries to restore lost forms of human dignity and value by enforcing strict codes of morality, facets of which are reminiscent of the theocratic tenor of premodern times. So is the ruthless dialectic of enlightenment capped by not one, but two, symmetrically opposed forms of repressive (albeit sharply contrasting) brands of authoritarianism: on the one hand, proto-totalitarian technocracy and the ideological program devolving from "liberalism" run amok, and, on the other, religious fundamentalism that represents a throwback to medievalism or the inquisitorial attitude of early modern times.

How do we redress this historic cul-de-sac that threatens to prove deadly as a Fourth of July parade with no exit?

Surely, it should be clear that no "small reasoning" will do to begin to address the cause of distress and disaster: that no partisanship, on either side, will likely do much but fan the ideological wildfires that (much like the natural variety) threaten to devour the land. The political impasse derives from deep sources: intellectual and spiritual causes related to the order of those "grand immovable" reasons that Emerson invokes in his "Lecture on the Times."

We are now, I believe, finally in a position to respond to the conundrum that underlies this book: the still pending question pertaining to the dual legacy of the Enlightenment. The above reference to religious dogmatism rearing its head once more may help highlight the enduring value of the Enlightenment heritage. That heritage, in its noblest aspect, bequeaths us intellectual freedom, and the courage to repudiate dogmatic and arbitrary forms of authority. It insists upon the value and dignity of the human being in the face of oppressive measures instituted in the name of God *or* privileged classes of man. It upholds the sacredness of individual liberty, *along with* an ideal of a universal spirit of humanity that might supply a *principled* ground of ethics in accord with Reason. It defends the irreducible value of life here, on this earth, and the truths revealed by patiently observant regard of the sacred book of nature.

All these Enlightenment initiatives retain their value as irreplaceable foundations of free society in a modern age. They consequently stand as cornerstones of any American democracy worthy of the name. What, then, corrupts this proud and enduring Enlightenment legacy? That question can finally be succinctly answered: *Mechanical Philosophy.*

It is true that certain forms of more or less mechanistic rationalism played an important part in Enlightenment-era thinking. Yet too many important texts make the tie between the Enlightenment and mechanistic rationality far too exclusive and absolute. Undoubtedly, the era's close engagement with material concerns evolved as a compensatory counterpoise to the otherworldly "spiritual" bias of Christian theology. Most likely, the materialism latent in the Cartesian *cogito,* and explicit in the elaboration of his philosophy, played a critical role in establishing the intellectual and spiritual independence of the individual human being. In so doing, it carried Renaissance initiatives inaugurated by the likes of Pico further in a specific subjective dimension, intensifying the centripetal force necessary for human powers of analysis to break from outworn theological constraint.

Even so, the mechanistic bent of the modern mind did not entirely define Enlightenment-era initiatives, as may be verified by the myriad facets of Enlightenment-era thinking not reducible to or even compatible with mechanical philosophy. Indeed, it may readily be perceived that the truly spiritual impetus of Enlightenment thought, one that bends the arc of history towards human freedom, must in fact be reckoned fundamentally and irrevocably at odds with any thoroughly mechanistic philosophy. If the natural scientific version of the latter appeared, at a certain moment or for a certain span of time, to sort with and, indeed, serve the higher cause, history itself is destined to dispel the illusion that it could do so for long. It is precisely the sticky oil of mechanistic materialism that jams the gears of the enlightened mind, and—transforming its full ensemble of salient initiatives into negative and destructive forms—throws humankind clear off track.

None of the points enumerated in my six-point synopsis of Enlightenment initiatives (with the possible exception of *Progress*) are intrinsically bound to or contingent upon a mechanistic materialism. Indeed, it is precisely interpreting them within that frame of mind that converts a nascent philosophy of freedom into its dark shadow form: a totalitarian dialectic of enlightenment.

Nature, no longer *Anima Mundi*, a dynamic, lawfully ordered cosmos manifesting the life and light of the *Logos*, becomes a soulless, mindless, meaningless mechanism that can, without compunction, be mercilessly mined for its material resource. Standing in this guise as representative of the underlying Reality of All Things (not excluding persons), all else irrevocably follows. Radical open-mindedness and the spirit of intellectual adventure (*Sapere aude!*) transforms into the dogmatic and narrow-minded religion of scientism, pridefully careless of truth and power, enslaved to ritualistic methods, and doomed to corruption. Genuine liberty metamorphoses into an egotistical form of consumer-driven statist individualism unconstrained by natural limits, the ideal of virtue, or religious aspiration. Wholesome culture of mind and soul shape-shifts into the monstrous Moloch of Progress, while the Party of Humanity morphs into a technocratic "New World Order" engineered, for "the greater good," by corporate and international organization. Finally, mirroring nature—or rather, its technological replacement— the human being herself is reconceived and recast as a glorified cogwheel in an internet of things, an inferior species of Machine, whose redemption ultimately lies in a cloud-form transhumanist heaven.

How may we imagine rectifying this situation in order to emancipate humankind from the vice-like grip of a killing ideology? How do we rekindle the still smoldering coals of true enlightenment? Clearly, we need a new philosophy, an "original relation to the universe" that sanctions a novel understanding of the nature of nature, of human being, of divinity, and of the formative relations between all these.

The call for a new philosophy is itself nothing new. It echoes and reiterates that high summons issued by Emerson already in *Nature,* a Declaration of *Intellectual* Independence issued sixty years after its political prototype. The beginning of the text merits recitation:

> Our age is retrospective. It builds the sepulchers of the fathers. The foregoing generations beheld God and nature, face to face; we through their eyes. Why should not we also enjoy an original relation to the universe? Why should we not have a poetry and philosophy of insight and not of tradition, and a religion by revelation to us, and not the history of theirs? Embosomed for a season in nature, whose floods of life stream around and through us, and invite us by the powers they supply, to action proportioned to nature, why should we grope among the dry bones of the past, or put the living generation into masquerade out of its faded wardrobe?[363]

Some of today's visionaries may maintain that we—or they, at least—can hardly be accused of wasting time "building the sepulchers of the fathers," and indeed have already proceeded far down the path Emerson recommends. "Look!" sayeth Yuval Noah Harari[364] and other prophetic proponents of the New Normal, "Look at the vistas opened by the Third, and now the Fourth Industrial Revolutions, brilliant developments that promise to usher us, in the blink of a digital eye, into a brave new world!"

The transhumanist agenda, however, represents no new philosophy, but an updated version of the old, mechanical one. It is a mutated variety, to be sure, as the transition from mechanical to electronic and digital power effects a quantum leap in technological capacity and artificial forms of intelligence.

Just so, all this progress proceeds—now, with breathtaking speed— along the same path first opened by Descartes: objectification (and now replacement) of nature; the absolutely sovereignty of "rational" human (and now, computer or artificial) intelligence; and God—any divinity not of our making—out of the question altogether.

That is not the "philosophy of insight" Emerson calls for; and it is profoundly antithetical to the first sketch of such he himself supplies in *Nature,* the apocalyptic "little book" that so stirred the pot then, and perhaps may do so again now. Certainly, in the pages of *Nature,* and in all of Emerson's almost endless references to the subject, we will find no dead mechanical, no objectively quantifiable (and of course no digitalized!) nature, but one instinct with life and wisdom, worthy of the enthusiastic homage paid to (as Emerson expresses it in his journals) "a living, leaping logos."[365]

Emerson could hardly be more forthright as to what he perceives as nature's defining character and deepest reason for being:

> It is essential to a true theory of nature and of man, that it should contain somewhat progressive. Uses that are exhausted or that may be...cannot be all that is true of this brave lodging wherein man is harbored, and wherein all his faculties find appropriate and endless exercise. And all the uses of nature admit of being summed in one, which yields the activity of man an infinite scope. Through all its kingdoms, to the suburbs and outskirts of things it is faithful to the cause whence it had its origin. It always speaks of Spirit. It suggests the absolute. It is a perpetual effect. It is a great shadow pointing always to the sun behind us.[366]

Shades of Plato once more. And yet, too, of Enlightenment initiatives, such as Emerson's own species of "progressivism."

Romanticism—which exerted a determinative influence upon Emerson[367]—figures prominently in the unfolding of non-mechanistic philosophies of nature in the wake of Enlightenment rationalism. Speaking of late 18th- and early-19th-century ideas of nature, a gloss under a painting in the Schiller Museum in Marbach reads: "In Schiller's time, [Nature is] as well a surrogate for Religion with a sacralizing and world-explaining character ("*Ver- und Erklärungschararacter*")."[368] *Nature's* next paragraph could hardly confirm this more explicitly: "The aspect of nature is devout. Like the figure of Jesus, she stands with bended head, and hands folded upon the breast. The happiest man is he who learns from nature the lesson of worship."[369]

How drastically different Emerson's attitude than that of Descartes, a man with a mind anxious to squeeze the clouds like a sponge so as to drain all awe and wonder from the skies. How different, too, from Lord Bacon, who is religiously wedded to the first and lowest of the several "uses" Emerson accords to nature:

> Whoever considers the final cause of the world, will discern a multitude of uses that enter as parts into that result. They all admit of being thrown into one of the following classes: Commodity; Beauty; Language; and Discipline.
>
> Under the general name of Commodity, I rank all those advantages which our senses owe to nature. This, of course, is a benefit which is temporary and mediate, not ultimate like its service to the soul.[370]

We will, in another chapter, briefly parse the other "uses." For now, bundling even the few cited quotations, we can arrive at a palpable sense of the crux of Emerson's preliminary "idea of creation." Nature, visible garment (*natura naturata*) and creative expression (*natura naturans*) of *Logos,* manifests as the revelation of a first and final spiritual cause of All. Its interest for man lies principally in its capacity to guide the soul on its path towards fuller participation in that divine origin proper to the genius of humankind.

Emerson's vision of nature coincides with and effectively authorizes a kindred interpretation of the constitution of the human soul. Rather than either an autonomous ego essentially *separable* from nature and divinity, or an even more alien biophysical machine, Emerson—eschewing not only mechanism, but a rigid mind/body or spirit/matter dualism— conceives man as a *soul* destined to find authentic identity in progressive discovery of the *confluence* of human consciousness, nature, and the creative power characteristic of divinity:

> [Man] shall look forward to an ever expanding knowledge as to a becoming creator. He shall see, that nature is the opposite of the soul, answering to it part for part. One is seal, and one is print. Its beauty is the beauty of his own mind. Its laws are the laws of his own mind. Nature then becomes to him the measure of his attainments. So much of nature as he is ignorant of, so much of his own mind does he not yet possess. And, in fine, the ancient precept, "Know thyself," and the modern precept, "Study nature," become at last one maxim.[371]

Let us look more closely into the idea of the human being characterizing the philosophical anthropology inscribed in—not only *Nature* and *The American Scholar*—but the whole of Emerson's *oeuvre.*

Philosophy and religion in the West have hardly neglected the question of the nature and constitution of the human being. As complex as the subject may at first appear, a relatively simple archetypal model of the essential lineaments of man crystallized in ancient times. The idea of the human being as a threefold unity of body, soul, and spirit boasts a long and distinguished heritage. In the Christian world, it formed the gist of the philosophical anthropology operative in official church doctrine until the Constantinople Council of 869 endorsed dualism instead. James Hillman:

> At that Council of Constantinople the soul lost its dominion. Our anthropology, our idea of human nature, devolved from a tripartite cosmos of spirit, soul, and body (or matter) to a dualism of spirit (or mind) and body (or matter).[372]

Hillman—a psychologist—bitterly laments this development because it elides the soul, and the forms of mediation (between spirit and body) proper to it.

In his book *An Endless Trace: The Passionate Pursuit of Wisdom in the West,* Christopher Bamford offers another account of this momentous change, one which he, like Hillman, regards as spiritually debilitating. Bamford confirms the universal pedigree of the threefold conception of the human being:

> As for "wholeness," traditionally and universally a human being was considered to be a whole of *three* parts, "body, soul, and spirit." In the West, however, at the Eighth Ecumenical Council of Constantinople (869 C.E.), the human being was reduced to two parts: body and soul only. Anyone who claimed that human beings had two souls (a soul and a spirit) was declared anathema, a heretic. This act crippled the metaphysical definition of the human being in the West. With the reduction to two parts, either the *spirit* was banned, in which case there was no organ of spiritual cognition, reducing knowledge to what was obtainable through the senses. Or else the *soul* was banned, in which case there was no interworld linking spirit and body, no imaginal realm, no realm of the dead or place of encounter with spiritual beings. One can look at it either way. No matter which one chooses, the consequences remain the same: literalism and abstraction.[373]

Bamford's last words here are no less significant than his first. It is the mechanical habits of a mind that traffics in "literalism and abstraction" that engender the reign of quantity, the dialectic of enlightenment, technocracy, and the leviathanic Great Reset. In order to understand the underlying intellectual conditions that led to the Covid crisis (as well as that of modernity more generally), we need to explore in what way the dualistic stream of thought that flows from the 869 Council (continuing through medieval nominalism into Cartesian mechanistic rationalism and on into the scientific materialism of the present day) demolishes the integrity of the idea of the three-fold human being and so corrupts and corrodes humanity as a whole.

To pursue this critical task, we shall, first of all, deepen our understanding of the nature of the three-fold of body, soul, and spirit. We can draw upon various sources (including the common store of human experience) in order to arrive at a working idea of these three integral aspects of our being and the dynamic of their relation to each other.

We have already lavished significant attention on the spirit, especially in connection with our discussions of the *Logos* and our preliminary encounter with the transcendental premises of Emerson's work. In fact, a positing of not only the reality of spirit, but open avowal of its ontological, epistemological and moral priority constitutes the very ground of American Transcendentalism.[374] It is in and through the spirit that the human being participates in the "invisible spiritual reality" Emerson invokes near the opening of his "Lecture on the Times." That reality may be construed as an "eternal uncreated" realm of archetypal ideas coincident with (the transcendent aspect of) divinity or the godhead.

This conception grounds Emerson's definition of Transcendentalism as Idealism in "The Transcendentalist," a noteworthy lecture delivered shortly after his "Lecture on the Times." The talk furnishes a good introduction to the characteristic profile of spirit as such proves a motive force in a major stream of post-Enlightenment philosophy:

> What is popularly called Transcendentalism among us, is Idealism; Idealism as it appears in 1842. As thinkers, mankind have ever divided into two sects, Materialists and Idealists; the first class founding on experience; the second on consciousness; the first class beginning to think from the data of the senses, the second class perceive that the senses are not final, and say, the senses give us representations of things, but what are the things themselves, they cannot tell. The materialist insists on facts, on history, on the force of circumstances, and the animal wants of man; the idealist on the power of Thought and of Will, on inspiration, on miracle, on individual culture.[375]

In Emerson's discourse, we are educated as to the essence of spirit and its primary relationship to what Platonic philosophy calls *nous,* the intelligible ground of all being and consciousness. We learn, too, of some of the essential attributes of *the body:* namely, its capacity not only to serve as a vessel and vehicle of organic life, but to function as the organ of sense-perception and the experience of a physical world.

If Emerson's predilections were not clear enough in that first passage, his continuation dispels any doubt as to the style and depth of his own philosophical commitment:

> These two modes of thinking are both natural, but the idealist contends that his way of thinking is in higher nature. He concedes all that the other affirms, admits the impressions of sense, admits their coherency, their use and beauty, and then asks the materialist for his grounds of assurance that things are as his senses represent them. But I, he says, affirm facts not affected by the illusions of sense, facts which are of the same nature as the faculty which reports them, and not liable to doubt; facts which in their first appearance to us assume a native superiority to material facts, degrading these into a language by which the first are to be spoken; facts which it only needs a retirement from the senses to discern. Every materialist will be an idealist; but an idealist can never go backward to be a materialist.[376]

To this perspective, it need be added that the spirit does not only ground the act of *knowing* in the human subject (in Bamford's words, our "organ of spiritual cognition"), but that of its very *being* as well, and thus represents the archetypal origin (or ideal form) of *humanity per se.* In Emerson's signature parlance, the spiritual dimension of being and consciousness goes by the name of Over-soul, and qualifies as the *transcendental* source of every individual person's authentic existence. It is, too, the ground of his or her participation in (the intrinsically universal) spirit of humanity.

Emerson on the Over-soul:

> I am constrained every moment to acknowledge a higher origin for events than the will I call mine. As with events, so is it with thoughts. When I watch that flowing river, which, out of regions I see not, pours for a season its streams into me, I see that I am a pensioner; not a cause, but a surprised spectator of this ethereal water; that I desire and look up, and put myself in the attitude of reception, but from some alien energy the visions come.
>
> The Supreme Critic on the errors of the past and the present, and the only prophet of that which must be, is that great nature in which we rest, as the earth lies in the soft arms of the atmosphere; that Unity, that Over-soul, within which every man's particular being is contained and made one with all other; that common heart, of which all sincere conversation is the

> worship, to which all right action is submission; that overpowering reality which confutes our tricks and talents, and constrains every one to pass for what he is, and to speak from his character, and not from his tongue, and which evermore tends to pass into our thought and hand, and become wisdom, and virtue and power and beauty. We live in succession, in division, in parts, in particles. Meantime within man is the soul of the whole.[377]

I think it quite likely that, given the temper of our times, many of my readers will look upon this passage, as a kind of intellectual relic of a bygone era, high-blown but empty rhetoric that—irrelevant at best, and dangerously "universalizing" at worst—soars high over the head of all that really matters. Yet the prior citation from "The Transcendentalist" anticipates such disregard. What, on the other hand, of the contradiction inherent in presuming to entertain social ideals while espousing a materialist philosophy that recognizes no transcendental ground of unity or shared humanity? A philosophy that tends, by its very nature, to exert an inexorable pull towards, not the unity that subsists and sanctions all true diversity, but ever more division, ever more parts, and particles, like the mechanical Cartesianism that cannot see God in a cloud for all the atoms in it? Failing to endorse a *real idea* of the spiritual ground of universal humanity, are we not inevitably saddled with degraded *ersatz* forms of the same: abstract and intellectualized notions of "the general welfare" or the "public good" that do not rest on principle, and—vaguely collectivist and vulnerable to ideological bias and partisan zealotry—cannot begin to see the universal in the individual, or vice versa?

It is time that, in the social as well as scientific spheres, the reality of the spirit, whether it be called Over-Soul, or *Logos*, or the universal spirit of humanity, or even Christ or the divine I AM or Holy Spirit—be acknowledged in order to cultivate a progressively more conscious relation to the same. Otherwise, despite all noble intent, we are left trafficking in ideologies that try to bear the fire of the spirit in beakers of cold glass, and the water of life in circuit boards and broken pots of clay.

That said, more or less exclusive identification of God and the Good with spirit, the "transcendent, eternal and uncreated" dimension of being, can lead to a denigration of the value, integrity, and even reality of both soul (or psyche) and body. Indeed, an almost irresistible inclination in that direction proves a powerful, if not definitive, feature of philosophy and religion in the West in its Greek and Judeo-Christian streams. That bias, itself to *some* degree derivative of the collapse of an integral three-fold ontology into a more simplified dualism (of spirit or mind and matter, heaven and earth, eternity and time) finds outlet in what Jacques Derrida critiques as the "logocentrism" inherent in the Western philosophical tradition. Platonism, in particular, typically regards the noetic realm of ideal form and eternal archetype as the locus of truth and real being, such that those who remain unduly attached to the markedly inferior and inherently deceptive realm of sense inevitably fall into falsehood and corruption. Augustinian-influenced Christian theology famously harps on a morally and imaginatively super-charged variations of the same theme. Life in the body and the sensual desires associated with it, devolving from original sin, feature as sources of temptation and corruption.

In many crucial ways, the modern age unfolds as a *reaction* against this otherworldly, transcendentally-inflected bias. Yet the strongly dualistic impetus deriving, in part, from Christian theology after Constantinople, has worked to shape this cultural and intellectual backlash in the form of an equally imbalanced and polarizing *reversal*: one that views material reality as, not only the principal locus of value and meaning, but the only authentically existent register of being. Accordingly, modern science, in its orthodox, post-Darwinian form, typically considers all psychic and spiritual phenomena—if, indeed, they are considered at all—as epiphenomenal derivates of the one fundamental and purely material reality. Correlatively, those who venture to attempt to credit immaterial powers and principles with authentic existence tend to be regarded as deluded adherents of a thoroughly "unscientific" frame of mind.

Imbalance of either kind inevitably leads to disastrous consequences. A theology one-sidedly committed to a transcendent God and the reality of spirit, one that denigrates the value of body and soul, proves easy prey for the dark shadow forces that revel, unmolested, in the recesses of the psyche. This results in diverse forms of irreligious violence that betray the spirit of God and humanity alike. Meanwhile, the devastation—soul-spiritual and material both—bred of a culture dedicated to unthinking worship of a purely materialistic science can hardly be denied today.

The remedy for these coordinated afflictions—which continue to coexist as polar forces in the contemporary world—may be resurrection of a philosophically conscious appreciation of the genuinely *three-fold* nature of the human being. That necessitates, not merely a sense of the sublimities of spirit, but like attention to the body and soul, without the cooperation of which no form of spirit—no *Logos*, no Truth, Beauty, or Goodness—can manifest on earth.

If the spirit represents the universal dimension of human life and being, *body* signifies the complementary opposite. Effect of the soul's mixture with matter and so incarnation in the realm of time and space, *body* represents the contraction of the soul into distinct, finite forms of (ontic) existence: any and every particular thing or creature. If the spirit abides in a transcendent, intelligible realm of being, the body provides for existence in a world of sense characterized—not by eternal verity—but constant change. For animate bodies especially, that means processes of growth and decay, life and death.

With respect to the human being in particular, the body thus serves as the vehicle of the human soul's earthly existence—its containment in a finite, temporally and spatially delimited form—and its sojourn in a realm of continual transformation. The latter manifests in magical conversion of food stuffs into nourishment; mineral substance into bone marrow and organs of sensation; motor skill and energy into motion and deed; child into adult, and in all the illimitable processes (disintegrative as well as constructive metamorphoses) of alchemical transformation that comprise the very essence of this world—not of everlasting *being*—but of *becoming*.

Body is thus no simple matter; far from it. If, moreover, we view the creation as a whole, we (limiting ourselves, for now, to the natural world) may quickly become aware of very different classes or kinds of things displaying very different types of bodies.

We encounter mineral nature: inanimate forms—rocks, for instance—comprised of various substances, and typically exhibiting very durable forms that remain fixed in place unless moved by some external force.

We encounter vegetable nature: plants that, rooted in place, nonetheless display tremendous forces of organic life and growth.

We encounter animal nature: living creatures that not only move at will, but—capable of sensation and emotion and even limited forms of cognition—display sentience or consciousness of a sort absent in plants and rocks.

Finally, *we encounter human nature*, a unique species of being classically regarded (as in *Genesis*) as the crown of creation.

Rudolf Steiner, in his book *Theosophy,* presents a lucid and straightforward account of the human being as a three-fold of spirit, soul, and body. In that text, Steiner presents the human body itself as exhibiting a three-fold nature reflecting the diverse characteristics of the mineral, vegetable, and animal kingdoms, each of which comprise distinct aspects of human nature. Thus the human being possesses:

1) ***A physical body*** made of (mineral) substances that provide the substrate of the whole of our anatomy and physiology, including the typical structural form (*Gestalt*) of the body, and all the sense organs through which we experience an outer world;
2) ***An etheric or life body*** responsible for:
   a) the hereditary genetic forces that include the formative power creative of embryological development and species type;
   b) all vital life processes, which include nourishment, circulation, maintenance or rejuvenative repair of organic function, growth and reproduction;
3) ***A soul or astral body*** that bears the instincts, drives, emotions and desires characteristic of our animal nature. It is this astral body that confers, too, the active power of *sensation* and sympathetic or antipathetic reactions often associated with specific sense impressions.

I am fully aware that the mechanistic bias of modern science—one that reduces the whole of nature to the physical dimension alone—does not permit it to recognize the life (etheric) or soul/astral bodies as independent realities any more than it acknowledges the existence of spirit or soul *per se*. This remains part and parcel of a larger problem.

By virtue of reference to *the astral body,* this discussion has already entered us into the realm of soul. That overlap is only fitting, for *psyche* and *soma* are indeed tightly interwoven and integrated. The body serves as the vessel of the soul, which cannot unfold its life on earth except in its couplement with the vehicle that grounds its existence in the world of sense and serves as the instrument of the soul's experience and interaction with that world. Additionally, the animal desires that constitute a basic dimension of soul consciousness reflect the instinctual wisdom—and compulsion—derivative of hereditary forces and the whole evolutionary background of physical existence. This includes, although is not limited to, habits responsive to the primal desire for *self-preservation.*

The human soul, however, cannot be reduced to the register of animal desires. In fact, in Steiner's discussion, *the soul, like the body, exhibits a threefold nature.* We know, of course, that the species of consciousness characteristic of our kind includes more than emotion and sensation; we are distinguished from other animals by our unique cognitive capacities. Human beings, in accord with the definition written into our name (*homo sapiens*), are *thinking* creatures. Not so exclusively ruled by instinctual proclivities as other creatures, human consciousness typically involves a constant stream of mental activity.

We are continually not only sensing and reacting, but reflecting and evaluating our experience in a manner responsive to the *self-reflexive awareness*—the sense of personal identity, ego, or "I-consciousness"—singularly characteristic of our kind.

Steiner associates our mental or cognitive process with the faculty of *understanding* in the soul, and names it accordingly *Verstandesseele,*[378] literally "Understanding-soul," in contrast to the *Empfindungsseele,* or "sentient soul," so intimately linked to the aforementioned soul body and responsible for the soul's sensitive and emotional nature.[379] Due to the awkwardness of any more literal translation, *Verstandesseele* has been variously rendered in English as "intellectual," "rational," or simply "mind-soul."[380] None of these translations, however, capture the resonance of the German word *Verstand.* Two reasons may be educed for the insufficiency, both of which are well worth mentioning because they bear upon larger concerns.

First, while the idea of understanding can, on the one hand, be restricted to the kind of exclusively conceptual/cognitive process implied by our usual sense of the words "intellectual" or "rational," it can also possess a deeper or broader meaning implying a genuinely feeling and far more soulful dimension. Steiner's recognition of that dimension finds expression in the alternative name he awards this register of soul: *Gemütseele.* The German *Gemüt* qualifies as one of those words that elude apt translation altogether; so much so, that my (generally excellent) English translation, rather than wrestle with the impossible task of a concise rendering, leaves out the relevant sentence entirely.[381] Generally speaking, the German world *Gemüt* suggests the mood or temper associated with a given place or a people. Applied in the present context, the word implies the deeper level of knowing engendered, not so much from rational or conceptual comprehension, but the wisdom born of shared experience, as might be implied in the sense in which we might say two persons *understand* each other well.

The second cause of translational deficiency does not necessarily contradict the first, but does stand in contrast to it insofar as it may imply a more restricted and purely rational notion of understanding. After its introduction by Kant, the distinction between "Understanding" (*Verstand*) and "Reason" (*Vernunft*) emerged as a theme central to Romantic critiques of Enlightenment rationalism.[382] In this context, "understanding," in its more reduced form, denotes the more usual mental processes by which we organize, interpret, and make sense of information within a more or less established, typically sense-based, frame of cognitive reference. The soul's own *left-brain* means of "data processing," it may loosely be associated with those "small reasons" Emerson alludes to in "The Lecture on the Times." *Vernunft,* on the other hand— *Reason* with a capital R—refers in this context to a higher *intuitive* faculty of mind that—participating directly in what I have called *Logos*—intrinsically involves a moral or spiritual dimension of consciousness akin to that underlying the "great, immovable reason" Emerson invokes in his lecture.

Reference to this higher or more exalted sense of the soul's mental capacities forms a natural segue to the third register of soul recognized by Steiner, one called *consciousness* soul *(Bewußtseinsseele).* Just as the sentient soul forms the bridge to the body, consciousness soul *represents the bridge to spirit.* In its purest and truest form, it connotes the soul or human subject's awareness of itself in relation to—and as a vessel of—some transcendent source of being and intelligence, a godhead or Oversoul that exceeds the limits associated with its own sense of personal or egoic identity, the finitude of a selfhood attached to the perishable vessel of the body.

Steiner first introduces the consciousness soul in connection with the idea of *duty* ("*Pflicht*"), and thus the *moral* obligation that stems directly from the human subject's sense of its relation to, and indeed existential dependence upon, a Being and Power infinitely greater than its own. In this wise, the consciousness soul can also be regarded as the basis of, not the psyche's sensing, feeling, or thinking capacities, but the primordial source of its *will.* The higher octave of the human will is thus transcendentally rooted in the ethical imperative to do what the soul regards as right and good, thereby fulfilling its obligation to serve a higher master.

These are descriptions of the consciousness soul in its purest register, and imply that human *consciousness*, at root and in origin, *transcends* what we usually think of as rational cognitive process centered in the human subject,[383] and functions as the ontological ground of the same. Indeed, all human soul-consciousness or awareness originates in the consciousness soul—the conduit of spirit and the ego's relation to the Oversoul—even if its "pure" or higher form, a rough equivalent of which is simply *conscience,* is all too often in the back rather than the foreground of our mind.

The foregoing discussion reveals that the *soul,* in its three-fold nature of the sentient, mind, and consciousness souls, links to the *body* on the one hand and the *spirit* on the other. In so doing, it bridges the worlds of eternity and time, transcendence and immanence, heaven and earth. The soul exercises its agent power in the form of its capacities of sensitive feeling, thinking, and willing, or—to employ rather more scientific terms—*affective, cognitive,* and *volitional* activity.

While the foregoing discussion suggests a tentative correspondence between the sentient soul and feeling, the mind soul and thinking, and consciousness soul and willing, that provisional correlation cannot be taken literally or in such a manner that discretizes functions which habitually weave and interpenetrate each other. In discussing, for instance, Steiner's alternative designation of the *Verstandesseele* as *Gemüt,* we have already recognized that a deeper comprehension of the idea of *understanding* implies a feeling as well as a thinking dimension. Moreover, the will, the ideal source of which I have identified as consciousness soul's connection to *spirit,* evidently works through the *body,* the vehicle of our deeds or action. Just as clearly, any higher thinking or intuitive reason is a gift of spirit and one with our moral consciousness. Nor, finally, is it at all difficult to comprehend how the drives and desires innate in the bodily nature (the astral body, primarily, but this in turn depends upon the etheric and physical bodies) can readily affect our thinking, *and* vice versa. If we come truly to understand something in a manner not in accord with habitual (perhaps inherited; perhaps culturally ingrained) patterns of perception, our feelings and associated reaction patterns will likely be transformed.

This differentiated, non-dualistic philosophical framework can help identify the salient impetus of the Enlightenment project as well as the ground of its failure. The three-fold vision makes clear that the soul's conduct, and indeed the moral compass that affords guidance and good judgment, depends upon its aspiration, not merely to satisfy any self-centered worldly desires, but to conform its thinking, feeling, and willing to the prerogatives of the spirit; the Oversoul that is, at one and the same time, the ground of our universal humanity and participation of the soul in *Logos*, divine law or Word.

The delineation of the three-fold character—at once anthropological and cosmological—suggests, too, that the aspiration to attain communion with and participation in the spirit cannot be an exclusive or one-sided endeavor, and that the demands of the body need also be recognized. The spiritual obligations of the soul extend "below" as well as "above" its central station, and so in equal measure to the ever-changing world of sense, finitude, limit, concrete form, and endless transformation as to the transcendent realm of eternal verity. The soul finds itself linked as much to the real as to the ideal; to the particular fact as much as universal principle; the *Stofftrieb* or drive for material actualization as much as the *Formtrieb* that draws the soul towards conformity to archetypal idea.

In Schiller's *Aesthetic Education of Mankind*, the tension between mind or spirit (*Formtrieb*) and body or matter (*Stofftrieb*) is mediated by the *soul*-infused *Spieltrieb* (creative play-drive), thus constituting a three-fold system that proved foundational for Rudolf Steiner's own thinking. As I have argued, however, the dualism that backgrounds early modern philosophy, most explicitly and decisively in Descartes, does not allow for a viable idea of any *Logos*—any kind of Reason or creative Imagination[384]—that effectively *mediates* between two distinct worlds of mind and matter, spirit and sense.

The framework provided by Steiner's exposition of the three-fold nature of the human being can aid a more detailed understanding of this critical deficiency, one that post-Enlightenment thinkers such as Schiller, Emerson, and Steiner sought to remedy.

Steiner confirms, first of all, that the ego consciousness specific to the human creature, our capacity to re-cognize our self and consequently affirm our existence, is a function of the *cognitive* faculty proper to *the mind soul.* Steiner additionally associates the I-thought with the "higher" grade of the consciousness soul; but we should remember that *consciousness soul forms the bridge to the spirit* which, by definition, represents a transpersonal source of the human being, one that transcends the limits of personal egoity. In Emersonian terms, consciousness soul thus taps into the Oversoul, the universal ground of our humanity commensurate, too, with the divine I AM. The deep mystery of Selfhood may thus be seen to inhere in the complex manner in which the *reflective* capacity of the mind soul (*Verstandes-* or *Gemütseele*) integrates into its (self-) understanding the *totality* of sense and experience supplied by the body (all three registers) and feeling (sentient) soul *along with* the moral intuition—the conscience, and concomitant noetic insight into principles—devolving from the spirit, the Oversoul, the transpersonal and universal ground of our human being and identity.

That is a mouthful, certainly, but nonetheless presents a more or less coherent vision of the human Self as an integral unity of body, soul, and spirit. That unity involves a perpetual dance between the personal and transpersonal registers of our consciousness, the ego and the Oversoul,[385] the limits intrinsic in embodied existence, and the illimitable horizon of the higher mind. The integrity of the Self, however, depends absolutely on the cooperation of all elements, and—most centrally—the power of soul, the three-fold nature of which itself centers on our capacity for understanding (*Verstandesseele*) to mediate the worlds of sense and spirit. Epistemologically speaking, this implies an integration of understanding based upon empirical observation and all the rich information provided by sense and the intuitive capacities of heart-felt imagination and higher reason that are the creative gifts of the spirit. Morally speaking, it connotes an aspiration toward virtue and a putting off of vice.

What happens, however, if the self, the ego, does *not* originally conceive of itself in relation to any higher intelligence, and, correlatively, *not* organically or morally beholden to the degree of salutary lawfulness inscribed in the natural order of things?

That is precisely the story I have been telling, for it is just this fatal splitting and collapse of the integrity of Self that is engineered by the mechanical philosophy that developed under the aegis of the *cogito*. Descartes's famous formula constructs the ego—human self-understanding—not as a delicate but strong and flexible suspension bridge between the worlds of bodily sense and a transcendent spirit, but as a solid wedge between these. The *Verstandesseele*—the human mind, organ of our understanding—ceases to operate in cooperation with the higher intrinsically moral form of Reason as *Vernunft;* nor does it embrace the wholeness of embodied sense and affective experience in the form of *Gemüt,* but functions as a cold, heartless, and unimaginative species of rationality on the model of the dead things it projects as nature.

Look, after all, at the preconditions of the *cogito,* as we have previously described them. Descartes *withdrew* all consciousness from the sense-world, on the one hand, *and* from any kind of divine *Logos* that transcended the logic of his own self-reflexive form of understanding. It is said "No Man Is an Island," but Cartesianism isolates the soul's understanding *(Verstand)* of its own being, cutting it adrift from both body and spirit, and effectively declaring Everyman exactly that—an island.

In Steiner's teaching, spirit, soul, and body are *each* comprised of three aspects: physical, etheric, and soul body; sentient, "rational," and consciousness soul; and spirit self, life spirit, and spirit man. The differentiations of the spirit are not so material here; but note that the "lowest" and "highest" registers of soul are intrinsically linked to the body, on the one hand, and the spirit, on the other. This means that our sensibility and affect cannot be sundered from the body that is the vehicle of sensation and experience; and our morality cannot be separated from our participation in the sphere of universal principle upon which we stake our very being, our consciousness of our own humanity.

The rational or mind-soul *(Verstandesseele),* however, has no intrinsic connection with the body or spirit, but only one mediated by the sentient and consciousness souls on either side, the vessels of (respectively) our sensibility and conscience. *If,* therefore, we choose to think and believe, as the very root of our human constitution, in the peculiarly solipsistic rationality of the *cogito* and construe our capacity for understanding (or knowing) to be separate from all that is below and above, on heaven and on earth, then, in fact, we are (whether we know it or not) *thinking* of every man, woman, and child as, indeed, *an island.* Each of us is then a mental world unto themselves: a world estranged from other human souls, nature as a whole, and divinity.

If I have been focusing upon the Cartesian frame of mind that sets conditions for the soul's relation (or lack thereof) to spirit and to sense, this style of *thinking*—best exemplified by but not limited to Descartes—profoundly informs modes of *willing* and *feeling* in the early modern era. As we are by now accustomed to thinking in threes, let me add Baconian and Hobbesian contours to fill out the soul(less) portrait of a certain less-than-ideal type of the modern self: one that, regrettably, remains all too prominent today.

First, the elements of the triad:

1) Descartes, author of the *cogito,* places a heavy accent upon capacities of human *thinking,* that faculty of the *mind* historically closely associated with the *spirit.* (In German, for instance, the same word, *Geist,* can be translated as either Mind or Spirit).

2) Lord Bacon, as we have seen, celebrated the capacity of knowledge to confer practical *power*; action in and upon the world representative of those forces of *will* that act through the vehicle of the *body.*

3) Thomas Hobbes takes as a point of departure for his political philosophy the necessity of the relationship of one human being to another. He finds himself required to reckon, up front, with the natural *passions* that so easily incite strife in any society, and so engages—even if somewhat obliquely—the *feelings* of either antipathy or sympathy that underwrite human society. In so doing, he addresses forms of consciousness proper to the human *soul.*

Now, these additional touches:

1) We have said more than enough about Descartes's *thinking* already, emphasizing how the *ego cogito* can effectively isolate a self-reflexive human mind from any divine or spiritual world, on the one hand, and nature, on the other.

2) The Baconian *will*, employing knowledge as a means of control, expresses itself primarily in the form of the mastery of and power over an objectified nature (and, by extension, other human beings) actualized through technology.

3) The identity of the Hobbesian soul is imagined, originally, in a state of nature, wherein it exists, in and for itself, in a state of isolation. While less than splendid, this state nonetheless defines *its essential nature as one of self-interested separateness from others.*

Society, for Hobbes, is a kind of necessary evil, and one that inevitably excites the antipathy to others inherent in the soul, which will always work to undercut the collaborative effort required by practical exigency. Hobbes thus builds his political philosophy on the premise of a state authority capable of controlling *the feelings of antagonism native to the soul.* Like his forerunner Machiavelli, Hobbes casts ideals of love and virtue—bonds of fellowship and sympathy—as noble, but contrary to nature. Ideas of self-governance or the cultivation of virtue cannot realistically furnish basis for sound government or political philosophy.

The point here is that the forms of thinking, feeling, and willing characteristic of the modern self *all hang together.* The killing social atomization and decay of moral consensus that afflicts American (and indeed world) society today cannot be separated from ways of thinking fostered, or precluded, by the prevailing philosophy—the dominant mechanistic/technocratic worldview that so profoundly conditions every aspect of human culture. It does so even in many who view themselves as religious, because religion, too often disconnected from reason or any intellectually self-conscious relation to a living *Logos,* may not provide an authentic connection with the source of those ethical principles and spiritual laws that are the Rosetta Stone of Goodness, Truth and Beauty. It may also (as history demonstrates all too clearly) depreciate the body and soul, and deny the spiritual imperatives inherent in the limits that attend upon our existence as physical and psychological entities.

Indeed, a certain mutually enabling symmetry and synergy inheres between more rigid forms of religious belief and scientific materialism: between imaginations of godhead typically divorced from nature, and nature study divorced from God. Both traffic in their own species of fundamentalism, the key signature of which is always a marked tendency towards the *literalism* that sidelines the agency of the soul and its mission of ever-creative, ever *novel translation between* intelligible and sensible worlds, spirit and matter, genuine principles or laws (not rules and regulations) representative of eternal verities and the changing phenomena of the times.

One may safely say that neither science nor religion, as these comprise dominant mainstream phenomena today, teach or preach what Emerson called, in early lectures, "the Doctrine of the Soul," by which phrase I understand him to mean the integral unity of the human being as spirit, soul, and body.

With respect, in particular, to the scientific materialism that remains the dominant intellectual force in our culture, we can see quite clearly how the Cartesian-Baconian-Hobbesian heritage leaves the human soul or psyche clueless as to what it should aspire toward in the yearnings of the heart, thoughts of the mind, or actions of the hand. Moreover, a science that reduces all reality to the physical level alone, and thus entirely lacks any genuine idea of soul or spirit, does not in the least do away with all the drives, instincts, passions, and desires inherent in the psychosomatic register of our nature. Such a science, in the guise of one or another psychology, may well strive to employ its characteristic methods to study such impulses in the same fashion it does the forces in nature, but—lacking any real philosophy—we are provided with no education in the spiritual laws that teach us how to culture those energies to serve the kind of principled ends conducive to, not only our own health and personal fulfillment, but the betterment of humanity. Instead, whatever psychological knowledge is gained is too often put to the usual kind of commercially exploitative ends that destroy souls rather than promote the mature alliance with body and spirit that alone can fulfill our soul's true human nature.

Indeed, our culture's training in atomic individualism and antagonistic competition positively fosters disintegration. A philosophy, a mode of *thinking,* envisioning society as composed of—not true whole Individuals—but separate human parts and particles, leaves the soul's innate desires at the mercy of our lower instincts. Without a spiritually informed *feeling* for truth, this frame of mind unleashes the *will* to act in the behest of those same instincts. Consequently, while we imagine ourselves as rational beings guided by an intellectually sound worldview, in fact the profound spiritual deficiency of our thinking life—our intellectual understanding (*Verstand*) of ourselves and our world—allows unconscious and undisciplined soul desires (including greed, the lust for power, and domination of others) to rule the roost and govern the thoughts and deeds productive of the profound disharmony evident everywhere in society today.

Steiner, in the course of his objective and low-key exposition of theosophy, describes this basic scenario in a period dominated by the influence of the First and Second Industrial Revolutions:

> Our sentient soul interacts with thinking, with the spirit, just as it does with the body. To begin with, thinking serves the sentient soul: we formulate thoughts about our sensations and thus explain the outer world to ourselves. For instance, a child who has been burned thinks about it and arrives at the conclusion that fire burns. We do not blindly pursue our drives, instincts and passions; we think about them, thus creating opportunities to gratify them. This is the direction taken by our material culture, which is the sum of the services rendered to the sentient soul by thinking. Vast amounts of thought power has created ships, railroads, telegraphs and telephones—all things that for the most part serve to satisfy the needs of sentient souls.[386]

Such an ideology (as Deneen points out) hardly conforms to the principles of self-governance characteristic of the classical notion of liberty. I would, in fact, propose that a spiritually and intellectually sound understanding of the idea of freedom or principle of liberty cannot well be attained without a basic understanding of the three-fold nature of the human being. In the absence, for instance, of a self-conscious relation to an idea of spirit, or respect for natural limits, the very idea of freedom inevitably suffers (like that of law) appropriation by human subjects that willy-nilly imagine all manner of desires or personal predilections as essential "rights" without any critical reflection on the relation of these to spiritual source or physical ground, while neglecting or rejecting others that may present more rightful claims.

The utter degradation and, indeed, occlusion of any real idea of the nature of the human being, and the consequent gross confusion pertaining to the province and authority of laws safeguarding or limiting civil rights and liberties, counts as *the* outstanding topic of the times, one that expresses itself in a wide array of controversial issues: Covid World, abortion, gun laws, voting rights, critical race theory, heteronormativity. The ideological polarization characterizing the passionate acrimony attending these issues threatens to tear the country apart. If we are, as a society, ever to address the underlying concerns represented by these issues in a fashion responsive, not to the undisciplined emotions that rule the more unenlightened state of the soul, or transhumanist dystopias, or religious dogmatism, but rather to the spirit of humanity we all share in the inviolable core of our being, we need strive to recapture a more integral vision of our human nature.

Only then may we be able to read the Times, not as an onslaught of chaotic sense-impressions, but as a text resonant with meaning, a "masquerade of the eternities."

Chapter 11

COVID AND THE RIDDLE OF THE SPHINX

I shall be telling this with a sigh
Somewhere ages and ages hence:
Two roads diverged in a wood, and I—
I took the one less traveled by,
And that has made all the difference.[387]

I concluded Part I of *Reset or Renaissance* (*Two Roads: An American Scholar's Covid Chronicle*) with these lines from Robert Frost's poem ("The Road Not Taken") in late July of 2021, roughly one year and many pages ago. Those lines are every bit as apropos now as then, and the choice they imply remains world-important. On one level, the book you are reading revolves around Covid-19. On another, deeper level, it concerns itself with the far broader subject of that fork in the road.

Like Frost's traveler, we are all at a crossroads, faced with a fateful decision. That decision does not so much focus upon one or another concrete matter (whether to vaccinate yourself, or your children, for instance), as critically important as such may be. The question posed is full of still more portent. As I contemplate the matter, the image of a *crossroads* (a classical topos) puts me in mind of Oedipus and his rendezvous with the Sphinx: a moment of destiny, if there ever was one.

From her cliff perch outside the city of Thebes, the Sphinx had been terrorizing the populace. Seizing upon any and all travelers to or from the city, she would pose a riddle ("What walks on four legs in the morning; two at noon; and three in the evening?") and mercilessly devour all who could not solve it. None could…until Oedipus, employing his keen intellect like a sharpened sword, responded: *Man. He crawls on all fours as a babe; stands firm and upright in the noon-tide of life; and when the dusk of age closes in upon his stooped shoulders, goes upon a staff or cane into the night.*

The Sphinx, her puzzle solved and power broken, cast herself down from her lofty perch, and so was destroyed.

Did Oedipus receive fit reward for his victory? Certainly. Having freed Thebes from the curse of the Sphinx, Oedipus becomes not only its King, but husband of the widowed queen, Jocasta.

A snappy, happy ending to the course of affairs? Hardly. This, after all, is Greek tragedy, Sophocles rocking the cradle of Western civilization. Oedipus, while a brilliant thinker, was also a passionate hothead with serious anger issues. Moreover, while very good at figuring out the kind of intellectual puzzle posed by the Sphinx, he was a far less insightful interpreter of the deeper sort of riddles pronounced as prophecy.

Before all of the above events, the oracle at Delphi had informed Oedipus that he was destined to kill his father and marry his mother. Appalled at the prospect, he had set out on the road to Thebes, venturing far from home in an effort to evade that sordid fate. Unfortunately, in so doing, Oedipus—mistaken as to his true parentage—unwittingly fulfilled it. En route to Thebes, Oedipus, on foot, encountered a chariot at a crossroads. The driver imperiously commanded Oedipus to yield the right of way and the royal-looking personage inside hurled callous insults at him when he would not. Oedipus, enraged, killed them both. Little did he know that the man inside was Laius, King of Thebes, Oedipus's own father.

The fatal altercation at the crossroads transpired not so very long before Oedipus met the Sphinx on her perch outside the city, solved her riddle, became King of Thebes and husband to Queen Jocasta. Even if you don't already know, I am sure you can guess the identity of Oedipus's real mother.

The gods (never mind that they had arranged the whole affair) do not look kindly upon patricide and incest. They granted Oedipus and Jocasta years of peace and prosperity as well as two daughters and two sons, but ultimately made sure that the wages of sin were paid. Mysteriously, without external sign or warning, disaster struck the city. If life in Thebes had been desperate on account of the Sphinx, the city now suffered a terrible plague inside its own limits. People sickened, and the broad hand of death covered the land in dark shadow.

The play itself opens as a chorus of afflicted citizens applies to the savior-hero King Oedipus—whose keen mind had saved them once before—for remedy. Their spokesperson describes the people's plight in this moving plea:

> A God that carries fire,
> a deadly pestilence, is on our town,
> strikes us and spares not, and the house of Cadmus
> is emptied of its people while black Death
> grows rich in groaning and in lamentation.[388]

This sounds (does it not?) like a description of Covid World in the early days in New York City; at least, as the story (complete with photos) was reported in *The New York Times*.

Oedipus, compassionate ruler that he is, promises to do all within his power to alleviate the plague. Soon, a messenger (Creon, Oedipus's brother-in-law and uncle) returns from the oracle and, at Oedipus's command, discovers to all present the source of the city's affliction: spiritual pollution stemming from the unavenged murder of late King Laius. This news encourages Oedipus, who publicly vows to undertake all necessary measures to identify the murderer, the culprit that has brought doom upon Thebes.

There is grand and fatal irony here. While intellectually clever Oedipus had solved the riddle of the Sphinx, and so answered the question pertaining to the nature of man *in the abstract,* he possessed no real knowledge as to his own personal identity. He did not know his place of birth, his parents, his lineage. Nor, blinded by pride, could he control his passions, which failing led him, senselessly, to kill his father in a fit of road rage. That trait, moreover, persists, as evidenced by his treatment of the blind seer Tiresias (who hints at Oedipus's own guilt) and Creon in the aftermath of Creon's return from the oracle. In every way that really counts, Oedipus Rex—despite his ability to problem-solve after a fashion that put the keys of power into his hands, and his capacity for decisive (even heroic) action—did not know himself, his true identity, his "I" at all.

That fundamental deficiency underwrites the play's tragic action. Until Oedipus discovers, and somehow comes to terms with the agonizing truth that he himself is the cause of its desolation, the great city of Thebes will continue to suffer the plague that spoils the fruit of life even on the vine.

The Sphinx, sporting the body of a lion, the wings of a bird, and the face of a woman, stands for the mysteries of nature and of man and the part each has in the other. Perhaps, so long as we—metaphorically suspended somewhere between New England and Thebes—find ourselves still in a terrain of paths and crossroads, we can imagine the fork in Frost's poem as representative of two distinct approaches to the enigma of the Sphinx; two different approaches, or ways of thinking about, the profound riddle of man and nature. The path many have been walking—or rather hastening down—for some four centuries, represents the first (by now more traveled) way.

Francis Bacon's book *The Wisdom of the Ancients*[389] consists of roughly thirty short essays on a variety of topics inspired by one or another ancient figure, among them "Cupid, or an Atom (Explained of the Corpuscular Philosophy)," "Daedalus, or Mechanical Skill (Explained of Arts and Artists in Kingdoms and States)," and "Dionysius, or Bacchus (Explained of the Passions)." No sterile experimentalist in the region of the mind, Lord Bacon evidently liked to read—and still more—interpret and *explain* the riddling meaning of myths and fables. Fortunately for us, one of the tales he undertakes to analyze involves the very subject at hand. Number XXVIII, titled "Sphinx, or Science (Explained of the Sciences)" conveniently provides us with Bacon's metaphorical distillation of the essence of the sciences—all couched in terms of an encounter with the Sphinx.

Telllingly enough, Bacon's is not just *any* Sphinx, but explicitly Sophoclean. He begins by rehearsing the story of Oedipus's contest with the Sphinx, and so links his own reflections to this ancient Greek tragedy. The first sentence of his commentary baldly states:

> **EXPLANATION.**—*This is an elegant, instructive fable, and seems invented to represent science, especially as joined with practice.*[390]

What could be more to the point of our present inquiry?

Proceeding initially (and rather provocatively) to identify, not Oedipus but the Sphinx herself, with science, Bacon predictably ends up lauding the heroic intellect capable of solving the riddles posed by the Sphinx-cum-science. At the same time, he acknowledges that those *not* up to the task will find themselves (or their minds) literally torn apart by the terrible enigma she (Nature/Science/Sphinx) poses. Casual contemplation of nature's mysteries may provide pleasure, but woe to the insufficient intellect nonetheless intent upon concrete, practicable solutions!

> Then it is that [the Sphinx's riddles] become torturing, severe, and trying, and unless solved and interpreted, strangely perplex and harass the human mind, rend it every way, and perfectly tear it to pieces.[391]

This disability, however, contrasts with the more successful man of science represented by Oedipus himself:

> All the riddles of Sphinx, therefore, have two conditions annexed, viz: *dilaceration* to those who do not solve them, and *empire* to those that do. For he who understands the thing proposed, obtains his end, and every artificer rules over his work.[392]

We are here in the familiar terrain of scientific knowledge as *power over nature*. The essay continues with a clear statement of that classic Baconian position:

> For the true and ultimate end of natural philosophy is dominion over natural things, natural bodies, remedies, machines, and numberless other particulars.[393]

A notion stated yet more explicitly in the note appended to the text:

> This is what the author so frequently inculcates in the *Novum Organum;* viz: that knowledge and power are reciprocal; so that to improve in knowledge is to improve in the power of commanding nature, by introducing new arts, and producing works and effects.[394]

So far, Bacon's riff on Oedipus and the Sophoclean Sphinx serves but to provide poetic expression for the view of science and project of knowledge we have already described. The truly telling part of the tale, however, involves what, by Bacon's own reckoning, counts as the *second* kind of riddle posed by the Sphinx to man: the riddle of man's own nature, which Bacon presents as quite distinct from the first:

> Sphinx has no more than two kinds of riddles, one relating to the nature of things, the other to the nature of man; and correspondent to these, the prizes of the solution are two kinds of empire,—the empire over nature, and the empire over man.... The riddle proposed to Oedipus, the solution whereof acquired him the Theban kingdom, regarded the nature of man; for he who has thoroughly looked into and examined human nature, may in a manner command his own fortune, and seems born to acquire dominion and rule.[395]

Thus Lord Bacon, who—after adding a few ancillary plaudits praising Oedipus's worthy feat—ends "Sphinx, or Science" on this high note.

So it is that, if we were to go by Bacon's account alone, we would presume that Oedipus, conqueror of Nature-qua-Sphinx and so King of Thebes, reigns happily ever after, his acute problem-solving mind destined to provide his realm with ever-increasing abundance and civilizational progress. We, however, know better. We know that this is *not* the end of the Sophoclean story. We know that where Lord Bacon lands us is *not* the end of the play, but rather its beginning; and that the "fable" of Oedipus's encounter with the Sphinx represents not the last, but the first act of what is—after all—*tragic* drama.

If we recall what in fact transpires some years after Oedipus assumes kingship of Thebes and marries Jocasta—the terrible plague that wraps, like the coils of a serpent, around the city—may we not have to reevaluate how well Oedipus can be said to know the nature of man? Can a man who does not know himself truly know anything of human nature?

If, moreover, Oedipus stands for the "Man of Science," what does his fate—and the fate of Thebes—say about the epistemological path we have been on, now, for centuries? What does it say about *the real source of the plague* upon the city, the polis, and what must be done so that the sore affliction may at last come to an end?

Think about it. Lives depend upon an answer to this riddle. If it seems too hard, take courage, and remember the Enlightenment motto that comes from Horace by way of Kant: *Sapere aude!*

How long are we, the People, going to suffer "health experts" to sit upon the throne of Thebes? How long will we continue to imagine that a science utterly and deliberately devoid of soul and of spirit can reveal to us the secret of nature, *or* the mystery of our own (three-fold) human being? Will modern science, like Oedipus, *ever* have the courage to confront the terrible blindness that lies behind its ascent to power and command?

One could well end this chapter with this question. Yet, given our lengthy prior discussions of Descartes, a related one arises. How do the premises implicit in Bacon's "Sphinx or Science" comport with the Cartesian ground of modern consciousness? That is not a particularly riddling question, and the answer is clear: *very well.* Recall to mind the starkness of the subject/object, man (*res cogitans*)/nature (*res extensa*), or mind/matter dualism that underlies Cartesian philosophy. Do we not find the same dualism operative in Bacon's explanations? It is explicit in the pains he takes to distinguish the two distinctly different kinds of riddles posed by the Sphinx. If the anatomy of the Sphinx herself belies such clear distinction and suggests the impossibility of drawing so clear a dividing line between man and nature, Bacon does not *see* this.

That blindness is of a piece with the manner in which he violently truncates Sophocles's text. Bacon turns a profound—and profoundly tragic—exploration of the relationship between *intellectual hubris and egotism,* on the one hand, and *the physical and spiritual health of the polis,* on the other, into a tidy "fable" neatly portraying the ascendancy of mind over matter and man over nature: a home-cooked recipe for science triumphant. A contemporary translation of this philosophy might read: *Operation Warpspeed. Lockdown. Test and Trace. Mask. EUA. Universal Vaccination.* And the rest.

Can a mythical creature like the Sphinx ever die or be destroyed? Is it possible that she may in fact be perched on her cliff outside the city gates once again? If so, we must question whether, this time around, the Oedipal Man who would command nature, and exercise "dominion over natural things, natural bodies, remedies" knows the answer to the riddle she is posing. The gods, after all, tend to get impatient when humankind refuses, again and again, to learn from history. From fact. Or from fiction.

~

Ralph Waldo Emerson—like Robert Frost, a native New Englander—sees things differently. As the whole of his "little book" *Nature* represents Emerson's cryptic answer to the riddle of the Sphinx, it should not be too surprising that she puts in a cameo appearance in this text as well.[396] Following upon "Commodity" and "Beauty" and preceding "Discipline" and "Idealism," Emerson's long discourse on "Language" represents the third and central chapter devoted to the "uses" of nature. Near its end, we find this passage:

> This relation between the mind and matter is not fancied by some poet, but stands in the will of God, and so is free to be known by all men.... When in fortunate hours we ponder this miracle, the wise man doubts, if, at all other times, he is not blind and deaf...for the universe becomes transparent, and the light of higher laws than its own, shines through it. It is the standing problem which has exercised the wonder and study of every fine genius since the world began; from the era of the Egyptians and the Brahmins, to that of Pythagoras, of Plato, of Bacon, of Leibnitz, of Swedenborg. There sits the Sphinx at the road-side, and from age to age, as each prophet comes by, he tries his fortune at reading her riddle.[397]

Thus does Emerson place the Sphinx squarely in the center of the perennial problem of philosophy.

While Lord Bacon appears in Emerson's inventory of luminaries, Emerson's approach to the matter strikes a resoundingly different chord than that of "Sphinx, or Science." Unlike Bacon, Emerson's chief concern does not lie with mind and matter construed as *separate estates*, but rather with the profound mystery of their intimate correspondence and connection. In exploring the issue, his tone—eschewing explanation that reduces image to concept—is not one of prospective intellectual conquest and dominion, but of wonder and astonishment. His own "prophetic" response to the Sphinx takes the form of metaphysical essay rather than scientific or solution:

> There seems to be a necessity in spirit to manifest itself in material forms; and day and night, river and storm, beast and bird, acid and alkali, pre-exist in necessary Ideas in the mind of God, and are what they are by virtue of preceding affections in the world of spirit. A Fact is the last issue of spirit. The visible creation is the terminus or the circumference of the invisible world.[398]

Such statement may well appear profoundly foreign to our modern scientific sensibilities. The materialist temperament that has reigned for hundreds of years disposes us to regard such sentences as incomprehensible and irrelevant. Neoplatonic effusions are not to be taken seriously by the scientist armored and plated in the epistemological and methodological presuppositions that equip him to smash the atom, crack the genetic code, muster the intelligence necessary to survey and control the whole world-wide net of human as well as inhuman things, and otherwise successfully answer the riddle of the Sphinx and rule the city of the world.

Yet, casting a glance at the world today, are there not good grounds for such confidence to falter, or even shrink back in horror? How far have we come, really, on the road to truth by interpreting facts as the consequence of so-called physical laws rather than endeavoring to comprehend them as "the end or last issue of spirit"?

This is the way I am endeavoring, here, to see the facts of Covid World: not as isolated phenomena caught up in chains of material and efficient causation, but *as symptoms of the state of the human soul that perpetually creates its world in the image of its own self-understanding.* As in *Oedipus Rex,* the health of the nation, the polis, does not reflect accidental events in some exterior "nature" supposed to have no essential connection with the consciousness of humanity. It reflects, instead, the mental and spiritual condition of the soul itself.

Covid-19, lab leak or no, can no more be an accident than is the plague that descends upon Thebes on account of the reign of Oedipus Rex, at one and the same time slayer of the Sphinx and unconscious murderer of father, mother, wife.

How do we seek alternative—perhaps less tragic—modes of knowing and understanding? I can offer only scattered clues culled from Emerson's gnomic text. Here are a few lines from the penultimate paragraph of "Language" that provide provocative hints as to another way one might approach the Sphinx; whether she be found by the side of the road outside the city, or in the pages of a book:

> "Every scripture is to be interpreted by the same spirit which gave it forth," is the fundamental law of criticism. A life in harmony with nature, the love of truth and of virtue, will purge the eyes to understand her text.[399]

This is not Lord Bacon's way; nor the path our civilization has chosen. Undoubtedly, many sincere scientists, natural as well as social, are moved by a deep reverence for nature (human as well as non-human), but the *language* of our preferred "scientific" method stems from philosophical assumptions incompatible with the congruence, or imaginative confluence, of subject and object implied here. More and more scientists—especially biologists—are recognizing and writing about this dilemma.[400]

While we cannot, unfortunately, proceed very far down this other way here, it is possible to mine even these few lines for a further hint as how better to *see* all that may be in store down what has, for so long, been our chosen path. A single Emerson phrase returns us, one last time, to Oedipus and the long-term consequence of his slaying of the Sphinx: "*Purge the eyes.*" That is, literally, what Oedipus does—*after* the fact. When Oedipus discovers the truth about himself, and finds his mother/wife Jocasta hung by her own hand, he seizes a brooch from the corpse and gouges out his own eyes. He gouges out those near-sighted, physical, literal, sense-bound eyes that—visible symbol of the egocentric "scientific" intellect that saw *nothing* even while imagining that it could see and command *all*—so betrayed him.

The saga does not end with Oedipus's terrible self-mutilation, his willful physical blinding. Banished by decree of Creon (now King) from the society, Oedipus wanders in exile, homeless and alone, except for the precious guidance and company of his two faithful daughters, Ismene and Antigone, feminine soul figures who become, literally, his two eyes. It is not, finally, any intellectual knowledge that will assuage his anguish, but the suffering borne alike by him and his daughters, which finally brings true self-understanding, dignity, redemption, and even holiness in death.

Greek drama qualifies as the historical origin of democracy, and citizens were once required to attend the great theatrical festivals where plays like those of Sophocles were staged. Evidently, law-givers recognized that the integrity of the polis depended upon citizens striving for deeper knowledge of self and society. Intellectual or "expert" knowledge alone would not suffice. Instead, civic integrity called for a mode of understanding that encompassed body, soul, and spirit; animal appetite, intellectual and moral vision, and passions of the heart. The theatre provided one chief means towards that end, one the community shared.

We stand today at a dramatic remove from such critical political self-reflection. Yet if we are to solve the lacerating problems that riddle our polis, we would do well to rethink the path we tread, not only on the floor of the Senate and down academic corridors, but in the yellow wood of our innermost hearts and minds. Perhaps someday, we will be able to say more of what we have seen and known along a road less traveled by. That could make all the difference.

Chapter 12

TROUBLE WITH THE UNIVERSE: THE MATTER OF NATURE

It is time to speak more plainly; to leave the tragic theatre, and venture back to the agora, where all sorts of people come and go. There, if we are fortunate, we may happen upon a philosopher; one of Socratic bent, stirring up trouble; posing questions the state may regard as seditious; kindling uncertainties the authorities sense must be stamped out like spot fires, lest they strike tinder, spread, and grow into an incinerating conflagration.

That might not be the worst that could happen. It could well be preferable to decay and destruction by way of an interminable process of internal corruption. What might *that* look like here, in America, today? Imagine Big Pharma lobbyists, unprincipled lawmakers, and others of their ilk crawling maggot-like about in the intestines of the House and Senate, eating out the guts of American democracy.

Why not, then, kindle the fire of the mind, the torch of enlightenment, once again? Why not relay, like a messenger running the flanks of mountains, the beacon of flame over the ridges of history, from Athens to Paris, to Boston, to Washington, where presidents to this day sit in state amidst classical columns? Few today have confidence that—if the purifying fire were allowed to burn—democracy in America might rise again, phoenix-like, from the ashes. But who knows? There is, after all, always *Nature*, human and Emersonian:

> The foundations of man are not in matter, but in spirit. But the element of spirit is eternity. To it, therefore, the longest series of events, the oldest chronologies are young and recent. In the cycle of the universal man, from whom the known individuals proceed, centuries are points, and all history is but the epoch of one degradation.
>
> We distrust and deny inwardly our sympathy with nature. We own and disown our relation to it, by turns. We are, like Nebuchadnezzar, dethroned, bereft of reason, and eating grass like an ox. But who can set limits to the remedial force of spirit?

The key question, as I have framed it, concerns *the dual legacy of the Enlightenment*, the two paths that lead in and out of the 18th century—and which of those paths we choose to follow. The American and French Revolutions represent the Age of Reason's most famous political progeny. Scientific Materialism and Romantic Idealism represent the philosophically-minded older and younger brothers that never can or will get along.

Before the mid-19th century, the doctrine of materialism had not decisively split science off from the humanities, relegating philosophy, arts and letters to the margins of mind and culture. Professionalization and specialization had not yet set in with the disciplined rigor that characterizes academic studies still today. Student at a university such as Jena (a horse ride away from Goethe's home in nearby Weimar, and a thriving center of intellectual inquiry in the last decade of the 18th and first decade of the 19th centuries) knew in the marrow of their bones that ideas mattered. Schiller's lectures on history drew rock concert-sized crowds. Schelling's deconstruction of scientific materialism in his *Naturphilosophie* (the *Philosophy of Nature* that flowed via its Coleridgean tributary into the woodland brooks and streams of Emerson's American mind) attracted heated controversy. Fichte required police protection for teaching the heretical philosophy of the Transcendental *I AM*.

Covid's great gift to the world may consist in dramatizing, on an unprecedented scale and with unheard-of political force, the profoundly *anti-intellectual* character of the philosophical materialism that underwrites the prevailing ideology today. The dark side of the dialectic of enlightenment licenses the likes of Dr. Fauci to lock down not only the world, but the doors of the mind because a computer modeler in England spills a souped-up bowl of numbers all over the globe.

I have critiqued the metaphysical premises underlying the Matrix (or Machine, or Leviathan), the sociopolitical effect of the dialectic of enlightenment. The list of luminaries (Horkheimer and Adorno, Guénon, Del Noce, Heidegger, Whitehead) who have levelled kindred analyses could go on and on. Nor should it be forgotten that science itself (quantum theory: Bohr and Bohm; systems theory: Bateson and Thom) long ago discredited any orthodox form of mechanistic determinism.

The tragic fact is that none of the vast trove of insightful critique has seemed to make much—if any—difference. The cancer of materialism and the scientistic technologism it breeds long ago entered deep into the body of the mind and (especially in the wake of the Third and Fourth Industrial Revolutions) metastasized there, continually affecting the patterns of thought and deed that produce and reproduce human culture. The religion of transhumanism represents the mythic apogee of this seemingly unstoppable juggernaut. Nonetheless, I cherish hope that the nightmare of the Covid moment may provide a window of opportunity for revisiting the intellectual premises that underlie the crises of modernity. Who knows what may grow from such reseeding?

It all begins—as does Enlightenment itself—with nature, humankind's view of which inevitably molds its own self-image.

In the introduction to *Nature,* Emerson defines his topic. Distinguishing it from Art, he acknowledges the popular sense of the word:

> *Nature,* in the common sense, refers to essences unchanged by man; space, the air, the river, the leaf. *Art* is applied to the mixture of his will with the same things, as in a house, a canal, a statue, a picture.

In addition to this colloquial vocabulary, Emerson recognizes a more philosophical one:

> Philosophically considered, the universe is composed of Nature and the Soul. Strictly speaking, therefore, all that is separate from us, all which Philosophy distinguishes as the NOT ME, that is, both nature and art, all other men and my own body, must be ranked under this name, NATURE.

Emerson further advises us that he does not intend to make much of this difference, and will employ the word in both senses more or less indiscriminately. A contemporary audience will receive his explanation concerning why with incredulous regret:

> [Man's] operations taken together are so insignificant, a little chipping, baking, patching, and washing, that in an impression so grand as that of the world on the human mind, they do not vary the result.[401]

Emerson clearly did not live in the age of climate change, mass extinction, continents of plastic afloat in the ocean. He did not live in the age some call the Anthropocene. How did we get from there to here, and what can we do about it?

It all begins (even if it does not end) with a *way of thinking.*

To gain clearer sight of that fork in the woods I wish to illumine, the divergent paths leading out of the Age of Reason, I will try to distinguish with still greater metaphysical precision the contrast between what Emerson, in *The Transcendentalist,* calls the *Idealist* and *Materialist* views of nature. Following Emerson, I suggest that we may conceive of nature, in the first place,[402] as the

Body of the World, of which our own human bodies are signal parts. A philosophy of nature thus hinges upon how we see and construe this World Body, how we understand its essential constitution.

If we are to grasp the essential difference between Idealist and Materialist views of nature, we may commence by stating that the Materialist starts by reducing the reality of the natural world to the physical (body) alone, imagining the laws of plant and animal life to be, in fact and principle, derivative of the laws of physics. Biologist Ursula Goodenough begins the first chapter of her book *The Sacred Depths of Nature* by stating: "Everything in our universe, including the Earth and its living creatures, obeys the laws of physics."[403] Near the beginning of chapter 2, "The Origins of Life," Goodenough writes, "Like everything else, chemistry is reducible to physics."[404]

Goodenough's claim here constitutes the foundational premise of science itself as such is conceived and practiced today. Modern science, does not (like Schelling or Coleridge) recognize Life as a metaphysical principle that transcends the sphere of *physical* causation. Only so is it possible for Goodenough to write, in her second chapter, "Life emerged from nonlife" and "Life can be explained by its underlying chemistry just as chemistry can be explained by its underlying physics."[405] Only so, is it possible for modern scientists to pursue "origin of life" experiments in their laboratories, fantasizing that, like Victor Frankenstein, the right combination of chemical matter vivified by the right sort of electromagnetic spark may magically produce Life. Any explanation other than "life emerged from nonlife" falls, today, outside of the realm of "science" and into the realm of irrational or occult belief.

If modern day materialistic science refuses to recognize the relative autonomy of the life body (which vital force is analogous if not identical to the "chi" in Tai Chi and traditional Chinese medicine), the astral or soul body fares no better. Biologists and psychologists alike recognize the drives, desires, and even emotions exhibited by higher non-human as well as human animals, but what respectable natural scientist acknowledges *soul* as an autonomous register of reality, linked with and yet irreducible to *any* physiological or neurobiological basis? The brain power and money flows today, copiously, in the other direction. We study states of mind as effects of the neurophysiological circuitry that are mapped with zeal, confident that such research will supply powerful new tools for understanding mental and psychological health.

As for the historic origin of this attitude, we can revert again to source. René Descartes regarded animals (including dogs, whom he tortured in experiments) as nought but unfeeling machines. Descartes's book on the human passions (his last) inclined to treat these similarly: not as thoughts of the heart, but as emotional machinery, traceable, always, like the tears that fall from the clouds, to rationally explicable (that means, material and efficient) causes.

Thus we have the typical materialist vision of nature, one characterized through and through by the *a priori* reduction of the reality of the World Body to the purely physical level alone, refusing to recognize either life or soul as autonomous registers of being and becoming.

Even this, however, is not wholly accurate; even this does not capture the full extent of the reductionism that characterizes materialism. Philosophically considered, the very idea of body—*including the physical body*—is integrally linked to that of life and soul. Eschewing altogether the latter two ideas, the materialist cannot, by definition, truly understand the body as such; as an entity, that is, a corporeal vessel, *organized by a living Idea not derivative of its purely material composition.*

Even in ordinary, commonsense parlance, the word *body* typically refers to a physical vessel imbued with *life.* Although exceptions no doubt may be cited,[406] we generally do not refer to dead or inanimate objects (a billiard ball, or a house, for instance) as a body in the same sense we apply the term to a person or animal. We do speak of a *body* of water, but most confidently when that refers to one naturally containing life; a sterile irrigation canal or even dead reservoir might not be so designated. We speak also of "a body of work," but that reflects our sense of the *living* intelligence that engendered and remains incorporated within it.

The wisdom thus inscribed in common usage points to a fundamental philosophical truth, one that we will discover to be of utmost import when we eventually return our attention (as we will) to Covid, vaccination and the transhumanist-inflected Great Reset agenda. I take as axiomatic that *the principle of body is fundamentally distinct from (and in critical respects contrary to) that of matter.* Correlatively, *the body is not, primarily or essentially, a material object or thing,* even if matter plays a role in the constitution of the body.

Clarifying this naturally requires a working idea of what, after all, *matter* really is, a riddle that science has, true to its colors, endeavored (unsuccessfully) to solve by breaking things down into ever smaller components. Quantum physics informs us that such rabid reductionism does not end in any definitive rational resolution of the question, but impenetrable enigma or poetic sallies of spirit. Niels Bohr writes, "When it comes to atoms, language can be used only as poetry."[407] Philosophy, however, *can* shed additional light on this matter.

Children of a resolutely materialist culture, we tend to think of "matter" as substance: that which functions as the ground of the actual existence of any and every thing. According, however, to Neoplatonic precept, nothing could be further from the truth. For the Platonist, all authentic existence and identity derives from the realm of ideal form: substance or real being is always *noetic* in essence. This holds for plant and mineral forms as well as animal bodies, but can be most readily comprehended in relation to the latter, including the body of most vital interest to us: our own human bodies. It is one or another archetypal form of intelligence that confers identity upon a soul *and*, correspondingly, the body that contains and reflects the genius or specific *nature* of that soul.

Neoplatonic tradition, the source of virtually all philosophical idealism in the West, saturates Emerson's thinking in *Nature* (the first edition of which featured an epigraph from Plotinus), and indeed all his major works. It is thus no surprise to find him elaborating the view of the body just expressed in his essay "The Poet." "The soul makes the body," writes Emerson, before quoting these lines from "the wise Spenser":

> So every spirit, as it is most pure,
> And hath in it the more of heavenly light,
> So it the fairer body doth procure
>
> To habit in, and it more fairly dight,
> With cheerful grace and amiable sight.
> For, of the soul, the body form doth take,
> For soul is form, and doth the body make.

Significantly, Emerson regards this metaphysical insight to be of profound *religious* import, illuminating, as it does, something of the underlying nature of creation as a whole.

> Here we find ourselves, suddenly, not in a critical speculation, but in a holy place, and should go very warily and reverently. We stand here before the secret of the world, there where Being passes into Appearance, and Unity into Variety.[408]

What, then, of *matter* itself? According to Plotinus, matter is not the substrate of substance, existence, or identity, but the opposite. *Matter, in essence, is nullity;* the absence of ideal form, or life, or any principle with indwelling intelligence or formative power. Plotinus:

> Matter is not Soul; it is not Intellect, is not Life, is no Ideal-Principle, no Reason-Principle; it is no limit or bound, for it is mere indetermination; it is not a power, for what does it produce?
>
> It lives on the farther side of all these categories and so has no title to the name of Being. It will be more plausibly called a non-being.... It is no more than the image and phantasm of Mass, a bare aspiration towards substantial existence...in itself invisible.[409]

More succinctly:

> Matter, is, so to speak, the outcast of Being, it is utterly removed, irredeemably what it was from the beginning: in origin it was Non-Being and so it remains....
>
> Matter, as the Actualization of Non-Being, is all the more decidedly Non-Being, is Authentic Non-Existence.[410]

Admittedly, absorbing this perspective, so contrary to the metaphysical prejudices long ingrained in our systems of thought, may require nothing short of a kind of radical *metanoia,* an intellectual revolution.

So be it.

It is crucial to recognize that the foregoing definition of matter does *not* mean that matter plays an inconsequential role in creation or nature in general; on the contrary. Plotinus himself is clear on this. Effectively a principle of negation (though not one with agent power), it is the entrance of soul-spiritual intelligence into the sphere of matter that enables particular forms of embodied being to exist as *distinct* corporeal entities and limited forms of consciousness. *Without* the admixture of matter, consciousness could not descend into the sensible sphere wherein many particular things come and go, arise, grow, decay, pass away, and evolve, as we know bodies (and, in their own way, psychic entities) certainly do.

As the ground of separation from the infinite soul-spiritual source of All, and so divinity itself, matter thus supplies the basis for finitude, and the manifest differentiation of the Many out of the One reflected in the multifarious character of our experienced world. In other passages, Plotinus calls attention to the non-being of matter as coincident with a sense of illimitable potential. Nothing in and of itself, it nonetheless serves as the ground of any and all forms of ontic existence:

> But what we think of as Matter, what we assert to be the potentiality of all things, cannot be said to be actually any one being among beings; if it were of itself any definite being, it could not be potentially all.[411]

One finds here the root relation of matter to the Latin word *mater,* and so (the idea of) *mother*, as in *Mother Nature.* It need be recognized, however, that matter can only serve in this wise in combination with soul, and the many Ideas that, as *logoi*, give rise to the myriad forms of embodied life, "all creatures, great and small." It is consequently those ideas, those many souls or *logoi* inherent in Nature (understood now as *anima mundi* or World Soul), that generate *real diversity,* not matter that—in and of itself or (so to speak) left to its own devices—is purely uniform, homogeneous, without form, identity, intelligence, direction, intent, character or meaning.

Crucially, it is precisely this non-form of non-being that Descartes, and Galileo after him, posits as the ontological ground of the sensible universe, as the essential nature of nature itself.[412] In Descartes, this purely material (and so essentially dead) nature takes formless form as *res extensa* (cf. Plotinus: "the image and phantasm of Mass"). In Galileo, it assumes form in the reduction of reality (or Being) to those *primary qualities* that lend themselves to exact measurement, precisely because they lack any qualitative or ideal form that would empower these qualities—or rather the bodies they characterize—to stand on their own as distinct beings or unique forms of authentic existence.

"The most abstract truth is the most practical."[413] So writes Emerson on the very first page of *Nature,* and the *practical and political resonance* of all these metaphysical concerns is, I hope, not unapparent. The whole dialectic of enlightenment, rich with nightmarish sociopolitical consequence, rests upon the basis of this reduction of the horizon of Being and Existence (including, ultimately, human being) to the species of non-Being implicit in the *purely material* dimension of *(non-)existence,* the perfect uniformity of which functions as the conceptual basis for all forms of (systematic) totalization, including, finally, totalitarian forms of political power.

Recall Adorno and Horkheimer's understanding of the metaphysical basis of the dialectic of enlightenment:

> For the Enlightenment, anything which cannot be resolved into numbers, and ultimately into one, is illusion.... In functional science the differences are so fluid that everything is submerged in one and the same *matter* [emphasis added].[414]

As here implied, integral to any system of totalization is the reduction of the reality of *number* itself from the *qualitative* dimension operative in Pythagorean philosophy—within which context "3," for instance, possesses a real noetic or ideal significance generative of all meaning associated with triangles, triads, trinities, etc.—to a *quantitative* sense of number, which abstraction coincidently reduces all reality to a single plane of (non-)existence. Things possess no "vertical" reference to any non-objectifiable realm of intelligible or spiritual essence or ideal form. Rather, all reality is strung out like numbers (or hung out like laundry) on a line.

Materialism, one might say, thus encourages us to believe that we might come to *know* the essence of a human being by purely quantitative analysis; a science of precise and painstaking measurement. This is the mode of thinking at work in the minds of those who believe that the identity of human persons can be comprehensively understood on the basis of a set of algorithms drawn from ever more sophisticated biometric data. That in turn presupposes the prior reduction of both psychological and organic to purely physical (and so ultimately measurable) function.

Naturally, once people are no longer seen as human beings possessed of a unique self-standing form of authentic existence, but instead are reduced to the status of data points, all bets are off with respect to any natural rights or liberties. We may grant human beings rights, but not statistics. Once the former is reduced to the latter, administrative governance clearly becomes more manageable and infinitely more efficient, and control duly optimized.

On the basis of the above discussion, we can draw these conclusions pertaining to the materialist construction of the nature of Nature:

1. In principle, *materialism repudiates the view that archetypal idea (ideal form or noetic essence), soul, life, and body are integral aspects of the constitution of Nature.* The Creation or the World Body—ontic existence in its entirety—is to be understood on the basis of an axiomatic *reduction* of all things to "primary qualities" amenable to a system of exact numeric measurement. All "wholes" are to be understood as an interactive ensemble of separable parts which are subject to quantitative analysis. All things are thus to be reduced to (abstract) quantities.
2. The basis of that system of measurement is *a single uniform plane* of material (non-)existence.[415] There is no difference (as in Platonism) between sensible and intelligible (or in any form supersensible) worlds or dimensions of being, as the Idea of the latter is unintelligible in the context of

materialism. Nor is there any essential difference between terrestrial and celestial spheres. The same laws (gravity, for instance) regulate both.

3. Given point #1 above, it may be postulated that "things themselves"(any and all natural entities, including plants, animals, and especially persons) do not possess authentic, essential, independent, ontic existence. (Even if we *imagine* they do possess such, the metaphysical premises of science do not allow it to understand or treat them accordingly.)
4. Instead, all things are to be understood as a function of "*laws*" which describe or model the behavior of phenomena as such can be measured, quantified, and plotted on that single uniform (quality-less) material plane which alone represents "reality."
5. That material dimension, itself lacking any inherent or authentic (noetic) substance, must itself be considered intrinsically "meaningless," as the very idea of meaning implies reference to another immaterial or spiritual plane of existence, which is not recognized as real within the materialist frame of reference. "*Representation gives way to universal fungibility.*"[416]
6. The so-called "laws of nature" are likewise not derivative of any intelligible dimension of being, or any divine *Logos* that supplies the *ratio* between intelligible and sensible dimensions of existence. The origin of the order and agency of these laws is assumed to inhere in the physics proper to the uniform material dimension alone and so to have no more *substantial* (intrinsically noetic) basis than the (non-)existent things the behavior of which these "laws" regulate.
7. Grasp of the "laws" of nature, while not affording insight into the *meaning* of anything (or all things together), nonetheless may suffice to predict, regulate, and enable manipulation of material things in order to produce certain material results. Application of the human will in the form of technology thus may be facilitated by a materialistic philosophy. As the physical laws of nature themselves do not, however, bear any intrinsic relationship to any immaterial principle (such as the Good), nature itself provides no moral guidance as to how technological power may *ethically* be employed. In this, man himself is left, literally, to his own devices, a most dangerous situation insofar as materialism teaches him to see himself—and other persons—as possessed of no more authentic existence than anything else.
8. Implicit in all of the above is the tenet that nature (and by logical extension, human nature) is intrinsically meaningless.

This strictly materialistic vision of nature is liable to instill terror and desolation in the souls of sensitive human beings aware of the full range of its implications. The first chapter of biologist Ursula Goodenough's 1998 book *The Sacred Depths of Nature* offers one poignant confirmation of this truth.

> I've had a lot of trouble with the universe. It began soon after I was told about it in physics class. I was perhaps twenty, and I went on a camping trip, where I found myself in a sleeping bag looking up into the crisp Colorado night. Before I could look around for Orion and the Big Dipper, I was overwhelmed with terror. The panic became so acute that I had to roll over and bury my face in my pillow.
>
> - All the stars that I see are part of but one galaxy.
> - There are some 100 billion galaxies in the universe, with perhaps 100 billion stars in each one, occupying magnitudes of space that I cannot begin to imagine.
> - Each star is dying, exploding, accreting, exploding again, splitting atoms and fusing nuclei under enormous temperatures and pressures.
> - Our Sun too will die, frying the Earth to a crisp during its heat-death, spewing its bits and pieces out into the frigid nothingness of curved spacetime.[417]

You can find the inscription of virtually all the key elements of the materialist vision of nature—and its logical psychospiritual consequences—in Goodenough's account of her youthful experience. Note that her "trouble with the universe" begins with the intellectual understanding of the nature of the cosmos conveyed in *physics* class. The account provided there (which she summarizes) describes nature exclusively in terms of the presumed facts of the physical matter of the universe. The behavior of that matter follows "laws" derivative of properties presumed intrinsic in that very matter.

None of the physical bodies, none of the stars, (including our sun), are supposed to have any distinctive essence or character that transcends and even shapes its defining material characteristics. Twenty-year old Goodenough may have known that our sun is effectively a source of life on the planet earth, but she had no concept, no dream that the radiant power of the sun might manifest a metaphysical or spiritual principle of Life that transcends its material constitution. She was hardly encouraged to imagine that the phenomenon of solar light and warmth might reflect the sun's participation in and emanation of a kind of Life that partakes of eternity.

In its traditional resonance, the idea of eternity intrinsically implies an *immaterial* dimension of Being: one not subject to the disintegration and death that so terrified young Goodenough. *As it should so terrify,* for the nature of the universe as it had been conveyed to her is ruled by impermanence, non-existence, and *death* unredeemed by any hint of meaningful transformation or new birth.

Note, too, that the scientific information, the *conception* of things delivered to the physics student, finds expression largely in terms of quantity: innumerable stars are part of *one* galaxy, and stars and galaxies are reckoned in the *billions*. The almost incomprehensible magnitudes do not, for Goodenough, translate into any kind of awe-inspiring sense of the sublime in a positive way. Because nothing possesses intrinsic being or quality, the immeasurable reaches of the cosmos do not magnify a sense of any sacred supersensible presence that may be the source of it all. What is conveyed instead is an overwhelming sense of the *absence* of any such presence: pure emptiness and nullity; the "nothingness" proper (cf. Plotinus) to the metaphysical nature of matter itself. Billions and billions and billions of shining stars, but as none partake of real being, it all adds up to zero—and pure, existential terror.

By extension, the "lawful" order of the universe itself, lacking real *logos* or *telos*, effectively amounts not to order, but chaos. The iron determinism of purely material laws extinguishes (rather than creates) meaning by persuading us that causation—some combination of chance and necessity mechanistic in essence—confirms the absence rather than the presence of conscious intelligence. No thing refers to any spiritual dimension of being; every thing is, literally, nothing other than its own purely contingent perishable entity.

The terror and desolation naturally lie in the implication that—since this is the nature of the universe itself—so too is it the essence of young Goodenough's identity, her own (in)human (non-)existence.

She continues:

> The night sky was ruined. I would never be able to look at it again. I wept into my pillow, the long slow tears of adolescent despair. And when I later encountered the famous quote from physicist Steven Weinberg—"The more the universe seems comprehensible, the more it seems pointless"—I wallowed in its poignant nihilism. A bleak emptiness overtook me whenever I thought about what was really going on out in the cosmos or deep in the atom. So I did my best not to think about such things.[418]

Ursula Goodenough's experience hardly qualifies as novel. Already in the 17th century, when the extent of science's challenge to religion was first beginning to gather formidable force, Blaise Pascal (who was both a devout Catholic and a brilliant mathematician and scientist) poignantly expressed the existential dread evoked by the nihilist tenor of modern science's reconstruction of the universe. In the Christian era, the heavens figured as the abode of God, the divine intelligence responsible for the order of the cosmos. The impending disappearance of divinity from the universe of human consciousness transformed the illimitable expanse of the heavens into an ominous void for Pascal no less than Goodenough. "I am terrified," wrote Pascal, "by the eternal silence of these infinite spaces."[419]

Philosophically speaking, scientific materialism surely does represent a negation of traditional theism. At the same time, these opposed viewpoints often share a deep (and deeply hidden) affinity: namely, the dogmatic certainty that attends their adherents' faith in the *literal* truth of their chosen account of the creation. Here is Ursula Goodenough herself, in search of the plausible grounds of a "global ethic":

> How things are is, well, *how things are*: our scientific account of Nature, an account that can be called The Epic of Evolution. The Big Bang, the formation of stars and planets, the origin and evolution of life on this planet, the advent of human consciousness and the resultant evolution of cultures—this is the story, the one story, that has the potential to unite us, because it happens to be true.[420]

There we are. The *truth*. No questions asked, or askable. No suspicion, even, that any reasonable, intelligent, and well-educated person could possibly argue with the "truth" of this story or criticize the metaphysical assumptions that underwrite the way of thinking that authorizes and legitimates it.

Would I disagree or dispute that life has undergone a process of evolution on our planet? Certainly not. Incontrovertible facts appear to verify this idea, one held by many (including Goethe and Emerson) long before Darwin. Would I contest that the universe "begins" with a Big Bang? Or disagree with the theory that life evolved from non-life, or that the nature of the human being can be rightly understood on the model of a theory of an evolutionary process driven exclusively by natural selection? Most certainly, as have many deeply intelligent persons hardly ignorant of modern science.

In the early 20th century, Bertrand Russell penned a passage that combines twenty-year old Goodenough's despair, aggressive assertion of the indubitable truth of the materialist worldview, and a tragically heroic attempt to "think about such things" in a manner that might rescue existential meaning from a cosmos that admits of none:

> Even more purposeless, more void of meaning, is the world which science presents for our belief. Amid such a world, if anywhere, our ideals henceforward must find a home. That man is the product of causes which had no prevision of the end they were achieving; that his origin, his growth, his fears, his loves and his beliefs, are but the outcome of accidental collocations of atoms; that no fire, no heroism, no intensity of thought and feeling, can preserve an individual life beyond the grave; that all the labors of the ages, all the devotion, all the inspiration, all the noonday brightness of human genius are destined to extinction in the vast death of the solar system, and the whole temper of Man's achievement must inevitably be buried beneath the debris of a universe in ruins—all these things, if not quite beyond dispute, are yet so nearly certain that no philosophy which rejects them can hope to stand. Only within the scaffolding of these truths, only on the firm foundation of unyielding despair, can the soul's habitation henceforth be safely built.[421]

Russell fantasizes that, despite knowing the human being to be no more than a pawn pushed around by senseless forces, we may still somehow find a way to build "the soul's habitation." Such a hope, however, can in no wise be squared with his own intellectual premises, which logically disallow even so much as passing reference to "the soul," any meaningful consequential idea of which is wholly incompatible with the *sovereign dominion* of matter and "accidental collocations of atoms."

Even so, Russell's gesture towards existential heroism nevertheless calls attention to the flip side of scientific materialism and the total objectification of nature inherent in it: the kind of (pseudo-)sovereignty materialism awards the human subject. We have discussed in prior chapters how the voiding of divinity and the objectifying of nature leaves the scientific mind in command of the whole field of being, its willful prerogatives unlimited by moral constraints devolving from either spirit or bodily nature. Yet as Russell's own words and world history amply demonstrate, that autonomous human subject's absorption of all responsibility for meaning-making into itself can quickly turn a sense of omniscience into meaninglessness, and practical omnipotence into spiritual impotence. The technological power afforded by materialistic science, while seductive, ultimately offers cold if not non-existent comfort to those whose human and spiritual sensitivities have not been numbed, or, more frighteningly, traduced and bedeviled (like one in possession of Tolkien's famous Ring) by an unbridled will to power and lust for control. Since the time of Lucifer's rebellion, *empire* has always offered a tempting alternative to willing recognition of a power greater than one's own.

The mature Goodenough herself—author rather than subject of her book—found her own (distinctly unimperial) way out of modernity's metaphysical impasse. Her book continues:

> But, since then, I have found a way to defeat the nihilism that lurks in the infinite and the infinitesimal. I have come to understand that I can deflect the apparent pointlessness of it all by realizing that I don't have to seek a point. In any of it. Instead, I can see it as the locus of Mystery.
>
> - The Mystery of why there is anything at all, rather than nothing.
> - The Mystery of where the laws of physics came from.
> - The Mystery of why the universe seems so strange.
>
> Mystery. Inherently pointless, inherently shrouded in its own absence of category. The clouds passing across the face of the deity in the stained-glass images of Heaven.[422]

Descartes, you will remember, fervently desired to achieve satisfactory mechanistic explanation of heavenly phenomena in order to *expunge* all mystery from the skies, eradicate the suspicion that nature manifests any reality that transcends the human subject's capacity for rational explanation. Nearly four-hundred years later (despite quantum theory and other related developments), Goodenough, like Weinberg, fancies that science has proceeded so far as to attain, to a significant degree, Descartes's goal. If questions remain—and of course they do—Goodenough and Weinberg exhibit a high degree of confidence that modern scientific knowledge, painting in broad brushstrokes here, and filling in with infinitesimal detail there, nonetheless suffices to provide a fairly comprehensive account of the origin and nature of the universe.

This does not, however, elicit delight or a sense of fulfillment. On the contrary: because their explanatory framework remains materialistic, the nihilism inherent in that philosophy rears its ugly head; so much so, that Goodenough, in order to preserve both her sanity and humanity, feels compelled to import mystery from sources that transcend the reach of science. "Clouds passing across the face of the deity in the stained-glass images of Heaven"? That is certainly a beautifully phrased image, but one completely inconsistent with the intellectual premises of her scientific world-view.

It is thus not surprising that Goodenough closes her chapter with the famous opening of the *Tao Te Ching*:

> The Tao that can be named is not the eternal Tao.
> The name that can be named is not the eternal name.
> The nameless is the beginning of heaven and earth.
> The named is the mother of the ten thousand things.[423]

My first spiritual teacher and practice was Taoist and, more than forty years later, I still do Tai Chi every morning. Due reverence for the Tao notwithstanding, we need be clear about the terms of what Goodenough calls "her covenant with mystery."

Her course of thought and contemplative action amounts to a confession of the total spiritual poverty inherent in her scientifically-informed materialistic understanding of Nature. Her recollection of her camping trip already made that as explicit and graphic as could be. Notice, however, that her solution to the problem as articulated here involves a move East that coincides with a surrender of the episteme, the Western project of knowledge itself.

Goodenough is no technocrat. Nor, clearly, is she at all an unfeeling or irreligious person. On the contrary, the whole purpose of her book is to disclose how modern natural science and the objective, transcultural truth she believes it achieves can serve as the basis for non-sectarian "religious" reverence and so a global ethos that can draw humanity together in its effort to face the terrible crises confronting it today.

Goodenough writes in her Introduction:

> It is therefore the goal of this book to present an accessible account of our scientific understanding of Nature and then suggest ways that this account can call forth appealing and abiding religious responses—an approach that can be called religious naturalism. If religious emotions can be elicited by natural reality—and I believe that they can—then the story of Nature has the potential to serve as the cosmos for the global ethos that we need to articulate.[424]

Natural reality *can* elicit religious emotion. Of that, there is no doubt. People all over the world, every day, experience this truth. Poets and artists have borne irrefutable witness to it for centuries, and at no time more profoundly than in the Romantic art and poetry that followed on the heels of the Enlightenment. "To me the meanest flower that blows can give/ Thoughts that do often lie too deep for tears"[425] wrote Wordsworth, famously testifying to the depths of human feeling inspired by a Nature he certainly regarded as sacred.

It was also Wordsworth, however, who wrote (again, famously), "we murder to dissect." The Goodenough passage preceding her annunciation of religious naturalism effectively acknowledges as much:

> We are moved to awe and wonder at the grandeur, the poetry, the richness of natural beauty; it fills us with joy and thanksgiving. Our response to accounts of the *workings* of Nature, on the other hand, is decidedly less positive. The scientific version of how things are, and how they came to be, is much more likely, at first encounter, to elicit alienation, anomie, and nihilism, responses that offer little promise for motivating our allegiance or moral orientation.[426]

Goodenough's book, her concept of religious naturalism, intends to remedy this failing, and her emphasis on "naturalism" signals her resolve to do so without invocation of anything supernatural. Despite her profound respect for traditional religion, and considerable knowledge and first-hand acquaintance with various streams thereof, the "supernatural" dimension prominent in those discourses seems to her at odds with her commitment to the beauty and truth of the natural world. Referencing her twelve years singing, reciting liturgy, hearing sermons, and participating in ritual in Trinity Presbyterian Church, Goodenough writes:

> All of it was happening in the context of ancient premises and a deep belief in the supernatural. What about the natural? Was it possible to feel such religious emotions in the context of a fully modern, up-to-the-minute understanding of Nature?[427]

Hence her project to meld science and religion in the form of "religious naturalism."

The endeavor to find real religious sustenance in nature even while distancing oneself from traditional religion (most pertinently, in a Western context, Christian theism) is not a new one. It is, in fact, a staple of Romanticism in both its European and American varieties. To be sure, some Romantics retained an allegiance to Christianity (Coleridge, Novalis, even Blake), but seldom in anything like an orthodox form. Many, however, did not, or did so tangentially, and deep reverence for nature qualifies as the more consistent defining characteristic.

One of the most important Romantic poets—Wordsworth—embraced a deeply religious naturalism like Goodenough's, that—resolutely immanentist—

repudiated the traditional supernatural apparatus of Christian religion. In the *Prospectus* to *The Excursion,* Wordsworth's truncated attempt to craft an epic comparable to Milton's theologically grounded *Paradise Lost,* Wordsworth explicitly sets God and his supernatural entourage aside:

> All strength—all terror, single or in bands,
> That ever was put forth in personal form—
> Jehovah—with his thunder, and the choir
> Of shouting Angels, and the empyreal thrones—
> I pass them unalarmed.[428]

Wordsworth does so in the name of the spiritual fulfillment available to the ordinary human being who duly honors the beauty and indeed "sacred depths" of Nature:

> —Beauty—a living Presence of the earth,
> Surpassing the most fair ideal Forms
> Which craft of delicate Spirits hath composed
> From earth's materials—waits upon my steps;
> Pitches her tents before me as I move,
> An hourly neighbor.[429]

Indeed, it is not only the supernatural trappings of traditional religion that Wordsworth wishes to put behind him, but those of classical mythology as well:

> Paradise, and groves
> Elysian, Fortunate Fields—like those of old
> Sought in the Atlantic Main—why should they be
> A history only of departed things,
> Or a mere fiction of what never was?[430]

Wordsworth ends this line of thought with what could almost qualify as the creed of religious naturalism, celebrating the spiritual communion Nature can offer the faithful adherent:

> For the discerning intellect of Man,
> When wedded to this goodly universe
> In love and holy passion, shall find these
> A simple produce of the common day.[431]

What it means for the human intellect to engage nature in a form commensurate with, and indeed guided by, "love and holy passion" counts as the outstanding question. For Wordsworth, the life of verse, at once creative and contemplative, fit the bill. Systems of mechanistic explanation, such as those more and more characteristic of the science of his day, did not.

Wordsworth may not have possessed an up-to-the minute understanding of the natural history and philosophy of his time. Other Romantics, however, including Ralph Waldo Emerson, certainly did. In the late 18th and early 19th centuries, nature study—not yet even called "science"—was not separated off from art, philosophy, and religion in anything like the way it is today; and it was common for persons of diverse walks of life to take a passionate interest in the latest development in natural philosophy. Indeed, in the aftermath of Emerson's decisive break from the Church, he became so enamored with the revelations of natural science—the botanical arrangements in the *Jardin des Plantes* in Paris, Herschel's astronomy, and much more—that he fleetingly entertained the idea of becoming a naturalist himself.

Emerson never lost interest in the perspective and insights proffered by science. Even so, he quickly came hard up against the limits of the brand of science which, in the course of his lifetime, turned decisively against the Romantic currents championed by Goethe, Alexander von Humboldt, Novalis and others who understood study of the natural world to be inseparable from artistic, philosophical, and spiritual concerns. If the culture of science in the West had taken a different path and chosen to incorporate rather than reject Romantic currents, a college physics class might not have ruined twenty-year-old Ursula Goodenough's experience of the night sky.

In light of this Romantic background, Goodenough's brand of "religious naturalism" must be regarded as a kind of rear-guard action, a modern form of a powerful earlier initiative. Unfortunately, I find her noteworthy attempt to bridge the schism between religion and science, the mind and the heart, reason and holiness doomed from the outset. For all her intelligence and eloquence, Goodenough never begins effectively to answer Wordsworth's charge that the reductionism inherent in scientific method "murders" nature; she never begins to answer the question as to why our intellectual understanding of nature's workings should initially induce *not* awe and wonder—nor even indifference—but rather "alienation, anomie, and nihilism."[432] Nor does anything she says effectively remedy the ground of such frankly devastating disaffection.

To phrase the matter more poetically—and tragically—Goodenough continues to assume an Oedipus-like attitude vis-a-vis the Sphinx of Nature. She may, unlike Oedipus, compliment the Sphinx on her surpassing beauty, yet nonetheless answers her in a way that throws her down.

As we have seen, the failure to recognize the history that lies behind her own way of being and thinking does not bode well for her hope that science, as she knows and tells its story, can help heal the affliction plaguing the city of the world.

Thus, although Goodenough aspires to head off in a new direction, her *relation to the universe* is not, in its essential lineaments, original. The philosophical materialism that constrains her understanding remains committed to the road traveled—the path trod, and trod, and trod—by the many comprising the mainstream for the last several hundred years.

How may we begin to think differently and set foot upon that road less traveled?

Less is not nothing; nor even near it. The road less traveled by is one that has been traversed by others: itinerant philosophers, Romantic poets—even one or two whose genius climbed the confines of the church like a rose bush peeking over the wall of a cloister. If nature is filled with wonder and beauty, why not begin by forthrightly confessing what must be the *divine source* of the very idea of beauty and the human capacity of its beholding?

> The world is charged with the grandeur of God.
> It will flame out, like shining from shook foil;
> It gathers to a greatness, like the ooze of oil
> Crushed. Why do men then now not reck his rod?
> Generations have trod, have trod, have trod;
> And all is seared with trade; bleared, smeared with toil;
> And wears man's smudge and shares man's smell: the soil
> Is bare now, nor can foot feel, being shod.

Who has said it better?

Yet Gerard Manley Hopkins concludes on a hopeful note:

> And for all this, nature is never spent;
> There lives the dearest freshness deep down things;
> And though the last lights off the black West went
> Oh, morning, at the brown brink eastward, springs —
> Because the Holy Ghost over the bent
> World broods with warm breath and with ah! bright wings.[433]

Such is the real nature of Nature, the innermost, true essence of nature in the poet's vision: no dead matter whirled about by senseless forces, no dreary book of numbers, but perpetual revelation of abiding divine presence.

The poet's vision is akin to Emerson's—himself both poet *and* scholar. Ill-content to rest with praise of the beauty of the world, Emerson desired to know its truth as well, and exhibited calm faith in the possibility of so doing. The second paragraph of *Nature* begins:

> Undoubtedly, we have no questions to ask which are unanswerable. We must trust the perfection of the creation so far, as to believe that whatever curiosity the order of things has awakened in our minds, the order of things can satisfy.[434]

Another Descartes fancying a mechanistic explanation of everything? Another Weinberg in the making, finding that he purchased knowledge and power at the price of meaning and value?

By no means, because Emerson holds a very different idea of what might constitute knowledge, and the kind of relationship to nature entailed in its pursuit or appropriate method. Emerson's "scientific method" centered around the effort to elevate the mind to understand nature's enigmas in a manner commensurate with, rather than antithetical to, the deepest laws and spiritual character of the Mind. While steadfastly refusing to reduce the mystery of the world to forms of rational-mechanical understanding, Emerson also declined to write it off as unknowable or beyond the pale of the higher, noetic, intuitive capacity of the mind Romantics liked to call Reason.

So is Emerson's *Nature* the annunciation of the quest for a *logos* filled not with spiritual darkness, but with Light; not with Death, but with Life; not with mute namelessness, but with the divine Word through which, in the beginning, all things were made. He sought a source of law that would command reverence and mystery-filled awe not because it is beyond science, but because it is the very source of knowledge that plumbs—not the uniform surface of a material cosmos—but "the sacred depths of nature" and the soul of man, at one and the same time.

Such a *logos* would naturally be anything but pointless. On the contrary, it would direct the human soul towards its spiritual destination; the ground of its own authentic being and identity, its covenant—yes—with mystery, but a mystery revelatory of the divine ground of existence.

Look at how Emerson begins the first chapter of his book *Nature*; how he speaks of his own experience of the stars:

> To go into solitude, a man needs to retire as much from his chamber as from society. I am not solitary whilst I read and write, though nobody is with me. But if a man would be alone, let him look at the stars. The rays that come from those heavenly worlds, will separate between him and what he touches.[435]

Emerson, like Descartes, takes as his point of departure a certain distancing of the human subject from any objective reality: the difference between the soul and nature, the "ME" and the "NOT ME" already articulated in his introduction. As this passage shows, however, that very detachment is itself catalyzed by *sympathetic relationship* with nature: in this case a contemplation (and even identification) of consciousness with the stars.

The act of contemplation, moreover, quickly leads Emerson's mind—his soul-spiritual consciousness—into remembrance of the divine source of creation and a sense of the immanent presence of divinity in the natural universe:

> One might think the atmosphere was made transparent with this design, to give man, in the heavenly bodies, the perpetual presence of the sublime. Seen in the streets of cities, how great they are! If the stars should appear one night in a thousand years, how would men believe and adore; and preserve for generations the remembrance of the city of God which had been shown! But every night come out these envoys of beauty, and light the universe with their admonishing smile.[436]

What a drastically different outcome than young Ursula Goodenough hiding her face in her pillows! For Emerson, like Kepler and others, nature bears witness, first and last of all, to the *presence* of divinity, of which Nature herself is the immanent or embodied expression. Later, he will call the starry skies the "the type of Reason," and indeed the whole of Emerson's "little book" strives to comprehend nature, not as objectified intrinsically meaningless matter, but as the ongoing creative agency and visible inscription of the Logos. Thus did Oliver Wendell Holmes call *Nature* "the Book of Revelation of our Saint Radulphus."[437]

Metaphysically speaking, (Mother) Nature, while not itself matter, does involve and shape matter. Recall the Plotinus quotation Emerson employed as a motto for the first edition of *Nature*: "Nature is the last thing of Soul, a thing that doth only do, not know." That last phrase sets Nature off from

Nous, the divine intellect that is the source of all ideal form and, ultimately, all Being and Knowing. In and of itself, *Nous,* however, represents the intelligible realm, the transcendent intellect, the noetic substance which acts on the visible or sensible sphere of things only in and through the Life of Soul, the last grade of which, as Plotinus tells us, we call Nature. Thus Nature—not in its various aspects, but as the unity and informing life-essence of the World Body—*is Soul*; not the individual human soul, but *Anima Mundi,* the Soul of the World.

In its creative agency, Nature as World Soul shapes and continually transfigures the matter that, in itself, is dead and formless. In so doing, it perpetually translates the transcendent power of the Logos, the divine Reason or Word that flows forth from *Nous* in an eternal fountain of Life and Light, into the myriad forms of immanent expression that comprise visible nature, the body of the world given to our senses.

> I find you in all these myriad things
> I love and care for like a brother.
> As seed, you sun yourself in the smallest
> and in the greatest, spread generously abroad.
>
> That is the wondrous play of powers
> that move selflessly, upward and down:
> rising in the roots, dwindling in the bough
> and blooming like resurrection in the crown.
>
> —*Rainer Maria Rilke*[438]

In the West, the word *God* has been closely associated with certain Jewish and Christian streams that commonly personify divinity in the masculine form often called (especially in Christianity) the Father. The exclusive identification of the very idea of divinity with what becomes, in organized religion, a very delimited and ideologically conditioned form, alienates and estranges many persons from the very idea of divinity itself. I do not say that any given characterization does not have its place and value, depending upon the authenticity of the relationship with the God-image in the soul and its practical fruit. Yet surely, no particular personification of an illimitable Being and Life can be definitive, a truth explicitly recognized in the Mosaic prohibition against the making of idols or graven images.

In modern as well as ancient times, human reverence for divinity in the form of the World Soul, or *Anima Mundi,* the Goddess *Natura,* assumes magnificent and infinitely varied expression. Rilke, in the above-cited poem from his *Book of Hours,* addresses God (explicitly and unabashedly named as such in earlier poems in the sequence) in a form that a "religious naturalist" like Ursula Goodenough might readily embrace, as it demolishes the permeable barrier between the "supernatural" and the "natural," the transcendent and immanent spheres of being and becoming.

For Emerson, nature as a whole—and the whole of nature as *Anima Mundi*—represents a life and creative agency continuous with godhead, and—as such—one manifestly superior to the finite human ego and its limited forms of "rational" understanding. A passage near the end of Chapter One of *Nature* makes the subordination of the human ego to God in/as Nature transparently clear:

> Standing on the bare ground,—my head bathed by the blithe air, and uplifted into infinite space,—all mean egotism vanishes. I become a transparent eye-ball; I am nothing; I see all; the currents of the Universal Being circulate through me; I am part or particle of God.[439]

Emerson, author of "Self-Reliance," is the last person one would accuse of any kind of pathological loss of personal identity. The evaporation of "mean egotism" does not imply any permanent sacrifice of authentic individuality. It does, however, suggests a theme elaborated in *Nature* and other Emersonian texts: namely, that the self rigidly identified with those forms of thought and perception that construct nature (the NOT ME) as objectified matter essentially extrinsic to the soul, and subject to measurement by the rational mind, must somehow be transformed—and indeed *transcended*—if the human subject is to arrive at an authentic sense of its own spiritual identity.

This re-orientation may well be the first step on the road less traveled, even if it is one recognizable in innumerable works of art, including many representative of the Romantic revolt against Enlightenment rationalism. No small portion of the best 19th-century works of American art and literature, including paintings belonging to the transcendentally-inflected Hudson River School, draw upon Romantic tradition even while exemplifying original, distinctly American developments. Much modern American nature writing, too, magnificently honors and renews this tradition—one regrettably off-limits within the precincts of science, the very language of which cannot admit soul-spiritual resonance as (not incidental but) integral to science itself.

Artists—visual or literary—are not so constrained. In his iconic painting *The Oxbow (View from Mount Holyoke, Northampton, Massachusetts after a Thunderstorm),* Thomas Cole makes graphically explicit the idea that

Nature represents the book of God, the page that bears the signature of divinity. The mountain rising just beyond the deep bend of the Connecticut River is tree-covered, but open swaths are patterned to form what can be read as Hebrew letters spelling *Noah,* or, if looked at upside down, *Shaddai,* which means "*the Almighty.*"[440]

What year was *The Oxbow* completed and first exhibited? 1836, the same year Emerson published a little book calling for "an original relation to the universe," his Book of Revelation, *Nature.*

CHAPTER 13

OUT OF THE WORDWORK: EMERSON'S ESOTERIC PEDIGREE

Transcendentalism is not mystical headiness or a vague sensation of oceanic unity, but concrete knowledge of the One in the Many, and the Many in the One: perception of *the underlying reality or truth of phenomena.* That truth—grounded in the "invisible spiritual reality" Emerson speaks of in his lecture on "The Times," is never literal in character, never "just how things are." In fact, precisely *that* assumption is how things (like those billions of stars in the galaxy of a physics student's mind) precisely are *not.* They are not, that is, understood as *participating* in an enduring dimension of being that *transcends* their perishable nature.

Literalism, the root of all fundamentalism (religious or scientific) is a way of seeing and understanding things that—by *reifying* material phenomena even while denying them any relation to a noumenal or intelligible level of existence— denies them intrinsic relation to archetypal verity, and so the representative significance constitutive of authentic identity. "Authentic identity"—mine, for instance—ultimately depends upon the way *I stand for something* that transcends my own perishable being.

We are back once again, to the difference between the sacrificial hind and the laboratory bunny. The significance of the first possesses a vertical as well as horizontal reference; the second does not. This is a problem of language or semiotics, and no minor one at that. Kin to the matter of the (mis)conception of *logos,* it is an issue inextricably bound up with the reigning anthropological premises that mold the character of society.

In his comment decrying the repudiation of the three-fold human being by the Church in the first millennium AD, Christopher Bamford remarks that the degradation thus effected issues in forms of culture characterized by "literalism and abstraction." It is precisely this combination that underwrites the discourse of scientific materialism. That discourse, however, often appears blissfully unconscious of the epistemological and moral deficiencies that attend these modes of signification, which are, perforce, also *styles of thought.* I have previously highlighted the literalism evident in scientific reasoning and, as well, explored a chief mechanism of abstraction: reductive forms of measurement and quantification. Rather than engage in further theoretical discussion of how literalism and abstraction cooperate in the construction of a reality that frames nature as well as human souls as a "substrate of domination," let me offer this prose-poetic rendering of this truth.

Literalism means:

God created the universe in seven days. On the first day, he created light. On the second, the firmament of heaven. On the third, dry land, the sea, and the grass. On the fourth, the sun, moon and stars. On the fifth, fish and fowl. On the sixth, cattle and man, male and female. And on the seventh day, he rested.

Literally.

Or *literalism* means:

How things are is, well, *how things are*: our scientific account of Nature, an account that can be called the Epic of Evolution. The Big Bang, the formation of stars and planets, the origin and evolution of life on this planet, the advent of human consciousness and the resultant evolution of cultures—this is the story, the one story, that has the potential to unite us, because it happens to be true.

Or *literalism* means:

How things are is, well, *how things are*: Our scientific account of nature. Of Covid-19.

Pacifica Graduate School: "*We are taking a fact-based approach.*"

Fact is reality. Covid is a deadly virus. It kills people. See these pictures of people dying? That is Covid. Nothing more and nothing less. That is all you need to know.

Pacifica: "*If we did what he said we should do, we'd all be dead in the streets.*"

Abstraction means:

The translation of "facts" into numbers; the reign of quantity.

Science. Studies. *Numbers.*

Numbers, and more numbers.

Don't bother about the person injured in an accident on the street. You are not allowed to help them, unless you happen to have a surgical mask and gloves on hand. It might spread the virus.

No, you're not allowed to see your ailing or dying mother or father in the hospital.
It might spread the virus, and then even more mothers and fathers might die.

Never mind the anguish of the vaccine-injured.
Never mind the marginalization of excluded others.
Never mind the principles of freedom of speech or bodily autonomy.
Never mind, never mind, never mind.
Numbers, numbers, numbers.
Case counts. Death counts. Vaccination percentages.
In the paper, every day. In red, black, and
bold.

Never mind that numbers lie.
Never mind they don't mean what they say.
Numbers, and more numbers.

That is all ye know on earth, and all ye need to know.

So shut up, lock down, mask up, and don't bother me with your transcendental nonsense.

~

Given the epistemological importance of the matter of language, it is hardly surprising that Emerson places a long chapter dedicated to the topic at the heart of his elaboration of the uses of Nature, one that functions as his book's central hinge. As we have seen, Emerson understands engagement with Nature as a means of realizing the human soul's innate connection with Spirit. Indeed, one could construe the "uses" inventoried by Emerson as ways and means by which the *bodily senses* as well as the *thinking, feeling, and willing* capacities of soul are guided by Nature (qua World Soul or *Anima Mundi*) towards cooperation with Spirit. Commodity serves the senses. Beauty educates the Feeling. Discipline trains the Will, and a study of Nature founded upon idealist premises cultivates the Thinking capacities of both Understanding and (higher, intuitive forms of) Reason. This transcendentalist schema represents a profoundly different relation of the soul to nature than that implicit in the Bacon-Hobbes-Descartes model that underwrites the modes of thinking, feeling, and willing characteristic of the modern type of self conditioned by a mechanistic philosophy.

In the center of his exegesis—between Commodity and Beauty on the one hand, and Discipline and Idealism on the other—Emerson devotes a chapter to

Language, or Word, the essentially *symbolic* (*not* literal or abstract) character of which functions as the ground of all of the soul's multifaceted interactions with the natural world. Here is the set of the unusually forthright declarations that begins that chapter:

> Language is a third use which Nature subserves to man. Nature is the vehicle of thought, and in a simple, double, and threefold degree.
>
> 1. Words are signs of natural facts.
> 2. Particular natural facts are symbols of particular spiritual facts.
> 3. Nature is the symbol of spirit.[441]

Emerson's philosophy, premised on the symbolic correspondences (never fixed, but fluid) between mind and matter, may be recognized as essentially *hermetic* in nature, responsive to the famous dictum attributed to ancient sage Hermes Trismegistus and inscribed on the legendary Emerald Tablet: "That which is above is like to that which is below, and that which is below is like to that which is above."[442] Giordano Bruno, whom Emerson recognized as a predecessor, stands as an early modern representative of the tradition, one whose signal contribution to intellectual history has been elaborated in Frances A. Yates's classic work *Giordano Bruno and the Hermetic Tradition.*[443]

Conscious acknowledgment of the hermeticist lineage and its consequential role in intellectual history lends symbolic resonance to the fact of Bruno's execution by the Church in 1600. The vision of a cohesive universe composed of symbolic correspondences did not die with Bruno (others carried the esoteric current forward), but his martyrdom on the cusp of the 17th century signifies—in a tragic wise—the sea-change to come. The objectification of nature written into the script of the Scientific Revolution augurs the loss of soul—the soul of nature, and of man himself—that accompanies the march of modernity.

Romantic idealism and American Transcendentalism represent countercurrents that envision a restoration of the unity of Nature, Divinity, and Humanity: a unity evident in the worldviews of the likes of Pico della Mirandola (whose syncretic philosophy drew, in part, upon the newly discovered *Corpus Hermeticum*, originally attributed to Hermes Trismegistus) and Giordano Bruno. Nor do bridges fail to connect Emerson's sources on the *near* and *far* side of the Scientific Revolution. Schelling, one of the chief influences on *Nature,* authored a book-length dialogue the very title of which speaks volumes: *Bruno, or On the Natural and Divine Principle of Things.*[444]

We touch here on the general topic of what today goes by the name of Western esotericism. The preface of an excellent book provides a synopsis of the purview of the subject, which achieved academic respectability only in the last three or four decades.

> It is still often regarded as self-evident that western culture is based on the twin pillars of Greek rationality, on the one hand, and biblical faith, on the other. Certainly, there can be little doubt that these two traditions have been dominant forces in cultural development. The former may be defined by its sole reliance on the rationality of the mind, the latter by its emphasis on an authoritative divine revelation. However, from the first centuries to the present day there has also existed a third current, characterized by a resistance to the dominance of either pure rationality or doctrinal faith.
>
> The adherents of this tradition emphasized the importance of inner enlightenment or gnosis: a revelatory experience that mostly entailed an encounter with one's true self as well as with the ground of being, God. In antiquity this perspective was represented by the Gnostics and Hermetists.... Starting with the Italian Renaissance of the late 15th century, the newly discovered "Hermetic philosophy" rapidly spread all over Europe. It found many adherents, in particular during the sixteenth and the first half of the 17th century. This so-called Hermeticist tradition and its later developments—the whole of which may be referred to as "western esotericism"—was characterized by an organic view of the world that assumed a strong internal coherence of the whole universe, including an intimate relationship between both its spiritual and material elements.[445]

The "Language" chapter of *Nature* resounds with the echoes of these ideas. "This radical correspondence between visible things and human thoughts"; "This relation between mind and matter is not fancied by some poet, but stands in the will of God"; "Visible nature must have a spiritual and moral side"[446]—these are assertions of a hermetic philosopher.

My aim in this brief chapter is merely to indicate that the philosophical vision that informs Emerson's *Nature*, while indubitably a highly original version of the so-called *perennial philosophy*,[447] does not come out of nowhere, or propose entirely unprecedented forms of thought and metaphysical imagination. On the contrary, the "third current" that so often weaves between Greek and biblical traditions, even while drawing upon ancient mystery wisdom and (at least since the turn of the 19th century) Eastern philosophy, has long flowed as a powerful subterranean stream below more widely accepted—and polarized—forms of science and religion.

In these troubled times, may this stream emerge once more into the daylight as it did (albeit in markedly different forms) in both the European and American Renaissance. May it help revivify a human soul parched from long sojourn in the desert of materialism; a soul thirsty for freedom and—spurred by dire need as well as inextinguishable aspiration—ready to strike out anew in search of oases of Truth and the Wisdom (*Sophia*) that preserves Life.

PART IV

SPIRITUAL DEMOCRACY

Chapter 14

DISQUIET ON THE WESTERN FRONT: BATTLEFIELDS OF FREEDOM

The affirmation of the human spirit that founds Transcendentalism shapes the lens through which one might view the Covid crisis. The whole of one's universe of thought bears upon material consideration of any given issue. To imagine otherwise is to fall prey to the very plague of atomization—mental as well as social—that is at the root of the wide array of problems confronting us today. Worldviews matter, and humankind will strive in vain to solve its problems if we persist, like Oedipus in Thebes, in considering them within the same ideological framework responsible for creating those problems in the first place.

Emerson, in an oration delivered before the Society of the Adelphi in Waterville College, Maine, August 11, 1841, defends the high office of the scholar:

> The land we live in has no interest so dear, if it knew its want, as the fit consecration of days of reason and thought. Where there is no vision, the people perish. The scholars are the priests of that thought which establishes the foundations of the earth. No matter what is their special work or profession, they stand for the spiritual interest of the world, and it is a common calamity if they neglect their post in a country where the material interest is so predominant as it is in America.[448]

He continues to warn against the dangers of materialism in terms as relevant (if not more so) today as then:

> We hear something too much of the results of machinery, commerce, and the useful arts. We are a puny and a fickle folk. Avarice, hesitation, and following, are our diseases. The rapid wealth which hundreds in the community acquire...enchants the eyes of all the rest; the luck of one is the hope of thousands, and the bribe acts like the neighborhood of a gold mine to impoverish the farm, the school, the church, the house, and the very body and feature of man.[449]

Emerson's oration—"The Method of Nature"— confirms that it is a peculiarly abysmal view of nature that grounds the *Weltanschauung* that dominates modern civilization. Covid World, for its part, manifests—all too vividly!—the helllish consequence of faithful adherence to the religion of scientism. Therein lies it epochal importance, and the unique opportunity for change it offers.

Yet how are we to see the Covid phenomenon whole? How trace the contours of the epic agon dramatized on the stage of the world?

In the last chapter of *Two Roads: An American Scholar's Covid Chronicle* I identified six war fronts characteristic of the official Covid response. After the philosophical excursions pursued in this second volume of *Reset or Renaissance*, it is plausible to see these six initiatives as the coordinated fronts of a Great War waged upon Nature, Man, and God, a global offensive mounted under the auspices of the Great Reset. The production (we now know) is sponsored by the Hobbes-Bacon-Descartes type of the modern self and its technocratic/ transhumanist mutation.

In order to pursue this line of thought systematically, the six chief war fronts can be arranged into distinct groupings.

> 1) ***The War on Nature*** stands on its own as the tip of the modern technocratic spear. Insofar as we have seen that Nature (or the Creation) frequently stands as representative, too, of divinity and the sacred, this war on Nature effectively doubles as a war on God or divinity. Insofar as our idea of the universe encompasses our idea of the nature of human beings themselves, this Western front supplies the philosophical beachhead for all the rest.
>
> 2) ***The Wars on Public Health***, on ***Society***, and on ***Science*** collectively comprise a coordinated, three-pronged assault on the integrity and authenticity of the Individual Human Being as a three-fold unity of Body, Soul, and Spirit. Thus:
>
> > a) ***The War on Public Health*** represents the endeavor to command and control the organic processes of *the body* by way of medical technology;
> >
> > b) ***The War on Society*** represents the effort to command and bring under centralized technological control *the soul,* including the emotional and affective dimension of human being (love, fear, friendship, animosity, etc.);
> >
> > c) ***The War on Science*** represents the endeavor to command and control *the spirit* as such finds expression in the right of bodily autonomy,

freedom of thought and will, personal agency, and the untrammeled quest for truth.

3) *The War on Medicine* synthesizes all of the above and makes concrete application of these other offenses to the practice of medicine in the private as well as public sphere. Given the state of technology today, it can easily function as a springboard for mechanisms of centralized control (via health IDs and related technology) that reach into most every aspect of existence.

4) *The War on Democracy* represents a direct assault on the foundations of democratic governance and the principles that underly free society. The most essential premises of such are: a) governance of, by, and for the people; b) the rule of law and respect for the unalienable rights and civil liberties of the sovereign individual; c) the foundational principle of *informed consent* as the basis of legitimate governance as well as medical practice.

Over the course of this book's remaining chapters, I will examine each of these battle fronts, more or less in turn.

1) The War on Nature

The official Covid policy is only conceivable within the context of an ideology that sees the human being (including the human body) as separate from nature. The ideology views nature itself, not as a source of life and deep wisdom, but as a foreign agent, an enemy force to be conquered and controlled by science, technology, and government regulation of human behavior.

The official Covid response system effectively condenses our idea of nature as a whole into the single, artificially isolated image of the SarsCoV-2 virus itself and its blindly malevolent capacity to occasion death and disease. The sun, sea, and stars are as if wiped off the screen of the mind as a big, ugly, protuberant thing—a grotesque caricature of Mother Nature that looks for all the world like the red rubber spiky massage ball bought at the local Pilates center—usurps our view of nature. This warped perspective authorizes policies that endorse a willful separation from the whole of nature (including other human beings) and indeed make coercive enforcement of such radical isolation the theoretical as well as practical core of the official Covid response.

This manifests in a number of obvious and easily recognized forms:

1) Lockdowns effectively quarantine entire populations, seeking to cut human beings off from almost all contact with the natural environment. While reducing contact with other human beings may have been the ostensible reason,

the policy implies that *all* of nature—not excluding the ocean beach, woodland path, or park trail—need be regarded first and foremost as the bearer of potentially deadly pathogens. With the limited exception of the need for ventilation in enclosed spaces, *none* of the vital health-giving properties of exposure to the elements—including sunlight as a crucial source of Vitamin D, or the vital ongoing retraining of immune response via contact with ambient germ-matter—figures into official policy. This policy was from the first, on the purely physiological (not to mention the psychological) level alone, itself a prescription for ill-health and increased susceptibility to disease.

2) This obsession with separation in fact extends to all surfaces—indoor as well as outdoor; man-made as well as natural. Thus the *disinfectant mania* that sought to further insulate the human being from any contact with surfaces not "cleansed" by man-made chemical germ-killers. These are also, of course, liberally applied to one's own body, especially the hands, the means through which human selves typically reach out to touch, feel, and connect with nature, with all that is "not me."

3) Masks serve further to cut off the human being from normal interchange with the very air we breathe, the most vital and constant medium of our interaction with the natural environment. Air passes through all but the most impermeable barriers, and so acts as the principal element of interdependence and physical, psychological, and spiritual exchange. Masking obstructs all of the above, further artificially and dangerously insulating the self from all aspects of the not-self. Masks made of microplastics, in particular, pose both special health and ecological hazards, the former on account of the effects of chemical inhalation, the latter resulting from the ongoing discard of millions and millions of plastic masks.[450]

4) Social distancing manifestly imposes additional forms of separation between one's own body and psyche and the bodies and souls of others. We will revisit this topic in the context of the War on Society and on the Soul.

Official policy thus sought to turn human beings into atomic particles or portable cubicles impervious to all environmental influence. As the *res extensa* was portrayed as invisibly deadly, *res cogitans* was charged with the (supposedly) self-preserving mission of concentrating all its powers on attaining a state of complete withdrawal and insulation. Fauci waved his magic wand, and—like Circe with her swine—turned people into frightened turtles, retreating into their shells as the shadow of death flickered darkly across the field of vision.

All of the above policies involve nature as such represents the environment—the external world—within which the human being moves and lives. Yet the official policy of regarding nature as a foreign agent inimical to human health and well-being does not stop there, but—astonishingly—views natural processes *internal* to the human body in a similar light. As in the case of locking down healthy individuals and precluding the ongoing immune-system training that depends upon contact with the environment, it does so in blatant violation of all traditional medical wisdom and precedent.

I refer here to the denial of the efficacy of natural immunity in particular, and, more generally, a reckless disregard for the natural action of the human immune system. That rationally inexplicable posture features as the central plank in the vaccine-centric official policy. The unprecedented and patently false declaration that natural immunity does not work, and that vaccine-induced immunity constitutes the only dependable means of securing protection from the virus, represents a flagrant and sacrilegious disdain of the natural wisdom inherent in the human body, a brand of living intelligence evolved and matured over aeons.

Some time ago, on a podcast I unfortunately can no longer locate, a German physician made the point that human medical intervention in and of itself never heals anything, because only Nature herself, the source of life and the body's innate wisdom, can and does actually heal. Good medicine always entails interventions that, one way or another, *release* and *facilitate* the healing potential latent in the body itself. In view of this insight, it would be fair to say that nothing better represents the jaw-dropping hubris of today's mad scientists and technocrats than the fantasy that vaccine-induced immunity might not *cooperate* with the forces of natural immunity, but rather can *supersede* and effectively *replace* the body's broad-based and flexible natural immunological defenses with biotechnologically manufactured machinery.

Such a notion—which scientific tradition might well brand as outright heresy—could only have emerged out of the matrix of the modern materialist worldview that culminates in a blind worship of human technological genius. Even so, it takes the Cartesian-inspired dogma of the separation of man from God and nature, and the putative replacement of the intelligence of the latter by the former, to a previously unheard-of-extreme.

All of the above-mentioned policies represent errors of *commission* stemming from a wholesale objectification of nature. Our official sins of *omission,* though, may be equally important. I refer here to the CDC and other federal agencies' failure to mention, let alone actively promote, all the basic health practices—good exercise, healthy diet, adequate hydration, etc.—that are essential to the maintenance of robust immune systems. Naturally, such egregious omission is only consistent with the Big Pharma-friendly vaccine-centrism that conditions every aspect of the official Covid response.

Predictably, the consequences of all of the above platforms and policies has been disastrous. Instead of a pandemic which, with sensible management (good health practices and strategic use of effective therapeutics) could have been tamed in a matter of months, our Big Pharma fantasy of Pfizer (or Moderna) as World Savior has saddled humankind with an enormous toll of unnecessary death and suffering, ever-evolving mutant strains that increasingly render their "vaccines" worse-than-useless, and impending immunological exhaustion in large portions of the human population.

So much for the success of philosophies and policies that abuse Mother Nature and treat her—like everyone else—as some *thing* that can and indeed must be improved upon by the wonders of technology and, finally, replaced.

Ecologist W. Aaron Vandiver puts the whole matter in perspective. Citing the ill-advised war mentality that fueled Big Ag/Big Pharma assaults on natural pests and predators (a mind-frame Vandiver himself ties to a *mechanistic* philosophy of nature), Vandiver sees the same disastrous scenario played out in the official Covid response. His words evoke the unquiet ghost of Francis Bacon in his modern "techno-utopian" mutation.

> The whole "war" concept is based on a militaristic, mechanistic way of thinking that is obsessed with exerting technological control over natural processes to achieve short-term aims—often eradication of a "threat" like a pathogen or a predator—but cannot recognize the long-term consequences of interfering in the complex set of biological relationships that support natural ecosystems, and that ultimately provide the basis for human health and wellbeing.
>
> Gates exemplifies this mindset, with his techno-utopian beliefs that human pathogens are like computer viruses, that human biology can be manipulated like computer code, and that vaccines can be regularly "uploaded" into the human body like software updates.[451]

2) The War on the Human Body, Soul, and Spirit

If the human being has traditionally been understood as an integral unity of body, soul, and spirit, the prevailing modern view consists of two contrary yet paradoxically complementary conceptions of man, both consistent with (and indeed premised upon) the underlying objectification of nature. On the one hand, we have the virtual deification of the scientific intellect, beneficiaries of which include the representatives of the Matrix—the technocrats in control of the Machine—who wield autocratic power largely unconstrained by any respect for divine, natural or even civic law. On the other hand, people are objectified and subjugated. Denied the basic rights and freedoms proper to a truly human existence (including bodily autonomy, rights of assembly and social association, and freedom of speech), erstwhile sovereign citizens are turned—body, soul, and spirit—into a "substrate of domination." Consequently, the three fronts I will now discuss may be construed as sites of conflict between the traditional idea of the human being and the transhumanist/Matrix agenda that strives to subordinate and control, if not effectively destroy, the bodily, psychological, and spiritual character of being human.

Because human beings are comprised of an integral unity of body, soul, and spirit, abuses of any one of these inevitably implicates the others, and my discussions of each of these terms necessarily interweave and overlap.

2a) The War on the Body

Nature and the human being intersect most tangibly in the human being's physical body. An overall view of nature as somehow essentially foreign to human health and welfare (on the face of it, a nonsensical notion) inevitably results in mistreatment of the body. Rather than relying and capitalizing upon the body's own natural intelligence for health and healing, the "new normal" view of medicine denigrates nature and attempts to artificially and technologically manipulate biochemical processes in order to commandeer the body's natural functioning for specific, limited purposes (for instance, manufacture of the pathogenic spike protein to combat coronavirus). This can be risky business, and the more drastic the manipulation, the riskier, because human knowledge of the finely-balanced cooperation of all the tremendously complex facets of human biology is necessarily limited. Given the elementary state of knowledge regarding the possible ramifications of mRNA gene therapy employed in the leading Covid "vaccines," the claim that such can possibly be known to be safe in the long as well as short term is contrary to all reason as well as a mountainous body of steadily accumulating evidence.

A materialistic conception of nature as a whole precludes real understanding of the physical body, which can only be truly understood as a vessel of soul and, still more proximately, as an organism shaped and maintained by the *etheric* forces that bear the *life* of the body and power all its vital functions. If the physical body is *not* construed in conjunction with the etheric or formative life forces (which mediate between the physical body and the soul), the physical body is perforce conceptualized and treated as an essentially *mechanistically driven* rather than an *organic* entity. The temptation to regard and treat the body as an elaborate piece of physical-chemical machinery rather than a living organism ultimately derives from the anti-metaphysical or nominalist prejudices characteristic of the modern worldview, which steadfastly refuses to believe in the reality of any immaterial principles or forms of existence, including Life, Soul, Nature, and Mind.

The essential difference between a machine and a living body inheres in the fact that the latter possesses an *indwelling* organizing power responsive to the informing idea—the *nature*—of the organism; whereas a machine does not contain the driving force of the principles of its operation within itself as integral to its own character or existence as a mechanical object. The nature and integrity of a living body consequently depends upon the organizing life and intelligence innate in the soul of which it is a vessel. The power to preserve the functional integrity of the organic type in accord with the wisdom built into the body in the course of a long history of evolution constitutes one of the defining features of that intelligence. A living body thus possesses the inborn capacity continually to draw upon the accumulated wisdom inherent in its nature (which nature is a kind of soul intelligence) to maintain, renew and heal itself from within. Capacities of both long and short-term memory, which are a function of, not mechanical processes, but the etheric body of the organism, are vital components of the strength, flexibility, and resilience of the natural immune system.

As Geert Vanden Bossche and others have emphasized, ill-advised vaccination regimes—including mass inoculation with leaky vaccines in the midst of the pandemic and repeated boosting in the context of ever-changing variants—risk *severe* compromise of the human population's natural immunological integrity. On account of this danger, as well as the terrible (if systematically denied and ignored) problem of vaccine injury and death, official Covid policy could well be seen to represent a reckless assault on the integrity of the human body: a policy only really conceivable within the ideological context of modern culture's idolatrous worship of the Man-made Machine and its contemporary correlate, Machine-made Man.

2b) The War on the Soul and Society

This involves the psychological (including the interpersonal or psychosocial) dimension of the human being.

In accord with the modern type of self, official Covid policy generally reflects the Hobbesian view of human nature as originally and essential *asocial.* Governance authorized by the social contract consequently assumes, as its chief obligation, the regulating of social behavior in such a way as to respect and protect the instinct for self-preservation that qualifies as *the* natural right or law and the basis of a sound ethics.

In the second chapter of his book *The Enlightenment (And Why It Still Matters),* Anthony Pagden offers a succinct synopsis of the gist of Hobbes's Leviathanic premises:

> For Hobbes...the only things that primitive[452] men shared in common—other than the "perpetual and restless desire of power after power that ceaseth only in Death"—was fear, the desire to avoid suffering and death for as long as possible, and the rational ability—as well as the collective will—to do something about it.[453]

Pagden continues, however, to detail the widespread reaction *against* Hobbes that set the tone for much 18th-century thought in England and Scotland as well as on the Continent. The kernel of that criticism—at one and the same time varied and consistent—revolved around the idea that the social character of man is not "added on" to an originally atomic human nature on account of practical exigency, but rather counts as inherent in our very constitution. The essence of that social nature was, moreover, considered as not antipathetic but sympathetic, based upon a kindred sense of shared humanity. Samuel Pufendorf's "sociality;" the "moral sense" Frances Hutcheson understood to be founded upon the imaginative capacity of *affective recognition;* the Earl of Schaftesbury's critique of Hobbes (and Locke) in the name of the "natural affection" innate to humankind; David Hume's regard for "sympathy" and the natural passions that (more than reason) ground morality; Rousseau's championing of "pity...a word that at the time had none of the patronizing inflection it has today—as the one universal, and universalizable human emotion ;"[454]—a wide array of Enlightenment era figures sought a more generously humane view of our nature than that proffered by Thomas Hobbes.

James Hillman, in his seminal work *Revisioning Psychology,*[455] insists that the soul is by nature not so much *subjective* as *intersubjective,* inevitably and always immersed in a field of affective interpersonal relationship.

In that respect, he follows the train of too-little acknowledged Enlightenment thinking that runs from Pufendorf to Rousseau and from Rousseau into Romanticism.

How does this bear on Covid World? Did not the official Covid Response prioritize, above all else, sympathetic regard for the other in preference to one's own self-interest? Duly honoring natural affection and displaying a Rousseau-esque pity for all who might suffer, did it not contradict rather than comply with the antisocial vision of human nature underwriting Hobbes's Leviathan?

Nothing could be further from the truth.

The official Covid response, in a fashion commensurate with the dynamic Matthias Desmet describes in his book *The Psychology of Totalitarianism*,[456] offers a narrative built *not* upon respect for real social bonds (which always involve *actual individualized human relationships* as opposed to abstract calculations of the general welfare) but rather upon group or collective opposition to a common enemy. In the case of Covid world, that enemy is not only Covid-19, but all those persons who refused (and continue to refuse) to fall in with the Party line prescribing the measures requisite for vanquishing the evil adversary. Official Covid policy involved an aggressive whipping up of a moral frenzy aimed at convincing all citizens to present a united front arrayed against—not only the virus—but any and all Covid dissidents.

Desmet explores the historical and philosophical ground of the psychological conditions that render people the world over vulnerable to mass formation and the forms of totalitarianism associated with it. *Social fragmentation and atomization; a sense of meaninglessness; free-floating anxiety; and pent up frustration and aggression:* Desmet ascribes principal responsibility for these soul conditions (the first of which functions as the ground and catalyst of all the others) to the ideology bred of the *Mechanical Philosophy*.

What I wish to highlight here, however, is that official Covid policy does not merely capitalize upon certain psychological conditions already prevalent in society and culture. Just as the Fourth Industrial Revolution seeks to accelerate the trend towards the increasing digitalization of life and society—and indeed exponentially so—so does Great Reset-influenced Covid policy not merely *reflect* social atomization, a sense of meaninglessness, anxiety, and frustration, but *works actively to produce and intensify these conditions, and to do so coercively by force of legal and sociopolitical compulsion.* The concrete measures implemented, as well as the social ethos endorsed, amount to an unprecedented, massive, no-holds barred assault upon the province of the soul.

That includes the social fabric of humanity and all the natural sympathies that bond human beings, enabling society to cohere.

Just as in the case of our relationship to nature, the watchword, the master key that *locks* all doors, is *distance* (the "D" component of the "VD" System of Response) or *separation.* Lockdowns, quarantines, masking, social distancing, preclusion of assembly in religious, professional, and cultural community, and (above all), the polarizing rhetoric that set friend against friend and brother against sister: such measures effectively aim to divide, divide, and divide yet further in order, finally, to conquer and control.

During the August 2020 commemoration of the 75th Anniversary of the Nuremberg Code in (where else?) Nuremberg, Germany, Lutheran minister Martin Michaelis parsed these soul-killing procedures:

> The way we treat each has mutated into a topsy-turvy world. We were supposed to be persuaded that distance is closeness; that not visiting someone is love.... People were excluded, isolated, imprisoned, driven into depression by diverse, inscrutable, constantly changing rules.

Michaelis has particularly choice words for one of the subtlest and most damaging mechanisms of social control:

> Masks in everyday life are not only useless, they are the organized disruption of social behavior. They are the finely dosed withdrawal of love, especially serious for child development.[457]

The *withdrawal of love*—this goes to the heart of the matter. The human soul exists by virtue of connection, and cannot live without the love that inspires the imaginative sympathy that is the life-blood of society. It may be supposed that Hate is Love's opposite and chief antagonist, but—in the form, at least, of Wrath—this actually stems from the same holy source. Love's more subtle, deep, and powerful opponent is the swiftest and sharpest arrow in Ahriman's[458] quiver: *Fear,* an emotion that so deeply hurts the soul it can scarce continue on its path toward freedom, without taste of which Love itself cannot long survive.

So is fear—principally of suffering and of death—the chief weapon of all authoritarian regimes. Fear cripples resistance and coerces compliance with orders that the conscience knows violate those first principles (the laws of nature and of nature's God) that confirm the spiritual integrity and so authentic existence of the soul.

I do not doubt that untold good and compassionate persons obeyed official edicts out of a genuine belief that, in so doing, they might best protect the lives and welfare of others as well as (and even more importantly than) their own. That claim naturally comprised the core of the controlling narrative, and endowed it with what *seemed* to pass for "moral sense." Yet that official narrative (one that some critics accuse of "weaponizing compassion") premises itself upon, not genuine regard for the affective bonds that tie one human being to another and so furnish the ground of society, but (as Michaelis succinctly states) perverse negation and destruction of the same.

If love cannot thrive without freedom, there is still another idea that freedom cannot, in any instance, do without, and which thus qualifies as indispensable to all psychological health and well-being. John 8, 32: *And ye shall know the truth, and the truth shall make you free.*

2c) The War on Spirit and on Science

To speak of the human spirit, one must grant that such exists; that, in the inviolable core of their being, as immaterial origin and ground, all persons participate in the archetypal idea of man (human being). This is an eternal verity, one with divinity in the beginning and ever present to us as the inextinguishable life and light of consciousness, however darkened by disuse or vain disputation. Emerson, as we have seen, calls the source of spirit *Oversoul.* That, however, is no exclusive designation. Elsewhere in Emerson, the same power and agency simply goes by the name of *spirit* or *soul,* or *the one mind*, or even *Holy Ghost.*

Apropros of the latter, note yet another instance of Emerson's ubiquitous references to the *eye* and *vision*—and so, obliquely, *enlightenment*—in his famous appeal to the young Harvard seminary graduates:

> Yourself a newborn bard of the Holy Ghost,—cast behind you all conformity, and acquaint men at first hand with Deity. Look to it first and only, that fashion, custom, authority, pleasure, and money, are nothing to you,—are not bandages over your eyes, that you cannot see,—but live with the privilege of the immeasurable mind.[459]

Affirmation of the spiritual origin and ground of human consciousness constitutes the founding axiom of American Transcendentalism.

Drenched in the element of spirit, Emerson himself typically eschewed intellectual system. You will find no doctrinaire explication of the metaphysical premises of Emersonian philosophy more accessible than his Orphic *Nature,* a text not difficult on account of any abstruse or technical language (on the contrary) but because of the sheer enormity of the sea of thought its author—aided by the very spirit of which we are speaking—manages to contain in that small volume.

A lesser and little-known Transcendentalist, Charles Mayo Ellis, exhibited no such scruples concerning systematic exposition. In an 1842 pamphlet titled *An Essay on Transcendentalism,* Ellis provides what may be the closest approximation we have to any plain statement of first principles. Ellis:

> Man has a body, wherein he is allied to the beasts; reason which is his peculiar endowment; a soul, which connects him with Deity. As an animal, he has instincts, love for food, pleasure, which we term appetites; as rational man, love for truth, intuitions of the understanding, sympathies as a member of the human family, affections of the heart; as a child of God, religious aspirations. His nature is triple—animal, rational, spiritual; and it is to those systems, on whatever subject, which contemplate him as a spiritual being, that we apply the term transcendental.[460]

Ellis's next short paragraph confirms the definition. Explicitly rejecting Locke's sensationalism, Ellis implies if he does not assert (as Emerson might) the commingling or even blending of the noetic emphasis of Platonic tradition and the prophetic element inherent in Levantine monotheism:

> That belief we term Transcendentalism which maintains that man has ideas, that come not through the five senses, or the powers of reasoning; but are either the result of direct revelation from God, his immediate inspiration, or his immanent presence in the spiritual world.[461]

Ellis draws repeatedly upon the three-fold nature of man even as he persistently endeavors to distinguish, as sharply and clearly as possible, the founding premises of Transcendentalism from those of (the more materialistic brands of) Enlightenment rationalism:

> Starting, then, with these, that man is and God is, which is involved in the first; the inquiry is, what has man? He has body, mind, spirit; affections, bodily, mental, religious; appetite, understanding, religion. And the latter he has and relies on as something distinct from the two former; not a combination of them. It is not because reason tells him that certain things are more for his animal comfort that he deems them right and beautiful, but because they answer the wants of the spiritual part of his nature.[462]

After describing how both the animal and rational nature of man obtain nourishment from physical and intellectual sources and so are sustained and developed, Ellis asserts that man's religious sensibility functions likewise, similarly employing the organs or faculties peculiar to it. In so doing, he sounds a theme central to American Transcendentalism: the *common vintage* of the human being's spiritual character. If the philosophy underlying American Transcendentalism is borne upon esoteric currents of thought, it is nonetheless equally an everyday affair, banking upon spiritual substance immediately available to all:

> This [religious] nature has the power of perceiving that which is independent of itself—true, good, and beautiful. For this it longs; this gives it strength and vigor. This is not doubted in everyday life—all act upon it. We call him whom we find destitute of it an incomplete man, insane. Everyone has the idea of God.[463]

In the era of mass shootings in America, we might well doubt Ellis's confidence on this last score, though the tragic fact might rather confirm than refute his thesis. Is it not highly likely that the violence endemic in American society today reflects a form of mental illness derivative of widespread estrangement from the soul-spiritual wellsprings of our being?

Ellis rehearses the gist of the Transcendentalist frame of mind in another forthright statement of doctrine that more or less clearly distinguishes the inalienable spiritual heritage of man from dependence upon any institutionalized form of religion. That distinction found historic expression in Emerson's resignation from his ministerial post in 1832, six years before he exhorted Harvard Divinity School graduates to "cast behind you all conformity." Ellis:

> This, then, is the doctrine of Transcendentalism—the substantive, independent existence of the soul of man, the reality of conscience, the religious sense, the inner light, of man's religious affections, his knowledge of right and truth, his sense of duty, the *honestem* apart from the *utile*—his love for beauty and holiness, his religious aspirations—with this it starts as something not dependent on education, custom, command, or anything beyond man himself.[464]

Ellis's premises are not seamlessly consistent with the conservative bent of Patrick Deneen's emphasis upon custom and tradition. At the same time, they hardly sort more readily with the secularism generally characteristic of modern liberalism. One would, however, be sorely mistaken if one were to imagine these Transcendentalist ideas as metaphysical notions with little real purchase on politics and morals. On the contrary, if Ellis constantly takes issue with the narrower forms of Enlightenment rationalism, that does not prevent him from invoking the Enlightenment-era concept of (what else?) *"the law of nature"* in his moral vocabulary. One can hear a stinging rebuke to our unprincipled Covid policy in Ellis's words here:

> Nothing can make that good which is wrong, nor that evil which is right. Nothing can deprive man of the sense of what is right. This is the law of nature—the same in all—the only foundation of practical religion, of government, laws, and the rule of right between man and man.[465]

In the concluding paragraph of the section fittingly titled "*Principles,*" Ellis explicitly presents Transcendentalist philosophy as a way of thinking, feeling, and doing that diverges, radically, from that offered by the materialism inherent in the dominant strains of Enlightenment thinking. Here is Ellis's endorsement of "the road less traveled":

> The results of the two systems show their comparative merits. The old deriving all ideas from sensation, leads to atheism, to a religion which is but self-interest—an ethical code which makes right synonymous with indulgence of appetite, justice one with expediency, and reduces our love of what is good, beautiful, true and divine, to habit, association or interest. The new asserts the continual presence of God in all his works, spirit as well as matter; makes religion the natural impulse of every breast; the moral law, God's voice in every heart, independent of interest, expediency or appetite, which enables us to resist these; an universal, eternal, standard of truth, beauty, goodness...to which every man can turn and follow, if he will.[466]

Like Emerson's, Ellis's is a direct appeal to the irreducibly spiritual nature of man. It affirms such, and forcefully evokes the dire consequences of its repudiation or neglect.

If Ellis sounds outdated to contemporary ears, who would contest the accuracy of his diagnosis? For all the intelligentsia's smug pride in its postmodern brand of nominalism, who is really fooling themselves as to the strength of the foundation upon which to build a house that might withstand the winds of time? If you say: *I have no God, and want none*, how then do you propose to believe in justice, or the power of beauty to move the soul? Leave popular God-images aside, but will you deny, too, the genius of the spirit of humanity?

The very first words of all of Emerson's essays (the first of which is "History") begins by invoking and affirming the same under the aegis of "the one mind":

> THERE IS ONE MIND common to all individual men. Every man is an inlet to the same and to all of the same. He that is once admitted to the right of reason is made a freeman of the whole estate. What Plato has thought, he may think; what a saint has felt, he may feel; what at any time has befallen any man, he can understand. Who hath access to this universal mind is a party to all that is or can be done, for this is the only and sovereign agent.[467]

In Emerson's understanding, this Mind or Spirit acts and speaks through men and women devoted to true and just cause, ennobling humanity in death no less than life.

Friedrich Schiller, born in 1759, proved a brilliant young firebrand. His rather sensational first play (*The Robbers*[468]) included trenchant social criticism of the monied classes. Schiller, a physician with a military unit, went AWOL to see his play's debut and ended up in prison. An honorary member of the French Republic, yet profoundly chastened and disturbed by the failure of revolutionary ideals, Schiller ultimately sought a surer path towards more enduring forms of liberty than external force deficient in inner soul-spiritual understanding of the human estate. In his *Aesthetic Letters*,[469] Schiller recognizes the quest for political freedom as the acme of human endeavors, and argues that humankind comes to freedom by way of beauty. Aesthetic judgment reconciles the realm of universal principle and the limits of bodily sense, and so cultivates the ethical ground in which the sensitive plant of human nature may safely grow to bear good fruit.

After a decade of struggle with tuberculosis and chronic pulmonary illness (during which time he composed much of his most notable work), Schiller died at the age of forty-five. His was no grand funeral, but a cold and rather poor affair. At Schiller's own direction, his coffin was borne—not by any of the aristocratic class—but by laborers, workmen who stood for the common people. According to a well-known poem by Conrad Ferdinand Meyer, the pall-bearers—despite the absence of elites—found themselves in a singularly distinguished company:

Schiller's Burial

A pair of poor and dimly burning torches that wind
and rain threaten every moment to put out.
A flapping pall. A simple coffin made of pine
without a wreath, not the meanest, and no procession.
As if one were hurrying to put a heretic in the ground.
The bearers hasten forward. Only one unknown figure,
wrapped in the swinging folds of a spreading cloak,
follows the coffin. It is the genius of humankind.[470]

~

Chapter 15

THE GENIE IN THE BOTTLE: VACCINE RITES

> *We hold these truths to be self-evident, that all men are created equal, that they are endowed by their Creator with certain unalienable Rights, that among these are Life, Liberty, and the Pursuit of Happiness.*

The integrity and coherence of the Declaration of Independence depends, transparently and indisputably, upon the reality of the human spirit. That spirit cannot be comprehended as a matter of opinion, a mere artefact of the mortal mind, or as a political football tossed around by the Left and the Right. The common person (the farmer, the trucker, the nurse, the pilot, the soldier) *knows* this intuitively; knows that the freedom they treasure, a quotient of liberty inseparable from their human dignity, flows from a sacred transcendental source. If they name this "God," the scholar will not disagree, though he may speak, too, of the participation of each and every individual in the Oversoul (or divine image, or Christ impulse, or eternal I AM). This same spirit is the origin and ground of an authentically *universal* dimension of human being and consciousness—a universality that does not impugn, but sanctions and protects individual difference and the uniqueness of every person.

The prerogatives guaranteed in the Bill of Rights clearly stand on the same transcendental ground. Dismiss or deny the human spirit—claim that it is (like everything else) nought but a social construct—and neither the Declaration of Independence nor the Bill of Rights makes any sense. Such brittle and dishonored papers may then be brushed off some president's or lawmaker's desk into the dustbin of history, along with the whole idea of democracy in America (or anywhere else).

Covid World effectively dramatizes just such careless disregard. It is, of course, much easier, much more natural, for such offense to be justified if the prevailing philosophy denies the very existence of a living nature, a truly rational soul, and (above all) a transcendentally grounded human spirit. Yet (as I argued in connection with the War on Society and the Soul), Covid policy, in line with the Great Reset agenda, does not merely *reflect* scientism, it aims to drive the technocratic agenda associated with that ideology (and, too, the transhumanism that goes along with the package) rapidly and decisively forward, sweeping away resistance on the religious and mythical as well as the practical and sociopolitical fronts.

The mechanistic paradigm cannot well be fully comprehended if we restrict our understanding to either its metaphysical or practical dimensions alone, crucial as these are. No ideological vision can achieve supremacy without offering some meaningful response to the primal fears and aspirations native to the soul. If scientific materialism lands humanity in the lap of meaninglessness, offshoots of that philosophy will evolve that assuage human fear and nourish dreams of spirit, even if the latter take unheard-of-forms, as in the case of transhumanist visions of a technologically "enhanced," no-longer-biologically-human kind. That is why Adorno and Horkheimer understand enlightenment *as myth*, stating: "Myth is already enlightenment, and enlightenment reverts to mythology."[471]

The religio-mythical system of Enlightenment Rationalist Fundamentalism marches forward under the banner of the familiar keywords: Science, Reason, Humanity, Freedom, Progress. In this book, I have not sought to reject salutary Enlightenment-era ideals, but to sketch how the materialism that came to govern the field of human concern drove forward the *deformation* of those ideals. In fact, the mind of enlightenment generates social institutions and praxes that reflect and entrench, in a hybrid fashion, both the genuine value of Enlightenment ideals and—increasingly—their destructive distortion.

Care for and healing of the body play a vital role in all cultures, and the institutions of modern medicine naturally play a central role in the social enactment of the myth of Enlightenment. Immersed in a scientific culture that effectively proscribes knowledge of any eternal spirit that *transcends* the span of an individual's material existence, the capacity of modern medicine *to preserve life* assumes an outsized, salvific function. So does the modern individual often invest a positively religious, often blind trust in the doctor. The physician or medical researcher stands as the priestly representative of mainstream culture's faith in the power of science to comprehend, master, and (via technology) control nature, including those inherently mysterious portals to the *other* world: birth and death.

Every system of belief has its rites and icons: symbolic and social enactments of trust in its ability to sustain body and soul, or otherwise bend human destiny in a favorable direction. Scientism and transhumanism are no exception, and modern technocratic society includes many such rites and symbols. Perhaps the single most important of these is the ritual act that, more than any other, links the ideology of the medical industrial past with that of the Machine's biotech dream of the future: *the vaccine.*

Insofar as the medical establishment represents a social institution reflective of the metaphysical ideology underlying the Matrix, performance of the ritual of vaccination continually underwrites the dominance of that system of belief. Indeed, for decades now—and all the more spectacularly and powerfully in Covid World—mass vaccination has served as an indispensable weapon in the Machine's ongoing attack upon the human spirit, an attack prosecuted by way of its invasion of the human body.

The body serves as the site of the ritual act. The unparalleled symbolic as well as practical importance of the body does not derive exclusively from its function as the vessel of *biological* life and health. This does bear great weight. Even so, the body's political privilege—the reason it emerges, again and again, as a flashpoint of conflict—derives still more vitally from its status as the vessel of the individual soul and the *spiritual* prerogatives that flow from sociopolitical recognition of that fact. The first and most fundamental of these is *the sovereignty of the individual over the body itself*, a prerogative often referred to today as "bodily autonomy."

The body qualifies as the original and paradigmatic piece of private property. Ownership rights to the body belong exclusively to the relevant individual soul, for whom the body is both physical vessel *and* visible insignia. This proprietary authority covers, as well, *actions* performed by the body. Actions express the *will* of the soul. Freedom—and therefore *spiritual agency*—is abridged when action is unduly coerced or restricted, as in the confinement and forced labor characteristic of slavery.

Still more primal, however, than coercion or restriction of physical activity is the instance in which some action is performed upon the body that the individual does not freely choose. Such represents, physically, psycho-spiritually, and politically, the most direct possible assault on the sovereignty of the individual because it most flagrantly robs the individual soul of its proprietary command over the physical vessel which belongs to that soul alone. As such, it represents a direct attack upon that freedom of will expressive of the spiritual identity of an individual; a direct attack, that is, upon *the essence of one's humanity.*

Vaccination, when compulsory or in any way coerced, falls into this category. Any vaccination program involving any degree of coercion (and the greater the coercion, the greater the offense) consequently amounts to an assault upon the human spirit. Inasmuch as the sovereignty of the individual human being inheres in the unalienable (or natural) right to bodily autonomy, coerced vaccination imperils the liberty integral to the spiritual marrow of humanity itself.

In this respect, coercive vaccination is—practically and psycho-spiritually—not unlike the institution of slavery, which today is recognized as an intrinsically dehumanizing practice. Because, however, compulsory vaccination involves an act performed directly upon the body (rather than confinement of that body, or compelling its labor), its violation of autonomy is of a distinct kind.

The more forceful, invasive, violent, and dangerous the deed performed upon the body, the more powerful the assault upon the sovereignty of the individual person. Corporal punishment of any kind violates the inherent dignity of human beings. Torture aims to break the human spirit by abusing the human body, crippling its form and impairing it function so it no longer so readily stands, upright, as vessel of immortal spirit.[472] By contrast, forced injection entails— no blows landed upon the surface of the body—but penetration of the physical interior of the person. Coerced vaccination forces entry into the figurative as well as literal bloodstream of the unwilling subject.

Physically or physiologically, such penetration with the injection of an unnatural substance poses real danger, carrying the possibility of death, or irreversible life-altering injury. Denial of the very possibility of such outcomes is counterfactual, and represents (not science, but) the blend of willful delusion and superstition characteristic of a religiously charged ideological formation. Moreover, adverse effects may manifest immediately *or* long after the injection itself, multiplying the psychological trauma inflicted by coerced vaccination. While short term reaction or lack thereof does provide a preliminary indication of whether or not the subject will be negatively affected, she can never be entirely confident that she has escaped unscathed. This naturally holds, too, of a parent deciding whether or not to vaccinate their child.

On a psycho-spiritual level, too, penetration into the interior of a person who does not wish to be vaccinated constitutes a peculiarly devastating form of violation. Insofar as unwanted injection effects alien entrance into the interior space phenomenologically experienced as the abode of the soul itself,[473] such a violation shares certain unmistakable features of rape. When coercively imposed by authorities at behest of the collective will (imposed on behalf of, and with the support of, the populace at large) the violation could be psychologically construed as akin to a kind of gang rape. The will of the many is imposed upon the will of the one, forcibly overriding the authority of the individual soul over the physical vessel that bears—or bares—its identity (in)to the world.

The analogy here, to be sure, is imperfect. Vaccination does not afford satisfaction of violently selfish lust on the part of the perpetrator(s); nor does gang rape proceed (as does vaccination) under the aegis of an act supposed to serve the general welfare; the good of the vaccinee as well as society at large. These significant differences serve to highlight the *ideological* underpinnings of compulsory or coerced vaccination. Deference to what is represented and imagined as a superior collective good justifies violation of what should be (in accord with the code of law requiring *informed consent* for any medical procedure) respected as a sacrosanct individual right. It is precisely this kind of social-scientific calculus—one inevitably vulnerable, as we have seen, to the willful corruption of relevant facts and perspectives—that has *always* served as the rationale for crimes against humanity committed by government authorities; crimes which often could not be ventured or sustained without popular support and collusion.

My perspective on these matters may seem extreme. Yet whole societies once viewed slavery as a perfectly acceptable practice. Many persons in such societies probably lacked the imagination to see themselves in the position of the slave. They were, in any event, subject to persuasive social, economic, and psychological reasons that disinclined them from even *trying* to do so. Similarly, many people today continue stubbornly to blind themselves to the physical, psychological, and spiritual violence written into the very idea of compulsory vaccination.

In the case of vaccination, those enabling reasons devolve from a regime built upon the myth of enlightenment. Practically as well as symbolically, the ritual of vaccination represents a rite central to the maintenance of what is *both* an economic *and* a religio-mythical system, It is coincidently the spearhead of the means by which those invested in that system compel others to recognize its authority and obey its edicts. Performed under the auspices of serving the public good, its popular sanction further supplies social confirmation of the sacrosanct character of the act. The rite of vaccination thus serves to seal the social contract in accordance with the terms set by technocratic powers-that-be.

If an infant is born into the community of the Catholic faith, soon after birth he or she will be welcomed into that community of believers by way of the rite of baptism, the first of the seven sacraments vital to Catholic religious practice. In the West, however, we have now long worshipped according to the tenets of "a new faith" (Tarnas). The baptismal rite of vaccination, performed soon after birth, consequently certifies the parents' belief in the creed of modern science and (bio)technology, and the unimpeachable authority of its white-frocked ministers.

In many states in the U.S., performance of the ritual is required by law as a condition of attendance of public (and often even private) school. In five states,[474] including California, the belief in scientism is politically so powerful that all children who wish to attend school are required to go through the prescribed ritual (and indeed repeatedly so). Faith in the truth and goodness thus enacted is so absolute, so immune from all reasonable question, that no contrary beliefs are acknowledged as possessing legitimacy: no "*religious exemptions*" are granted.

To believe that this is wrong, to contend that the state should have no such authority over sovereignty of my or my child's body, does not qualify as an opposing viewpoint worthy of respectful consideration. Rather, it is branded and prosecuted as unlawful heresy. The truth that vaccines are "safe and effective" at saving lives and alleviating suffering can no more be questioned within the context of this ideological framework than can the salvific power of Jesus within the context of Christian belief. It is, in the religious sense of the term, *dogma.*

Of course, proponents of the policy would claim that my line of argument here is specious, because it is no religious belief that authorizes the propriety of vaccination, but duly tried and tested scientific truth. Here I beg to differ, and do so with good reason—the same fact-based, enlightened reason that casts the safety and efficacy of the Covid vaccines in such grave doubt.[475]

I do readily acknowledge one essential difference between a religious sacrament and the rite of vaccination. The latter bears a certain superficial resemblance not only to the act of baptism, but—insofar as both involve the taking of a magical substance into the interior of the body, and indeed one's own life-blood—to the act of communion. The rites of baptism and communion, however, qualify as authentically *religious* rites, because they are consciously performed as acts of *spiritual* transmission. Even while working with physical substances (consecrated bread, wine or water, for instance) and so involving the body, these rites explicitly address and seek to nourish the human spirit. No one showers in a baptismal font or eats the host for breakfast.

The rite of vaccination, on the other hand, has no such explicit soul-spiritual intent. As befits the worldview it exemplifies, its purpose is the purely physical/physiological prevention of illness. The *psychosocial* implications of the ritual I have discussed are not overt or explicit, but covert. The resultant effects consequently are not so much authentically spiritual or religious (in which case they would need to be in accord with human freedom) but *ideological* in nature.[476]

With the advent of the Covid pandemic, the leviathanic powers-that-be upped the vaccine ante exponentially. No longer may parents restrict tribute to the God of Science by vaccinating their children with an ever-increasing number (currently 72 in the U.S.) of injections. Now adults, too, have been required to pay obeisance by way of their own bodies, to bend their knee before the biotechnology-driven Machine that promises to protect us from death, disease, and each other, and "get the jab." Only so could adult persons inhabiting Covid World certify, not only their requisite faith in scientific authority, but their moral integrity and social conscience, the respect for their fellow citizens that verifies (such is the consummate irony) *their very humanity.*

As we have seen, the the "reign of quantity" (Guénon) helped set the Great Reset agenda in motion. The human body—that sacred temple of spirit, that privileged site of the sovereign freedom of the individual person—was mercilessly reduced to sets of numbers. Those numbers were calculated so as to translate into one unambiguous message: vaccinate, or suffer and die. If you did not follow that commandment, you may not have died a physical death, but would nonetheless have suffered social and professional decease, or exile, at the hands of all the duly faithful. *Mass* formation indeed!

So might the Matrix, the Machine, the leviathanic Deep State that extends far beyond national borders, work its will. The vaccine campaign and all that went along with it ultimately prosecutes a war upon the bodies, souls, *and* spirits of human beings—all three, at once, in their integral unity.

Rudolf Steiner:

> The time will come—and it may not be far off—when...people will say: It is pathological for people to even think in terms of spirit and soul. "Sound" people will speak of nothing but the body. It will be considered a sign of

> illness for anyone to arrive at the idea of any such thing as a spirit or a soul. People who think like that will be considered to be sick and—you can be quite sure of it—a medicine will be found for this. At Constantinople the spirit was made non-existent. The soul will be made non-existent with the aid of a drug. Taking a "sound point of view," people will invent a vaccine to influence the organism as early as possible, preferably as soon as it is born, so that this human body never even gets the idea that there is a soul and a spirit.[477]

One can read this passage in different ways. One can take Steiner literally, and imagine that certain vaccines may physiologically produce a de-spiritualizing and dehumanizing effect. One can also understand the passage to reference the critical moral and spiritual conflict I have sought to highlight: that the violation of essential human freedoms inherent in any campaign of compulsory or coerced mass vaccination itself constitutes a "breaking" of persons: a potentially fatal wounding of the soul-spiritual core of humankind.

If the vaccine needle represents the icon of the technocratic religion and its transhumanist mythology, mass vaccination additionally serves (and this can in no wise be overlooked) the Matrix in very crucial practicable ways. First, and most obviously, once the prevailing ideology has thoroughly materialized the human body (effectively divorcing it from life, nature, soul, and spirit), that body can serve as a gold mine for pharmaceutical profiteering.

In an earlier chapter, I addressed the dramatic growth of the bioweapon industry in past decades, but the use and distribution of such is inherently restricted. Not so vaccines, the successful promotion of which can make the perceived health, safety, and security of entire populations dependent on Big Pharma and the state-sponsored medical establishment. The economic implications of that scenario are obvious, and, in the context of Covid World, the potential for financial bonanza has been realized on a previously unimaginable scale. Pfizer alone sold over *35 billion* dollars worth of Covid vaccine in 2021.[478] This is *pharmacolonialism*, indeed, but not restricted to or even concentrated in developing nations (many of which do not have the infrastructure that enables maximal distribution) but implemented on a global scale.

Vaccination and proof thereof can also function as a technological and administrative portal by means of which people may be subjected to unheard-of degrees of surveillance and administrative control. *Identification* functions as ground zero for the functionality of any administrative state, and—if engineered and used inappropriately via vaccines passports, health IDs, green cards, etc.—prepares the way for unholy programs of social control. Why did God punish King David for taking a census? Even in antiquity, religiously-inspired minds recognized that counting people—reducing persons to facts and figures—risks fatal disregard of the irreducibly *spiritual* identity of *individual* human beings. Rather than recognized as a sovereign individual possessed of inalienable rights, citizens can readily be identified as someone duly subservient to the Matrix technocracy, *or not,* and "privileges" (the technocratic substitution for unalienable rights), such as access to bank accounts, granted or withheld accordingly.

This explains why mass vaccination has emerged as (on the one side) the tip of the spear of the Great Reset agenda and (on the other) the chief catalyst of a burgeoning, non-partisan global health freedom movement. That movement centers on bodily autonomy and informed consent as the locus of the sovereignty of the individual human being and so an essential condition of free society. In accord with the precedent of American Transcendentalism and its philosophical kin in other lands and times, that movement might also prove the springboard of a transformative reclamation of those transcendentally-sourced ethical principles that serve as the ground of—not some indiscriminately collectivist and readily manipulated notion of "the welfare of humanity"—but a true Party of Humanity: that *authentic universality* grounded in the spiritual identity of every human being.

We thus stand, once more, at that fork in the road, and are perhaps gaining ever greater understanding of the nature and import of the choice before us. As early as the second decade of the 20th century, Rudolf Steiner possessed a very clear view of the situation in which we find ourselves. In the passage following those cited earlier, and which brings to a close his 1917 lecture on "Changes in Humanity's Spiritual Make-up," Steiner presents humanity with the choice between two fundamentally opposed historic trajectories:

> The two philosophies of life will be in complete opposition. One movement will need to reflect how *concepts and ideas may be developed to meet the reality of soul and spirit* [emphasis added]. The others, the heirs of modern materialism, will look for the vaccine to make the body "healthy," that is, makes its constitution such that this body no longer talks of such rubbish as soul and spirit, but takes a "sound" view of the forces which live in engines and in chemistry and let planets and suns arise from nebulae in the cosmos. Materialistic physicians will be asked to drive the souls out of humanity.[479]

Alternatively, should we not ask *idealistic* physicians (be these physicians of the body or soul; doctors or farmers, poets or teachers) to *do the opposite*: to think, work, live and dream so as to *care* for the soul in the temple of the body, so the spirit of humanity may rise and (in death no less than life) walk alongside us once again.

Chapter 16

YARDWORK: IS SCIENCE REAL?

I have singled out faith in modern science as the central plank of the ideology underwriting the Great Reset and its technocratic agenda. Some early sections of this book, however, strike a different chord, condemning our Matrix-inspired Covid World for its *betrayal* of science. Is science then (part of) the problem, or the solution? Am I talking out of two sides of my mouth when speaking of science?

The answer to the first question above is: *both*. To the second: *yes*, and *no*. Much depends, after all, upon what "science" one is speaking about, and how one understands "science" in the first place.

Let me clarify.

IN THIS HOUSE WE BELIEVE
BLACK LIVES MATTER
WOMEN'S RIGHTS ARE HUMAN RIGHTS
NO HUMAN IS ILLEGAL
SCIENCE IS REAL
LOVE IS LOVE
KINDNESS IS EVERYTHING

I am sure you have seen this sign posted in a yard somewhere—at least, if you live in a blue state. As stated in the initial phrase, it represents an overt statement of *belief.* The yard sign gives popular expression to what passes today as the liberal creed.

While one comes across a few different versions of the sign, variations are typically minor. In most instances, the phrase **SCIENCE IS REAL** appears, as here, very prominently, in eye-catching bright green near the center. In some, it is featured, with like visibility, as the *first* clause of the creed.

But what does it mean to say that "SCIENCE IS REAL"? It is supposed to mean that science reliably delivers truths about the world, facts discovered and verified by its vaunted method. Science goes about its business impartially and objectively. Its pursuits are not driven by politics, and its results are substantiated by Nature herself. In the words of Ursula Goodenough, science faithfully tells us "how things are."

Anyone who has not been doped silly today—anyone who has been paying any attention to sources other than mainstream propaganda, including *real* life, during the pandemic—knows how profoundly flawed this plank is. Covid politics has revealed it to be rotten to the core, so that anybody standing on this plank (including Anthony Fauci, self-proclaimed representative of science itself) is liable, sooner or later, to suffer a fall, perhaps even a deep plunge.

Long ago (in 2021), when I was writing the first volume of this book, the credibility of the science touted by our public health officials and agencies (Fauci as well as other "health experts" at the NIH, CDC, FDA, and all who fell in line behind their lead) was more or less intact—at least in the minds of the majority of the public, including almost all of "liberal" persuasion. When it was stated that the Pfizer vaccine was 95% effective, or (later) that unvaccinated persons were suffering hospitalization and death at far higher rates than the vaccinated so that we were in the midst of "a pandemic of the unvaccinated," or that "rigorous" testing had proven the vaccines to be safe, or that natural immunity was not reliably effective, most persons tended to take this as authoritative, "scientifically" proven information as opposed to the "mis- and disinformation" disseminated by Covid dissidents and disreputable "conspiracy theorists." On account of the huge reservoir of firm belief in revered methods of acquiring knowledge, when health experts and policy makers told us that they were "following the science," this lent their words the ring of truth, and their actions the aura of legitimacy.

For many persons (even as authorities backtrack on virtually all of their chief claims, and tell us that the "science" was *never* black and white, but always one or another shade of gray) this remains the case. It does so, however, for fewer and fewer every day, and only against the weight of both reason and and an avalanche of evidence.

It is little exaggeration to say that pharmaceutical companies and public health agency experts have all but given up on producing anything more than the thinnest pretense of doing science in any way, shape, or form consonant with historic standards and criteria. Hair-raising examples abound, and the first volume of *Reset or Renaissance* documents diverse instances of the shoddy "science" today routinely passed off as the real thing. In accord with the present theme of the War on Science and Medicine, I here offer a few additional, particularly telling examples.[480]

According to diagnostic pathologist and former NHS[481] physician Dr. Clare Craig, the 2022 Pfizer trial aimed at securing EUA authorization for Covid vaccines for infants and the very young (six-months to five-years-old) performs a shocking parody of (so-called) science. Craig emphasizes that the trial should never have been conducted in the first place. EUA authorization is reserved for meeting medical emergencies that pose imminent risk of serious injury and death. As very young children are not at such risk from Covid, an EUA application lacked both legal and rational justification. Of course, given a governmental policy that has automatically and baselessly extended a state of medical emergency in the country as a whole, the government's willingness to entertain and approve the application was hardly surprising.

As far as the results of the ill-advised and ill-fated trial itself are concerned, even hardcore Covid skeptics may well be taken aback by Pfizer's appalling doctoring of relevant data and its performance of a hatchet job that obfuscated results clearly demonstrating not the safety and efficacy of the vaccine, but the opposite.

Pfizer initially recruited 4,526 children between the ages of six months and four years for the trial. The first red flag? 3,000 did not make it to the end of the trial. *Why?* We have no idea. Pfizer provides no information as to why fully *two-thirds of the trial subjects were dropped.* Craig reasonably asserts that in the absence of any explanation of this conspicuous lacuna, the entire trial should be deemed null and void.

The results that *were* obtained, however, were indeed notable. Pfizer tested for both contraction of "severe Covid" (defined as a slightly raised heart rate or respiratory irregularity) as well as "any Covid." With reference to the former category, *six* vaccinated children contracted severe Covid, whereas only *one* child in the placebo group did so.

Not even Pfizer could do much with those simple, damning numbers; their real "creativity"—and callousness—revealed itself in the handling of the *any* Covid statistics. "What they did was to utterly twist the data." Craig's account of the matter, in her words:

> They vaccinated the children and then waited three weeks after the first dose before the second dose. In that three-week period, 34 of the vaccinated children got Covid and only 13 in the placebo group which worked

> out as a 30% increased chance of catching Covid in this three-week period if you were vaccinated. So they ignored that data. And then there was an eight-week gap between the second dose and the third dose, when again children were getting plenty of Covid in the vaccine arm. So they ignored that data. There was then several weeks after the third dose which they also ignored, which meant that in the end, they had ignored 97% of the Covid that occurred during the trial. And they just looked at tiny numbers—so tiny. In the end, they were comparing three children in the vaccine arm who had Covid with seven in the placebo arm, and they said that this showed that the vaccine was effective.[482]

One might wish that this were all. Yet—as if omitting 97% of relevant data were not enough to torpedo a scientific study—Pfizer also evidently ignored the fact that, in the two-month follow-up after the initial trial period, twelve children contacted Covid a second time, all but one of whom (eleven) were vaccinated.

To cap off the catastrophic experiment, the conduct of which blows any semblance of "science" to smithereens, Pfizer *vaccinated the entire placebo group* six weeks after the end of the trial, thereby *destroying any control group* that might permit assessment of any long-term consequences, including, of course, any adverse effects that might be attributed to the vaccine.

Not only does the trial incriminate Pfizer, the FDA's approval of the EUA on the basis of such data makes the capture of the agency by the pharmaceutical industry all too obvious. *Corrupt if not incompetent, and incompetent if not corrupt.* Probably both.

Another instance of scientific malfeasance and agency capture involves more current events. This story centers upon the June 2022 approved and now (September 2022) available bivalent Covid boosters, supposedly modified to mount resistance against omicron variants rather than just the ancestral Wuhan strain of the virus.

Dr. Paul Offit is anything but an anti-vaxxer. He has long been a leading supporter of the government's vaccine program and a critic of its detractors. Yet sitting on the VRBPAC (Vaccine and Related Biological Products Advisory Committee) review board responsible for recommending approval for Emergency Use Authorization and government buy-in for additional R&D for a new bivalent Covid vaccine, Offit found himself only one of two of twenty-one committee members that voted NO. Not only did he consider evidence of efficacy scanty and singularly unconvincing; he found the order of official proceedings highly unusual. The way the hearing was conducted seemed, to

Offit, deliberately designed to render impossible or preempt any scientifically meaningful review. Offit:

> I've seen nothing like this. I guess the thing that's most upsetting to me is normally when you get something from the FDA when we have these meetings, you usually get it a few days before you meet. You usually get a couple hundred pages.
>
> Here on the other hand, normally you get the EUA submission from the company, which is 85 to 100 pages long, and then you get the FDA's review of all those data. It's a very thorough review. Not here, though. Here, it was 22 pages from the FDA, which included a half-page on Pfizer's data and a half-page on Moderna's data.
>
> You could get that from the press release. In fact, it was no more detail than the press release provided.[483]

The dearth of relevant and timely documentation was not the only irregular feature of the proceeding. Offit further observed that, because VRBPAC fulfills a purely advisory function, the normal course of events involved nothing more than presentation of relevant evidence; there is no "lobbying" for one result or another. The government can, after all, decide to ignore VRBPAC's recommendation. Yet Offit noted that during the June 28, 2022 meeting a representative of the WHO made a presentation advocating approval, as did a representative of the FDA itself. Offit:

> That's unusual. Then the next day you read a press release from HHS [U.S. Department of Health and Human Services] that says the government has decided to purchase at least 105 million doses from Pfizer.... So you just kind of felt like the fix was in.... It was something they [the Biden administration] wanted and I felt like we were being led here and with a critical lack of information.[484]

The evidence of efficacy Dr. Offit found wanting pertained to a bivalent vaccine targeting the Ba.1 omicron variant. As Ba.4 and Ba.5 eventually superseded Ba.1, the bivalent booster that finally became available involved a reformulation of that vaccine. Many persons, however, expressed particularly keen skepticism about the safety and efficacy of the newly formulated boosters because—in yet another display of the kind of corner-cutting that scissored the heart out of public trust in science—these new bivalent boosters were *never* clinically tested on human beings. Not only, moreover, was this vaccine—one the government hopes millions and millions of persons would receive—never tested on humans, it was only tested on a grand total of *eight* (8) mice!

Health experts excused the haste by citing an analogous practice (lack of human testing between reformulations) with flu shots. The situation, however, cannot be considered the least bit comparable, given the safety profile and decades of experience with flu shots versus the still novel Covid vaccines, and the many red flags (including incidence of myocarditis) already raised in connection with their use.

Not surprisingly, critics do not think the "SCIENCE" that classifies these vaccines as adequately tested, and recommends them for use against what is (for most) a relatively mild disease, is (to cop a phrase from a yard sign) "REAL" at all. We have heard a great deal about "fake news." What about the Covid World complement of the same: "fake science"?

Responding to a September 4 San Francisco Chronicle article titled: "New COVID Booster Shows 'Tremendous Promise.' Can It Prevent the Next Surge?,"[485] Jay Battacharya wrote:

> In 2021, the Biden administration, Fauci, and the CDC made a bet on the basis of incomplete randomized trial data that the vax would stop Covid transmission. Vax mandates and discrimination followed. For the new booster, some are making the same bet, based on data from 8 mice.[486]

Dr. Richard Urso refused to receive the tidings in good humor...

> Today, the FDA approved "Bivalent Ba.5 Booster" because of an unspecified "emergency." The booster was tested on, drumroll, 8 mice. That's it. It will be given to millions of people next week. This is not gallows humor, just gallows.[487]

...while, true to her office, Representative Mary Miller emphasized the political angle:

> The last time the FDA approved boosters, 2 senior FDA officials resigned. It is time for serious oversight and reform at the FDA.[488]

So, the *first* part of the answer to the *first* question raised at the outset of this chapter rehearses the theme highlighted earlier. Official Covid policy premises itself upon a profound and methodical betrayal of REAL science, and entails a systematic corruption of the salient Enlightenment-era ideals (open-minded freedom of thought; reasoned resistance to entrenched dogma and arbitrary authority; impartial and objective inquiry; evidence (nature)-based research; individual genius and original inquiry) that inaugurated the Scientific

Revolution and lent science its unparalleled prestige and authority; its sinecure as the West's new faith.

Just as *internal decay* pointed towards the eventual demise of the Catholic Church's hegemonic hold on European culture in early modernity, so does the systematic corruption evident in the world of science today (could one speak of the *ecclesiasticization* of science?) augur a like transformation. We are just at the beginning of what promises to be a complex and lengthy process of metamorphosis.

Of course, science pursued with integrity and respect for impartial truth, does have its defenders and champions today. It is in good measure due to the *spirit* displayed by the likes of Richard Urso, Jay Battacharya, Peter McCullough, Robert Malone, Tess Lawry, Paul Marik, Pierre Kory, Geert Vanden Bossche, and many, many others that the portion of the public that "dares to know" *does* know much of the true—and truly sordid—story behind Covid World "science."

The ongoing vilification and persecution of such individuals on the part of the Matrix amounts to an ongoing war on the human spirit, science, medicine, *and* the rights basic to *real* democratic governance. It is an assault on *all* of these related fronts because it is, above all, a War on Truth, the very idea of which falls under the jurisdiction of the Spirit.

This war oppresses not only those who speak out or act in a manner contrary to official edict but all those who so much as imagine doing so. So does the War on Truth translate into a government-sponsored attack upon the very foundation of the science and art of medicine.

AB2098, a bill passed by California lawmakers, currently sits on Governor Gavin Newsom's desk, waiting to be signed into law with a stroke of his pen. As of today (September 12, 2022) Newsom has not indicated whether he will, or will not, do so.

The key provision of the law reads as follows:

> It shall constitute unprofessional conduct for a physician and surgeon to disseminate misinformation or disinformation related to COVID-19, including false or misleading information regarding the nature and risks of the virus, its prevention and treatment; and the development, safety, and effectiveness of COVID-19 vaccines.[489]

Like Dr. Paul Offit, media personality Drew Pinsky—better known as "Doctor Drew"—can hardly be counted amongst the ranks of Covid dissidents. True, very early in the pandemic, Dr. Drew played down the seriousness of the illness, but soon changed his tune, apologized for being wrong on Covid, and largely toed the party line. At least, he refrained from raising his (very loud) public voice in protest...until AB2098, having passed both houses of the California legislature, landed on Governor Newsom's desk.

That got Dr. Drew riled up, and rightfully so:

> I want to explain how draconian this law is, this AB2098 in the state of California.... Let's say you come in, you're my patient.... If you were 30 years old, and I say: "You know, there's a study that just came into circulation last—this—week, that suggested that in men under 40, the risk of myocarditis is five times higher from the Moderna vaccine than from Covid itself...." RIGHT THERE, *that* would qualify as *misinformation,* even though it is *factually accurate.* It is merely me discussing what is available in the medical literature with my patient.[490]

Dr. Drew goes on to say that if, for any reason, that patient had a bone to pick with him, he could file an anonymous complaint to the state, as could (on their own initiative or even at that annoyed patient's urging) anyone else, and it would be

> as though a police report had been filed for a criminal action. It will require a full response, with citations, and will take months and months, and may require an attorney for each case. THAT is what they are doing. It is totally out of control.
>
> It will be absolutely chilling for the practice of medicine. It will become almost impossible to practice medicine the way we are trained to...which is to use our objective reasoning, share our ideas with our patients, and come up with the best possible recommendation for *that particular patient* for *that particular circumstance* [emphasis added].[491]

The formula here reads: Centralized Control of Science → Government Overreach → Destruction of Professional Prerogative, Doctor-Patient Relationships, Informed Consent and Individual Rights and Freedoms. In short, the scenario promises (as Dr. Drew suggests) destruction of the practice—the science and the art—of medicine, as we know it; or have known it, once upon a time.

This War on Medicine is manifestly also a War on the Body, Soul, and Spirit of the human being. The traditional sacredness (*spiritual* basis) of the doctor-patient relationship derives, in the first place, from the particularity of the individual body, which expresses the uniqueness of the individual soul and forms the basis of the value—the irreplaceable value—of any and every *particular* doctor-patient relationship. That relationship is grounded in emotional dynamics of trust and compassion; knowledge of personal history; and innumerable other factors brutally sacrificed on the altar of technocratic obsession with uniformity and centralized control.

Even as—metaphysically speaking—the *soul* constantly translates between the universal level of knowledge and principles characteristic of the *spirit* and the contingency of any and every particular (psychological as well as physical) instance, a good doctor (always a physician of the soul as well as the body) does the same. He draws upon his general knowledge of the pertinent science and all relevant principles in order to apply these to the unique case at hand, an interpretive act of translation that is—in every case of any complexity—as much art as science.

The total incapacity of any sort of centralized or standardized system of care to honor the irreducible individuality intrinsic to the practice of medicine—the science and art of healing—provides a vividly concrete instance of the danger inherent in any model of top-down, centralized, bureaucratic control. It exhibits with special clarity the core of the dialectic of enlightenment: namely, the *erasure of the human individual* (both doctor and patient) in body, soul, and spirit. As Dr. Drew suggests, a law such as AB2098 not only betrays the truth *in* and *of* science, it breeds distrust and division between human souls, dividing us against each other, and cutting the heart as well as the mind out of the practice of medicine.

I hope and pray by the time these words see the light of day, Governor Newsom has not signed AB208, but consigned this egregious affront to science, medicine, and the citizens of California to ignominious oblivion.[492]

Before proceeding to a last example of the corruption of science that leads, in a flash, to interference—violently destructive interference—with the practice of medicine, I wish for a moment to address some of the larger concerns implicit in the critique of the ideological basis of mass vaccination leveled in the last chapter. Doing so may be called for insofar as that critique passed beyond the bounds of Covid World to engage the matter of mass or compulsory vaccination in general. I expect that many persons will find fault with my arguments, and reject my transcendentally-inflected defense of individual bodily autonomy as egocentric and inhumane, despite my arguments to the contrary.

While it is now evident for all to see that the Covid "vaccines" do not prevent infection or transmission, the same—so the argument runs—cannot be asserted with similar confidence for childhood vaccines.[493] The historic case for mass vaccination hinges on the principle of herd immunity. Vaccine catechism teaches that it is indeed necessary to vaccinate a high percentage of young children and infants in order to prevent the spread of dangerous infectious diseases in the population as a whole. One may tout one's individual right to bodily autonomy, but that hardly holds water in this special case. Whether any parent does, or does not, vaccinate their child affects—not only that child's body—but (albeit indirectly) that of countless other children and even adults, who may be put at risk by such recalcitrance. When speaking of infectious disease, the boundary of the body does not stop at any one person's skin, but extends to the collective, the body politic as a whole.

While I cannot enter into a full-fledged discussion of the pros and cons of childhood vaccination, I can (in line with the drift of my larger historical argument) contend that the dogmatic claim that the approved vaccination schedule does *more good than harm* for public health does *not* rest upon conclusive scientific evidence. It is a product, not of exhaustive study undertaken in the spirit of impartial objectivity that meets traditional criteria of scientific verification, but of a potent combination of ideological investment, religio-mythical belief, financial interest and raw sociopolitical power (including control of educational, professional and governmental institutions).[494] While individual physicians who have been trained in the system may naturally embrace vaccination in the sincere belief that they are performing a deed shown (and even proven) by science to protect the health and well-being of their patients and the populace as a whole, one could question whether they have any more substantial and rational grounds for that belief than did colonial-era Christian missionaries who imagined that they served the bodies and souls of indigenous populations by the forced imposition of their faith. Indeed, it may well be that the upper echelons of the pharmaceutical industry and the public health personnel intimately acquainted (and often entangled) with those interests have more conscious and concrete knowledge of the potential for serious harm inflicted by the manufacture and mass distribution of their products than any clergy, which traffics in less tangible elixirs. In the wake of multiple felony convictions, including recent ones stemming from the opioid crisis, it is inconceivable that they do not.

Anyone, in fact, who imagines that the spirit of truth, real science, and genuine concern and love for humanity drive the vaccine agenda today need only look at the case of Dr. Paul Thomas to find compelling evidence to the contrary.

After leaving a mainstream group practice on account of his own first-hand experience of patients suffering vaccine harm, Oregon doctor Paul Thomas opened his integrative pediatrics practice fourteen years ago. Doctor Thomas did not, however, turn wholly against vaccines, but sought to provide truly *informed* consent for all his patients. His well-known 2016 book, *The Vaccine-Friendly Plan*,[495] rejected a one-size-fits-all approach to vaccines, offering guidance facilitating "thoughtful individualized decisions based on research and collaboration between parents and clinicians—a plan to optimize a child's immune system and minimize any risks."[496] Evidently, the Oregon State Medical Board did not look kindly upon a physician intent upon providing his pediatric patients with the opportunity for truly informed consent, or upon the author of a book that contains data revealing that unvaccinated patients are far less susceptible to chronic disease than vaccinated patients. After relentlessly badgering Dr. Thomas, the CDC, in a January 2019 letter, insisted that Dr. Thomas *prove* that his "vaccine-friendly plan" was as "safe" as the CDC schedule. Dr. Thomas rightfully regarded that as an irregular and even irrational request, insofar as the CDC itself has never taken pains to perform any kind of comparative studies proving the "safety" of its vaccine schedule.

After his initial bafflement, Dr. Thomas hit on an ingenious strategy for doing what he could to fulfill the CDC's request. He hired an outside expert who helped design and run a comparative study drawing (without any selective exception) on the pool of over 3,000 patients born into Dr. Thomas's practice since its inception. That pool included 561 children who had received no vaccinations and 2,763 children who had received one or more vaccines. The study stratified the latter group according to the number of vaccinations received.

Here is Dr. Paul Thomas himself on the results, which were duly published in the International Journal of Environmental Research and Public Health in November of 2020:[497]

> What we found was actually even mind-boggling for myself. I've had a sense—I've had a practice now for fourteen years, where patients get to decide. The one thing I am absolute on is informed consent. You, the patient, get to decide what gets injected into your body, if anything. You

> should always insist on that or else walk out of that doctor's office. But because we do informed consent, we had a growing number of unvaccinated patients, and I was clearly seeing: These kids don't get sick. They don't get chronic conditions. The data spoke for itself. Over time, over that ten-and-a-half years, the more vaccines you had, the worse you were, whether we looked at infections, ADD/ADHD, neurodevelopmental issues, eczema, allergies—it doesn't matter what we looked at, even just plain old anemia—*skyrockets* in the vaccinated as compared to the unvaccinated.[498]

If the medical establishment and our public health agencies behaved responsibly, the publication of the results should have been cause for genuine consternation. The study should have prompted additional research so as to *either refute or corroborate* the results. The data, after all, poses compelling public health concerns, whether or not vaccines effectively eliminate or reduce incidence of the diseases they target. Given the range and number of vaccinations typically administered today, medical and public health institutions—in accord with the humane and enlightened spirit of "real" science—cannot afford to take anything for granted, or act on the basis of dogma and vested interests like some arrogant papacy. In fact, rather than fantasy, such institutions should encourage rigorous examination of all evidence, and go so far as to entertain, with utmost seriousness, the *possibility* that mass vaccination could be a prime cause for the dramatic rise in chronic illnesses afflicting the American public over the last decades, most especially since the explosion of the vaccine schedule in the late 1980s.

Unfortunately, the all-too-predictable response of our Matrix-controlled medical machinery followed a very different script. Dr. Thomas:

> The data is so powerful that, within five days of it being available online, they yanked my license. On December 3, 2020, the Oregon Medical Board had an emergency meeting, and suspended my license. I was supposedly a threat to public health.[499]

Dr. Paul Thomas, the soft-spoken integrative pediatrician and author of the popular book *The Vaccine-Friendly Plan;* a profoundly ethical physician, committed, above all, to fulfilling the first and cardinal principle of the Nuremberg Code—*informed* consent—a threat to public health? I don't think so. Dr. Thomas and his ilk, however, certainly *do* represent a threat to the prevailing regime, and its increasingly dogmatic and repressive rule, just as Wycliffe, Hus, and Luther posed a threat to an ever more degenerate Catholic Church. Perhaps today, Dr. Paul and other defenders of the law of informed consent will be instrumental in holding the West's no-longer-new faith to account so that the leviathan Machine cannot mine the bodies and control the minds of the many, take the names of science and of medicine in vain, and spit in the face of the Spirit of Truth that is the real healer of humankind.

Chapter 17

OF KINGS, QUEENS, AND MUSIC HALLS

It is time—high time—to speak about government; to devote concerted attention to the foundation stone of this nation, the intellectual principle integral to (if I may follow presidential rhetoric) its very *soul.* In his impassioned September 1 (2022) speech on "The Continued Battle for the Soul of the Nation" from Philadelphia's Independence Hall[500] (site of the signing of both the Declaration of Independence and the United States Constitution), President Biden railed against lawless parties that pose a grave threat to the idea that defines America's political and spiritual identity. After finishing his delivery of the prepared text, the President evidently felt he had still not made his chief point forcefully enough. Like some aged warrior sounding a rallying cry, Biden, clenching his fist and bringing it down hard upon the wooden podium, let fly a last, single exclamation:

"*Democracy!*"

Obviously, the President cherishes the idea signified by this word. Nor is he alone in that. All true Americans—Democrats and Republicans alike—hold it in esteem.

Very well, but does *he*—do *we—know what it means?*

In the long, agonizing wake of the Covid-19 debacle, one must wonder. America was born in the throes of a struggle to throw off the shackles of a tyrannical king, but throughout the nation, the ghastly visage of despotic power has risen again and freedom once more been chained by callous indifference, arbitrary edict, and lawless force.

Need I again rehearse the litany of abuse in key ways comparable to the long inventory of grievances enumerated in the Declaration of Independence itself?

We have been locked up (or down), imprisoned in our own houses and rooms for months on end without reasonable cause; our shops have been shuttered, our jobs lost, our children shut out of school and separated from family and friends; our mouths have been inhumanly muzzled, as if the American people were nought but a pack of dangerous dogs; we have been forbidden to assemble and worship—not the skinny idol of the scientific tribe—but the one true God (or Buddha, or Shiva, or...) in mosque, church, or temple; suffering affliction, we have been mercilessly denied treatments that heal even while sickness chokes our lungs; our good physicians have been cruelly discredited, and foul poisoners obeyed like officers of the law; our press has been perverted, our voices suppressed and censored, our books effectively banned; we have been prevented from seeing, hearing, and touching loved ones, the heartlessness proceeding to the door of death itself.

The defenders of the authorities, our modern *ancien régime,* protest: "All for cause!" To which one might reply: "Their throat is an open sepulchre; with their tongues they have used deceit; the poison of asps is under their lips.... Destruction and misery are in their ways."[501]

Did even King George ever so severely, so intimately, so methodically afflict colonists on distant Atlantic shores? Did any barbaric Roman tyrant—any Caligula or Nero—ever inflict such rationally *systematic* violence upon the bodies, minds, and souls of his own people, licensing abuse by avaricious fraud that tears at the contract of civil society, the very fabric of the law?

On this all-important score, Jefferson's complaints against King George hold good, too, in the heyday of Covid World:

> He has combined with others to subject us to a jurisdiction foreign to our constitution, and unacknowledged by our laws; giving his Assent to their Acts of pretended Legislation...
>
> ...Declaring themselves invested with power to legislate for us in all cases whatsoever...
>
> Taking away our Charters, abolishing our most valuable Laws and altering fundamentally the Forms of our Governments...[502]

The "*Forms of our Governments*"? Pray tell, what may that be? As we remember American history in the Independence Hall of today, we need rehearse that most pressing question and seek answer, not with self-assured complacency, but a critically informed conscience.

Democracy: The Greek roots of the word clue us into its meaning. *Demos* means the people—not of any aristocratic or elite or otherwise special class—but the common person. *Kratos* means rule or strength. Put these together, and one grasps the essential concept of democracy: a form of government led by no king or monarch, nor by any privileged few, but rather one wherein the people are empowered to rule and so govern themselves.

It is indeed a revolutionary idea. While by no means without ancient precedent (as its Greek roots and the Athenian example shows), it nonetheless emerged anew in the modern era, representing a dramatic and decisive break from traditional forms of sovereignty exercised by both church and state. I have already attempted to sketch the multifold transformations that led, finally, to the emergence of the democratic idea and its eruption in the birth of this nation; yet few have put the gist of the matter as cogently as yet another American Transcendentalist, Theodore Parker. Parker did so, moreover, on a most fit occasion: an Independence Day celebration in Boston, roughly four score years after the ratification of the Constitution of these United States.

On July 4, 1858, Parker, a reform-minded Unitarian minister, gave a sermon in Boston's Music Hall on "The Effect of Slavery on the American People." Proposing, as necessary background, to "look a minute at some of the chief peculiarities of our political institutions," Parker provides historical perspective relevant to the advent of the democratic idea in the modern world. He vividly portrays the primacy of ecclesiastical and political hierarchy and the correlative subservience—indeed servility—of the people in the medieval era:

> In the Middle Ages, through the greater part of Europe, there prevailed a form of government which looks strange to you and me. Vicariousness was the general rule in religion, and politics; neither Church nor State was amenable to the people.
>
> First, the clergy were responsible for the Religion of the People; that is, one man in three or four thousand was thought answerable for the future welfare of all the rest. The clergy made an ecclesiastical theology, and called it Divine Revelation; they established ecclesiastical ceremonies, which they named the Ordinances of God. The people were only to believe the one and practise the other, and their calling and election was made sure; for the priest claimed to speak with authority superior to human consciousness. "Believe" and "Obey" were his two commands; "trust our office, and not your own soul!"[503]

After having thus illustrated the key principle of vicariousness with respect to ecclesiastical institution, Parker proceeds to its political analogue:

> Second, the King and the Aristocracy were responsible for the Politics of the people; they made, expounded and administered the statute law, claiming authority above the collective interests or collective conscience of the people. The magistrate's statutes were a finality, the people's Need and Right was none. The official did not *propose* statutes; he *made* them and enforced.[504]

Parker proceeds to place accent upon the ultimate, the divine ground assumed by both ecclesiastical and political authority, which origin naturally placed such power beyond popular grievance or reproach:

> Then the church and state were both accounted divine,—that is, the final and ultimate authority. The priest, king, or noble all claimed to hold of God, not of mankind; they were feudatories under Him, responsible to God, not to man. The ecclesiastical or political ruler had all the command and right; only obedience and duty belonged to the ruled. The king or noble was the state, the priest the church.... Such was once the theory of Divine State and Divine Church, the two-fold kingdom of God on earth.[505]

"So much for these Vicarious Institutions," declares Parker:

> Now in America, we have somewhat changed that state of things. The political and ecclesiastical functionary is the servant, the People master now.

True to the American Transcendentalist ethos and the genius of humanity that informs it, Parker continues to gives a *spirited* rendition of this dramatic inversion, first in its religious context:

> The ecclesiastical Ezekiel stands in the church valley of dry bones, and says, "Come from the four winds, O Spirit! and breathe upon these slain, that they may live!" But the Angel of Humanity answers, "Son of man, not so! Let the dead bury their dead! Follow thou me; behold I make all things new. Egyptian and ecclesiastical mummies come not back again. Forward, O son of man! Forward!"

...and, subsequently, in its political setting:

> In the State the political man counts himself servant, not master. Let President Voted-in say in his proclamation to the people, "Gentlemen, I am your superior, and you are my servants; you are to do as I say;" if he should try to act thereon, there would be a state of things presently. The People alone are primitive and final, the magistrate derivative, provisional and responsible. The American Legislative, Judiciary or Executive, is only an attorney of the manifold and thirty-million-headed People; a servant hired express to make, expound and administer certain statute laws, which are amenable to the people and reversible thereby.[506]

Finally, before turning to his announced subject (you will note that Parker delivers his sermon a few short years before the onset of the Civil War, and in the role of an abolitionist dedicated to that cause), Parker utters a series of noteworthy sentences which capture, as well as any three or four, the essence and epochal force of the democratic idea:

> Theocracy, the priest power, and monarchy, the one-man power, and oligarchy, the few-men power, are three forms of vicarious government over the People,—perhaps for them, not by them. Democracy is Direct Self-government, over all the people, for all the people, by all the people. Our institutions are democratic: theocratic, monarchic, oligarchic vicariousness is all gone. We have no divine vicar who is responsible to God for our politics and religion; only a human attorney, answerable to the people for his official work. The axis of rotation has changed: the equator of the old civilization passes through the poles of the new.[507]

Government "of the people, for the people, by the people." The reader will probably be familiar with that (more succinct expression of the) phrase from another context: the conclusion of Lincoln's Gettysburg Address. Lincoln borrowed the phrase from Parker, who in turn may have copied it from John Wycliffe who, in 1384, wrote in the Prologue of his translation of the Bible: "The Bible is for the Government of the People, by the People, for the People."[508]

The phrase thus claims distinguished pedigree. If Hus was the Luther before Luther, Wycliffe was the Hus before Hus. They were all of them dauntless heralds of the *principled* religious revolution that transfigured the world. Parker's "axis of rotation" sentence confirms my earlier statement: "*The modern emergence of the democratic Idea represents the political complement and correlative of the Reformation, contributing to the profound civilizational change marking the modern era.*"

As the occasions of both Parker's and Lincoln's speeches attest, however, the light of that Idea, as bright as it may shine in the pristine heaven of the mind, has from the first been obscured by violent prejudice. In the wake of Covid World and other contemporary developments, whether the genius of democracy be more or less assured today than in Parker and Lincoln's time counts as a question that not only *may*, but *must* urgently be asked. If slavery threatened the integrity of democratic ideals, other discriminatory, dehumanizing and even lawless forms of social and political praxes—many documented in this book—do so now. In the face of that frightening reality, it may be well to rehearse the resolve to preserve American democracy and the civil liberty essential to that idea memorialized in the concluding sentence of Lincoln's Gettysburg Address:

> It is rather for us to be here dedicated to the great task remaining before us–that from these honored dead we take increased devotion to that cause for which they gave the last full measure of devotion—that we here highly resolve that these dead shall not have died in vain—that this nation, under God, shall have a new birth of freedom—and that government of the people, by the people, for the people shall not perish from the earth.

Thus democracy: the word, its meaning, its storied and endangered heritage. Yet now, after paying due homage to it, we must perform a sharp pivot in our exploration of its import. If the principle of governance "of, by, and for the people" qualifies as the gist of democracy, it is only a part—and indeed, even a potentially misleading part—of the political character of the country: a character not finally wholly comprehended by the strict sense (semantic or political) of the heralded word itself.

Nor are the reservations I am about to detail without momentous historic precedent; on the contrary.

It may be surprising to discover that several of the founders were not ambivalent about the value of democracy (taken, now, in the strict sense, as they properly understood the term) and not because they knew they desired it, but because they knew they did not.

In a June 21, 1788 speech at a ratification convention[509] in New York, Alexander Hamilton declared:

> It has been observed by an honorable gentleman, that a pure democracy, if it were practicable, would be the most perfect government. Experience has proved, that no position in politics is more false than this. The ancient democracies, in which the people themselves deliberated, never possessed one feature of good government. Their very character was tyranny; their figure deformity.[510]

These are harsh words. How are we to understand them? By "pure democracy" Hamilton means (as his speech implies) *direct,* rather than *representative,* democracy; and so a system wherein people do not elect *representatives* to perform the business of government, but conduct this themselves.

Theodore Parker lauds democracy, indeed, as "Direct Self-government," ignoring that, as a matter of fact, the American government was not instituted in that pure form and has never operated in that fashion.

As Hamilton implies, "pure" or direct (rather than representative) democracy is only generally practicable in a community of manageable size, such as existed in ancient Athens. Whether Hamilton's unqualified condemnation of the system can be historically justified is debatable and one may well suspect the arch federalist of harboring a peculiarly critical view of the matter. Nonetheless, the remainder of the passage does fill out the picture Hamilton wishes to paint of the risk of *depravity* inherent in pure democracy, and its tendency to incline towards—not liberty—but tyranny.

> When they assembled, the field of debate presented an ungovernable mob, not only incapable of deliberation, but prepared for every enormity. In these assemblies, the enemies of the people brought forward their plans of ambition systematically. They were opposed by their enemies of another party; and it became a matter of contingency, whether the people subjected themselves to be led blindly by one tyrant or by another.[511]

The dynamic Hamilton describes here repels rather than appeals, and conjures a specter of repeated mass formations (or at least, kindred manifestations of herd instinct). In so doing, it highlights the outstanding vulnerability of the idea of democracy in anything like its pure form. Responsible debate may all too easily degenerate into divisive acrimony and demagoguery, ultimately enabling one or another partisan faction to obtain oppressive power.

Viewing matters from the standpoint of contemporary American politics, one might venture to suggest that these dangers are not altogether ameliorated, but in fact persist (albeit in a modified form) within the framework of a representative democracy such as that characteristic of the United States Congress today. One may well maintain that our Congress, mercilessly torn by partisanship, has largely ceased to function as a body suited to constructive deliberation of the topic of the times.

Hamilton was not the only founder to recognize the potential for such malfunction of democratic systems. Madison did so as well, and his more detailed sketch of the dangers of factionalism resonates all too well with our current state of political affairs. In his influential 10th Federalist Paper, penned in 1787, Madison sets the principal danger of democracy in stark relief:

> Complaints are everywhere heard...that the public good is disregarded in the conflicts of rival parties, and that measures are too often decided, not according to the rules of justice and the rights of the minor party, but by the superior force of an interested and overbearing majority.[512]

...before continuing to paint a scene almost uncannily pertinent to the present day:

> Some of the distresses under which we labor have been erroneously charged on the operation of our governments; but it will be found…that other causes will not alone account for many of our heaviest misfortunes; and particularly, for that prevailing and increasing distrust of public engagements, and alarm for private rights, which are echoed from one end of the continent to the other. These must be chiefly, if not wholly, effects of the unsteadiness and injustice with which a factious spirit has tainted our public administration.[513]

Madison, in another passage especially relevant to current affairs, develops his definition of factionalism so as to recognize that it is not always the majority party that attains undue power:

> By faction, I understand a number of citizens, whether amounting to a majority or minority of the whole, who are united and actuated by some common impulse of passion, or of interest, adversed to the rights of other citizens, or to the permanent and aggregate interests of the community.[514]

Madison believes these serious (if not fatal) ills are endemic to pure democracy, and so irremediable within the framework of that system:

> A pure democracy, by which I mean a society consisting of a small number of citizens, who assemble and administer the government in person, can admit of no cure for the mischiefs of faction. A common passion or interest will, in almost every case, be felt by a majority of the whole; a communication and concert result from the form of government itself; and there is nothing to check the inducement to sacrifice the weaker party or an obnoxious individual. Hence it is that such democracies have ever been spectacles of turbulence and contention…incompatible with personal security or the rights of property; and have in general been as short in their lives as they have been violent in their deaths.[515]

If the principle written into the word "democracy" does not effectively preclude the tendency toward tyranny or despotism, but may even invite it, how can it legitimately qualify as the lodestone of political aspiration, the shining idea illuminating the American city on the hill? Government of, by, and for the people may be part of the equation, and an inspiring substitute for the power of popes and kings, but what must be added to that ingredient to create and preserve—even theoretically—that cherished political identity?

Despite his dire diagnosis, Madison does not propose reversion to any "vicarious" form of government, but rather endorses a time-honored variation of the democratic idea, one that introduces another historic term:

> A *republic,* by which I mean a government in which the scheme of representation takes place, opens a different prospect, and promises the cure for which we are seeking.[516]

As this sentence makes clear, Madison views *representation* as the key and defining element of a *republicanism* that might ameliorate the ills of democracy. Most of the remainder of Federalist #10 entails discussion of the *kind* of representative scheme best suited to that end. That discussion revolves principally around the number of representatives. Madison recommends choosing a number large enough to be truly representative and not readily subject to the formation of elite cabals, yet small enough to be manageable and not lost in undue multiplicity.

Representation undoubtedly functions as an indispensable element of democracy in the modern world, one that enables America and other nations to attempt a form of government of the people, by the people, for the people. Crucial questions, however, remain. Does the scheme of representation finally settled upon and inscribed in the Constitution indeed suffice largely to eradicate the dangers Madison exposes? If not, does the error lie in a miscalculation as to how to achieve equitable representation, or derive from some other source? Does the idea of *a republic* in fact promise a cure for the ills of democracy? Has Madison rightly articulated the key idea of republicanism *per se,* and the chief means by which it may effect that cure?

My prior references to present day politics imply that, if the scheme of representation has served well enough in the past (American democracy has, after all, proved remarkably stable for well over two centuries), its adequacy must nonetheless be diminishing, and dangerously so. We hear more and more of imbalances written into the electoral system that appear to bend it further and further away from the democratic ideal of a truly representative democracy. The recurrent election of presidents who have lost the popular vote, sometimes by substantial margins, represents one manifestation of this flaw. Corruption in government additionally constitutes a mortal threat to the representational core of democratic governance, rendering elected officials and candidates for office subject to intense pressure from powerful special interests careless if not disdainful of the public weal.

While these are real and pressing problems, I would suggest that another threat to democracy inheres in an element neglected or (more plausibly) taken for granted by Madison; an element that pertains to the very gist of what constitutes not so much the idea of democracy per se, as that of a *republic.*

As seminal as its core idea may be, the word "democracy" appears in neither the Declaration of Independence nor the Constitution. The word signifying Madison's suggested "cure" for the ills of factionalism does so, albeit only once. Article IV, Section 4, declares "The United States shall guarantee to every state in this union a *republican* form of government." As the text gives no further information as to the precise meaning of the key phrase, one might well assume that the Constitution, like Madison (who was, after all, one of the framers) understands *republicanism* to mean, essentially, one or another form of representative democracy. Yet another, quite distinct meaning has been attributed to this storied word, and that by yet another founder; one especially well-versed in the annals of political history.

In the lengthy debate preceding formulation and ratification of the Constitution, John Adams undertook systematically to inquire into the concept of a republic. Adams begins by acknowledging the historic *confusion* obscuring the term:

> But of all the words in all languages, perhaps there has been none so much abused in this way as the words *republic, commonwealth*, and *popular state*.[517]

After denying that (contrary to certain attributions) France, Spain, Portugal and "the four great empires, the Babylonian, Persian, Greek, and Roman" can rightfully be called republics, Adams complains:

> If, indeed, a republic signifies nothing but public affairs, it is equally applicable to all nations; and every kind of government, despotisms, monarchies, aristocracies, democracies, and every possible or imaginable composition of them are all republics.[518]

One might think, in this context, of the (distinctly undemocratic) regime of what is today called the People's *Republic* of China.

After rejecting several deficient definitions, Adams gives us the kernel of what appears to him the true core of the republican idea:

> Others, again, more rationally, define a republic to signify only a government, in which all men, rich and poor, magistrates and subjects, officers and people, masters and servants, the first citizen and the last, *are equally subject to the laws* [emphasis added].[519]

This definition of "republic" reflects an idea quite distinct from the gist of the idea of democracy, in either its pure or representational sense. Whereas the latter centers upon the power and prerogatives of the people, republicanism, as described by Adams here, hinges upon the preeminence of no people, but rather that of the order of the law, the authority of which exceeds that of any and all persons. Correlatively, a *constitution* (such as that of the United States) represents a privileged or primary set of laws, a relatively comprehensive charter that establishes the foundations of the government as well as fundamental principles underlying its administration. The form of government thus established comprises a *constitutional democracy* or democratic republic.

The idea of the rule of law can and indeed must be distinguished from that of governance (of, for, and) by the people. Even so, while a certain tension and even conflict can subsist between these ideas, they may also cooperate. In fact, just such coherence comprises the foundation of the form of governance most usually called simply "democracy." A constitution, after all, will typically be framed by representatives of the people and be ratified by either the people themselves or those representatives, while the principal laws thus established may subsequently protect the prerogatives of the people.

Adams himself provides an account of this *crucial synergy between the people and the law* in the course of an etymological discussion of the nature of a republic:

> The word *res,* every one knows, signified in the Roman language wealth, riches, property; the word *publicus*... signified public, common, belonging to the people; *res publica,* therefore, was publica res, the wealth, riches, or property of the people.... The original meaning of the word *republic* could be no other than a government in which the property of the people predominated and governed; and it had more relation to property than liberty. It signified a government, in which the property of the public, or people, and of every one of them, was secured and protected by law.[520]

Articulating the reciprocity inhering in the relationship between the people and the law, Adams touches the core of the popular idea of (constitutional) democracy. At the same time, this passage (as well as the next, which we will shortly peruse) illuminates the reason why no few persons view the founders' formulations of the principles of democratic governance with skepticism if not outright disdain.

One could consider Adams's whole line of thought somewhat suspect on account of the jealous (indeed, quasi-religious) valuation of *property* central to it, an investment characteristic of aristocratic Enlightenment thinkers, including Locke and most (if not all) of America's founders. I do not wish to attempt to rebut the notion that a zealous regard for the wealth and privilege of the propertied class affected (if it did not indeed infect) much of the founders' thinking. At the same time, I do not believe that a selfish desire to protect their own status and assets altogether controlled and corrupted the founders' political deliberations,[521] so that nought of real value may be culled from their ruminations on fundamental questions pertaining to the self and society.

Adams's discourse here, on the all-important subject of the nature of republic, may serve as a case in point. For our own purposes, I propose to understand "property" here in a manner at once both more immediate and more philosophical than its narrow, normal construction, and one more in line with the whole sense of the Latin word *res* by means of which Adams introduces the concept of property here. I mean, that is, to understand "property" in the sense suggested earlier, as pertaining *primarily* and *originally* to that sole and exclusive *possession* which lends *physical substance* to the *identity* of (not any privileged class of monied persons) but each and every human being: namely, the *human body.* Such a reading, I would suggest, can make good and moral *spiritual* sense out of the early modern preoccupation with "property," wresting both the fact and basic idea from the uneven field of classist concern to the bare and equal level of sheer existence common to *every* living person.

I do not deny that such a hermeneutic turn represents a "strong reading" of Adams's text, and so may be judged to effect a significant transformation of its intended meaning. All interpretations do the same to a greater or lesser extent, and I propose that reading Adams from this angle *preserves,* even as it may *transfigure*, the salient political philosophy inscribed in his prose, and the important insight into the essence of democracy it contains. In particular, this passage, and its continuation, conveys the crucial idea that it is not the principle of popular representation alone, but the combination of that idea with the rule of constitutional law that may prove an effective antidote to factionalism and the abuse of power it breeds:

> [The word republic...] signified a government, in which the property of the public, or people, and of every one of them, was secured and protected by law.

> This idea, indeed, implies liberty; because property cannot be secure unless the man be at liberty to acquire, use, or part with it, at his discretion, and unless he have his personal liberty of life and limb, motion and rest, for that purpose. It implies, moreover, that the property and liberty of all men, not merely of a majority, should be safe; for the people, or public, comprehends more than a majority, it comprehends all and every individual; and the property of every citizen is a part of the public property, as each citizen is a part of the public, people, or community. The property, therefore, of every man has a share in government, and is more powerful than any citizen, or party of citizens; it is governed only by the law.[522]

If we attempt to read this passage in light of my proposed modification of the essential meaning of property, one phrase may seem to lose sense. While one should certainly be at liberty to "use" one's own body as one sees fit (short, of course, of the commission of criminal acts), no one can "acquire" or "part with it" in any normal, or normally acceptable, sense. Yet such illicit ownership is precisely the issue in, not only slavery, but trafficking of various sorts. Furthermore, key phrases of the rest of the passage may well be felt to *gain* sense and more powerfully convey meaning basic to the very idea of a constitutional democracy and the rights of the citizens inherent therein.

If there be any doubt as to whether Adams himself understands his rehearsal of the meaning of republicanism to apply to democracy per se—insofar as that word or concept does not appear in the above-cited material—his conclusions allay any such concern. "There is," writes Adams,

> a peculiar sense in which the words *republic, commonwealth, popular state,* are used by English and French writers; who mean by them a democracy, or rather a representative democracy; a "government in one centre, and that centre the nation"; that is to say, that centre a single assembly, chosen at stated periods by the people... the whole legislative, executive, and judicial power, to be exercised in a body.[523]

One can hear certain collectivist overtones in Adams's emphasis upon the public weal in the citation preceding this last one. Even so, that emphasis is not only over-balanced but indeed premised upon rights of the individual, the sacred character of "the property and liberty of *all* men." Adams does not, after all, endorse any controlling notion of "the greater (public) good," or anything like majority rule that might contravene the lawful rights of the individual. To repeat:

> The people or public comprehends *more than a majority*, it comprehends all and *every individual*.... The property...of *every* man has a share in government, and...*is governed only by the law* [emphasis added].[524]

Adams's philological excursion illuminates the idea of "the People" that functions as the bedrock of democracy, and, correlatively, the essential cohesion of this idea with that of law in the kind of constitutional democracy or republic characteristic of the U.S. (and most modern democracies). The idea of a people is not one of the simple *mass* of persons, one indistinguishable from the other in the formation of that larger entity. On the contrary, it is the public interest of the *ensemble of individual human beings*, the character and identity of which depends upon the rights and prerogatives accorded by force of law to each and every single (and singular) citizen. The authority of the people thus does not derive from any numeric or quantitative source at all, but from the realm of principle—the principles, first of all, of liberty and equality under the law.

This theoretical foundation receives its most explicit formulation in the language of the Declaration of Independence, but finds fit reflection too, in the spirit as well as the letter of the Constitution and, especially, the Bill of Rights.

As the realm of principle represents an intrinsically transcendental realm of universal form or intelligible idea, we may duly recognize that the very idea of a democracy rests upon premises that are, at one and the same time, irreducibly transcendental and spiritual. That means that the ground of authority in a modern democracy does not ultimately cease to depend any less upon (a notion of) divinity than the preceding medieval model, be these theological or monarchical; but only that the recipient or seat of that authority has been transferred from church or king or nobility to the common person; the spiritual character and identity of each and every individual human being.

That, indeed, represents a radical, indeed a revolutionary idea in the history of humanity; one which as prescient a writer (and incisive critic of the Machine) as Paul Kingsnorth has not entirely caught up with.

Kingsnorth is British, and while no loyal subject of any tyrannical king, he (like millions of other Britons) evidently considered himself such in relation to the Queen.

Until, of course, last month.

At the age of ninety-six, and after a reign of over seventy years (the longest of any monarch in British history) Queen Elizabeth II died on September 8, 2022. Her funeral took place on September 19th in Westminster Abbey, a cathedral that dates back to the 13th century, and so to the heart of the Middle Ages. Kingsnorth, watching the ceremony on TV, found himself deeply moved; his sense of the sacred character of the proceedings epitomized by a particularly stirring moment. Kingsnorth:

> The Abbey is, of course, laid out in the shape of the cross, and the coffin was set down at the meeting point of the nave and the transept, where the two arms of the cross meet. At one point in the proceedings, the camera showed us this view, and then focused in on the scene, and the impression was that of some energy flowing down from above and into the coffin, then out across the marble floor and into the gathered crowd.[525]

Upon reflection, Kingsnorth identified the symbolic gist of that image...

> What we were seeing as the camera panned down was a manifestation, through technological trickery, of the ancient notion of sacral kingship.

...elaborates its historic reach and essential structure or ideal form:

> This notion was the rock upon which the political structure of all medieval societies was built, and in theory at least it is still the architecture which supports the matter of Britain.... Authority, in this model of society, flows downward, from God, and into the monarch, who then faces outward with that given power and serves—and rules—his or her people.

...and, finally—combining history and ideality—its archetypal or universal significance:

> This notion—that any power exercised by a human ruler ultimately derives from the spiritual plane—is neither British nor European. It is universal. Pharaonic Egypt recognized it, and so did Native America. The Anglo-Saxons believe it and so did the Japanese Emperors. Cultures large and small, imperial and tribal, on all continents over many millennia, have shared some version of this understanding of what the world is.[526]

Kingsnorth finally enthusiastically affirms the *transcendent* ground of our specifically political existence as such is both signified and supplied by (the idea of) sacral kingship:

> Power, it tells us—politics, it insists—is no mere human confection, because the world is no mere human confection. There is something—someone—else beyond it, and if we are silent, in these cathedrals or in these forests, we can hear it still. Those who take power in this world will answer to it at the end.[527]

Kingsnorth's keen religiously-informed perceptions bear us back, once more, to the divine ground of ultimate authority so forthrightly identified by Theodore Parker. In dramatic contrast to the latter, however, Kingsnorth's attachment (for the moment, anyway!) to the old idea of the divine right of kings and queens, and, too, his countervailing sense of the historic ascendancy of the profane Machine, blinds him to the equally sacred foundation of the revolutionary Democratic Idea announced in the American Declaration of Independence and articulated by the likes of both Jefferson and Parker. Kingsnorth continues:

> What is meaningful about this royal death is that the late Queen really believed this [model of sacral kingship]. So, I think, does her son, the new King. But the society around him very much does not. The understanding now is that authority flows upward from below, from "the people" and into the government, which supposedly governs on our behalf. In this model there is no sacred centre, and there is no higher authority to whom we answer. There is no heavenly grant of temporary office which will one day be returned, and a tally made. There is only raw power, rooted in materiality, which in itself has no meaning beyond what we ascribe to it. There is only efficiency. There is only management. There are only humans.[528]

Kingsnorth wrote this Substack piece ("Intermission: Last Post for Christian England") on the very day, or evening, of the Queen's funeral. I can certainly sympathize with his nostalgic desire for the return of a kind of medieval order of things, but cannot share it. As an American heir of Parker and Emerson, I could also not let pass without comment his implicit equation of the idea of democracy (government legitimated by consent of the governed) with the profane and materialistic leveling characteristic of no truly inspired vision of the New World, but rather the diabolical dialectic of enlightenment that (admittedly) holds the majority in thrall today. That same night, I penned and posted this response:

> *Thanks for the moving picture you painted of the Queen's funeral, and more generally, for all your valuable insights. In a time of great darkness, I have often found windows of light in your posts. I do, however, have some real questions about your line of thought in this one.*
>
> *I certainly recognize the catastrophic loss of the sacred in the modern period. That loss can—generally and retrospectively speaking—be linked to the transition from the medieval to the modern era, especially*

the Enlightenment and its widespread repudiation of (often dogmatic and violently intolerant) forms of traditional authority, including that of the Church and monarch (or King). I am somewhat distressed, however, at your suggestion that this transformation—so basic to modernity—necessarily bears with it a purely materialistic secularism and repudiation of divine law. To be sure, such has emerged as the dominant worldview in the course of the last two centuries, but this represents, in my mind, a betrayal of the real spiritual impulse that catalyzed modernity.

One notable fruit of that impulse was the birth of my nation (yes, I am an American) and the modern vision of democracy. Recall the first sentences of the Declaration of Independence:

> We hold these truths to be self-evident, that all men are created equal, that they are endowed by their Creator with certain unalienable Rights, that among these are Life, Liberty and the Pursuit of Happiness.—That to secure these rights, Governments are instituted among Men, deriving their just powers from the consent of the governed…

Your piece contains a more or less explicit criticism of this epochal initiative, at least insofar as democracy hinges upon the idea articulated in that last phrase. Yes, the democratic vision premises itself upon the principle that government precisely is NOT the locus of sacral authority, but is "of the people, by the people, for the people."

The language of the Declaration itself naturally goes back to the writings of an Englishman (Locke), the first of whose two Treatises on Civil Government *consisted entirely of a potent critique of the tradition of the divine right of kings. Yet Locke was no atheist, and few of the more truly enlightened 18th-century thinkers after him (with, of course, notable exceptions) were. As the language of the Declaration itself makes explicit, democracy, in essence, does not predicate itself upon repudiation of godhead or divine law, but sees the seat of that throne not in the person of a King or Pope, but in the spiritual humanity, the divine nature, inherent in each and every individual.*

In this political vision, it is precisely the chief function of government to guarantee those freedoms that enable the individual citizen rightfully to pursue the realization of that spiritual humanity (which, if you wish, you could associate with the Christ force, or divine I AM) by virtue of the school of life; his or her experience of the world as "the vale of soul-making." You find apt representation of this principle of the sacred character of the "I"—which is not merely the personal ego—in the writings of American Transcendentalists, who give cultural and literary expression to this idea. Two of the most representative, of course, are Emerson and

Whitman; the former the ex-preacher turned prophet of the Oversoul; the latter, the great singer of the "Song of Myself" and poet of the Democratic Idea.

I believe this recognition of the divine spirit inherent in each and every individual to be the true impulse behind, not only American Romanticism, but European Romanticism as well. It finds its own unique, and uniquely powerful, expression in (among others) Wordsworth.

No, as both a real democrat (I mean spiritually, not the degraded political party carrying the name at present) and real Romantic—and, of course, an individual not born into a country with a royalist tradition—I cannot feel any nostalgia for the age of the divine right (or sacral sovereignty) of kings and queens. Is it not rather the mission of the modern age to redeem the broken promise of Romanticism, in all its multiple forms, and realize that the throne of God is no royal seat, but the heart and soul of the individual human being?

Montesquieu said that the principle of monarchy, the true principle, was honor. And Queen Elizabeth, it seems, served her country and her people with great and admirable honor. Yet he likewise said that the principle of democracy was virtue: that it could not function, unless the People themselves aspired to the realization of the spirit of humanity; the logos *inherent in each and every individual. Call the spiritual quest what name you will, and style it after your own fashion, but in one way or another is not that the path toward a more human future, and a recovery of the sacred in everyday life? Is not the real crisis of the present day not the demise of royalty, but the distortion and decay of the true democratic idea; what one writer called "spiritual democracy,"*[529] *in America, in England, and indeed across the globe?*

Respectfully Yours,
Daniel Polikoff[530]

Kingsnorth responded to this comment generously and thoughtfully. His reply concludes:

Looking at America from over here, and talking to American friends, it looks like the decay of your democracy into consumerism, individualism and empire must result precisely from the fact that "virtue" has virtually disappeared. How could it be otherwise given the pressures? There can be no good society anywhere without that notion of virtue being widely shared. Again, the late Queen seemed to embody it in a very old-fashioned way, which might explain some of the feelings.

If we're going to have spiritual democracy, we need recover it—right? That has to start within, I think.[531]

This exchange brings us back to Patrick Deneen's discussion of the interdependence of the ideas of *liberty* and *virtue* in classical as well as Christian sources, and the consequent teaching that good governance of society goes hand in glove with self-governance, the one relying upon and strengthening the other. The whole project, as Kingsnorth suggests, must "start within." *Virtue* manifests individual *character*, the strength of—not the body—but the *soul* of the human being. "Spiritual democracy" might thus be considered an essentially redundant phrase, insofar as there can be no real, sustainable democracy that does not rest firmly upon the ethical and psychological culture of its citizens, the quality of the individuals comprising the whole of society, not excluding those comprising the government itself.

This simple, yet profound and all too easily neglected, perspective again sets in stark relief the dramatic contrast between the guiding principles of monarchy and democracy, construed as political philosophies. As both Montesquieu and Kingsnorth suggest, in any enlightened monarchy, order, harmony, and resonance with heaven devolves from the honor and wisdom of the sovereign. The sacral rule of the king or queen distributes the benefits of divine favor to the society at large. In a democracy, on the other hand, the operative relation to the divine source of existence depends radically upon each and every individual person's cultivation of their own soul nature; their striving to bring their thinking, feeling, and willing into attunement with Spirit, the unique form of the divine image innate in every person, the *Logos* or Overself that functions as the ground of each and every individual's authentic existence.

The first and foremost function of government in democratic society, as reflected (if incompletely and imperfectly) in America's Bill of Rights, thus consists not in the passage of any set of lesser laws or promotion of any given social program, or (still less) the imposition of measures suited to impose a specific code of moral or religious conduct upon the populace as a whole, but rather in the provision and protection of that essential liberty of thought, feeling, and action that best enables the individual to pursue the end of the realization of their authentic identity unconstrained by undue hindrances imposed by other persons or the government itself. Practically speaking, this translates into the jealous guardianship of certain fundamental principles that comprise the arsenal of freedom, ethical ideas reflected in concrete provisions of the Bill of Rights. Freedom of religion, speech, press, assembly, franchise, privacy and the rest, serve to honor and preserve the God-given spiritual prerogative of the individual human being, ensuring not only the liberty to pursue the winding pathways of one's private or inner life, but protecting, too, the free and full exercise of the soul's faculties in the joint pursuit of fit ends alongside others in society, so long as one's words and deeds do not unfairly cripple or fatally truncate the like endeavor of fellow citizens.

It is, of course, this last necessary clause that can complicate matters, and often supplies seemingly rational and even legal justification for the infringement of basic rights by the government. In the complexity of social existence, grey areas will inevitably emerge, yet judgment in any given instance may be aided by faithful recollection of the founding principles of constitutional democracy, the first and foremost of which is—*not* the granting of any power of government to act proactively on behalf of any *perceived* interest of society—but the government's obligation to respect and protect the unalienable rights of the individual human being. That responsibility naturally extends to those rights—such as the rights of speech and assembly—essential to the individual's participation in political process and, consequently, to the legitimacy of any government presuming to be truly representative; government of, by, and for the people.

American democracy, as verified by the language and laws of the founders, thus represents a political philosophy that premises itself upon, not the purely temporal authority of government, but *the spiritual sovereignty of the individual human being*. The ground of that sovereignty rests in the immediate relationship to godhead explicitly endorsed by American Transcendentalists, and, correlatively, to the universal spirit of humanity inherent in the soul of every single person—a direct relationship *not* enjoyed in any kindred fashion by the organ of government or indeed any group or mass of persons.

To put the gist of the matter simply, conscience and moral responsibility inhere in the very character and composition of the individual human being as an integral unity of body, soul, and spirit. It does *not* so inhere in the conglomerate construction of the state, the just administration of which always depends upon the conscience and character of its members. The irreducible unit of spiritual authority remains, in the first and last analysis, the human self.

In this respect, the revolution in political philosophy represented by modern democracy strictly parallels that of the Protestant Reformation. Martin Luther repudiated the idea that religious authority rested with the institution of the Catholic Church insofar as the individual believer enjoys her own direct relationship to the godhead. The refuge and sanctuary of man in Christ and Christ in man consequently lies, not in the perfumed chamber of ceremony, but in the recesses of the human heart and in the faith and conscience of the adherent of Christian Liberty. Likewise, the Democratic Idea wrests the scepter of real power from all external office, investing it in the souls of the People, and reconceiving government as the organ and instrument of the People's free and sovereign will.

The two revolutions are correlative and coordinate, and may be regarded as distinct aspects of one and the same historical—and uniquely modern—impulse.

It is thus in no wise incidental that the maturation of the philosophy of democracy should, in the post-revolutionary century that saw America striving for cultural as well as political independence, feature numerous more or less radical Protestant ministers, including Theodore Parker and (at the onset of his public career) Ralph Waldo Emerson. America's *political* founders were, per force, embroiled in the heat of political controversy, and destined to expend their genius on the complexities entailed in establishing a working government. Precisely because of their firsthand knowledge of the inherent tendency of government to abuse the power accorded to it, the founders, as we have seen, inscribed the primacy of the Rights of the People in the law and canon of the land. Even so, it was only natural that our free-spirited Transcendentalists—less consumingly concerned with affairs of state—would speak and write still more explicitly, eloquently, and unequivocally of the sovereignty of the individual, and the place of the same as not only the foundation stone of the temple of democracy but also the touchstone of the national ethos.

While the Transcendentalists did not need to concern themselves with a revolutionary war or the original formation of a government, they did find themselves involved in political matters of grave, even existential import; above all, the still unsettled and deeply unsettling issue of slavery. Theodore Parker uttered the phrase "government of the people, by the people, for the people" in the context of a speech on slavery in 1858. Henry David Thoreau had already written an eloquent attack on the inhuman institution in his 1854 piece *Slavery in Massachusetts*.[532] Five years before that, Thoreau had penned a still more famous essay, one centrally if not quite so exclusively concerned with slavery and forthrightly addressing our present theme: the sovereignty—at once both spiritual and political—of the individual human being.

Thoreau's essay *Civil Disobedience* counts as one of most influential in all of modern history. The text served as a source of inspiration for Mahatma

Ghandi's non-violent overthrow of British rule in India and Martin Luther King, Jr.'s leadership of the Civil Rights Movement in the United States. The whole essay may be considered a tutorial in the reliance of the public upon the private conscience and the power of moral force. Early on, Thoreau zeroes in on the heart of the matter, subordinating not only the rule of any "pure democracy," but also that of civic (as opposed to natural or divine) law, to the supreme court of individual conscience:

> A government in which the majority rule in all cases cannot be based on justice, even as far as men understand it. Can there not be a government in which majorities do not virtually decide right and wrong, but conscience?—in which majorities decide only those questions to which the rule of expediency is applicable? Must the citizen ever for a moment, or in the least degree, resign his conscience to the legislator? Why has every man a conscience, then? I think we should be men first and subjects afterward. It is not desirable to cultivate a respect for the law, so much as for the right. The only obligation which I have a right to assume, is to do at any time what I think right.[533]

This may sound radical, and so it is. Yet the ground of Thoreau's position—at once intellectual, moral, and spiritual—defines him as anything but an anarchist.

> To speak practically and as a citizen, unlike those who call themselves no-government men, I ask for, not at once no government, but *at once* a better government. Let every man make known what kind of government would command his respect, and that will be one step toward obtaining it.[534]

Worthy advice, to be sure. Today, one must wonder how, exactly, the partisans of either major party—so-called "Republicans" or "Democrats"—might answer that question, and whether (whatever lip service they pay to the democratic idea) their conduct does not lead one legitimately to question whether they do not in fact incline towards one or the other varieties of "vicariousness" enumerated by Theodore Parker: theocracy, monarchy, or (technocratic?) oligarchy.

In the concluding paragraph of the essay, Thoreau takes his own advice, and does his part to set forth, as clearly as possible, the foundational principles of democratic governance worthy of the name:

> The authority of government, even such as I am willing to submit to... is still an impure one: to be strictly just, it must have the sanction and consent

> of the governed. It can have no pure right over my person and property but what I concede to it. The progress from an absolute to a limited monarchy, from a limited monarchy to a democracy, is a progress toward a true respect for the individual.[535]

It would be difficult to state the gist of the political developments characteristic of modernity and its trajectory towards the democratic ideal any more clearly and simply. Thoreau, though, does not stop there, but continues to articulate the Enlightenment ideal of universal humanity (kin to that informing the 1948 United Nations Universal Declaration of Human Rights) even while emphasizing that any valid initiative in that direction must be premised upon explicit recognition of the unimpeachable spiritual sovereignty of the individual human being:

> Is a democracy, such as we know it, the last improvement possible in government? Is it not possible to take a step further towards recognizing and organizing the rights of man? There will never be a really free and enlightened State, until the State comes to recognize the individual as a higher and independent power, from which all its own power and authority are derived, and treats him accordingly.[536]

Emerson's emphasis on the character and culture of the individual as the axis upon which the world—its political sphere not excluded—turns is predictably no less direct and forceful. He begins his essay "Politics" with a sharp cutting down of the state to human size. He does so in a fashion fit to make any modern-day Hobbesian statist shudder:

> In dealing with the State, we ought to remember that its institutions are not aboriginal, though they existed before we were born; that they are not superior to the citizen: that every one of them was once the act of a single man: every law and usage was an expedient to meet a particular case.[537]

Later in that same paragraph, Emerson, after a feint in the direction of recognizing the real and fundamental import of political enterprise, quickly refers any possibility of external or practical accomplishment to the hidden springs of more inward moral and spiritual culture:

> Politics rest on necessary foundations, and cannot be treated with levity. Republics abound in young civilians, who believe that the laws make the city, that grave modifications of the policy and modes of living, and employments of the population, that commerce, education, and religion, may be voted in or out; and that any measure, though it were absurd, may

> be imposed on a people, if only you can get sufficient voices to make it law. But the wise know that foolish legislation is a rope of sand, which perishes in the twisting; that the State must follow, and not lead the character and progress of the citizen; the strongest usurper is quickly got rid of; and *they only who build on Ideas, build for eternity* [emphasis added]; and that the form of government which prevails, is the expression of what cultivation exists in the population which permits it.[538]

In the concluding passages of "Politics," Emerson, incorrigible in faith and optimism, dreams of a future state run, not by force, but by the power of virtue and love:

> We live in a very low state of the world, and pay unwilling tribute to governments founded on force. There is not, among the most religious and instructed men of the most religious and civil nations, a reliance on the moral sentiment.... There never was in any man sufficient faith in the power of rectitude, to inspire him with the broad design of renovating the State on the principle of right and love. All those who have pretended this design, have been partial reformers, and have admitted in some manner the supremacy of the bad state.[539]

One can find many more such fine and high-minded passages in both Thoreau's and Emerson's essays. Both are well worth reading entire. I, however, shall consider the point made, and wish to return, for now, to rather grim realities at hand today.

I believe both British and American citizens—or rather those amongst the privileged classes of persons—have, over the course of time, grown into the habit of taking a critical quotient of political liberty for granted, a luxury that affords (if the soul is so disposed), a certain concentration on private virtue largely shielded from concerted public assault. Thoreau might choose—and admirably and courageously so—to speak out on slavery in Massachusetts; he might, on another occasion, choose to refuse to pay the few pennies of tax he owed, and so unexpectedly spend a (not uncongenial) night in the local jailhouse. Direct threat to his life and livelihood as a consequence of such actions was, however, likely minimal, short of his undertaking violent action (such as participation in the Harper's Ferry slave rebellion instigated by John Brown). Emerson could speak heresy at the Harvard Divinity School, ruffle the polite feathers of the religious or academic elite, and preclude his reinvitation to Harvard for thirty years; but he was not burnt at the stake for it, as were Hus or Bruno. In short, Thoreau at Walden, and Emerson in the Manse, could largely choose to *ignore* the Government, or the Church, if they so preferred, and, for most of their productive hours, did so prefer. We have rich and rare fruit from those private orchards.

In the revolutionary period, America's founders enjoyed no such peace and security. Lives and essential liberties were perpetually at stake, and the founders bore the heavy burden of seeking to secure life and liberty for the people of a nascent nation. For this reason, some words of the founders retain, in certain respects, a sharper political edge than those of our Transcendentalist authors; words that therefore may more cuttingly apply to the present hour when, once again, the physical as well as soul-spiritual foundations of life and liberty are put at risk by a hostile, if seemingly protective, paternalistic force.

In the face of the incessant indignities Jefferson inventories in the Declaration, virtue itself summoned John Adams and his brethren to the revolutionary cause. Only active rebellion would serve to defend the rightful liberties and so human dignity of the colonists. Even so, then, as now, there were harbored in the bosom of statehouse and commons those who saw the whole matter in a dramatically different light. No few Loyalists took the part of the Crown, and lobbied against any disturbance of the existing order, the apparent safety, security and stability supplied by the reigning British authority. Thomas Hutchinson, Governor of Massachusetts, was one notorious Tory. Another royal apologist was an eminent Massachusetts lawyer named Daniel Leonard, an erstwhile friend of Adams, "seduced" (according to Adams) by Hutchinson to turn against the revolutionary cause.

In the turbulent time when the question of whether or not to sever ties with Britain consumed the colonists, a series of letters, authored by Leonard but appearing under the eponymous authorship of one *Massachusettensis,* presented the case for continuing fealty to the Crown. The widely read epistles were eloquent and persuasive, and—lest *Massachusettensis* exert undue influence—called for a fit response from partisans of the revolutionary movement.

Writing under the alias of one *Novanglus,* John Adams undertook the formidable task. He discharged it (and here I must feel rather more sympathy for our author than most) at great, and greatly learned, length. Perhaps a brief excerpt of his erudite disquisitions—as a whole, rather too scholarly to serve very well the cause of liberty in 1775—may do so in some small but consequential manner now.

I choose here a portion of Adams's first Novanglus letter. I hold it to be acutely relevant to the present state of affairs concerning Covid World and the

Great Reset agenda in America, in Britain herself, and indeed the free world at large. It is so relevant because official Covid policy spectacularly conflicts with what I have called Spiritual Democracy. In America in particular, many if not all of those policies constitute flagrant abrogation of laws the government is bound by oath to uphold, and thus egregious violation of the constitutional rights of the citizens that government is supposed to represent and to serve.

The details of those violations have been sufficiently documented in these pages. Before entering into Adams's spirited response to a not wholly dissimilar situation in revolutionary times, let me say a word as to the general political-philosophical logic that may help explain how such a state of affairs could have come about today.

It is inherent in the nature and function of government that its formation entails the concentration of sizeable political as well as physical/military force. The people award to government the power to legislate and to exact taxes that support police and military units capable of enforcing the country's laws and defending the nation from external threat. In addition to these forces, the government inclines to assume a high degree of moral authority on account of its representative status. In a democracy, after all, the elected government stands—in theory, at least—for the voice and will of the people.

The combination of political (legislative, executive, and judicial) power, material and military force, and the presumption of moral authority inevitably tends to magnify the might of the government to such a degree that it is liable to lose sight of its true status vis-a-vis the citizenry, imagining itself as *master* rather than *servant* of the people. The Hobbesian dynamic in and through which the very act of constituting the state necessarily awards it nigh absolute power, inscribes itself as an endemic tendency in *all* government, even the democratic form founded upon directly contrary principles and deliberately designed (as in the separation of powers) to avert the emergence of the leviathan State from the sea of the People.

The pull in that monstrous direction is primeval in strength. There is no more commonplace and no more universally and powerfully applicable principle of political philosophy than that reflected in the precept: *power corrupts.* The axiom finds magnificent imaginative representation in Tolkien's epic *The Lord of the Rings.* Diabolical Gollum aside, noble Boromir's mind is twisted and he himself driven to destruction by the temptation inherent in the sheer power of the Ring and his own sense of its limitless capacity to empower the glorious triumph of Good over Evil. Even modest Christ-like Frodo suffers possession by the dark side of the psyche when the Ring is on his finger, and his salvific mission is almost sabotaged at the last, critical moment by the possessive egotism evoked by the Power of the Ring.

How may any democratic government resist falling prey to similar temptation and abusing the power vested in it by the people? I here suggest one crucial political philosophical corrective: conscious remembrance of and due respect for the ultimate ground of authority in a democracy, which lies—not with the government itself, and its intrinsic superfluity of power— but with the individual human being and the natural rights inherent in the spiritual character of the nation's citizens.

The government, or fallible officials that man the ship of state, should wear a talisman inscribed with the words of the Declaration of Independence, or last line of the Gettysburg address, if they do not wish the albatross of tyranny to be hung around the neck of civic memory. The talismanic formula may be: the *excess* of the power of government is linked, on the one hand, to an intrinsic *deficiency of sovereignty*. (The government is formed to serve the People, and not the other way around.) On the other hand, the *deficiency of power* of the individual should not obscure the *efficiency* (practical force) of the *spiritual sovereignty* inherent in the humanity of each and all of its citizens, and so the People as a whole.

It is not that the government is not charged to act in the interests of the People, but it is despotic folly to imagine it can do so while heedlessly violating the covenant of our Constitution; the charter of the Republic writ in the blood, sweat, and tears of the founders, and protecting the essential liberty of the People.

Who put the ring on Dr. Fauci's hand?

Who will reclaim it, and embark upon a perilous journey to toss it into the volcanic fires of the common heart?

In order to better remember that commission, we can take a page from John Adams and his Novanglus letters. The following is from the first of those.

John Adams begins:

> 23 January 1775
>
> My Friends,
>
> A Writer, under the signature of Massachusettensis, has addressed you, in a series of papers, on the great national subject of the present quarrel between the British administration and the colonies.... I will take the liberty, in the spirit of candor and decency, to bespeak your attention, upon the same subject.[540]

The passage of present interest for us begins with reference to the text of Massachusettensis:

> It is true as this writer observes, "that the bulk of the people are generally but little versed in matters of state, that they rest the affairs of government where accident has placed them." If this had not been true, the designs of the Tories had been many years ago, entirely defeated. It was clearly seen, by a few, more than ten years since, that they were planning and pursuing the very measures, we now see executing. The people were informed of it, and warned of their danger: But they had been accustomed to confide in certain persons, and could never be persuaded to believe, until prophecy became history. Now they see and feel, that the horrible calamities are come upon them, which were foretold so many years ago, and they now sufficiently execrate the men who have brought these things upon them. Now alas! when perhaps it is too late. If they had withdrawn their confidence from them in season, they would have wholly disarmed them.[541]

"*They had been accustomed to confide in certain persons, and could never be persuaded to believe, until prophecy became history.... If they had withdrawn their confidence from them in season, they would have wholly disarmed them.*" What apt, what pregnant words! Never believe for a moment, we are living today a dull reality that will creep tamely toward tomorrow, and tomorrow, and tomorrow. No. If we wake and open our eyes, we will find ourselves playing lead roles in high Shakespearian drama. Tragedy, or some other genre—it is for us to do and say.

Adams continues:

> The same game, with the same success, has been played in all ages and countries, as Massachusettensis observes. When a favourable conjuncture has presented, some of the most intriguing and powerful citizens have conceived the design of enslaving their country, and building their own greatness on its ruins. Philip and Alexander, are examples of this in Greece—Caesar in Rome—Charles the fifth in Spain—Lewis the eleventh in France—and ten thousand others.[542]

Who today may we count amongst that ten thousand? Fauci, Bourla, Gates? Schwab, Tedros, Trudeau?

Adams continues with another citation from Massachusettensis, his arch apologist-for-the-crown antagonist:

> "There is a latent spark in the breasts of the people capable of being kindled into a flame, and to do this has always been the employment of the disaffected."

The *disaffected?* Who may that be at present? The vaccine-injured? Dissident doctors who wish to cure rather than kill their patients? Or those political untouchables, those dreadful conspiratorial "anti-vaxxers," who have the *heretical* audacity to doubt the Almighty Wisdom of the God-Man of Modern (so-called) Science, preferring to worship instead at the altar of the laws of Nature and of Nature's God, and so refusing to *believe*—to take on *faith*—that recurrent infusions of (largely untested) biochemical concoctions do not only line the pockets of the criminally rich but as well prove genuine elixirs of health and happiness?

Adams links *liberty* and *virtue* together under the aegis of the *God-given* character of natural law:

> What is this "latent spark"? The love of Liberty? *a Deo, hominis est indita naturae.* [*It is given to the nature of man by God.*] Human nature itself is evermore an advocate for liberty. There is also in human nature, a resentment of injury, and indignation against wrong. A love of truth and a veneration for virtue. These amiable passions, are the "latent spark" to which those whom this writer calls the "disaffected" apply.[543]

Adams finally stands up for the discernment, conscience and courage of the People, as opposed to the machination of those canny forces that draw strength from the darkest corners of the soul:

> If the people are capable of understanding, seeing and feeling the difference between true and false, right and wrong, virtue and vice, to what better principle can the friends of mankind apply than to the sense of this difference. Is it better to apply, as this writer and his friends do, to the basest passions in the human breast, to their fear, their vanity, their avarice, ambition, and every kind of corruption?[544]

Is it, or is it not? A question at once political and existential, and very like another that may and must be asked by every person: *To be, or not to be...*

> God is a circle whose center is everywhere and whose circumference is nowhere. Nice mathematical model of God! I like it a lot. There's something about it that is *really* true. We interact with one another as if there's a spark of the divine within us. You say: "Well, no we don't." We certainly do interact with the people we value, when we're acting in a manner we

regard as appropriate, as if there's something about them that is of transcendent, and in some sense eternal, value. You might say: "Well, you don't believe that." Well, do you believe in natural rights? Because the notion of natural rights is predicated on that underlying presupposition or observation, and if you don't believe in natural rights.... Then *where* are you exactly? And *who* are you, exactly? Those are questions very much worth posing.

—Jordan Peterson,
Cambridge, England, April 2022

CHAPTER 18

FROM LONDON TO MAIN STREET: ROGER WILLIAMS AND THE SEED OF DEMOCRACY

Each one of us has our stories; our personal history. In a very real way, we *are* our stories. Our identity is ineluctably shaped by the narratives written into the places we inhabit. If you or I take the time to explore some of the many threads that, crisscrossing space and time, weave the fabric of our being, we can garner the power to rediscover and create anew the texture of our existence, the very fiber of consciousness and character.

Given the country of my birth, the strands of my personal story inevitably braid with those composing the quilt of American history.

I am today a scholar and poet living (as I have done for the last twenty-plus years) in the headlands of Marin County, north of San Francisco. The greater Bay Area includes not only the redwoods and ocean shores of Marin and the steep, storied streets of San Francisco, but the heady culture of Berkeley, historic hotbed of radical protest, free speech and—still today—an epicenter of Progressive politics.

When I first moved to the Bay Area in 1997, I planned to live in Berkeley. The city's renowned university, complete with soaring clock-tower, reminded me of Cornell, my alma mater some 3,000 miles east in Ithaca. At a time of challenging personal transition, Berkeley appeared to offer a reassuringly familiar environment, one colored by academic interest and intellectual sophistication.

After an intensive search (housing was not easy to come by), I all but signed two separate leases in Berkeley. For reasons outside of my control (a cousin showing up from nowhere; a landlord's sudden change of plans) both fell through. Balked and annoyed, I set off on a daytrip to the beach in Marin County for respite, and—just for the heck of it—looked into an apartment for rent up the road from Tennessee Cove in Tamalpais Valley. Not only did I like both the apartment and its live-in owner, I initially mistook the square yardage for the (significantly higher) price. So was the die of destiny cast. I moved into the house on Pine Street off Shoreline in Tam Valley, and was soon carrying forty boxes of books down a long flight of outdoor stairs to the entrance of my new abode.

While I did not end up living there, Berkeley remained a prominent presence on my Bay Area map. I secured a card affording admittance to the UC Berkeley library, and, over the years, spent countless hours researching Rilke and other subjects in its stacks. Then there were the theatres—the Berkeley Rep, the Ashby Stage, the Aurora—venues where I have enjoyed some of the most intellectually stimulating and politically engaged theatre I have ever seen.

Berkeley qualifies as one of those places that embodies its own unique version of the American Spirit: the keen aspiration to *the ideal* that breaks down the barriers—moral, social, legal, material—erected, again and again, to stand in the way; the radical affirmation of freedom and of principle that worships conscience, love and liberty even—indeed especially—in the face of oppression and fear, despair, affliction, and strife; the never-ending quest for *enlightenment* in that word's Western as well as Eastern sense; an impassioned search for Truth and Beauty answering to the call of that ineffable presence some call God, that illimitable Power that ever transcends the frangible bounds of mortal being even while illuminating it in flashes of light from within, indwelling the fabric of the mind and the chamber of the heart as an ever-kindled and ever-enkindling flame.

Yes, Berkeley has been one of the places that harbored such Spirit, a place where, in 1955, two years before I was born, Allen Ginsberg, disciple of Whitman and of Blake, could see a dead flower rising out the rubble of the crude mechanical debris of modernity (image of the Machine, old-style) and conceive a remarkable poem, scribe the marvelous…

Sunflower Sutra

I walked on the banks of the tincan banana dock and sat down under
the huge shade of a Southern Pacific locomotive to look at the sunset
over the box house hills and cry.
Jack Kerouac sat beside me on a busted rusty iron pole, companion, we
thought the same thoughts of the soul, bleak and blue and sad-eyed,
surrounded by the gnarled steel roots of trees of machinery.
The oily water on the river mirrored the red sky, sun sank on top of final
Frisco peaks, no fish in that stream, no hermit in those mounts, just
ourselves rheumy-eyed and hungover like old bums on the riverbank,
tired and wily.

Look at the Sunflower, he said, there was a dead gray shadow against the
sky, big as a man, sitting dry on top of a pile of ancient sawdust—

I rushed up enchanted—it was my first sunflower, memories of Blake—
my visions—Harlem and Hells of the Eastern rivers, bridges, clank-
ing Joes Greasy Sandwiches, dead baby carriages, black treadless
tires forgotten and unretreaded, the poem of the riverbank....
and the gray Sunflower poised against the sunset, crackly bleak and dusty
with the smut and smog and smoke of olden locomotives in its eye—
corolla of bleary spikes pushed down and broken like a battered
crown...leaves stuck out like arms out of the stem...broken pieces
of plaster fallen out of the black twigs, a dead fly in its ear,
Unholy battered old thing you were, my sunflower
O my soul, I loved you then!
The grime was no man's grime but death and human locomotives, all
that dress of dust, that veil of darkened railroad skin, that smog
of cheek, that eyelid of black mis'ry, that sooty hand or phallus
or protuberance of artificial worse-than-dirt—industrial—mod-
ern—...spotting your crazy golden crown....
Poor dead flower! when did you forget you were a flower? when did you
look at your skin and decide you were an impotent dirty old loco-
motive? the ghost of a locomotive? the specter and shade of a once
powerful mad American locomotive?
You were never no locomotive, Sunflower, you were a sunflower!....
So I grabbed up the skeleton thick sunflower and stuck it at my side like
a scepter, and deliver my sermon to my soul, and Jack's soul too, and
anyone who will listen,
—We're not our skin of grime, we're not our dread bleak dusty image-
less locomotive, we're all beautiful golden sunflowers inside, we're
blessed by our own seed and golden hairy naked accomplishment-
bodies growing into mad black formal sunflowers in the sunset, spied
on by our eyes under the shadow of the mad locomotive riverbank
sunset Frisco hilly tincan evening sitdown vision.

~

I am not, like Ginsberg, a beat Poet, but I am, like him, profoundly indebted to William Carlos Williams, poetic elder of Paterson, New Jersey, where Ginsberg grew up, and who concluded his brief introduction to the latter's infamous *Howl and Other Poems* (which contains "Sunflower Sutra") with the words: "Hold back the edges of your gowns, Ladies, we are going through hell."

We have all been there—been through hell—during Covid; some more than others. Yet within the confines of our house across the Richmond Bridge from Berkeley, the monstrous Machine could *more or less* be kept at bay. I wrote my own far more modest sunflower poem in a more domestic Williams-esque vein, one nonetheless infused with the same heavenly light Ginsberg cries for and passionately summons us to recall as the birthright of our human being.

Suns

fresh-cut
in a green-glazed
vase

adorned
with blue
butterflies

gold petals lift
from stiff
stalks

aspiring to ascend
to the light that
raised them

one
sun
holy

father
whom they
look up to from

the depth of their dark

eyes

~

Although living, now, in the Bay Area, I grew up (as mentioned) in the Midwest, in the North Chicago suburban town of Highland Park. Just yesterday (October 11, 2023), I came across a piece offered by a guest contributor on Dr. Aaron Kheriaty's Substack that brought my attention to a bit of history—an important cairn on the trail of Spirit in America—that made its mark on my childhood without my being in the least aware of its rich significance.

We lived in a section of Highland Park named Ravinia, best known as the home of the summer music festival by that name. Ravinia has its own little business district, all of which is concentrated on a single street running through the midst of the small suburban village.

Ravinia Elementary School, which I attended from kindergarten through fifth grade, stood about three-quarters of a mile away from our home on the far side of town. For six years of my childhood, I would—after a brief saunter down our own Broadview Avenue—walk three long blocks down that main street, past a hair-salon on the corner, past the doctor's office where my grandmother (who lived with us after the sudden death of my grandfather the year before I was born) worked as a receptionist; past Vogue Dry-Cleaners with its racks of plastic-wrapped clothes visible through the window; past a dim-lit cafe with red leather upholstered bar stools that bore the surname of Mrs. Shelton, the ageless crossing guard who escorted us over the train tracks that carried commuters (like my father) to work in Chicago, and whose expressionless face I could easily recognize to this day—before continuing on down the street to the crushed gravel play yard and red brick building of Ravinia School, where I first learned to read and write and play line-ball and ice-hockey.

In those days, we walked home for lunch, so I walked up and down that long, not-so-busy main street at least four times a day, five days a week, for six years. Nor did the street lose its prominence when I finished fifth grade at Ravinia and went on to Edgewood Middle School. As the chief artery to Lake Michigan, the Ravinia Festival, Green Bay Road, and all destinations beyond, I continued to walk—or ride—down it countless times thereafter. In referring to that street, we never employed the appellation "street" or "avenue." We'd just say, simply, "Go down Roger Williams to get to the Lake."

From a very early age, "Roger Williams" was a household name, a faultlessly steady friend who could, more often than not, get you where you needed to go.

Growing up, I knew vaguely that *our* Roger Williams was named after a man who had lived long ago; maybe even one of those "pilgrims"[545] who came over from England. A boy far more interested in butterflies and baseball than history, I never thought or wondered much about him; never inquired into the character and destiny of the man who gave Ravinia's chief thoroughfare, my own personal Main Street, its name. That ignorance remained largely in force until very recently; until, that is, I conceived the notion of writing something about the history of spirit in America, and happened to come across a blog about the first and only "pilgrim" whose name, for as long as I can remember, I have known by heart.

Everyone knows (or should know) that the seed of the nation that would become America was planted in the soil of religious freedom. The original pilgrims, after all, were religious separatists: heirs of Wycliffe and Luther, they were persons who believed that they could not in good conscience pursue their Protestant faith within the confines of the Church of England. Many separatists viewed the latter as a kind of Anglican equivalent of the Catholic Church, one originally formed—*not* on account of authentically spiritual motives responsive to the Reformation's principled rejection of the papacy and all that implied (top-heavy hierarchy, rigid dogma and elaborate ritual that put infinite distance between the believer and her God) but in order to enable King Henry VIII to divorce one wife (Katherine of Aragon, who proved incapable of producing an heir to the throne) to marry a woman he fancied more, Ann Boleyn.

There's ample evidence to support that view. When Luther first nailed his theses to the church door, Henry VIII took it upon himself to defend the Church by rebutting Luther's arguments, moving the Pope officially to declare Henry *Defensor Fidei* ("Defender of the Faith"). After separation from Rome, the Church of England did retain a distinctly Catholic flavor in terms of iconography and ceremonial practice. Henry's estrangement from the Catholic Church was thus clearly sourced—not in substantive religious difference—but in his unyielding desire for a divorce that the Pope would not grant.

This notorious episode of European history culminated, finally, in Henry the VIII's entire break from Rome, one aided and legally enabled by support from influential Protestant members of the English Parliament. In 1534, Parliament passed The First Act of Supremacy, declaring the English King to be—not only the nation's monarch but, as well, the supreme head of the Church of England.

Thus was the bond between church and state formally cemented in England at the close of the first third of 16th century.

Everyone knows (or *should* know) that the United States of America does not embrace, but rather forbids, any official alliance between church and state. That interdiction is of such foundational importance to the charter of the country as to find expression in the first clause—the very first words—of the Bill of Rights: "Congress shall make no law respecting an establishment of religion, or prohibiting the free exercise thereof."

Roger Williams is chiefly known as the American who first articulated this underlying principle, recommending a "wall of separation between the Garden of the church and the wilderness of the world."[546] Not only did he formulate it in theory, he implemented it in practice. Williams founded Providence Plantations, which later became the Colony, and subsequently the State, of Rhode Island. Upon Williams's securing of Royal Charter for the Colony in 1644, Rhode Island became the first colony formally to institute a democratic form of governance, one that—contrary to the Puritan as well as English norm, but in accord with ideas of religious liberty promoted by Williams—practiced strict separation of church and state.

If Williams had contributed little more to American history than this idea, he would remain a figure of signal importance. While the principle of separation of church and state constitutes one kernel of Williams's contribution to our political history, we err if we tie his significance to an overly narrow construction of that key concept. It is not only the idea of the separation of church and state that Williams inaugurates and champions, but (more generally) the modern idea of liberty itself. That idea need be comprehended in all its many ramifications, including those that do not involve direct reference to organized religion.

The title of John M. Barry's 2012 book, *Roger Williams and the Creation of the American Soul,* conveys that author's settled conviction that no single individual played a more seminal role in the formation of the national ethos than a man who lived a century-and-a-half before the nation's official founding. Alluding not only to the contour of Williams's intellectual and political career generally, but, as well, to the particular role he played in the founding of Providence and Rhode Island, Barry writes:

> [Williams] was not the first person to call for religious freedom, but he was certainly the first to link that call to individual liberty in a political sense and to create a government and a society informed by those beliefs.... It would be he, not Thomas Jefferson, who first called for a "wall of separation" to describe the relationship of church and state.... It would be he who created the first government in the world that built such a wall. And it would be he who first defined the word "liberty" in modern terms, and saw the relationship between a free individual and the state in a modern way.[547]

Barry appears relatively confident that Americans today share a widely accepted idea of the "modern" idea of liberty, and so "the relationship between a free individual and the state," one evolved over the course of the four or five hundred years that have passed since the Renaissance, Reformation, and Scientific Revolution. I am not so sure. Rather, it seems to me that whatever consensus may have formed as to the essence of the "modern" idea of liberty has been subject to severe erosion, and perhaps never more so than today. We will thus hardly be remiss if we aim to recall to mind the historic origin of that idea insofar as such may be linked to the exceptional life and radical thought of Roger Williams, the man John Quincy Adams (eldest son of the author of the Novanglus letters) once called "altogether revolutionary."[548]

Williams enjoyed—or suffered—the rather dubious fortune of living at a time of turbulent religious and political upheaval. Given the cultural landscape of 16th- and 17th-century Europe, the profound changes unfolding in those two dimensions of culture inevitably intertwined. The very idea of liberty belongs precisely to the problematic interface of just this intersection of spiritual and sociopolitical concern. One can contemplate the idea of truth in a manner thoroughly detached from political or social aim; indeed, the *telos* of pure science demands precisely such divorce. The idea of liberty, on the other hand, necessarily involves the domain of human will along with a host of fraught questions revolving around the relation of the individual to the collective and—correlatively—the use and abuse of power in society.

Born in London in 1603, the same year Queen Elizabeth's death ended her forty-five year reign and King James ascended to the English throne, Roger Williams grew up in the eye of civic and religious storm that shaped the history of early modernity. Taken on at the age of only thirteen as the assistant of England's most eminent jurist, young Roger regularly witnessed epic power struggles between Parliament and King, Protestants and Catholics, Puritans and Anglicans, Common Law and the Crown. Before long, Williams would be no passive observer of such momentous affairs, but an active player in those deadly serious games that set the course of history, first in England, then in America, and finally (for what corner of the world remains unaffected by what happened here?) the world at large.

In the early 17th century, the gale force winds of change released by the Protestant Reformation of 1517—abated only imperfectly and temporarily by the 1555 Peace of Augsberg—were blowing fiercely yet. The bitter acrimony between the Protestant and Catholic factions of Christendom had reached one peak of destructive intensity in the 1572 Bartholomew Day Massacre, an exclamation point punctuating the French Wars of Religion that scarred that country in the latter half of the 16th century.

England harbored its own internal conflicts. The confusing legacy of Henry the VIII's imperfect break with Catholicism had long proved a seedbed of endless, and endlessly bitter, strife. It imported the worm of religious contention into the intestines of the English state. Henry VIII retained allegiance to much Catholic doctrine and ritual after a fashion that sorely rankled the Protestant faction of England. His son, Edward, who acceded to the throne upon Henry's death in 1547, represented the first King raised as a Protestant. Edward took that destiny to heart. Although only nine-years-old upon becoming King, the precocious Edward—who would live but six more years—formed strong religious convictions early. In concert with influential Protestant officials (most notably, Thomas Cranmer, Archbishop of Canterbury) and regents appointed to rule in his name, Edward and his regime instituted many notable anti-Catholic reforms (the abolition of the Latin Mass; elimination of the institution of celibacy for the clergy; the proscription of image and ornamentation in churches; and the confiscation of Catholic property in the name of the crown) that effectively transformed the ecclesiastical institution in England from a quasi-Catholic Anglicanism to something much closer to a dyed-in-the-wool form of Protestantism.

This did more than rankle many in England still wedded to the power and glory of the Catholic Church. It infuriated them. Catholics, however, had grounds for believing the political winds might shift once more, for amongst their number they counted Edward's half-sister Mary, putative heir to the throne.

After Edward's untimely death by illness at age fifteen, a Protestant faction led by the Duke of Northumberland sought to block Mary Tudor's accession to queendom. Yet Henry's writ of succession (which Edward had sought to cancel at Northumberland's advice) and some of the Duke's repressive policies (including land enclosure) weighed heavily against him. In 1553, Mary—backed by popular support as well as a militia she'd assembled—succeeded in taking the crown by force. Northumberland was executed.

Northumberland would be among the first of many to meet that fate under Mary's rule.

A zealous Catholic, Queen Mary avenged the wrongs against her sect with a kind of fatal passion. Applying her power—now joined with that of her Spanish/Catholic husband Phillip—Mary worked intensively to reverse the institutional and legal transformation of the English Church effected by Edward. In significant measure, she succeeded, though at terrible cost.

One of the pro-Catholic measures instituted by Mary (in collaboration with Rome) entailed the revival of heresy laws. The laws could be employed to punish religious offense against the joint powers of church and state with death. After its passage in 1554, hundreds of influential Protestants fled London. Not few of those who remained and refused to renounce their beliefs were burned at the stake. These included Thomas Cranmer, chief architect of the Protestant conversion of the Church of England.

Under threat of execution, Cranmer had in fact recanted and attempted officially to rejoin the Catholic, the "true faith." According to law, he *should* have been absolved and accepted as a convert, but Mary made a special exception in his case. Cranmer dramatically revoked his recantation just before his burning, salvaging, perhaps, some semblance of honor, if not his skin.

Queen Mary's legacy found apt expression in her nickname, one that survives as a household term in our language. The very first reigning Queen of England was, indeed, *Bloody Mary.* The historic violence Mary perpetrated—effect, in good measure, of an unholy alliance of church and state—remained material to the bitter conflicts that tore at England during the reign of King James a half-century or so later.

True, one might contend that the strong hand of Mary's successor—the more famous Elizabeth I—curbed, perhaps, the worst effects of internal religious strife during the forty-five years intervening between Queen Mary and King James. A Protestant, Elizabeth (more the pragmatist than the zealot) nonetheless retained aspects of Catholicism in state-sanctioned forms of worship. Declaring that she sought to "open no window into men's souls," Elizabeth tolerated some measure of religious nonconformity.

Even so, the Queen's moderation on this score knew strict bounds. Catholic agitation aimed at undermining or overthrowing her—and history reveals no lack thereof—would be neither overlooked nor endured. Under her governance, heresy laws were not abolished, but effectively reversed, and Elizabeth executed several hundred Catholics in the course of her reign.

The degree of religious freedom present in Elizabethan England should thus not be over-estimated; nor should one imagine her rule as one that loosened the alliance of church and state or lifted the repression such a bond empowered. Nor was the Queen alone in upholding the system of non-separation.

Parliament—more aggressively anti-Catholic than Elizabeth herself—certified her reign of both church and state by passing a *second* Act of Supremacy, one that declared the Queen "Supreme Governor" of the Church of England. This second act was needed because Elizabeth's sex precluded her from direct rule of the Church. She could and did, however, rule it through appointed officials.

John Barry provides details that paint a vivid picture of the practical force of the church-state unity in Elizabethan England. Not only did the government require many to swear loyalty to Queen in her dual role as civic *and* religious leader; her government—despite Elizabeth's own gestures of respect for freedom of conscience—demanded a significant measure of active conformity in worship, criminalizing disobedience:

> To assure loyalty to both the crown and the church, Parliament required all office-holders, all members of Parliament, all priests, and even all university students to swear the Oath of Supremacy, stating, "I do utterly testify and declare in my conscience" to affirm the monarch as "the only supreme Governor of the Realm...as well as in all Spiritual or Ecclesiastical things or causes as Temporal, &c. &c. &c. So help me God." With the Act of Uniformity, Parliament also required all subjects to attend weekly worship at their parish church. "Recusancy"—failure to attend worship or even refusal to participate in the full liturgy—became a crime and a subversive act.[549]

If Catholics represented the chief target of such policy, they were not the sole party of concern. Influential Protestants, most of whom were strict Calvinists, reviled the persistently Catholic features of the Anglican Church: its ecclesiastical hierarchy, for instance, as well as regular use of the Book of Common Prayer (the text of which Calvinists regarded as composed of the dead letter rather than the living Word of God). Vigilant adherents of simpler forms of worship based more exclusively on scripture (*sola scriptura),* these stricter types became known as "Puritans," an initially derogatory term that dates all the way back to the sixth year of Elizabeth's reign (and, too, the birth year of both Shakespeare and of Galileo) in 1564.

While these Puritans could, for the most part, remain more or less peaceably within the Anglican Church because Elizabeth did tolerate nonconformity on the Protestant as well as Catholic side, such liberality, and the relative stability it afforded, would not endure. Eventually the factionalism within Protestant ranks would become as bitterly divisive as that between Catholics and Protestants. This transpired in part because—in the eyes of the more radical

Puritans that ultimately became confirmed separatists—the line between the Catholic and the Anglican Church blurred to the point of invisibility.

The deep sectarian differences dividing English society thus had been, at best, thinly papered over during the reign of the Virgin Queen. In the wake of King James I's accession to the throne, that paper tore badly. Under the rule of his son and successor, Charles I, it ripped off altogether.

James, like Elizabeth, was a Protestant; yet never puritanically so. He was, after all, the only son of Mary Stuart, the Catholic Queen of Scots.[550] Over the long course of his own twenty-two-year reign as King of *both* England and Scotland, James's policies antagonized both Catholics and Protestants. While his early persecution of Catholics led to the Gunpowder Plot, his own increasingly evident Catholic sympathies stirred bitter resistance amongst Protestants. I will discuss that source of tension soon; even so, in confronting the complex and historically pivotal reign of King James, questions of religion—while indisputably critical in their own right—should not preempt our whole attention, or even claim center stage.

James I of England, unlike Edward just over one-half century before, was no boy-king. By the time James was crowned King of England in 1603, he was thirty-six-years old; more importantly, he had already ruled as King of Scotland for thirty-five years, including over twenty as an adult monarch.[551] James proved to be a passionate and intelligent sovereign. He was, moreover, one who took a conscious interest in political theory—at least, inasmuch as such may be construed to revolve around the nature and role of kingship itself.

James wrote two books on that subject: *The True Law of Free Monarchies* was published in 1598 and *Basilikon Doron* the following year. Both works (the second composed in the form of a letter to his son as future sovereign) are indicative of the truth that James's consuming interest—the cause to which he most passionately dedicated his considerable active and intellectual powers—was no religious agenda but the institution of kingship itself. Through his words and deeds, James strove not only unequivocally to assert the sovereign power of the royal throne, but to certify its *essentially illimitable* scope. James maintained the power of the King to be absolute, and effectively coincident with that of God himself.

The True Law of Free Monarchies declares as much in no uncertain terms. James did not invent the theory of the divine right of kings, but he was the first Scottish (and subsequently English) king self-consciously to affirm it as doctrine, and conduct his royal affairs accordingly. In a country with a parliamentary system of government, and one wherein the people had long been accustomed to certain rights by power of the law, James's absolutism—especially when coupled with the religious schisms that scored the realm—could not but lead to pitched conflict. The battles that ultimately ensued shaped not only the future of England, but that of America as well. John Barry cites historian Alan Simpson declaring:

> It is in the midst of the struggles between king and Parliament that the English [Puritan] discovers his mission. The confused strivings became fused with a providential purpose: a way is being opened for the establishment of Zion.[552]

...before adding his own noteworthy assertion:

> This English history laid the foundations of American history: in particular, it built the infrastructure of American culture.[553]

One might imagine that the church itself might have cause to leash James's extravagant claims of sovereign spiritual as well as temporal authority. As we have seen already, however, the First and Second Acts of Supremacy had officially wed the English church and English state. Resistance to James's exercise of unchecked sovereignty did indeed mount amongst moderate Protestants as well as rather more radical (and increasingly influential) Puritans, especially when—almost immediately after his coronation—James forcefully rejected an official petition (the so-called Millenary Petition, named in reference to its thousand signatories) aimed at reforms promoting simpler forms of worship. Not only did the provocation of the Millenary Petition motivate James to commission a Bible more sympathetic to the institution of kingship than the Geneva Bible then in general use (the famous King James version appeared in 1611[554]), the confrontation with the petitioners revealed the degree to which King James was willing to put his theory of the divine kingship into material practice despite the damage such absolutism might inflict on the realm.

Barry articulates the long-term consequences of James's short-sighted absolutism:

> [King James's] refusal to make any substantive accommodation with reformers and—more importantly—his subsequent choice of bishops slowly bent the Church of England back toward Catholicism, which in non-conformists built a reservoir of ill-will. He was not only widening but deepening the fissures within the church. Only force could hold it together. He was quite content to apply the force necessary to do so. Believing his

own authority came directly from God, James warned Puritans to comply "or else I will harrie them out of this land, or else do worse, only hang them, that's all."[555]

In time, it would come to hanging, and to harrying, as, first the Pilgrim, and consequently, the Puritan exodus to America would prove. In the meantime, however, King James's appetite for unbridled power encountered a more powerful opponent than any the church might provide: namely, the law. That power found embodiment in, first, Parliament itself, without whose power and consent James could not tax or raise funds for his royal enterprises.

Secondly (but by no means subsidiarily), it resided in the law itself; especially, English common law, the rights and prerogatives of which were, for decades, ably elaborated and championed by the young Roger Williams's revered elder and mentor, Sir Edward Coke.

English common law is a complex phenomenon with a complex history. Sir Edward Coke interpreted it in his own unique—and uniquely powerful—way, leaving his own inimitable stamp upon it in the process. Whether accurately or not, Coke understood common law to be rooted in the Magna Carta, a document that attained almost mythic status as a first great check upon royal prerogative in the annals of European history. The Carta itself (first acceded to by King John in 1215, and finalized by King Edward in 1297) probably grew out of earlier, related initiatives, one of which (The Charter of Liberties) declares:

> No free man shall be taken, or imprisoned, or disseized, or outlawed, or exiled, or in any way destroyed; nor will we go upon him, nor send upon him, but by the lawful judgment of his peers or by the law of the land. To none will we sell, to none will we deny or delay, right or justice.[556]

By its very nature, the force of law possesses the power to constrain the willful and arbitrary excesses of royal authority. Common law possesses special power in this regard on account of its difference from so-called civil or statuary law. Whereas the latter (deriving from Roman law, and historically favoring monarchal rule) establishes law by way of the issue and enforcement of legal statute, common law *builds upon precedent.* It depends upon the (sometimes centuries old) body of prior judicial rulings, many of which are often closely bound up with local custom, tradition and (sometimes recondite) legal language.

In the English context, all of those features—as well as the traditional connection between common law and property rights—contribute to a palpable sense of the "antient Rights and Liberties" of the English people, the guardianship of which hardly comports with the ambitions of a king who regards himself—and his authority—as divinely ordained. Elaborating the rich mix of ingredients that constitutes the fiber of common law, John Barry suggests, too, the ground of the nigh inevitable conflict between the Crown and those who (like Williams's mentor) sought to uphold the rights of the people:

> All this comprised the English "inheritance" of rights. All elements of this English inheritance imposed concrete limits on the crown which inherently contradicted the theory of the divine right of kings. And all this James, like all English monarchs for centuries, had in his coronation oath sworn to confirm and sustain. James brought his new views on royal power, royal prerogative, to an England which had come to value the stability of common law and fear the danger of arbitrary power, and to an England already disturbed by high Anglican worship pushing toward Catholicism.
>
> He had all the awesome magnificence of the monarchy on his side.... But as he pitted the majesty of the crown against the majesty of the law, he encountered Sir Edward Coke.[557]

Sir Edward Coke was fifty-one years old, and already a man of great eminence, when James assumed the throne in 1603. Ten years earlier, Queen Elizabeth had made Coke her Attorney General, preferring him to another distinguished candidate—Coke's life-long enemy and rival on diverse private as well as professional fronts—Francis Bacon.

Ironically, Coke's early, dramatic confrontation with King James took place not long after James elevated Coke to the post of chief justice of the Court of Common Pleas (the common law court), "the most powerful judgeship in England," in 1606. Coke's initial confrontation with the King entailed maintaining and indeed elevating the status of the Commons Court vis-a-vis the two other English court systems, the ecclesiastical and the so-called "prerogative" court. Both of these systems reflected the power of the Crown, and were increasingly used by James's minions to oppress subjects disfavored—often for religious reasons—by the King and his officers. One method of such persecution involved the notorious oath *ex officio*, by means of which those accused were effectively compelled to incriminate themselves, forced, as they were, into the impossible choice of betraying their own religious convictions (regarded, by many, as mortal sin punishable by eternal damnation) or professing tenets interpretable as treasonable disloyalty to the King.

To curb such practices, Coke, in his role as chief justice, undertook legal maneuvers (including issuing "writs of prohibition" as well as writs of *habeas corpus*) that effectively hamstrung the power of the ecclesiastical and prerogative courts. That was accomplished by diverting the flow of cases to his own Court of Common Pleas, which court disdained the oath *ex officio* and like practices, and generally offered layman a reasonable semblance of fair trial.

The maneuver did not please James. The King soon seized upon the unwonted provocation to assert his doctrine of royal supremacy—the King's superiority, not only to Parliamentary procedure, but to the Law itself.

The King was not without support in that endeavor. A new legal dictionary opined that "the king was above the law by his absolute power,"[558] and James's own Lord Chancellor, Sir Thomas Egerton, memorably proclaimed, "The monarch is the law. *Rex est lex loquens*, the king is the law speaking."[559] James himself affirmed his own post as—not only both a royal sovereign and head of the church, but England's sovereign judicial officer as well. Asserting his privilege to sit upon and decide any case he chose, the King was (in his own words) "the supreme judge; inferior judges [are] his shadows and ministers.... The King being the author of the Lawe is the interpreter of the Lawe."[560]

Sir Edward Coke, summoned to a council before the King days after James issued this statement, had the audacity to disagree. In his respectful yet forceful rebuttal, Coke argued that knowledge of the common law and its complex history could not be replaced by mere reason, royal as that might be. "True it was," Coke opined, "that God had endowed his Majesty with excellent Science, and great endowments of nature, but

> his Majesty was not learned in the Lawes of his Realm of England...and judgment of Law requires long study and experience, before that a man can attain to the cognizance of it. And that Law was the Golden metwand and measure to try the Causes of the Subjects, and which protected his Majesty in safety and peace.[561]

James was not amused. The King and his chief justice engaged in a barbed repartee, the latter reminding the King that even Henry de Bracton, a revered 13th-century scholar and defender of royal prerogative, had declared "*Quod Rex non debet esse sub homine, sed sub Deo et Lege*" (The King should not be under man, but under God and the Law).[562] The King, accusing Coke of "traitorous speech," finally flew into a thunderous rage, even threatening to strike Coke.

He did not do so. Neither did Coke give way, or concede an inch of legal ground. Instead, the next day, he instituted new measures limiting the authority of the ecclesiastical court to prosecute cases against laymen and officially outlawing the oath *ex officio*. The terms in which he performed the latter office—though pronounced when three-year-old Roger Williams was yet a small child—might well be considered a template for the latter's own "altogether revolutionary" thought:

> No man ecclesiastical or temporal shall be examined upon secret thoughts of his heart.... The Ecclesiastical judge cannot examine any man upon his oath, upon the intention and thought in his heart.... *Cogitationis poenam nemo emeret* [no man may be punished for his thoughts]. For it hath been said in the Proverb, "Thought is free."[563]

Coke issued this edict a full ten years before he took Roger Williams into his employ around 1616. Yet the 1606 episode, if it may have been the first, was by no means the last time Coke contested King James's assertions of royal power. In fact, though fourteen years older than James, Coke outlived him by almost a decade, and played a kindred—and equally dramatic—role in the early years of King Charles's (James's son and successor) reign. Roger Williams, who Coke attached to himself as not only a scribe, but as a kind of surrogate son, thus enjoyed ample opportunity to see his revered elder in action.

The lessons to be learned from Coke's example were not lost upon Roger Williams. Long after his mentor's death, he remembered Coke as

> his much honored friend, that man of honor, and wisdom, and piety.... How many thousand times since I had the honorable and precious remembrance of his person, and the life, the writings, the speeches, and the example of that glorious light.[564]

John Barry provides another rendition of the same theme, expanding its significance so that it touches upon our chief interest here: namely, the words and deeds of Roger Willliams in the New World:

> [Coke's] work, his life, and his example...embedded themselves within Williams, for Williams took all this in as he took notes, and he inscribed it not on paper but into his own fiber. Later he would take it with him to the New World, where he would translate the inscriptions into what amounted to a new language.[565]

Many tales can and need be told of the years between Williams's initial apprenticeship to Coke (circa 1616) and his departure for the American colonies in 1630. John Barry tells them well in his book, and I cannot embark upon any summary of all the compelling details here. I can, however, identify the themes common to the most pertinent events, whether such took place during the remainder of King James's rule until his death in 1625, or under King Charles thereafter.

The Coke versus King episode exhibits the signal leitmotif. Typically, we witness religious difference of opinion which threatens to escalate to open and even violent conflict, and, concomitantly, a pitched power struggle between the King or High Church, on the one hand, and Parliament, defenders of the law, and the rights of the English people (including those persons holding religious or political opinions disfavored by the crown) on the other. On occasion, however, Parliament itself (most often inspired by anti-Catholic sentiment) acts the role of the oppressor, urging measures that infringe upon religious liberty.

It bears mention that the tumultuous political and spiritual battles of those times (which, as Barry contends, "laid the foundations of American history [and] built the infra-structure of American culture") revolved around rights later singled out in the First Amendment of the U.S. Constitution. Those rights—especially religious freedom and freedom of speech—may all be regarded as variations of the *freedom of thought* defended by Coke in his early face-off with the King.

Let me cite one outstanding example. In 1621, the Protestant-controlled Parliament delivered a petition to King James. The petition consisted of fourteen grievances, each and every one of which concerned itself with religion and the inadmissible (from the Protestant Parliament's point of view) pro-Catholic policies of James and his Government. That the grievances included not only a plea that young Charles, King James's son and heir, *not* marry a Catholic (it was known that James in fact planned to marry Charles to the daughter of the Catholic King of Spain), but insisted as well upon strict enforcement of existing anti-Catholic laws, discloses that religious intolerance was hardly limited to the throne or High Church. Even so, the King's angry response to the petition met one excess with another, perhaps still more egregious one.

Refusing to consider or even read any clause of the petition (the very scribing and submission of which James regarded as an act of insubordination), James moved, effectively, to *silence* or censor Parliament altogether, denying the body its liberty to debate select matters of state, or bring grievances against his government.[566] James ordered the Speaker of the House of Parliament:

> to make known in our name unto the House, that none therein shall meddle henceforth with anything concerning our government or deep matters of state, and namely not to deal with our dearest son's match with the daughter of Spain, nor to touch the honour of that King or any other our friends and confederates. Such issues (the King asserted) were "far beyond your reach and capacity."[567]

Sir Edward Coke was, at that point in time, no longer Chief Justice.[568] He was, however, a member of the Privy Council and colleague of the Parliamentarians sitting in the House of Commons. Coke advised Commons that the King's action was unprecedented, and so void of legal standing. Commons members accordingly re-submitted a second, very similar petition, upholding, in terms resonant with Coke-inspired undertones, its own most cherished right of free expression. In answering James, Commons cited:

> the ancient liberty of Parliament for freedom of speech...a Liberty which, we assure ourselves, so wise and just a King will not infringe, the same being our antient and undoubted rights and an inheritance from our ancestors, without which we cannot freely debate nor clearly discern of things in question before us.[569]

In the face of such articulate opposition, James remained obdurate. Disputing that freedom of speech qualified as the "antient and undoubted right and inheritance" of Englishmen, he claimed that it rather "derived from the grace and permission of our ancestors and us"[570]—meaning, the grace and permission of his own kingly sovereignty, a permission James informed the House he now sought fit to revoke.

Coke himself did not back down, invoking, in his reply, both the historic and mythically charged root of all constraint of executive power (Magna Carta), and the fount of the very idea of representative government, a mode of rule charged—not to serve the willful desires of the sovereign—but to listen to the voice and express concerns of the people. Coke:

> The privileges of this House is the nurse and life of all our laws, the subject's best inheritance....If my sovereign will not allow me my inheritance, I must fly to Magna Carta and entreat explanation of his Majesty.... When the King says he cannot allow our liberties of right, this strikes at the root. We serve here for thousands and ten thousands.[571]

The House of Commons added its own formal Protestation, emphatically reaffirming

> That the liberties, franchises, privileges and jurisdiction of Parliament are the ancient and undoubted birthright and inheritance of the subjects of England, and that the arduous and urgent affairs concerning the King...and the maintenance and making of laws and redress of mischiefs and grievances which daily happen within this realm are proper subjects and matters of counsel and debate in Parliament; and that in the handling and proceeding of those businesses every member of the House of Parliament hath and of right ought to have freedom of speech.[572]

James's response was immediate. He ripped up the Protestation. He dissolved Parliament, pledging never to convene it again. The next day, he summoned Coke to a meeting of the Privy Council. James not only castigated Coke for his insouciance, but ordered him to be arraigned and deposited in the royal prison. Sixty-nine-year-old Sir Edward Coke, the most eminent English jurist of that (if not all) time, thus spent the next four months confined in the Tower of London.

Roger Williams, whose apprenticeship with Coke ended (very congenially[573]) in the midst of this turmoil, experienced all of this—and much more—first-hand.[574]

When Charles acceded to the throne after James's death in 1625, the new King followed in his father's footsteps, entertaining like concepts of royal power and steering the Church of England towards ever greater intolerance of Puritanism. As before, economic issues (the need for the King to collect funds) forced Charles to convene Parliament. Upon one such notable occasion, in 1629, a number of contentious matters came to a head in a manner eerily kin to the fateful events eight years earlier. As was the case then, the King (Charles, this time!) and Parliament could find no common ground. The King refused to address diverse grievances. Parliament refused him critical monies. An angry King once more dissolved Parliament, which would not be called into session again for eleven years—a span of time later designated "the era of Personal Rule."

After dismissing Parliament, Charles took his father's attack upon freedom of speech to a new level, issuing an interdiction directly affecting not only Parliamentarians but any and all Englishmen who sought to express an opinion on matters of import. Charles's new "Royal Instructions" demanded that:

> hereafter none do presume to print or publish any matter of new relations, histories or other things in prose or in verse that have reference to matters and affairs of state, without the view, approbation and licence of the government.[575]

So much for freedom of thought and speech, and all those "antient rights and Liberties" comprising the "inheritance" of the English people! Blanket censorship became, not only practice, but official government policy.

Matters in the domain of freedom of religion were—if such is imaginable—even worse. Charles not only wed a Catholic wife in the same year as he assumed the throne, he chose William Laud—a peculiarly intolerant High Church Anglican—to officiate at his coronation, and awarded him clerical and advisory positions of singular power thereafter. Charles himself, cementing still more solidly the powers of church and state, regarded Puritans as "enemies of monarchs."[576] He had, moreover, academic support for his extremism; the master of Trinity College, Cambridge (Roger Williams's own *alma mater*) deemed Puritanism "the roote of all rebellions and disobedient intractableness in parlieaments, &c., and all schisme and sauciness in the countrey."[577]

It was Laud, however, who initiated diverse practical means of religious oppression.

Under the future Archbishop of Canterbury's[578] aggressive leadership, the crown initiated policies anathema to Puritans. John Barry provides details that convey a palpable sense of the real, weighty, and—in many respects—unbridgeable differences between the Puritans and those High Church Anglicans whom Puritans increasingly regarded as Protestants in Name Only:

> All about them, then, Puritans could see the church changing, and all the changes were away from simplicity, away from, in their view, Scripture. Even the physical church was changing. Laud moved the communion table out of the nave to the east end of each church, which forced changes in the sitting of family pews and gave great offense, railed it off, which separated priest and congregation and gave greater offense still, and renamed it the altar, which smacked of Catholicism. These tangible changes exemplified the enormous theological gap between Charles and Laud on one side, Puritans on the other, for those changes shifted the emphasis in worship away from each worshipper's relationship with God toward the sacraments and priestly power. And while Puritans complained of crosses and demanded simplicity, Laud relished the great cathedrals, relished stained glass, relished crucifixes, and relished formal ceremony, all of which he called the "beauty of holiness."

To Puritans, this so-called beauty represented corruption.[579]

These at once material and spiritual offenses were compounded by legal and political ones that made England not only inhospitable, but positively oppressive for conscientious Puritans. By requiring that all Church officials formally swear that the whole of the High Church of England Service was in every respect aligned with Scripture—an opinion inimical to the most basic of Puritan premises—Laud rendered it impossible for any conscientious Puritan (Williams included) to obtain a church post.

Any critic of the High Church, however, had reason for—not merely weighty personal concern—but fear and terror. Barry again provides a sense of what are, in this case, the truly gory details:

> The High Church tolerated no criticism. If its pursuit of noncomformists did not equal the Spanish Inquisition in brutality, if the English church burned no one at the stake after 1612, it still executed at least some "heretics" and it still used violence to discipline critics. Alexander Leighton attacked bishops as "unChristian and satanic." The High Commission had him arrested and kept in Newgate prison in an open cell, exposed to rain, frigid temperatures, and snow for fifteen weeks.[580]

Leighton was eventually condemned to life in prison. Before that term began, however, he was subjected to unspeakable torture:

> Before Leighton's life term began, he was to enjoy another briefer sentence: he was tied to a stake to receive thirty-six-stripes with a heavy cord upon his back, then placed in the pillory for two hours, then branded in the face with "SS" for "Sower of Sedition." Then his nose was split and his ears cut off. This was no clean dissection; the executioner sawed off his ears in a slow, bloody, mess. Only then did he go to prison.
>
> Reportedly, when this sentence was pronounced, Laud pulled off his cap and gave God thanks for it.[581]

Nor was it the case that Puritans more prudently discreet than Leighton possessed no grounds for concern. Today, "content moderation" algorithms, increasingly powered by AI, surveil the words and deeds of web users. In 17th-century London, spies—most in Laud's employ—performed a similar function. Puritan ministers who did not follow the prescribed rules (which included practices inimical to their belief, such as wearing surplices and extensive use of the Book of Common Prayer) were always in danger of discovery and harsh punishment.

By this time, Roger Williams was a Cambridge graduate and devout Puritan cleric. He had escaped answering for his beliefs in part by taking a post as a tutor in a prestigious private household, but the protection that offered was becoming increasingly uncertain. More importantly, Roger Williams—like his mentor Sir Edward Coke—was not one who readily bowed to any superior authority, nor one inclined to keep his opinions to himself. As the reign of Charles and of Laud wore on in the late 1620s, it became increasingly clear that, if young Roger Williams wished to live and to think freely, he would have to leave England.

Nor was he, of course, the only Puritan who had come to that inescapable conclusion.

The Mayflower, the vessel of the Pilgrims,[582] had sailed for the American colonies and founded the Plymouth Colony as early as 1620. The (England-based) Massachusetts Bay Company, motivated in part by commercial ambitions and yet committed, too, to the Puritan cause, sent ships over to found the Massachusetts Bay Colony near the end of the decade. John Winthrop, elected by the Company to become Governor of the colony, sailed over on the Arbella—one of a fleet of eleven ships carrying roughly seven hundred migrants—in April of 1630. The colony initially struggled mightily, and may never have survived if another ship (the *Lyon*) captained by William Peirce had not made the risky trans-Atlantic voyage in December, 1630, at the most perilous time of year.

In addition to desperately needed supplies, the ship carried some twenty passengers. One of those was Roger Willliams. The twenty-eight-year-old Williams first set foot in the New World on February 5, 1631.

It was in the New World that Roger Williams began his career as a truly independent actor on the world stage. Even so, it had been all he had witnessed and experienced in England, in which place he had received a rich education in government, law, religion, and—above all—the psychology and the politics of power—that had formed the lineaments of his conscience and character. By force of fate (or destiny), Williams had been granted a box seat from which to view how the unwonted exercise of excessive and intolerant power—especially royal or executive power, super-charged by religious authority and justification in the name of God (the unholy alliance of church and state)—could and did compromise the cherished rights of a people, and shred the covenant of a historic culture. He had seen, too, how human dignity ruled when matters of import were not arbitrarily decided by fiat, but—by virtue of the freedom (those "antient rights and liberties") enjoyed by diverse parties—thoughtfully debated, and considered from varying, often conflicting, points of view. He'd even seen how, on occasion, the force of reason and eloquence combined with custom and the wisdom of a law common to all could stand up against—and even put down—a King, *if* given the opportunity to speak, and be heard.

Roger Williams had seen and felt, too, the violently divisive force of religious schism. He'd seen man trip and fall, again and again, when claiming privileged access to infallible truth or unquestionable right. Devoutly religious himself, he saw all too vividly how religion too often served the temporal ends of man rather than the eternal ends of God, especially when (as so often happened within the confines of a spiritual culture heavily invested in religious institution) the one was habitually confused with the other.

Correlatively, he'd witnessed how a morality born of an inflexible ideological self-righteousness hollowed out the heart, turning a religion of love into crusades of intolerance and hate, and breeding forms of authority bent upon hallowing the most depraved acts of violence as holy acts. Before he was yet thirty years old, Roger Williams had seen worthy men, both nobles and commoners, literally drawn and quartered by the ruthless force of prejudice.

Roger Willliams had seen all this. He had seen it in England, in the Old World, and he had seen enough. Disembarking the *Lyon* in 1931, Roger Williams did not want to see it again in the New.

From the first, however, the odds were stacked against the young cleric and his enlightened attitudes. To be sure, the Puritans had come (most of them, anyway) to the American colonies to gain religious freedom. For most Puritans, however, this meant the freedom to worship as *they* saw fit, and to build society accordingly, so that they, and their endeavor, would be found worthy in the eyes of God. The Puritans came to build—in Massachusetts Bay Colony Governor John Winthrop's famous words—a shining city on a hill; a new world that conformed to the tenets of righteousness, and so worthy of God's (predestined) Grace and serving as a beacon of God's light to the world.

One didn't pull off such high ends carelessly, or by easily suffering religious or moral aberration. Consequently, it was by no means clear that there was room, in that shining city, for substantial difference of opinion on matters of religious doctrine and observance, or the moral and social norms that comprised the civic expressions of Puritan beliefs. Barry:

> Conformity was central to Winthrop's city upon a hill. More than in any other English-speaking society, the idea and ideals of this society were

> well-defined. Massachusetts was purpose-driven and its purpose was to advance God's interests upon earth. The definition of that interest was nearly universal within Massachusetts.[583]

Such dedication can ennoble; it can also endanger. In England, the physical as well as spiritual space that might permit Puritans to pursue their own form of worship had been mercilessly constricted until it had vanished altogether. Given the straight and narrow goal of the Puritan's vision, what was to prevent the same pattern from repeating itself, in a different guise, in the American colonies?

The sources of religious division were, after all, already present, imported whole cloth from England. Despite the trouble at home, many influential Puritans—including Winthrop and the leaders of the Bay Colony—still regarded themselves as faithful servants of both the Crown and the Anglican Church. Separatists there were, however, who felt otherwise, and strongly so. The ships bound for the New World had thus borne, not only the host of new emigrants, but—along with them—the seeds of religious conflict.

If, as Barry states, the definition of "God's interests upon earth" could be considered "nearly universal within Massachusetts," significant schism did emerge both within Massachusetts as well as between Massachusetts and other locales, including two that would become important for Williams: Salem and Plymouth. Indeed, even before the *Lyon* sailed, Salem, under the leadership of Samuel Skelton, had become uncompromisingly separatist. The differences within the Protestant/Puritan faith were not merely nominal. When John Winthrop desired to take communion in Skelton's church soon after his arrival in Massachusetts, Skelton saw fit to deny him that privilege on account of Winthrop's continuing ties to the Church of England. In time, the differences between distinct sects—theological as well as ritual in nature—would virtually rival those dividing Catholics and Protestants in England.

The intensity of religious mission that informed the founding of the colonies lent itself to a repetition of Old World wrongs in another crucial respect as well. The eschatological imperative so basic to the Puritan mentality encouraged a *de facto* merger of the powers of church and state. True, such a merger was never officially authorized by any Act of Supremacy or declaration of the divine right of Kings. Indeed, the Bay Colony specifically proscribed certain means of amalgamating ecclesiastical and civic authority:

> Technically, the Bay was not a theocracy. Consistent with the admonition to render unto Caesar the things that were Caesar's, and to God those

which were God's, the plantation prohibited a minister or church officer from simultaneously holding a government office.[584]

Such check, however, noteworthy as it might be, did not forestall significant consolidation of political and religious power. If ministers could not serve as magistrates, other laws helped established the theocratic character of colonial governance; for instance, the limiting of franchise (which included election of chief civic and church officials) to church members.[585] Church control was, moreover, not only bolstered by such legal strictures, it was implicit in the sheer power held by clergy leaders and the (unofficial as well as official) way the colony conducted its business:

> Those who controlled both church and state never forgot their goal: to build the New Jerusalem. And those who controlled both church and state also worked in perfect unison to build that perfect society, defined by them as a society which perfectly obeyed God. Before any consequential decision, the governor and magistrates actively sought the opinion of the leading ministers; they sought out Cotton, sought out Wilson, sought out Hooker, Nathaniel Ward, Richard Mather, and others.... Hubbard, a contemporary and official historian of the plantation, said of Cotton, "Whatever he delivered in the pulpit was soon put into an Order of Court, if of a civil, or set up as a practice in the church, if of an ecclesiastical concernment."[586]

John Cotton, who would emerge as one of the most (if not the most) influential ministers in the colonies, had fled England in 1633, and had been quickly elected to a ministerial post in Boston. The post may well have been open, in part, on account of a decision the young Roger Williams had made upon his own arrival in the colonies some two years earlier. That pivotal decision qualifies as the first of many acts that represent Williams's campaign on behalf of religious liberty, an idea that cut sharply against the grain of the Puritan mentality.

By the time he left England, Williams had earned the respect of many Puritan leaders, John Winthrop among them. As fate would have it, John Wilson, the minister of the Boston church, was due to leave for England to collect his family soon after Williams's arrival. Winthrop and other community leaders consequently offered Williams a teaching post at the Boston church, the nerve center of the Bay Colony. The offer represented quite an honor for the young Williams. It promised him not only a degree of material security but—more importantly—a position of prestige and influence in the fledgling community.

Even so, after lengthy conversation with Winthrop and other church leaders, Williams declined the offer. He did so on the grounds that the Boston church was insufficiently separated from the Church of England. Williams had come to the New World to breathe the air of religious liberty. The Bay Colony and Boston's ties to Laud's Church—an institution Williams now considered irretrievably corrupt—constituted an unacceptable affront to his conscience and sense of spiritual autonomy.

Willliams's refusal of the Boston post counts as the first of his many consequential acts of nonconformity in the New World. It suggests not merely how thoroughly Williams had already become his own man—one who (like Sir Edward Coke) stood upon no authority but that of his own character and conscience—but, as well, how uncompromisingly original his thought, word and deed would prove to be.

Williams's first dramatic "declaration of independence" may, at first glance, be construed as simply one more act of a strong-willed individual or group that wants the world in which they lived to reflect their own peculiar set of beliefs—Catholic or Calvinist, Anglican or Separatist. Williams, however, did not decline the post in Boston with an eye towards establishing his own preferred form of orthodoxy there or elsewhere. Though inwardly committed to his own religious beliefs and forms of worship, Williams never looked to encourage or enforce uniformity in the realms of thought and conscience. If he sought to separate himself, and decisively so, from the Church of England, this symbolized his desire, not to advance the fortunes of one or another sect, but to distance himself from all species of governance—ecclesiastical or civic, or (most especially) any church-state jointure—that sought to impose one or another form of spiritual belief upon the human community, or coerce obedience in matters of conscience.

Predictably, that initial deed of refusal proved consequential in more ways than one. Williams preserved his freedom, but did so at the high cost of alienating the Bay Colony's most eminent religious and political leaders. They had, after all, effectively invited him to become one of them, and his careful considered "no thank you" represented critical rejection of far more than the post itself.

Still, it was not only Williams's refusal of the position that most surprised and offended Winthrop and his influential Bay Colony peers. Not content with any quiet demurral, Williams soon made the underlying reasons for his position more explicit. Revealing the extraordinary outspokenness that would come to distinguished his career, he proceeded to criticize a fundamental premise of the Puritan program in America: the right, and indeed, necessity, to enforce—by means civic as well as religious—conformity with God's law.

In the eyes of all concerned (Williams included), the Ten Commandments represent the first authoritative promulgation of that law. It was commonly believed that no Puritan society could succeed if it proved permissive with respect to the matter of adherence to the Commandments, rock solid foundation of holy scripture. Roger Williams, however, had his own, strikingly original ideas as to how the force of scripture should—or should not—be applied within the context of the governance of civil society.

Tradition divides the Ten Commandments into two so-called tables, considered by some as representative of the two tablets of stone Moses received from the Lord at Sinai. Though there is some variation in numbering, the First Table consists of the initial commandments—in Williams's numbering, the first four—which pertain to man's relation to God. These include the exhortation to restrict worship exclusively to the one true God; to make no graven images; to refrain from taking God's name in vain; and to maintain reverent observance of the sabbath. The Second Table, by contrast, pertains to the social sphere, the relation of one human being to another. These prescribe the honoring of parents, and proscribe theft, murder, adulterous conduct, covetousness, and the bearing of false witness.

Williams's radical idea consisted in seeing in the two tables a difference that underwrites a corresponding division between the rightful domains of church, on the one hand, and the state on the other; between, that is, religious (First Table) and civic (Second Table) duty. In accord with his evolving concept of religious freedom, Williams opined that the state should deliberately restrict the purview of its lawful governance to Second Table (civic) concerns. Matters involving the relationship of the individual to God—those specifically religious issues addressed in the First Table—should be neither monitored nor regulated, nor interfered with in any way, by state power.

This idea may well seem perfectly logical and natural to us. Its essential import, after all, finds indelible inscription in the first clause of the First Amendment ("Congress shall make no law respecting an establishment of religion, or prohibiting the free exercise thereof.") The idea was, however, anything but natural or logical for Williams's contemporaries. Not only did it contradict the historic norms of social praxis the world over (as exemplified, for instance, by the window into English history provided in this chapter), it contravened the very premises of the Puritan vision as so memorably articulated by Winthrop, and cherished by most all religious and civic leaders in the New World, whether separatist[587] or still attached to the Church of England.

Barry sets in relief the radical force of Williams's critique when such is viewed within the context of prevailing Puritan norms:

> Obedience to God was the very foundation of Winthrop's city on a hill. That obedience meant conforming to God's laws, and those laws began with the Ten Commandments. The government intended to enforce these commandments.
>
> Williams attacked this intent. He stated that magistrates had no authority to enforce "the First Table"....
>
> All in Massachusetts, Williams included, considered duties to God infinitely more important than duties to man. Still, Williams was asserting that these most important duties lay outside the sphere of government. The state, he said, had no authority to inject itself in any way into an individual's relationship with God.[588]

It is unclear how Williams arrived at his stance. No doubt his experiences in England played a formative role, but other Puritans (Winthrop included) had been through the mill of the same religio-political perturbations. In one respect, however, Williams, *had* enjoyed a singular privilege. Only he had been Sir Edward Coke's assistant, and so been party to most all of the momentous currents of history that implies.

Barry, though, brings us round to the main point:

> Whatever the source of Williams's views, this very first criticism of the Bay authorities expressed the essence of his later thought. That thought would eventually develop into a systematic and comprehensive formulation of religious and political freedom, of the appropriate exercise of power by the state and by the church, and of an individual's rights and the limits on those rights. [589]

There is more—much more—to Roger Williams's story. There is his exodus to Salem and, subsequently, Plymouth, after the Boston episode, smaller locales that entertained their own differences with the Bay Colony's leaders and would, in the long run, prove central to Williams's destiny. There is Williams's resourceful homesteading, and the remarkable saga of his relationship with the Indian tribes (Wampanoag, Narragansett, Pequot and others), whose tongue[590] he learned, whose friendship he earned, and whose land rights he championed—to the ever more vexed consternation of the colonial authorities. There is the story of the escalation of that vexation leading, finally, to the judgment that Williams—whose ideas about religious liberty and native land rights hacked at the root of the Puritan project—represented an existential threat to orderly rule in the colonies. That judgment found expression in Williams's conviction in the General Court in Boston (Williams was not present at the proceedings) on charges of sedition and heresy in 1635, and the consequent sentence of banishment levied by authorities. There is the secret message (sent by Winthrop who, for all their differences, liked and respected Williams) warning Williams that the law was coming for him (Willliams was to be apprehended and shipped back to England, where he could well have been imprisoned or executed). There is Williams's consequent flight into the wilderness in the dead of winter in January, 1636, and the preservation of his life enabled by his Indian friends. There is his eventual return to favor in the eyes of *some* influential allies, the spreading of his ideas, his founding and governance and securing (by return to England) of a charter for the colony of Providence, in Rhode Island, a demesne governed in accord with his principles of religious liberty, and thus serving as a beacon of light to the world—albeit one founded upon ideas fundamentally at odds with those underlying Winthrop's vision of the City on the Hill.

Williams elaborates those ideas most famously in his 1644 text, *The Bloody Tenent of Persecution for Cause of Conscience,* which he composed while back in England about the thorny and politically contentious business of securing legal charter for the Colony of Rhode Island. That he succeeded in that endeavor is remarkable given the tumult of the times. England was sunk in the throes of the first stages of the Civil War (fueled, naturally, by religious conflict) that would result in the execution of the King, and transform politics in England forever.

That under such trying circumstances, Williams succeeded in completing the *Bloody Tenent*—a book of more than four hundred pages—and ensuring the printing of the same, is also remarkable. It is so all the more, given that the book's message of church/state separation and religious freedom was no more congenial to quarreling Protestant factions in England than it had been to Puritan leaders in America. As one historian wrote:

> No voice had yet been raised in Parliament for a toleration of all Protestant groups. Men's hearts were attached by the tuition of conviction and by habits to the ideal of a national Church which would permit of no dissent. One inflexibility was to be replaced by another, one uniformity by another quite as rigorous and infallible.[591]

Nor was the conflict limited, by any means, to differences internal to Protestantism. Rather "It was clearly the intention of Parliament to destroy Catholicism in England."[592]

Roger Williams, though, begged to differ. He did so passionately, articulately, with great erudition, and at great length.

While the main text of *The Bloody Tenent* is cast in the form of a dialogue between Truth and Peace, an introductory section enumerating the treatise's arguments provides an abstract of Williams's main ideas. The First Argument acknowledges and abhors the religious violence that tragically scars so much of European history and ignited Civil War in England.

> First, that the blood of so many hundred thousand souls of Protestants and Papists, spilled in the wars of present and former ages for their respective consciences, is not required nor accepted by Jesus Christ, the Prince of Peace.[593]

The Second offers a succinct statement of Williams's foundational premise, the ground floor of his philosophy of religious freedom:

> Second, pregnant Scriptures and arguments are...proposed against the doctrine of persecution for cause of conscience.[594]

The Fourth fuses the First and Second even while already making good on the author's promise to provide a scriptural basis for his arguments:

> Fourth, the doctrine of persecution for cause of conscience is proved guilty of all the blood of the souls crying for vengeance under the altar.[595]

Notably, the allusion here is to *The Apocalypse* (or *Book of Revelation*):

> And when he had opened the fifth seal, I saw under the altar the souls of them that were slain for the word of God, and for the testimony which they held. And they cried with a loud voice, saying, How long, O Lord, holy and true, dost thou not judge and avenge our blood on them that dwell on the earth?[596]

Williams's Fifth Argument amounts to a cogent formulation of the principle of separation of Church and State:

> Fifth, all civil states, with their officers of justice in their respective constitutions and administrations, are proved essentially civil, and therefore not judges, governors, or defenders of the spiritual or Christian state and worship.[597]

The Sixth represents a formal statement of religious tolerance:

> Sixth, it is the will and command of God that (since the coming of his Son the Lord Jesus) a permission of the most pagan, Jewish, Turkish, or Antichristian consciences and worships be granted to all men in all nations and countries, and they are to be fought against with that sword which is only (in soul matters) able to conquer, [that is] the sword of God's Spirit, the Word of God.[598]

...while the Twelfth reprises the Sixth even while striking a peculiarly modern note:

> Twelfth and last, true civility and Christianity may both flourish in a state or kingdom, notwithstanding the permission of diverse and contrary consciences, either of Jew or Gentile.[599]

Given that Williams's twelve arguments exhibit significant redundancy, the six cited provide a fair picture of the whole, and so a sense of the foundations of Williams's idea of religious freedom and its application to legitimate forms of governance.

Around the time he wrote *The Bloody Tenent*, Willliams coined and began employing his own term for the concept of essential religious and political freedom: "*soul liberty.*"

~

My brief meditation upon soul geography at the beginning of this chapter described how I first came to know and rely upon Roger Williams, the exemplar of American spirit remembered in the name of a street in my home town. My reminiscences also singled out Berkeley—traditional locus of beat poetry, radical protest and free speech—as a historic hot-spot of spirit in America. Post-Covid Berkeley, however, exemplifies all too well the tragedy that has befallen the nation since the era when the torch of spirit was ably borne by the liberally-minded branch of our polity.

Nothing better epitomizes that decay—that profound betrayal of Roger Williams's legacy of soul liberty—than what happened (and to some extent is still happening) in the theatres.

By fall of 2023, with the peak of the pandemic far behind us, most places in the world had long since lifted vaccine, mask, and social distancing restrictions. Cultural venues such as theatres and concert halls had been welcoming back art-starved patrons for some time. Given its liberal complexion, the Bay

Area moved more slowly. Still, things had loosened up considerably. Wasn't it past time for me to break my fast, and consider something as risqué as going to a play?

One grey day November 2023, for the first time in a very long time, I browsed the theatre listings. Neither the Berkeley Repertory nor the Shotgun Theatres had anything particularly interesting, but the small Aurora (another one of my favorites) was staging what looked to be a compelling drama. I logged onto the Aurora's site and began scrolling to check relevant information.

As far as its mission is concerned, the Aurora first had these words to share:

THEATRE FOR EVERYONE

At Aurora, we believe that **theatre belongs to everyone.** We ask that our staff, our artists, and our audience work together to make all people feel welcome here.

- **Be respectful of others.**
- **Avoid making assumptions** about people based on age, race, gender, religion, disability, gender identity and expression, sexual orientation, physical appearance, or any other status or characteristic.
- **Remember that making comments or asking questions about the factors listed above—even with good intentions—can have a harmful impact.** This is especially true about factors that have been connected with marginalization.
- **Please let us know** if you feel marginalized in any way. We take all such issues seriously and will do our best to address such concerns in a timely, respectful, and conscientious manner.
- We have all kinds of people on our stage, behind the scenes, on our staff, and in our audience, and **Aurora belongs to all of us.**

Thank you for being a part of the Aurora Family! [600]

This was all very reassuring, and made me feel right at home.

Soon, I found the write-up for the play:

> Adapted from George Orwell by the Bay Area's own Michael Gene Sullivan, 1984 is a ferocious and provocative retelling of the prescient and iconic novel. Big Brother's surveillance state seeks to control not just our bodies but our minds as well, reaching into every corner of our lives. Accused of Thoughtcrime, Winston Smith faces an interrogation that will

> reveal his struggle for scraps of love and freedom in a world awash with paranoia and violence. Can the yearning for freedom be extinguished? Or is our shared humanity more powerful than any forces of repression? Experience the novel come to life with shocking relevance in this brilliant adaptation on the Aurora stage.[601]

What, I thought, could possibly be more timely? Many had already drawn upon Orwell's classic novel to critique our modern Covid World, especially after the Biden Administration had proposed a Disinformation Governance Board that looked, for all the world, like an Orwellian Ministry of Truth.

For a moment, I allowed myself to imagine a return to the theatre, that most human of art forms which, at its best (as in Elizabethan England) has been the looking glass of society, and even (as in ancient Greece) the school of democracy.

The moment did not last.

Most venues that, in the past, had required vaccination, only carded you, if at all, at the door. Never mind that it was November 2023, and everyone knew (or *should* have known) that the Covid vaccines did *not* stop infection or transmission and in fact rendered one more rather than less likely to contract (and so spread) the bug—still, the usual procedure wasn't good enough for the Aurora. The Covid-19 Safety link on the website (which, of course, I should have checked first, as had long been my habit) had this to say:

> Beginning August 1st, 2023, with the start of our 2023/2024 Season:
>
> **We require that all audience members and Aurora Theatre Company employees be fully vaccinated against COVID-19. As of October 2023, this requirement includes the new 2023–2024 Pfizer-BioNTech or Moderna COVID-19 vaccine. All patrons will be asked to provide affirmation of up-to-date vaccination status for their entire party at the time of ticket purchase.**[602]

"Shocking relevance" indeed. What is most shocking, perhaps, is that the Aurora could stage *1984,* publish their "THEATRE FOR EVERYONE" pitch alongside this write-up of the play, *and* exclude every human being who had exercised their right of informed consent to decline vaccination—*and do all of this, without the least hint of the irony involved.*

Did I say that Berkeley once stood for the antithesis of group-think: critical reflection, nonconformity, questioning authority (especially government authority), and (above all) freedom of thought, speech, and conscience?

So much for that proud tradition. So much for bodily autonomy across the bay. So much for the *soul liberty* Roger Williams so courageously fought for. So much for spirit in America in these days, in these parts.

Chapter 19

PAST AS PROLOGUE: MONARCHY, TECHNOCRACY —OR SOUL LIBERTY?

In the prior chapter, I offered a glimpse into politics and religion in England in the years leading up to the turn of the 17th century and its crucial early decades. I touched more lightly upon the interface of politics and religion in the new American colonies. I lent significant attention to the English context because (as John Barry's book makes so vividly clear), the power plays involving the Crown, Parliament, various factions of the Church, and the law formed the soil in which the seed of what would eventually emerge as American democracy was planted. That seed owed no small quotient of its germinal force to the life and mind of Roger Williams.

Williams's radical ideas developed as a kind of alchemical abreaction to the abuses of power he witnessed, particularly that enabled by the melding of church and state. A devoutly religious man himself, Williams's clear view of the marked distinction between the realm of the spirit (the Kingdom of God, biblically speaking) and that of the world of men and their doings on earth formed the basis of his idea of soul liberty. By contrast, King James and Puritan divines both harbored the settled conviction that direct translation between the spiritual and the worldly sphere was not only possible, but necessary, and indeed comprised the needful task—and special privilege—of those chosen (by God or man) to govern.

I do not mean here to imply that translation between the spiritual and material realm is not possible. On the contrary, such "translation" is the defining task of the soul. By "direct translation" I mean here the kind of *unmediated* identification of a spiritual with a material content that effectively elides the intervening interpretive act of the soul. That is exemplified in both the doctrine of the divine right of kings and papal infallibility. In both cases, a spiritual content is identified with a worldly office in a rigid manner that acknowledges no space or distance between (on the one hand) the spiritual and (on the other) a temporal political reality.

The doctrine of the divine right of kings to which James adhered fuses the realms of God and man, annihilating any interval between the divine and the royal will. If James acknowledged that England should be ruled in accordance with God's law, he as king served as God's proxy on earth. It follows that (as Egerton put the matter with admirable concision) "the King is the Law speaking"—not man's law only, but God's as well.

In kindred fashion, Puritans saw their charter in the New World as the analogue and sequel to the holy covenant that bound the Hebrew People to their God. "The Lord will be our God" declared Winthrop in his famous sermon,

> and delight to dwell among us, as his oune people, and will command a blessing upon us in all our ways.... Wee shall finde that the God of Israel is among us, when ten of us shall be able to resist a thousand of our enemies; when hee shall make us a prayse and glory that men shall say of succeeding plantations, "the Lord make it like that of New England."[603]

The words that follow articulate both Winthrop's iconic formulation of the American ideal, and the dire consequences (expanded upon at length in the continuation of the passage) of falling short in the effort to fulfill the sacred covenant:

> For we must consider that wee shall be as a city upon a hill. The eies of all people are uppon us. Soe that if wee shall deale falsely with our God in this worke wee haue undertaken, and soe cause him to withdrawe his present help from us, wee shall be made a story and a by-word through the world. Wee shall open the mouthes of enemies to speake evill of the wayes of God.[604]

Puritan leaders differed dramatically from James in matters of theology and religious observance. They differed not at all with respect to at least one fundamental premise of political philosophy. As Winthrop's words demonstrate, he and others of his ilk firmly believed that those in charge of the fortunes of the colonies were charged with the mission, and the power, to discern the Word of God, and to act so as to ensure its fulfillment. That meant establishing and enforcing both the laws and social norms ensuring that Puritan society conformed to the Will of God as expressed in holy scripture, thus qualifying the New World fitly to represent the Kingdom of God on earth.

For Winthrop and his Puritan brethren no less than for James (and after him, Charles), religious and political authority were viewed as essentially indivisible.[605] That authority, moreover—that *sovereignty*—properly belonged to the annointed leader or leaders of the realm, be he King, Governor, Archbishop of Canterbury, or Minister of the church in Boston.

Recall Theodore Parker's description of the "vicarious" character of medieval political and religious philosophy, in which context "the church and state were both accounted divine." Review of the history presented in the prior chapter enables us not only to know whereof Parker speaks, but to recognize that the system he describes endured well into the early modern period, including 16th- and early 17th-century England and the mainstream of Puritan colonial culture.

In his speech, Parker maintained:

> Now in America, we have somewhat changed that state of things. The political and ecclesiastical functionary is the servant, the People master now.[606]

That is to say, America is (in principle) a land of religious freedom, *and* a democracy, a nation the government of which is of, by, and for the people.

How then did we get from there to here? That is obviously a complex story, but this much can be said: *the idea of soul liberty constitutes the seed of American democracy.*

Roger Williams knew first-hand the consequences of the philosophy described by Parker and practiced in both England and the colonies. He had seen the excess of power and religious intolerance result in oppression, persecution, torture, and murder. The threat thereof drove him first from England and—not long thereafter—likewise harried him, posthaste, from the safety of his home in Salem into the bitter-cold winter wilderness as he fled colonial authorities charged with arresting and deporting him.

It did not matter that Williams's *theology* differed little from that of the Bay Colony leaders who banished him. That his *political* philosophy did—and that Williams endorsed freedom of thought, speech, conscience, and worship, and actively agitated for the observance of the same—mattered a great deal. If the seed of democracy finally landed, along with the *Mayflower* and the *Lyon*, upon American soil, that soil could at first hardly be judged to be anything other than harsh and unyielding.

The reigning political philosophy in both England and the colonies as here described was positively—and deliberately—*antithetical* to democracy. "The idea of democracy was entirely foreign. The idea that authority and sovereignty came from below, from the governed, as opposed to from above, from God, was entirely foreign."[607] Barry paints the fuller picture, first with respect to the English context in the 1640s when Willliams published *The Bloody Tenant:*

> In England, despite the fact that Parliament was waging a civil war against the king, no member of Parliament was advocating democracy. Creating rule from below was neither the announced nor unannounced goal of Parliament. The predominant view of the relationship between the state and the subjects was that the state held sovereignty over and was separate from its subjects—hence the use of the word "subject" as opposed to "citizen." And although the theory of the divine right of kings—which as advanced by James and Charles gave them virtually dictatorial powers—was much disputed, the idea that authority came from God was not disputed.[608]

When Barry speaks of "authority" here, he means the authority—and consequent practical power—vested in *offices* of governance in both a civic and religious context. (Parker again: "Believe and obey . . . trust our *offices*, and not your own soul.") Again, the very idea thus expressed extinguishes *effective—politically* relevant—difference between the spiritual and material realm. Very much as in the traditional doctrine of papal infallibility, divine sanction and worldly office (the authority wielded by the state, whether that state be ruled primarily by King or Parliament) coincide.

The same political philosophy reigned in the American colonies. Barry continues:

> New England Puritans differed not at all. The goal of creating a democracy had never stirred the leadership of Massachusettes—except to opposition. Winthrop believed that the magistrates, even though "being called [elected] by you [freemen], we have our authority from God." Therefore they must be obeyed.[609]

Paradoxically, Winthrop imagined that the people's *liberty* consisted in just such unquestioned *obedience to authority*: "So shall your Libertyes be preserved, in upholding the honor & power of Authoritye amongst you."[610]

Winthrop recognized that the principles of democratic governance were antithetical to his political philosophy and to all he considered conducive to good and holy rule. "Democracy," stated Winthrop, "is, among most civil nations, accounted the meanest and worst form of government...history records that it hath always been of least continuance and fullest of troubles."[611] John Cotton, minister of the Boston church and arguably the most prominent preacher in the colonies, concurred:

> Democracy, I do not conceyve that ever God did ordeyne as a fitt government eyther for church or commonwealth. If the people be governors who shall be governed? As for monarchy, and aristocracy, they are both of them clearly approved, and directed by scripture.[612]

"If the people be governors..." Cotton's dismissive query states the core of the prevailing anti-democratic attitude with memorable concision.

The world of difference between Williams and Puritan leaders like Winthrop and Cotton begins with Williams's willingness to take the distinction between the spiritual and material realms seriously, and to draw out the practical consequences of that substantive difference. The first and foremost of such consequence was, for Williams, ready recognition of the *fallibility* inherent in mortal judgment and his refusal to grant exception to that cardinal rule. To a far greater degree than his contemporaries, Williams showed himself keenly aware of the fact that all public offices—royal, magisterial, and ecclesiastical not excepted—are eminently human institutions, and that those who fill such offices are in no wise immune to man's gross imperfections and ineradicable tendency to err. Indeed, Williams could draw on a wealth of experience to bolster the premise that—contrary to the reigning presupposition—the possession of authority did not constitute proof of virtue, wisdom, and divine sanction, but in fact tended to provoke presumption, prejudice, arrogance, and error. Like Tolkien's famous ring, the keys of power magnify pride and self-righteous disrespect for the spiritual autonomy and indeed very humanity of those "who shall be governed," and so readily translate into words and deeds that betray the spirit of love and beneficence official measures typically pretend to serve.

John Cotton likely did not mistake the raw state of Massachusetts for the Garden of Eden. Nonetheless, he, unlike Williams, insisted upon believing that he and his fellow clerics were, not only specially privileged, but *ordained* for the task of deciding how the people of the colony should think and act in order to make fertile New England into an American Paradise. Knowledge of the right way depended, of course, on knowledge of scripture and skill in its interpretation. Cotton seemed little impressed by the fact that learned and devout men and women throughout the ages had arrived at very different constructions of the meaning and intent of the Good Book, and that such differences had all too often led—as the Civil War tearing England at the time clearly demonstrated—to violence of almost unimaginable extent.

Williams, however, as his arguments in *The Bloody Tenent* make clear, *was* impressed and horrified at the gruesome consequence: "The doctrine of persecution for cause of conscience," he wrote, "is proved guilty of all the blood of the souls crying for vengeance under the altar." Williams was not speaking abstractly but referring concretely to (as his First Argument declares) "so many hundred thousand souls of Protestants and Papists." He professed astonishment that Cotton (like so many others) could so blithely ignore the grisly consequences of Cotton's hermeneutic absolutism.

Williams, in fact, had special reason to accuse Cotton of what he called a "monstrous Partiality": the refusal to admit the possibility of one's own error. Shortly before Williams wrote *The Bloody Tenent,* an old letter of Cotton's—written shortly after Williams's official banishment—was published without Cotton's knowledge or consent. In it, Cotton justifies his endorsement of the fateful sentence. In *Mr. Cotton's Letter Examined and Answered,* a pamphlet-sized precursor of *The Bloody Tenent,* Willliams responded to Cotton's arguments. Cotton's rationalization of an act that could easily have resulted in Williams's death provided Williams (whom Cotton knew as a religious man of intelligence and integrity, albeit holding different opinions than himself) with a dramatic case in point as he critiqued the doctrine of persecution for the cause of conscience and elaborated his defense of religious freedom.

Yet if Williams denied the offices of religious institution any absolute authority, how much less would this devout man of God be inclined to award the state any right to pretend that its wisdom and right in governance could be considered beyond question? Once Williams had separated religious from civic authority, any possible ground for absolutism in politics or undue obeisance to the state was dissolved. Supreme authority derived from God, not man, and if the church could not be trusted infallibly to interpret the Word of God, neither could any form of civil government rightly claim the mantle of unimpeachable sovereignty. The state could and must exercise practical administrative power, but could claim no unquestionable transcendental or superordinate source of sanction for its policy.

Williams—forerunner of Emerson and Thoreau—thus held individual conscience as the sacrosanct refuge of the human spirit and an agent power that could not be commanded by the mortal and fallible offices of church or state. The logic of his heart and the force of his mind consequently led him to embrace the only political philosophy commensurate with that belief. "Foreign" as it might be to the prevailing temper of the times, if Roger Williams were to remain true to the principles that constituted the moral substance of his being, he could not but become a democrat. "I infer," wrote Williams in *The Bloody Tenent,* "that the sovereign, original, and foundation of civil power lies in the people."[613]

One could hardly imagine an inference more at odds with the temper of the time, and so more revolutionary. This sovereignty of the people, Williams alleged, was:

> distinct from the government set up. And if so, that a people may erect and establish what form of government seems to them most meet for their civil condition, it is evident that such governments as are by them erected and established have no more power, nor for longer time, than the civil power of people consenting and agreeing shall betrust them with. All true civil Magistrates have not the least inch of civil power, but what is measured out to them from the free consent of the whole.[614]

Williams's words fly in the face of the prevailing political philosophy. The offices of government did not lend government officials authority. Officials could rightfully claim "*not the least inch* of civil power, but what is measured out to them from the *free* consent of the whole."

Williams wrote these words almost half a century before John Locke penned his *Two Treatises of Government*, a work widely interpreted as justifying the Glorious Revolution's overthrow of the monarchy in England in 1689. He wrote them well over a hundred years before Rousseau's 1762 *The Social Contract,* a book regarded as a chief source of the ideas that fueled the French Revolution. Williams anticipated them both. Directly or indirectly, his current of influence runs deep. One way and another, *The Bloody Tenent* helped tune the instruments of America's future revolution.[615]

It bears emphasis that Williams's historic defense of religious and political liberty go hand in hand. Just as one and the same First Amendment of the U.S. Constitution protects both religious liberty and the freedom of speech, the text of *The Bloody Tenent* complements its defense of the former with kindred championing of the latter. Arguing that social progress hinged, not upon the rigid imposition of conformity, but the open questioning of accepted beliefs, Williams wrote:

> If it shall be a crime, humbly and peacably to question...whatever is publickly taught and delivered, you will certainly find yourselves...enslaved and captivated in the Chains of those Popish Darknesses, (to wit Ignorance is the mother of Devotion, and we must believe as the church believes, &c).[616]

In England at the time, it was indeed a crime to question official opinion. In 1643, Parliament (revealing once more that abuse of power lay not only on the side of the Crown) passed an *Ordinance for the Regulating of Printing* which required writers to procure a license—and so official governmental approval—before publishing printed matter.

Willliams defied the law. *The Bloody Tenent* was published anonymously and secretly by Williams's friend Gregory Dexter, who later followed him to Providence.

Censorship laws notwithstanding, Williams's book was widely read in influential circles—and widely reviled. His opinions on religious and political liberty, though cherished by a few kindred spirits (Henry Vane and John Milton, for instance) were not popular. *The Bloody Tenent* was not only verbally condemned. If mid-century England no longer burned heretics at the stake, it did burn their books. Great public display was made of watching seized copies of *The Bloody Tenent* go up in flames.

Today's censors pursue the opposite course, preferring to keep their work—and so, too, the work of those whom they persecute—as invisible as possible. While I expect all would agree that book-burning in the public square makes far better theatre than deplatforming or shadow-banning, it may well be less effective. Devouring flames notwithstanding, *The Bloody Tenent* found its readers. It may be a bit of a stretch to apply what Rilke wrote of Jan Hus ("The glowing stake wrote his name / in the illumined book of fame") to the burnings of *The Bloody Tenent,* but the conflagrations and their effects bear some comparison.

Nor is it an accident that *The Bloody Tenent* appeared in the same year as Milton's *Areopagitica*, perhaps the most famous—and certainly most erudite—defense of free speech ever written.[617] Milton's pamphlet, written in direct response to the 1643 censorship laws (and circulated as a pamphlet to evade them), contains innumerable choice passages. One in particular addresses the spiritual and intellectual arrogance and stupefaction of society implicit in any state-sponsored control of information. That would include the whole woeful industry of "fact-checking" and policing of "misinformation" as practiced today:

> And how can a man teach with authority, which is the life of teaching, how can he be a Doctor in his book as he ought to be, or else had better be silent, whenas all he teaches, all he delivers, is but under tuition, under the correction of his patriarchal licencer to blot or alter what precisely accords not with the hidebound humor which he call his judgement.... I hate a pupil teacher, I endure not an instructer that comes to me under the wardship of an overseeing fist. I know nothing of the licencer, but that I have his own hand here for his arrogance; who shall warrant me his judgment? *The State Sir*, replies the Stationer, but has a quick return, *The State shall be my governours, but not my criticks* [emphasis added].... For though a licencer should happ'n to be judicious more than ordinary...yet his very office and his commission enjoyns him to let passe nothing but what is vulgarly received already.[618]

Still more than his friend Milton, Williams was not only a strikingly original thinker, but a man of action, one who consistently employed his formidable will and political acumen to put his ideas into practice, whatever the odds against him. Not only did Williams secure the desired charter for Rhode Island, the same charter granted the inhabitants of the colony the power to form whatever government they chose.

Under Williams's guidance, they chose democracy. Barry:

> In May 1647, representatives from Providence, Newport, Portsmouth, and Warwick/Shawomet met for three days and produced a sixty-one-page constitution and legal code. Williams led the Providence delegation.... This document created the freest society in the world, built around a structure of law, endorsing every man's "peacable and quiet enjoyment of his lawful right and Libertie." It of course confirmed that the government established freedom of religion.... And the government was reaffirmed as "Democraticall: that is to say: a Government held by ye free and voluntarie consent of all, or the greater parte of the free Inhabitants."[619]

The seed had sprouted. Thus did the Rhode Island settlements—Providence chief among them—debut democracy in America. Thus did its body politic become the prototype of the revolutionary idea that underlay the founding of a new nation, a sovereign country that—even if not exactly that shining city on the hill—nonetheless represented, in fact as well as imagination, a New World.

Such is the precious legacy of Roger Williams, the man who gave his name to the Main Street of my childhood.

~

It is, however, a legacy, an inheritance, We, the People, are in grave danger of losing. We find ourselves in that predicament because too few Americans recollect their own history. I speak here not just of the facts which comprise the body of memory, but of the spiritual gist of the matter: this nation's soul history, and the idea of liberty at its core. That forgetfulness, that ignorance, threatens to carry us back to a new version of former times: times when the people were not governors, but the governed; when we were not citizens, but subjects; when the minds, souls, and bodies of the people were captivated and enslaved in chains of popish darknesses.

Popish Darknesses? Have not we long since separated church and state; and so left such medievalism behind?

It is a cliché—yet a deep truth nonetheless—that those who do not remember history are doomed to repeat it. If history never repeats itself literally, it does so nonetheless, as old forces take on new, permuted forms. So it is today, in America, and in Europe, in what I have been calling Covid World.

As citizens of a modern democracy, it is easy to imagine that we live in a society that—for all its manifest imperfections—nonetheless reflects an essentially enlightened frame of mind. Prejudice and strife remain, to be sure, and ghost our dreams of liberty, justice, and love. Still, we cherish those dreams. Still, we strive, against the odds, to make them real. In so doing, we imagine our conduct and our conscience to be ruled by no oppressive dogma, no gross superstition, no diabolical illusion, no unholy will to power, but by common sense; by fact and reason; by science, ethical principle, and the rule of law; by bonds of fellowship and compassionate regard for the other; by the holy creed of our shared humanity. These are the modern values cultured in the crucible of the Enlightenment, the storied Age of Reason that put the nightmare of religious intolerance ("persecution for cause of conscience") and the contumely of kingship behind us.

In particular, we may hold that momentous revolutions—scientific *and* political, linked by the elixir of reason, and the appeal to Nature—put the crushing absolutism, the chronic oppression, the seemingly unstoppable violence borne of the unholy marriage of church and state in the rear view mirror. *Those* "Chains of Popish Darknesses" have been banished forever.

Or so we thought. Or so we hoped. Yet Covid World opened our eyes to the truth that we stand, even now, engulfed in another, yet more fearsome wave of those same darknesses.

What, after all, does Roger William mean by the memorable phrase I have been repeating? On a literal level, of course, "Chains of Popish Darknesses" refers to the reign of the Catholic hierarchy and its infallible head, whose religious authority—imposing itself between the individual and his God—brooks no question.

Williams, though, employed the phrase in the context of discoursing upon the freedom of thought and expression in the civic or public as well as religious sphere ("if it be a crime...peacaeably to question...whatever is publickly taught and delivered"). The phrase thus has a wider orbit of meaning. It implies the oppression implicit in any form of rule that presumes to authority that cannot be questioned—inhering, not in the contestable truth or objective *merit* of acts performed and continued free and informed consent of the governed, but rather in the relevant *office* itself.

Such rule exhibits "a monstrous partiality," rejecting, as it does, the very possibility of its own error while taking for granted that of all who oppose its commands. "Popish darknesses" thus implies absolutism, especially forms thereof that (like the emblematic marriage of church and state) combine spiritual and political power. Such conjunction enables those who govern not only practically to impose their will by virtue of the force of law and of might, but also to command and control the channels of moral justification.

Since the beginning of the Common Era, two forms of discourse have achieved dominance in Western culture. Both religion and science derive their authority from one or another transpersonal (one could say transcendental) source. Within the context of the West's monotheistic religions, that source is God. In Science, it is Nature understood in the form of an objective order of utterly impersonal law. Both religion and science thus point to an order of being or power *not subject to the will of man*. In essence and conception, religion and science may thus be construed as originally *apolitical* in character. Paradoxically, it is this that lends these discourses the power of *ideological* legitimation. It is precisely the capacity for a truth to stand above and beyond the sphere of partial opinion that lends it unique authority when invoked in the worldly or political sphere which it, in essence, transcends.

Nonetheless, religion and science—construed not as ideal forms of knowledge or faith, but as concrete forms of social praxis actualized in human history—obviously can and do fall short of their ideal ends. This is glaringly obvious in the case of religion. No particular ritual form of observance ensures the attainment of spiritual felicity; and it is difficult if not impossible to construe the hateful violence perpetrated in the name of religion as service to a loving God rather than the benighted escapade of this or that faction of a tragically warped humanity. In many contexts, including that of early modern Europe, the tainting of religion by its patent—and patently unholy—mixture with politics counts as the rule rather than the exception.

As far as tangible attainment of its putative ends is concerned, science appears to have been far more successful than religion. Its vaunted method—practiced the world over, and not subject to the kind of diversity evident in forms of religious observance—earns a good deal of credit for its evident accomplishments. Viewed from a certain perspective, those successes can be seen to form a striking contrast with religion's at best questionable and at worst disastrous historical record. That contrast has moved people to believe that their trust—while perhaps sorely misplaced if invested in religious authority—may be more securely and responsibly put in the hands of science and its practitioners.

After all, if interpreting the will of God may often appear a vexed enterprise doomed to error and disaster, discovering the more objective laws of nature has certainly seemed a safer, surer and far more profitable bet. So long as this or that scientist follows the prescribed "method" of discovery and verification, one can have faith that what science deems to be true is indeed so. We practice and confirm that belief every time we switch on a light bulb, step on a plane, or boot up our computer. To doubt the truth of what science has to say today would, it seems, not only disqualify one as a rational being, but entirely incapacitate one as a functional member of society.

Nonetheless, real science—contrary to political theory and practice today—no more lends itself to forms of institutionalization that can safely be soldered to the governance structures of the state than does religion. In the one case no less than the other, the alliance poses a severe threat to the soul liberty of the people, and so democracy itself. In the case of science in particular, this is so, not because the spirit of science is incompatible with democracy, but because science suffers profound corruption when made an organ of state or global political power. Nothing bears this truth out more spectacularly than Covid World.

Science, in its true form, begins with *asking questions,* and the inquiry thus initiated continues being science only so long as questions are invited and treated with the respect they deserve. Science hinges upon radical doubt, and ("*Sapere aude!*") the courage and genius of independent minds. If music be the food of love, the food of science is doubt, dissent, and difference of opinion. It is thus democratic, not autocratic, by nature. In its unquenchable quest for knowledge and for truth, science demands originality and hates authority—especially arbitrary and entrenched authority. Dogma is its death and antithesis. In its radical integrity and disruptive force, science represents the *antidote* to Popish Darknesses and indeed all forms of authoritarianism. It does so because science flows from the indomitable agency of the human spirit, and cannot be controlled by precedent, or contained within any given institutional form.

All this may be affirmed of science, truly understood and practiced. All this is why science, as the handmaid of reason, contributed to the overthrow of medieval forms of rule, the abuses of monarchy, and the interminable bloody wars bred of religious persecution.

So it is the tragedy of modernity, and the cursed plague of our transhumanist present, that science today—at least the mainstream medical science that created Covid World—displays *none* of the above defining characteristics. Science today—much like true religion perverted into narrow-minded orthodoxy, hollow ritual, and sectarian prejudice—is not, in the main, science at all, but rather the sinister shadow of itself. Consequently, the very endeavor that inaugurated the Enlightenment and helped dispelled the religious intolerance that spread violence, terror, and murder throughout Europe for centuries on end, has now become the agent of like—and indeed still more devastating and deadly—abuse.

A point of law contributes to this deformity. The First Amendment prohibits any contract between the religion and the state, but no such law checks the leviathan state from swallowing science whole, or vice versa. Attached more fixedly than the church ever was to the formidable political and financial power of the state, science is a principal instrument of that global technocratic Matrix that engulfs the state itself. Mercilessly beat into submission, reduced to servile whoredom, science—*political* from the first to the last statistic—no longer serves Wisdom, but rather the *ideological* as well as *technological* ends of the Machine. It is, not the Word of God, but the Edict of Science that, invested with imperial rule in the realm of nature, authorizes the state—proxy of the Matrix—to vomit illusion in the name of truth even while issuing diktats that spread fear, superstition, intolerance, division, poverty, sickness, torture. and death across the face of the globe.

What was the cost of the lockdowns? How many businesses closed, for good? How many depressions, suicides, substance abuse cases, or instances of domestic violence did the lockdowns contribute to or cause? What was the educational cost, extracted at the expense of our children? How many livelihoods were lost from lockdowns, and from coercive vaccine mandates? How many good physicians have lost their licenses or their jobs for the heresy of questioning the party line (a.k.a. spreading "misinformation")? How many excess deaths since the vaccine roll-out? How many died because they were put on remdesivir or ventilated rather than treated early with safe, effective, inexpensive vitamins and repurposed drugs? How many vaccine-injured are suffering horribly, their very existence disputed as they are denied medical and financial assistance? What percentage of people suffer from chronic illness in America today? What has been the rate of rise in autism over the last forty years?

How then do we account for the dramatic and disastrous shift from science as vanguard of an enlightened era to science as an ethically and politically *regressive* if not *reactionary* force in culture?

In early modernity, "science" did not own the authority it does today. Nor was the enterprise of scientific inquiry embodied in an extensive array of prestigious and wealthy institutions. "Science" as we know and think of it did not exist. Natural philosophy remained the pursuit of amateurs as much or more than "professionals" (if one could employ that latter term properly at all before the 19th century) as Benjamin Franklin's career so colorfully illustrates.

That has all changed dramatically. When we speak of "science" at present, the very word tends to conflate a certain method of inquiry (itself associated with a specific philosophy or worldview) with the institutionalized forms responsible for the vast majority of scientific research. Those institutions are often intimately intertwined with government agency and funding as well as private industrial and commercial enterprise. That extensive entanglement of science with other sectors dedicated, not to pure truth-seeking, but to political and commercial ends is habitually occluded and disguised by use of the word after a fashion that picks the bone of "science" clean of its worldly flesh, and pretends that one can imagine "science" today—even that performed by parties with vested interests in certain results—to be completely or largely impartial. So it is that the very invocation of the name of "science"—like that of the Word of God in earlier times—resounds with the overtones of an absolute authority, any questioning of which (contrary to the spirit of science itself) is too often considered beyond the pale.

If Covid has taught us nothing else, it has revealed this imagination to be a fatal delusion. It is also one that Roger Williams would recognize as akin to those delusions of grandeur—that damnable hubris exhibited by kings and clerics alike—that led him to propose a Wall of Separation between Church and State.

Williams's doctrine of separation served a two-fold purpose. On the one hand, it precluded the state from claiming the excess of power—the absolute sovereignty—that derives from its identification with the Word and the Will of God: an authority which, when invoked, trumps all human reason, and invites inhumane assertions of power. While this probably qualifies as the more generally recognized function, it was not necessarily the one uppermost in Williams's mind. For him, the protection of the purity and sanctity of religious consciousness from its contamination by worldly concern may well have been of equal if not greater importance.

Those invested in the integrity of science will readily recognize that—in deference to the objective, impersonal truth science purports to serve—the principle of separation ideally *should* apply to science no less than religion. Real science is not supposed to take orders from politics.[620] We know the moment it does so, it is corrupted, and quickly ceases to be science at all in anything but name because it then no longer pursues a Truth from which an auxiliary Power *may* flow, but instead subordinates Truth itself to the demands of Power. In the moment such corruption sets in, science is transformed from a discourse of transpersonal truth-seeking into a vehicle of ideological legitimation and—potentially—social violence.[621]

Covid World revealed that such corruption constitutes the rule rather than exception in science today, at least in those domains (which today includes virtually the whole of the science of medicine) that naturally overlap public policy. As I have written before, it appears that this fate has befallen America's prestigious schools of public health,[622] which—in the area, at the very least, of vaccine science—long ago ceased even *to ask* relevant and indeed urgent questions. Heavily subsidized by government funds, such schools function, in this area, as "ideological state apparatuses" (Althusser) rather than politically impartial academic institutions.

The extent of such corruption—predictable given the pervasive mingling of scientific, political and commercial institutions and interests—is not widely recognized, and naturally soundly denied by those invested in the status quo. The capacity of science to maintain authority today derives in no small measure from the systematic means by which the extent of the corruption plaguing it is consistently covered-up and hidden by the workings of the Matrix.

The Wuhan cover-up is just one extreme instance of what is no gross anomaly but an ugly snapshot of the all-too-pervasive machinations of an irresponsible technocracy.

It is true, of course, that one can hardly lay the blame for all our Covid World ills at the door of the use and abuse of science alone. The Matrix, as I have described, exists as an *integrated array* of power structures, comprised of not only academic and research institutions, prestigious journals, and all the organs of science, but also industry, government, financial and health care institutions, media, tech, international organizations, NGOs, even public schools (now increasingly the locale of school-based health centers) and more. Corruption spreads like a cancer throughout the array, and is perhaps especially conspicuous in the government and media, which control the flow of information and saturate public consciousness with the propaganda ("vaccines are safe and effective") that "science" passes off as truth. Meanwhile, corporate industry (first and foremost, Big Pharma) lurks in the background, mining the human body for money and using that lucre to pull puppet strings.

The picture is complex, and it makes no sense to single science out for blame—*except* for the cardinal truth that it is what is called "science" now that provides the intellectual basis for the "rational"—and so moral—legitimation of so much that is done in the name of the "welfare of humanity." That includes securing "Public Safety"—the new code word for what Hobbes called the first (and only) law of Nature: the desire to live rather than die, which primordial instinct the Matrix loves to employ as a lever of control and pull again and again, constantly subjecting the People to the rule of Fear, and the oppressive strictures of the Biosecurity State.

So it is that history does, and does not, repeat itself. People are indeed—as in the 16th and 17th centuries—increasingly under the thumb of autocratic rule. We are, in this sense, increasingly back where we came from before Roger Williams lived and braved the wildernesses of the world for the cause of freedom; before Enlightenment philosophers inspired American revolutionaries to wrest political as well as spiritual sovereignty from the Crown, and claim it in the name of the People. The democracy so valiantly fought for, the sovereignty dearly bought in the name of We, the People, is slipping away—not slowly now, but quickly, like the last bit of water that, after a long gradual draw, drains down the sink with a whirl and a final emphatic *whoosh*.

That said, the rules of the game *are* different today.

~

Neither King James nor the likes of Winthrop and Cotton pretended to be servants of the people, but rather reigned as their superior masters. They did not question the basis of their own authority, and certainly did *not* aspire to govern in accord with enlightened principles of "democraticall" government. They openly disdained the same, avowing that power—their power—came from God, and that they possessed the divinely appointed right to govern the people in accordance with *their* sovereign will. In this, at least, they were open and forthright about the premises of the authority they claimed to own.

The post-Enlightenment, post-revolutionary landscape looks very different. America was founded—as Theodore Parker so vividly sketched—on the principle of the sovereignty of the People. The "antient rights and libertyes" long ago encoded in Magna Carta and common law, so courageously defended by Sir Edward Coke, have been magically transmuted into the statutory form of the Bill of Rights, and so been written into the charter of the nation. As exhibited in that document, the democratic principle of popular sovereignty did not crown the people *en masse*, and cannot be sundered from the charge of jealous guardianship of individual civil rights and liberties.

Yet from where do We—the individual citizens who comprise "the People"—derive our sovereignty?

Recall John Barry's sentence describing the state of political philosophy in the early 17th century: "The idea of democracy was entirely foreign. The idea that authority and sovereignty came from below, from the governed, as opposed to from above, from God, was entirely foreign."[623] I do not doubt the truth of Barry's assertion, but do take exception to one inference that may be drawn from his phrasing: namely, that the people, occupying the "lower" rungs of social hierarchy (and constituting, in one apt metaphor, the "grassroots") do *not* derive their authority and sovereignty from God, whose power Barry pictures as descending from above. Barry's phrasing mistakes the separation of the institutions of church and state inscribed in the Constitution to imply that, in principle, the political philosophy of democracy is intrinsically secular in nature, originally linked, as it is, to the historic repudiation of forms of authority that devolve "from above, from God."

As I have vigorously argued, nothing could be further from the truth. The language of the Declaration (worth citing, again and again) demonstrates as much, stipulating that—in accord with the belief of the founders in natural law and the rights such law affords—American citizens derive their sovereignty from a quintessentially spiritual, a divine source:

> We hold these truths to be self-evident, that all men are created equal, that they are endowed by their Creator with certain unalienable Rights, that among these are Life, Liberty and the pursuit of Happiness.

The individual human being's spiritual sovereignty and concomitant right to political liberty underlies the philosophy of democracy. It is indeed an overthrow of prior medieval political and theocratic philosophies, but by no means a product or prescription of godlessness, as the free exercise clause displays. What spiritual democracy does not and cannot condone is any *state*-sponsored establishment of religion. It cannot do so because such mixing of church and state awards to temporal institutions and organs of worldly power the privilege reserved for private conscience, violating the sacredness that properly belongs to that first and last refuge of the spirit.

Over the course of more than two centuries, a felt and lived sense of that sovereignty has steeped in the blood of "Americans of all nations."[624] It has unbent the knees of entire citizenries once subservient to kings, nobles, and clergy, and made people the world over unamenable to the yoke of servitude and subjection to illegitimate autocracy

That is one-half—the bright half—of the dual legacy of the Enlightenment.

The other is darker, and striving for ascendency. Today, it is making a concerted and unprecedented effort to bend those knees again.

To seize and hold power now, however, the Dark need overcome the Light. To do so, requires a degree of subtlety, a science and art of illusion, largely if not entirely unnecessary for a king, a pope, or for aristocrats sure of their ancestral rights and of the serfdom (psychological as well as socioeconomic) of commoners, or of the Third Estate.

Exactly here is where science—or rather, its dark, shadowy double—comes in, bidding to succeed where religion in the West can no longer tread: joining with the state in unholy marriage to provide ideological sanction for authoritarian forms of rule. The task: to maintain, by hook and by crook, the *semblance* of democracy and of the reign of reason; of the rule of law and the civil liberties that law guarantees; and of a deeply humanitarian code of ethics—even while violently subverting and indeed destroying the same.

Why such a campaign? It is precisely the bright side of our Enlightenment heritage that resists seduction by the Myth of Progress. It is precisely the form of critical conscience nursed in the Age of Reason that stands squarely in the way of the Matrix agenda of top-down, total control, enrichment of the few at the expense of the impoverished and dispossessed many, and (perhaps most compellingly) fulfillment of the transhumanist dream of re-creating God in the image of the scientific Mind of Man and its own monstrous offspring: the (AI driven) Machine, the intelligence and power of which knows no limits.

Not so long ago, Schwab and Gates and Johns Hopkins sponsored Event 201, gathering together elite Matrix forces to plot strategy for the upcoming pandemic—strategy and tactics that constituted the wholesale violation and indeed annihilation of democratic methods of civic dialogue and decision making. Not so long ago, Covid-19 was heralded by Klaus Schwab and his ilk as a golden opportunity for the reimagination and reconstruction of the world christened (in suitably mechanistic lingo) *The Great Reset*.

So religious zeal finds its way into the power centers of the modern world—but through a back door, and in a disguised form no less fanatical, and more powerful and well connected, than any medieval popedom. Not that our modern-day scientific clergy has not taken a page from that prior chapter! If the Catholic Church could sell salvation of the soul in the form of indulgences, passing off filthy lucre as a ticket to the Kingdom of Heaven, why should not our modern priesthood peddle the salvation of the body in the form of another financially remunerative yet fraudulent rite: the taking of a shot incapable of producing the desired effect, and more likely to kill or injure than save you?

This much, at least, is clear: religious appeals to the power of God are by no stretch of imagination the only means of justifying tyrannical authoritarianism. In certain respects, whether a system of belief holds of God or of the laws of a purely material nature matters less than the dogmatic absolutism shared by literal-minded species of both religious and scientific beliefs. As different as the bases of the pre- and post-Enlightenment autocracies are, both revolve around the common center that defines authoritarianism per se: denial of the spiritual sovereignty of the individual, and so—the *soul liberty* synonomous with *human freedom*.

~

So the power mongers of the present have sought—and found—their new way to the throne. Predictably, that way builds upon the premises of "the West's new faith." Predictably, it builds, with devilish cunning and power, upon that other, darker side of the Enlightenment heritage: the *mechanistic materialism* that has infiltrated and indeed conquered modern science, and which that science now sponsors and promotes.

We are back, then, to the theme announced near the beginning of this book—back, that is, to the *dialectic of enlightenment.*

Unless bowing to naked dictatorship and rule by pure force—an extreme always lurking on the margins of authoritarian forms of rule—the exercise and maintenance of state power requires ancillary ideological (and that means, too, moral) justification. In an earlier chapter of our history, when the name of God carried ultimate authority, this ideological legitimation was supplied by various forms of the fusion of church and state: Acts of Supremacy, declarations of divine kingship, or the imprimatur of religious mission. Making room for soul liberty, and the sovereignty of the people, required break-up of that coupling. Thus the doctrine, first formally articulated by Roger Williams, of the Wall of Separation between Church and State.

Today the seal of truth no longer rests in the treasure box of the Church. In the ruling mechanistic worldview, nature—material nature—is all in all. God is not, and man— merely animal, as he is—is likewise nothing essentially other than nature, albeit an exceptional form thereof, capable, perhaps, of mastering, transcending, transforming, and even replacing nature by virtue of…*the scientific intellect.* It is thus science, not religion, that rules this world, the field of nature, and—*since this constitutes the whole of reality in the materialist paradigm*—necessarily becomes the court of ultimate appeal. Science today, as the West's new faith, is thus in a position to fulfill the ideological function once served by religion: namely, dictation of what constitutes ultimate truth, and bestowal of a species of authority *not subject to question.*

In a recent e-mail exchange, a colleague of mine with ties to the public health establishment asserted that, in the context of Covid World, "there were many assertions made, including by people with respectable credentials, which were 100% factually wrong and which had the affect of killing people." In his mind, the absolute certainty of his conviction fully justified wide-ranging censorship of what he deemed dangerous "misinformation."

So it is that scientific certainty—*absolute* (100%!) surety—parallels the species of *unquestionable* authority claimed by religionists who profess to know the Word of God. In one case no less than the other, ultimate ends (saving lives, or the salvation of souls) are cited to justify *coercive* suppression of dissenting views. In both instances, those in positions of authority regard their *office* as legitimation of their prerogative to treat the people not as citizens entitled to know diverse opinions on a matter closely concerning their own welfare, but as servile subjects.

Of course, one would like to hope that the objectivity and impartiality proper to the essence of science, and responsible for its rise to eminence in the first place, would limit the capacity of any centralized power to wield science as an ideological tool. Unfortunately, we have seen not only in Covid World, but in the Third Reich and other instances as well, how the unholy alliance of science and the state can readily make the former all too malleable to the political ends of the latter.

Nor is it necessary to presume nefarious or self-serving intent on the part of *all* concerned for the linkage of scientific and politically authority to darken clear vision of the principles underlying democratic governance, and turn even well-meaning citizens into little Napoleons. Very much as is the case with religion, the certainty of the truth claims inherent in modern science seduces those who believe in its authority to fall prey to a "monstrous partiality," imagining the official representatives of scientific opinion to be incapable of error and entitled—in gross violation of the tenets of democracy—to govern accordingly.

No matter that this species of authority (historically reserved for religious *revelation*) is antithetical to science and therefore transmogrifies into dogma and endemic corruption.

No matter that, in marked contrast to religion, no doctrine of separation precludes the fusion of science and the state.

Americans (especially left-leaning ones) possess an instinctive repugnance to the notion of theocracy, an innate spiritual resistance that builds upon and confirms the legal prohibition inscribed in the Constitution. Yet no such guards, legal or psychospiritual, defend against the rule of a technocracy that (as Covid shows) constitutes a new brand of autocracy, one that wrests power from the people, exerts an unheard degree of technological and social power, and shreds the fabric of democracy. Matrix-approved "health experts" count as the privileged few in possession of knowledge inaccessible to the uninitiated, unordained many. We thus have no right to doubt the edict handed down from on high in the name of science and those who stand for it by virtue of—not their truth-saying—but their office.

No matter evident lies and the breaking of laws. No matter that it may be clear that proper scientific procedures were not followed. No matter that results do not bear out today's prophecy, nor tomorrow's. No matter the notable defections (and consequent condemnations and exile) from the elite order. If We, the People doubt, dissent, question, or disagree, we are guilty of the crime of spreading "misinformation."

That is a new name for an old offense. It used to be called...*heresy.*

~

Governments never had any legitimate authority to close the Covid debate before it was ever really opened. If our supposedly democratic government had, in good faith, sought not to dictate truth but to find it, approved "health experts" would not have summarily silenced, vilified, discredited, and persecuted those conscientious and knowledgeable persons who expressed alternative viewpoints on lockdowns, masks, vaccines, and all the rest. Instead, authorities would have welcomed and indeed *sponsored* responsible public debate.

Covid World, however, made it evident that—contrary to the founding tenets of democracy—leading public health authorities were never really interested in *serving* the people at all. Instead, the agents of the Matrix were—and are—interested in *ruling* us.

King James, for all his enormous flaws, was no fool. He possessed a keen mind capable of sharp insight; so much so, that Roger Williams saw fit to cite his pithy saying, "Persecution is the true mark of a false religion." So it is, and so it is too with science today, the counterfeit character of which is advertised by nothing so much as the systematic censorship perpetrated in its name.

On March 18, 2024 (the day the Supreme Court heard oral arguments in *Murthy v. Missouri*[625]), defenders of freedom of speech held a rally in front of the steps of the Court. Houston-based doctor Mary Talley Bowden shared her story:

> I am an ears, nose and throat doctor in Houston, Texas, and I want to give you a perspective on what it's like to be the neighborhood doctor during this pandemic. Four years ago, the government decided they knew better than your doctor. Fauci, Birx, Jha, Collins, Walensky, Cailiff, Murthy collectively decided that your doctors—no matter how many years in practice, papers published, lives saved—were not competent. These doctors hijacked our exam rooms, hijacked your right to bodily autonomy and informed consent, and—without a vote—declared themselves the experts. *They* were the science, and they were *in charge.*

> Remarkable, given their experience—or lack of it. Despite the degrees, none of them practice medicine. How many Covid patients did they examine? How many histories did they take? How many prescriptions did they write? Zero! None of them have cared for a single Covid patient, but because they had the full support of Big Pharma, the government, and most importantly, the media, they became the scientific authorities on a novel disease they had zero first-hand experience in treating. They dictated who would get treated and how—all from the safety of their homes, over zoom calls, never risking their lives to care for a single Covid patient.
>
> Reasonable scientists with good intentions would remain open-minded to other opinions, would have welcomed other suggestions, would have collaborated with anyone able to contribute and would have engaged in debate with those they disagreed with. But there was far too much invested in a predetermined plan for that to happen. Moving "at the speed of science," the Covid shot agenda was too big to fail. Nothing would stand in its way.[626]

Bowden goes on to detail the Biden administration's astronomical investment (on the people's dollar, of course) in a PR campaign to convince people to take the shot, including *ten billion dollars* targeting people of color. That phase of the campaign, in particular, entailed involving cultural "influencers" from entertainment and other sectors to condition, by emotional appeal, perceptions of the shot.

Bowden describes, too, the excruciating story of the relentless persecution she continues to be subjected to as a consequence of sharing her empirically grounded[627] disbelief in the efficacy and safety of the Covid-19 vaccines: loss of employment, reputational ruin, and *blanket censorship*. She cannot even speak to independent journalists who might wish to interview her, because experience shows they will be immediately deplatformed.

William Laud's vicious campaign against Protestant recusants, as thorough as it was, could hardly compare with the resources the technologically adroit and financially fearsome Matrix employs to enforce uniformity of belief, silence unapproved voices, and punish dissenters. It is true that our modern day thought police generally (with notable body-slamming exceptions) eschew physical violence. Quietly marginalizing and neutralizing Mary Talley Bowden is safe enough. Hanging her, splitting her nose, or sawing off her ears for the *heresy* of disbelieving in the safety and efficacy of the Covid-19 vaccine would probably command unwanted attention.

Bowden's experience reveals that anyone who believes we live in a country that abhors the persecution of persons because they do not ascribe to some officially ordained system of belief, simply does not know the score. Moreover, this entire book (both its first and second volumes) reveals that scientistic system of belief to be no less irrational, arbitrary, and intolerant than the most offensive forms of religious prejudice.[628] There are grounds for imagining that it may be even more so.

~

Within the context of a religious worldview, the human being lends priority to ideal and spiritual dimensions of being and consciousness. God, not man rules, and king or priest purport to draw their worldly authority from a divine source, shaping temporal goals so that these reflect spiritual ends. We know that the deference to ideal or spiritual dimensions, including invocation of the name and power of God, hardly guarantees wise, compassionate, and humane governance. Every light casts a shadow, and by virtue of reference to the absolute (God), religious imperatives can all too readily justify authoritarianism, oppression, and violent persecution.

Even so, religious worldviews—especially those, like American Transcendentalism, that are *philosophically self-conscious*—recognize the spiritual ground of human existence, and so can provide ample metaphysical room for what we would recognize as a human and enlightened *ethics*. The relation between the spiritual and material worlds remains, always, a problem to be solved (unless it is imperiously swept away by declarations of divine kingship or some other simple formulaic solution), but the ongoing address of that inexhaustibly rich mystery remains, precisely, the core of what can naturally unfold in the form of the soul-spiritual culture of man and woman. All sorts of compelling questions—the nature of love, of virtue, of liberty, of the True, the Good, and the Beautiful—remain *questions* one seeks to answer in the vocabulary of life itself. Nothing ranks as more important than addressing those profound concerns. The freedom to contemplate and address them in the refuge of one's own conscience, and (if one so desires) share one's perspective in the public forum, comprises the essence of the spiritual sovereignty of the individual and the essential correlate thereof: what Roger Williams calls *soul liberty.*

The situation is altogether altered once we complete the transition to the modern scientific worldview. To be sure, there is no longer any danger that the

Word or Power of God will be invoked to authorize sins against humankind. At the same time, what I have called the eclipse of the *Logos* imports nullity into the spiritual marrow of the human being. The repudiation of the very *idea* of any order of being and intelligence superior to that of mortal man—any spiritual realm that transcends the sphere of our worldly affairs and the diverse and competing interests that comprise it—deprives our moral nature of intellectual and spiritual nourishment, effectively starving, degrading, and (if not countered) finally destroying it.

This assault upon the moral and spiritual fiber of the soul goes hand in hand with the tendency of materialist philosophy to transfer, in accord with the dialectic of enlightenment, ever-increasing power to the state, or its overseer—the global technocratic Matrix.

The proponents, witting or unwitting, of our modern technocracy, of all the versions and ramifications of the Great Reset, imagine that they are heading us towards a future unlike anything humankind has known before. In certain respects, that is undoubtedly the case. In others, our modern technocratic oligarchs are leading us straight back to *serfdom.*

So it is that religion and science can both serve as potent ideological bases for authoritarianism and persecution of disfavored persons. Even so, the most aggressive evangelical campaign *should* hear, whispering in the recesses of the religious conscience, Jesus's response to the Adversary upon his temptation in the desert. Not only did Jesus refuse to turn stones into bread (the principal occupation of much science these days), when offered mastery of the kingdom of this world if he would bow down, Jesus—with a sweeping gesture—declined.

Technocrats today appear more than willing to make the deal. They naturally expect that we will—in our turn—bow to the new Princes of the World. If We, the People, remember ourselves—if we treasure our soul liberty—we will not comply.

~

I wish to conclude by citation of words written, and spoken, by an American living abroad in Germany. Satirist C. J. Hopkins's book *The Rise of the New Normal Reich*[629] sports a cover image featuring a barely visible swastika superimposed over a medical mask. Hopkins's collection of essays does not shy away from drawing some parallels between what transpired during the Covid pandemic and violations of essential rights and liberties associated with the Nazi rise to power. Ironically—and after a fashion that shows the deep perversion of logic involved in the Covid regime—Hopkins was charged with the offense (criminal in Germany) of public display of Nazi symbols so as to promote National Socialist ideology.

Hopkins—as everybody knows who knows anything of him and his work—was, of course, doing nothing of the kind but just the opposite. Still, he was charged and (as he naturally contested the ludicrous allegation) brought to trial.

Hopkins's closing statement, fittingly delivered in Germany, the homeland Horkheimer and Adorno were forced to flee, contains this powerfully frank gloss on the dystopian end of the dialectic of enlightenment:

> Not every form of totalitarianism is the same, but they share common hallmarks. Forcing people to display symbols of conformity to official ideology is a hallmark of totalitarian systems. Declaring a "state of emergency" and revoking constitutional rights for no justifiable reason is a hallmark of totalitarian systems. Inundating the public with lies and propaganda designed to terrify people into mindless obedience is a hallmark of totalitarian systems. Segregating societies is a hallmark of totalitarian systems. Censoring dissent is a hallmark of totalitarianism. Stripping people of their jobs because they refuse to conform to official ideology is a hallmark of totalitarian systems. Fomenting mass hatred of a "scapegoat" class of people is a hallmark of totalitarianism. Demonizing critics of the official ideology is a hallmark of totalitarian systems. Instrumentalizing the law to punish dissidents and make examples of critics of the authorities is a hallmark of totalitarianism.[630]

Nor is it surprising that Hopkins—though knowing nothing of the first volume of *Reset or Renaissance*—echoes, verbatim, the theme of *Two Roads:*

> We are, once again, at a crossroads. Not just here in Germany, but throughout the West. People went a little crazy, a little fascist, during the so-called Covid pandemic. And now, here we are. There are two roads ahead. We have to choose...you, me, all of us. One road leads back to the rule of law, to democratic principles. The other road leads to authoritarianism, to society where authorities rule by decree, and force, and twist the law into anything they want, and dictate what is and isn't reality, and abuse their power to silence anyone who disagrees with them.
>
> That is the road to totalitarianism. We have been down that road before. Please, let's not do it again.[631]

Hopkins was acquitted by a judge who—despite damning Hopkin's words as "ideological drivel" and theatrically donning a mask as she left the courtroom—nonetheless could not justify a guilty verdict.

For a moment, Hopkins—like so many of us—thought that this phase, at least, of his ordeal was over. Yet, like it or not (and I do *not* like it) Covid World and the New Normal Reich remains very much with us.

The German government—acting in the best interest of the once proud nation of *Dichter und Denker*, of Schiller and Schelling—appealed the decision.

Hopkins's trial—and ours—continues.[632]

CODA: AN AMERICAN TRANSCENDENTALIST'S REQUEST FOR RELIGIOUS EXEMPTION

(as such pertains to ANY existing or proposed vaccine mandate)

I hold the human being to be a creature made in the image of a divine intelligence that is the source and origin of the universe entire. I regard this godhead as no anthropomorphic phantom of an all-too-human imagination but, on the contrary, a virtually inconceivable Creative Life and Wisdom that acts as the real and effective ground of all authentic existence, and of all the Laws that order that existence.

I hold Nature, understood (not merely phenomenally as the apparent world but) as the creative and ordering World Soul (*Anima Mundi*) immanent in the physical universe and all the bodies therein, to be continuous with and indeed an aspect of this godhead. As such, Nature acts as the divine living intelligence that animates and orders bodily existence, including human anatomy and physiology.

This view in no wise contradicts the principle of evolution insofar as I understand the divine idea of the human being gradually to have assumed its current form as a consequence of a process of development guided by archetypal wisdom (not driven *solely* by blind, unintelligent mechanism). Timeless idea and evolutionary unfolding thus both contribute to the beauty and integrity of the human being in anatomical form and in most every aspect of physiological function.

I thus hold the human body and its workings—including that of the *enormously complex human immune system*—to be expressions of the wisdom inherent and agent in Nature. Correlatively, I regard the human body as (no mere piece of machinery but) the sacred temple of the human soul and spirit, which soul-spiritual essence is itself participant in the *Logos* or reasoning life of the godhead.

The act of vaccination entails a dramatic intervention in the natural functioning of the human immune system. As a rule, as promoted today, it is premised upon the assumption that—in both the short and long run—the *eminently fallible* human understanding, which did not design or organize the body or its systems of vital function, possesses a quotient of knowledge and protective power equaling or surpassing that of the sacred life and wisdom inherent in Nature (and so the godhead) itself, and can positively guarantee that its intervention *enhances* rather than *degrades and endangers* human health.

In the context of my sincerely held philosophico-religious beliefs, this represents a tragically sacrilegious act of hubris, one that directly contradicts the tenets of my spiritual worldview. In accordance with the First Amendment, I should not be compelled to perform or undergo an act contrary to my religious conscience, and so, as an American citizen vested with all the rights lawfully guaranteed therein, be exempted from *any and all vaccine mandates,* as should all children in my charge.

Footnote 1: I do not see that the First Amendment right of religious freedom contains any clause that allows reference to (conclusions drawn from) a scientific system of belief to suspend or negate that right. In case the state would argue that it *does* possess the power to compel my vaccination because the hypothesis that overwhelming public good would thereby be effected is supported—*not* by what can rightly be called an alternative system of belief, but rather by facts or truths *demonstrably proven* by modern science—it should be compelled *to make transparent the terms of that demonstration.*

In the absence of such demonstration (the conditions of which are no wise satisfied by mere citation of accepted opinion or specious dependence on "scientific consensus," the very notion of which is oxymoronic), no court has any power to differentiate between responsible science and myth, sound conviction and the "hag of superstition." At a bare minimum, the safety and efficacy of vaccines would therefore have to be shown to have met the standards for safety and efficacy required of other drugs, which include *long term placebo controlled double blind trials.*

The government has performed *no* such trials for *any* of the vaccines on the official schedule. Nor has it availed itself of the ready opportunity afforded to compare the health of vaccinated and unvaccinated populations, or performed other studies that might materially contribute to transforming what is at present no more than popular opinion ("vaccines are safe and effective") into what might then rightfully be regarded as scientifically proven Truth... *or* Falsehood.

In lieu of the failure of the relevant governmental bodies to pursue, encourage, or even tolerate such studies, it can only be assumed that the weight of extant reputable evidence disinclines them from that course, and that the consistent refusal to sponsor or even allow substantive debate of the relevant issues by knowledgeable parties, relying instead upon putative "consensus," censorship, and casuistic mud-slinging, only strengthens the suspicion that the official position does not have so much as one solid scientific leg to stand on, let alone the three or four necessary to uphold the balance of TRUTH.

Footnote 2: My reverence for Nature does not depend upon naive denial of the fact of sickness, affliction and death in the natural order, or translate into a belief that most any human medical (or technical) intervention necessarily impugns sacred wisdom. Nonetheless, I believe that the best medicine proceeds in the context of a healthy respect for the God-given integrity of the human organism and generally succeeds by cooperating with and marshaling the healing forces inherent in the body itself. The vaccine schedule today, however, as exhibited by the sheer number of recommended injections (over 70) and the delivery of many soon (if not immediately) after birth or in very early life, often for diseases to which infants or children evince no or very little susceptibility, displays a blatant disregard for the natural integrity of the body and its immune system, as does the mass administration of largely untested vaccine platforms (such as the mRNA technology employed in the Pfizer and Moderna Covid shots). It is by way of such practices, along with the coercion implicit in mandates, that modern public health policy forces the issue, provoking conscientious objection to programs of compulsory vaccination.

Footnote 3: Such conscientious objection, I would claim, is eminently rational, and indeed the only position commensurate with the truly enlightened values at work in the birth of both modern science and America herself. When viewed in the light of facts and reason, the contrary position (support of a program of compulsory vaccination) may well be regarded as neither rational nor truly modern, but rather one based upon a positively medieval web of superstition as well as institutions which are ideologically entrenched, centralized, hierarchical, and riddled with corruption—much like the Catholic Church before the Reformation.

Insofar as what is called "science" today, as that term is applied in the context of the vaccination debate, is more properly understood *not* as *real* science at all, but as a system of quasi-religious belief, mandatory vaccination indeed functions as a form of religious oppression. It thus represents an unlawful subjugation of the spirit that exerts its sway through concrete material practices and prescribed quasi-magical rituals, including the cultic rite of vaccination. Such a perspective makes transparently clear that—*if, contrary to an enlightened regard for fact and reason, such practices are mandated*—the constitutional protection of freedom of religion absolutely requires the right of religious exemption from all such ritual procedures.

We no longer require persons to profess belief in the God of our fathers and partake of holy communion, and punish failure to do so with expulsion from the community. Americans the world over should likewise no longer require their fellows to prostrate themselves before the God of the Needle, and punish refusal to vaccinate with castigation and social exclusion.

It is time, *high* time, to assume a more *enlightened* stance: to modernize (truly!) and move towards a future that remembers the sovereign dignity of the individual human being, and respects the Constitutional rights that inscribe cognizance of that sovereignty into the highest law of the land, the charter of our national identity.

The contrary stance is incommensurate with the American spirit, and betrays the regard for liberty that catalyzed the founding of this nation. Upon that rock We, as a People, must stand, if we are not to fall.

AFTERWORD

This book raises more questions than it answers. That, I believe, is a virtue. The version of modernity critiqued here hinges upon a closing of the doors of the mind. It entertains the benighted notion that (while lacunae remain to be filled in) modern science has essentially solved the riddle of Nature and so, too, of Man.

In truth, however, we have triumphed no more than Oedipus did in the moment he solved the riddle of the sphinx and cast her down from her pedestal. Do we need rehearse again the plot of that true story? The play begins with a city (Thebes) ravaged by pestilence, a plague caused by its king's (Oedipus's) *overweening pride and utter lack of self-knowledge.*

Nor are plagues (and other forms of diabolical afflictions that devour whole swaths of humanity whole) missing from the biblical book alluded to in the title of this one. Indeed, the *Revelation* verses immediately preceding the one cited by Roger Williams in the opening salvo of his *Bloody Tenent (*decrying the souls under the altar "that were slain for the word of God") speak of the famous four horsemen of the apocalypse. The figures mounted upon the white, red, black and pale horse signify terrific destruction wrought upon humankind by the forces of conquest, war, famine, and death, the last of which is often associated with plague.

Many hear the hooves of the horses beating hard upon the earth today. Some contend these have been saddled by the forces of which we have constantly been speaking: the Matrix, or Moloch-like Machine.

Apocalypse, however, does not only denote the destruction of the world. Etymologically, *apocalypse* means a tearing away of the veil, and so an act of *revelation.* Such disclosure may be terrible while exhibiting, too, elements of supreme beauty, as the *Book of Revelation* indubitably does. When we address ourselves to life and death or other matters that are in essence sublime, terror and beauty go hand in hand.

So it is that along with the shadowy delusion, noxious corruption, and gruesome arrogance featured in Covid World—all those Popish Darknesses that have wrought such unimaginable harm and suffering—there glimmers in these times as well the rejuvenating light of the Spirit. For all its horror, the Covid crisis has stirred newly awakened dreams of—not AI-driven transhumanist Frankensteinian monsters—but a new humanity, one risen from the ashes of the burnt-out souls of modern men and women.

Alongside the poet in Berkeley, the deathless imagination catches a revivifying glimpse of a radiant sunflower—the virginal glory of the human soul now choked and buried beneath the thick grime of a century (or two, or three) of dead thoughts.

In this book, this radiance shows as but a sliver of light, a crack of dawn piercing heavy darkness. Like a host of angel faces, unanswered questions crowd in to beckon from the other side of the window, gesturing towards the path, the way to be followed if the first thread of sun is to be woven into the broader light of day.

The features of this or that question may be fairly well defined: what is the philosophical ground of what I (following Roger Williams into the virgin wilderness of the New World) call "soul liberty"? Can that idea be elaborated in the context of the threefold nature of man that, drawing upon the deepest roots of metaphysical tradition, underlies American Transcendentalism, and finds modern form in Rudolf Steiner's anthroposophical vision?

Such particular query invites more expansive exploration. If, in accord with the tenets of soul liberty and the doctrine of separation of church and state, effective antidote to the pervasive materialism of our modern age and the spiritual wasteland it produces does not lie in recourse to traditional forms of religious institution—if we cannot respond to an ascendant technocracy by flirting with monasticism or theocracy (or, of course, monarchy newborn)—how are we to begin to see the contours of the path forward? If, in accord with Emerson's emblematic departure from the church, we need no outworn religious forms, but "an original relation to the universe"; "a poetry and philosophy of insight and not of tradition" and "a religion of revelation to us, and not the history of theirs," how are we to begin to understand what such might be and mean? How can we learn to read Emerson in the light of the *Logos* (that One Mind or Oversoul) that inspired his text and manifests itself in his Word?

I first conceived this *Reset or Renaissance* project when I realized that the letter writing catalyzed by the Covid crisis was not only going to overflow the bounds of a reasonable epistle, but was going to expand, too, beyond the limits of one or even two lengthy volumes. As recorded in the Preface to *Two Roads*, I imagined that (pursuing my own version of Emerson's project of "a natural history of the intellect") I would say what I could of modernity in this second volume before turning to the ancient roots of Western culture in subsequent work.

That more distant remembering remains a compelling charge. Even so, upon finally arriving at the end of this book, I realize I have barely begun to say what need be said on the topic of modernity itself. I am consequently as yet unsure of where the next bend in the road will take those generous and patient readers who have accompanied me so far, and wish to walk further along the untraveled path I seek to find. Yet I am willing to wager that, if we persevere in good faith and hope, we will find a table laid for us in the midst of dark valleys, and shall be served the bread of life even in the lap of adversity.

Past is prologue. So has it been, and so shall it ever be.

~

NOTES

1 Paul Brunton, *The Spiritual Crisis of Man* (1952; reprt., New York: Samuel Weister, 1970), 7.

2 Eric Klinenberg, 2020: *One City, Seven People, and the Year Everything Changed* (New York: Knopf, 2024).
Mill Valley is a town in Marin County, just over the Golden Gate bridge north of San Francisco. It is an affluent community virtually synonymous with what passes for liberal or progressive politics today.

3 Daniel Joseph Polikoff, *Reset or Renaissance, vol 1.: Two Roads: An American Scholar's Covid Chronicle* (Spencertown, NY: Portal Books, 2024).

4 By the time this book is published, this sentence may require revision.

5 Charles Eisenstein, "The Human Family," Dec. 4, 2021, https://charleseisenstein.substack.com. Eisenstein collected his Covid-related writings in his book *The Coronation, Essays on the Covid Moment* (White River, VT: Chelsea Green Publishing, 2022).

6 Ibid.

7 The "war fronts" described and discussed are: nature, science, medicine, public health, democracy, and society.

8 Klaus Schwab and Thierry Malleret, *COVID-19: The Great Reset* (Geneva, Switzerland: Forum Publishing, 2020).

9 Richard Ramsbotham, "COVID-19 and 'The Great Reset': What Is It All About and Where Is It Heading?" *New View*, issue 97, autumn 2020, 4.

10 Schwab and Malleret, *The Great Reset*, 12.

11 Ibid., 15.

12 Schwab and Malleret (16–17), as cited in Ramsbotham (4).

13 For a definitive treatment of this subject, see Robert F. Kennedy Jr., *The Wuhan Coverup* (New York: Skyhorse Publishing, 2023).

14 "Event 201: A Global Pandemic Exercise," co-sponsored by The John Hopkins Center for Health Security, The World Economic Forum, and The Bill and Melinda Gates Foundation, https://www.centerforhealthsecurity.org/event201/.

15 Ibid.

16 Ibid., "Recommendations" tab.

17 Ibid.Hotwash and Conclusions video clip of the Communications discussion.

18 Matthew Harrington on Linkedin, https://www.linkedin.com/in/matthew-harrington-558987b.

19 Kennedy, *The Real Anthony Fauci*, 428.

20 Event 201 website, Highlight Reel.

21 In the aftermath of the 2024 election, Mark Zuckerberg of Meta confessed to widespread censorship implemented (in his account) at the behest of the government, and initiated reversal of some of the offending policies.

22 Brianna Dresser, testimony before the U.S. Senate Expert Panel on Vaccine Mandates, Nov., 2, 2021, https://www.youtube.com/watch?v=lkVN3KwDfvI.

23 Kennedy, *Fauci*, 429.

24 Ibid., 428.

25 Ibid.

26 Ibid., 429.

27 Ibid., 427.

28 Ibid.

29 Ibid.

30 Mercola and Cummins, *The Truth About Covid-19* (White River, VT, and London: Chelsea Green, 2021), 44.

31 Ibid., 45.

32 Ibid.

33 Ibid., 48.

34 Schwab and Malleret, *The Great Reset*, 96.

35 Ibid., 97.
36 Ibid.
37 Ibid., 89.
38 Ibid., 91–92.
39 "What Will It Take to Defeat the Coronavirus," Zany Minton Beddoes interviews Bill Gates, *The Economist* podcast, August 20, 2022, https://www.economist.com/podcasts/2020/08/20/what-will-it-take-to-defeat-the-coronavirus.
40 Ramsbotham, "COVID-19 and 'The Great Reset,'" 6.
41 Beddoes/Gates interview, *The Economist.*
42 Schwab and Malleret, *The Great Reset,* 220.
43 Ibid., 224.
44 Ibid., 217.
45 Kennedy, *Fauci*, xix.
46 Ibid., xx.
47 Schwab and Malleret, *The Great Reset,* 156–57.
48 Charles Eisenstein, "The Coronation," March, 2020, https://charleseisenstein.org/essays/the-coronation/.
49 Ibid.
50 Ibid.
51 Ibid.
52 George Orwell, *1984,* as cited in Charles Eisenstein, "A Path Will Rise to Meet Us," Dec. 17, 2020, https://charleseisenstein.substack.com/p/a-path-will-rise-to-meet-us.
53 Luke Kemp, "The 'Stomp Reflex': When Governments Abuse Emergency Powers," *BBC Future,* April 17, 2021, https://www.bbc.com/future/article/20210427-the-stomp-reflex-when-governments-abuse-emergency-powers.
54 Ibid.
55 Interview with Dr. Robert Malone, *The Joe Rogan Experience* #1757, Dec. 2021, https://open.spotify.com/episode/3SCsueX2bZdbEzRtKOCEyT.
56 Eisenstein, "A Path Will Rise to Meet Us."
57 Christine Anderson public statement, replayed on "A Slippery Slope," *The Highwire* #245, Dec. 9, 2021, https://thehighwire.com/videos/episode-245-the-slippery-slope/.
58 Russell Brand, "This is What History Warns Us", *Under the Skin* podcast, Nov. 25, 2021, https://www.youtube.com/watch?v=_8ZcOWYsE7M.
59 Ralph Waldo Emerson, "Self-Reliance," in *Emerson: Essays and Lectures* (New York: Library of America, 1983), 282.
60 Henry David Thoreau, "Civil Disobedience" in Owen Thomas, ed. *Walden and Civil Disobedience,* (New York: W.W. Norton,1966), 230–31.
61 *Holy Bible,* King James Version, I Corinthians 13:11.
62 See *Reset or Renaissance* vol. 1, ch. 34.
63 Tennessee Liberty Network website, https://tnliberty.com.
64 *The Highwire,* #249.
65 Federal document as displayed on *The Highwire,* Episode #249.
66 *The Highwire,* #249.
67 See, for instance, Darragh Roche, "Fauci Said Masks 'Not Really Effective in Keeping out Virus' Email Reveals," *Newsweek,* June 2, 2021, https://www.newsweek.com/fauci-said-masks-not-really-effective-keeping-out-virus-email-reveals-1596703.
68 See *Reset or Renaissance,* vol 1, ch. 20 ("ICU Interlude: In-Hospital (Mis) Treatment").
69 *The Highwire,* #249
70 Kennedy, *The Real Anthony Fauci,* 63–70.
71 Ibid.
72 *The Highwire,* #249.
73 Eisenstein, "A Path Will Rise to Meet Us."
74 Joseph Cambray retired from his post as President in 2022.
75 Some have fittingly called this tactic "the weaponization of compassion."
76 See *Reset or Renaissance*, vol. 1, 308.
77 Cf. Interview with Dr. Robert Malone, *The Joe Rogan Experience* #1757, Dec. 2021, https://open.spotify.com/episode/3SCsueX2bZdbEzRtKOCEyT. Malone's source for his discussion of "mass formation," and mine for

the identification of its chief enabling conditions, is Belgian psychologist Mattias Desmet. See Mattias Desmet, *The Psychology of Totalitarianism* (White River, VT: Chelsea Green Publishing, 2022).

78 Desmet, *The Psychology of Totalitarianism.*

79 John Stuart Mill, *On Liberty.*

80 "Pope Emphasizes 'Moral Obligation' to Get Vaccinated," *San Francisco Chronicle,* Jan. 11, 2021, A5.

81 Cf. Interview with Dr. Robert Malone, *The Joe Rogan Experience* #1757.

82 Charles Eisenstein, "Mob Morality and the Unvaxxed," Aug. 1, 2021, https://charleseisenstein.substack.com/p/mob-morality-and-the-unvaxxed.

83 Cf. for instance Gerard Gallagher, "No Doubt Trump Will Face Surprise Infectious Disease Outbreak," *Healio,* Jan. 11, 2017, https://www.healio.com/news/infectious-disease/20170111/fauci-no-doubt-trump-will-face-surprise-infectious-disease-outbreak; and Bill Gates, "The Next Outbreak? We're Not Ready," *Ted* talk, March 2015, https://www.ted.com/talks/bill-gates-the-next-outbreak-we're-not-ready?

84 Kennedy, *Fauci,* 357.

85 Ibid.

86 Ibid., 358.

87 Ibid., 359.

88 Ibid., 357, 359.

89 Ibid., 359.

90 Ibid., 358–9.

91 Ibid., 359.

92 Ibid., 131.

93 Ibid., 360.

94 Ibid., 361.

95 Ibid.

96 Ibid.

97 Ibid., 363.

98 Ibid., 365.

99 Ibid., 378.

100 Ibid.

101 Ibid., 378–9.

102 Ibid., 379.

103 Ibid., 381, 380.

104 Ibid., 380ff.

105 Ibid., 381.

106 Ibid., 393.

107 Ibid., 392.

108 Ibid., 393.

109 Ibid.

110 Ibid., 392.

111 Cf. An e-mail sent Jan. 31 from Andersen to Fauci, which states, "I should mention that after discussions earlier today, Eddy, Bob, Mike, and myself all find the genome inconsistent with expectations from evolutionary theory." These e-mails were acquired via FOIA requests by ICAN. See Fatal Flaws, *The Highwire* #251 (The Jaxen Report), Jan. 20, 2022.

112 Ibid., 380.

113 K. G. Andersen, A. Rambaut, W. I. Lipkin, et al., "The Proximal Origin of SARS-CoV-2," *Nature Medicine* 26, 450-452 (20202).https://doi.org/10.1038/s41591-020-0820-9.

114 Jerry Dunleavy, "Fauci Worked Behind the Scenes to Cast Doubt on Wuhan Lab Leak Hypothesis," *Washington Examiner,* June 2, 2021, https://www.washingtonexaminer.com/news/fauci-worked-behind-scenes-cast-doubt-wuhan-lab-leak-hypothesis.

115 Charles Calisher, Dennis Carroll, Rita Colwell, Ronald B. Corley, Peter Daszak, Christian Drosten et al, "Statement in Support of the Scientists, Public Health Professionals, and Medical Professionals of China Combatting COVID-19," *The Lancet,* V 395, 10226, E42–43, March 7, 2020, DOI: https://doi.org/10.1016/S0140-6736(20)30418-9.

116 I have only scratched the surface of available evidence in these few paragraphs. Both Megyn Kelly ("The Truth About Fauci and Collins," *The Megyn Kelly Show,* Jan. 14, 2022, https://www.youtube.com/watch?v=aa6-EFoJoV4) and Jeffrey Jaxen on *The Highwire* (*The Highwire,* #251, Jan. 20, 2022) give detailed reports on the extensive evidence documenting a carefully orchestrated cover-up. The whole episode suggests that charges of "conspiracy theory"

are often a vain pretext encouraging us to divert our gaze from those with blood on their hands.

117 https://en.wikipedia.org/wiki/Johns_Hopkins_Center_for_Health_Security.
118 Johns Hopkins Center for Health Security Website, https://www.centerforhealthsecurity.org/our-people/inglesby/.
119 Kennedy, *Fauci,* 382.
120 Cited in Tom Inglesby, "Letter from the Director," UPMC Center for Biosecurity 2010–2011 Annual Report, https://www.centerforhealthsecurity.org/who-we-are/annual_report/pdfs/2011-CHS-annual-report.pdf.
121 Ibid.
122 Kennedy, *Fauci,* 382.
123 Ibid.
124 Ibid., 384.
125 Ibid., 384–85.
126 Ibid., 404.
127 Ibid., 405.
128 Ibid.
129 Neo is the nickname of the protagonist in the 1999 Wachowski Brothers film *The Matrix.*
130 Ibid., 407.
131 "Bill and Melinda Gates Pledge $10 Billion in Call for Decade of Vaccines," Bill and Melinda Gates Foundation Press Release, January 2010, https://www.gatesfoundation.org/ideas/media-center/press-releases/2010/01/bill-and-melinda-gates-pledge-$10-billion-in-call-for-decade-of-vaccines.
132 Kennedy, *Fauci,* 303.
133 Ibid.
134 Ibid., 257.
135 Ibid., 385.
136 Kennedy, *Fauci,* 389.
137 Ibid., 405.
138 Iibd., 407.
139 ibid., 407–8
140 Schwab, *The Fourth Industrial Revolution* (New York: Crown Publishing, 2016), 7
141 Ibid., 409.
142 Ibid.
143 Ibid.
144 The WEF cited in Ramsbotham, "Covid-19 and 'The Great Reset,'" 4.
145 Schwab and Malleret, *Great Reset,* 151–52.
146 Ibid.
147 Pierre Teilhard de Chardin, *The Phenomenon of Man* (New York: Harper and Row, 1959). First published in 1955 as *Le Phenomene Humain* by Editions du Seuil in Paris.
148 Genesis, 1:27
149 Aldous Huxley, "Transhumanism," in *New Bottles for New Wine* (London: Chatto and Windus, 1957), 13–17.
150 Max More, "Transhumanism: Towards a Futurist Philosophy," https://web.archive.org/web/20051029125153/ http://www.maxmore.com/transhum.htm.
151 Ibid.
152 Bostrom and Pearce, "FAQ: What is Transhumanism?," https://whatistranshumanism.org.
153 Kennedy, *Fauci,* 410. It need be noted that one may easily read Kennedy as introducing Jacques Ellul as an early proponent of transhumanism. Ellul was, to the contrary, an early critic of the capacity of technology to bend society towards authoritarianism.
154 Ibid.
155 The term "religio-mythical" implies that any system of belief necessarily entails a certain way of narrating the human adventure, and so revolves around a given *mythos*, or emplotment of human destiny.
156 Paul Kingsnorth, "The Cross and the Machine," *First Things*, June, 2021.
157 I. K. Taimni, *Man, God, and the Universe* (Wheaton, IL: The Theosophical Publishing House, 1969).
158 Ralph Waldo Emerson, "Nature" in *Emerson, Essays and Lectures* (New York: Library of America, 1983), 21.
159 From Kepler, *Harmonia Mundi,* as quoted in Edouard Shuré, *From Sphinx to Christ* (Kessinger Publishing), 18.
160 These had previously been segregated, the former regarded as a branch of the liberal arts and the latter belonging to the study of natural

philosophy.
161 Ibid.
162 Richard Dawkins, *The God Delusion* (New York: Houghton Mifflin, 2006), 36.
163 William Wordsworth, "Lines Composed a Few Miles above Tintern Abbey," l. 78.
164 Richard Tarnas, *The Passion of the Western Mind* (New York: Harmony Books, 1991), 278.
165 Ibid.
166 Michael Pollan, *How to Change Your Mind: The New Science of Psychedelics* (London: Allen Books, 2018), 12.
167 Ibid., 279.
168 Ibid., 280.
169 Raymond Kurzweil, *The Singularity is Near: When Humans Transcend Biology* (New York: Penguin Books, 2005) as cited in Romanyshyn, *The Frankenstein Prophecies,* 58.
170 Robert D. Romanyshyn, *Victor Frankenstein, the Monster and the Shadows of Technology* (London and New York: Routledge, 2019), 58.
171 Ibid.
172 Ibid.
173 Kurzweil, *Singularity* as cited in Romanyshyn, 57
174 As cited in Kingsnorth, "The Cross and the Machine."
175 Kingsnorth, "The Cross and the Machine."
176 Ibid.
177 Ibid.
178 While the sharp edge of Covid crisis has been blunted, Matrix forces remain intent on kindred Great Reset-related initiatives, including the proposed amended International Health Regulations and indeed the entire WHO-sponsored One Health initiative. Similarly, as the 2024–2025 bird flu fuss demonstrates, the public health (fake) pandemic machinery can still rev up even with Dr. Fauci no longer at the wheel.
179 The time period referred to would be the three or four months following the emergence of omicron, and so the last months of 2021 and the beginning of 2022.
180 Kingsnorth, "The Cross and the Machine," *First Things*, June, 2021.
181 Patrick J. Deneen, *Why Liberalism Failed* (New Haven and London: Yale University Press, 2018).
182 Max Horkeimer and Theodor W. Adorno, *Dialectic of Enlightenment*, trans. Edmund Jephcott (Redwood City, CA: Stanford University Press, 2002), The authors began the text in 1942; German editions appeared in 1944 and 1947.
183 Horkeimer and Adorno, *Dialectic of Enlightenment,* 1
184 Ibid., 2
185 BigTech moguls like Bill Gates, Jeff Bezos, and others, whose enormous wealth affords them significant political clout, offer unmistakable examples. I have already referenced many of Gates's activities; Bezos's ownership of *The Washington Post* is just one of the Amazon founder's avenues of political influence. Yet the principle applies broadly, and—opening fields of creative entrepreneurship—can have constructive as well as negative consequences.
186 Ibid.
187 Ibid., 4–5.
188 Ibid., 6–7.
189 Ibid., 7.
190 These are all vaccine-injured persons. See Polikoff, *Reset or Renaissance*, vol. 1, 262–273.
191 I do not here imply any temporal evolution moving from Descartes to Bacon. Bacon was born in 1561, and Descartes in 1596; Bacon published his first major work (*Essays*) the year after Descartes' birth. Nonetheless, they were intellectual contemporaries in the first decades of the 17th century, and the currents of their thought flow together in the genesis of the modern scientific mind.
192 Adorno and Horkheimer, *Enlightenment*, 5–6.
193 Ibid., 6.
194 Ibid.
195 Ibid., 21.
196 Ibid.
197 Ibid., 21–22.

198 Ibid., 18.
199 Ibid., 24.
200 Voltaire, *Traité sur la Tolérance, A l'occasion de la mort de Jean Calas*, 1763. Recently translated by Desmond M. Clarke as *Treatise on Toleration* (UK: Penguin Classics, 2016).
201 John Locke, *Two Treatises of Government and A Letter Concerning Toleration* (Digireads Publishing, 2015).
202 Charles de Secondat Baron de Montesquieu, *The Spirit of the Law* (New York: Hafner Publishing, 1949). Original publication: 1748.
203 Kant, *Toward Perpetual Peace and Other Writings on Politics, Peace and History*, Ed. Pauline Kleingold, Tr. David Colclasure (New Haven, CT: Yale University Press, 2006).
204 Thomas Paine, *Common Sense and Selected Works of Thomas Paine* (San Diego: Word Cloud Classics, 2014).
205 Patrick J. Deneen, *Why Liberalism Failed* (New Haven, CT, and London: Yale University Press, 2018).
206 Deneen, *Liberalism*, 179.
207 Horkheimer and Adorno, *Enlightenment*, 9.
208 Deneen, *Liberalism*, 180.
209 The "deep state" Deneen refers to may be regarded as another name for what I call the Matrix, especially if the concept is not limited to the government of discrete nation states but includes global networks.
210 Deneen, *Liberalism*, 182.
211 Ibid., 21.
212 Ibid., 21–22.
213 Ibid., 22.
214 Ibid., 23–4.
215 Ibid., 24.
216 Bacon was, however, deeply involved in politics for virtually his entire life, and certainly (as is consistent with his view of knowledge as an avenue to power) ambitious of advancement. It can hardly be a coincidence that Thomas Hobbes was, at one point, Lord Bacon's secretary. Some of Bacon's political dealings enter our story in the concluding chapter of this book.
217 Tarnas, *Passion*, 279–80.
218 Deneen, *Liberalism*, 25.
219 Ibid.
220 Ibid., 26.
221 Ibid., 25.
222 Ibid.
223 Ibid., 26–7.
224 Ibid., 27.
225 Each of these figures was actually born in the 16th century: Bacon in 1561, Hobbes in 1588, and Descartes in 1591. I nonetheless think of them as 17th century thinkers as virtually all of their significant work (with the exception of Bacon's *Essays*, published in 1597) appeared in that century and features as an integral part of its intellectual character.
226 Ibid., 31.
227 Thomas Hobbes, *Leviathan* (Oxford: Oxford University Press, 1909), 99.
228 Ibid., 128.
229 Ibid., 48–9.
230 Ibid., 49.
231 Ibid.
232 Ibid., 51.
233 That is, my liberty to value the preservation of my life may be recognized—that cardinal "natural law" is observed—but there is no ideal value placed upon my freedom to make that decision for myself, at least in cases where my action or inaction may affect others. In other words, freedom of choice or bodily autonomy are not really recognized as *principles* that possess an intrinsic worth as ideals. In the liberal system, once I have consented to award authority to the state, my opinion as to what may preserve (my) life does not carry real weight. It is the state's decision as to what measure may preserve the *most* lives that matters; the numeric count or *calculation*, so familiar in Covid World today, of how many lives mass vaccination, or masking (etc.) may "save."
234 Here it is not only the apparatus of the nation state, but, as well, that of international organization (as represented, for instance, by WHO) that is relevant. Indeed, it is possible

for the nation state itself to become subject to and dominated by the globalist apparatus represented by organizations like the WHO and WEF.

235 Other, equally crucial dimensions of Locke's philosophy, honoring "natural rights" that cannot be reduced to material or utilitarian terms and which help found "spiritual democracy," will be amply discussed in later chapters.

236 Recall the rhetoric employed by Bill and Melinda Gates as they called for a "Decade of Vaccines" (see Chapter 3). "Vaccines" declared Melinda Gates, "are a miracle."

237 Horkheimer and Adorno, *Enlightenment,* 22.

238 Ibid., 23.

239 Ibid.

240 Ibid.

241 Ibid.

242 The irony, of course, is that such "rationality" tends, by virtue of the logic intrinsic to the system, to culminate in a flood of patent irrationality that breeds either chaos, or totalizing conformity, or both. Many instances from Covid World could be cited: the imposition of compulsory vaccine mandates despite knowledge that vaccination does not stop transmission; compelling even those who have natural immunity—and so superior protection—to undergo vaccination; locking down access to the outdoors; requiring masks in restaurants, which nonetheless are removed for eating and drinking; etc.

243 Ibid.

244 Ibid., 23–24.

245 Thomas Hobbes, *Leviathan* (Oxford: Oxford University Press, 1909), 8.

246 Ibid.

247 Ibid.

248 Deneen, *Liberalism,* 183–84.

249 Ibid.192.

250 Ibid., 183.

251 William Wordsworth, *The Prelude,* 1805, Book VI, l. 352–55.

252 William Wordsworth, "The Prelude," 1805, Book X, l. 692–702.

253 Thomas Paine, *The American Crisis.* Written in Dec. 1776. https://www.ushistory.org/paine/crisis/c-01.htm.

254 The fourth chapter (122–134) of my book *In the Image of Orpheus: Rilke—A Soul History* (Asheville, NC: Chiron Publications, 2011) analyses the language in which Augustine describes the all-important conversion experience that grounded his theology. I discuss in some detail how Augustine's version of the "fundamental tenets of the Christian soul," as inscribed in the Pauline passage that catalyzed his conversion, consists of renunciation of sin, moral aversion to the world. belief in doctrine, and reliance upon prior (scriptural and priestly) authority.

255 Many have taken issue with this Petrarchan coinage, and with justification. Even so, in the early phase of the Middle Ages—which one could define as the many hundreds of years succeeding the fall of Rome up until the 12th or 13th centuries—one could find good reason to credit the relevance of Petrarch's phrase.

256 Carl L. Becker, *The Heavenly City of the Eighteenth-Century Philosophers,* (New Haven, CT, and London: Yale University Press, 1932), 47.

257 Tarnas, *The Passion of the Western Mind,* 147.

258 Ibid., 146.

259 Augustine's almost decade-long involvement with Manichaeism, a dualistic gnostic doctrine that sees the material world as inherently fallen or evil, likely also contributed to Augustine's understanding of original sin.

260 Pagden, *The Enlightenment,* 49.

261 Ibid., 45.

262 Aquinas, *Summa Theologica*, Part II (First Part), Q, XCI, art ii, as cited in Becker, *The Heavenly City,* 3.

263 Padgen, *The Enlightenment,* 47.

264 Ibid.

265 Tarnas, *Passion,* 201.

266 Ibid., 202.

267 Stephen Jay Gould, *Rocks of Ages: Science and Religion in the Fullness*

of Life (New York: Ballantine Books, 2002).

268 Unfortunately, I cannot locate the source of this translation. It is inscribed in my book *Rue Rilke*, which I wrote in 1993. When that book was finally published in 2016, I sought the source of the translation transcribed in my travel journal, soliciting aid from a Petrarch scholar at my alma mater, but to no avail.

269 Ibid., 211.

270 Pico della Mirandola, *Oration on the Dignity of Man*. Translated by Mary Martin McLaughlin in *The Portable Renaissance Reader*, edited by J. B. Ross and M. M. McLaughlin (New York: Penguin, 1977), 478.

271 Tarnas, *Passion*, 224

272 Of course, Columbus's voyage of discovery represents another, decidedly worldly, dimension of the expansion of European consciousness that transpired in this historic period, one entailing the atrocities—both material and spiritual—associated with the whole project of colonization. It is only to be expected that the darker side of the desire to know and master the whole of the world characteristic of modernity would be present at its inception; that the nefarious dialectic of enlightenment can already be glimpsed in the shadow of the sun-lit brilliance of Renaissance man.

273 As cited in Klaus Schwab and Thierry Malleret, *Covid-19: The Great Reset* (Geneva, Switzerland: Forum Publishing, 2020), 15. The citation is from Barbara Tuchman's *A Distant Mirror: The Calamitous 14th Century* (New York: Random House, 1987).

274 Ralph Waldo Emerson, "Martin Luther," *The Early Lectures of Ralph Waldo Emerson,* ed. Stephen E. Whicher and Robert E. Spiller (Cambridge, Mass: Belknap Press, 1966), 120.

275 Generally speaking, purchase of indulgences offered, not absolution, but reduction of time spent in Purgatory.

276 The Catholic Church traditionally administers seven sacraments: baptism, confirmation, confession, communion, marriage, ordination, and last annointing.

277 As presented in Tarnas, *Passion,* 239. In his Luther lecture, Emerson renders the last lines: "It is neither safe nor prudent to do aught against conscience. Here stand I; I cannot do otherwise." This is, of course, closer to Churchill's text.

278 Not that Luther himself exhibited any propensity to ascetism. On the contrary, Luther was known for his hearty manner and down-to-earth humor, as well as attachment to his wife, Katharina von Bora. In all of this, a kind of separation between the sacred and profane and the laws and manners proper to each—after a distinctly un-Catholic fashion—may be discerned.

279 New York Governor Hochul's early claim that the vaccine was a gift from God represents one notable exception.

280 The full title is *De revolutionibus orbium coelestium (The Revolution of the Heavenly Spheres).*

281 Tarnas, *Passion,* 252.

282 Ibid., 263.

283 Becker, *Heavenly City,* 47.

284 https://x.com/wef/status /983378870819794945.

285 Thomas Paine, "The Age of Reason", in *Common Sense and Selected Works of Thomas Paine* (San Diego: Word Cloud Classics, 2014), 335.

286 Alexander Pope, "Epigram on Sir Isaac Newton."

287 Tarnas, *Passion*, 270.

288 There is ambiguity here. As discussed, the nominalist tradition stemming from Ockham—while acknowledging the epistemological power of science in the natural sphere—did not credit reason with the capacity to comprehend theological or religious truth, and so prepared the splitting of religion and science.

289 Pagden, *The Enlightenment,* 43.

290 Ernest Gellner, *Postmodernism, Reason and Religion* (London and New York: Routledge, 1992), 80.

291 Ibid.
292 "Party of Humanity" is a term coined by historian Peter Gay. Peter Gay, *The Party of Humanity: Essays in the French Enlightenment* (New York: W.W. Norton, 1971). The aristocratic character of Enlightenment figures such as Voltaire do not necessarily contradict this perspective.
293 Ibid., x.
294 Hobbes, Locke, Montesquieu, Rousseau, and Kant, to name a few.
295 Tarnas, *Passion,* 243–44.
296 Ibid., 244.
297 Ibid.
298 John Locke, *Two Treatises of Government and A Letter Concerning Toleration* (Digireads Publishing, 2015).
299 Locke's *Two Treatises* were actually written well before their publication in 1690, and were intended to affect the course of events that eventually led to the so-called Glorious Revolution in England in 1688. The Glorious Revolution, like the English Civil Wars which transpired mid-century (1642–1651) diminished the power of royalty in Britain. One could say that, whereas the American and French revolutions took place in the 18th century, the 17th qualifies as England's "revolutionary" century. The sociopolitical profile in each country differs profoundly.
300 Locke's *First Treatise of Civil Government* mounts a point-by-point rebuttal of a contemporary (1680) defense of that doctrine presented in Sir Robert Filmer's *Patriarcha.*
301 There are naturally notable exceptions, especially among the French, such as d'Holbach, de la Mettrie. A strong argument can be made that others, including Helvetius and even Diderot, were effectively atheists, but prevented from open avowal of their views by the danger that might incur.
302 Isaac Newton, *Philosophiae Naturalis Principia Mathematica* as cited in Robert Westfall, "The Rise of Science and the Decline of Orthodox Christianity: A Study of Kepler, Descartes, and Newton," in *God and Nature: Historical Essays in the Encounter between Christianity and Science,* Ed. David C. Lindberg and Ronald L. Number (Berkeley: University of California Press, 1986), 239.
303 Margaret L. Jacob, "Christianity and the Newtonian Worldview" in Lindberg and Number, *God and Nature,* 245.
304 Baron de Montesquieu, *The Spirit of the Laws* (New York: Hafner Publishing, 1949), 1.
305 "Consent" here is largely a theoretical condition of participation in society rather than any concrete act performed by actual citizens. However, as we will see, the notion of consent assumes a different practical force with Locke, not because it is necessarily supposed to actually have been given by citizens, but because (despite that hypothetical status) it may in concrete fact be *revoked.*
306 Locke, *Two Treatises and a Letter Concerning Toleration,* 102.
307 Ibid.
308 John Locke, *Two Treatises of Government: A Critical Edition with Introduction by Peter Laslett* (London: Cambridge University Press, 1960), 289.
309 Scholarship can indeed verify a line of significant influence here, one mediated by Locke's reliance on the writings of late sixteenth-century theologian Robert Hooker. Cf. Frederick Copleston, *A History of Philosophy* (New York: Doubleday, 1964), V. 5, Part I, 137.
310 James MacGregor Burns, *Fire and Light: How the Enlightenment Transformed Our World* (New York: St. Martin's Press, 2013), 37.
311 As cited in Frederick Copleston, *A History of Philosophy* (Garden City, NY: Image Books, 1959), vol. 5, Part I, 137.
312 Ibid.
313 https://www.archives.gov/founding-docs/declaration-transcript.
314 Pagden, *The Enlightenment,* 8–9

315 Ibid., x–xi.
316 Gellner, *Postmodernism, Reason and Religion*, 80.
317 Jean Le Rond d'Alembert, *Preliminary Discourse to the Encyclopedia of Diderot* (Chicago: University of Chicago Press, 1995). The *Preliminary Discourse* was originally published in 1751.
318 Immanuel Kant, "An Answer to the Question: What is Enlightenment?" in *Towards Perpetual Peace and Other Writings on Politics, Peace, and History*, ed. Pauline Kleingold (New Haven, CT: Yale University Press, 2006), 17.
319 The way Plotinus speaks of this "authentic Human-Principle" as the "We," in deliberate contrast to the "Ours," makes clear the universality we are speaking of here is not a function of collectivity or similarity conceived as an extrapolition from a multiplicity of persons, but a real ideal or spiritual factor. In the first Ennead, Plotinus writes: "...before this there was only the 'Ours'; but at this stage stands the We (the authentic Human-Principle)..." He goes on to speak of human nature as "mingled in a lower phase, but above that point [is] the beginning of the veritable man, distinct from all that is kin to the lion..." Plotinus, *The Enneads* (Burdette, NY: Larson Publications, 1992), 28.
320 Kant, *Toward Perpetual Peace.*
321 Pagden, *Enlightenment,* xii.
322 *Puer Papers,* ed James Hillman (Dallas: Spring Publications, 1989).
323 T.S. Eliot, "Tradition and the Individual Talent" in Eliot, *The Sacred Wood: Essays on Poetry and Criticism* (London, New York: Methuen, 1960), 47–60.
324 These and the following references allude to events discussed in the first volume of *Reset or Renaissance.* For Cait Corrigan, see pp. 28–31; for Donald Walsh, p. 33; for Paul Marik, 106, 322.
325 Karl Popper, *The Logic of Scientific Discovery* (1959; reprt., Eastford, CT: Martino Fine, 2014). Popper actually maintains that scientific truth can never properly or logically verified, only falsified. Scientific "truth" is thus never absolute, but a form of imaginative conjecture which best fits available evidence. Popper was not a positivist.
326 The Spirit will be discussed at length in the further course of this book, especially in chapters 10, 14, and 15.
327 "Superavit" is a poem in Rilke's first book of poems, *Larenopfer* (*Offering to the Lares*). For a discussion of the poem in this (my) translation, see Daniel Joseph Polikoff, *In the Image of Orpheus: Rilke, A Soul History* (Wilmette, IL: Chiron Publications), 17.
328 Paul Kingsnorth, *Real England* (London: Granta Publishings, 2009).
329 Paul Kingsnorth, "In the Desert of the Real," May 3, 2022, https://paulkingsnorth.substack.com/p/in-the-desert-of-the-real?s=w.
330 Ibid.
331 Ibid.
332 Paul Kingsnorth, "What Progress Wants," May 24, 2022, https://paulkingsnorth.substack.com/p/what-progress-wants?s=r.
333 Allen Ginsberg, *Howl and other Poems* (San Francisco: City Lights, 1956–59), 17.
334 Ibid.
335 René Guénon, *The Reign of Quantity and the Sign of the Times* (1945; Hillsdale, NY: Sophia Perennis, 2001).
336 Ibid.
337 Ibid.
338 Ralph Waldo Emerson, "The Method of Nature" *in Lectures and Essays* (New York: Library of America, 1983), 130
339 Rainer Maria Rilke, "The Young Workman's Letter," in *Where Silence Reigns: Selected Prose*, trans. G. Craig Houston (New York: New Directions, 1978), 69.
340 Ralph Waldo Emerson, "The Method of Nature," in *Emerson, Essays and Lectures* (NY: Library of America, 1983), 130.
341 Ralph Waldo Emerson, *Nature* in

Emerson, Essays and Lectures, (NY: Library of America, 1983), 5. *Nature* was originally published in 1836.

342 Ibid.

343 Philosophy distinguishes between created things in their passive ontic existence (*natura naturata*) and the active formative agency that creates things as they are (*natura naturans*). I follow tradition in using "nature" here, and throughout this text, as inclusive of both aspects.

344 Michael Pollan, *How to Change Your Mind: The New Science of Psychedelics* (Allen Books, London: 2018), 12.

345 Samuel Taylor Coleridge represents a post-Enlightenment philosopher who thought deeply about the nature of law and the development of the idea of law in intellectual history. For Coleridge, a "law" possesses the status of a unitary property or principle, intrinsic in which is the causative power that ensures the activity exhibited by particular phenomena diverse in time, place, and contingent condition, conform to the same pattern. Coleridge phrased the matter thus: "This antecedent cause or principle...it has since the time of Bacon and Kepler been customary to call a law.... We derive from it a progressive insight into the necessity and generation of diverse phenomena." Cited in Owen Barfield, *What Coleridge Thought* (Middlefield, CT: Wesleyan University Press, 1971), 44, note 7.

346 Montesquieu complains of this paradoxical logic in the second paragraph of his *Spirit of the Laws*. "They who assert that a blind fatality produced the various effects we behold in this world talk very absurdly: for can anything be more unreasonable than to pretend that a blind fatality could be productive of intelligent beings?" The modern person, of course, smiles at such naive incredulity, secure in the knowledge that Montesquieu published his book a century before Darwin introduced his ideas of evolution by natural selection. Intelligent persons after Darwin, however, have considered the latter, in particular, as a *deus ex machina* insufficient to account for all the miracles (inclusive of the miracle of life itself) attributed to it. Nor does any argument from biology answer the questions posed by physics and cosmology pursued in the continuation of my text.

347 Ursula Goodenough, *The Sacred Depths of Nature* (Oxford: Oxford University Press, 1998), 11.

348 Aristotle identified four causes: material, efficient, formal, and final. These pertain, respectively, to the material substance involved in causation; the agent force; the form or idea implicated; and the motivating purpose or telos. As a general rule, modern science does not recognize or think in terms of formal and final causes.

349 The critique pursued here cannot be effectively answered by contending that modern science no longer embraces the mechanical philosophy per se, and that its understanding of the world is premised upon complex forms of probability, the emergent properties of natural systems, and the like modifications of the classic paradigm. The critique remains applicable and in force unless and until science explicitly recognizes immaterial or spiritual forces or intelligences as the source of order and law in nature. Premodern forms of knowledge or science that antedate "the reign of quantity" do so (medieval alchemy represents one instance). Resort to such esoteric or "occult" streams cannot, however, be accommodated within the forms of rationality definitive of modern conception and methods of what remains normative for "science" today.

350 Plato, *The Republic,* Bk. VI, 528e, trans. Thomas Taylor (V. 1, 373-374) as cited in Anthony Damiani, *Astronoeisis* (Burdette, NY: Larson Publications, 2000), 9.

351 Ibid.
352 Anthony Damiani, *Astronoeisis* (Burdette, NY: Larson Publications, 2000), 9.
353 As cited in Adorno and Horkheimer, *Dialectic of Enlightenment*, 1.
354 Richard Westfall, "The Rise of Science and the Decline of Orthodox Christianity," 227. It's mentioned earlier.
355 Damiani, *Astronoesis,* 9.
356 Tarnas, *Passion*, 307–08. The famous citation at the end refers to the French astronomer and mathematician LaPlace's reply to Napoleon when the latter inquired after the role of God in LaPlace's astronomical cosmology.
357 *Politically speaking,* the left-leaning heirs of Enlightenment Rationalist Fundamentalism consequently often come to view belief in God as obstructive of the rationally and humanely oriented technological applications of the scientific intellect that supposedly leads to "progress" in the social as well as material world.
358 Psychologically speaking, maximum inflation transforms into maximum deflation; excessive pride converts, even, to self-loathing.
359 Referring to *Two Roads,* Volume I of *Reset or Renaissance*
360 Ralph Waldo Emerson, "Lecture on the Times" in *Emerson: Essays and Lectures* (New York: Viking, 1983), 151.
361 Ibid.
362 Born in Chicago, I grew up in the northern suburb of Highland Park. My parents continued to reside there, in the family home, for 65 years, so that I revisited Highland Park throughout my life. My parents finally moved to a senior residence near my sister in Keene, New Hampshire, in January 2022. My 92-year-old mother died nine days after arrival in Keene. In May, we held a memorial for her in the Community Center of the town we had all shared, and so were back in Highland Park again. On July 4th, Central Avenue, where I had loved to go to Baskin and Robbins for coconut ice cream when a child, and where we had walked and breakfasted a little over a month earlier, was the scene of yet another horrific mass shooting. I do not know if I shall ever visit Highland Park again.
363 Emerson, *Nature,* in *Essays and Lectures*, 5.
364 Yuval Noah Harari is the author of two best-sellers. *Sapiens: A Brief History of Humankind* (New York: Harper, 2015) and *Ecce Deus: A Brief History of Tomorrow* (New York: Harper, 2018). Harari may well be the favorite intellectual of the WEF crowd, and speaks often of the immeasurable possibilities opened by new technologies. While occasionally warning of their dangers, Harari generally touts the inevitability of one or another version of a transhumanist future. The title of *Ecce Deus* ("Behold, God") expresses the gist of the modern worldview as I seek to elucidate it.
365 I cite the catchy phrase in part on account of my own emphasis on logos in this book, yet it need be acknowledged that in this context Emerson did not employ the phrase to refer to Nature so much as to the riches of continental philosophy conveyed to him in the form of an article by Frederic Henry Hedge. See Joel Porte, *Representative Man: Ralph Waldo Emerson in His Time* (New York: Oxford University Press, 1979), 56. The relevant journal entry (as cited by Porte) dates from late Dec. 1833.
366 Ibid., 40.
367 By the time Emerson wrote *Nature* in 1836, he could draw on decades—almost half-a-century—of Romantic philosophy that offered both rigorously systematic as well as imaginatively vital critiques of mechanical constructions of nature and the species of rationalism associated therewith. Even so, Emerson's own book, while profoundly influenced by, especially, Schelling and Coleridge, certainly

possesses its own unique zest, one especially strongly flavored by Emerson's Neoplatonic and Hermeticist inclinations.

368 I recorded this statement in notes taken upon visiting the museum. I did not record information as to the name of the associated painting.

369 Ibid.

370 Ibid., 12.

371 Emerson, "The American Scholar," in *Essays and Lectures,* 56.

372 James Hillman, "Peaks and Vales: The Soul/Spirit Distinction as Basis for the Difference between Psychotherapy and Spiritual Discipline," in *Puer Papers* (Dallas: Spring Publications, 1989), 54.

373 Christopher Bamford, *An Endless Trace: The Passionate Pursuit of Wisdom in the West* (New Paltz, NY: Codhill Press, 2003), 107–8.

374 At least in its Emersonian inflection. I believe it remains essentially true, though in markedly distinct forms, in the case of other major figures.

375 Emerson, "The Transcendentalist," in *Essays and Lectures*, 193.

376 Ibid.

377 Emerson, "The Oversoul," in *Essays and Lectures,* 385–6.

378 Rudolf Steiner, *Theosophie: Einführung in übersinnliche Welterkenntis und Menschenbestimmung* (Dornach, Switzerland: Rudolf Steiner Verlag, 1904), 35.

379 To be most precise, Steiner represents the soul body and sentient soul as distinct but intimately interwoven; so much so, that he employs the term "astral body" to refer to the blended functioning of the "highest" register of body and the "lowest" register of soul (Ibid., 48).

380 Rudolf Steiner, *Theosophy* (Hudson, NY: Anthroposophic Press, 1994), 42.

381 On page 35 of the cited German edition of *Theosophie*, Steiner writes: "*Man könnte sie auch die Gemütseele oder das Gemüt nennen*" (One can also name this the Gemüt-soul or Gemüt). The sentence is omitted in the translation cited above.

382 Emerson was well versed in this distinction, and employed it liberally in *Nature* and other texts.

383 Instrumental reason—reasoning towards a given determinate end—is an aspect of this brand of understanding, and one not infrequently identified with reason itself.

384 Within the context of a materialistic rationalism, reason and imagination are often conceived as disparate or antithetical (even if it is often acknowledged that scientific breakthroughs are imaginative triumphs). In Romantic philosophy, Reason (as contrasted with the Understanding) and Imagination are close kin. "The Imagination," writes Emerson in *Nature,* "may be defined to be the use the Reason makes of the material world."

385 One may also speak of the Overself, the term employed by Paul Brunton, one of the pioneers of the importation of Eastern philosophy (including yoga and meditation) to the West, and a great admirer of Emerson. Correlatively, it is certainly no coincidence that Emerson's idea of the Oversoul resonates with tenets of Indian philosophy. Emerson was a great reader of the Bhagavad Gita and other select classics, and these exercised a direct influence upon his conceptualization of the Oversoul. Emerson's poem "Brahman" represents a well-known poetic expression of that influence.

386 Steiner, *Theosophy,* 41.

387 Robert Frost, "The Road Not Taken," https://www.poetryfoundation.org/poems/44272/the-road-not-taken.

388 Sophocles, *Oedipus the King,* trans. David Greene, in David Greene and Richmond Lattimore (eds.), *Greek Tragedies,* (Chicago: Chicago University Press, 1960) V. 1, 112.

389 Francis Bacon, *Bacon's Essays and Wisdom of the Ancients* (Las Vegas: Digibooks, 2020).

390 Ibid., 254.

391 Ibid., 255.
392 Ibid.
393 Ibid.
394 Ibid., 322.
395 Ibid., 255.
396 *Nature* by no means includes Emerson's only or most important reference to the Sphinx. Emerson chose a long and thematically representative poem on the theme (titled, simply, "The Sphinx") to be the first and leading work in the collection of his own poetry that he himself compiled and edited.
397 Emerson, *Nature,* in *Essays and Lectures,* 24–5.
398 Ibid., 25.
399 Ibid.
400 Cf. Robin Wall Kimmerer, *Braiding Sweetgrass: Indigenous Wisdom, Scientific Knowledge, and the Teachings of Plants* (Minneapolis: Milkweed Editions, 2013), or Andreas Weber, *Enlivenment: Towards a Poetics for the Anthropocene* (Cambridge, MA: MIT Press, 2019).
401 Emerson, *Nature* in *Essays and Lectures*, 8.
402 I emphasize first place here because ultimately, as will become clear, I understand Nature as the World Soul (*Anima Mundi*) that enlivens, and represents the unity of, this World Body.
403 Ursula Goodenough, *The Sacred Depths of Nature* (New York: Oxford University Press, 1998), 4.
404 Ibid., 18.
405 Ibid., 27, 28.
406 It is true, certainly, that we speak of planetary or celestial bodies, but I believe the traditional understanding—expressed, for instance, by Kepler—that these represent, not masses of dead matter, but living intelligences, underwrites this usage.
407 As cited by Werner Heisenberg in Werner Heisenberg and Arnold J. Pomerans, *Physics and Beyond: Encounters and Conversations* (New York: Harper and Row, 1972), 41.
408 Emerson, "The Poet," in *Essays and Lectures,* 453.
409 Plotinus, *The Enneads: A New, Unabridged, and Definitive Edition of the Classic Translation by Stephen MacKenna* (Burdett, NY: Larson Publications, 1992), Ennead III.6, "The Impassivity of the Unembodied," 235.
410 Ibid., Ennead II.5 "Potentiality and Actuality," 138–139.
411 Ibid.
412 Clearly this identification of nature as purely material does *not* understand the generative agency inherent in the principles of Life and Soul, or the ideal form intrinsic in the logoi embodied in and through nature's creative activity, as indwelling (Mother) Nature.
413 Emerson, *Nature* in *Essays and Lectures,* 7.
414 Adorno and Horkheimer, *Dialectic of Enlightenment,* 4–5, 7.
415 This contention remains valid no matter how many "dimensions" of existence science recognizes since all remain within the metaphysical universe (or "multiverse") of an essentially materialistic physics.
416 Adorno and Horkheimer, *Dialectic of Enlightenment,* 7.
417 Goodenough, *Sacred Depths*, 9–10.
418 Ibid., 10.
419 Cited in Tarnas, *Passion of the Western Mind*, 301.
420 Goodenough, *Sacred Depths*, xvi.
421 As cited in Charles Eistenstein, *The Ascent of Humanity* (Berkeley: North Atlantic Books, 2007, 2013), 162.
422 Goodenough, *Sacred Depths*, 14.
423 Ibid.
424 Ibid., xvii
425 William Wordsworth, "I Wandered Lonely as a Cloud" in *William Wordsworth: The Oxford Authors* (Oxford: Oxford University Press, 1984), 303.
426 Goodenough, *Sacred Depths*, xvii.
427 Ibid., 11.
428 William Wordsworth, *Prospectus* to *The Excursion*, l. 31–35 in *English Romantic Writers,* ed. David Perkins (New York: Harcourt Brace, 1967), 301.

429 Ibid., l. 42–47.
430 Ibid., l. 47–51.
431 Ibid., l. 52–55.
432 Clearly, this was not the case with the likes of a Kepler or Newton. The difference here is undoubtedly what I called "the eclipse of the logos." For those early moderns, the pattern and order discerned in nature manifested, not mindless merciless mechanical laws, but divine intelligence; Reason qua Logos.
433 Gerard Manley Hopkins, "God's Grandeur" in *The Poems of Gerard Manley Hopkins* (London: Oxford University Press, 1967), 31.
434 Emerson, *Nature,* 7.
435 Ibid., 9.
436 Ibid.
437 Cited in Joel Porte, *Representative Man: Ralph Waldo Emerson in His Time* (New York: Oxford University Press, 1979), 69.
438 Untitled poem contained in the first volume of Rilke's *Book of Hours, The Book of Monastic Life*, as translated in Polikoff, *In the Image of Orpheus,* 159.
439 Emerson, *Nature* in *Essays and Lectures,* 11.
440 John K. Howat, Introduction, *American Paradise: The World of the Hudson River School* (New York: Metropolitan Museum of Art, 1987), 125.
441 Ibid., 20.
442 A version presented in Gary Lachman, *The Quest for Hermes Trismegistus* (Edinbrugh: Floris Books, 2011), 100. This book offers a good introduction to the figure of Hermes Trismegistus.
443 Francis. A. Yates, *Giordano Bruno and the Hermetic Tradition* (Chicago: University of Chicago Press, 1964).
444 Schelling's *Bruno oder über die göttlichen und natürlichen Prinzip der Dinge* appeared first in 1802. For an English version, see F.W.J. Schelling, *Bruno, or On the Natural and Divine Principle of Things*, ed. Michael G. Vater (Albany: SUNY Press, 1984).
445 Roelof van den Broek and Wouter J. Hanegraff, sds., *Gnosis and Hermeticism: From Antiquity to Modern Times* (Albany: SUNY Press, 1998), vii.
446 Emerson, *Nature* in *Essays and Lectures.* The citations are from pages 22, 24, and 25 respectively. An exploration of the *esoteric* origins of the American Renaissance in general, and Emerson's work in particular, exceeds the bounds of this volume, but will be dealt with in succeeding ones, and those interested in pursuing the topic presently may wish to consult Arthur Versluis's seminal texts on the topic.
447 While the phrase may be most familiarly associated with the 1945 book so titled by Aldous Huxley, it was originally coined by Agostino Steuco in 1540, and so is of Renaissance vintage. Steuco employed it in the title of a work attempting synthesis of diverse philosophies and religions in a manner reminiscent of Pico della Mirandola's syncretism.
448 Emerson, "The Method of Nature," in *Essays and Lectures,* 115.
449 Ibid.
450 W. Aaron Vandver, "The 'World War' on COVID: An Arsenal of High-Tech 'Weapons' of Social Control," *The Defender,* Sep. 1, 2022, https: //childrenshealthdefense.org/defender /world-war-covid-tech-social-control/.
451 Ibid.
452 Following 18th-century usage, Pagden uses the world "primitive" to refer, not to any tribal or indigenous culture, but to the Enlightenment concept of man "in the state of nature."
453 Pagden, *The Enlightenment,* 92.
454 Ibid., 93.
455 James Hillman, *Re-Visioning Psychology* (New York: Harper Collins, 1975).
456 Mattias Desmet, *The Psychology of Totalitarianism* (Whit River Junction, VT, and London: Chelsea Green Publications, 2022). See also Charles Eisenstein on "Mob Morality and the Unvaxxed," as well as the second

chapter in this book.

457 Martin Michaelis, Speech in Nuremberg, *The Nuremberg Code: The 75th Anniversary Commemoration,* CHD.TV, Aug. 20, 2020, https://live.childrenshealthdefense.org/75th-commemoration-of-the-nuremberg-code?utm_ b.

458 In ancient Persian doctrine, Ahriman was the evil or dark twin of the benevolent solar deity, Ahura Mazda, God of Zarathustra. In modern times, Rudolf Steiner has revived aspects of the ancient teaching, understanding the dark aspects of the divine—in Christian theology, identified with the devil or satan—with two distinct beings called Lucifer and Ahriman. Whereas Lucifer ("the light-bringer") tempts the human by way of diverse forms of illusion and spiritual inflation, Ahriman is the counterforce of contraction and the materialization of consciousness, as well as the will to power that accedes to supremacy in the absence of authentic spiritual consciousness. Transhumanism, the imagination that human beings can transcend the condition of material existence by virtue of matter-based technology that enables total control over nature, represents the acme of the dangerous cooperation of Lucifer and Ahriman. Paul Kingsnorth draws on Steiner's depiction of Ahriman in the first of his set of substack essays on the Internet (Paul Kingsnorth, "The Universal," April 13, 2023, https://paulkingsnorth.substack.com/p/the-universal?utm_source=publication-search).

459 Emerson, "The Divinity School Address," *Essays and Lectures*, 89.

460 Charles Mayo Ellis, "An Essay on Transcendentalism," in Perry Miller, ed. *The American Transcendentalists: Their Prose and Poetry* (Baltimore: Johns Hopkins University Press, 1957), 22–23. One should not be confused by Ellis's identification of "soul" with what, according to our prior exposition, might better be spoken of as "spirit." In accord with Neoplatonic philosophy, Ellis, like Emerson, employs the term "soul" very generally, and its aegis can include all that may be spoken of as "spirit." By contrast, what I (following Steiner and others) identified as "soul" in a sense distinct from spirit would here correspond to what Ellis addresses as the middle, "rational" aspect of the three-fold human being.

461 Ibid.

462 Ibid., 25.

463 Ibid.

464 Ibid., 26.

465 Ibid., 26.

466 Ibid., 27.

467 Emerson, "History" in *Essays and Lectures,* 237.

468 Friedrich Schiller, *Die Räuber* (Stuttgart: Reclam, 2017).

469 Friedrich Schiller, *On the Aesthetic Education of Man,* English and German, ed. Elizabeth M. Wilkinson and L.A. Willoughby (New York: Clarendon Press, 1967).

470 Conrad Ferdinand Meyer, "Schiller's Bestattung" (Schiller's Burial). Translation by Daniel Joseph Polikoff.

471 Adorno and Horkheimer, *Dialectic of Enlightenment*, xviii.

472 The strategy can backfire, because if an individual survives or somehow "stands up" (physically or morally) to torture, the stature of their humanity in the eyes of others can be magnified rather than reduced. The apogee of this logic is the crucifixion.

473 Esoterically as well as exoterically, the blood, and the stream that carries it, is closely associated with essential identity; with the heart and soul of "who I am."

474 In January, 2025, new Governor Patrick Morrisey issued an executive order reinstating the right of religious exemption in West Virginia. Corresponding legislative action is expected to follow. The number of states not allowing religious exemption is thus down to four.

475 See the first volume of *Reset or Renaissance* (including the section on

vaccine safety and efficacy in the first postscript) as well as the next chapter in this book.

476 Of course, it is true that religious sacraments are themselves not protected from contamination by ideology, and religious form does not guarantee spiritual integrity in any given instance. Even so, it is clear that the sacraments express a religious and spiritual—not merely a medical—intent. There is, as well, the question of freedom. I do not believe anyone in America is forced to take communion.

477 Rudolf Steiner, "Changes in Humanity's Spiritual Make-up" in *The Fall of the Spirits of Darkness: Fourteen Lectures by Rudolf Steiner... given in 1917* (Forest Row, UK: Rudolf Steiner Press, 1993), 85.

478 Spencer Kimball, "The Covid pandemic drives Pfizer's 2022 revenue to a record $100 billion," CNBC Health ans Science, Jan. 31, 2023. cnbc.com/2023/01/31/the-covid-pandemic-drives-pfizers-2022-revenue-to-a-record-100-billion.

479 Ibid.

480 Not wishing to break the time frame of the book, I do not here delve into the evidence of overwhelming malfeasance recently revealed by systematic review of the (2020/2021) clinical trial data submitted by Pfizer in its successful attempt to secure EUA for its original Covid-19 mRNA vaccine. Pfizer resisted release of the relevant data, but a lawsuit brought by ICAN and Aaron Siri resulted in the court-ordered release of tens of thousands of pages of test data. Systematic review of this data by independent (mostly volunteer) researchers revealed the shocking truth that Pfizer, and all government agency officials charged with review of the findings, knew that the vaccine triggered a frightening range of (often devastating) adverse effects in significant numbers of trial participants. For a comprehensive review of this story, which definitively rebuts any claim of the "safety and efficacy" of the Pfizer Covid-19 vaccine and reveals a massive Matrix-engineered coverup of the damning results, see Naomi Wolf, *The Pfizer Papers* (NY: Skyhorse Publishing, 2024). This story, in conjunction with those told in this chapter and my prior volume, exhibits three distinct ways of abusing or corrupting science: 1) Not doing or permitting the most relevant studies; 2) Conducting inadequate, clearly deficient or misleading studies; 3) Performing relevant studies, but hiding, obfuscating, or falsifying relevant results. All play a major part in Covid World.

481 The National Health Service, England's publicly funded health care service.

482 Chief Nerd, "BOMBSHELL: Dr Clare Craig Exposes How Pfizer Twisted Their Clinical Trial Data for Young Children," *Rumble,* June 17, 2022, https://rumble.com/v18s66i-bombshell-dr.-clare-craig-exposes-how-pfizer-twisted-their-clinical-trial-d.html.

483 Megan Redshaw, "Paul Offit: It 'Felt Like the Fix Was in' before FDA Panel Voted to Reformulate Covid Booster Shots." *The Defender,* July 9, 2022, https://www.theepochtimes.com/paul-offit-it-felt-like-the-fix-was-in-before-fda-panel-voted-to-reformulate-covid-booster-shots_.

484 Ibid.

485 Catherine Ho, Erin Allday, *San Francisco Chronicle,* e-edition, Sept. 4, 2022

486 @DrJBattacharya , Twitter, Sept. 4, cited on "The Fine Line," *The Highwire,* # 284, Sept. 8, 2022, https://thehighwire.com/watch/.

487 @richardurso.md, Aug. 31, 2022, cited on *The Highwire* (Ibid.).

488 @RepMaryMiller, Aug. 31, 2022, cited on *The Highwire* (Ibid.).

489 California Legislative Information, AB 2098: Physicians and Surgeons: unprofessional conduct, Oct. 3, 2022. https://leginfo.legislature.ca.gov/faces/billTextClient.xhtml?bill_id=202120220AB2098.

490 Dr. Drew Pinsky in a clip replayed on *The Highwire* (Ibid.).

491 Ibid.

492 Governor Newsom did, to his undying shame, sign AB 2089 into law. However, lawsuits challenging the legality of the measure were immediately filed, and enforcement of the law soon enjoined by the court injunction. As a consequence of these suits and ongoing pressure, AB 2098 was officially repealed in September 2023. However, the spirit of this law (if not the letter of this particular piece of legislation), continues to be pervasive.

493 According to testimony provided by ICAN attorney Aaron Siri, the widely held assumption that the vaccines on the childhood schedule (including polio and measles) provide a very high degree of protection against infection and transmission is just that—an assumption. It is, moreover, one more assumption contradicted by the facts conveyed in relevant study results in the possession of government health officials. "Aaron Siri Testifies: New Hampshire," *The Highwire,* Episode #404, Dec. 6, 2024, https://thehighwire.com/ark-videos/siri-testifies-new-hampshire-the-transmission-paradox/.

494 See, for instance, Zoey O'Toole and Mary Holland (eds.), *Turtles All the Way Down: Vaccine Science and Myth* (Washington, DC: Children's Health Defense, 2022). The book was published anonymously.

495 Paul Thomas, M.D. and Jennifer Margulis, *The Vaccine-Friendly Plan: Dr. Paul's Safe and Effective Approach to Immunity and Health-from Pregnancy Through Your Child's Teen Years* (New York: Ballantine Books, 2016).

496 Elizabeth Mumpert, M.D., editorial review, https://www.amazon.com/Vaccine-Friendly-Plan-Effective-Health-Pregnancy/dp/1101884231.

497 James Lyons-Weiler and Paul Thomas, "Relative Incidence of Office Visits and Cumulative Rates of Billed Diagnoses Along the Axis of Vaccination," *International Journal of Environmental Research and Public Health* 2020 Nov. 22;17(22):8674. doi: 10.3390/ijerph17228674. The article, it should be noted, was retracted by the journal editors in July, 2021. Does this call into question the validity of the results? Not necessarily. No reason was provided for the retraction by the IJerph in the published notice. Given the sensitive nature of the material and the sway of the NIH, one could imagine the retraction derives from political rather than scientific reasons.

498 Dr. Paul Thomas, interview with Del Bigtree, *The Highwire,* https://thehighwire.com/ark-videos/doctor-sues-oregon-medical-board-for-35-million/.

499 Ibid.

500 President Biden, "Remarks . . . on the Continued Battle for the Soul of the Nation," Independence Hall, Philadelphia, Sept. 1, 2022, https://www.whitehouse.gov/briefing-room/speeches-remarks/2022/09/01/remarks-by-president-bidenon-the-continued-battle-for-the-soul-of-the-nation/.

501 Romans 3:13, 16.

502 The Declaration of Independence (full text), https://www.ushistory.org/declaration/document/.

503 Theodore Parker, "The Effect of Slavery on the American People," a sermon delivered in the Boston Music Hall, July 4, 1858, p. 3–4. https://archive.org/details/SPC0001893300/page/n1/mode/2up?view=theater.

504 Ibid., 4.

505 Ibid.

506 Ibid.

507 Ibid.

508 James A. Langley, "Who Coined 'Government of the people, for the people, by the people'?", *Washington Post,* March 3, 2017, https://www.washingtonpost.com/opinions/who-coined-government-of-the-people-by-the-people-for-the-people/.

509 The United States Constitution was drafted in 1787 in Philadelphia.

Ratification was a complex process not completed until acceptance by all states of the original Bill of Rights in 1791.

510 Alexander Hamilton, New York Ratifying Convention, June 21, 1788 (Francis Child's version), https://founders.archives.gov/documents/Hamilton/01-05-02-0012-0011.

511 Ibid.

512 James Madison, Federalist Paper #10, Bill of Rights Institute, https://billofrightsinstitute.org/primary-sources/federalist-no-10.

513 Ibid.

514 Ibid. In this connection, and viewing matters from the perspective of October 2023, one might well note the remarkable instance of the influence wielded by a small group of extreme Republicans, which influence threatened a government shut-down and realized the unprecedented removal of the Speaker of the House (Kevin McCarthy).

515 Ibid.

516 Ibid.

517 John Adams, Defence of the Constitution, *The Founders Constitution* V. 1, ch. 4, no. 10, https://press-pubs.uchicago.edu/founders/documents/v1ch4s10.html.

518 Ibid.

519 Ibid.

520 Ibid.

521 It is well to remember that the preeminence of the idea of private property, and its protection by law, need to be viewed against the background of medieval and monarchal societies in which context personal property could often be lawfully usurped by royalty, nobility, or even clergy. The sanctity of property thus does have a historic and valid connection with the idea of the sovereignty of the individual basic to democracy. This perspective tends to get lost on account of the excess accumulation of wealth permitted or encouraged by capitalism as well as the neo-Marxist tendencies on the left that (rightfully) abhor those excesses and see them as tied to a history of classist, racist, sexist, and ethnic prejudice. Still, the tie between property and the liberty and sovereignty of the individual should not be forgotten or carelessly written off. See the following discussion of property in relation to the body.

522 Ibid.

523 Ibid.

524 Ibid.

525 Paul Kingsnorth, "Intermission: Last Post for Christian England," *Substack,* Sept. 19, 2020, https://paulkingsnorth.substack.com/p/intermission-last-post-for-christian/.

526 Ibid.

527 Ibid.

528 Ibid.

529 Stephen Herrmann, *Spiritual Democracy: The Wisdom of Early American Visionaries for the Journey Forward* (Berkeley: North Atlantic Books, 2014). As Hermann notes (see note #1, p. 349), the phrase originated in commentary upon Walt Whitman's poetry and his ideas about what he called "Religious Democracy."

530 https://paulkingsnorth.substack.com/p/intermission-last-post-for-christian/comment/9168948.

531 Ibid.

532 Henry David Thoreau, "Slavery in Massachusetts" in *Thoreau: The Major Essays,* 130–145. Thoreau delivered the material as a lecture on July 4, 1854 at an anti-slavery convention in Framingham, MA and published it in the abolitionist journal *Liberator* two-and-a-half weeks later.

533 Henry David Thoreau, "Civil Disobedience" in Owen Thomas, ed. *Walden and Civil Disobedience* (New York: W. W. Norton, 1966), 225.

534 Ibid.

535 Ibid., 242–43.

536 Ibid., 243.

537 Emerson, "Politics," in *Essays and Lectures,* 559.

538 Ibid., 560.

539 Ibid., 570.

540 John Adams, *The Letters of Novanglus, No. 1* "To the

Inhabitants of the Colony of Massachusetts-Bay," January 23, 1775, Massachusetts Historical Society, Adams Papers, Digital Edition, V. 2, https://www.masshist.org/publications/adams-papers/view?&id=PJA02dg5.

541 Ibid.

542 Ibid.

543 Ibid.

544 Ibid.

545 Williams was, in fact, a Puritan but not a Pilgrim.

546 As cited in James Calvin Davis, *On Religious Liberty: Selections from the Works of Roger Willliams*, (Cambridge, MA, and London, Belknap/Harvard, 2008), 1.

547 John M. Barry, *Roger Williams and the Creation of the American Soul* (New York: Viking, 2012), 6.

548 Ibid.

549 Ibid., 11.

550 If anyone were to doubt that tension between Protestant and Catholics continued to simmer under the surface during Elizabeth's rule—often threatening to boil over—Catholic plots to depose Elizabeth and place her cousin Mary on the throne should dispel that skepticism. Queen Elizabeth's well-founded suspicion that Mary herself was party to such scheming led to the latter's execution—by order of her cousin Elizabeth—in 1587. Those interested in a dramatic interpretation of the dynamics of that storied relationship may enjoy Schiller's powerful play *Mary Stuart*.

551 When James was a year old, his mother Mary was forced to surrender the crown. As the infant James was incapable of governance, Scotland was effectively ruled by a series of four different regents (a complex story that cannot be related here) until the end of James's minority in 1578, although he did not assume full control of the government until 1583. James married Anne of Denmark in 1589, who bore him three children, including Charles I, who succeeded his father as King of England upon James's death in 1625.

552 Alan Simpson, *Puritanism in Old and New England* (Chicago: University of Chicago Press, 1955), 61.

553 Barry, *Roger Williams,* 10.

554 The Geneva Bible in wide usage before (and still, to some degree, after) the King James version includes annotations that are Puritan and Calvinist in tenor, and employs language that tends to cast monarchy or the institution of kingship in a less than favorable light. The Authorized (KJV) actually doesn't have any annotations for precisely that reason.

555 Barry, *Roger Williams,* 17.

556 Ibid., 20.

557 Ibid., 21–22.

558 Ibid., 29.

559 Ibid., 30.

560 Ibid.

561 Ibid., 30–31.

562 Ibid., 31.

563 Ibid., 31.

564 Ibid., 23–24.

565 Ibid., 25.

566 Submitting a petition of grievances represented a chief method by which Parliament sought to represent its interest, and that of the people, to the King. Although I have not researched the matter, I would expect that it was this practice, in its English context, that gave rise to the language in the last clause of the First Amendment: "Congress shall make no law . . . abridging the right of the people . . . to petition the Government for a redress of grievances."

567 Cited in Barry, *Roger Williams,* 54.

568 He had been ousted from that post by the machinations of Francis Bacon, whom Coke, in turn, ultimately brought down by exposing the Lord Chancellor's (Bacon's) habit of accepting bribes. As bribery of various sorts was common practice, whether Bacon was or was not particularly culpable in this respect is a matter of some debate.

569 Barry, *Roger Williams,* 54.

570 Ibid., 55

571 Ibid., 55.

572 Ibid.
573 Coke funded Williams's further education at the highly reputed Charterhouse School. Williams excelled in his studies and went on to graduate from Pembroke College at Cambridge.
574 Williams—versed in shorthand—was charged with the task of recording Coke's public statements, and so accompanied Coke in all the latter's public engagements. He would thus himself have been "in the ring," a bodily witness to the momentous political wranglings of the time.
575 Barry, *Williams,* 81.
576 Ibid., 73.
577 Ibid.
578 After officiating at James's coronation, Laud quickly became Bishop of Bath and Wells and, too, Dean of the Chapel Royal. In 1628, Charles made him Bishop of London and a member of the Privy Council. Yet even that does not do justice to the power he wielded. Barry: "Though the nominal leader of the church remained the archbishop of Canterbury, Laud ruled in fact." Laud became the Archbishop of Canterbury in 1633.
579 Barry, *Roger Williams,* 82.
580 Ibid.
581 Ibid., 83.
582 The Pilgrims were English separatists (Protestants who could not reconcile their faith with obedience to, or indeed any association with, the Anglican Church) who had fled to Holland to escape persecution already in 1608. They were not content with their lot in Holland, however, for a variety of economic and cultural reasons. Thus their voyage to America, via England, in 1620, and the resultant founding of Plymouth Colony which, in time, would become Roger Williams's own.
583 Barry, *Roger Williams,* 168–69.
584 Ibid., 169.
585 In time, such membership became increasingly difficult to secure. Church membership was regarded as more of a privilege than a right, ultimately requiring loyalty oaths and like encumbrances for those not already in the fold.
586 Ibid., 169–70.
587 "Williams's position did not come from any sympathy for Separatists. Most Separatists believed the government should enforce the First Table and blamed government's failure to do so for corruption in the church. Henry Barrows, an early Separatist leader... wrote, 'Yet now if I be asked who ought to abolish this idolatry... and to depose these antichristian priests; to that I answer, the prince, or state.... Only the magistrate may pull down the public monuments of idolatry.'" Barry, *Roger Williams*, 152.
588 Ibid., 151
589 Ibid., 152
590 Williams had extensive contact with a number of Indian tribes, including the Wampanoag (reputed to be the tribe that aided him when he fled his banishment order), Pequot and the Narragansett. He learned, at least, Narragansett, the language featured in the first book devoted to understanding a Native American language, Williams's *A Key into the Language of America* (1643).
591 W. K. Jordan, *The Development of Religious Toleration in England* as cited in Barry, *Roger Williams,* 320.
592 Ibid.
593 "The Bloody Tenent of Persecution for Cause of Conscience" in *On Religious Liberty: Selections from the Works of Roger Williams*, ed. James Calvin Davis (Cambridge and London: Belknap/Harvard, 2008), 86.
594 Ibid.
595 Ibid.
596 *Holy Bible*, King James Version, Revelation VI: 9-10
597 Williams, "Bloody Tenent," 86.
598 Ibid.
599 Ibid.
600 Aurora Theatre website, https://www.auroratheatre.org/mission. Accessed Nov. 2024.
601 Aurora Theatre website, https://www

.auroratheatre.org/1984. Accessed Nov. 2024.

602 Aurora Theatre website, https://www.auroratheatre.org/covid19safety. Accessed Nov. 2024.

603 As quoted in Barry, *Roger Williams,* 125.

604 Ibid.

605 The caveat here is the colonial ban against ministers serving as magistrates. As previously discussed, however, actual social praxis proved this a rather ineffective check on the consolidation of religious and political power.

606 Theodore Parker, "The Effect of Slavery on the American People," a sermon delivered in the Boston Music Hall, July 4, 1858, 3–4. https://archive.org/details/ASPC0001893300/page/n1/mode/2up?view=theater.

607 Barry, *Roger Williams*, 334.

608 Ibid.

609 Ibid.

610 Ibid.

611 Ibid.

612 Ibid.

613 Ibid., 335.

614 Ibid.

615 For avenues of Williams's influence on the founding fathers, see Barry 333–34.

616 As quoted in Barry, *Roger Williams,* 345.

617 Roger Williams and John Milton were friends, and tutored each other in foreign languages. Williams instructed Milton in Dutch and Native American tongues in exchange for help polishing his Greek and Latin.

618 John Milton, *Areopagitica, A Speech of John Milton for the Liberty of Unlicens'd Printing*, Dartmouth College John Milton Reading Room, https://milton.host.dartmouth.edu/reading_room/areopagitica/text.shtml.

619 Barry, *Roger Williams*, 352–53.

620 Nor should politics take orders from science. Abuse in one direction tends, as in Covid World, to converge and meld with abuse in the other.

621 Paul Feyerabend is one of the most insightful and prescient critics of the common deification of science and the role it plays—subversive of democracy—in contemporary society. Feyerabend's classic *Against Method* (1975; reprt., London: Verso, 2010) calls into question many of the epistemological canards underlying our understanding of how real science actually is done. In Feyerabends's view, that has precious little to do with either reason or rationality as usually construed or the hallowed "scientific method." His book *Science in a Free Society* extends his arguments into the political domain in a manner deeply commensurate with the thrust of this last chapter of *Apocalypse.* The resonance with Williams's church/state position sounds in a single sentence that expresses the gist of Feyerabend's position: "A free society insists on the separation of science and society." Paul Feyerabend, *Science in a Free Society* (London: Verso, 1978), 31.

622 See pp. 380–95 in the first volume of *Reset or Renaissance.*

623 Ibid., 334.

624 Walt Whitman, *Preface* to *Leaves of Grass,* in *The Portable Walt Whitman* (New York: Penguin Books, 1973), 5.

625 Formerly *Missouri v. Biden.*For discussion of that case, see *Reset or Renaissance*, vol. 1, 355ff.

626 Mary Talley Bowden, Remarks at the Rally to Reclaim Free Speech, March 18, 2024, Washington, DC. https://live.childrenshealthdefense.org/chd-tv/events/rally-at-the-u-s-supreme-court-to-reclaim-and-protect-free-speech-or-mar-18/.

627 Bowden relates how, in her considerable experience with patients, vaccinated patients fell sick as frequently as the non-vaccinated and—if anything—suffered more rather than less severe Covid symptoms. Many of her patients did not wish to get the jab, but mandates forced their hand. That background

led Bowden, at one point, to tweet "Vaccine mandates are wrong" multiple times, attaching patient testimonials to each tweet. This led to a media fire storm, her loss of privileges, and the ongoing campaign of censorship and persecution continuing to this day.

628 France, indispensable ally of the American Revolution and bestower of the Statue of Liberty, is promoting a law that would punish subjects (including doctors) simply for discouraging an ailing patient from using a therapeutic that the state (in cooperation with the medical establishment) deems appropriate. The proposed punishment is brutal, entailing imprisonment as well as a hefty fine: a year in jail and 30,000 euros for a first offense, and three years and 45,000 euros if it is confirmed that the person in question was harmed by the unlicensed counsel. David Thunder, "French Parliament Passes a Bill Criminalizing 'Intent to Non-Treatment,'" Feb. 18, 2024, https://davidthunder.substack.com/p/french-parliament-passes-a-bill-criminalising.

629 C. J. Hopkins, *The Rise of the New Normal Reich* (consentfactory.org: Consent Factory Publishing, 2022).

630 C. J. Hopkins, Closing Statement, Berlin District Court, Jan. 23, 2024. https://consentfactory.org/2024/02/04/ the-verdict/.

631 Ibid.

632 After Hopkins endured terms of incarceration worthy of a terrorist and other repressive measures, on October 1, 2024, the Berlin Appellate Court reversed Hopkins' acquittal and found him guilty of the crime of hate speech. His remaining recourse is an appeal to the Constitutional Court (the German equivalent of the U.S. Supreme Court). Hopkin's September 30 statement to the Appellate Court is very direct and well worth reading. C.J. Hopkins, "Statement to the Berlin Appellate Court," Sept. 30, 2024. https://consentfactory.org/2024/10/01/guilty/.

INDEX

Note: References followed by "n" refer to endnotes.